Palgrave Studies in Financial Services Technology

Series Editor
Bernardo Nicoletti, Rome, Roma, Italy

The Palgrave Studies in Financial Services Technology series features original research from leading and emerging scholars on contemporary issues and developments in financial services technology. Falling into 4 broad categories: channels, payments, credit, and governance; topics covered include payments, mobile payments, trading and foreign transactions, big data, risk, compliance, and business intelligence to support consumer and commercial financial services. Covering all topics within the life cycle of financial services, from channels to risk management, from security to advanced applications, from information systems to automation, the series also covers the full range of sectors: retail banking, private banking, corporate banking, custody and brokerage, wholesale banking, and insurance companies. Titles within the series will be of value to both academics and those working in the management of financial services.

More information about this series at
http://www.palgrave.com/gp/series/14627

Bernardo Nicoletti

Banking 5.0

How Fintech Will Change Traditional Banks in the 'New Normal' Post Pandemic

palgrave
macmillan

Bernardo Nicoletti
Temple University
Rome, Italy

ISSN 2662-5083 ISSN 2662-5091 (electronic)
Palgrave Studies in Financial Services Technology
ISBN 978-3-030-75870-7 ISBN 978-3-030-75871-4 (eBook)
https://doi.org/10.1007/978-3-030-75871-4

This Palgrave Macmillan imprint is published by the registered company Springer Nature Switzerland AG
The registered company address is: Gewerbestrasse 11, 6330 Cham, Switzerland

Foreword

I have known Bernardo for quite a long time now—we have worked together in many countries, across many professional roles. Some years ago, he wrote another inspiring book, *The Future of Fintech*. I consider this book to be an outstanding sequel. Bernardo now tackles a new, yet connected, topic—how to push and support digital transformation in banking.

It was about time for such a book. The beginning of the so-called "Fourth Industrial Revolution" goes back to 2012. In 2021, however, many financial institutions continue to operate almost unchanged and seemingly unaware of what is happening around them. A few of them launched new companies and business models. Others failed, sometimes dramatically. The digital world has disrupted entire sectors, such as publishing, media recording, commerce, and manufacturing, among others. The financial services sector is not being spared.

"Digital transformation" has been on the agenda of many executives and board rooms for quite a long time. But beyond the buzzword, it is often not clear what "digital transformation" means. Financial services have often interpreted "digital transformation" only as a means to provide access to some products via digital channels, online or mobile, or, alternatively, as a pure cost reduction initiative. Digital transformation is much more than that: it is an entire change in the company's business model. It involves putting the customer at the center and using digital platforms to build a new business and operating model around that, using both own or external products and services. Such a transformation involves all dimensions such as products, processes, people, partners, and platforms.

In the last few years, we have heard statements such as: "banking is necessary, but banks are not." This approach has spurred a number of studies to understand what digital transformation means for banks. Surprisingly, some financial institutions have yet to embrace the change.

Bernardo advocates putting the customer and their needs at the center and building on that using three steps: intuition, demonstration, and experiment. He also introduces certain exciting ideas about how "banking" should change, emphasizing the evolution from offering "products" to "services," and the fundamental importance of "platforms." The text is also full of insightful cases in which digital transformation has been experimented with and implemented.

The book also stresses another critical aspect: the increasing importance for financial institutions of data and data management. The crisis caused by the pandemic has underscored this point by not only giving it a new sense of urgency, but also by showing that banking can operate in a much more digital and agile way than we thought.

To date, bankers must use all available tools to grow, protect themselves, and better plan for the future. The most effective way to do this is through the strategic use of data, artificial intelligence, and robotic process applications in symbiosis with our talents. These solutions are essential in order to understand the customer and protect the institutions from exposure, as well as mitigate the associated risks. Unfortunately, in some cases, the probability of fraudulent transactions, dictated by despair, increases as well.

At the same time, bankers must do responsible banking, taking into account the ESG—Environment, Society, and Governance.

Analysis tools will play an essential role in this recovery, providing bankers with all the information they need to limit their exposure, promote new offers, and enrich their services.

It is fascinating to go through the various chapters of this book because the financial institutions that have started implementing the digital transformation state that their work is only the beginning of what is to come. There is a need for a continuous digital transformation.

A financial institution's question is not "if" to do it, it is "when" to do it. The time is now, and the success will be with the hard work pioneers.

Madrid, Spain
March 2021

Ramon Billordo
Senior Global Banking Executive, Financial Services, Digital Transformation, Global Fintech

Contents

Acronyms, Abbreviations, and Currencies

3P	Planet, Persons, Profit
ABA	American Banking Association
ADA	American with Disabilities Act
ADAS	Advanced Driver Assistance Systems
AGI	Artificial General Intelligence
AI	Artificial Intelligence
AIFM	Alternative Investment Fund Managers
AMA	American Marketing Association and American Management Association
AML	Anti-Money Laundering
ANN	Artificial Neural Network
API	Application Programming Interface
AR	Augmented Reality
ATI	Attitude Toward Innovation
ATM	Automatic Teller Machine
AUM	Assets Under Management
AVR	Automatic Voice Recorder
B2B	Business-to-Business
B2C	Business-to-Customer
BaaP	Banking as a Platform
BaaS	Bank as a Service
BC	Behavioral Control, Before Christ, or Business Continuity
BCP	Business Continuity Plan
BI	Business Intelligence or Business Interruption
BPaaS	Business Process as a Service
BPI	Business Process Intelligence

BPM	Business Process Modeling
BPO	Business Process Outsourcing or Business Process Optimization
CAGR	Compounded Annual Growth Rate
CBDC	Central Bank Digital Currency
CBR	Case-Based Reasoning
CC	Cognitive Computing
CCPA	California Customer Privacy Act
CDO	Chief Digital Officer
CEO	Chief Executive Officer
CERT	Computer Emergency Response Team
CES	Customer Engagement Score
CEV	Customer Engagement Value
CIC	Contract Inconsistency Checking
CIO	Chief Information Officer
CLM	Contract Lifecycle Management
CNN	Convolutional Neural Network
CNY	Chinese Yuan Renminbi
Cobot	Collaborative Robot
CPC	Customer Proximity Center
CPS	Cyber-Physical System
CR.AA.M	Compliance Risk & Audit Activity Management
CRM	Customer Relationship Management
CSAT	Customer Satisfaction Score
CSF	Critical Success Factor
CSR	Corporate Social Responsibility or Customer Service Representative
CTO	Chief Solutions Officer
CtQ	Critical to Quality
CTR	Click-Through Rate
CX	Customer Experience
DB	Data Base
DFS	Digital Finance Services
DM	Data Management
DNN	Deep Neural Network
DPI	Digital Performance Index
DR	Disaster Recovery
DRP	Disaster Recovery Plan
DRS	Disaster Recovery Site
DT	Design Thinking
EC	European Commission
ECB	European Central Bank
EDI	Electronic Data Interchange
EESC	European Economic and Social Committee

EP	Equator Principle
EPC	European Payments Council
ERP	Enterprise Resource Planning
ERPB	Euro Retail Payments Board
ESG	Environmental, Social, and Governance
ETF	Exchange-Traded Fund
EU	European Union
EUR	Euro
FC	Financial Crime
FCR	First Call Resolution
FDS	Fraud Detection System
FICO	Originally Fair, Isaac and Company
Fintech	Financial Solutions
FSB	Financial Stability Board
FTE	Full-Time Equivalent
G20	Group of Twenty
GAFAM	Google, Amazon, Facebook, Apple, and Microsoft
GBP	British Pound Sterling
GDP	Gross Domestic Product
GDPR	General Data Protection Regulation
GPT-3	Generative Pre-Trained Transformer
GPU	Graphics Processing Unit
GUI	Graphical User Interface
HCI	Human Computer Interaction
HFT	High Frequency Trading
HITL	Human-in-the-Loop
HNW	High Net Worth
HPC	High Performance Computing
HR	Human Resources (Department)
HRM	Human Resource Management
IA	Integrated Analytics or Intelligent Automation
IaaS	Infrastructure as a Service
IAM	Identity and Access Management and Innovation Acceptance Model
ICT	Information and Telecommunication Solutions
IDS	Intrusion Detection System
IEC	International Electrotechnical Commission
IEEE	Institute for Electrical and Electronics Engineers
IoC	Indicator of Compromise
IoT	Internet of Things
IP	Internet Protocol or Intellectual Property
IPS	Intrusion Prevention System
ISO	International Standard Organization

IVR	Interactive Voice Response
JPEG	Joint Photographic Experts Group
KPI	Key Performance (or Process) Indicators
KYC	Know Your Customer
LOC	Loan on blockchain Contract or Line of Credit or Line of Code
M&A	Merger and Acquisitions
MCD	Mortgage Credit Directive
MFA	Multi Factor Authentication
MICR	Magnetic-Ink Character Recognition
MIFID	Markets in Financial Instruments Directive
MIS	Management Information Systems
MIT	Massachusetts Institute of Solutions
MNO	Mobile Network Operator. And Maintenance and Operations
MP3	Moving Picture 3
MPC	Secure multi-party computation
MSMEs	Micro, Small, and Medium Enterprises
MSP	Multi-Sided Platform
NBO	Next Best Offer
NFC	Near Field Communication
NGFW	Next-generation Firewall
NGW	Next Generation Web
NIST	National Institute of Standards and Solution
NLG	Natural Language Generation
NLL	Natural Language Understanding
NLP	Natural Language Processing
NPS	Net Promoter Score
ODA	Operational Data Analytics
OECD	Organization for Economic Co-operation and Development
OT	Operations Solution
P&C	Property and Casualty
PaaS	Platform as a Service
PEF	Perceived Economic Factor
PROU	Perceived Ease of Use
PSP	Payment Service Provider
PSU	Payment Service User
PT	Perceived Trust
PU	Perceived Usefulness
R&D	Research and Development
RATER	Reliability, Assurance, Tangibles, Empathy, and Responsiveness
RBI	Reserve Bank of India
RE	Real Estate or Reputation
Regtech	Regulatory Solutions Organization
RFM	Recency, Frequency, and Monetary Value

RMB	Yuan renminbi
ROI	Return on Investment
ROPO	Research Online, Purchase Offline
RPA	Robotic Process Automation
RRSP	Registered Retirement Savings Plan
SCT	SEPA Credit Transfer
SCT inst	SEPA Instant Credit Transfer
SDG	United Nations Sustainable Development Goals.
SEC	Securities and Exchange Commission
SEPA	Single European Payment Area
SIEM	Security Information and Event Management
SLA	Service Level Agreement
SME	Small and Medium Enterprises
SMS	Short Message Service
SOC	Security Operations Center
SP	Social Pressures
STEM	Science, Solution, Engineering, Mathematics
STP	Straight Through Processing
Swift	Society for Worldwide Interbank Financial Telecommunication
SWOT	Strengths-Weaknesses-Opportunities-Threats
TAM	Solution Acceptance Model
TCM	Total Cost Management
TEG	Technical Expert Group
TIPS	TARGET Instant Payment Settlement
TQM	Total Quality Management
UCITS	Undertakings for Collective Investment in Transferable Securities
UD	Universal Design
UGAI	Universal Guidelines on Artificial Intelligence
UI	User Interface
UK	The United Kingdom
UMTS	Universal Mobile Telecommunications System
UN	United Nations
UNEP-FI	United Nations Environment Programme—Finance Initiative
UNICEF	United Nations Children's Emergency Fund
UPS	Uninterruptible Power Supply
US or USA	United States of America
USD	United States Dollar
UX	User Experience
VoC	Voice of the Customer
VR	Virtual Reality
VUCA	Volatile, Unpredictable, Complex, and Ambiguous

List of Figures

List of Tables

CHAPTER 1

Introduction

Banking is necessary; banks are not.
Bill Gates

The global recession and the pandemic hit hard. They have affected all organizations and functions. After these crises, it is vital to develop and manage innovative strategies in banking. Except for fintech organizations, banking has almost remained outside of the trend of digital transformations.[1] Some financial institutions have begun to innovate, create new business models, invest in emerging technologies, and partner with fintech organizations, either financing or buying them.[2] Accenture, in a survey, found that only 1 in 10 banks were committed to digital transformation; 4 in 10 were trying to transform but had no integrated strategy, and 5 out of 10 were not making any progress.[3] Meanwhile, an IDC analysis estimates that 70% of all digital transformation initiatives do

[1] Uusitalo, J. (2019). *Strategic insurance in the face of uncertainty* (Master's Thesis). University of Jyväskylä, Finland.

[2] Generali. (2018, February). *Le assicurazioni tutto connesso*. www.generali.com/it/info/discovering-generali/all/2018/A-fully-connected-insurance. Accessed 2 November 2019.

[3] https://newsroom.accenture.com/news/only-half-of-banks-globally-are-making-significant-advancements-in-digital-transformation-resulting-in-lower-market-valuations-accenture-report-finds.htm. Accessed 3 March 2021.

B. Nicoletti, *Banking 5.0*, Palgrave Studies in Financial Services Technology, https://doi.org/10.1007/978-3-030-75871-4_1

not reach their goals.[4] Of the USD 1.3 trillion spent on digital transformation in 2018, it was estimated that more than $900 billion went to waste. If this is the scenario, financial institutions need to design and offer customers products and services relevant to them. At the same time, they did not base most of their innovations on customer centrality. This book has the objective to present this approach and calls it banking 5.0.

Bill Gates was clear: "Banking is necessary, banks are not."[5] This statement forecasts potential scenarios. These innovative approaches or visions are banking 5.0. This book underlines that the functions, disciplines, and activities of banking 5.0 can change financial institutions to support organizational efficiency, effectiveness, ethics, and economics within a long-term and sustainable perspective.

The sequence of industrial revolutions is:

- The steam engine characterized the first industrial revolution. The engine initially revolutionized the textile industry and then other sectors.
- The introduction of electricity brought about the second industrial revolution. It, combined with the introduction of mass production, created another change that spread from industry to social and political environments.
- The computer characterized the third industrial revolution, which again revolutionized work and extended into the social world.
- The mass diffusion of the internet characterized the fourth industrial revolution. It allowed the introduction of devices such as mobile phones with enormous impacts not only in the industry but in the social and political spheres.

At this point, one might wonder what the probable fifth industrial revolution will be. The answer is not easy and might tempt to say: let complete and use the full potential of Industry 4.0 and then think about the future. What the sequence of industrial revolutions proves is that their life cycle

[4] https://thefinanser.com/2020/10/the-difference-between-cloud-based-and-cloud-native.html/. Accessed 3 March 2021.

[5] Amberber, E. (2015). Banking is necessary, banks are not. *7 Quotes from Bill Gates on Mobile Banking*.

is getting shorter. It is therefore likely that the fifth industrial revolution is upon us.

The fifth industrial revolution can be expected to be characterized by the spread of solutions such as Artificial intelligence (AI), robots, and actions on sustainability. A broad fifth industrial revolution, based on technologies, such as robots, attention to sustainability, mobile phones, AI/cognitive computing, and predictive modeling, would affect the entire banking business model. These innovative solutions enable new ways of communicating, information sharing, and banking. There is a need for a new vision of banking. This vision is called banking 5.0 in this book. Innovative solutions have generated researchers' interest in very different fields: computer and management science, organization theory, law, and economics. An integrated vision is missing. This book shows why and how banking 5.0 can change in an integrated way banking. Banking 5.0 is potentially the engine and starting point of the customers' increasing need for innovative banking services and solution models.

This book analyzes the significance, development, and application of banking 5.0, to banking's digital transformation. The word digital in digital transformation might be misleading. A digital transformation is a definition and implementation of a new business model. In implementing this new business model, a digital solution will be relevant but not exclusive. This innovative approach should be transparent (almost invisible). As in the famous Turing test,[6] the customer should not understand if a person, a robot, or a mix of the two supplies banking.

There are important messages in this book. The first one is that banking is not necessarily done in banks. Banking should become part of the business activities and functions of all organizations and individuals. Ordinary activities should incorporate banking, whenever and wherever necessary. Non-financial transactions should embed banking transactions transparently to the customer. This situation does not mean that all the business or individuals should become banks. It means that the banking transaction should be part of their ordinary activities. The provision and processing of this transaction should be made usually by an external entity that, if necessary to the transaction, would have a banking license to assure the customer of the reliability and trust in the transaction. In other words,

[6] The Turing test was born as a criterium to determine if a machine is can behave as a person. Alan Turing suggested this criterium in the article Turing, I. B. A. (1950). Computing machinery and intelligence-AM Turing. *Mind, 59*(236), 433.

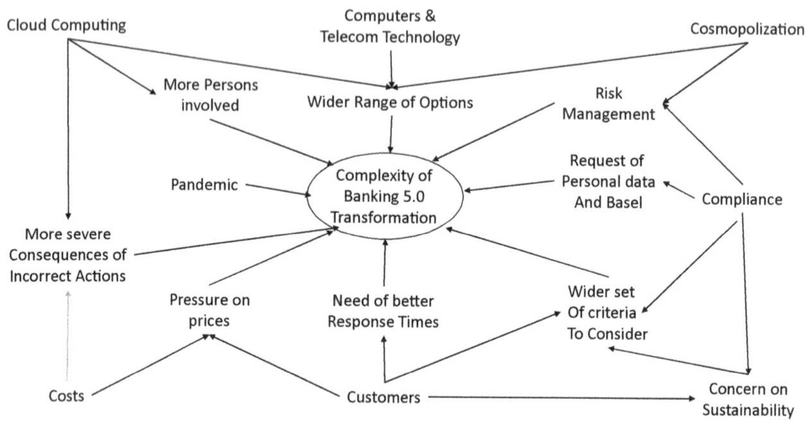

Fig. 1.1 Impacts of transformation on banking (simplified)

at the center of a transaction, there should be a customer and his/her needs, not the bank.

From an internal point of view, the operations should be provided by an actor who could be a robot, a person, and in most of the cases, a combination of the two (a cobot). The robot should have Artificial intelligence (AI). This vision implies the importance of person–machine collaboration. In this new vision, AI is fundamental. Banking 5.0 is born out of an industrial revolution determined by AI, like the earlier four industrial revolutions were determined by other enabling technologies.

The 2020 pandemic is pushing even more to embark on the banking 5.0 transformation and become more agile, responsive, and connected enterprises. In a survey of Fortune 500 CEOs, 63% said that the Covid-19 crisis would accelerate their technological investment despite financial pressures.[7] One legacy of the pandemic could be the acceleration of the financial institution's transition to banking 5.0. This transition entails challenges.[8] Figure 1.1 summarizes some of these challenges.

[7] Jacobides, M. G., & Reeves, M. (2020). Adapt your business to the new reality. *Harvard Business Review, 98*(5), 74–81.

[8] Iansiti, M., & Lakhani, K. R. (2020). Competing *in the age of AI: Strategy and leadership when algorithms and networks run the world*. Harvard Business Press, Brighton, MA.

Banking 5.0 will bring a cultural transition to the customers.[9] The growth of banking for a financial institution will come from a change of approach. This approach must be transformed from merely passive to preventive and proactive, with a range of new services and products, new business models, and more considerable attention to prevention for defaults. Customer needs, knowledge, and expectations have expanded exponentially over the past years. Financial institutions need to adapt to their customers' needs. In an age of immediacy, continuous changes, and overwhelming choices in which loyalty is no longer a certainty, the sector must extend beyond its main products and services if it wants to keep and increase its customer base. It must innovate and change its approach. It is critical to understand who the banking customers are, and their needs expressed or implicit.[10]

In a highly competitive environment, current financial institutions can no longer rely on organic growth or internal innovation. As a result, mergers and acquisitions, equity partnerships, and collaborations are essential. The winners are the financial institutions able to launch and grow an ecosystem, with alliances with innovative start-ups, teaming up with fintech organizations, and joining even with some of their competitors. Merger and acquisitions (M&A) activity will focus on key markets and products. Access and use of solutions that allow improvements within the sector will come through acquisitions or partnerships. These potential opportunities require a holistic view of innovation. It would include distribution, new products, credit management ability, or improvements in the default settlement process.

The winners will be the ones which would invest in innovative platforms. They should rethink and revise their business model. A rapidly changing market and evolving industry require an unprecedented ability to do banking. Technological changes are essential. They are not enough. Knowing these changes and using them in the best way are different things. Financial institutions should use analytics, AI, and robots to benefit and use them as a basis for a radical banking 5.0 transformation.

[9] www.insuranceup.it/it/opinioni/deloitte-4-trend-per-le-assicurazioni-nel-2020/. Accessed 25 December 2019.

[10] Parasuraman, A., Berry, L. L., & Zeithaml, V. A. (1991). Understanding customer expectations of service. *Sloan Management Review, 32*(3), 39–48.

Financial institutions are pure service providers that are highly data-founded. Digitization can influence financial institutions.[11] Already, large parts of the banking industry are robustly affected by digitization. In particular, the distribution is becoming heavily digitized. Digitization should strengthen the entire value network of the banking industry.[12] Digitization will change the profit and loss account of the financial institutions in three ways through new business models:

- Lower costs.
- Added revenues.
- More agility.

Digitization can impact pricing and competition. The real question is whether digitization-driven changes such as distribution accesses, competition types, and so on, be allowed under new regulations. The compliance framework should not restrict competition. Instead, the customer and data protection should be at the center of considerations.

A close relationship between the persons and the robots will characterize the fifth industrial revolution. The word robot in this book does not refer to the humanoid robots seen in the movies. Robots can be physical but also virtual. They can allow operators to act more rationally and with less operational effort. The joint and integrated work between the persons and the robots can supply the maximum benefits. This book considers industry 5.0 as the personalization of a solution and the need of a new relationship between persons and machines from this perspective. From the customer's point of view, the ultimate benefit is mass personalization. The two words are apparently in contrast, but they represent a goal not far in the future.

[11] Prognos, A. G. (2017). *Digitalisierung in der Versicherungswirtschaft*. Studie. Hg. v. vbw Vereinigung der Bayerischen Wirtschaft e.V. München, Germany.

[12] In the case of banking, the traditional concept of the value chain does not apply. Due to the importance of the information, it is necessary to consider a value network of banking. The term value "network" emphasizes the notion that a critical determinant of value to any particular user is the set, or network, of other users that are connected. In a value network, value is created through linking: the organization and facilitation of exchange between users (Stabell, C. & Fjeldstad, Ø. [1998]. *Configuring value for competitive advantage: On chains, shops, and networks*. Wiley, Hoboken, NJ).

Banking 5.0 is not only a component of an industry 5.0 initiative.[13] It is much more. It is a new original vision of banking that makes it more agile, integrated, responsive to the customers, and adds value to the organization. Banking 5.0 is the set of solutions that can support managers at all stages of the banking processes. Banking 5.0 refers to an organization that uses the fundamental principles of complex adaptive systems and innovative science to achieve success. Banking 5.0 is not an improvement in banking 4.0. It is a disruptive innovation. The pandemic has given the important lesson that the future is not a minor change of the past. The future will be drastically different, and innovative solutions need to be disruptive.

This book explores the problems and solutions in how banking 5.0 can add more value to the customers, manage relationships, improve processes, and better manage resources internally and from partners.[14] For analyzing these challenges, this book uses the business model canvas framework.[15] This framework is a powerful tool for the analysis of organizations and helps in modeling their strategies. Banking 5.0 considers that future customers will not be the same as today. The "normal" will be "new."

The aim of this book is not only to present what banking 5.0 could be. It aims to show how it should work and how to reach that target. Three imperatives will position banking well against the disruptive world of tomorrow. They must embed speed and agility, find the best parts of their response to the crisis, and find ways to preserve them.[16] It is necessary for banking institutions to fundamentally reinvent their business models to sustain an extended period of very low interest rates and strong economic challenges.[17] Simultaneously, they must adopt the best

[13] Lasi, H., Fettke, P., Kemper, H. G., Feld, T., & Hoffmann, M. (2014). Industry 5.0. *Business & Information Systems Engineering, 6*(4), 239–242.

[14] This book uses the terms vendor or intermediary. It replaces them with partners as if the relationship fails, both the customer and the vendor/intermediary are damaged.

[15] Osterwalder, A., Pigneur, Y., Oliveira, M. A. Y., & Ferreira, J. J. P. (2011). Business model generation: A handbook for visionaries, game changers, and challengers. *African Journal of Business Management, 5*(7), 22–30.

[16] McKinsey's Global Banking Annual Review. www.mckinsey.com/industries/financial-services/our-insights/global-banking-annual-review. Accessed 30 December 2020.

[17] www.mckinsey.com/industries/financial-services/our-insights/global-banking-annual-review. Accessed 10 December 2020.

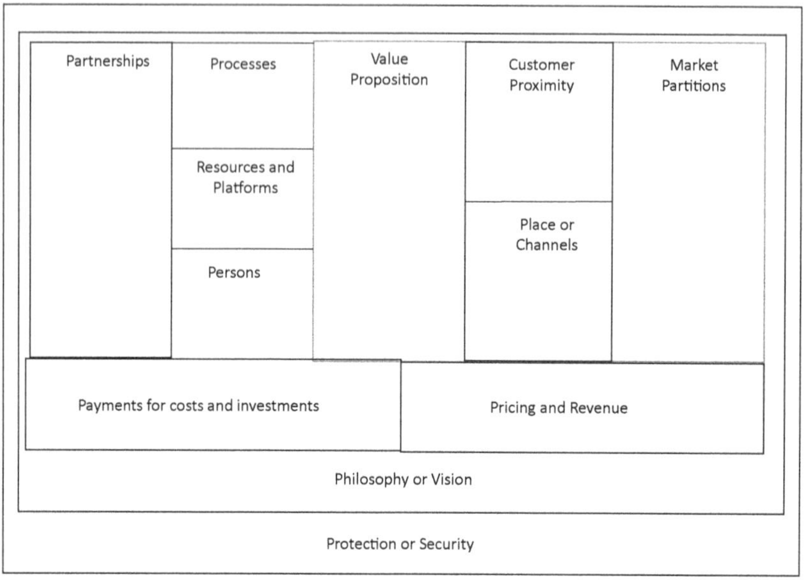

Fig. 1.2 Business model canvas

innovative ideas from digital challengers. They must bring purpose to the fore, environmental, social, and governance (ESG) issues. They must work together with the communities they serve to redefine their contract with them.[18] In doing so, they should understand that society 5.0 will be entirely different from the current society.

AI, person-machine collaboration, and sustainability will be the bases of industry 5.0. It is time to deeply analyze these banking solutions since the sector is in dire need of a digital transformation. This book presents an integrated conceptual model of banking 5.0. It then details its implementation on methods and techniques, dealing with banking 5.0 as an agile business model. The organizations' transformation must cover all the components in the business model canvas, which this book calls the 12 Ps (Fig. 1.2):

[18] McKinsey's Global Banking Annual Review. www.mckinsey.com/industries/financial-services/our-insights/global-banking-annual-review. Accessed 4 January 2021.

- Philosophy or vision
- Value proposition
- customer Proximity
- market Partitions
- Processes
- Place or accesses
- resources and Platforms
- Persons
- Partnerships
- Pricing and revenues
- Payments for costs and investments
- Protection or security.

The chapters of this book precisely follow the sequence of these twelve Ps. The book also includes how to manage the digital transformation of banking 5.0 and discuss the future of banking 5.0.

The book introduces innovative solutions. These solutions are embedded in the business model components. They are justified and create transformation as part of these components. For each solution, there is a section that presents the basic architecture of the solution. A second section discusses banking 5.0 applications of the solution of that specific component of the business models. Finally, there is a discussion on the benefits and the challenges connected with those innovations to the business model component under consideration.

This introduction analyzes the significance, development, and application of banking 5.0 about banking's digital transformation.

Chapter 2 defines the goal of this book on banking 5.0 and its relationships with industry 5.0. It presents a model of the Critical success factors (CSF) of banking 5.0.

Chapter 3 aims to define the philosophy or vision of the organization's business model concept. It is one of the main factors at the base of banking 5.0 and introduces the business model's general framework in this book. The chapter begins with an introduction to banking that is helpful for those unfamiliar with this world. This chapter introduces the concepts of digital transformation. There is also an introduction and a general picture of managing a project to transform banking 5.0.

Chapter 4 deals with the proposition of value for the customer through banking 5.0. It underlines the products and services supplied or potentially offered by financial institutions within the framework of banking 5.0.

Chapter 5 deals with customer proximity. It underlines the importance of communication with the customer and building their User experience (UX) and journey. It examines in detail customer relationship applications.

Chapter 6 underlines the partition or segmentation of the market, how to assure customers' delight, and target one customer segment.

Chapter 7 deals with distribution. It underlines the characteristics of the digital distribution typical of banking 5.0. The digital distribution must be a revolution for traditional distribution. Banking 5.0 transformation has an impact on distinct aspects of customers' lives and organizations. The latter needs to adapt to customers' new and increasingly demanding needs (such as e-commerce).

Chapter 8 deals with digital platforms. It examines in detail the technological innovations at the base of banking 5.0. The chapter's final part deals with technological innovations and the compliance aspects in their double role of challenges and opportunities.

Chapter 9 deals with the processes, with particular attention to the onboarding. It underlines the importance of using proper methods and tools for supporting the transformation, such as design thinking, and lean and digitize.

Chapter 10 deals with persons. It underlines the importance of person robot collaboration. It goes into the details of the new e-competencies and the need for education 5.0.

Chapter 11 deals with partnerships and examines the aspect of banking ecosystems, whose importance is growing.

Chapter 12 considers revenues and underlines the support to manage and innovate pricing in banking 5.0.

Chapter 13 deals with costs and investments. It underlines the importance of correct and automated management of contracts.

Chapter 14 examines the protection of the business models. It goes into details of cybersecurity, compliance, and resilience.

The following chapter explores the future of banking 5.0. It underlines the characteristics and the perspective of the threat of bigtech organizations.

Table 1.1 Banking 5.0 model

Business model components	*Traditional bank*	*Digital model*	*Banking 5.0 model*
Philosophy	Service provision	Digital banking	Embedded banking, personalization, humanization
Value proposition	Limited service of the branch network and staffing, carried out at clearly defined times, Service depends on the qualification and experience of the Bank employee	Unlimited, can go beyond the geographical location of the banking institution and round the clock-access	Instantaneous service, Fintech, sustainability, + services
Proximity	Requires time and cost	Quick service, communication via SMS and e-mail newsletter	Advanced CRM
Partition	Segmentation	Online. In branch	One customer segment
Place	Flexible, however, is limited to a small variety of service channels	Flexible and carried out through any convenient channel for the client	Online, Mobile, chatbots
Platforms	Legacy systems	Digital and automation	Multi Serice Platforms, Artificial intelligence, API
Processes	Bureocratic	Bureocratic	Flexible and lean
Persons	Functions of the operator is performed by an employee of the bank	Functions of the operator are performed by the bank's client or automated	Human-robot collaboration, robo-advisors, RPA
Partnerships	Limited to bancassurance	Alliances and partnerships	Ecosystem, Fintech, Bigtech

(continued)

The last chapter concludes and opens to future research on the subject.

The book reports several references to real organizations in quite different sectors.

A detailed glossary, a bibliography of recent works on the subject, and a sitography complete the book.

Table 1.1 (continued)

Business model components	*Traditional bank*	*Digital model*	*Banking 5.0 model*
Pricing	High, taking into account the bank's costs for the personnel and maintenance of departments	Low, often services are provided free of charge	Risk-pricing, Machine Learning
Payments	The key models are articles on the staff and maintenance of departments	The key articles are articles for the purchase and maintenance of servers and software package	Pay as you go
Protection	Physical protection	Passwords and pins	Cyber security

Table 1.1 shows in synthesis the banking 5.0 model, developed in this book.

CHAPTER 2

Industry 5.0 and Banking 5.0

There is nothing permanent except change.
Heraclitus of Ephesus.

Introduction

A saying attributed to Darwin argues that[1]: "*It is not the strongest species or the most intelligent which survived, but one that is best suited to change.*" This statement applies to banking. Financial services need innovation. Otherwise, the organizations would suffer or simply disappear. This chapter examines innovation in banking and calls it banking 5.0.

Innovation is necessary to face new challenges for organizations. It is essential to improve the organizations' effectiveness, efficiency, ethics, and economics and meet the growing needs of adding value and supplying delights to customers by each component of its business model.

It is possible to summarize the innovation goals in three aspects[2]:

[1] Huxley, T. H. (2018). *The Darwinian hypothesis*. Amazon Digital Press LLC, Bellevue, WA.

[2] Hammer, M., & Champy, J. (2009). *Reengineering the corporation: Manifesto for business revolution, A*. Zondervan, Grand Rapids, MI.

B. Nicoletti, *Banking 5.0*, Palgrave Studies in Financial Services Technology, https://doi.org/10.1007/978-3-030-75871-4_2

#1. Using the potential of innovative solutions:

- Innovating by using solutions such as Artificial intelligence (AI), robotic process automation, and sustainability, in all operations and channels.
- Standardizing wherever possible.

#2. Saving in resources:

- Creating centers of excellence where it makes sense in the organization.
- Optimizing relationship with the customers and the partners.
- Automating and outsourcing, where the benefits/cost ratios are more significant.
- Assuring sustainability with responsible banking.

#3. Doing fewer transactions and adding more value in each of them. This aspect involves:

- Focusing on areas that contribute more to adding value to the customers and the organization.
- Collaborating with partners and relating with them in an ecosystem vision.
- Outsourcing or automating the administrative parts of banking and focusing on high value-added activities.

The move in these directions requires to push on better governance of the banking business model and to define an innovation plan to:

- Be more integrated and accessible to the customers and the entire ecosystem.
- Define better priorities of the organization.
- Create efficiencies, increase revenues, and achieve agility for the organization.

Innovation has characterized the last few centuries through some industrial revolutions. At the base of each of them, there was the introduction of general-purpose solutions.[3] These technologies can be used in many sectors and have an overall impact on economics, society, and a wide range of complementary innovations they support.[4]

- The steam engine characterizes the first industrial revolution. This innovation initially revolutionized the textile industry and then transportation and other industries.
- Electricity brought to the second industrial revolution. It combined with the introduction of mass production and created another cycle of a revolution that spread from industry to social and political environments.
- The computer characterizes the third industrial revolution. This innovation again revolutionized work and extended into the social.
- The mass diffusion of the internet characterized the fourth industrial revolution. This innovation introduced mobile phones with an enormous impact not only in the industry but also in the social and political spheres.

A new general-purpose solution, AI, will characterize the fifth industrial revolution. A close relationship between the persons and the robots will also characterize the fifth industrial revolution. Robots can be physical and virtual. The joint and integrated work between the persons and the robots assures the maximum benefit. From the customer's perspective, the ultimate benefit is the full personalized service through mass customization. Society requires sustainability from industry 5.0 (Fig. 2.1).

Banking 5.0

Banking is the exchange of value (and trust) between an individual or an organization and a financial institution.[5] Banking is an industry that

[3] Helpman, E. (Ed.). (1998). *General purpose technologies and economic growth*. MIT Press, Cambridge, MA.

[4] Lechman, E., & Marszk, A. (2019). *ICT-driven economic and financial development: Analyses of European countries*. Academic Press.

[5] Zhou, C. (2009, December). Are banks too big to fail? Measuring systemic importance of financial institutions. *Measuring systemic importance of financial institutions*.

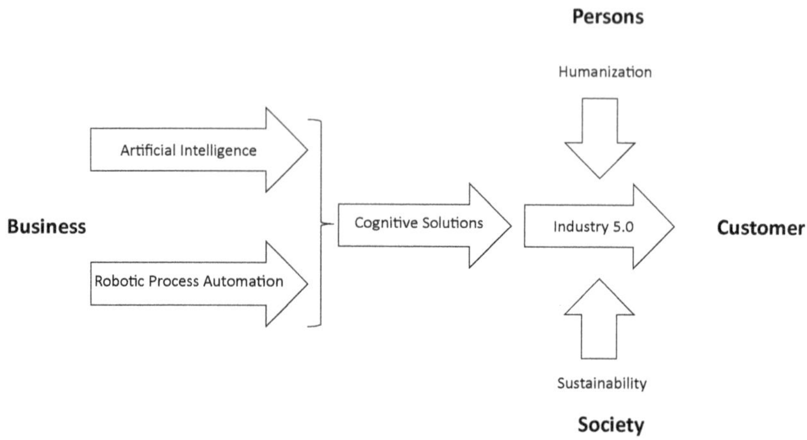

Fig. 2.1 Industry 5.0 framework

handles cash, credit, and other financial transactions.[6] Financial institutions supply a safe place to deposit extra cash and get credit. Banking offers savings accounts, certificates of deposit, and checking accounts. Financial institutions use these deposits to supply credit. These loans include home, asset, and car loans. Financial institutions manage information, therefore, are highly influenced by innovation in information and communication technologies.[7]

Banking organizations have continuously transformed over time. It is possible to divide the macro changes into five main periods to mimic the so-called industrial revolutions.[8] These changes have been significant and have led to economic and social changes. In between subsequent disruptive changes, there has been a continuous improvement. The following pages detail these five innovative waves in the industrial and banking sectors (called in this book banking 1.0, 2.0, 3.0, 4.0, and 5.0) (Table 2.1).[9]

[6] www.thebalance.com/what-is-banking-3305812. Accessed 8 September 2020.

[7] Some authors call banks "information systems." See for instance Ocampo, J. A. (2018). International asymmetries and the design of the international financial system 1. In *Critical issues in international financial reform* (pp. 45–74). Routledge, London, UK.

[8] Schwab, K. (2017). *The fourth industrial revolution*. Currency, London, UK

[9] Domingo Galindo, L. (2016). *The challenges of logistics 4.0 for the supply chain management and information solution* (Master Thesis, NTNU), Trondheim, Norway.

Table 2.1 Industry and banking generations

Generation	*Industry no. X*	*Banking no. X*
1	Steam engine	Central banks
	Industrial production and transportation	Clearing house
2	Electricity	
	Telegraph	Branch networks
	Division of labor	
3	Computer	Banking applications
	Telecommunication network	MICR
	ERP	Credit cards
	Telex	Dematerialization
	Minitel	Electronic financial markets
		Electronic payments
4	Cloud	Fintech
	Internet of everything	Online/mobile banking
	Convergence of industrial automation and ICT	Virtual global market
		ETF
		Cryptocurrency
		High Frequency Trading
5	Artificial Intelligence	Cognitive banking
	Robotic Process Automation	Robo-advisors
	Humanization	Hybrid Robo-advisors and bots
	Sustainability	Responsible banking
		Embedded banking

First Industrial Revolution: Banking 1.0

The need for banking was born a long time ago. In prehistoric times, the person created food reserves to cope with the winter. Subsequently, with the coins' introduction, the simple saving of assets was improved to cope with potential risky events.

Banking began in ancient Assyria and Babylonia well before banks were born. The merchants accepted to loan grain as collateral within a barter system. Lenders in ancient Greeceand during the Roman empire accepted deposits and changed money.[10] In the same period, archaeology in ancient China and India shows traces of money lending.

[10] www.liquisearch.com/history_of_banking. Accessed 8 September 2020.

Banking in the modern sense started in medieval and early Renaissance Italy, in the prosperous cities in central and northern Italy, like Florence, Lucca, Siena, Venice, and Genoa. The Bardi and Peruzzi families' banking was the most important in fourteenth-century Florence, setting up branches overall Europe.[11] The Medici family set up one of the most famous Italian banks. Giovanni di Bicci de' Medici set it up in 1397.[12] The earliest known state deposit bank, Banco di San Giorgio was founded in 1407 in Genoa, Italy.[13]

The advent of the printing press created the basis for transforming traditional coins into paper money. This innovation was one of the first examples of the close relationships between the financial world and innovative solutions.

The first industrial revolution with the introduction of the engine supported transportation and traveling. The banking management began working increasingly on a regional scale. There was the need for diverse ways to exchange money. The Bank of England started to issue banknotes in 1695.[14] The Royal Bank of Scotland set up the first overdraft facility in 1728.[15] The start of the nineteenth century saw the birth of the first bankers' clearing house in London. It allowed multiple banks to clear transactions. The Rothschilds pioneered international finance widely. They financed the purchase of the Suez Canal for the British government.

Thanks to the better transportation network, central banks were born and started to grow during the first industrial revolution. The Bank Charter Act of 1844 gave the Bank of England a monopoly over banknotes. Initially, the banknote was simply a promise to the bearer that they could redeem it for its value *in species*. In 1833, a second Bank Charter Act stated that banknotes would be considered as legal tender during peacetime.[16]

[11] The Bardi and Peruzzi families dominated banking in fourteenth-century Florence, establishing branches in many other parts of Europe

[12] www.themedicifamily.com/The-Medici-Bank.html. Accessed 20 January 2020.

[13] www.bank6.wordpress.com/history/. Accessed 20 January 2020.

[14] www.bankofengland.co.uk/about/history. Accessed 4 November 2020.

[15] www.natwestgroup.com/heritage/history-100/objects-by-theme/serving-our-customers/overdraft-authorisation-1728.html. Accessed 4 November 2020.

[16] www.britannica.com/topic/Bank-Charter-Act. Accessed 4 November 2020.

Second Industrial Revolution: Banking 2.0

Electricity introduction was at the base of the second industrial revolution. Several other discoveries characterized the second industrial revolution. These innovations made possible radical developments in transportation and communication. Materials such as steel, copper, or aluminum became relevant in the construction of machinery and products. The chemical industry expanded in a significant way.[17] Other innovations characterized the second industrial revolution. These innovations helped to reduce the purchase price of many products. The introduction of the division of labor meant a revolution in the industry with mass production. It was the model for industrial plants for several decades. Simultaneously, Henry Ford pushed the idea of the assembly line.[18]

The second industrial revolution affected banking with the introduction of the telegraph. This device allows delivering commands at a distance. The original purpose of building a telegraph network in many countries (for example, in China) was to send military information and not support financial activities.[19] Banks gained benefits from the economic development that was stimulated by the telegraph.[20] This situation created an entirely new possibility for remote banking. That was a real "fintech" revolution, since thanks to the telegraph, it became much easier to exchange information, including financial information. The telegraph was at the base of expanding the banks' branch networks both in number and in geographic scope.[21]

The telegraph innovation was the beginning of globalization in financial services. The Fedwire Funds Service used the telegraph to make

[17] Schwab, K. (2017). *The fourth industrial revolution*. Currency, London, UK.

[18] *The second industrial revolution*. www.ushistoryscene.com/. Accessed 28 December 2018.

[19] The Telegraph and Modern Banking Development, 1881–1936. https://chichengma.weebly.com/uploads/9/4/2/0/9420741/telegraph_jfe_final_paper_web.pdf. Accessed 4 January 2021.

[20] The Telegraph and Modern Banking Development, 1881–1936. https://chichengma.weebly.com/uploads/9/4/2/0/9420741/telegraph_jfe_final_paper_web.pdf. Accessed 4 January 2021.

[21] The Telegraph and Modern Banking Development, 1881–1936. https://chichengma.weebly.com/uploads/9/4/2/0/9420741/telegraph_jfe_final_paper_web.pdf. Accessed 4 January 2021.

money transfers between banks in 1918. The use of telegraphs continued until the 1970s.

Third Industrial Revolution: Banking 3.0

The introduction of the computer marked the third industrial revolution. It is a device that separates hardware and software.[22] This separation allows excellent flexibility, solution innovations, and the introduction of entirely innovative solutions: Computer-based applications started to support the organization's functions.

In the 1950s, the US population reached 150 million. The economic boom after the Second World War expanded the gross national product. There was a growth of the middle class.[23] The number of new personal checking accounts increased substantially.[24] Bank of America processed more checks than any other financial institution. Checks are popular and convenient, but they present a severe problem to the bank's back-offices. It took a huge Bank of America's workforce and many hours to process millions of checks per month and more than a billion per year. All checks had to be cleared manually, and banks were closing by 2:00 p.m. to process them overnight. In 1950, the Bank of America introduced the world's first computer used in banking. Its name was ERMA, Electronic Recording Method of Accounting. It was used to process checks and automate account management.

Simultaneously, General Electric, Stanford Research Institute, and Bank of America partnered and introduced Magnetic-ink character recognition (MICR). It uses a string of numbers at the bottom of the checks still today.[25] MICR solved one of the biggest challenges when developing ERMA: how to enable a machine to read the necessary information from

[22] Rifkin, J. (2011). *The third industrial revolution: How lateral power is transforming energy, the economy, and the world*. Macmillan, London, UK.

[23] Bank of America revolutionizes the banking industry. https://about.bankofamerica.com/en-us/our-story/bank-of-america-revolutionizes-industry.html. Accessed 30 March 2021.

[24] Bank of America revolutionizes banking industry from Bank. https://about.bankofamerica.com/en-us/our-story/bank-of-america-revolutionizes-industry.html. Accessed 4 January 2021.

[25] Bank of America revolutionizes banking. https://industry.about.bankofamerica.com/en-us/our-story/bank-of-america-revolutionizes-industry.html. Accessed 4 January 2021.

checks, deposit slips, and other routine banking documents.[26] The American banking association (ABA) in 1956 adopted MICR as the industry standard. Bank of America made the MICR solution available to all banks without royalty charges.[27]

By 1954, the first computer for business use was available. It was called Remington Rand UNIVAC-1. Magnetic tapes fed data into this factory-sized computer.[28] Actuarial and statistical applications were among the first applications of the computer. Later, other applications were introduced for the management, support, and control of banking processes.[29] As computers became widespread in the banking workplaces, new ways for their potential use developed. Smaller computers became powerful. Over time, they become the standard workstation for financial institution employees.[30]

Diners Club in 1950 introduced another "fintech" innovation: the credit card. Credit cards' introduction and success continued to open the way to introduce many other new technological products, such as Automatic teller machines (ATMs) in 1960. This innovation allowed people to withdraw their money directly from an ATM (Automatic teller machines) rather than going to a branch.

The first electronic system, called Quoton, was introduced at the end of 1960.[31] It had large computer screens to support brokers and communicate prices in the stock market. In 1966, another "fintech" revolution launched the global telex network. In 1970, the first electronic exchange trading was founded and commissioned. In the 1980s, large financial institutions installed mainframe computers to ensure the safe and best storage and processing of substantial amounts of data.

[26] Bank of America revolutionizes banking. https://industry.about.bankofamerica.com/en-us/our-story/bank-of-america-revolutionizes-industry.html. Accessed 20 March 2021.

[27] Metaminds. www.metaminds.com/. Accessed 4 January 2021.

[28] Bank of America revolutionizes banking. https://industry.about.bankofamerica.com/en-us/our-story/bank-of-america-revolutionizes-industry.html. Accessed 4 January 2021.

[29] Nicoletti, B. (2014, May). Lean and digitize e-procurement, proceedings of the *Public e-procurement in Europe: Public management, technologies and processes of change*, Lisbon, Portugal.

[30] A Brief History of Automation. www.insurancejournal.com/magazines/mag-coverstory/2000/05/15/21633.htm. Accessed 30 May 2020.

[31] How Fintech Industry Is Changing the World. www.theseus.fi/bitstream/handle/10024/123633/TRUONG_OANH.pdf?sequence=1. Accessed 4 January 2021.

Fourth Industrial Revolution: Banking 4.0

The widespread use of the internet marked the beginning of a new revolution.[32] Industry 4.0 is the convergence of industrial operations technologies and information and communication technologies.[33] Industry 4.0 also relates to the merge of the internet of things (IoT), the internet of persons (IoP), and the internet of everything (IoE).[34]

The fourth industrial revolution is not only smart and connected machines and systems. It has a much broader scope. There have been waves of breakthroughs in areas ranging from mobility to nano-solutions, from renewables to advanced sensors.[35]

The internet allows reliable communication among machines, persons, and digital applications in real time and cheaply.[36] This situation enables the implementation of what is known as "smart banking,"[37] and advanced digitization within and between organizations or service operations websites.[38]

Banking 4.0 is a disruptive innovation as the three earlier revolutions. They have in common the support not by a single solution but by the interaction of several technologies whose effects have changed the business models. The results have influenced the organizations, the environment, and the social functions.[39]

[32] Kagermann, H., Helbig, J., Hellinger, A., & Wahlster, W. (2013). *Recommendations for implementing the strategic initiative INDUSTRIE 4.0: Securing the future of German manufacturing industry; Final report of the Working Group 4.0 Industries*. Forschungsunion, Essen, Germany.

[33] Skilton, M., & Hovsepian, F. (2017). *The 4th industrial revolution: Responding to the impact of artificial intelligence on business*. Springer, Cham, Switzerland.

[34] Hermann, M., Pentek, T., & Otto, B. (2016). Design principles for industrie 4.0 scenarios. In *2016 49th Hawaii international conference on system sciences* (HICSS) (pp. 3928–3937). IEEE.

[35] Skilton, M., & Hovsepian, F. (2017). *The 4th industrial revolution: Responding to the impact of artificial intelligence on business*. Springer, Cham, Switzerland.

[36] Stock, T., & Seliger, G. (2016). Opportunities of sustainable manufacturing industry in 4.0. *Procedia CIRP, 40*, 536–541.

[37] Mcclellan Jr, R. E. (2006). Smart insurance. *Grower Talks, 70*(5), 76–78.

[38] Stock, T., & Seliger, G. (2016). Opportunities of sustainable manufacturing industry in 4.0. *Procedia CIRP, 40*, 536–541.

[39] Schmidt, R., Möhring, M., Härting, R. C., Reichstein, C., Neumaier, P., & Jozinović, P. (2015). Industry 5.0-potentials for creating smart products: Empirical research results.

Over the last few decades, solutions have drastically affected the banking industry, raising a new concept called e-banking or online banking. Online banking became popular in the late 80s when systems could be accessed via fixed or mobile phone lines.[40] Online banking was launched in New York in 1981, where major banks like Citibank, Chase, and others started supplying home banking services via a system called videotext. Stanford Federal Credit Union was the first service provider of online banking.

Internet or online banking characterized the fourth industrial revolution in banking. Online banking can be defined as an "internet portal, through which customers can use different types of banking services ranging from bill payment to making investments."[41] Online banking removes cash, and it allows customers to access almost any type of banking operation in a secure way.

From banking of individuals, online banking started to extend to banking of businesses.[42] Online banking by organizations is beneficial for both organizations and financial institutions. Customers can access the service 24*7 hour, retrieve any information, and make a certain number of transactions easily. It is affordable for both large and small organizations. A new way of marketing financial services was created. It was also possible to share mutual support and guidance within a virtual community.[43]

Banks used online banking as a business strategy to increase market share rather than making profits. Capgemini, UniCredit Group, and the European Financial Management and Marketing Association carried out a study which concluded that most banks use online banking as a strategy

In *The international conference on business information systems* (pp. 16–27). Springer, Cham, Switzerland.

[40] Housel, T. J., & Davidson, W. H. (1991). The development of information services in France: The case of public videotex. *International Journal of Information Management, 11*(1), 35–54.

[41] Pikkarainen, T., Pikkarainen, K., Karjaluoto, H., & Pahnila, S. (2004). Consumer acceptance of online banking: An extension of the solution acceptance model. *Internet Research, 14*(3), 224–235.

[42] Faroughian, F. F., Kalafatis, S. P., Ledden, L., Samouel, P., & Tsogas, M. H. (2012). Value and risk in business-to-business e-banking. *Industrial Marketing Management, 41*(1), 68–81.

[43] Sharma, H. (2011). Bankers' perspectives on e-banking. *Global Journal of Research in Management, 1*(1), 71.

aiming to attract more customers by offering lower prices for products and services. It was not beneficial for all banks in all countries.[44] For example, in Russia, supplying online banking facilities to customers was very expensive.[45] This situation caused an impact on the financial institution's market share as customers being unable to receive help from lower prices moved to other financial means where costs were lower.

There are benefits and challenges in online banking. The system available for accessing the services may be discouraging since there is poor control in some cases. There is the threat of hackers at whichever level of security available.[46] There is no direct contact between customers and banks, which can be overcome introducing the possibility of chatting with an operator.[47] Whatever be the challenges faced by online banking, many new entrants are supplying the above services worldwide, and they are trying to manage the services effectively, efficiently, and economically.

Banking 4.0 is supported by innovative solutions whose quantitative effects create new services, processes, modes of operations, and business models. All of them support the customization of the products and services.[48] The gradual movement of financial institutions toward digitization earmarks the fourth industrial revolution. In a banking 4.0 environment, organizations can increasingly connect and integrate with partners (upstream) and intermediaries and customers (downstream) through the internet of everything. Transparency of information can create virtual twins of the banking processes.[49] Cyber-physical systems can

[44] Capgemini, UniCredit Group and EFMA, World Retail Banking Report 2009, www.de.capgemini.com/m/de/tl/World_Retail_Banking_Report_2009.pdf.

[45] History About the Internet Banking Marketing Essay. www.ukessays.com/essays/marketing/history-about-the-internet-banking-marketing-essay.php. Accessed 4 January 2021.

[46] Souflis, D. (2002). The CLR &. NET. *Dr Dobbs Journal, 27*(12), 10.

[47] Baldock, R. (1997). The virtual bank: Four marketing scenarios for the future. *Journal of Financial Service Marketing, 1*(3), 260–268. Daniel, E. (1999). Provision of electronic banking in the UK and the Republic of Ireland. *The International Journal of Bank Marketing, 17*(2). Ramsay, J., & Smith, M., (1999) Managing customer channel usage in the Australian banking sector. *Managerial Auditing Journal, 14*(7). Saeidipour, B., Ranjbar, H., & Ranjbar, S. (2013). Adoption of internet banking. *IOSR Journal of Business and Management, 11*(2), 46–51.

[48] Riecken, D. (2000). Personalized views of customization. *Communications of the ACM, 43*(8), 26.

[49] Helms, M. E., Vattam, S. S., Goel, A. K., Yen, J., & Weissburg, M. (2008). *Problem-driven and solution-based design: Twin processes of biologically inspired design*. ACADIA.

enable decentralized decision-making. Decision support systems (using mobile apps) can help and support. These principles are the basis of design principles for further digitizing banking.[50]

The implementation of these types of processing solutions will take place over time. They need significant investments and special programs and training. The results are a substantial improvement in the banking processes' performance and costs, speed, flexibility, banking services customizations and extensions.

Fifth Industrial Revolution: Banking 5.0

AI, cobots, and sustainability will characterize the fifth industrial revolution. Each one of these aspects will have a profound impact on banking. Banks will not disappear significantly, because some will transform profoundly and partner with the start-ups. The competition will be fierce. New types of banking will spread, thanks to the fifth-generation technologies. Andrew Ng compared the transformative power of AI to that of electricity, saying, "Just as electricity transformed almost everything 100 years ago, today I have a challenging time thinking of an industry that I do not think AI will transform in the next several years."[51]

The analysis of industry 5.0 shows a lot of uncertainty about what it will bring and how it will disrupt business. It is going to break down barriers between the real world and the virtual one.[52] The next step of the industrial revolution will be to respond to the customers' high demand for individualization in the products and services they buy.[53]

[50] Tham, C. K., & Luo, T. (2013). Sensing-driven energy purchasing in smart grid cyber-physical system. *IEEE Transactions on Systems, Man, and Cybernetics: Systems, 43*(4), 773–784. Klötzer, C., & Pflaum, A. (2015). Cyber-physical systems as the technical foundation for problem solutions in manufacturing, logistics and supply chain management. *October 2015 5th international conference on the Internet of Things (IoT)* (pp. 12–19). IEEE.

[51] Lynch, S. (2017, March 11). Andrew Ng: Why AI is the new electricity. *Insights by Stanford Business*. www.gsb.stanford.edu/insights/andrew-ngwhy-ai-new-electricity. Accessed 22 December 2020.

[52] https://gadget.co.za/now-prepare-for-the-5th-industrial-revolution/. Accessed 22 August 2020. Østergaard, E. H. (2018). Welcome to Industry 5.0.

[53] www.machinedesign.com/automation-iiot/article/21835933/yes-industry-50-is-already-on-the-horizon. Accessed 22 December 2020.

Successful organizations increasingly do not just add value. They reinvent it. The critical strategic task is to reconfigure roles and relationships among an ecosystem of stakeholders (vendors, partners, and customers) to create value by new combinations and integrate players and services. This new organizational paradigm has been called value constellation.[54] This new logic of value breaks down the distinction between products and services. It combines them into activity-based "offerings" from which customers can create value for themselves. As potential offerings grow complex, so do the relationships necessary to make them. This concept can be generalized.[55]

Banking 4.0 involves a change not only in operations but in the entire organization. An essential function is marketing/sales. The continuous increase of global e-commerce requires cross-functional integration and even complex integrative processes across the organization.[56]

Another vision describes industry 5.0 as faster, more scalable, and with more people concerned than earlier revolution.[57] This situation will take place, thanks to the push toward more advanced person–machine interfaces with improved integration, better automation of robots paired with the power and creativity of persons' brains.[58] This innovation will lead to improved productivity.

Banking 5.0 will be increased collaboration between persons and intelligent systems like robots. The European Economic and Social Committee (EESC) describes Industry 5.0 as "focused on combining persons' creativity and artisanship with the speed, productivity, and consistency of robots."[59] With this development, automation takes over most monotonous, repetitive tasks while persons will be engaged in the work's

[54] Normann, R., & Ramirez, R. (1993). From value chain to value constellation: Designing interactive strategy. *Harvard Business Review, 71*(4), 65–77.

[55] Nicoletti, B. (2017). *Agile insurance. Volume I: Adding value with lean processes.* Springer International Publishing, London, UK. ISBN 978-3-319-61082-5.

[56] Castillo, F. (2016). *Managing information solution.* Springer International Publishing, Cham, Switzerland.

[57] Rundle, E. (2017). The 5th industrial revolution: When it will happen and how.

[58] Shelzer, R. (2017). *What is Industry 5.0 and how will it affect manufacturers?* https://blog.gesrepair.com/industry-5-0-will-affect-manufacturers/.

[59] www.mdpi.com/2078-2489/11/2/124/htm#:~:text=Thepercent20Europeanpercent20Economicpercent20andpercent20Social,percent2Cpercent20andpercent20consistencypercent20ofpercent20robotspercentE2percent80percent9D.

emotional and creative side. Persons will take on more responsibility and increased supervision of systems to elevate service quality across the board. This idea is not new, as Accenture's survey with 512 manufacturing execs worldwide showed. Eighty-five percent of the participants foresee a collaborative production line between persons and robots in their plants by 2020+.

The customers will choose and be willing to pay more for the services and products with distinctive marks of personal care and professionalism like in wealth management consultancy.[60] This demand for individualized touch will be rising in the future much more because customers look to express their individuality through the products and services they buy.[61] Financial institutions will satisfy this demand efficiently, effectively, and economically by combining humans and intelligent robots.

The efficient cooperation between persons and solutions will affect the economy, ecology, and the social world.[62] On the other side, AI and robots will need more electrical energy for their computers to run. Hence the importance to take all the possible actions to assure sustainability of the environment with a green approach.[63]

There are other social and economic consequences connected with banking 5.0, called by some authors Globotics.[64]

Business Model

The term Business model (BM) is widely used and applied to the organization, information solution, and entrepreneurship literature since the

[60] Østergaard, E. H. (2018). Welcome to Industry 5.0. https://ww2.isa.org/intech/20180403/. Accessed 22 December 2020.

[61] Østergaard, E. H. (2018). Welcome to Industry 5.0. https://ww2.isa.org/intech/20180403/. Accessed 22 December 2020.

[62] Shelzer, R. (2017). What is Industry 5.0—And how will it affect manufacturers? https://blog.gesrepair.com/industry-5-0-will-affect-manufacturers/.

[63] Rada, M. (2018). Industry 5.0 definition. https://medium.com/@michael.rada/industry-5-0-definition-6a2f9922dc48. Einstein, A. (2020). *Parsimony*. PRMIA Institute, Northfield, MN.

[64] Baldwin, R., & Forslid, R. (2020). *Globotics and development: When manufacturing is jobless and services are tradable* (No. w26731). National Bureau of Economic Research.

advent of the internet between the 1990s and today.[65] In principle, the words "business model" show how an organization pursues its goals, and all processes are part of it. The term business model has taken a particular relevance and usage in the last decades, even if the term is born from Drucker's studies.[66] According to Drucker, a business model can support the analysis and transformation of organizations: It helps to answer questions such as[67]: who are the target customers, what is the organization selling, how to make the selling, and how to realize a margin?

A business plan covers the planning of activities necessary to achieve a goal. A business model clarifies the functioning of the organization's various components and how they can be successful in adding value to the customers and the organization.

There is no single definition of business model. The consensus is on the reasons why to use this term, that is, to explain how an organization generates value for its stakeholders, especially the customers. There are different definitions of these words based on the point of view of those who use it. A meaning for a business model is: "a statement, a description, a representation, an architecture, a conceptual tool or model, a structural template, a method, a framework, a pattern, and a set."[68]

Fundamentally, a business model performs two essential functions[69]:

- Value creation. It defines a series of activities that generate a new product or service so that there is net value created all along with the various activities.
- Value capture. It captures value from some of those activities for the organizations developing the model.

There are some standard features of a business model: Rappa, for example, highlights the monetary aspect of the business model concept,

[65] Zott, C., Amit, R. & Massa, L. (2011). The business model: Recent developments and future research. *Journal of Management, 37*(4), 1019–1042.

[66] Drucker, P. (1994, September–October). The theory of the business. *Harvard Business Review*, 95–104.

[67] Gassmann, O., Frankenberger, K., & Csik, M. (2017). *Develop business models. 55 innovative concepts with the St. Gallen Business Model Navigator* (2nd ed.). Carl Hansen, Miinchen, Germany.

[68] https://timreview.ca/article/807. Accessed 30 May 2020.

[69] Chesbrough, H. W (2006). *Open business models*. Harvard Business Press.

which is present in some other definitions.[70] Chesbrough, Rosenbloom, and Magretta connect the concept of business model to organizational strategy.[71] Chesbrough and Rosenbloom stress the mentioned concept in a technological innovation perspective, stating that "the business model is an intermediary between solution development and economic value creation."[72] Chesbrough states that it is critical that the business model itself is essential in helping to make revenue through the market.[73] Consequently, business models are "stories that explain how enterprises work [...]. A good business model begins with an insight into personal motivations and ends in a rich stream of margin."[74] With this statement, Magretta refers to Drucker and defines "a good business model" can supply answers to his two questions mentioned before. Other scholars, who focus on e-business, stress the value creation related to this specific type of business. They describe the business model "as the design of transaction content, structure, and governance transactions."[75] They analyzed a sample of US and European e-business models to define the value creation drivers. They say that: "A business model depicts the content, structure, and governance of transactions designed to create value through the exploitation of business opportunities."

Most of these scholars developed a specific explanation of a business model based on a particular context. In this sense, Drucker described the

[70] Afhua, A., & Tucci, C. L. (2000). *Internet business models and strategies* (1st ed.). McGraw-Hill College, New York, NY. Mullins, J. W., Mullins, J. W., Mullins, J., & Komisar, R. (2009). *Getting to plan B: Breaking through to a better business model.* Harvard Business Press, Brighton, MA. Teece, D. J. (2018). Business models and dynamic capabilities. *Long-Range Planning*, *51*(1), 40–49.

[71] Magretta, J. (2002, May). Why business models matter. *Harvard Business Review*, 3–8. Chesbrough, H. & Rosenbloom, R. S. (2002). The role of the business model in capturing value from innovation: Evidence from Xerox Corporation's solution spin-off financial institutions. *Industrial and Corporate Change, 11*(3), 529–555.

[72] Chesbrough, H., & Rosenbloom, R. S. (2002). The role of the business model in capturing value from innovation: Evidence from Xerox Corporation's solution spin-off financial institutions. *Industrial and Corporate Change, 11*(3), 529–555.

[73] Chesbrough, H. (2007). Business model innovation: It is not just about solution anymore. *Strategy & Leadership, 35*(6), 12–17.

[74] Magretta, J. (2002, May). Why business models matter. *Harvard Business Review*, 3–8.

[75] Zott, C., & Amit, R. (2013). The business model: A theoretically anchored robust construct for strategic analysis. *Strategic Organization, 11*(4), 403–411.

theory of the business. This theory relates to the underlying assumptions on which the organization is built. Or it is associated with the organizational behavior, organization's business scope, customers, competitors, values, actions, solution, dynamics, and the organization's strengths and weaknesses.[76] Most of the later literature on the definition and use of business models was developed, starting from this definition.

Until this point, the focus has been on the economic and monetary meaning of a business model. Other authors gave a different definition for all those organizations in which margin plays a less relevant role (such as socially oriented organizations and government organizations).

Nature, necessity, and context are at the base of a diversified use of the business model concept. This situation explains why there is not an agreed-upon definition.

Business Model Architecture

Before examining the relationship between business models, strategy, and competitive advantage, it helps go through the components that an organization must define to develop a good/excellent business model.

One of the most used tools is visual thinking, which uses visual tools like Post-it, notes, pictures, sketches, and diagrams to build and define business models.[77] It becomes simpler to discuss, brainstorm, and make changes to the model because in this way it becomes visually concrete and tangible.

Figure 2.2 is the typical structure used to design a Business model canvas (BMC), which could serve as a reference for every organization type. It supplies a standard method of describing, evaluating, planning, thinking, and developing the activities necessary to add value to the customers.[78] It is based on Osterwalder's book[79] and his later research on

[76] Drucker, P. (1994). *The theory of the business*. Books, Google.com,

[77] Fielt, E. (2014). Conceptualizing business models: Definitions, frameworks and classifications. *Journal of Business Models, 1*(1), 85–105.

[78] Osterwalder, A. Pigneur, Y., & Clark, T. (2010). *Business model generation*. Wiley, Hoboken, NJ.

[79] Osterwalder, A. (2004). *The business model ontology a proposition in a design science approach* (Doctoral dissertation), Université de Lausanne, Faculté des hautes études commerciales. Lausanne, Switzerland.

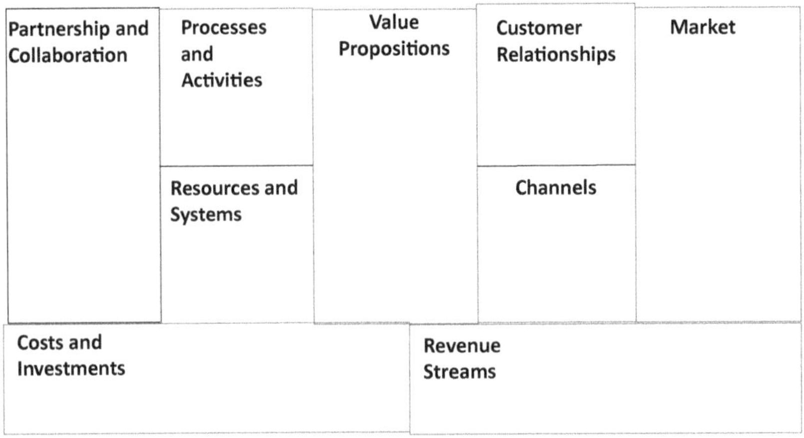

Fig. 2.2 Traditional business model canvas

business models.[80] This scholar supplies a template (a canvas) to define and explain business models easily. Ten building blocks compose it. Each one must be "answered," considering the specific organization. For this reason, it is critical to understand the meaning of each component of the canvas correctly. This book uses the business model canvas version, as changed by the Author (Fig. 2.3).[81]

The basic BMC is composed of ten segments. For a reminder reason, the components start with ten Ps.

- Proposition of Value or Products or Portfolio strategy
- Proximity with the Customer
- Partition of the Customers
- Place or Accesses
- Platforms and Resources
- Processes and activities
- Persons
- Partnerships

[80] Osterwalder, A. Pigneur, Y., & Tucci, C. L. (2005). Clarifying business models: Origins, present, and future of the concept. *Communications of the Association for Information Systems, 16*(1).

[81] Nicoletti, B. (2016). *Digital insurance.* Palgrave-Macmillan, London, UK.

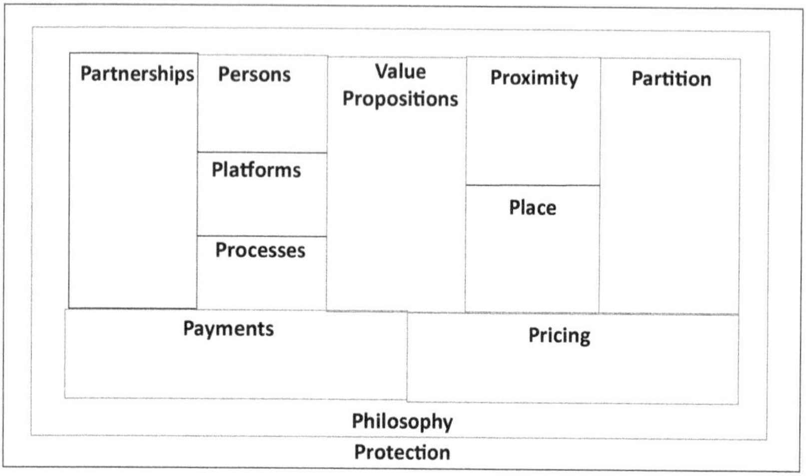

Fig. 2.3 Modified business model canvas

- Pricing and Revenues
- Payments for Costs and Investments.

There are two other Ps that are essential, even if not mentioned in the traditional business model canvas (Fig. 2.3).

- Philosophy—It should be the envelope of the business model canvas. Philosophy defines the long-term vision. The vision is related to business or management strategies.[82] This vision is what all organizations need to implement new initiatives, strategies, or solutions to be integrated with the existent business model or be aware and prepared in case of a disruption with the past. The business model canvas does not consider it explicitly. Certainly, it is essential since it is the integration of all the other components of the BMC in such a way to have a consistent strategy for the organization.

[82] Liker, J. (2004). *The Toyota way*. Esensi, San Francisco, CA.

- Protection. In the modern world, security is essential. It must be security by design.[83] Hence it should be part of the business model of the organization. It should wrap around the traditional BMC.

The remaining parts of this chapter analyze each component of the BMC.

Business Models Philosophy

Based on the earlier overview of the business model's components, it is interesting to consider the strategies designed for a business model and the possible competitive advantages. To this end, it helps to start with the concept of strategy.

"*A satisfied customer is the best business strategy of all.*"[84] A good strategy is firmly customer oriented. A robust organization achieves the same result by satisfying all aspects of a business, above all customer delight.[85]

The beginning of the modern study of strategy dates to the 1960s. There is still no unique definition of strategy. In general, the strategy is creating a unique and valuable position, involving a distinct set of activities.[86] From this definition, the strategy is nothing more than a set of critical actions to position the organization in the market and achieve a solid and sustainable competitive advantage. The concept is to diversify with the competitors so that the organization can keep and improve its position. What is needed is to introduce innovations that can attract more customers. On the other hand, when one organization successfully presents a change in the market, other organizations tend to replicate it. An organization must be good at planning its strategy. Even if the competitors imitate what it proposes, it should be able to always supply something more than the others or introduce a new strategy that supplies a sustainable competitive advantage.

[83] Geismann, J., Gerking, C., & Bodden, E. (2018, May). Towards ensuring security by design in cyber-physical systems engineering processes. In *Proceedings of the 2018 international conference on software and system process* (pp. 123–127).

[84] Panda, S., & Rao, K. S. N. (2019, October). Customer acquisition and retention in non-banking finance financial institutions (NBFC). *Journal of Mechanics and Continua and Mathematical Sciences, 14*(5). https://doi.org/10.26782/jmcms.2019.10.00045.

[85] Schneider, B., & Bowen, D. E. (1999). Understanding customer delight and outrage. *Sloan Management Review, 41*(1), 35–45.

[86] Porter, M. (1996). What is strategy. *Harvard Business Review, 74*(6), 61–78.

In this sense, Porter said that the essence of strategy formulation is "coping with competition."[87] Peter Drucker explains strategy through three assumptions[88]:

1. The environment in which position the organization.
2. The mission of the organization.
3. The core competencies needed to reach the mission.

Mintzberg defines strategy as a pattern in a stream of decisions.[89] Consequently, it is critical to define the goals of these decisions.

Porter introduced the concept of competitive advantage. Porter starts from the following basic premises.[90]

- "The nature of the competition is different among industries and even among the segments of the same industry."
- "In the globalization context, a country can offer different competitive benefits for an organization, depending on if it is an origin country or a host country."

Porter, with his five forces model, explains the functioning of the competition in the market. He supplies an essential basis for organizations to refer to, when necessary, develop the business strategy. The five forces are (Fig. 2.4)[91]:

1. The threat of new entrants depends on how high are the barriers to entry into a market. Some classic barriers to entry are:

[87] Porter, M. E. (1989). How competitive forces shape strategy. In *Readings in strategic management* (pp. 133–143). Palgrave Macmillan, London, UK.

[88] Drucker, P. (1994). *The theory of the business*. https://publicpurpose.com.au/wp-content/uploads/2016/05/Theory-of-the-Business-HBR-Sept1994.pdf. Accessed 20 April 2020.

[89] Mintzberg, H., & Waters, J. A. (1985). Of strategies, deliberate and emergent. *Strategic Management Journal, 6*(3), 257–272.

[90] Porter, M. E. (1990). *The competitive advantage of nations: With a new introduction*. Free Press, New York, NY.

[91] Porter, M. E. (2008). The five competitive forces that shape strategy. *Harvard Business Review, 86*(1), 25–40.

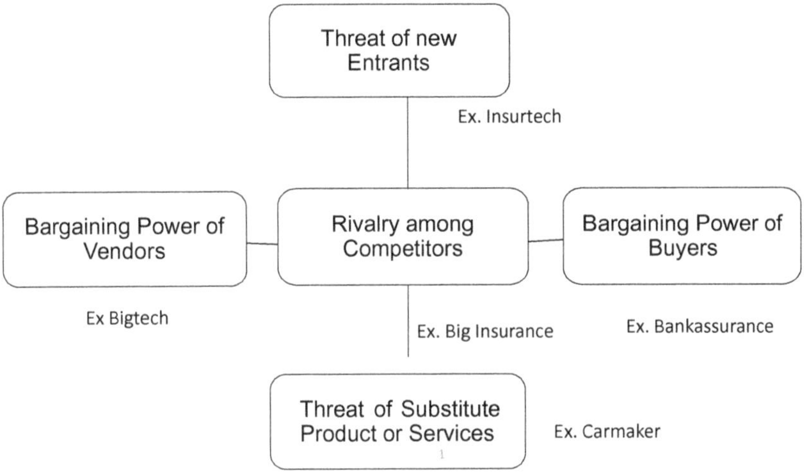

Fig. 2.4 Porter's five forces of competitive advantage for insurance

- Government policy.
- Regulations.
- Capital needs.
- Economies of scale.
- Product differentiation.
- Switching costs or sunk costs.
- Access to distribution.
- Customer loyalty to proven brands.[92]
- Industry profitability.

2. The threat of substitute products or services is about:

   - Buyer propensity to substitute.
   - Buyer switching costs.
   - Number of substitute products available in the market.

3. Regarding buyers' bargaining power, it is so much higher as the more options the buyers have.

[92] 75% consumers stay loyal to a brand even if they can get a better deal (Edelman Trust Barometer. [2020, November]. A Catalyst Known as COVID, Part III | Believe in Banking. Accessed 25 January 2021).

4. Bargaining power of vendors: the power of organizations is less when they have only one (or at least a few) vendor available.
5. The intensity of competitive rivalry. It decides the competitiveness of a market.

These are the factors that play an essential role in the achievement of competitive advantages[93]:

- Cost leadership: the goal is to become the lowest-cost producer in the industry (achieved by producing on a large scale).
- Cost focus: it is about a lower-cost specific advantage (for example with innovative solutions).
- Differentiation focus: by differentiating within just one or a small number of target market segments. Organizations that want to achieve this type of advantage must be sure that customers have diverse needs. It is a niche marketing strategy.
- Differentiation leadership: it is about charging a premium price that covers the added operational costs of a smaller production scale and gives customers clear motivations to prefer a product over the others.

Value Propositions

The customer value propositions (CVPs) represent the portfolio of the products and services that an organization offers to its customers in all their uses. Customer satisfaction, or better customer delight, is a critical component of the business model to make an organization successful. The customers generate revenues, but they do also words of mouth, thus bringing other customers, and should assure continuous supporting behavior to the organization.[94] A successful value proposition must be unique. It must be clear to the decision-makers. It is about conquering the customer, influencing his/her choice, taking him/her to choose

[93] Porter, M. E. (1985). Solution and competitive advantage. *The Journal of Business Strategy*, 5(3), 60.

[94] Hassan, A. (2012). The value proposition concept in marketing: How customers perceive the value delivered by firms. A study of customer perspectives on supermarkets in Southampton in the United Kingdom. *International Journal of Marketing Studies*, 4(3), 68.

a product or service rather than another.[95] This essential component serves to distinguish one brand from another. The CVP (customer value propositions) is about all those benefits that an organization promises to the customer when she/he chooses its service/product in exchange to his/her loyalty. It is critical to understand this concept and make value propositions an integral part of the business strategy. Without the economic return from the customer, an organization cannot last for long.

There are several indicators for measuring the customer delight, such as Customer Satisfaction Score (CSAT),[96] Customer Engagement Score (CES)[97], and Net Promoter Score (NPS).[98]

On the other side, the offer of products and services must assure value also to the organization. In this case, the margin is the measure of success.

N26

Valentin Stalf and Maximilian Tayenthal decided in 2013 that they wanted to disrupt the financial sector by offering banking services that follow you around wherever you go. They created a simple, transparent, and mobile banking solution. After one year and a half of development, in 2015, they introduced their first products in Germany and Austria. With the acquisition of a European banking license in 2016, they extended their business to several European Union countries and later to the USA. N26 became one of the most valued fintech organizations in Europe, with a valuation of £2.8 billion in 2019.[99] Their vision is to offer banking services that a customer can enjoy using all of them worldwide. The founders decided that their mobile bank should not be an institution that the community is obliged to use instead of a service that is provided to them. This approach helps their customers and make their lives easier.

[95] Zhang, T. C., Gu, H., & Jahromi, M. F. (2019). What makes the sharing economy successful? An empirical examination of competitive customer value propositions. *Computers in Human Behavior, 95*, 275–283.

[96] Mansoor, M., Awan, T. M., & Alobidyeen, B. (2020). Structure and measurement of customer experience management. *International Journal of Business and Administrative Studies, 6*(4), 171–182.

[97] Bexelius, E., & Diklev, J. (2020). Customer experience without customer contact: DSOs adapting to a supplier centric market: A multiple case study of Swedish DSOs.

[98] Ganesh, L. S. (2020). An overview of banking sector. In *Lean six sigma in banking services* (pp. 23–28). Springer, Singapore.

[99] Lehmann, S., & Nilsson, A. (2020). Make banking simple again: A multiple case-study about the internationalization of the largest online retail banks in Europe.

N26 has always been extremely passionate about customer delight. They are growing through being referenced by other customers. When they started, they focused first on customer delight and then on growth. For the first one year and a half after launching N26, they did not use any key performance indicator on monetary terms.[100] They claim that traditional banks outsource their platforms to ICT companies. They are an ICT organization that is also a fully licensed bank. They have an ultra-modern, cloud-hosted core banking system and do not rely on any legacy system.

Customer Proximity
This component of the BMC includes three essential aspects: the 3 Cs:

- Target Customer: for whom does the banking 5.0 initiative aim to create value?
- Competition: who are the competitors for the target customers?
- Compliance: Which are the rules the organization must respect?[101]

(1) Customers are the central components of an organization. They are specific types of persons, organizations, or financial institutions to whom propose products or services. The customer is the person who is willing to pay for the financial institution's services and products. It is critical to understand what type of products/services to develop, deliver during an organization's lifecycle, and include in an offering portfolio.

Customer proximity describes the relationships an organization sets up with specific customers and/or customers' segments. These relations impact distribution. Customer proximity strongly influences the overall customer journey (a key component of competitive advantage). Empathy is an essential component of customer proximity in services like banking.

Some questions necessary to define the right customer relationship are:

[100] www.mckinsey.com/business-functions/mckinsey-digital/our-insights/building-and-scaling-one-of-the-worlds-fastest-growing-mobile-banks?cid=other-eml-alt-mip-mck&hdpid=cf37cfab-0327-4dce-9213-c03e862cb942&hctky=9204549&hlkid=31d0489bd238481daa2361c8774c0735. Accessed 28 February 2021.

[101] Osterwalder, A., & Pigneur, Y. (2010). *Business model generation: A handbook for visionaries, game changers, and challengers*. Wiley, Chichester, UK.

- What type of relationship each customer or customer segment expects to set up with the organization, and how should this relationship continue over time?
- How expensive is the development and maintenance of the relationship?
- How and how much does this relationship integrate within the organization's business model?

Types of relationships could be[102]:

- Personal help refers to the interaction between the customer and a representative of the organization. The latter supplies customer support for any need during the sales process and after the sale. This type of interaction can occur physically at the point of sale (POS) or through physical or virtual channels, such as chats, emails, customer proximity centers, and so on.
- Long-term help means that long-lasting and even deep proximity exists between the organization and the customer. The organization interacts with the customer on a periodical basis and for the long term.
- Dedicated personal help refers to continuous interactions between the customer and a representative of the organization. In this case, the representative is always the same for the same customer. The relationship becomes more personal, and the customer has more trust, setting up a long-term relationship.
- Self-service allows customers to choose, buy, and use products and services without an employee's help. In addition to helping the customer, the self-service enables the organization to reduce the operating costs, but it loses customer proximity.
- Automated services are a more advanced form of self-service because there is a customization component. The customer's characteristics are detected, and based on these characteristics, specific information and support are provided.

[102] www.strategyzer.com. Accessed 9 March 2020.

- Communities are virtual multiple users which can talk with each other and exchange opinions and experiences about the products/services. To date, more organizations make these communities available to other persons, which is a way to know their customers.
- Co-creation requires the involvement and experience of the customer. It is an active, creative, and social process that involves customers in creating new products and services. For example, Amazon.com invites customers to write reviews.
- *Ad hoc* transactional basis is when there is no relationship between the organization and its customers, but only for specific transactions.

Switching costs show how easy or difficult it is for a customer to switch to a different alternative; It is contrary to lock-in, where the customer is tied to a financial institution:

The following motivations may drive customer proximity[103]:

- Customer acquisition.
- Customer retention.
- Boosting sales (up-selling or cross-selling).
- Customer loyalty programs.

(2) Competitors offer the same or comparable products or services within the same market sector.[104] The competition triggers a price lowering mechanism to increase the market share. Consequently, organizations must try to be more efficient in reducing their costs and improving quality.[105]

(3) Compliance shows that organizational behavior is consistent with the laws, internal business policies, procedures, and any other regulation.[106] Innovative solutions supply financial institutions with the

[103] Geib, M., Reichold, A., Kolbe, L., & Brenner, W. (2005, January). Architecture for customer relationship management approaches in financial services. In *Proceedings of the 38th annual Hawaii international conference on system sciences* (p. 240b). IEEE.

[104] Porter, E. M. (1990). *Competitive advantage of nations*. Macmillan, New York, NY.

[105] www.businessdictionary.com/definition/competitor.html. Accessed 30 May 2020.

[106] www.businessdictionary.com/definition/compliance.html. Accessed 30 May 2020.

possibility to free by the burdensome regulatory costs imposed by a fast-changing regulatory framework.[107]

Allstate[108]

For Allstate Business Insurance, Earley Information Science developed ABIe, a context-aware virtual assistant. It works through an online avatar (called "Abby") and provides Allstate agents with answers to questions.

Customer Partitions

To serve its customers better, an organization needs to segment its customers with a target of one customer segment.[109] Cluster analysis can help in this segmentation.[110] This analysis method creates groups that are homogeneous, that is, they have similar characteristics. Business-to-customers marketing organizations make the first segmentation based on a few necessary information: age, marital status, gender, and area of interest. Business-to-business marketing focuses on industry, the number of employees, products previously bought, and location. Customer groups stand for separate segments if[111]:

- Their needs justify different offers.
- The organization reaches them through a differentiated distribution.
- They need distinct types of relationships.
- They have different profitability.
- They are willing to pay for distinct characteristics of the offer.

To be able to define these characteristics, an organization must collect information from customers. Several methods are used for this scope:

[107] Dzhaparov, P. (2020). Application of blockchain and artificial intelligence in bank risk management. *Икономика и управление, 17*(1), 43–57.

[108] *KM World*. (2016, January). www.kmworld.com/Articles/Editorial/Features/Allstates-Intelligent-Agent-Reduces-Call-Center-Traffic--and-Provides-Help-During-Quoting-Process-108263.aspx. Accessed 10 January 2020.

[109] Ericson, R. V., Doyle, A., Barry, D., & Ericson, D. (2003). *Insurance as governance*. University of Toronto Press, Toronto, Canada.

[110] Romesburg, C. (2004). *Cluster analysis for researchers*. Lulu. Com.

[111] www.shopify.com/encyclopedia/customer-segmentation. Accessed 30 May 2020.

surveys, telephone interviews, face-to-face, and so on.[112] Big data analytics can help a lot with this segmentation.[113] Choosing a customer segment to serve is a scoping decision that helps organizations focus on customer opportunities most likely to generate success. The choice of the specific type of customers to serve is the first decision to be taken.

Place or Accesses

The distribution channels are the go through whereby an organization decides to supply its products and services to a specific customer type.[114] Depending on the type of customers, an organization can choose a specific distribution channel. The choice of access is pivotal in strategic marketing decisions. This choice affects the timing and costs of the distribution. It depends on several factors like[115]:

- Typology of target customers
- Type and size of the market
- Value proposition
- Type of products/nature of services and the need for support/interactions
- Type of operations
- Costs and benefits
- Competition
- Geography
- Culture.

The organization chooses accesses which should be flexible, efficient, economical, and consistent with the organization type. The goal in selecting an access is to reach as many customers as possible at the

[112] Sarstedt, M., & Mooi, E. (2014). A concise guide to market research. *The Process, Data, and, 12.*

[113] Salem, S. B., & Mansour, N. Examination of Big Data Analytics and customer segmentation in the banking sector: Learning for BNP Paribas Bank of France. In *Econder 2020 3rd international economics, business and social sciences congress* (p. 283).

[114] McDonald, M., & Wilson, H. (2016). *Marketing plans: How to prepare them, how to profit from them.* Wiley, Hoboken, NJ.

[115] Müller-Lankenau, C., Wehmeyer, K., & Klein, S. (2006). Strategic channel alignment: An analysis of the configuration of physical and virtual marketing channels. *Information Systems and e-Business Management, 4*(2), 187–216.

lowest possible cost. Online accesses are more used for their interesting characteristics.[116]

Platforms and Resources

Platforms and resources are critical assets of an organization. They are the resources (physical and non-physical) a financial institution needs to run its banking, keep relations with the different customers' segments, earn revenues, and build a valid value proposition. The essential resources can be of four types: physical, intellectual, personal, and financial[117]:

- Physical resources are the most natural resources to find. Tangible resources can be equipment, inventory, buildings, and operational or service locations.
- Intellectual resources have a value higher than physical ones. Brands are one of the essential resources of organizations. There are other intangible resources like banking and market knowledge, brands, copyrights, patents, and solution competencies in addition to the trademarks.
- Person resources refer to employees and contractors who are the engine of each organization.
- Financial resources include funds, cash, lines of credit, and stocks, including stock option plans for employees.

The organization must answer the following question:

- What are the essential resources the organization's value propositions/distribution accesses/customer proximity/revenue streams require?

Platforms are how to enhance the resources. They are both information and communication platforms and automation support.

[116] Soopramanien, D. G., & Robertson, A. (2007). Adoption and usage of online shopping: An empirical analysis of the characteristics of buyers, browsers and non-internet shoppers. *Journal of Retailing and Customer Services*, *14*(1), 73–82.

[117] www.cleverism.com/key-resources-building-block-in-business-model-canvas/. Accessed 20 October 2020.

Essential Processes and Activities

The essential processes are a set of interrelated activities carried out within the organization that creates value for the customers and the organization. They contribute to building customer proximity. Depending on the type of business model, the activities are different. While defining these activities, an organization should consider:

- Value propositions.
- Customer proximity.
- Place and Distribution accesses.
- Characteristics of the marketing, operations, and support.
- Revenue, costs, and investments streams.

The essential activities create a bridge between value propositions and customer partitions' needs. Some types of crucial activities engaged by the organizations are:

- Research & Development (R&D) is commonly used to describe all the activities an organization performs to create new processes/products/services or improve current ones.[118] R&D's typical functions are a new product and process development, current product and process updates, quality assurance, and innovation.
- The marketing department of an organization plays an essential role in its growth and promotion.[119] By managing various promotional activities and coordination, the financial institution can attract more customers (or investors). It can increase its market share. Depending on the portfolio of products/services offered by an organization, the marketing function may include different activities, such as designing and preparing promotional materials, checking and managing social media, producing external and internal communications, conducting campaign management for marketing initiatives, and so on.

[118] Hall, B. H. (2006). *Contribution to the international encyclopedia of the social sciences* (2nd ed.).

[119] Epetimehin, F. M. (2011). Achieving competitive advantage in insurance industry: The impact of marketing innovation and creativity. *Journal of Emerging Trends in Economics and Management Sciences, 2*(1), 18–21.

- A systematic approach to sales involves a series of steps that enable a sales force to close deals, increase revenue and margin contribution, and make more sales through referrals.[120] The series of steps are customer-centric and help a financial institution's sales force keep customers and increase sales volumes and revenues. A sales process involves six steps: prospecting, qualifying, proposal presentation, handling negotiations, closing, and follow-up for repeat business.[121]
- The operational activities create value for the customer through the production of the products or services. Operations are a process that transforms inputs into outputs. This process is composed of person, machinery, virtual activities, and so on. Operations is a value addition process. Every operational activity must add value or be necessary for regulatory reasons.[122] Classical activities related to this function are selecting product, design, and operations processes, selecting the right operations ability, operations scheduling and planning, operations, quality, cost, and inventory controls, maintenance, and replacement or disposition of assets and systems.

Partnerships and Collaboration

Partnerships are the network of equity and capital vendors, suppliers, and intermediaries that make the business model work. A collaborative relationship between two or more organizations (irrespective of their size or how long they are on the market) that want to carry out joint projects or complement each other is essential in the business model.[123] A contract typically defines the partner relationship. From an economic point of view, the contract specifies how much each partner contributes to the costs and receives in earnings percentage.[124] When considering a partnership, the

[120] www.nasp.com/article/D6BC485A-B705/how-to-define-a-sales-process-for-sales-success.html. Accessed 29 December 2019.

[121] Viio, P., & Grönroos, C. (2014). Value-based sales process adaptation in business relationships. *Industrial Marketing Management, 43*(6), 1085–1095.

[122] www.newagepublishers.com. Accessed 30 May 2020.

[123] Example of collaboration between two or more organizations. https://florencedouglascenter.org/rocky-river/example-of-collaboration-between-two-or-more-organizations.php. Accessed 30 May 2020.

[124] www.businessdictionary.com. Accessed 20 April 2020.

starting point is the services that such an agreement can bring to the business. The possible benefits connected with a partnership are[125]:

- Bridging the gap in ability, knowledge, and experiences. Collaborating with other parties can supply a broader range of knowledge to various parts of the organization.
- Bringing the availability of cash and investments into the organizations.
- Allowing one financial institution to share the financial burden for expenses and capital expenditures needed to run a business. This situation could result in considerable savings.
- Affording the ease and flexibility to start banking opportunities. It could reduce the downside of opportunity costs.[126]
- Bringing new perspectives, vision, and culture can help an organization complement what they have or even replace it. A partnership can simplify the competitive environment or bring new customers, markets, and services.

It is possible to set up diverse types of partnerships[127]:

- A general partnership involves many partners, all equally active in the management, earnings, and expenses. If only one of the partners is liable, everyone else must contribute. It is precisely for this reason that this type of partnership is the least used.
- A limited partnership is a mix of general partners and limited partners. The latter has limited participation in comparison to the other partnerships.
- A limited liability partnership (LLP) is a mix between general partnership and corporation. All partners have a limited responsibility regarding losses, omissions, negligence, incompetence, or malpractices committed by other partners or by their employees.

[125] www.americanexpress.com/us/small-business/openforum/articles. Accessed 20 April 2020.

[126] What Are the Advantages and Disadvantages of a Partnership? www.americanexpress.com/en-us/business/trends-and-insights/articles/what-are-the-advantages-and-disadvantages-of-a-partnership/. Accessed 4 January 2021.

[127] www.thebalancesmb.com/selecting-a-business-partnership-398880. Accessed 20 April 2020.

- A joint venture, or temporary groupings or associations of enterprises, is typically a partnership of different businesses. It is set up for a specific purpose (like making a special deal) or for a limited time.

The components to consider when deciding whether an organization wants to make a partnership or not are[128]:

- Key partners.
- Types of partners.
- Key services.
- Essential resources or knowledge that an organization can pool with the partners.
- Key activities that a partner can perform.
- Key markets on which it might be possible to enter.
- Key competitors in the market space.
- Customer portfolio.
- Key investments possible.

Pricing and Revenues

This business model component describes the organization's earnings from selling products or services to the customers. The variables to be considered are the prices (fixed or dynamic) and the methods of payment. These are two essential aspects to make the business model sustainable. Revenue streams may be different and be generated from varied sources: from the sale of products to the payment of a fee, from the transfer of a license to brokerage commissions. At this stage of the business model definition, an organization can find customers' preferred payment systems. Revenue streams are in two categories[129]:

- Transaction revenue is a one-time payment for the product or provision of a service.

[128] www.uwplatt.edu/files/entrepreneurship/Businesspercent20Modelpercent20Canvaspercent20Explainedpercent20Handout.docx. Accessed 30 May 2020.

[129] https://expertprogrammanagement.com/2012/01/types-of-revenue-streams/. Accessed 19 November 2020.

- Recurring revenue is an on-going payment provided to the organization.

The following questions should have an answer[130]:

- What benefits are customers now paying for?
- What benefits will convince customers to pay more for the organization's products and services?
- How are they paying for these benefits?
- What mode of payment would they prefer?
- What percentage of the total revenue is each revenue stream?

Payments for Costs and Investments

This business model canvas component defines the fixed and variable costs and the investments that the financial institution must support for the essential resources, activities, and partnerships. This component can be defined in smaller units, such as by-product, service, product line, customer, cost center, or geographic region.[131] For specific organizations, cost reduction may be an essential aspect, mainly if one of the financial institution's goals is to offer competitive prices.

The cost structure concept is a management accounting concept.[132] The critical components of the cost structures are[133]:

- Product cost structure

  Fixed costs: Direct labor, operations overhead, general management dedicated to a product.
  Variable costs: Direct costs, commissions, operations supply, and piece-rate wages.

[130] Revenue Streams in Business Model Canvas. www.cleverism.com/revenue-streams-in-business-model-canvas/. Accessed 30 May 2020.

[131] Cost structure. Accounting Tools. www.accountingtools.com/articles/what-is-cost-structure.html. Accessed 30 May 2020.

[132] www.accountingtools.com/articles/what-is-cost-structure.html. Accessed 15 April 2020.

[133] Cost structure definition—Accounting Tools. www.accountingtools.com/articles/what-is-cost-structure.html. Accessed 20 March 2021.

- Service cost structure

  Fixed costs: Administrative overhead.
  Variable costs: Staff wages, bonuses, payroll taxes, travel, and entertainment.

- Product line cost structure

  Fixed costs: Administrative overhead, operations overhead, and direct labor.
  Variable costs: Direct materials, commissions, and operations supplies.

- Customer cost structure

  Fixed costs: Administrative overhead for customer service and credits.
  Variable costs: Costs of products and services sold to the customer, product returns, credits taken, and advance payment discounts.

Protection
Protection is the set of safety and security measures to protect the organizations from risks, external attacks, and dangers. There is a saying, "expect the unexpected," and that phrase takes some specific meaning regarding organizations. It is necessary to cover the organization from losses. Insurance is a way to get protection from a financial point of view. It is also critical to protect all the assets of the organization. This book will not consider the most important protection: the one for the persons. So, safety is not included. The remaining assets must also be protected. While the industrial revolutions have changed the organizations completely, new types of protections have become important. Cyber security takes care of the protection of computers, the internet, and other resources.

Business Model and Banking 5.0

The banking world is too varied to build one business model capable of fitting each of the organizations included in that definition. The value proposition, the market, the culture, and the structure of revenues and costs are distinctive aspects of every organization. This chapter does not discuss them. Figure 2.5 shows an example of a business model canvas

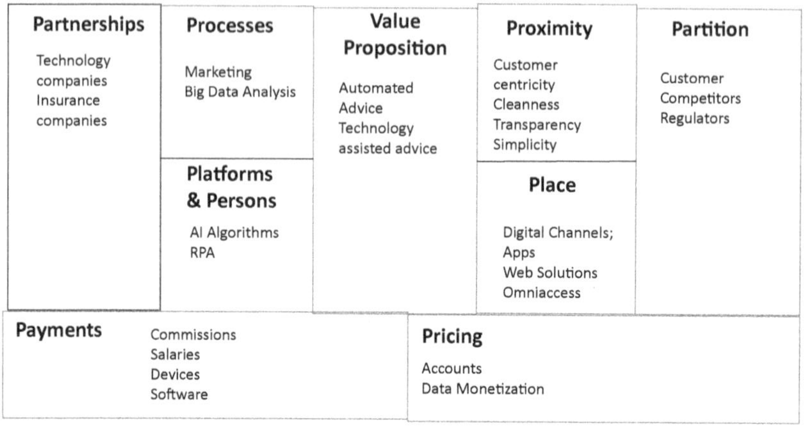

Fig. 2.5 Business model in a fintech organizations (example)

for a financial institution. Banking and fintech organizations have several points in common. Although the former's economic base usually is significantly higher than the one of the latter, fintech organizations are the Darwinian evolution of banking.[134]

The business model canvas aims to supply any banking organization with general and practical guidelines for being a successful organization. This banking 5.0 approach is important for prospering and even surviving due to the drivers that can disrupt the banking industry (Fig. 2.5)[135]:

- Poor engagement: "Financial institutions have struggled to engage prospective customers and nurture proximity with current ones. The product purse high customer interest but low engagements, leading to significant untapped demand."[136] The whole industry's low digitization does not match the new types of expectations, especially

[134] Darwin, C. (2004). *On the origin of species, 1859*. Routledge, London, UK.

[135] www.mckinsey.com/~/media/mckinsey/industries/financialpercent20services/our percent20insights/timepercent20forpercent20insurancepercent20financialinstitutionspe rcent20topercent20facepercent20digitalpercent20reality/digital-disruption-in-insurance.ashxx. Accessed 30 May 2020.

[136] Nicoletti, B. (2017). A business model for Insurtech initiatives. In *The future of FinTech* (pp. 211–249). Palgrave Macmillan, Cham, Switzerland.

by the new generation of customers, such as the millennials or the Generation Y.[137]

- Legacy cost and investment structures: New start-ups can deliver cutting-edge propositions without incurring transformation as the incumbent organizations.
- Legacy ICT (Information and Communication Technologies) systems: The rigidity of the banking processes and systems goes together with old methods and ICT systems. The combination of legacy cost structures and legacy ICT systems has caused financial institutions' total expense ratio to decline by more than 0.5% points (2000–2013) in several European markets.[138]
- Risk aversion. The banking industry has often been static, hostile to change and innovation: high product development cycles, low ICT investments, and slow delivery decisions have been severe bottlenecks for many financial institutions trying to prosper or at least survive.[139]

As the first step, it is interesting to position the four issues listed before into the business model canvas's associated components. This macro-area of the business model affects (positively or negatively) the case considered (Fig. 2.6). The figure can supply insights into the factors that have or could create difficulties for the whole sector. If it is possible to single out the adverse factors, it should be possible to find the possible remediation.

Benefits and Challenges of Business Model

Though the banking industry has been one of the slowest sectors in adopting digital transformation, the digitization process significantly affects financial institutions. It forces them to radically change corporate culture, services and procedures, customer relationships, and relations with the sector's various stakeholders and competitors. Still, too few

[137] Brodmann, J., Rayfield, B., Hassan, M. K., & Mai, A. T. (2018). Banking characteristics of millennials. *Journal of Economic Cooperation & Development, 39*(4), 43–73.

[138] Average expense ratio (expense per GWP) from 2000 to 2013; unweighted average expense ratios of Austria, Belgium, France, Germany, Ireland, Italy, Netherlands, Portugal, Spain, Sweden, and the United Kingdom (McKinsey Global Insurance Pools).

[139] Nicoletti, B. (2017). A business model for Insurtech initiatives. In B. Nicoletti (Ed.), *The future of Fintech* (pp. 211–249). Palgrave Macmillan, Cham.

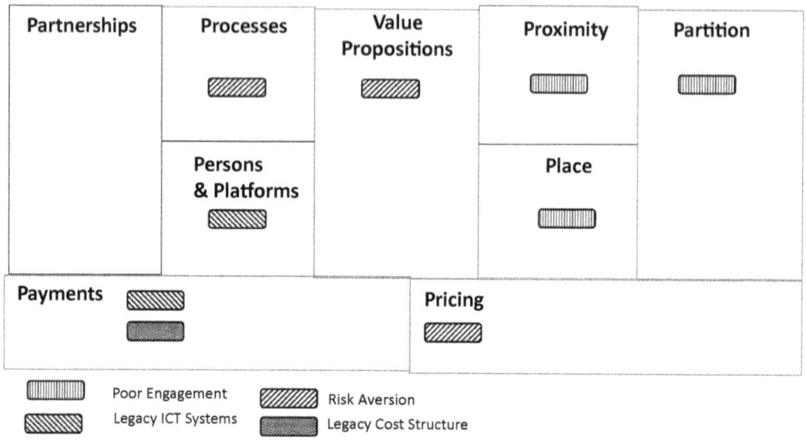

Fig. 2.6 Traditional financial institutions issues

financial institutions are working on updating their business model with a fundamental digital transformation. This book has the goal to change this situation. This attitude is already changing. 42.62% of surveyed financial institutions said they have permanently changed their strategy after the pandemic.[140] Several papers and studies try to investigate the impact of banking digitization.[141] There is some analysis of the strategic implications of innovative solutions on cost structures, banking

[140] www.thefinanser.com/wp-content/uploads/2020/12/The_Omniaccess_Future.pdf. Accessed 4 January 2021.

[141] Segev, I., & Vickers, A. (2017). *What the new world of insurance could look like*. McKinsey and Financial Institution. www.mckinsey.com/business-functions/mckinsey-digital/our-insights/digital-blog/what-the-new-world-of-insurance-could-look-like. Accessed 26 February 2020. Muller, F., Naujoks, H., Singh, H., Schwarz, G., Schwedel, A. et al. (2015). Global digital insurance benchmarking report. Bain and Financial Institution. McKinsey. (2016). *Making digital strategy a reality in insurance*. www.mckinsey.com/business-functions/mckinsey-digital/our-insights/making-digital-strategy-a-reality-in-insurance. Accessed 26 February 2020. Willis Towers Watson. (2017). New horizon: How diverse growth strategies can advance digitization in the insurance industry.

processes,[142] customer delight,[143] person resources,[144] and newly emerging risks.[145]

Banking 5.0 transformation will profoundly modify the financial and banking ecosystem, impacting all banking value network activities, from product development to credit scoring/pricing, sales and distribution, policy and credits management, and asset and risk management.[146] The new banking 5.0 scenario can enable traditional financial institutions to set up or become part of unique ecosystems generated by the development of connections among traditionally separated sectors and new partners and competitors.

Conclusions

This chapter presents the revolutions in banking, along with the five industrial revolutions. This chapter presents a model for industry 5.0 and its application in the case of banking 5.0.

[142] Kpmg (2019). Insurtech 10: Trend for 2019. EY. (2018). Can commercial financial institutions transform, cut costs and accelerate growth?

[143] Larsson, A., & Broström, E. (2019). Banking customer retention: Financial institutions' perception of customer loyalty. Market. *Intelligent Planning*. https://doi.org/10.1108/mip-02-2019-0106. Moneta, A. (2014). The customer-centric financial institution in the digital era. *Accenture White Paper*.

[144] Johansson, S., & Vogelgesang, U. (2015). Insurance on the threshold of digitization: Implications for the life and P&C Workforce. *McKinsey and C. Whitepaper.*

[145] Singh, A., & Akhilesh, K. B. (2020). The insurance industry-cyber security in the hyper-connected age. In K. Akhilesh & D. Möller (Eds.), *Smart technologies* (pp. 201–219). Springer, Singapore. Egan, R., Cartagena, S., Mohamed, R., Gosrani, V., Grewal, J., Acharyya, M., Dee, A., Bajaj, R., Jaeger, V. J., Katz, D., & Meghen, P. (2019). Cyber operational risk scenarios for insurance financial institutions. *British Actuarial Journal, 24*, 1–34. https://doi.org/10.1017/s1357321718000284. Biener, C., Eling, M., & Wirfs, J. H. (2015). Insurability of cyber risk: An empirical analysis. *Geneva Papers Risk Insurance-Issues Practice, 40*, 131–158. https://doi.org/10.1057/g2014.19.

[146] Eling, M., & Lehmann, M. (2018). The impact of digitization on the insurance value chain and the insurability of risks. *The Geneva Papers on Risk and Insurance. Issues and Practice, 43*, 359–396. https://doi.org/10.1057/s41288-017-0073-0.

CHAPTER 3

Business Model Philosophy in Banking 5.0

Vision without execution is just hallucination.
Henry Ford

Introduction

Ernst & Young surveyed in 2019 several Swiss financial institutions.[1] Most of the banks were convinced that a fundamental structural change has begun in the financial industry. In 2007, 73% were of this opinion. The figure was 88% in 2019 and very likely much more in 2020+. Most banks (60%) agree that the most significant lever for profitable income growth is improved customer focus. Twenty-five of the surveyed banks believe that the key is product-centric measures such as bundling different services (19%). This thesis is at the base of this book, which strongly believes that financial institutions must review their customer focus and business models.

The survey showed different opinions about the most critical levers for profitable income growth. Customer experience (17%), increasing the conversion rate through better customer understanding (13%), and the systematization of customer acquisition, development, and retention (30%) can be grouped in a single category as a customer-centric lever.

[1] Ernst & Young. (2020). *Ey-banking_barometer_2020* (EY Report).

B. Nicoletti, *Banking 5.0*, Palgrave Studies in Financial Services Technology, https://doi.org/10.1007/978-3-030-75871-4_3

Regional banks (75%) and cantonal banks (69%) want to place a stronger emphasis on customer interests going forward.

Customer focus means increasing value creation for the customers. Recent research has found business model innovation and design as critical tools in implementing organizational strategy.[2] This book uses the business model canvas, as introduced by Osterwalder[3] and applies it to banking 5.0.

Digital transformation shows the changes in the business model associated with digital solutions in all aspects of society.[4] There are four essential dimensions in a digital transformation: technologies, value creation changes, structural changes, and financial aspects.[5]

This chapter focuses on the application of banking 5.0 transformation to financial institutions. The approach is general, covering the entire business model. It underlines the relevance of three features in this banking 5.0 transformation[6]:

- Light touch processes structured to be changeable rather than rigidly fixed.
- Flexible infrastructure that allows for continuous flows and configurability of process flows.
- Mindful actors to define the business models, evaluate them, and take actions based on the relevant context.

This book considers business model innovations according to the classification proposed by Edward.[7] This author divided business model

[2] Pfeffermann, N., Minshall, T., & Mortara, L. (Eds.). (2013). *Strategy and communication for innovation*. Springer, New York, NY.

[3] Osterwalder, A., Pigneur, Y., Oliveira, M. A. Y., & Ferreira, J. J. P. (2011). Business model generation: A handbook for visionaries, game changers and challengers. *African Journal of Business Management, 5*(7), 22–30.

[4] it.wikipedia.org/wiki/Trasformazione_digitale, Accessed 30 May 2020.

[5] Matt, C., Hess, T., & Benlian, A. (2015). Digital transformation strategien. *Business & Information Systems Engineering, 57*(5), 339–343.

[6] Baiyere, A., Salmela, H., & Tapanainen, T. (2020). Digital transformation and the new logics of business process management. *European Journal of Information Systems*, 1–22.

[7] Edward, G., Berman. S., Bell, R., & Blitz, A. (2007). Three ways to successfully innovate your business model. *Strategy and Leadership, 35*(6), 27–33.

innovation into efficient business model innovation and novel business model innovation. The former refers to redesigning content, design, and governance elements to reduce overall costs and improve efficiency. The latter refers to the generation of creative content, structure, and governance of the system with changes to the existing business model. Most of the book is devoted to the latter type of innovation.

According to a McKinsey Global Survey, 99% of executives claimed that they had pursued a large-scale transformation in the past two years.[8] While doing so, many executives experienced cultural and talent gaps and weak partnerships between ICT and the rest of the business. Overcoming these issues requires financial institutions to reskill persons, reset culture, produce closer ICT–business relationships, and rigorously measure innovations' value-added capabilities.

Digital Transformation

Many scholars have tried to explain the impacts of a digital transformation in organizations.[9] Dehning et al. defined some criteria about this phenomenon, based on the organizational function/process impacted[10]:

- Business capabilities, processes, and relationships.
- Acquisitions.
- ICT uses in internal and external processes.

[8] www.mckinsey.com/business-functions/mckinsey-digital/our-insights/managing-the-fallout-from-solution-transformations?cid=other-eml-alt-mip-mck&hlkid=bf4d7318cabc44d99ce3ad00689ae9fc&hctky=2743882&hdpid=eac0bc3c-8635-4f36-a0ed-4322b51bbc6a. Accessed 9 March 2020.

[9] Lucas, H. C., Agarwal, R., Clemons, E. K., El Sawy, O. A., & Weber, B. (2013). Impactful research on transformational information solution: An opportunity to inform new audiences. *MIS Quarterly*.

[10] Dehning, B., Richardson, V. J., & Zmud, R. W. (2003). The value relevance of announcements of transformational information solution investments. *MIS Quarterly*.

The so-called digital (r)evolution[11] is often (but not only) implemented through digitization.[12] It is "the ability to turn current products or services into digital variants and offer benefits over tangible products."[13] This situation took place in the media industry. It experienced a digital shift with the dematerialization from physical products to online products. Internet and social networks enable direct access to potential customers and strengthen ties with current customers. Digital transformation has an organizational impact on persons. Job roles evolve in line with the change of activities. Decision-makers must consider the evolution and, in some cases, the revolution on knowledge and competencies connected with a digital transformation.[14]

When working on digital transformation, it helps consider the experiences done by other organizations. Some statistics are impressive. According to a McKinsey study, the rate of change is "unprecedented."[15] Eighty percent of the financial institutions in a survey have started a path in this direction over the last few years. Fifty percent believe they will have to change even more by 2023. In the motor, engineering, and aerospace sectors, 85% of respondents expect innovative solutions based on Artificial intelligence (AI), the internet of things, and data-driven business models to completely transform their businesses.

[11] Cappiello, A. (2020). The digital (r)evolution of insurance business models. *American Journal of Economics and Business Administration*. https://doi.org/10.3844/ajebasp.2020.

[12] Dapp, T., Slomka, L., AG, D. B., & Hoffmann, R. (2014). Fintech—The digital (r)evolution in the financial sector. *Deutsche Bank Research*, 1–39.

[13] Gassmann, O., Frankenberger, K., & Csik, M. (2014). *The St. Gallen business model navigator*. www.im.ethz.ch/education/HS13/MIS13/Business_Model_Navigator.pdf. Accessed 3 January 2020.

[14] Kohli, R., & Johnson, S. (2011). Digital transformation in latecomer industries: CIO and CEO leadership lessons from Encana Oil & Gas (USA) Inc. *MIS Quarterly Executive, 10*(4), 141–156; Liu, D. (2012). Competitive business model in audio-book industry: A case of China. *Journal of Software, 7*(1), 33–40.

[15] McKinsey. (2018, October). Unlocking success in digital transformations. *McKinsey White Paper*.

Digital Transformation Architecture

Digital transformation is not limited to the adoption of innovative solutions.[16] Digital transformation is a change in the corporate culture and the definition of an innovative business model. The digital transformation consists in a radical shift in the organizations, from processes and information flows to business models that fully exploit the opportunities offered by innovative solutions, distribution, media, and communication accesses. It is a radical change that impacts the entire organization. It needs a robust approach, a rigorous method, and proper application tools. It requires a long-term vision and an in-depth analysis of the short, medium, and long terms steps that the organization should take. Without a redesign of the business model, there is a danger to using these extraordinary means in a much less efficient, effective, and economical way than their potential.[17]

The implementation of innovative solutions is not sufficient to ensure the success of the organization. It is vital to redesign the basis of the business model, adapting it to the digital age customers and regulations. It is necessary to imagine a new organization able to capture the opportunities that digital transformation makes available. This process must cover every aspect of the organization, from the organization chart to the corporate culture, from the business model to the leadership style, starting with the financial institution's vision and culture.

In a VUCA world (Volatile, Unpredictable, Complex, and Ambiguous), financial institutions need to rethink how they interact with digital solutions to overcome environmental challenges and exploit market opportunities.[18] An example is that some organizations mix different generations of personnel to create a digital knowledge pool with experienced resources. This approach can change the organization's whole culture and amplify how persons work in teams, both with internal staff and partners.

[16] Why Digital Transformation Matters. www.bons.io/blog/why-digital-transformation-matters. Accessed 20 June 2020.

[17] www.hyphen-italia.com/cosa-significa-trasformazione-digitale/. Accessed 30 May 2020.

[18] www.mindtools.com/pages/article/managing-vuca-world.htm. Accessed 4 March 2020.

Lucas et al. propose seven specific dimensions for describing a digital transformation: change in processes, creation of new organizations, change in relationships, change in user experience, change in markets, change in the number of customers, and disruptive impact. A solution must affect three or more of these dimensions to be transformational.[19]

For succeeding in the digital transformation, it is essential to have clear what it means, and the goals in the specific organization and status examined. Digital transformation can impact the whole ecosystem. The impacts in operational processes can be of two types[20]:

- Transformation of processes necessary for exploiting innovative solutions: digitization creates the opportunity to transform the organization, both in user experience and business model.
- Organizations can decide to undertake the digitization of a specific process in full.

The Altimeter Group, referring to organizations that have made or are making efforts to implement the digital transformation, states that the first and most significant goal is to supply a better digital customer journey. It is about "the realignment of, or new investment in, solutions and business models to more effectively engage digital customers."[21] Digital transformations require to rethink how to connect with the customers, offering an experience aligned with their needs. Customers now have more information on banking services than in the past, at least in some cases. They can use and compare many sources with increasing ease. They know the characteristics of the services and the competition. They buy with a higher awareness than in the past. The phases of the banking process previously occurred at separate times and through different accesses. There is now an immersion in an almost continuous process that takes place

[19] Lucas, H. C., Agarwal, R., Clemons, E. K., El Sawy, O. A., & Weber, B. (2013). Impactful research on transformational information solution: An opportunity to inform new audiences. *MIS Quarterly, 37*(2), 371–382.

[20] Henriette, E., Feki, M., & Boughzala, I. (2015). Information systems: In a changing economy and society. *MCIS Proceedings*.

[21] Solis, B., Li, C., & Szymanski, J. (2014). Digital transformation: Why and how financial institutions are investing in new business model to *Lead Digital Customer Experience, Altimeter Group* (2014). www.altimetergroup.com/disclosure. Accessed 12 December 2019.

more in the virtual world.[22] When it is not closed in the digital environment, the customer needs consistency and continuity across all accesses. An omnichannel, or omniaccess, approach should supply this feature.[23]

According to Accenture, digital is re-imagining the person's experience.[24] It is remaking how persons live, work, play, and connect. Everything is being rethought, simplified, and improved, even what persons have taken for granted in the past. Digital transformation is revolutionary in the face of life in all its aspects. It is a model that can potentially bring significant benefits for organizations and to persons. It is challenging, requiring a considerable effort from individuals who were used to different processes, streams, and work activities before the advent of digitization.

Similarly, and especially after the pandemic, many things have changed: sociality, connection with persons, trends, ways of working, and so on. The innovative solutions have become part of life in a brief time and without realizing it, changing their habits thoroughly. Through the mobile network, persons are in continuous connection with the rest of the world. With a mobile phone, it is possible to access information everywhere and share thoughts and communication with friends, contacts, and anyone interested. A revolution of this size results in a parallel change in customer manners and product usage. It is precisely the realignment toward new and increased customer expectations, which is the primary driver of the digital transformation in banking.

The digital transformation can generate fresh players to create markets that did not exist before. These new realities are born out of business opportunities made possible from innovative solutions and creative approaches.

The success of a digital transformation can come from providing a better user experience for the digital customer through realignment and investment in solutions and banking models to engage more effectively,

[22] https://docplayer.it/6872-La-trasformazione-digitale-aggiungere-tecnologia-al-business-per-ottenere-l-effettomoltiplicatore.html. Accessed 30 May 2020.

[23] Juaneda-Ayensa, E., Mosquera, A., & Sierra Murillo, Y. (2016). Omnichannel customer behavior: Key drivers of solution acceptance and use and their effects on purchase intention. *Frontiers in psychology*, *7*, 1117.

[24] www.accenture.com/t20160128t000639__w__/us-en/_acnmedia/accenture/conversion-assets/dotcom/documents/global/pdf/solution_7/accenture-interactive-digital-transformation.pdf. Accessed 12 December 2019.

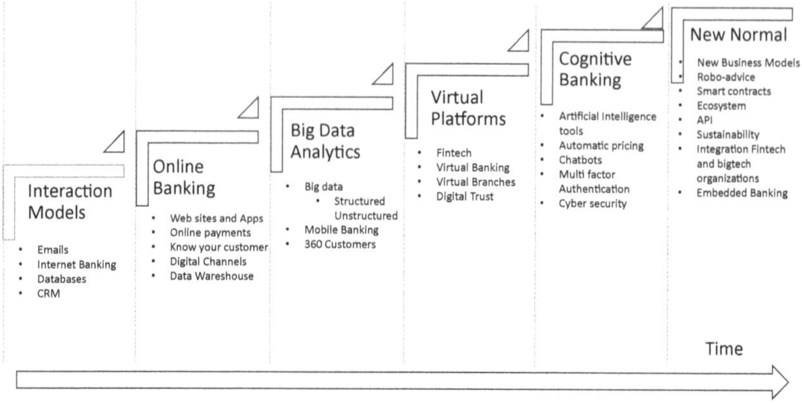

Fig. 3.1 Digital banking evolution

efficiently, and economically with the customer at every touchpoint in the customer journey.[25] One of the first reasons for digital transformation is the need to rethink the interactions with the customer. A customer journey must align with his/her expectations formed in the daily and almost continuous use of innovations. It changes rapidly, and that changes how the customers interpret the services they use.

In this digital age, customers are much more aware of the characteristics of the product/service they are interested in. They often know the competing products/services. This trend leads organizations to revise their marketing strategies completely. It was possible to push a sale by talking to the customer and showing the products and services available, in the past. Online interactions cannot easily replicate this type of selling approach. It is necessary to find new ways to convince the customer to buy. Efforts can no longer be directed only to increase customer awareness concerning banking services or make them accessible online. They must be able to catch customer interest through an ever-increasing social and economic approach and journey.

The development of digital banking follows a certain number of stages (Fig. 3.1)[26]:

[25] Edelman, D. C., & Singer, M. (2015). Competing on customer journeys. *Harvard Business Review, 93*(11), 88–100.

- Digital banking initially meant essentially emails, internet banking, databases, and CRM.
- The second digital banking phase refers to Web sites and apps, online payments, Know your customer, digital accesses, and data warehouse.
- The third phase of digital banking was to move to big data (both structured and unstructured data), mobile banking, and 360 customers' interactions.
- The fourth phase of digital banking was characterized by fintech banking, virtual banks, virtual branches, and digital trust.
- The fifth phase of digital banking will be based on AI, automatic pricing, chatbots, multifactor authentication. cybersecurity, and robot process automation.
- The sixth phase (to come) will be based on new business models supported by robo-advisors, smart contracts, ecosystems, APIs, integration with fintech and bigtech organizations, and embedded banking.

This book examines these last two phases. In most of the cases, it will require a jump of two or three of the phases described.

Digital Transformation in Banking 5.0

The banking 5.0 digital transformation depends on AI solutions. They are reaching more in-depth into the work environment, replacing, and augmenting mundane jobs, and changing or augmenting those that stay. On the other side, less than half of machine learning (ML) models make it to production; and if they do, it is often a lengthy process.[27] Consequently, it is essential to follow a rigorous project method in introducing AI in financial institutions.

[26] Mat Rahim, A. R., Mohamad, Z. Z., Abu Bakar, J., Mohsin, F. H., & Md Isa, N. (2018). Artificial intelligence, smart contract and Islamic finance. *Asian Social Science, 14*(2), 145.

[27] Gartner. (2020). *Debunking myths and misconceptions about artificial intelligence, 2021* (Gartner Report).

There are three significant transformation models in a successful financial institution-wide digital transformation[28]:

- Stepwise. Transforming to a banking 5.0 organization can appear as a step into the dark for senior management. This transformation model is the most common. Many organizations run multiple rounds of pilots and iterations before fully committing to scaling up across the organization's entire or substantial parts.
- Big bang. An increasing number of organizations get firm convictions on going on with a complete digital transformation.[29] They fully commit upfront to move the whole organization into banking 5.0.
- Emergent. It is impossible to plan a banking 5.0 transformation in detail from the start. Most banking 5.0 roadmaps have innovative approaches. Some organizations have chosen to implement their entire transformation through an agile, dynamic, stepwise, bottom-up approach.[30]

This last approach assures the highest levels of success in pursuing digital transformations.[31] In defining their transformations' scope, successful organizations boldly set up financial institution-wide efforts and build a new organization. They create an adaptive design that allows the transformation strategy and resource allocation to adjust over time. They adopt banking 5.0 execution practices and mindsets by pushing risk-taking and collaboration across all organizations. In these successful efforts, leadership and accountability are clear for each stage of the transformation.

[28] www.mckinsey.com/business-functions/digital-mckinsey/our-insights/five-moves-to-make-during-a-digital-transformation. Accessed 20 May 2019.

[29] The journey to an agile organization | McKinsey. www.mckinsey.com/business-functions/organization/our-insights/the-journey-to-an-agile-organization. Accessed 10 May 2020.

[30] The journey to an agile organization | McKinsey. www.mckinsey.com/business-functions/organization/our-insights/the-journey-to-an-agile-organization. Accessed 20 June 2020.

[31] www.mckinsey.com/business-functions/digital-mckinsey/our-insights/five-moves-to-make-during-a-digital-transformation. Accessed 19 May 2019.

JPMorgan Chase surveyed digital banking attitudes among its customers. Some of the findings are[32]:

- Fraud alerts, digital bill payments, and mobile deposits are their most important digital banking features.
- Fifty-four percent of customers said they use digital banking tools more than they did last year due to the pandemic.
- JPMorgan Chase's customers expected to continue to use digital banking tools more often in the following years.
- Eighty percent of the customers preferred to manage their money digitally.
- Thirty percent of respondents signed up for Peer-to-Peer (P2P) payment options in six months.

Benefits and Challenges of the Digital Transformations

Banking 5.0 can supply significant benefits to financial institutions. Digital transformation has not been successful only in some organizations.[33] According to a McKinsey survey, more than three-quarters of the initiatives pursued have yielded some or significant cost reductions and improvements to employee experiences. More than two-thirds of respondents say these change efforts increased revenue from existing streams, and more than half cite the creation of new revenue streams: a new product line or new business.[34]

The financial institution consultant Bain & Company recommends that organizations invest in digital transformation.[35] A survey of the Digital performance index (DPI)[36] on 343 organizations in eight industrial

[32] www.jpmorgan.com/insights/solutions/2020-digital-banking-survey. Accessed 20 January 2021.

[33] Bughin, J., LaBerge, L., & Mellbye, A. (2017, February). The case for digital reinvention. *McKinsey Quarterly*.

[34] Dhasarathy, A., Frazier, R., Khan, N., & Steagall, K. (2021, March). Seven lessons on how technology transformations can deliver value. *McKinsey Digital*.

[35] www.bain.com/insights/rebooting-a-digital-solution-to-trade-finance/. Accessed 29 February 2020.

[36] Digital Performance Index is an Accenture index that assesses the level of digital investment and progress across four business functions: planning, manufacturing, selling,

sectors found that in 2018 only 6% of organizations improved their financial performance due to their digital investments or converted them into revenue growth. There are several reasons why this happened. According to a Bain & Company study, most organizations do not have a holistic digital transformation strategy.[37] According to the same study, the organizations with this comprehensive strategy grow at 50% more than their competitors. They are 30% more profitable. The ICT costs are reduced by 20% on average. The lessons learned are that it is possible to succeed in digital transformation. The condition is that the organizations, including financial institutions, must have a clear philosophy in this regard. This philosophy must be holistic. It must consider all the components in the business model canvas.

There are challenges associated with digital transformation. They must be analyzed and considered. Most of the challenges are connected with operational risks.[38] The main risk is the occurrence of a disaster that could put the organization's continuity at risk. The more an organization depends on digital and automation technologies, the more it is necessary to protect the financial institution. The organization is in danger of cyber-attacks. Advanced solutions can produce data losses. It is possible to lose data due to the interruption of processes for human errors and problems in the software and hardware. Hackers can cause damages to ICT systems and operational automation. The risks can also be internal to the organizations. The risks can depend on a slowing down of procedures, with long transaction responses and batch jobs. That can be due to infrastructural sizing problems or buggy software development and implementation.

Digital transformation involves migration from manual procedures or old ICT procedures. These migrations can lead to errors or interruptions of the processes. The consequences can be significant for the organization. The use of new methods requires training of the operators who must use and manage them. This process is neither easy nor immediate.

and management. www.accenture.com/_acnmedia/pdf-64/accenture-digital-performance-index.pdf. Accessed 20 April 2020.

[37] www.bain.com/insights/leading-360-degree-digital-transition/. Accessed 29 February 2020.

[38] According to Basel regulations, operational risk is the risk of losses deriving from inefficient or broken processes, personnel, internal systems, or external events. 10 November 2029. www.bis.org/list/bcbs/tid_28/index.htm. Accessed 10 November 2029.

All the mentioned causes can create much damage due to the increasing dependence on ICT. The temporary use of manual procedures in the absence of ICT procedures can be simply impossible, or information is forgotten. ICT procedures cannot be easily changed or updated. Such difficulty is in the case of internally developed applications (so-called legacy applications). These difficulties of updating are fundamental in the case of ICT solutions bought from outside. In these cases, the vendor's dependency can be very punishing if software updates, or custom changes are needed.

The situations described require an effort to manage risks, both in projects and in the business as usual. The analysis of operational risks is an integral part of the activity of the financial institution. Its prompt and correct management minimizes potential negative impacts on critical financial institution assets and adverse consequences on the corporate strategy. The following activities are necessary:

- Risk assessment on all areas subject to risk (with particular attention to cross-departmental risks) at least once a year.
- Creation of a risk register. The operational risk committee should revise and approve the content regularly.
- Creation and follow-up activities by an operational risk committee on the strategies implemented to mitigate the vulnerability areas.

ISO 9000[39] and ISO 27000[40] have implicit the concept of risk. Data can be lost due to human errors and problems in the systems and processes. Risk-based thinking is essential and must be part of the culture of prevention and improvement. It is necessary to manage the business's challenges and consequences, the processes, and the entire organization. The activities for risk assessment are part of the cycle[41]:

- Definition of risk management policies.

[39] A Risk Based Thinking Model for ISO 9001:2015. https://rube.asq.org/audit/2015/01/a-risk-based-thinking-model-for-iso-9001-2015.pdf. Accessed 10 May 2020.

[40] ISO/IEC 27000—Key International Standard for information security revised. www.iso.org/news/ref2266.html. Accessed 30 June 2020.

[41] Boneva, M. (2018). Challenges related to the digital transformation of business financial institutions. In *Innovation management, entrepreneurship and sustainability (IMES 2018)* (pp. 101–114). Vysoká škola ekonomická v Praze, Prague, Czeck Republic.

- Identification, assessments (probability of occurrence and impact), and risk analysis.
- Risk treatment and remediations.
- Monitoring and measurement.
- Evaluation of the performance of the processes (to find residual risks).
- Continuous improvement.

This process is not easy. Planning and governance may need resources outside the organization. It is essential not to forget that there are challenges in digital transformation. If the risk becomes real, the consequences might be high. In most of the cases, management considers risks only in a negative sense. Risk-based thinking can help find opportunities, while risk-by-design[42] can help to prevent issues.

Innovation Roadmaps

A well-conducted digital transformation is successful. This aspect underlines the importance to dedicate particular care to the Business model canvas (BMC) of the digital transformation, its roadmap, and its implementation.

Roadmap for a Digital Transformation

It is interesting to analyze how innovative solutions can become banking as usual in an organization. A study suggests how foundational technologies and their banking use cases evolve.[43] The first factor to consider is change. This factor is how the solution is innovative. The more radical the change is, the more effort is necessary to ensure that users understand how to use it. The second factor is complexity. Its measurement depends on the number and diversity of parties needed to add value to the new solution.

It is essential to have a framework that maps innovations against these two factors, dividing them into quadrants. Each quadrant is a stage of

[42] McKnight, W. (2017, Spring). Risk by design. *Electrical Connection*, 48.

[43] Iansiti, M., & Lakhani, K. R. (2017). The truth about blockchain. *Harvard Business Review, 95*(1), 118–127.

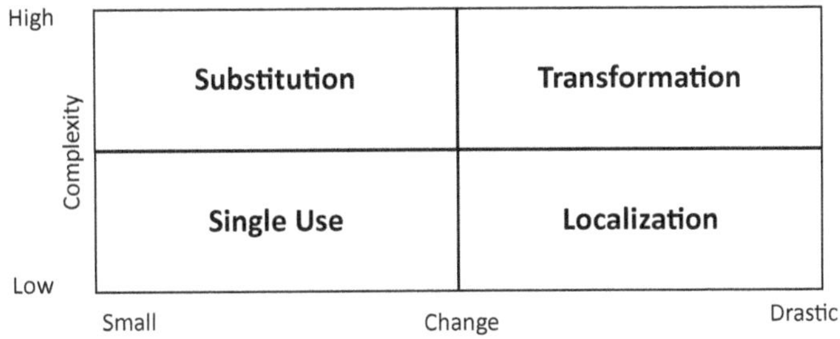

Fig. 3.2 Innovation types (*Source* Iansiti, M., & Lakhani, K. R. [2017]. The truth about blockchain. *Harvard Business Review, 95*[1], 118–127)

innovative solutions.[44] Identifying how a change falls into one of them can help managers understand its challenges, the level of collaboration and consensus needed, and the regulations and compliance requirements.[45] Managers can use this model to assess the state and to evaluate strategic investments in innovation.

In this model, the stages in an innovative solution introduction are (Fig. 3.2)[46]:

- Single use. The first quadrant refers to the small change and low complexity of an innovation able to save costs and being a highly focused solution.
- Localization. The second quadrant includes innovations that are drastic in change and low in complexity. They need only a limited number of users to generate immediate value. Consequently, it is easier to promote their adoption.
- Substitution. The third quadrant has applications that are small in change because they build on current single-use and localized applications. They need high coordination since they involve broader and

[44] Blockchain for and in Logistics: What to adopt and where. www.mdpi.com/2305-6290/2/3/18/htm. Accessed 20 June 2020.

[45] The truth about blockchain. *Harvard Business Review*. https://hbr.org/2017/01/the-truth-about-blockchain. Accessed 10 May 2020.

[46] Iansiti, M., & Lakhani, K. R. (2017). The truth about blockchain. *Harvard Business Review, 95*(1), 118–127.

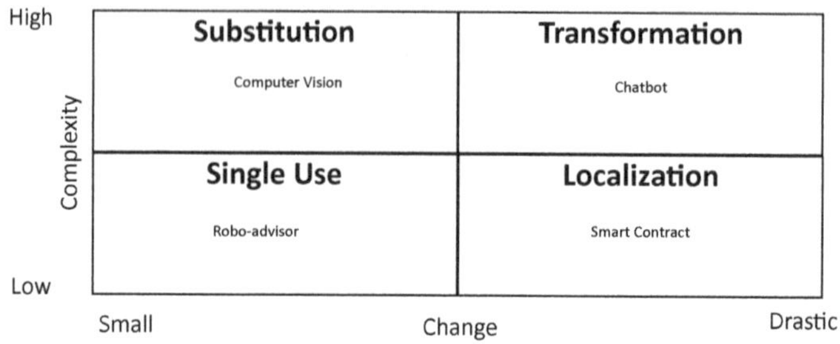

Fig. 3.3 Innovation types in banking

increasingly common uses. These innovations aim to replace whole ways of doing banking. There are high barriers to their adoption.

- Transformation. The last quadrant includes completely innovative applications that, if successful, could change the very nature of economic, social, and regulatory systems. They involve the coordination of the activities of many actors and institutional agreement on standards and processes.[47] Their adoption requires significant social, legal, regulatory changes, and challenges.

Examples of potential use cases of each one of innovation types for AI solutions applied to banking 5.0 could be (Fig. 3.3)[48]:

- Small Change and Low Complexity—Single Use. A use case is computer vision. Image processing enables processing, and analyzing images and video for recognition, algorithm development, and system design.
- Drastic Change and Low Complexity—Localization. Natural language processing is an example of this use of AI. It is a computer program designed to implement computer conversation with human users, especially over the internet.
- Small Change and High Complexity. Substitution. Robo-advisors is a use case of this innovation. They are digital platforms that supply

[47] Logistics Blockchain. www.mdpi.com/2305-6290/2/3/18/htm. Accessed 30 March 2021.

[48] Definition of these solutions from www.investopedia.com. Accessed 10 November 2020.

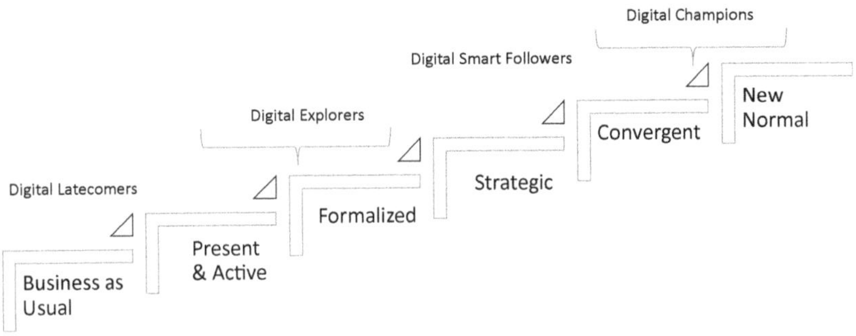

Fig. 3.4 Digital transformation stages (Adapted by the author from https://www.slideshare.net/briansolis/the-six-stages-of-digital-transformation-by-brian-solis)

automated, algorithm-driven financial planning services with little to no human supervision. Robo-advisor potentially replaces human consultants in wealth management and extends the diffusion of these services thanks to their lower costs.

- Drastic Change and High Complexity—Smart contracts are an exciting application of AI. A smart contract is a self-executing contract. The terms of the agreement between buyer and seller are in the code lines and are verified by using AI.[49] A distributed, decentralized blockchain network hosts the code and the data. It involves different parties, and, in many cases, it might require compliance with potentially new legislative regulations.[50]

In terms of generations, Altimeter defines six stages of digital transformation (Fig. 3.4).[51] It is possible to combine this model with a maturity model for digital banking presented by Deloitte.

[49] Smart contracts definition. www.investopedia.com/terms/s/smart-contracts.asp. Accessed 4 January 2021.

[50] www2.deloitte.com/content/dam/Deloitte/ce/Documents/financial-services/ce-digital-banking-maturity-2020.pdf. Accessed 20 January 2021.

[51] Solis, B, (2016). Six stages of digital transformation. www.slideshare.net/briansolis/the-six-stages-of-digital-transformation. Accessed 4 March 2020.

Digital Latecomers

- Banking as usual. The organizations run with a legacy perspective of customers, processes, metrics, business models, and solutions, believing that there is no reason to change.

Digital Explorers

- Present and Active. Small experiments foster digital literacy and creativity throughout the organization. Simultaneously, they aim to improve and amplify specific touchpoints and processes. In this generation, it is necessary to find processes that need a change, decide which of them to innovate, start searching for solutions, and test the possible new ways of working.
- Formalized. Experimentations become intentional while executing in more promising and capable levels. Innovations become more challenging. As a result, change agents need executive support for innovative solutions

Digital Smart Followers

Strategic. Individual groups recognize collaboration strengths since their research, work, and shared insights contribute to new strategic plans for digital transformation ownership, efforts, and investments.[52] In this generation, it is necessary to define the various areas of action and the financial resources needed to support the planned implementation.

Digital Champions

- Converged. A dedicated digital transformation team leads to strategy, development, and operations based on banking and customer-centric goals. The organization's new structure takes shape as roles, ability, business models, processes, and systems support and sustains the change.

[52] Digital transformation: A guide to digital transformation. https://rejolut.com/digital-transformation/. Accessed 20 June 2020.

- New normal. Digital transformation becomes business as usual, with executives and operatives recognizing that change is permanent. There is the implementation of new ecosystems to find and act upon solutions and market trends in pilots and, eventually, at scale. There is an extension of the innovations to other financial institutions in the group or the partners.

Collectively, these generations act as a digital maturity model to drive a successful digital transformation.[53]

Implementing a full digital transformation is not easy for traditional financial institutions since they must devote most of the available resources to supporting current heavy, sometimes broken, processes and attending the existing banking.[54] Transforming a financial institution requires moving front and back offices in a synchronized fashion to ensure that the innovative approach has high acceptance and becomes live fast. On the other side, traditional financial institutions potentially can afford a full digital transformation since they have the funds and the resources to invest in a full-scale digital transformation. The issues are legacy systems and culture.

Critical Success Factors

There are several critical success factors (CSF) for banking 5.0. initiatives, CSFs ensure successful competitive performance for the banking 5.0 initiative.[55] Since these factors are critical, the management needs sufficient information to allow her/him to find whether events are progressing well in each CSF.[56]

[53] www.prophet.com/2016/04/the-six-stages-of-digital-transformation/. Accessed 29 February 2020.

[54] Albrecher, H., Bommier, A., Filipović, D., Koch-Medina, P., Loisel, S., & Schmeiser, H. (2019). Insurance: Models, digitization, and data science. *European Actuarial Journal, 9*(2), 349–360.

[55] Bullen, C. V., & Rockart, J. F. (1981). *A primer on critical success factors*. Sloan School of Business. MIT, Cambridge, MA.

[56] Bullen, C. V., & Rockart, J. F. (1981). *A primer on critical success factors*. Sloan School of Business. MIT, Cambridge, MA.

Critical Success Factors for Industry 5.0

Industry 5.0 includes a set of solutions enabling AI solutions and processes integrated with robotic process automation. These solutions change products, processes, business models, organizations, and systems significantly.[57] They should also aim to increase sustainability.

The critical support factors for industry 5.0 are several.[47] This book lists them for mnemonics reasons with words starting with "C": Collaboration, Cognition, Confidence, Contribution, Conservation, Competence, Content, Customization, and Creativity.

The model classifies the industry 5.0 factors in hard and soft from the point of view of measurements. Measures can be either "soft," meaning subjective and qualitative, or "hard," meaning objective and quantitative. All these factors require strict management tools (or Command to continue with words starting with C). In turn, specific solutions support them.

Soft

- Collaboration refers to the need to have all the applications, robots, and operators working together.
- Confidence or trust must be the cornerstone of the industry 5.0 solutions. The basis of trust is a stringent security policy. Cyber attacks would be extremely dangerous for a system based primarily on non-human agents, highly integrated factors, and fragile units.
- Creativity is a set of characteristics that lead to the definition of innovative solutions.[58] It is an individual characteristic, but in the case of industry 5.0 must not be a one time effort but it should be a process and a team design thinking.[59]

[57] Schmidt, R., Möhring, M., Härting, R. C., Reichstein, C., Neumaier, P., & Jozinović, P. (2015). Industry 5.0-potentials for creating smart products: Empirical research results. In *The International Conference on Business Information Systems* (pp. 16–27). Springer, Cham, Switzerland.

[58] Hassan, M. U., Malik, A. A., Hasnain, A., Faiz, M. F., & Abbas, J. (2013). Measuring employee creativity and its impact on organization innovation capability and performance in the banking sector of Pakistan. *World Applied Sciences Journal, 24*(7), 949–959.

[59] Amabile, T. M. (1988). A model of creativity and innovation in organization. In B. M. Staw & L. L. Cumming (Eds.), *Research in organizational behavior* (Vol. 10, pp. 123–167). JAI Press, Greenwich, CT.

- Competence in the case of industry 5.0 refers to e-competencies.[60]

Hard

- Content, such as price, stock market, financial, and customer-related information, needs to match information needs.[61]
- Customization aims to satisfy as many needs as possible of each customer, in contrast to conventional tools, which try to reach as many customers as possible while meeting a limited number of customer needs.[62]
- Cognition means the intelligent use of data. All information systems, sensors, and controls (all thanks to the integration connection tools) generate vast numbers of data, referred to as big data. These data should be analyzed. Big data analytics is essential in industry 5.0.[63] Data analytics, data mining, analysis, and distribution of big data are critical supports for big data analytics. They have the 9Vs characteristics: (Veracity, Variety, Velocity, Volume, Validity, Variability, Volatility, Visualization, and Value) needed to process the banking 5.0 data adding value to the organization.[64]
- Conservation in all the sectors is crucial to achieving sustainability and improving the triple bottom line of commercial, environmental, and social success.[65] Important are all the actions and policies for

[60] Smit, J. (2016). *e-Competency of Practitioners: A grounded theory*.

[61] Wu, J. H., Hsia, T. L., & Heng, M. S. (2006). Core capabilities for exploiting electronic banking. *Journal of Electronic Commerce Research, 7*(2).

[62] Coelho, P. S., & Henseler, J. (2012). Creating customer loyalty through service customization. *European Journal of Marketing*; Simonson, I. (2005). Determinants of customers' responses to customized offers: Conceptual framework and research propositions. *Journal of Marketing, 69*(1), 32–45.

[63] Chiang, R. H., Grover, V., Liang, T. P., & Zhang, D. (2018). Strategic value of big data and business analytics. *Journal of Management Information Systems, 35*(2), 383–387. https://doi.org/10.1080/07421222.2018.1451950.

[64] Owais, S. S., & Hussein, N. S. (2016). Extract five categories CPIVW from the 9V's characteristics of the big data. *International Journal of Advanced Computer Science and Applications, 7*(3), 254–258.

[65] Jeucken, M. (2010). *Sustainable finance and banking: The financial sector and the future of the planet*. Earthscan.

improved performance that will contribute to sustainable development and operations.[66]

- Contribution to the organizations' financial results is important in banking 5.0 as in many other business activities.[67]

The following pages examine each of the nine "C"s in banking 5.0 in an integrated and consistent way.

Collaboration

Traditional ICT applications have provided some support for the exchange of information with the customers and the intermediaries.[68] Solution advances in a banking 5.0 initiative significantly increase the potential to do so. The critical change is the transition from an "exchange of information" to the "free flow of information" in the value network between the products, services, and related organizations.[69] It is necessary to coordinate this exchange effectively.[70] A free movement implies a higher degree of exchangeability of the data, a higher degree of automation in the exchange of information, and integrated use of the data in the approach to big data analytics.[71] Application programming interfaces (API) significantly contribute to the collaboration.

In banking 5.0, both the depth of integration (among financial institutions and customers) and the entire banking process's automation potential is much more than those in traditional banking services. The latter is limited to supporting the tasks using a computer application based

[66] Jeucken, M. (2010). *Sustainable finance and banking: The financial sector and the future of the planet*. Earthscan.

[67] Van Leeuwen, G., & Klomp, L. (2006). On the contribution of innovation to multifactor productivity growth. *Economics of Innovation and New Solution, 15*(4–5), 367–390.

[68] Kollmann, T. (2011). *E-Business: Grundlagen elektronischer Geschäftsprozesse in der Net Economy*. Gabler, Wiesbaden, Germany.

[69] Schlick, J., Stephan, P., Loskyll, M., & Lappe, D. (2014). Industries 4.0 in der praktischen Anwendung. In T. Bauernhansl, M. T. Hompel, & B. Vogel-Heuser (Eds.), *Industrie 4.0 to Produktion, Automatisierung und Logistik: Anwendung. Technologien. Migration* (pp. 57–84). Springer, Wiesbaden, Germany.

[70] Van Weele, A. J. (2010). *Purchasing & supply chain management: Analysis, strategy, planning and practice*. Cengage Learning EMEA. Andover, UK.

[71] Lee, J., Kao, H. A., & Yang, S. (2014). Service innovation and smart analytics for industry 5.0 and big data environment. *Procedia CIRP, 16*, 3–8.

on the personalized information and documents exchange. The automation process, a higher degree of integration, and AI characterize banking 5.0. Banking 5.0 is based on digitization and advanced automation within the organizations and functions of the ecosystem. It is not limited to new and improved solutions inside the specific institution. The collaboration is within the ecosystem.

Next to the degree of integration, relationships with partners will be different in banking 5.0 (for example, around new services complementary to the banking services[72]).

Considering what was mentioned before, collaboration is the main factor for the survival of the banking environment. Eventually, organizations that will not be part of a collaborative ecosystem will tend to disappear.

Collaboration in the case of banking 5.0 has a more generalized meaning, including human–robot collaboration. This collaboration is a fundamental challenge for banking 5.0. AI can play a crucial role in performing organizational tasks more efficiently and empowering operators through symbiotic interactions with persons. Operators must take part in the analysis and interpretation of AI-generated results dynamically.

Confidence

Highly integrated, continuous/porous networks are vulnerable to systemic risks such as total computer applications collapse in case of failure of one of its parts, due to some events such as hacking or internet viruses that can fully invade integrated systems.

"Smart banking" shares real-time information among all stakeholders in the ecosystem. They make banking processes visible, perfect and transparent, but they must be secure.

Security will require an entirely diverse set of capabilities and competencies to cope with cyber-attacks.[73] To find these talents requires finding new sources with the help of partners, such as partnership programs with universities and research centers. It helps explore new accesses such as social networks, social media, and similar.

[72] Essig, M. (2006), Electronic Insurance. Konzeption und Anwendung, In. J. Zentes (Ed.), *Handbuch Handel* (pp. 735–758). Gabler, Wiesbaden, Germany.

[73] Zhu, B., Joseph, A., & Sastry, S. (2011, October). A taxonomy of cyber attacks on SCADA systems. In *2011 International conference on internet of things and 4th international conference on cyber, physical and social computing* (pp. 380–388). IEEE.

Creativity

The success of banking 5.0 is mostly decided by factors like the management entrepreneurial quality (e-competencies technological ability, leadership, banking skills, the capacity to assess and respond to risk, and market knowledge) and resource and product-based factors like the product-market fit and the market acceptance.[74] In this economic environment, creativity generates values and ensures sustainable development centered on the person's capital. Persons can use their imagination to increase the significance of an idea that might add value to the banking ecosystem.[75]

More specifically, innovative ideas, not money or technologies, are the source of economic success in banking 5.0 and, more importantly, the source of customer delight. A creative economy improves new production lines, services, and trading, innovating social and financial environments. An economy that has adopted creativity as a development factor will expand fast, thanks to prosperity and diverse and sustainable labor and robots.

There are several ways to approach a creative economy. It is possible to use the same indicators as other economic systems, such as production, customer expenditure, employment, and trade. Businesses use assessments, value networks, prices, or transactional data.[76] The concept of creativity is the defining element of the twenty-first-century economy, playing an essential role in the banking 5.0 transformation.

Competence

Competence is the ability to do something well.[77] In the case of banking 5.0, the interest is for the so-called e-competencies.[68] The personal e-competence describes his/her knowledge, competencies, and other

[74] Kakati, M. (2003). Success criteria in high-tech new ventures. *Technovation, 23*, 447–457.

[75] Ungureanu, A. V. (2020). The transition from industry 4.0 to industry 5.0. The 4Cs of the global economic change. *LUMEN Proceedings, 13*, 70–81.

[76] Hervani, A., & Helms, M. (2010). Increasing creativity in economics: The service-learning project. *Journal of Education for Business*, 267–274.

[77] Technical competence definition and meaning | Collins. www.collinsdictionary.com/dictionary/english/technical-competence. Accessed 4 January 2021.

abilities in using for example ICT tools to perform a function to respect a given standard in professional and or personal settings.[78]

Only if the professionals who work in banking have digital competencies, an organization can fully exploit the opportunities offered by banking 5.0.[79]

Content

Content means product/service offering, a portfolio strategy. It would include information combination, brokerage, currency exchange, financial services and products, infrastructure, financial education, financing, investments, payment service, lending/credit, fraud prevention, and user identification. Content is a critical success factor.[80]

Customization

High-tech ventures are likely to be more successful if they implement product customization strategies to target existing customers rather than addressing only new markets.[81]

Customization of products and services supports delight in the customers and get more of them. This relational component "can be a mean of affirmation of a social identity, inducing a sense of distinction from a social group."[82] Personal and individual treatment of the customer can be very positive on the customer, if they perceive to be

[78] www.igi-global.com/dictionary/employability-entrepreneurship-economic-recovery/8660.

[79] Competence is an ability to apply knowledge, skills, and attitudes for achieving observable results. The European model of e-Competence (e-CF) provides a reference of 40 skills, as required and applied to the digital workplace transformation, using a common language for skills, abilities, and ability levels. For details, reference can be made to: Sanz, L. F., Gómez-Pérez, J., & Castillo-Martinez, A. (2018). Analysis of the European ICT competence frameworks. In *Multidisciplinary perspectives on human capital and information solution professionals* (pp. 225–245). IGI Global, Hershey, PA.

[80] Roeder, J., Cardona, D. R., Palmer, M., Werth, O., Muntermann, J., & Breitner, M. H. (2018). Make or break: Business model determinants of FinTech venture success. *Proceedings of the Multikonferenz Wirtschaftsinformatik, Lüneburg, Germany.*

[81] Kakati, M. (2003). Success criteria in high-tech new ventures. *Technovation, 23*, 447–457.

[82] Halstrick, T. (2020). *Determining a bank's customer value proposition based on customer value dimensions* (Bachelor's thesis). University of Twente.

treated personally and individually. The effect is an exciting customer journey.[83]

Cognition

Data analytics are an essential enabler for banking 5.0.[84] Intelligent (innovative) technologies and related algorithms allow the combination, processing, and analysis of large volumes of data from many heterogeneous sources. Using all this big data in machine learning models, the organization can improve its knowledge of the customers, partners, and markets, forecast market trends, and improve processes and products' shortcomings. Big data analytics can allow managers to make better and more informed decisions. Big data analytics can automatically take operational decisions about banking in a growing number of cases, such as interests on loans or pricing decisions.[85]

Analysis of the data and their intelligent use are critical success factors for the organizations that want to exploit the potential of banking 5.0. The data analytics tools can support the organization and its partners in improving marketing, sales, design, and operations. Predictive analysis on where and when to expect the next event, relevant from the financial institution's point of view, offers the possibility to perfecting the services.[86]

Conservation

Sustainability connects with conservation. Unfortunately, financial institutions did not have a strong focus on environmental protection, nor have they focused on technologies to improve the earth's ecological sustainability. This situation should change with banking 5.0. Many different AI techniques have been used to investigate sustainability in the

[83] Determining a Bank's Customer Value Proposition based on. https://essay.utwente.nl/81278/1/Halstrick_BA_BMS.pdf. Accessed 4 January 2021.

[84] Koch, V., Kuge, S., Geissbauer, R., & Schrauf, S. (2014). Industry 5.0: Opportunities and challenges of the industrial Internet. Strategy & PwC. www.strategyand.pwc.com/media/file/Industria-4-0.pdf. Accessed 30 May 2020.

[85] Nicoletti, B. (2014, February). Using operational analytics to achieve to digitized, visible supply chain. *Inbound Logistics*.

[86] Lee, J., Kao, H. A., & Yang, S. (2014). Service innovation and smart analytics for industry 5.0 and big data environment. *Procedia CIRP, 16*, 3–8.

last decade.[87] Current studies linking AI algorithms with environmental management have paved the way. There is still a lack of solid focus and action to the need for a better and fast solution to save the environment and increase sustainability. Banking 5.0 will change this approach.

The Task Force for Climate-related Disclosure and the Sustainability Accounting Standards Board standardized corporate social responsibility reporting and made it mandatory.[88] These international initiatives have found a set of conditions that may help organizations and financial institutions act in a socially responsible corporate behavior that prioritizes sustainability, the health of the environment, and the planet's future.[89]

Contribution

The definition of contribution is the part played by a person or an asset in bringing about a result or helping something to advance. In the case of banking 5.0, it refers to the financial contribution and the contribution to anything connected with the innovation.

The productivity benefits resulting from traditional ICT application initiatives are a reduction in transaction and process costs. Banking 5.0 allows the financial institution to turn paper-based processes into digital ICT applications. There is a transformation from a labor-intensive activity into automated workflows and sustainable ICT processes.

Banking 5.0 should support critical activities like the process of managing relationships with partners, such as insurance organizations in the bancassurance. The driving factors of banking 5.0 contribution

[87] Chen, S. H.; Jakeman, A. J., & Norton, J. P. (2008). Artificial intelligence techniques: An introduction to their use for modelling environmental systems. *Mathematics and Computers in Simulation, 78*, 379–400; Yetilmezsoy, K., Ozkaya, B., & Cakmakci, M. (2011). Artificial intelligence-based prediction models for environmental engineering. *Neural Network World, 21*, 193–218; Papadimitriou, F. (2912). Artificial intelligence in modelling the complexity of Mediterranean landscape transformations. *Computer Electronic Agriculture, 81*, 87–96; Alzoubi, I. Almaliki, S. & Mirzaei, F. (2019). Prediction of environmental indicators in land leveling using artificial intelligence techniques. *Chemical and Biological Technologies in Agriculture, 6*, 4.

[88] Truant, E., Corazza, L., & Scagnelli, S. D. (2017). Sustainability and risk disclosure: An exploratory study on sustainability reports. *Sustainability, 9*(4), 636.

[89] Federal Reserve. (2020, December). *Federal Reserve Board announces it has formally joined the Network of Central Banks and Supervisors for Greening the Financial System, or NGFS, as a member* (Federal Reserve Report).

are the improvements in sales, operations, and new services design.[90] Banking 5.0 enables the development of faster processes of sales and operations. The organization can activate new product-service functions and improve the banking revenue.[91] Traditional ICT applications are focused on process efficiency. The goals of banking 5.0 are increased productivity, flexibility, and performance, which meet today's customers' high customization needs.[92]

Significant Challenges

All these factors of the model pose a substantial challenge and a potential change in financial institutions' work. They need a critical and complete digital transformation of the organization and competencies, both of which should change synergistically.[93] Organizations need to create new job profiles, for example, AI experts, contract experts on intellectual property, or data scientists, to analyze relevant data, their management, and their use.

A characteristic of banking 5.0 is the increasing digitization and networking of products, processes, organization models, and value-adding activities. It requires significant investments.

Banking 5.0 requires integration with the information systems of other organizations in the banking ecosystem.[94] All partners must have access to the relevant data and process them to support decision-making. Linked

[90] Schuh, G., Powerful, T., Wesch-Powerful, C., Weber, A. R., & Prote, J. P. (2014). Collaboration mechanisms to increase productivity in the context of industries 4.0. *Procedia CIRP, 19*, 51–56.

[91] Schuh, G., Powerful, T., Wesch-Powerful, C., Weber, A. R., & Prote, J. P. (2014). Collaboration mechanisms to increase to productivity in the context of industries 4.0. *Procedia CIRP, 19*, 51–56.

[92] Kagermann, H. (2014). Von Industries 4.0 Chancen nutzen. In T. Bauernhansl, M. T. Hompel, & B. Vogel-Heuser (Eds.), *Produktion Industries 4.0. Automatisierung und Logistik* (pp. 603–614). Springer, Wiesbaden, Germany.

[93] Geissbauer, R., Weissbarth, R., & Wetzstein, J. (2016). Banking 5.0: Are the organisation ready for the digital revolution? www.strategyand.pwc.com/reports/insurance-4-digital-revolution. Accessed 20 March 2021.

[94] Nicoletti, B. (2019). Digital transformation via open data in insurance. In A. L. Mention, *Digital innovation harnessing the value of open data*. World Scientific, Singapore.

data offers a solution in this respect.[95] Linked data is a method that allows to aggregate and collect data from distributed sources. To make this data accessible on the web,[96] the data must be published under the condition of "open" use for a specific user category. This publishing allows the organizations to browse and navigate the data by any media through deep linking[97] and aggregate them. Linked data is now a mature solution with exciting potential. It requires large numbers of data linked together. Linked data can supply a powerful representation of the investigation into the banking activities in terms of relationships (links).[98]

Innovation Acceptance Model

It is relevant in the introduction of banking 5.0 to analyze a model developed to assess innovative solutions' acceptance: the Innovation acceptance model (IAM). The model is a development of the Technology acceptance model (TAM).[87] Some studies have used this model to assess the acceptance of internet and mobility innovations,[99] and supply chain.[100] Authors have applied TAM to innovative solutions for the banking sector.[101] It also applies to the introduction of AI-based innovations.

[95] Data, L. (2014). Connect data distributed across the Web. linked data.org. Accessed 29 May 2020.

[96] Tomassetti, F., Rizzo G., Glass, A., Hardy, L., Torchiano, M., & Morisio, M. (2011). Linked data approach to the automation of the selection processes in systematic reviews. In *The assessment and evaluation in software engineering (EASE 2011), 15th Annual Conference* ((pp. 31–35)). EIT.

[97] Azim, T., Riva, O., & Nath, S. (2016, June). uLink: Enabling user-defined deep linking to app content. In *Proceedings of the 14th Annual International Conference on mobile systems, applications, and services* (pp. 305–318).

[98] Bizer, C., Heath, T., & Berners-Lee, T. (2011). *Linked data: The story so far. In Semantic services, interoperability and web applications: Emerging concepts* (pp. 205–227). IGI Global, Hershey, PA.

[99] Kim, Y., Park Y. J., & Choi, J. (2016). The adoption of mobile payment services for Fintech. *International Journal of Applied Engineering Research, 11*(2), 1058–1061; Chen, M. C., Chen, S. S., Yeh, H. M., & Tsaur, W. G. (2016). The critical factors influencing internet services finances satisfaction: An empirical study in Taiwan. *American Journal of Industrial and Business Management, 6*(6), 748–762.

[100] Kamble, S., Gunasekaran, A., & Arha. H. (2019). Understanding the blockchain solution adoption in supply chains-Indian context. *International Journal of Production Research, 57*(7), 2009–2033.

[101] Tzanis, S. (2012). *Direct insurance: The determinants of success* (Dissertation). University of St. Gallen, Switzerland.

IAM states that the critical determinants for the adoption and use of innovations are[102]:

- Perceived usefulness (PU) is the degree to which the decision-makers think that using a specific innovation allows their organization to improve its performance. The PU measures include the increase in performance, economics, productivity, efficiency, overall usefulness, time savings, and work productivity.
- Perceived ease of use (Peou) is the degree to which the decision-makers believe that an innovative solution requires little effort. The Peou measures include ease of control, ease of use, simplicity, clarity, and flexibility.

It is possible to generalize the IAM (Innovation Acceptance Model) model.[103] There are other factors to consider when analyzing banking 5.0 from an IAM perspective. Despite the benefits of banking 5.0, overcoming the trust issues in the customers is, for example, a significant challenge for the adoption of banking 5.0. To overcome this type of challenges, in the case of organizations, small- and medium-sized enterprises, the IAM model can be expanded to include the theory of planned behavior,[104] and the influence of several other potential factors.[105]

A comprehensive model for IAM should include (Fig. 3.5)[106]:

[102] Song, Y. W. (2019). *User acceptance of an artificial intelligence (AI) virtual assistant: An extension of the solution acceptance mode* (Doctoral dissertation). The University of Texas at Austin, Austin, TX.

[103] Nicoletti, B. (2017). *The future of FinTech*. Palgrave Macmillan, Cham, Switzerland; Bin, M. A., Pyeman, J. B., Ali, N. B., Abdul, N. B., & Khai, K. G. (2018). Determinants of supply chain finance adoption among Malaysian manufacturing Financial institutions: A proposed conceptual framework. *International Journal of Education and Research, 6*(4), 237–248.

[104] Ajzen, I. (1991). The theory of planned behavior. *Organizational Behavior and Human Decision Processes, 50*(2), 179–211.

[105] Bin, M. A., Pyeman, J. B., Ali, N. B., Abdul, N. B., & Khai, K. G. (2018). Determinants of supply chain finance adoption among Malaysian manufacturing financial institutions: A proposed conceptual framework. *International Journal of Education and Research, 6*(4), 237–248.

[106] Schierz, P. G., et al. (2010, May–June). Understanding customer acceptance of mobile payment services: An empirical analysis. *Electronic Commerce Research and Applications*, 9(3), 209–216; Nicoletti, B. (2014). *Mobile banking*. Palgrave Macmillan, London, UK.

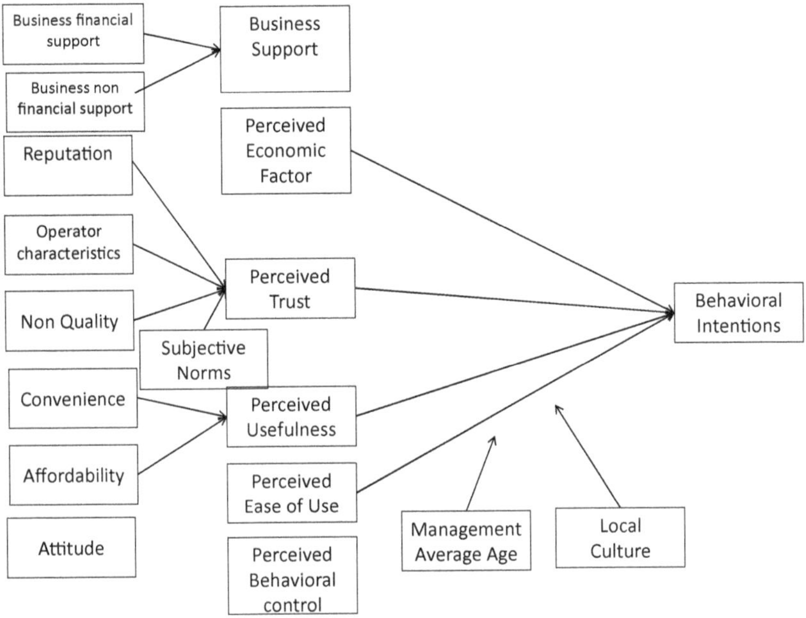

Fig. 3.5 Innovation acceptance model

- Behavioral intentions (BI) arise from the adoption of banking 5.0, namely the propensity to embrace innovative solutions.
- Perceived economic factor (PEF) has a substantial and immediate effect for small- and medium-sized enterprises in adopting banking 5.0.
- Perceived usefulness (PU) has a significant and direct impact on an organization's intention to adopt an innovation. It is decided by the level of convenience (CON) and the affordability (AFF) arising from moving to banking 5.0.
- Perceived trust (PT) has a significant and direct effect on an organization's intention to adopt banking 5.0.
- Characteristics of the digital operation (Maintenance and Operations—MNO).
- Non-quality (NQ) depends on the services provided by the vendor of the innovative solutions.

- Awareness and knowledge (AK) show the realization, perception, or inside of a situation or fact.
- Support organizations can be of two types. (1) Financial assistance, such as the availability of subsidies, working capital, and concessions. (2) The non-financial support includes training, consulting, management, distribution, research, and development.[107]
- Reputation (RE) is based on the perception of reliability, credibility, social responsibility, and reliability of the organizations offering to support the transformation to banking 5.0.[108]
- Attitude toward innovation (ATI) refers to the favorable or unfavorable results of the organization's evaluation towards the innovation.[109]
- Subjective norms relate to perceived social pressures that influence an organization's behavioral intention (Social Pressures SP).[110]
- Perceived behavioral control (BC) refers to the ease or difficulty of performing the specific innovation's behavior.[111]

Conclusions

The implementation of banking 5.0 requires a philosophy: a strategy and an integrated design of all the business model canvas components. It is a vision that should cover its entire business model, including besides "Philosophy" (the integrated vision):

- Proposition of Value.
- Proximity.
- Partition of the Customers.
- Place or Channels.

[107] Yusoff, M–N. H., & Yaacob, M. R. (2010). The government business support in the new economic model. *International Journal of Business and Management, 5*(9), 60–71.

[108] Fombrun, C. J. (1996). *Reputation: Realizing value for the corporate image*. Harvard Business School Press, Cambridge, MA.

[109] Ajzen, I., & Fishbein, M. (1980). *Attitude understanding and predicting social behavior*. Prentice-Hall, Upper Saddle River, NJ.

[110] Ajzen, I., & Fishbein, M. (1980). *Attitude understanding and predicting social behavior*. Prentice-Hall, Upper Saddle River, NJ.

[111] Ajzen, I. (1991). The theory of planned behavior. *Organizational Behavior and Human Decision Processes, 50*(2), 179–211.

- Processes.
- Platforms.
- Persons.
- Partnerships.
- Correct Pricing.
- Payments for costs and investments.
- Protection.

This book looks at all these aspects. It analyzes the changes necessary for the overall design and implementation of banking 5.0. By defining the business model canvas components, an organization should select its business model and strategy. From that moment on, based on the choices made, the organization's positioning in the market may, or may not, result in competitive advantage (sustainable or not). From time to time, the financial institution needs to rethink its philosophy and then adapt and improve its business model to avoid being overwhelmed by competitors. It is not a simple goal because, speaking of transformation, other factors (mostly persons) arise, deciding an organization's ability to adapt to new situations and transform in a new business model.

A business model reflects the goals of an organization and its vision. It produces results through the market, in which the organization can gain a competitive advantage. Banking 5.0 changes how financial institutions and customers interact (in marketing, sales, operations, customer service, and similar).[112] Banking 5.0 combines digitization (through AI) and automation (through robotic process automation) and influences all business and decision-making processes, including risk protection. Digitization changes current products and allows new product offerings. The correct way to analyze such changes is by considering a business model canvas and working on it to benefit the customers and the organization.

This chapter shows the components that support banking 5.0 and how banking organizations can spread and integrate them. The adoption of banking 5.0 is different from the adoption of traditional innovations. In this type of change, there is a need for redefining the banking business model. This change is made possible through restructuring and aligning all the different sectors such as marketing, sales, and operations. The

[112] Eling, M., & Lehmann, M. (2018). The impact of digitalization on the insurance value chain and the insurability of risks. *The Geneva Papers on Risk and Insurance-Issues and Practice, 43*(3), 359–396.

reorganization of these sectors should push toward the effective adoption of banking 5.0. This adoption is a new concept for many financial institutions. Over time, this adoption should become business as usual.

Until now, few organizations have been able to achieve the results expected. McKinsey Global Survey confirms that the rate of success of digital transformations is alarmingly low.[113] About eight in ten respondents in one of its surveys stated that their organizations had begun digital transformations in recent years. Just 14% say their efforts have reached sustained performance improvements. Only 3% of the respondents report complete success at supporting their transformation. This situation will change over time, but the innovators need to consider and implement all the critical success factors that, as shown in this chapter, can assure success.

Based on the topics discussed in this chapter, it becomes clear the importance and impact of the banking 5.0 transformation in banking organizations' life cycle. Simultaneously, banking 5.0 transformation becomes more critical to the distribution of services and their accesses. The banking regulators recognized the increasing incidence of digitization in internal and external processes to banking organizations issuing new regulations to consider these changes and, so doing, pushing organizations to take the necessary actions.[114]

Improving the innovation process is the basis for the financial institutions' competitive advantages, be they incumbent or start-ups. Combining lean and digital technologies helps make organizations faster and more effective, efficient, and economical than their competitors. In this way, it creates the basis for competitiveness and success. In this context, the application of the lean and digitize principles are the correct approach to meeting these challenges.[115] It seems particularly helpful to extend its applications to the innovation in processes, organizations, and business models for banking 5.0.

[113] www.mckinsey.com/business-functions/digital-mckinsey/our-insights/five-moves-to-make-during-a-digital-transformation. Accessed 19 May 2019.

[114] www.ivass.it/pubblicazioni-e-statistiche/pubblicazioni/relazione-annuale/2017/Relazione_IVASS_2016_en.pdf?language_id=3. Accessed 14 March 2020.

[115] Nicoletti, B. (2015, March). Optimizing innovation with the lean & digitize innovation process. *TIM Review*.

Banking 5.0 has a positive and meaningful relationship with customer delight. With the changing times and solutions, there is a need to continuously reinterpret and reorganize the banking 5.0 dimensions in a cross-country and industry analysis. It is necessary to consider that customers of every economy and every industry have their unique needs about the quality of service demanded.

CHAPTER 4

Proposition of Value and Fintech Organizations in Banking 5.0

The purpose of the business is to add value to the customer.
Kiichiro Toyoda

Introduction

Value is essential to meet customer needs[1] and to find the best value network.[2] A customer can choose an organization rather than another based on the value-adding of a financial institution's solution. It should be an invitation so attractive that the customer cannot refuse it.

The starting point in innovation is to adopt a systematic method to define and handle target values and needs about innovation as an enabler for an agile development process: the value system. The value system is a framework for mapping value in a complete, hierarchical, dynamic,

[1] Soliman, M., & Saurin, T. A. (2017). Lean production in complex socio-technical systems: A systematic literature review. *Journal of Manufacturing Systems, 45*, 135–148.

[2] Welo, T. & Ringen, G. (2012). NPD practices in the Norwegian manufacturing industry: Assessing the relationship between key dimensions and performance. In *ISPIM Innovation Symposium, the International Society for Professional Innovation Management.*

B. Nicoletti, *Banking 5.0*, Palgrave Studies in Financial Services Technology, https://doi.org/10.1007/978-3-030-75871-4_4

and transparent way.[3] The value system defines structures, and prioritizes "values" adaptively for specific innovation projects. It is the basis for a value-alignment of innovation projects and processes. Maximizing customer value is a core principle in innovation, but the value definitions often used are based on logical reasoning rather than real-life observations.[4] The method presented in this chapter integrates emotional customer value into the traditional model, based on minimizing running costs and reducing time-to-market.

Several studies detail how to find and measure customer value.[5] A financial institution's real value comes from the customer, without which the financial institution would not exist. "Satisfying customers is the source of sustainable value creation."[6] For this reason, value propositions are vastly different across organizations and customers within an organization. Only when an organization receives revenue through the customer's payment can consider having sustainable sales financing.

One of the reasons business models have become popular is that persons want to discover the best way to manage their banking to add value to the customers and the organization simultaneously. Peter Drucker pointed out that making a profit is very often mentioned as the purpose of a company. It "is not only false; it is irrelevant."[7] It may even be harmful. For Drucker, "there is only one valid definition of business purpose: to create a customer."[8] An organization can get customers only if it can deliver what the target customers need. An organization defines its business through the value proposition it offers to its customers. This

[3] Schuh, G., Lenders, M., & Hieber, S. (2008). Lean innovation: Introducing value systems to product development. In *PICMET 2008 Proceedings*, 27–31 July, Cape Town, South Africa 2008.

[4] Gudem, M., Steinert, T., Welo, T., & Leifer, L. (2013). Redefining customer value in lean product development design projects. *Journal of Engineering, Design & Solution, 11.*

[5] da Luz Peralta, C. B., Echeveste, M. E., Lermen, F. H., Marcon, H., & Tortorella, G. (2020). A framework proposition to find customer value through lean practices. *Journal of Manufacturing Solution Management.*

[6] Kaplan, R. S., & Norton, D. P. (2004). The strategy map: Guide to aligning intangible assets. *Strategy & Leadership, 32*(5), 10–17.

[7] Swaim, R. W. (2011). *The strategic Drucker: Growth strategies and marketing insights from the works of Peter Drucker*. Wiley, Hoboken, NJ.

[8] Zehner, W. B., & Zehner, J. A. (2019). Marketing for science based organizations perspectives and questions. *Marketing of Scientific and Research Organizations, 32*(2), 77–106.

approach is precisely the bridge between the organization's purpose and the customers' needs and desires. The business model is a vehicle to drive the employees, the management, the partners, and the financial institution's stakeholders in this direction.

An Accenture study found several patterns among customers. Five key findings characterize them[9]:

- Customers want integrated propositions addressing their core needs.
- Customers increasingly want a fully personalized offering also from their financial providers.
- Customers are willing to share data with their vendors in return for better advice and more attractive deals.
- Customers want better integration across all accesses, be them physical or digital.
- Customers desire a financial institutions in which to trust.

The value proposition could improve thanks to smart solutions. For further improvements, alliances are possible, for instance, with AI developers and service providers that may supply an excellent customer value proposition.[10] Financial institutions can take the orchestrator roles of an ecosystem that can add more value to the customers.[11]

Many financial institutions have not considered a priority to supply value to their customers versus their shareholders. The consequence has been the birth of fintech organizations. These are start-up financial institutions that rely on innovative solutions to improve banking customer journeys. Fintech organizations are emerging rapidly[12] to collect on opportunities to disrupt the banking market in areas where traditional financial institutions' legacy systems do not satisfy/delight customers.

[9] www.accenture.com/_acnmedia/pdf-95/accenture-2019-global-financial-services-consumer-study.pdf. Accessed 11 October 2020.

[10] www.iotinsobs.com/. Accessed 20 May 2020.

[11] Smart Home Insurance. LinkedIn SlideShare. www.slideshare.net/matteocarbone/smart-home-insurance-14443835. Accessed 30 March 2020.

[12] Design, Websight. Financial Solution Partners. The Only Investment Bank Focused Exclusively on Financial Solution. FT Partners | Financial Solution Investment Bank, San Francisco, CA. www.ftpartners.com/fintech-research. Accessed 10 January 2021.

Banking 5.0 and Value Network

The literature defines six value dimensions of a customer journey.[13] They are (1) Sensorial; (2) Emotional; (3) Cognitive; (4) Pragmatic; (5) Lifestyle; (6) Relational. The definition and implementation of a customer value proposition for financial institutions based on these value dimensions are essential. It should be based on values that financial institution managers consider most important to their specific customers in their experience. Functional, emotional, and symbolic customer value dimensions tend to be most valuable to financial institution customers in their customer journey. A survey found that these value dimensions, based on the six aspects of the service offering are what financial institutions' employees think their customers find most valuable.[14] The most often mentioned aspects were: (1) Accessibility of products/services, (2) Security-related elements, (3) Personalized products and services, (4) Comprehensive product range, (5) Convincing online appearance, and (6) Corporate Social Responsibility.

It is interesting to analyze the relationships between banking 5.0 and the value network of a financial institution. Because of banking 5.0, information is becoming more relevant for financial institutions than operational factors. Many financial institutions have started to move part of their business to the web to cope with this digital development. They have developed a type of relationship with customers based on innovative solutions and advanced communication tools.

Online banking means starting, arranging, and carrying out online banking processes. It brings interacting and exchanging services with the internet's help to achieve added value for the customers and the organization. Organizations, public institutions, and customers can be both service providers and service customers in a vision of Banking as a Service.[15] What is essential is that the online banking relationship generates added

[13] Halstrick, T. (2020). *Determining a bank's customer value proposition based on customer value dimensions* (Bachelor's thesis), University of Twente.

[14] Gentile, C., Spiller, N., & Noci, G. (2007). How to sustain the customer experience: An overview of experience components that co-create value with the customer. *European Management Journal, 25*(5), 395–410.

[15] Attanasi, V. (2018). *The value generation in the Bank. Organization and process performance monitoring-Intesa Sanpaolo case study* (Doctoral dissertation), Politecnico di Torino, Turin, Italy.

value, bringing either a direct or indirect financial benefit or an intangible contribution to the customers and the organization.[16]

The dematerialization of products, made possible by the online and mobile approach, transforms how financial institutions position themselves in the value network due to reduced operational and interaction contacts and costs, and the diverse ways the financial institution can engage with customers. These new market conditions can strengthen downstream organizations. Upstream financial institutions can still gain added value through the digital service if they include distinctive components in their service offerings that are difficult to replicate or imitate from the competition.[17]

Value Network Architecture

A classification of the value-added functionalities by a financial institution to its customers is based on the banking philosophy, considering Porter's generic strategies: Cost leadership, Cost focus, Differentiation; Differentiation focus (Fig. 4.1)[18]:

Banking 5.0 can support all these strategies, making it possible for financial institutions also to choose a hybrid strategy. Banking 5.0 can[19]:

- Reduce costs by increasing productivity or making available solutions, for example, robo-advisors, at a low price. Innovative solutions allow automatizing, standardizing, and improving the effectiveness, efficiency, and economics of banking processes. For example,

[16] Meier, A., & Stormer, H. (2009). *eBusiness & eCommerce: Managing the digital value chain*. Springer Science & Business Media, Berlin/Heidelberg, Germany.

[17] Vendrell-Herrero, F., Bustinza, O. F., Parry, G., & Georgantzis, N. (2017). Servitization, digitization and supply chain interdependency. *Industrial Marketing Management, 60*, 69–81.

[18] Porter, M. (1985). How information gives you competitive advantage. *Harvard Business Review, 63*(4), 149–160.

[19] Eling, M., & Lehmann, M. (2018). *The impact of digitization on the insurance value chain and the insurability of risks*. Springer, New York, NY.

Strategy	Goal	Characteristics	Tools
Cost Leadership	Economics	When the financial institution has the goal of charging low prices to attract a high volume of low-margin customers	Cognitive Computing
Cost Focus	Efficiency	When the financial institution strips out frills not valued by its customers, such as loyalty programs,	Language Systems, Computer Vision
Differentiation	Effectiveness	When the financial institutions decide to compete on quality, they charge a premium on a lower volume of high-margin customers.	Machine Learning, Rule-based Reasoning; Predictive Analytics
Differentiation Focus	Expertise	The focus is on supplying a specialized product offering, which allows the financial institution to charge a premium.	Machine Learning

Fig. 4.1 Porter's generic strategies

smart contracts, that is, programs that automatically execute the payments under predefined conditions stored in a blockchain, are entirely digital and automatic products, implementing Straight-through processing (STP), a characteristic of banking 5.0.[20]

- Cost focus by stripping out frills not valued by the target segment, such as using chatbots for rich customer servicing. This impact regards the digitization of all processes of the value network, leading to the automation of banking processes (that is, the automated processing of transactions, automatic reporting, help desk support, and so on) and decisions (that is, portfolio optimization, automated credit scoring, product offerings, and so on).
- Improve differentiation by assuring high quality, such as 24*7 service: Innovative solutions change how financial institutions and customers interact. This impact on the value network is how banking organizations can interact with their customers (for example, in marketing, sales, operations, and customer service) and adapt to their behavior. Customers traditionally needed personal interactions for product information or transactions. They can now get information online, which allows them comparing products and prices via

[20] Eling, M., & Lehmann, M. (2018). *The impact of digitization on the insurance value chain and the insurability of risks*. Springer, Cham, Switzerland.

marketplace comparators.[21] It is possible to buy more products and services online without any personal interaction. A survey by Accenture done in 2019 probed several markets. The result is that 68% of persons prefer to use online access to get info on banking products and services.[22]

- By supporting new specialized product offering, such as strongly customized products, such as trade finance, with own differentiation focus.[23] Innovative solutions create opportunities to change current portfolio strategy and products and to develop new services.

The following chapters detail how banking 5.0 can help to plan and implement these strategies.

Value Network in Banking 5.0

This section aims to clarify how financial institutions should deal with their customers' empowerment and, simultaneously, use them to achieve a competitive advantage.

Some incumbent organizations have some negative characteristics[24]:

- Poor engagement.
- Risk aversion.
- Legacy systems and processes.

Incumbents may face significant transformation difficulties. They could end up with negative consequences if the transformation would not be professionally managed. For new entrants and recent start-ups, it may be easier to design their businesses following the banking 5.0 model.

[21] Saffer, D. (2010). *Designing for interaction: Creating innovative applications and devices*. New Riders, Indianapolis, IN.

[22] www.accenture.com/_acnmedia/pdf-95/accenture-2019-global-financial-services-consumer-study.pdfAccessed. Accessed 1 January 2021.

[23] Nicoletti, B. (2018). *Procurement finance*. Springer International Publishing, London, UK.

[24] www.mckinsey.it/idee/culture-for-a-digital-age. Accessed 20 March 2020.

Fujitsu commissioned a European-wide study[25] to understand the dimension of the change in the interaction between financial institutions and their customers.[26] This study underlines that[27]:

- More than a third of European customers would consider moving to a competing financial services institution if they did not get up-to-date solutions to help interactions.
- A third of customers are already using mobile payments. A fifth pay using wearables and cryptocurrency.
- A fifth of customers would be ready to buy banking services from challengers such as Google, Facebook, and Amazon.

Benefits and Challenges in Value Network

Banking 5.0 offers the benefit of building a value proposition around what today customers care about[28]:

- On-demand availability when s/he needs help or have questions.
- Speed and simplicity with any event or transactions or problem resolution or remediation.
- Total costs and customer journey, combined with trust.
- Effective innovation on respect their needs.

[25] Fujitsu EMEIA. (2016, May). Banking on change: Customers drive digital charge in financial services. www.fujitsu.com/fts/about/resources/news/press-releases/2016/emeai-160504-banking-on-change-customers-drive-digital.html. Accessed 25 August 2019.

[26] Seven thousand online customers across the UK, France, Benelux, Spain, Germany, Switzerland, and Eastern Europe understand customers' habits, views, and opinions towards traditional financial services.

[27] Fujitsu EMEIA. (2016, May). Banking on change: Customers drive digital charge in financial services. www.fujitsu.com/fts/about/resources/news/press-releases/2016/emeai-160504-banking-on-change-customers-drive-digital.html, Accessed 25 August 2019.

[28] https://advisorevolved.com/insurance-agency-value-proposition/. Accessed 28 March 2020.

There are several challenges in adding value in banking 5.0. Five categories are essential[29]:

- Services in the banking proposition are fundamental. Bankers have an opportunity to solve customer problems by delivering a comprehensive value proposition for banking services (and potentially non-banking). Especially, bankers can embed banking activity in the operational tasks of their customers.
- Loss control. The prevention and mitigation potential of innovations can help in predicting non-performing credits and improve relationships. If carefully selected, banking 5.0 solutions bring tangible economic benefits to banking based on real time, data-driven processes.
- Behavioral change. The more a financial institution links customer behaviors and losses, the higher the opportunity to understand and promote more secure practices while discouraging riskier ones.
- Risk selection and pricing. Banking 5.0 solutions are helpful, directly or indirectly, to analyze risks during the credit approval and pricing process, improving credit scoring activity effectiveness. Data collection tools can enhance the overall quality of the credit scoring/pricing process.

Banking 5.0 transformation is tied with obstacles that may hamper the smooth implementation of digital transformation. It is important to find and analyze the main barriers to digital transformation in the retail and corporate banking sectors. The findings of a group of researchers reveal some clustering of the obstacles. Elements of strategy and management, solutions and regulatory compliance, customer, and employee should receive a high degree of attention within digital transformations.[30] Further main barriers can be found in market, knowledge and product, the participation of employees and customers, and public benefits. Several sub-barriers characterize each main barrier with different importance for the digital transformation of banking.

[29] www.slideshare.net/matteocarbone/smart-home-insurance-144438351

[30] Špaček, F., & Diener, M. (2020, September). Implementation barriers in digital transformation: A qualitative perspective on German banking. *The 14th International Days of Statistics and Economics*, Prague, Czech Republic.

New Banking Business Models

There are several new business models for digital banks. This chapter examines some of them.

The requirements for new business models in financial institutions are the following ones[31]:

- Faster e-Know your customer (eKYC) and more comfortable onboarding.
- Around the clock customer service.
- Innovative and targeted services aligned with customer needs.
- Rapid credit processing and use of sophisticated credit scoring systems.
- Proactive and competitive pricing of products and services.

There are legal and regulatory challenges.[32] The biggest initial challenge faced by digital banks is the limitation in increasing capital due to regulatory restrictions and bad economic situations.

There are also market challenges:

- Despite the widespread adoption of online banking in the world, digital banks struggle to achieve primary bank status.
- Digital banks face competition from payment service providers especially if backed by bigtech organizations.
- The competition will increase with new opportunities on the horizon.

The positive impacts of digital banks on banking are[33]:

- Bringing the catfish effect in the local banking industry.[34]
- Contributing to expanding credit to the underserved.

[31] Choi, Y. (2020). *Digital banks*. World Bank Report.

[32] Choi, Y. (2020). *Digital banks*. World Bank Report.

[33] Choi, Y. (2020). *Digital banks*. World Bank Report.

[34] Yuting, X. J. Z. (2007). How Chinese banks respond to the entry of foreign banks. *Finance & Economics, 10*.

Challenger Banks

A challenger bank is: "... a bank that is smaller than a national brand and that is specifically designed to compete with the big traditional banks, be it through offering superior service, better deals, or more often than not, a combination of the two."[35]

Online banking increased the competitive playing field for financial institutions. Adding to the financial crisis of 2008 and the pandemic of 2020+, the environment has and will change dramatically.[36] Plenty of physical branches across a country does not make sense anymore. The branches and their employees consume valuable resources. It is wiser to spend those resources improving solutions to delight the customers.

Returns for a typical challenger bank tend to be better with respect to traditional financial institutes. Costs are lower than the big traditional banks.[37] Challenger banks have more advanced and up-to-date software than traditional banks. They have user-friendly websites and a small management structure. Consequently, senior management knows what is happening on the shop floor.

Challenger banks usually supply a more personalized service to customers than traditional banks. However, the new licensing laws and the preference for online banking by customers have changed the market. Small and specialized institutions have a better and more up-to-date environment today in which they thrive and grow. It has become more challenging to compete for customers than in the past. The market is becoming progressively more crowded.

In the past, a typical challenger bank had a business model of targeting profitable lending niches. Competition within these niches has intensified.[38] Margins are diminishing. To respond effectively, challenger banks have created new product lines. They are becoming more complex and will take on more staff. They will slowly become like traditional banks.

[35] https://moneyfacts.co.uk/savings-accounts/guides/what-are-challenger-banks/. Accessed 11 November 2020.

[36] https://marketbusinessnews.com/financial-glossary/challenger-bank-definition-meaning/.

[37] Lu, L. (2018). How a little ant challenges giant banks? The rise of ant financial (Alipay)'s fintech empire and relevant regulatory concerns. *International Company and Commercial Law Review (2018), Sweet & Maxwell*. ISSN 0958-5214.

[38] https://marketbusinessnews.com/financial-glossary/challenger-bank-definition-meaning/. Accessed 30 March 2021.

The challenge faced by the big traditional banks is the entirely different business model used by challenger banks.[39] These banks target millennials who rely heavily on modern solutions such as mobile banking. They aim to fill the student loan needs, some mortgage categories, and lending to small- to medium-sized businesses.[40] Challenger banks tend to be asset-light and leverage customer data and solutions to drive their customer-centric strategy. Algorithms, predictive analytics, and machine learning are present on many challenger banks' business models.

Some challenger banks have introduced chatbots to communicate with their customers.[41] With the support of machine learning, some challenger banks offer a system that makes recommendations to customer service agents for customer queries.[42] This solution speeds up the resolution process and improves the customer journey. Customers get the answers quickly. They enjoy not having to listen to automated responses that might not specifically resolve their problems. Some challenger banks have deployed AI to allow customers to access financing in seconds.

Neobanks

Neobanks are financial institutions that offer internet-only financial services and products and do not have physical branches. Neobanks appeal to customers who accept doing most of their banking through a mobile phone. The characteristics of neobanks are:

Philosophy

- Not chartered with state or federal regulators as banks.
- Real-time data integration and management.

[39] Lui, A., & Lamb, G. (2018). Artificial intelligence and augmented intelligence collaboration: Regaining trust and confidence in the financial sector. *Information and Communications Solution Law*. ISSN 1360-0834

[40] https://voxeu.org/system/files/epublication/The_Future_of_Banking_2.pdf. Accessed 12 November 2020.

[41] www.firstsource.com/challenger-vs-established-banks-in-ai-machine-learning-and-data-analytics/. Accessed 4 January 2021.

[42] Challenger vs Established banks in AI, machine learning. www.firstsource.com/challenger-vs-established-banks-in-ai-machine-learning-and-data-analytics/. Accessed 4 January 2021.

  - In some cases, they are owned by traditional financial institutions which want to diversify or try new business models.

Value Provision

- Offerings are like those at traditional banks, even if more limited.
  - Checking and savings accounts.
  - Payment and money transfer services.
  - Financial education tools, including budgeting help.
  - Do not supply credit extensions to limit their risk. This approach helps them to keep costs down.

Proximity

- Customer-centric organizational design.
- Customer needs data-driven architecture.

Place

- Be an online-only financial institution.

Platforms

- Supply open banking through APIs.
- Open ecosystem with access to external developers.
- Open architecture technology stack.
- Ability to "plug and play" best-in-class tools/services.

Processes

- Supply a streamlined process designed for use with a mobile phone.

Persons

- Limited internal staff, mostly commercial and technical.

Partnerships

- Tend to partner with more prominent chartered financial institutions to enjoy deposit accounts and get government agencies to ensure customer deposits.
- Current accounts generate key data for third parties.
- Some neobanks link with traditional bank accounts, especially with open banking. This link assures the best of both business models.

Pricing

- Data powers business model also through third party affiliation fees.

Payments

- By cutting physical branches and moving everything online, neobanks save on the costs of banking. This approach allows them to reduce fees and expand services to underbanked persons.

Traditional banks have recognized the demand for neobanking services. They started rolling out similar offerings to compete. For example, Bank of America offers an AI-driven virtual financial assistant dubbed "Erica" in its mobile app.[43]

Neobanks have benefits and challenges.

The most relevant benefits are:

- Low costs.
- Convenience.
- Fast processing time.

The most relevant challenges are to be:

- Comfortable with their solutions.
- Less regulated than traditional banks.

[43] https://builtin.com/artificial-intelligence/ai-in-banking. Accessed 11 November 2020.

- No physical bank branches: It is becoming increasingly easy to do everything online. Usually, neobanks often include the use of other financial institutions ATMs.

The rise of new types of data and analysis techniques from Artificial intelligence (AI) to machine learning drives the decisions behind the neobanks systems. Neobanks are competitive for the following reasons[44]:

1. Credit decisions: AI allows more sophisticated rules which address the sparse data problems by factoring in alternate and behavioral data such as mobile phone usage and lifestyle behavior.
2. Risk Management: AI can use both quantitative and unstructured data for risk management. AI supports fraud management. It creates triggers when contradictory spending patterns are met.
3. Trading: AI allows customers to manage their entire portfolios by finding stock price movement trends and performance from both unstructured and structured data sources
4. Personalized banking and advice: Chatbots can manage customer queries. Robo-advisors can support wealth management and build customized plans for savings and investment management.

Digital Payment Instruments

The increased use of digital solutions explains the reduction of physical financial institution branches and subsidiaries. The market has shifted toward online payment instruments, defined as any personalized device and/or set of procedures agreed upon by the Payment service user (PSU) and the Payment service provider (PSP) and used by the PSU to start a payment order.[45] Payment cards followed by credit transfers, direct debits, and e-money payments were the more popular non-cash payment instruments in the EU in 2016. According to the European Central Bank (ECB) statistics (2017) on payment instruments, the total number of non-cash payments increased by 8.5% to €122 billion in 2016 compared

[44] https://bridgei2i.com/neobanks-the-new-age-tech-revolutionizing-ai-in-banking/. Accessed 4 January 2021.

[45] www.ebf.eu/wp-content/uploads/2020/01/EBF-PSD2-Guidance-Final-v.120.pdf. Accessed 20 October 2020.

to 2015. Payment cards accounted for 48.9%, followed by credit transfers with 25.1%, direct debits with 20.4%, and e-money with 2.3%. All together, these four payment methods accounted for 96.7% of all cashless payments.[46] The pandemic fueled a larger use of these instruments.

AI and machine learning are valuable tools for payments organizations and financial institutions to help reduce fraud in all environments, particularly in e-commerce transactions.[47] Most critically, systems can learn from each transaction, continually improving and becoming more effective thanks to machine learning and AI.

One of the most significant areas that AI can improve is the customer journey for payments organizations and financial institutions. According to a Juniper Research analysis, the presence of chatbot programs will save financial institutions billions of dollars in operating costs and hundreds of millions of workforce hours when applied to a customer-facing setting like customer service and dispute resolution.[48] The study puts the figure at USD 7.3 billion globally by 2023, up from USD 200 million in 2019. That is a staggering 862 million hours (about 98,000 years) saving.

For payments solutions organizations and financial institutions, AI quickly could become an invaluable tool for securely resolving chargebacks, helping their merchant customers, and streamlining merchants' onboarding in a very cost-effective way. The application of AI in these mobile banking settings can assure convenience in digital banking. Juniper Research's chatbot study found that the dominant channel for chatbot integration will be mobile banking, accounting for 79% of successful integrations in 2023. The implementation of chatbots in settings, including mobile banking apps, will result in a 3,150% increase in banking chatbot interactions between 2019 and 2023.

Industry estimates growth of AI-powered voice commerce in double digits in the near term.[49] AI opens a new channel for banking. Payments

[46] www.ecb.europa.eu/press/pr/stats/paysec/html/ecb.pis2018~c758d7e773.en.html. Accessed 20 October 2020.

[47] www.fintechnews.org/the-crirital-role-of-artificial-inteliigence-in-payments-tech/. Accessed 4 January 2021.

[48] www.juniperresearch.com/press/press-releases/bank-cost-savings-via-chatbots-reach-7-3bn-2023. Accessed 4 January 2021.

[49] The Critical Role of Artificial Intelligence in Payments Tech. Fintech News. Accessed 4 January 2021.

organizations can use this channel to create more digital touchpoints to make buying convenient and secure.

AI can drive digital transformation for merchants of all sizes by taking payments data to the next level. For example, machine learning algorithms can analyze transaction data to find patterns (for example, seasonal decrease in revenue) and help business owners plan and compensate down to details. Further, they can supply targeted marketing capabilities like rewards programs and analytical dashboards to help business owners manage their inventory, capture recent sales, and perfect their businesses with each customer.

Fintech Organizations

A fintech organization is a financial start-up, which uses innovative technology solutions to improve financial performance.[50] Fintech organizations improve applications, procedures, products, processes, business models, and ideas in the financial sector.

The term fintech organizations include any solution-driven innovation in banking: software, applications, processes, products, and services.[51] Fintech organization start-ups have rigorously targeted some areas of financial services in payments. They are now directing their efforts directly to financial institutions' services. Nine out of 10 banking executives surveyed by Price Waterhouse Coopers reckon that at least part of their business is at risk, a higher proportion than in any other finance area.[52]

[50] Nicoletti, B. (2017). *Future of FinTech*. Palgrave Macmillan, Basingstoke, UK.

[51] Baumann, N. (2018). A catalyst for change. How fintech has sparked a revolution in insurance. www2.deloitte.com/content/dam/Deloitte/global/Documents/Financial-Services/gx-fsi-cataylst-for-change. Accessed 20 March 2020. Chester, A., Hoffman, N., Johansson, S., & BraadOlesen, P. (2018). *Digital insurance in 2018. Commercial lines InsurTech: A pathway to digital*. McKinsey. Swiss Re Institute. (2017, June). Solution and insurance: Themes and challenges.

[52] https://blogs.reuters.com/breakingviews/2016/07/13/fintech-bigger-and-dicier-for-financialinstitutions-than-financialinstitutions/. Accessed 29 July 2016.

Fintech organizations are the main competitors of traditional financial institutions.[53] They use innovative methods to improve financial performance. Modern devices, investment services, and cryptocurrencies are examples of innovations aimed at modernizing and improving the financial world. Fintech organizations are not only start-ups but successful organizations that can improve the economic status. Fintech organizations introduce solutions and innovative solutions. In this way, they improve and develop the provision of services and increase competitiveness.

Before the advent of the e-commerce models in the financial industry in the 1980s, solutions and innovations in most of the cases supported financial institutions, retail, and businesses. The overwhelming success of the e-commerce model followed. It increased the importance and necessity of innovation also for the global financial industry. With the diffusion of the internet, the world's first fintech organization appeared, performing online brokerage services that supported the e-commerce sales model. A turning point marked the internet boom in the 2000s for the formation and widespread dissemination of online banking among customers. The pandemic in 2020 pushed even further the model. The internet has been widely used worldwide, reducing consultations, and turning all actions into fast tasks. It has supported the growth and diffusion of fintech organizations. Many fintech organizations appeared and offered new functions and highly developed services. The areas more interested were risks, financial management, money management, data analysis systems, and automated online trading.

Fintech organizations contributed to creating a new face for the global financial sector. They offered many improvements to solve customers' problems and challenges in their financial transactions with traditional financial institutions. PayPal is one of the typical examples of a fintech organization. It was one of the organizations at the forefront of innovation, changing transaction and money management through online trading and payment service. Another example of the growth of fintech

[53] Price Waterhouse Coopers. (2016). Insurtech: A golden opportunity for financial institutions to innovate.www.PwC.com/us/en/insurance/publications/assets/PwC-top-issues-insurtech.pdf. Accessed 31 July 2016. Scheuffel, P. (2016). Taming the beast: A scientific definition of fintech. *Journal of Innovation Management*, 4(4), 32–54.

organizations was the emergence of the e-commerce platform eBay. It is a website that allows customers to buy, often via auctions on its website, a wide range of products and quickly makes secure payments via the network.

Compared to 2008, where global investments in fintech organization amounted to 930 million USD, the global fintech market is expected to grow gradually and reach a market value of approximately USD 305 billion by 2025, growing at a compound annual rate of about 22.17% over the forecast period 2020–2025.[54] The global fintech industry is growing despite the pandemic, although results vary across geographies and verticals.[55] Fintech organizations have been adapting to fluid market conditions by revamping product and service offerings but still face significant operational challenges.

The USA, Europe, Asia, South America, and the rest of North America have successful fintech organizations.[56] The number one position in the list of established players trying to change the finance industry comes from China. More than half of the fintech organizations clustered in North America, Europe, and Asia are evolving quickly. The rest of the world is trying to shatter the *status quo* and is catching up to the fintech organizations.[57]

Regulations protect financial institutions, but the wave of start-ups makes global banks unite in recent years. Former bank secrecy rules and bank transfer rules pose a threat to fintech organizations. The International Monetary Fund and the World Bank Group launched the Bali Fintech Agenda, a set of 12 policy elements to help member countries get the benefits and opportunities of rapid advances in financial solutions. These initiatives are transforming the provision of banking services

[54] www.marketdataforecast.com/market-reports/fintech-market. Accessed 20 October 2020.

[55] www.weforum.org/agenda/2020/12/global-covid-19-data-tracks-fintechs-progress-through-unchartered-waters/. Accessed 4 January 2021.

[56] https://home.kpmg/xx/en/home/insights/2019/11/2019-fintech100-leading-global-fintech-innovators-fs.html. Accessed 20 October 2020.

[57] From Brazil to China, how the rest of the world is trying. https://news.yahoo.com/from-brazil-to-china-how-the-rest-of-the-world-is-trying-to-reopen-their-economies-as-the-coronavirus-pandemic-continues-203353029.html. Accessed 4 January 2021.

while simultaneously managing the inherent risks.[58] A significant problem that regulators face due to the threat of hacking is data security and the protection of confidential financial data of customers and corporations.

Fintech organizations are growing despite the elevated level of regulation characterizing the banking sector. The presence of entry barriers instead is slowing the market's access to the so-called bigtech organizations such as Google, Facebook, and Amazon.[59] Without players in a powerful dominant position, the sector can develop gradually and widely, giving fintech organizations the time and space to grow, get funding, and develop innovative solutions.

Customer expectations are relevant components as drivers of disruption. The solution affected the so-called tech-barriers, which has lowered them and allowed several fresh players access to banking.[60] The diffusion of open-source frameworks, development, on-demand, and cloud computing are other examples of solution facilitators for the new entrants. The results are causing unexpected disruptions and turbulence in the financial services market that was, by its very nature, stable and stationary in all its components.[61]

Fintech organizations' lending platforms allow customers to shop for, apply, and obtain loans online in short times. They supply lenders with the usual credit report data (including payment history, amounts owed, length of history, number of accounts, and so on). Fintech lenders also use alternative data sources, such as e-commerce, social media activities, online shopping information from marketplaces such as Amazon, shipping data from postal services, browsing patterns, and type of telephone

[58] www.worldbank.org/en/news/press-release/2018/10/11/bali-fintech-agenda-a-blueprint-for-successfully-harnessing-fintechs-opportunities. Accessed 20 October 2020. www.imf.org/en/News/Articles/2018/10/11/pr18388-the-bali-fintech-agenda#:~:text=Thepercent20Internationalpercent20Monetarypercent20Fundpercent20and,servicespercent2Cpercent20whilepercent20atpercent20thepercent20same. Accessed 20 October 2020.

[59] Nicastro, A. (2018). Strategic alternative for financial institutions to seize fintech revolution opportunities: Cases of successful M&As and alliances.

[60] Barry, C., Hogan, M., & Torres, A. M. (2011). Low-cost financial institutions and high-tech barriers: User views on questionable web design practices in Ireland. *Irish Journal of Management, 31*(1), 43.

[61] Nicoletti, B. Future of Insurance 4.0 and Insurtech. In *Insurance 4.0* (pp. 389–431). Palgrave Macmillan, Cham.

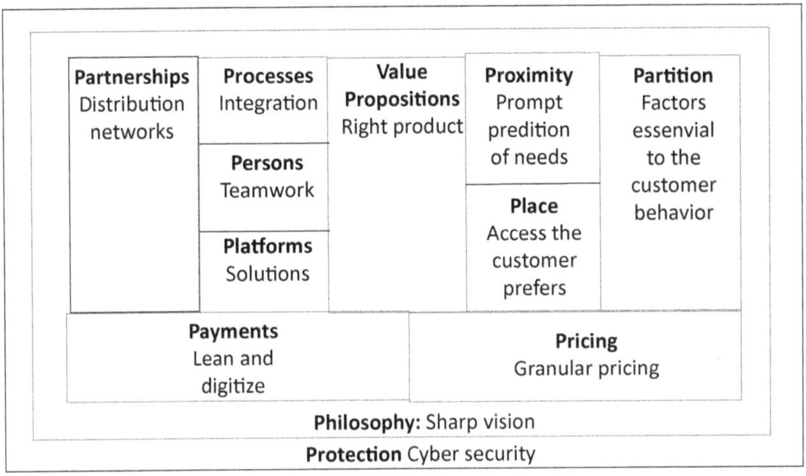

Fig. 4.2 Business model canvas in a fintech organization

or browser used.[62] Alternative data processed by fintech organizations using AI can ease credit access for persons or SMEs without a traditional credit history. They can lower the costs associated with lending both for customers and lenders.[63]

Fintech Architecture

The definition of a business model for fintech organizations can start with the general model for banking organizations presented in this book, making the necessary adjustments.[64] Every start-up should address its focus toward these essential components to effectively engage with today's knowledge-empowered customers (Fig. 4.2)[65]:

[62] Jagtiani, J., & Lemieux, C. (2019). The roles of alternative data and machine learning in fintech lending: Evidence from the LendingClub consumer platform. *Working Paper*, No. 18-15. Federal Reserve Bank of Philadelphia.

[63] Vives, X. (2017). The impact of FinTech on banking. *European Economy* (2), 97–105.

[64] Nicoletti, B. (2017). *The future of fintech*. Springer International Publishing, London, UK. ISBN 978-3-319-51414-7.

[65] Nicoletti, B. (2017). *The future of fintech*. Springer International Publishing, London, UK. ISBN 978-3-319-51414-7.

- Philosophy. A sharp vision of the goals of the organization.
- Proposition of value. Focus on the right products that suit evolving needs and preferences across the customer lifecycle.
- Proximity to the customer. Focus on prompt communication when customers perceive banking as valuable; predict customers' life situations, and offer services when they need it most.
- Partition of the market. Focus on the factors essential to define customer behavior about buying banking: social behavior and shopping preferences.
- Place or accesses. Focus on the right access that customers prefer and use most. Define an omnichannel (or better omniaccess[66]) strategy.
- Platforms. Focus on solutions, not on technologies.
- Processes. Focus on banking process integration.
- Persons. Focus on new ways of working, new roles, and teamwork,
- Partnership and collaboration. Focus on financial institutions and distribution networks. Be part of an ecosystem to offer a full range of services.
- Pricing and revenue. Focus on customer lifetime value and granular pricing.[67] based on better data capture.
- Payments on costs and investments. Focus on lean and digitize.[68]
- Protection. Focus on cyber security, which tends to be a weak point for fintech organizations.[69]

This framework fits well with the environment for a start-up working in financial services. Considering various categories in fintech organization initiatives, their difference would be the specific items' weight in the previous list and their specific aims and goals. Regarding the "partnership and collaboration" area, for example, the financial institutions' weight is quite different if referred to as a fintech organization or a traditional financial institution. The focus is not on "financial institutions" but rather "financial institutions and other strategic partners."

[66] https://thefinanser.com/wp-content/uploads/2020/12/The_Omniaccess_Future.pdf. Accessed 19 December 2020.

[67] Berger, P. D., & Nasr, N. I. (1998). Customer lifetime value: Marketing models and applications. *Journal of Interactive Marketing, 12*(1), 17–30.

[68] Nicoletti, B. (2016). *Lean and digitize: An integrated approach to process improvement*. Routledge, London, UK.

[69] Pedersen, N. (2020). *Financial solutions: Case studies in fintech innovation*. Google.

Fintech organizations have targeted all parts of the value network of traditional financial institutions. Although these start-ups are present in every part of the value network, their focus to date has been on the more easily accessible parts of the value network: credit and especially payments. Since fintech organizations' innovation aims to contribute to the banking value network, many financial institutions view partnerships with fintech organizations positively.

It is possible to develop a classification of fintech organization business models.[70] It is possible to build this classification on (a) theoretical foundations of the business model concept and (b) data from available databases aggregating information about innovative organizations, such as Crunchbase.[71] It is possible to consider the dimensions of fintech organization business models with the characteristics shown in Table 4.1.

It is possible to define the models of fintech organizations.[72] By using the organization tags of the database Crunchbase, it is possible to define a cluster dendrogram and find ten clusters of fintech organization business models: (1) Cryptocurrency; (2) Payment Service; (3) Financial Markets Intermediary; (4) Information Aggregator; (5) Information Extractor; (6) Insourcer of Sub-Processes; (7) Lending Community; (8) Alternative Trading Venue; (9) Robo-Advisor; and (10) Co-Creator of Financial Analysis.

Fintech organization business model component "Product and Portfolio strategy" plays a significant role in a fintech organization's success. Studies have found that product-specific factors are crucial determinants of venture success. They rely on innovation to generate competitive advantages.[73] The fintech organizations that are more likely to succeed

[70] Roeder, J., Cardona, D. R., Palmer, M., Werth, O., Muntermann, J., & Breitner, M. H. (2018). Make or break. Business model determinants of FinTech venture success. *Proceedings of the Multikonferenz Wirtschaftsinformatik, Lüneburg, Germany.*

[71] Ferrati, F., & Muffatto, M. (2020, June). Using Crunchbase for research in entrepreneurship: Data content and structure. In *20th European Conference on Research Method for Business and Management Studies: ECRM 2020* (p. 342). Academic Conferences and Publishing International, Reading, UK.

[72] Eickhoff, M., Muntermann, I., & Weinrich, T. (2017). What do fintech organizations actually do? A taxonomy of FinTech business models.

[73] Kakati, M. (2003). Success criteria in high-tech new ventures. *Technovation, 23*, 447–457.

Table 4.1 Fintech activities

Sector	*Fintech activities*
Credit	Credit scoring Direct lending Peer-to-peer lending Microfinance Crowdfunding
Asset management	Quantitative and asset management Digital banking
Personal finance	Chatbots Virtual assistant Robo-advisor
Payments clearing settlement	e Wallet Digital payment services
Market analysis	Market research Market intelligence Sentiment analysis
Commercial and corporate	Business finance Trade finance Expense reporting
Capital markets	Trading Do.it.yourself funds Alternative data
Cryptocurrencies	Financial activities related to cryptocurrencies
Risk	Credit scoring and underwriting Pricing Risk management
Security	Fraud detection Identification Biometrics and KYC AML
Collection	Debt collection
Insurance	Insurtech business models
Legal	Smart contracts
Regulations	Regtech organizations to support compliance
Suptech	Suptech to support supervisory
ESG	ESGtech in support of the environment, Social And Governance
General purpose	Semantic and natural language Predictive analytics

target existing markets with growth potential like credit markets.[74] Fintech organizations adopt simple business models focused on specific areas and rich in technological aspects. Several of them use Artificial intelligence (AI), often machine learning. They have a vast ability for big data analysis and processing. Fintech organizations can seize the market opportunities more swiftly than traditional financial institutions, thanks to digitization and automation and their small size. They often have a culture that recognizes innovation and a mentality that places them in an excellent position in sector change.[75]

Fintech and Banking 5.0

The relevance of fintech organizations comes from Bill Gates' statement on financial institutions: "Banking is necessary, banks are not.[76] or "banks are the steel industry of the [nineteen]nineties."[77] Fintech organizations play a fundamental role in developing solutions that address the financial service's needs. Higher customer loyalty, new income sources, and more operational efficiency are some of the benefits that make fintech organizations attractive partners for traditional financial institutions.

In terms of solutions, most investments target fintech organizations active in AI and mobile application fields. Compared to other sectors, these solutions help more in customer value creation. They attract investors interested in new business models.[78] Other investments focus on technologies, such as big data analytics, cloud computing, the internet of things, and blockchain solutions.

Investment in AI-based start-ups multiplied during 2016–2018. Investment levels in the AI sector were 665% higher than during the

[74] MacMillan, I. C., Siegel, R., & Narasimha, P. S. (1985). Criteria used by venture capitalists to evaluate new venture proposals. *Journal of Business Venturing, 1*, 119–128.

[75] Catlin, T., & Lorenz, J. T. (2017, March). Digital disruption in insurance: Cutting through the noise. *Digital McKinsey*.

[76] Angelshaug, M., & Saebi, T. (2017). The burning platform of retail banking. *The European Business Review, 5*, 30–35.

[77] Beck, H. (2001). Banking is essential, banks are not. The future of financial intermediation in the age of the internet. *Netnomics, 3*(1), 7–22.

[78] Ntt Data & Everis. (2019). Publish InsurTech Outlook. www.marketscreener.com/NTT-DATA-CORP-6491233/news/NTT-DATA-and-everis-Publish-InsurTech-Outlook-2019-29215636/. Accessed 10 May 2020.

previous five years.[79] This investment focus underlines the importance of being a data-driven organization able to construct personalized offers, attract and keep customers, and achieve more effective, efficient, and economic processes across all business lines. The pandemic has not slowed down this growth.[80]

Evolution of Fintech Organizations

There are four waves in the development of fintech organizations (Fig. 4.3).[81] In the first wave, around 2016, fintech organizations were mostly challengers and disruptors. As new entrants, they were attacking the established order. The mantra was disruption. New entrants took the lead in smart and innovative solutions and data, designing innovative solutions that solved customers' dissatisfaction with traditional financial institutions. Their focus on fewer frictions and excellent service levels has changed the expectations of customers. New entrants set new standards.

This sense of urgency fueled the second wave. The second wave's fintech organizations, the enablers, aimed to impact the top line and bottom line of the traditional financial institutions. Many fintech organizations explored the potential of new data streams to improve pricing, automate credit scoring, and reduce fraud. They launched all sorts of new proactive services, especially in the online and mobility space. Many traditional financial institutions realized that partnering with fintech organizations is vital to accelerate innovation.

The third wave characteristic is ecosystems beyond banking. The third wave of fintech organization is about increasing relevancy and opening. This trend is essential for the years after the pandemic. More fintech organizations realize that the most effective way to reach out to customers is

[79] www.nttdata.com/global/en/media/press-release/2019/september/ntt-data-and-everis-publish-insurtech-outlook-2019. Accessed 20 May 2020.

[80] Ntt Data and Everis Publish. (2019). InsurTech Outlook. www.marketscreener.com/NTT-DATA-CORP-6491233/news/NTT-DATA-and-everis-Publish-InsurTech-Outlook-2019-29215636/. Accessed 22 June 2020.

[81] Peverelli, R., & de Fenika, R. (2019). The four waves of Insurtech organization. https://xprimm.com/The-Four-Waves-of-Insurtech-articol-117,149-13848.htm. Accessed 30 May 2020.

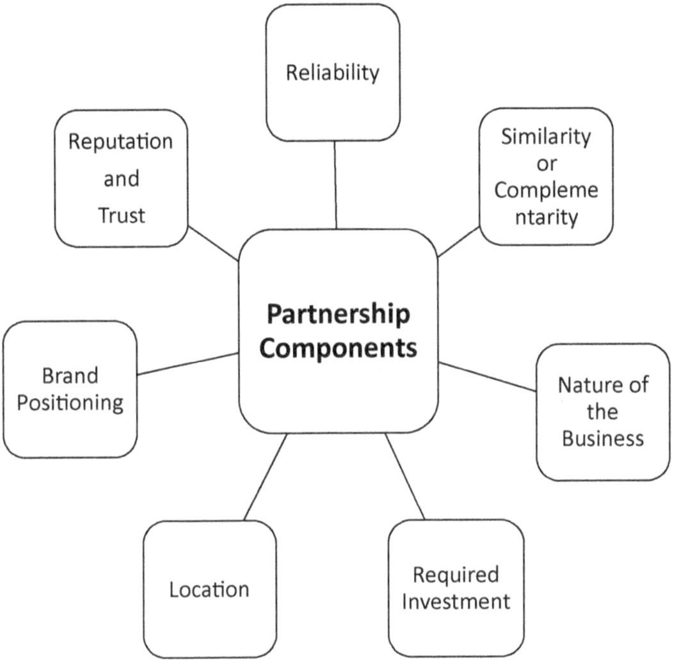

Fig. 4.3 Partnership components

to be part of essential platforms and ecosystems.[82] These platforms are not only platforms around the home, mobility, work, and health. They are around significant life events such as study, weddings, birth, divorce, and retirement, in individuals. It is around transportation, procurement, manufacturing, and so on, for commercial banking. All those events require significant financial and risk decisions. More fintech organizations partner in financial ecosystems with traditional financial institutions or with other fintech organizations.

[82] The Number 1 Insurtech Trend for 2019: Ecosystems beyond. https://wwwdigitalinsuranceagenda.com/thought-leadership/the-number-1-insurtech-trend-for-2019-ecosystems-beyond-insurance/. Accessed 20 December 2020.

The pandemic generated the fourth wave.[83] Pandemic created uncertainty about everything. Many fintech organizations have been under stress on several fronts.[84] It was already becoming not easy to get funds for fintech organizations, especially for some early stage ventures. Many investors preferred to focus on established fintech organizations with sound and proved business models. Interest rate cuts and the economic slowdown have changed the scenario in which to act for putting the basis for new business models.

The fourth wave sees fintech organizations as social challengers. They can grab the opportunity to increase their social and economic impact and position themselves as a Force for Good.[85] More and more fintech organizations set up the mission to tackle critical global challenges: applying new sustainable solutions with significant social and economic impact.

The pandemic created new opportunities for some fintech organizations. For example, as social isolation has taken hold worldwide, this situation generates big growth in online financial services and e-commerce. Forty-two percent of respondents surveyed in 2020 said they used at least one fintech services.[86] More than six percent of all financial decision-makers surveyed became a fintech user since the start of the pandemic. The fintech organization sector, based on innovation, can generate new and transformative solutions. The added value of the fourth wave is different from the earlier waves. The possibilities to increase banking's social and economic impact with innovative solutions seem almost endless.

Given their differentiated capabilities, namely adaptability, and innovation, many fintech organizations are well-positioned to survive the crisis and contribute to the business and society in meaningful ways. Adversity inspires creativity.

Maintaining operational resilience is top of mind as well. Lending fintech organizations are being overwhelmed with customer requests for

[83] www2.deloitte.com/us/en/pages/financial-services/articles/beyond-covid-19-new-opportunities-for-fintech-companies.html. Accessed 20 January 2021.

[84] www2.deloitte.com/us/en/pages/financial-services/articles/beyond-covid-19-new-opportunities-for-fintech-companies.html. Accessed 20 January 2021.

[85] Taddeo, M., & Floridi, L. (2018). How AI can be a force for good. *Science, 361*(6404), 751–752.

[86] Krivkovich, A., White, O., Zac Townsend, Z., & Euart, J. (2020, December). How US customers' attitudes to fintech are shifting during the pandemic. McKinsey Paper.

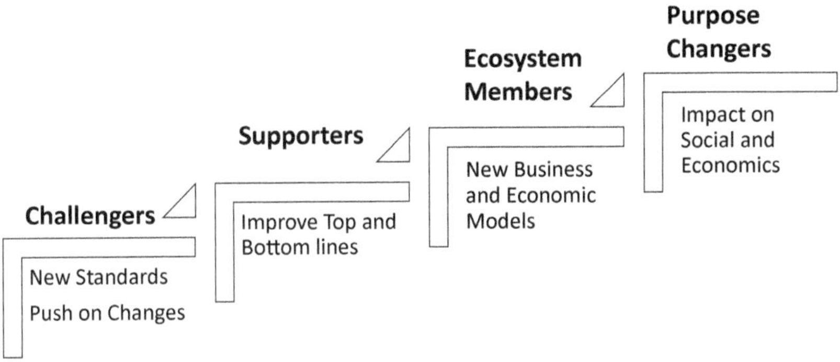

Fig. 4.4 Waves of fintech organizations (Adapted from https://www.digitalinsuranceagenda.com/thought-leadership/the-four-waves-of-insurtech/)

tolerance and relief from the damages of the pandemic. They secure the small business loans established by the pandemic aid, comfort, and economic security acts, implemented in many countries.[87] Payment- and wealth-focused fintech organizations expand ability or invest in added resources to withstand their systems' stress from higher transaction volumes. These actions are especially challenging for fintech organizations that depend on transaction volumes for revenue and were thus cash-starved at the time of the pandemic.

It is necessary to consider that most fintech organizations still realize now the past waves' promise. Figure 4.4 lists the different waves of fintech organizations over timeessential components to consider in a partnership.[88]

Collaboration Between Fintech Organizations and Traditional Financial Institutions

Financial institutions are collaborating with fintech organizations to face technological challenges and benefit from new opportunities. This collaboration does not always appear positive: Nine out of ten financial

[87] An example is the CARES Act in the USA, but similar programs are present in many countries. https://home.treasury.gov/policy-issues/cares. Accessed 20 October 2020.

[88] Nicoletti, B. (2017). A business model for insurtech initiatives. In B. Nicoletti (Ed.), *The future of FinTech* (pp. 211–249). Palgrave Macmillan, Cham, Switzerland.

institutions consider fintech organizations a risk to their existing business.[89] On the other hand, start-ups value the chance to get close to traditional financial institutions since access to the customer databases, getting funding, and addressing compliance issues are critical factors in scaling their businesses.

To improve their products and customer service, and limit the damage deriving from the new entrants' arrival, financial institutions have started signing partnership agreements with fintech organizations. The goal is to build profitable partnerships with new operators and defend and increase their market share. These initiatives prove that traditional operators are beginning to understand the fintech organization sector's potential and consider the digitization of their business model as essential and positive.[90]

Fintech organizations attract traditional financial institutions to buy their knowledge. The partnerships with fintech organizations allow the partners to extend and improve their banking services and bring new competencies, value, effectiveness, efficiency, and economics. This collaboration can help reach faster results for traditional financial institutions, such as creating a research and development center or building a corporate culture of innovation, which would otherwise be expensive in money, internal resistance, and time.

The fintech organizations are interested in collaborating with traditional financial institutions because the latter have more banking experience, a large customer base, and financing availability.[91] Some surveys report that customers do not seem ready to leave traditional banking providers. They trust them for security and protection against fraud. The customers attribute excellent value to brand reputation and personal interaction.[92] Radical disintermediation of financial institutions would imply

[89] www.nttdata.com/global/en/media/press-release/2019/september/ntt-data-and-everis-publish-insurtech-outlook-2019. Accessed 20 May 2020.

[90] Munich, R. E. (2016, January). Reinventing insurance for the digital generation. www.munichre.com/topics-online/en/html. Accessed 30 March 2020.

[91] Kumaresan, A., Saurav, S., & Raghunanda, K. (2017). Top 10 trends in property & casualty insurance. www.capgemini.com/wpcontent/uploads/2017/12/property-and-casuality-insurance-trends_2018.pdf. Accessed 14 March 2020.

[92] Capgemini & Efma. (2019). World Insurance Report 2019. www.efma.com/study/detail/30818. Accessed 30 May 2020.

profound innovation of the traditional business models. This change is unlikely in the short-to-medium term.[93]

The main differences between traditional financial institutions from the fintech organizations are interactions with the customers and the service's characteristics.[94] Financial institutions' marketing approach is often product-oriented since they focus on offering a better product/pricing than their competitors. There is an indirect connection with the customer. The service provision focuses on product development and its distribution.

The marketing goals of fintech organizations are process oriented. The emphasis is on offering the best experience during the customer journey. The relationship with the customer is direct.[95] The automation of processes allows for higher proximity: The development of alliances with fintech organizations allows the traditional institutions to profit from the ability, dynamics, and ways of doing banking. By its very nature, banking has not often developed. There is a strong trend in a mixture of partnership and acquisition by financial institutions of fintech organizations. From 2016 to 2018, the fintech organization ecosystem attracted investments totaling USD 11.2 billion; more than double the USD 5.5 billion raised between 2010 and 2015.[96] Most of the investments in fintech organizations are in more mature start-ups. There are regional differences, with the Western world executives preferring to invest at an early stage of the start-up life cycle. In Latin America, the favorite is investing in a more advanced phase of the fintech organization's life cycle. Big data analytics and blockchain solutions are the most attractive developing areas in the medium term for the banking sector.[97] AI and robotic process automation will be relevant for moving into banking 5.0.

[93] Braun A., & Schreiber, F. (2017). The current InsurTech landscape: Business models and disruptive potential. In *Institute of insurance economics*. University of St. Gallen. St. Gallen, Switzerland.

[94] Svetlana, V. (2016). InsurTech: Challenges and development perspectives. *International Journal of Innovative solutions in Economy, 3*(5).

[95] Cappiello, A., & Cappiello, A. (2020). The digital (R)evolution of insurance business models. *American Journal of Economics and Business Administration, 12*(1), 1–13.

[96] www.nttdata.com/global/en/media/press-release/2019/september/ntt-data-and-everis-publish-insurtech-outlook-2019. Accessed 25 April 2020.

[97] Braun A., & Schreiber, F. (2017). The current InsurTech landscape: Business models and disruptive potential. In *Institute of insurance economics*. University of St. Gallen. St. Gallen. Switzerland.

The banking sector still needs to have a consistent approach to fintech organizations' disruption. Their executives should think forward, inserting innovation at the heart of their strategies.[98] They need to decide how, and not if or when, to take part in the fintech organization ecosystems. There are several forms of collaboration between traditional financial institutions and start-ups[99]:

- Exploration, by actively watching the latest trends and innovations.
- Collaboration with start-ups and building pilot solutions to test in the market with strategic partnerships.
- Invest in a venture capital fund is the most common of the partnership between traditional financial institutions and start-ups. The goal is to purchase fintech organization shares, get control over the organization, and take advantage of the innovations developed.
- Enter a strategic partnership with fintech organizations that aims to outsource or improve some stages of the value network. New product development in fintech organizations can help traditional financial institutions to discover emerging service needs and threats that require new banking business models.
- Set up accelerators and business incubators to create and develop creative solutions and promote innovative ideas and business models. These mechanisms to fund financial institutions and strategic acquisitions may result in financial institutions' readiness to address specific problems, those that otherwise would not be considered necessary in the short term.

The expectation is that investments in the next few years in fintech organizations will significantly outweigh investments in banking and capital markets, much of which has been compliance-driven.[100] Fintech organization acquisitions by traditional financial institutions have taken place. Investment strategies will move toward mergers and acquisitions

[98] Cappiello, A. (2020). The digital (R)evolution of insurance business models. *American Journal of Economics and Business Administration, 12*(1), 1–13.

[99] PwC. (2016, June). Opportunities await: Global Fintech Survey. www.PwC.com/gx/en/financial-services/assets/fintech-insurance-report.pdf. Accessed 15 July 2016.

[100] www.insurancenetworking.com/news/innovation/insurtech-financialinstitutions-are-the-new-fintech-leaders-37470-1.html. Accessed 23 August 2016.

in the short term to preempt competitors and get better control over the technological innovation needed.[101]

Financial institutions use different parameters to select the fintech organization model corresponding to their strategic goals[102]:

- Short- and medium-term evaluations are carried out by analyzing the value-added impact on customers, consequences on banking lines, simplicity of integration, opportunity costs deriving from the failure to collaborate, and modular nature of offers.
- Long-term evaluation allows analyzing the market potential, generation of profits over time, meeting regulations, and integrating into an ecosystem.

The difficulty is finding the right combination of collaboration between these two types of businesses. Future business models will have the characteristics of close partnerships, in which traditional financial institutions will focus their activity on customer proximity. Simultaneously, fintech organizations, as innovators and carriers of innovative solutions and applications, will act on the value network. The result of this collaboration is a reorganization of the traditional banking value network.[103]

Once, based on these components, the financial institution has opted for single or multiple partners, different scenarios are possible:

- The fintech organization has a leading position.
- The traditional institution has a leading position.
- Creation of a joint venture with equal positions.

This differentiation aims to explain the strategic rationale behind every choice.[104] There are several reasons why financial institutions and fintech

[101] Deloitte. (2018). A catalyst for change: How fintech has sparked a revolution in insurance. www2.deloitte.com/content/dam/Deloitte/global/Documents/Financial-Services/gx-fsi-cataylst-for-change.pdf. Accessed 22 June 2020. www2.deloitte.com/content/dam/Deloitte/global/Documents/Financial-Services.pdf. Accessed 20 March 2020.

[102] Capgemini & Efma. (2019). World Insurance Report 2019. www.efma.com/study/detail/30818. Accessed 20 March 2020.

[103] Swiss Re Institute. (2017, June). Solution and insurance: Themes and challenges.

[104] Oliynyk, H., & Sabirova, A. (2013). Insurance financial institution and bank partnership as a distribution channel of insurance products. *Economics & Economy*, *1*(2), 131–141.

organizations set up business relationships in each of the three scenarios. Each partner can cooperate or compete according to the context and the moment, becoming a competitor.[105] As far as collaboration is concerned, Ernst & Young suggest helping distribution partners to develop digital capability by sharing resources and expertise.[106]

Ant Fortune[107]

Fintech organizations have used emerging technologies, including AI, big data analytics, cloud computing, and blockchain solutions, to supply technical support for financial services such as customer services, risk management, marketing, investment management, and credit assessment.[108] AI has become a leading trend in finance, making financial products and services brighter by mining data from massive information stores.

The core engine of Alibaba's financial affiliate, Ant Financial, is the world's largest third-party payments platform. AI is used in its businesses, including intelligent customer service, transaction risk control and marketing, virtual damage assessment for car insurance, loan approval, and anti-fraud processes.[109] Alipay's smart customer service, which can handle 2–3 million user queries per day, only needs one second to complete five rounds of requests, 30–60 times more efficient than any human service. More than 120 customers in the insurance, securities, government, and e-commerce industries use Ant Financial's AI solutions.

Ant Financial opened its AI capabilities to 10 financial institutions on 14 June 2017, setting up virtual shops at its independent wealth management platform Ant Fortune. The average daily trading volume of its cooperative fund organizations increased 243% in just one month after they set up their Fortune Accounts on the platform. Such growth and the relative dominant position has created problems with regulatory bodies.

[105] Bouncken, R. B., Gast, J., Kraus, S., & Bogers, M. (2015). Coopetition: A systematic review, synthesis, and future research directions. *Review of Managerial Science, 9*(3), 577–601.

[106] EY Report, Insurance in a digital world: time is now (2013). www.ey.com/Publication/vwLUAssets/EY_Insurance_in_a_digital_world:_The_time_is_now/$FILE/EY-Digital-Survey-1-October.pdf. Accessed 20 August 2016.

[107] www.chinadaily.com.cn/a/201811/07/WS5be25b2da310eff303287227.html. Accessed 4 January 2021.

[108] Fintech reimagines new service models—Chinadaily.com.cn. www.chinadaily.com.cn/a/201811/07/WS5be25b2da310eff303287227.html. Accessed 04 January 2021.

Benefits and Challenges of Fintech

Four crucial effects of fintech organizations on the financial system are[99]:

- Changes in entry barriers (usually easing them, but in some cases, the development of fintech organizations may stiffen such obstacles, say, by imposing higher technological requirements),
- Decreased significance of traditional financial institutions (outdated by distinct types of networks for, say, payment processing).
- Blurred boundaries between distinct types of financial markets or institutions (banks and nonbank organizations, say).
- The emergence of new (often complex) challenges for financial authorities (owing to the provision of financial services and products by previously unregulated organizations outside the financial industry).

Each category of fintech organizations is matching to some unique and dynamic needs of the market. Due to the pandemic, many online lenders tighten their credit rating to keep the quality of their balance sheets and mitigate any potential defaults increase.[110] It is possible that the historical data used for underwriting credit decisions could be less reliable in today's environment. They will need to revise, in some cases, their models accordingly. Many fintech organizations use machine learning applications for credit scoring. It is helpful since it learns from recent events and continuously updates policies and rules.

Fintech organizations have some unique benefits that allow them to create new ways of adding value in the current environment and position themselves to thrive in the longer term. Fintech organizations have several attributes that supply them the agility needed to create and deliver innovative solutions rapidly[111]:

[109] Fintech reimagines new service models. Chinadaily.com.cn. www.chinadaily.com.cn/a/201811/07/WS5be25b2da310eff303287227.html. Accessed 20 December 2020.

[110] Beyond COVID-19. www2.deloitte.com/content/dam/Deloitte/us/Documents/financial-services/us-beyond-covid-19-new-opportunities-for-fintech-companies.pdf. Accessed 4 January 2021.

[111] www.bank-as-a-service.com/BaaS.pdf

- Good at exploiting and analyzing distinct types of data.
- Not being dependent on complex, disparate, legacy systems, they can build platforms using a cloud-native approach, fully exploiting the Application programming interface (API) with the ecosystem.
- Innovators in customer journeys.[112]
- Focus on specific, little-regulated businesses. They target processes where the traditional financial institutions have the most significant ineffectiveness and inefficiencies. These processes are the ones primarily connected with customer proximity.
- Knowledgeable and comfortable with partnering within the broader financial services and beyond.
- Used to collaborate and work remotely.

Many fintech organizations are re-examining their mission and business models to adapt to the new normal. A key question is how to use both existing and new opportunities. It might be essential to think big and act boldly. For example, the pandemic's economic disruption has stressed serving unbanked and immigrants, especially in emerging countries. At present, there are 1.7 billion, and growing, unbanked individuals worldwide, according to the World Bank.[113]

On the other side, social isolation is accelerating customers' online, especially mobile, access to view and manage their finances. Because many fintech organizations are purpose-built for mobile access, they often excel in offering impressive presentations, onboarding, underwriting, data visualization, and supplication of the right context for transactions.

In the first stages of their market entry, the innovative business model of fintech organizations raised concerns about whether they would be a threat to traditional financial institutions due to their digital disruptors' characteristics.[114] Fintech organizations are now experiencing a significant shift in their environment. This shift involves the nature of the environment itself (regulations, new entrants, and boundaries), the kind

[112] Hartung T., & Rohatsch, N. (2018). *Einfluss der Digitalisierung auf die Unternehmensstrategie*. München University, München, Germany.

[113] www.liquisearch.com/history_of_banking. Accessed 8 September 2020.

[114] Naylor, M. (2017). *Insurance transformed: Technological disruption*. Springer, Cham, Switzerland.

Value-Adding	Cases in Banking
Improving the Value Proposition	Fintech Challenger Bank Neobank Instant Payments Request to Pay
Expand the value proposition	Open Banking Digital Wallet P2P Banking
Cross Selling	Other Services

Fig. 4.5 From banks to banking

of risks, and customers' needs. Fintech organizations need to adapt to the new rules of the market.

New Products to Add Value

Most financial institutions do not have sufficient tools and methods to help them understand and forecast when to push appropriate products.[115] It is critical to the basics of banking to understand the products and the portfolio of success. The synthesis of some banking products under this philosophy is in Fig. 4.5.

In the analysis of new products supported by banking 5.0, it is possible to use two criteria. The first one is based on cost leadership. The second criterion is based on differentiations. This section analyzes these two opportunities.

New Banking Products for Cost Leadership

Innovative solutions can support product development. They can be based on big data analytics and AI. In particular, the collection, analysis, and use of big data analytics ease a better knowledge of potential

[115] https://worldinsurancereport.com/. Accessed 39 May 2020.

customers and find their risk profiles. They improve the competitiveness of the products and services offered by customizing customers' needs in quality and price.[116] Big data analytics allow for processing, correlating, and analyzing the data available and drawing added information and forecasts from real-time processes and with an estimated probability. The ability to collect and use big data analytics is crucial for analyzing the vast quantity of information, structured and unstructured,[117] collected by social networks and other sources (customer feedbacks, market research, and so on). Machine learning algorithms can extract beneficial information from big data analysis and use them for customer segmentation and risk allocation.

New Banking Products for Differentiation

This categorization considers the goals that the financial institution wants to reach with new services:

- Acting on the demand for banking by improving the value proposition.
- Keeping the same value proposition and making incremental changes to the implied promises.
- Cross-selling products for banking.

In the first category, there are currently mainly two types of products:

- Instant Payments.
- Request to Pay.

The second category expands the value proposition: keeping the same value proposition but making the implied promise more in-depth or broader for customers. In this category, there are three types of products:

[116] Cappiello, A., & Cappiello, A. (2020). The digital (R)evolution of insurance business models. *American Journal of Economics and Business Administration, 12*(1), 1–13.

[117] Anchen, J., & Dowe, A. (2019). Advanced analytics unlocking new frontiers in P&C insurance. *Sigma, 4*, 2–30.

- Open Banking.
- Digital Wallet.
- P2P Banking.

The third category is for cross-selling products of diverse types, not necessarily financial. It creates entirely new value propositions: The organization makes a new promise to its customers about a portfolio of products and/or services. In this category, it is possible to list:

- Other services

The following pages consider each one of these products.

Open Banking
Open banking is known as "open bank data."[118] Open banking is a banking practice that supplies third-party unrestricted access to customer banking, transaction, and other financial data from banks and non-bank financial institutions through Application programming interfaces (APIs). Open banking will allow the networking of accounts and data across institutions for use by customers, financial institutions, and third-party service providers, such as fintech organizations and online financial service vendors. Open banking is becoming a significant source of innovation, potentially able to deeply innovate banking. On the other side, open banking raises the potential for customers' risks as more of their data is shared widely.

Customers must consent to let the financial institution allow such access. Third-party providers' APIs can use the customer's shared data. Use cases include comparing customer's accounts and transaction history to a range of financial service options.[119] It is possible to aggregate data across participating financial institutions and customers to create marketing profiles. If authorized, third parties could make new transactions and account changes characteristics on the customer's behalf.

[118] Benmoussa, M. (2019, December). Api application programming interface banking: A promising future for financial institutions (international experience). *Revue Des Sciences Commerciales, 18*(2), 31–43. Open Banking Definition—Investopedia. www.investopedia.com/terms/o/open-banking.asp. Accessed 30 December 2020.

[119] Open Banking. Opening New Avenues in Banking (Part-1) | IFBI. www.ifbi.com/node/2457. Accessed 4 January 2021.

Open banking APIs can help customers switching from using one bank, checking account service of another financial institution, or finding the best financial products and services for them.

Through networked accounts, open banking could help lenders get a correct picture of a customer's financial position and risk level to be able to offer more customized credit terms. An open banking app for customers who want to buy a home could automatically compute what customers can afford based on all the information in their accounts. In this way, it is possible to supply a more reliable picture than mortgage lending guidelines currently offer. Open banking can help small businesses save time through online accounting and help fraud detection organizations better monitor customer accounts and find problems or opportunities sooner. Broader concerns would be data breaches due to inadequate security, hacking, or insider threats that have become common.

Open banking is likely to affect the competitive landscape of financial services and products. This situation could help customers by increasing competition. It is necessary to consider that market concentration and associate pricing power could more than offset customers' cost benefits.

It is now time to move from open banking to open finance. The issue is not to limit openness to banking accounts but also to mortgages, investment accounts, pensions, and insurance if they are all included on APIs. Customers could quickly move money between accounts and manage their entire financial footprint, in one central place.[120]

Instant Payments

Instant payments are digital retail payment solutions that process payments in real time, 24*7, with funds made available at once for the recipient.[121]

In December 2014, the Euro retail payments board(ERPB) proposed that at least one pan-European solution for instant payments in euro should be available to all payment service providers in the European

[120] www.fintechfutures.com/2020/07/from-open-banking-to-open-finance/. Accessed 20 February 2021.

[121] www.ecb.europa.eu/paym/integration/retail/instant_payments/html/index.en.html. Accessed 8 September 2020.

Union.[122] The goal was to ensure cross-border payments availability and compatibility. To avoid any fragmentation and increase in competition, instant payment solutions should have the following layers[123]:

- End-user solution layer: cooperatively or competitively developed in the market (for example, for person-to-person mobile payments).
- Scheme layer: underlying payment schemes.
- Clearing layer supporting the clearing of transactions between payment service providers.
- Settlement layer supporting the settlement of transactions between payment service providers.

Eurosystem developed an instant payment solution called. TARGET Instant Payment Settlement (TIPS). The base of the scheme is on the European Payment Council (EPC)'s existing Single European payment areas (SEPA) and credit transfer (SCT) scheme. It is called SEPA Instant Credit Transfer (SCT Inst). Critical features of SCT Inst are that services should be available 24*7 and that it should not take more than ten seconds for the recipient's Payment service provider (PSP) to inform the payer's PSP if the money has been received. The SCT Inst scheme became operational in November 2017.

Digital Wallet or e-Wallet

A digital wallet or e-wallet allows customers to conduct financial transactions quickly and securely. The digital wallet functions as a physical wallet. There is digital money in a digital wallet. The application is installed on a mobile device. Cash is loaded on the wallet from a customer banking account. The transactions from the wallet can be done anywhere and anytime. The digital wallet allows Peer-to-Peer (P2P) transactions, including payments for utility bills, fees, money transfer to other people's wallets, and other online and offline payments.

122 Instant payments. European Central Bank. www.ecb.europa.eu/paym/integration/retail/instant_payments/html/index.en.html. Accessed 4 January 2021.

123 www.ecb.europa.eu/paym/integration/retail/instant_payments/html/index.en.html. Accessed 14 November 2020.

In a digital wallet, AI chatbots can execute and automate basic transactions with the customers' approval.[124] AI can handle voice instructions and execute payments for routine tasks such as account number verification.[125]

There are some excellent local solutions, specifically in the Nordic region, but no available wallet is widely used in Europe. Apple Pay or Android Pay, and similar are exciting exceptions. Payments with the two most famous American mobile wallet systems amounted to around 0.25% of the total payments processed in America in 2019 and are growing.[126] Cards, with 58% of the market, are still dominating. China's mobile wallet and payments processed near USD 50 trillion in 2019.[127]

There are considerable differences in the use of digital wallets among China, Europe, and America. As of 2019, only 9% of American customers had adopted Apple Pay, while 81% of Chinese customers used AliPay.[128] Key strategic drivers for these differences are: (1) Create value for all parties, not only for the customer, and (2) Monetize the ecosystem, not just the product.

In summary, the mobile wallet has been rising for a decade, but the system struggles in Europe and America. Card payments are still predominant. The issue is that the form factors and infrastructure are not as right or developed for mobile wallets as the environment that supports the big players in China. Those factors are infrastructure, ease of use, incentives, and ubiquity.[129]

[124] www.business2community.com/mobile-apps/top-5-major-digital-wallet-trends-of-2020-02287450. Accessed 2 October 2020.

[125] https://thefinanser.com/2020/09/the-rise-of-the-mobile-wallet.html/. Accessed 14 November 2020.

[126] https://thefinanser.com/2020/09/the-rise-of-the-mobile-wallet.html/. Accessed 4 January 2021.

[127] www.google.it/url?sa=t&rct=j&q=&esrc=s&source=web&cd=&cad=rja&uact=8&ved=2ahUKEwiDzd2q0oLtAhWlmFwKHVf2BnoQFjABegQIARAC&url=httpspercent3Apercent2Fpercent2Fthefinanser.compercent2F2020percent2F09percent2Fthe-rise-of-the-mobile-wallet.htmlpercent2F&usg=AOvVaw3VNDsmXrX_5tJ19dhMbspp. Accessed 14 November 2020.

[128] Gross, I., Perez, K., & Quah, B. (2020). Why hasn't apple pay replicated Alipay's success? *Harvard Business Review*.

[129] Skinner, C. (2020). *Doing digital: Lessons from leaders*. Marshall Cavendish, Singapore.

Paytm[130]

Paytm is an acronym for "pay through mobile." It is the first Indian company to be financed by the Chinese e-commerce company Alibaba. Alibaba is the largest stakeholder in Paytm parent company.[131] Paytm, started as a recharge platform in 2010. It then changed into a virtual bank business model. It is one of the cashback business model pioneers. Over time, it became India's most significant mobile payment operator. It offers an Indian digital wallet serving 100 million registered users through mobile payments, banking services, the marketplace, gold, recharge, and bill payments. Paytm has a semi-closed wallet approved by the Reserve bank of India (RBI) to store money in digital form. The stored cash is available to buy products and services in specific market locations, establishments, or entertainments like stores, petrol pumps, movie tickets, and so on, of the organizations that have contracted to accept this payment instrument. It is a digital payment platform that allows users to transfer cash into the integrated wallet via online banking.[132] It was ahead of its digital payment competitors with 100 million users even before the Cashless Indian Economy initiative.[133] Paytm new model helps small merchants to get a better profit margin by buying directly from manufacturers.[134]

Request to Pay

Request to pay is a secure messaging service framework launched in 2020.[135] It overlays on top of existing payments infrastructure as a

[130] www.paytm.com/. Accessed 20 September 2020.

[131] Sahoo, S. (2017, April). Application of ICT In Indian Banking sector: An empirical study. *International Journal of Innovative Research and Advanced Studies (IJIRAS), 4*(4).

[132] Venkatesan. (2018) Usage of Paytm—A study in Madurai city. *Bodhi International Journal of Research in Humanities, Arts and Science, 2*, 141–144

[133] Joshi, D., & Parihar, S. (2017). Digitalization & customer perception towards the banking services. *Aweshkar Research Journal, 23*(2), 133–141.

[134] Vikas, D., & Kumar, A. A. (2018). What Indians think about Paytm. *World Scientific News, 110*, 184–196.

[135] www.requesttopay.co.uk/#:~:text=Requestpercent20topercent20Paypercent20ispercent20a,aspercent20wellpercent20aspercent20amongpercent20friends.&text=Especiallypercent20forpercent20thosepercent20needingpercent20morepercent20flexibilitypercent20withpercent20payments.

new flexible way to manage and settle bills between businesses and organizations and among personal friends.

For each request, the payer will be able to pay in full, pay in part, ask for more time, or decline to settle and begin a dialogue with the requestor. It supplies more control to the person asked to pay. It gives the biller all the information they will need to reconcile the payment when it arrives.

The framework helps fintech organizations and PSPs develop services that interoperate to deliver Request to pay to their customers.

P2P Banking

Peer-to-Peer (P2P) banking is an online system that allows individual members to complete financial transactions by using an auction-style process.[136] The process lets members offer credit for a specific amount and a special rate. Buyers have the option to search for an amount and quality of interest that meets their needs. Their risk level categorizes all members. Members can browse for other people based on several demographic information.

This product has always existed in the shadow economy and often becomes usury. Thanks to the web, it can become visible and hopefully respect the correct code of conduct.[137]

In traditional banking, the spread between deposit rates and lending rates finances the financial institution's costs and margins. Both lenders and borrowers get to save such costs while paying specific commissions to the P2P portal provider and/or the credit rating agency when used.[125]

Other Services

Ernst & Young surveyed Swiss banks in 2019. A total of 83% of the banks surveyed believe that they will need to tap into new revenue sources in the future to keep their earnings power.[138] This situation is present in almost one-half of all banks (48%) saying they "entirely agree" with this statement and a further third saying they "partially agree" (35%).

[136] Bachmann, A., Becker, A., Buerckner, D., Hilker, M., Kock, F., Lehmann, M., & Funk, B. (2011). Online peer-to-peer lending-a literature review. *Journal of Internet Banking and Commerce, 16*(2), 1.

[137] Winn, J. K. (Ed.). (2016). *Consumer protection in the age of the 'information economy'*. Routledge, London, UK.

[138] www.ey.com/en_ch/news/2020/01/bank-barometer. Accessed 14 November 2020

One exciting new opportunity for financial institutions is to change the service model. The change could be in the direction of offering new services to improve its banking activities' attractiveness. The banking service would become a type of virtual assistant: moving from banking to services. Thanks to this customer proximity, there could be an increase in the retention of the best-performing customers and the acquisition of new ones.

Services within the banking proposition are essential. Financial institutions can support the solution of customer problems by delivering significant value propositions for their customers. Banks have plenty of exciting options to choose from to harness this added source of revenue. These opportunities range from product and service innovations (for example, growing real estate brokerage and management, managing digital data, supplying credit rating tools., and so on) to upgrading the business model for retail and mass affluents (for example, digital platforms).

The most significant contribution to expanding banking into services is integrating the banking transactions in operational business activity. This integration is a real transition to banking 5.0.

The classification of value-added services in banking is[139]:

- Self-Service: This category includes services where financial institutions support customers with tools and manage their customer risks better, including their assets or health.
- Advice and help: This category includes services that supply customers with fast support in case of need and information that can help them manage their lifestyles, property, or funds better.
- Anticipation of customer needs: Some value-added services can fill gaps in the customers' journey by predicting their needs and taking care of those needs by supplying credit and support for new events.[140]

[139] Radwan, S. M. (2019). The impact of digital technologies on insurance industry in light of digital transformation. www.joif.org/SystemFiles/Assets/Thepercent20Impact percent20ofpercent20digitalpercent20Technologiespercent20onpercent20Insurancepercent 20Industrypercent20.pdf. Accessed 30 May 2020.

[140] Insurance Reinvented: Value-Added Services. www.capgemini.com/wp-content/upl oads/2017/07/value_added_services_in_insurance_2017_2_web.pdf. Accessed 22 April 2020.

- Collaboration and engagement: Value-added services for collaboration and engagement can support better customer proximity. By supplying differentiated services, financial institutions can improve customer acquisition and retention.

Combining these value-added services can enable financial institutions to play a more significant and consistent role inside the customer journey.[141]

There are several options for increasing the value-adding services offered by financial institutions to their customers. Services are an exciting possibility for cross-selling efforts. Financial institutions could monetize their ability to analyze data and manage risks. Financial institutions have robust analytics capabilities compared with other industries. Analytics and actuarial sciences have been a standard component of the traditional banking business model.[142] Digital ecosystems offer traditional financial institutions valuable opportunities to use analytics to evolve and expand their business models. They could help the evolution of current banking businesses by advancing risk assessments, for example, by considering security measures. Other organizations could use banking analytics tools to enhance pricing and risk-accumulation control.

As different organizations generate large volumes of data, risk management will demand increasing data modeling and advanced analytics.[143] Because of their established analytics capabilities, financial institutions in new digital ecosystems could offer analytics-as-a-service to other players.[144] These offerings could include predictive modeling and optimization services that enable faster and wiser banking decisions across other industries within the entire value network.

[141] Lemon, K. N., & Verhoef, P. C. (2016). Understanding customer experience throughout the customer journey. *Journal of Marketing, 80*(6), 69–96.

[142] Davenport, T., & Harris, J. (2017). *Competing on analytics: Updated, with a new introduction: The new science of winning*. Harvard Business Press, Brighton, MA.

[143] Insurance beyond digital: The rise of ecosystems and platforms. www.mckinsey.com/industries/financial-services/our-insights/insurance-beyond-digital-the-rise-of-ecosystems-and-platforms. Accessed 30 December 2020.

[144] www.mckinsey.com/industries/financial-services/our-insights/insurance-beyond-digital-the-rise-of-ecosystems-and-platforms. Accessed 20 March 2020.

Many studies have found services as an essential topic for the banking sector.[145] It is exciting if the ecosystems involving digital platforms deliver an interconnected set of services to the customer in one integrated platform. A financial institution capable of distributing innovative property banking propositions to its customer base strengthens the customer relationship by offering, for example, credit or mortgage. It could get access to more precious customer insights and orchestrate its ecosystem of partners. This financial institution will compete as a platform sponsor capable of defining the platform strategy and the degree of openness that fits its corporate goals.[146]

A classic example of services possible in an ecosystem is bancassurance: the sale of insurance services in banks. This process involves the insurance organizations piggybacking on bank accesses to sell insurance products. Most banks' vast network supplies a veritable and extensive distribution mode that can reach millions of people both in rural and urban centers.[147]

For the mortgage sector, machine learning tools can improve compliance, cost structures, and competitiveness. These tools, algorithms, and technologies are helpful to review, analyze, and assess assets in pictures, videos, and voice conversations. For example, one immediate benefit is checking better and understand interactions between customers and sales agents to improve controls over selling of the products and services. [148]

Idea Bank and ING have extended into banking adjacencies by supplying services like accounts-receivable management, factoring, and cash-flow analysis to small and medium enterprise customers.[149] Bancoposta, for example, has become the largest provider of mobile phone

[145] Lepetit, L., Nys, E., Rous, P., & Tarazi, A. (2008). The expansion of services in European banking: Implications for loan pricing and interest margins. *Journal of Banking & Finance, 32*(11), 2325–2335. Bouquet, C., Hebert, L., & Delios, A. (2004). Foreign expansion in service industries: Separability and human capital intensity. *Journal of Business Research, 57*(1), 35–46.

[146] Parker, G., & Van Alstyne, M. W. (2014, April). Platform strategy. *Boston U. School of Management Research Paper No.* 2439323, p. 14.

[147] Singh, R. K., Singh, A., & Chavan, S. (2020). Distribution channels in life and general insurance: A conceptual analysis. *Studies in Indian Place Names, 40*(27), 590–609.

[148] Minelli, M., Chambers, M., & Dhiraj, A. (2013). *Big data, big analytics: Emerging business intelligence and analytic trends for today's businesses* (Vol. 578). Wiley.

[149] Wewege, L., Lee, J., & Thomsett, M. C. (2020). Disruptions and digital banking trends. *Journal of Applied Finance and Banking, 10*(6), 15–56.

services in Italy.[150] Large and traditional banks can create significant value by rapidly executing an innovative business model to deliver a service-as-infrastructure. They could enter new market segments via digital accesses based on back-end-infrastructure of banking platforms, capital assets, banking licenses, core banking products, servicing balance sheet to small fintech organizations. At the same time, they could supply credit-card processing to retailers, instead of competing with non-financial bigtech organizations on the customer-facing front end of platforms or apps.[151]

Wells Fargo[152]

Wells Fargo upgraded digital experiences in its core banking products by adding a predictive banking feature to guide existing customers. Predictive banking is a powerful solution that simplifies the access to the data from a customer's account into easy-to-understand, tailored insights. By instantly calculating and recalling a customer's past and present transactions, the feature forecasts expenses, and deposits, flags potential shortages or fees, and suggests potential savings.[153]

This feature supplies customers with an integrated view of their finances and increased control to advance their financial health and meet financial goals.[154] Insights range from flagging higher than normal automatic monthly payments, so that customers may investigate a change to a reoccurring bill, to reminding a customer to transfer money from savings to a checking account to avoid a possible upcoming overdraft. Conversely, if a customer has more money than usual in a particular month, they may be prompted to transfer money into savings. There are over 50 different prompts a customer can receive based on past and expected future activity.

[150] Lukac, B. C., Gallo, A., & Rodriguez-Tous, F. (2017). Making the case for a post bank. *Report Prepared for the Communications Workers Union*, 1–46.

[151] Cleary, S., Röhrig, M., Rouhana, R., Schaette, C., Sukumar, N., & Voelkel, M. (2018). Fintech decoded: Capturing the opportunity in capital markets infrastructure. *McKinsey & Company*.

[152] Barakina, E. Y., & Ismailov, I. S. (2020, November). Legal regulation of using the artificial intelligence solutions in the banking. In *Innovative economic symposium* (pp. 40–47). Springer, Cham.

[153] https://stories.wf.com/seeing-financial-future-ai/. Accessed 20 January 2021.

Sustainability

Sustainable banking is a strategic approach where all banking value network activities, including interactions with stakeholders, are done in a responsible and forward-looking way.[155] It is necessary to find, assess, manage, and watch for risks and opportunities associated with environmental, social, and governance issues[156]:

Corporations face pressure from responsible stakeholders to move toward sustainable investments that have a higher risk yet keep the balance between achieving economic gains and creating positive social and environmental returns.[157] Managing sustainability agendas can be a critical competitive advantage for corporations and financial institutions. Governing sustainability agendas should supply better financial institutions results but not only, from enhanced risk management tools. [158]

Sustainable banking aims to reduce risks, develop innovative solutions, improve banking performance, and contribute to environmental, social, and economic sustainability; the so-called 3 Ps[159]:

- Planet. The environment and earth.
- Persons. Everyone inhabiting the earth, from domestic and international workers to families and children.
- Profit. The financial and overall long-term viability of the organization.

[154] www.businesswire.com/news/home/20180213005588/en/Wells-Fargo-Adds-AI-Enhancement-to-Mobile-App-Giving-Personalized-Account-Insights-to-Customers Nation wide. Accessed 20 January 2021.

[155] PSI Principles for Sustainable Insurance. www.unepfi.org/fileadmin/documents/PSI_document-en.pdf. Accessed 10 May 2020.

[156] The Principles «UNEP FI Principles for Sustainable Insurance. www.unepfi.org/psi/the-principles/ The Principles «UNEP FI Principles for Sustainable Insurance. www.unepfi.org/psi/the-principles/. Accessed 10 May 2020.

[157] Weber, O., & Feltmate, B. (2016). *Sustainable banking: Managing the social and environmental impact of financial institutions*. University of Toronto Press, Toronto, Canada.

[158] Weber, O. (2012). Environmental credit risk management in banks and financial service institutions. *Business Strategy and the Environment, 21*(4), 248–263.

[159] www.e-education.psu.edu/ba850/node/643. Accessed 15 March 2020.

Banking's core business is to follow and manage money. Through risk prevention, risk mitigation, and sharing risks over many operators, the banking industry should also protect society, foster innovation, and support economic development. These are critical contributions to a well-functioning and sustainable social banking business.

There is an increase in environmental, social, and governance (ESG) challenges. These dynamic environments bring diverse, interconnected, and complex risks. It also presents opportunities, which banking 5.0 needs to analyze and pick up. The banking industry needs to cope with these non-traditional risk factors. They can have a significant impact on banking's viability. Resilient banking depends on integrated and forward-looking risk management considering ESG issues.[160] Better management of these issues supports the banking contribution to building a resilient, inclusive, and sustainable society. Many ESG issues are too big and complex. They need widespread actions across society, innovation, and long-term solutions. It is necessary to build banking 5.0 on a new foundation.

Sustainability Architecture[161]

Financial institutions have been involved in environmentally responsible investments for many years, particularly after the United Nations Environment Programme—Finance Initiative (UNEP FI) statement on financial institutions and sustainable development, which recognized the role of financial institutions in "making our economy and lifestyles sustainable."[162] Many financial institutions have developed environmentally responsible investment portfolios such as green stocks, bonds, and money market accounts. These portfolios finance projects aimed at supporting the conservation of natural resources and the implementation of ecologically responsible banking practices. Such investments, however,

[160] Nogueira, F. O., Lucena, A. F. P., & Nogueira, R. (2017). Sustainable insurance assessment: Towards an integrative model. *The Geneva Papers on Risk and Insurance. Issues and Practice, 43*(2), 275–299. https://doi.org/10.1057/s41288-017-0062-3.

[161] ElAlfy, A., & Weber, O. (2019). Corporate sustainability reporting: The case of the banking industry. Centre for International Governance Innovation. *CIGI Papers No. 211*, Waterloo, ON.

[162] www.mainstreamingclimate.org/unepfi/. Accessed 26 October 2020.

have remained minor when compared to other conventional banking portfolios.

The Principles for Responsible Banking[163] have the aim to define banking's role and responsibilities in creating a sustainable future. The UNEP FI appeared in 1992 as an alliance between the United Nations and the private sector to position sustainability at the forefront of financial institutions' banking. Today, it includes more than 240 financial institutions worldwide.

UNEP FI organizes biennial round tables that set out the international financial community's sustainable plans and set up the critical criteria that decide what it means to be a responsible bank. Together with the 2016 adoption of the SDGs (Sustainable Development Goals), the UNEP FI activities aim to end poverty, protect the planet, and ensure that everyone enjoys peace and prosperity. The world action plans to limit global warming, adopted at the Paris conference on climate, and defines six Principles for Responsible Banking.

The six principles are commitments to embracing sustainability through[164]:

- Aligning banking strategies with the goals expounded in the SDGs and the Paris Agreement.
- Increasing the positive impacts and decreasing their banking activities' adverse effects, concentrating on those areas where the result is most significant.
- Working responsibly with their customers to develop sustainable practices and foster shared prosperity for current and future generations.
- Proactively consulting, engaging, and partnering with relevant stakeholders to achieve society's goals.
- Setting public goals and implementing them through an effective and efficient governance system and a responsible banking culture, looking to address the most negative impacts that result from their banking.

[163] UNEP, F. (2019). Principles for responsible banking. *United Nations Environmental Programme-Finance Initiative: Geneva, Switzerland.*

[164] UNEP, F. (2019). Principles for responsible banking. *United Nations Environmental Programme-Finance Initiative: Geneva, Switzerland.*

- Periodically reviewing the implementation of these principles, committing to openness, and assuming full responsibility for positive and negative impacts.

It is necessary to use all intellectual, operational, and investment abilities to implement the responsible banking principles across spheres of influence, subject to applicable laws, rules, regulations, and duties owed to shareholders and customers.

Three thousand investors have signed up for these principles as of 2020.[165]

Chui et al.,[166] working on a McKinsey project, created a library of 160 use cases covering ten significant domains of human life where AI can be used to address current social challenges.[167] In information verification and validation, Vinuesa et al. examined AI's potential impact on the 17 Sustainable Development Goals (SDGs) of the United Nations (UN) 2030 plan.[168] Specifically, they map all 169 targets of the 17 SDGs, and they find that AI could have positive effects on 134 targets, while it may have adverse effects in 69 marks. AI can have both positive and negative impacts on the same target. For example, AI can decrease poverty by finding areas of poverty using satellite images and guiding international and financial actions accordingly. AI needs specific competencies and training, thus increasing inequalities among the population.[169] Another potential negative aspect of AI is that its development takes place in

[165] https://cib.db.com/insights-and-initiatives/flow/trust-and-agency/bridging-the-sustainability-gap.htm?kid=nl2020. Accessed 10 November 2020.

[166] Chui, K. T., Lytras, M. D., & Visvizi, A. (2018). Energy sustainability in smart cities: Artificial intelligence, smart monitoring, and optimization of energy consumption. *Energies, 11*(11), 2869.

[167] Tsekeris, C., & Mastrogeorgiou, Y. (2020). Contextualizing COVID-19 as a digital pandemic. *Homo Virtualis, 3*(2), 1–14.

[168] Vinuesa, R., Azizpour, H., Leite, I., Balaam, M., Dignum, V., Domisch, S., & Nerini, F. F. (2020). The role of artificial intelligence in achieving the sustainable development goals. *Nature Communications, 11*(1), 1–10.

[169] Vinuesa, R., Azizpour, H., Leite, I., Balaam, M., Dignum, V., Domisch, S., & Nerini, F. F. (2020). The role of artificial intelligence in achieving the sustainable development goals. *Nature Communications, 11*(1), 1–10.

advanced countries, thus reflecting their needs and values, and not so much the needs and values of emerging ones.[170]

Sustainability in Banking 5.0

Financial institutions' areas of interest in sustainability are essential[171]:

- Environment risk management is essential to understand environmental risk exposure and incorporate environment consideration into risk management.
- Disclosure of environment-related effects (for instance, climate change) over some transition period,
- Environment-related stress testing.

Financial institutions and other financial institutions have started to implement sustainable operations internally that vary from energy conservation practices and recycling programs in branches and offices to reduce their operational footprints. The financial sector can favor investments in low-carbon portfolios and green energy.[172] This push can be with financial institutions offering mutual funds that invest in green organizations. Several financial institutions have now adopted the risk management framework, called Equator Principles,[173] to manage environmental and social risks in project financing. Within the sustainable-lending operations domain, financial institutions have worked collaboratively with customers to minimize their ecological footprints.

ESG is becoming increasingly crucial to both funds and their investors. Every year, more investors are incorporating ESG targets into their investment decisions. Deutsche Bank Global Markets Research suggests that by the end of 2020, close to 50% of global assets under management will

[170]Vinuesa, R., Azizpour, H., Leite, I., Balaam, M., Dignum, V., Domisch, S., & Nerini, F. F. (2020). The role of artificial intelligence in achieving the sustainable development goals. *Nature Communications, 11*(1), 1–10.

[171]www.mckinsey.com/business-functions/risk/our-insights/banking-imperatives-for-managing-climate-risk. Accessed 8 February 2021.

[172]Nassiry, D. (2019). The role of fintech in unlocking green finance. In *Handbook of green finance, 545* (pp. 315–336). Springer, Berlin. Germany.

[173]www.equator-principles.com/. Accessed 20 October 2020.

incorporate ESG factors.[174] With current growth rates, potentially 95% of global Assets under management (AUM) (USD 130 trillion) will have an implicit or explicit ESG mandate by 2030.[175]

Banking has been increasingly aligned with sustainability goals. Organizations should move toward the banking 5.0 model to enhance resource conservation in support of circular economy efforts.[176] Organizations with a robust banking strategy and valid banking 5.0 review processes can perfect their banking processes and improve circular economy performance.[177] Organizations with a banking 5.0 model can use the performance review process and maximize their sustainable banking processes. Banking 5.0 applications can speed up banking transactions by developing information processing capabilities to support organizational processing aimed at a more effective, efficient, and economical ESG-compliant organization.

Financial institutions play an essential role in leading sustainable development. Some aspects are critical in this relationship[178]:

- The financial sector has large control over access to funds, which directly affects investments in specific sectors or indirectly through their lending activities.
- Stakeholders can influence, through their pressures, the actions to improve the reputational risks of financial institutions.
- With global warming, for example, floods and hurricanes are spreading in many areas in the world. Financial institutions started to respond to sustainability risks by incorporating shadow prices.

[174] http://cib.db.com/insights-and-initiatives/flow/trust-and-agency/bridging-the-sustainability-gap.htm?kid=nl2020. Accessed 10 November 2020.

[175] Bridging the sustainability gap—Deutsche Bank. www.cib.db.com/insights-and-initiatives/flow/trust-and-agency/bridging-the-sustainability-gap.htm. Accessed 30 December 2020.

[176] Geissdoerfer, M., Savaget, P., Bocken, N. M., & Hultink, E. J. (2017). The circular economy—A new sustainability paradigm? *Journal of Cleaner Production, 143*, 757–768.

[177] Murray, A., Skene, K., & Haynes, K. (2017). The circular economy: An interdisciplinary exploration of the concept and application in a global context. *Journal of Business Ethics, 140*(3), 369–380.

[178] Weber, O. (2005). Sustainability benchmarking of European banks and financial service organizations. *Corporate Social Responsibility and Environmental Management, 12*(2), 73–87. *Corporate Sustainability Reporting:* http://issuu.com/cigi/docs/paper_no.212web. Accessed 20 March 2021.

Sustainable development requires substantial investments in renewable energy, environmentally friendly infrastructure, and green solutions. While governments and public-sector institutions can supply financing for green investments, financial institutions could remove bureaucratic challenges to accessing required investment funds. Financial institutions could find green assets as an opportunity to improve the quality of their operations.

One of the challenges that sustainable banking faces is that customers do not perceive significant differences between financial institutions and available banking services.[179] Such beliefs about financial institutions have increased after the financial scandals of the late 1990s and the 2008 financial crisis, which led to a decline in customers' confidence in the financial system and banking institutions.[180]

Responsible financial institutions should acknowledge the direct environmental impacts of their operations and the indirect impacts that result from their lending activities. The financial sector is a critical enabler in sustainability because it serves several industries and sectors such as insurance, asset management, and retail, especially small- and medium-sized enterprises. Each of these sectors plays a role in shaping the global economy. Annual impact reports can help in setting benchmarks. In this way, it should be possible to improve the financial institutions' performance and push investors on their investment's ecological footprints.[181]

The European Commission (EC) issued a Disclosure Regulation.[182] Its purpose is to achieve transparency on how financial market participants and advisers consider sustainability risks in their investment decisions and insurance or investment advice. A sustainability risk is an environmental, social, or governance event or condition that, if it occurs, could have an adverse material impact on the value of an investment.

The Disclosure Regulation lays down harmonized rules applicable as from March 2021 to financial market participants and advisers about:

[179] Chousa, J. P., Castro, N. R., & Vizcaíno-González, M. (2009). Riesgo de reputación y responsabilidad social empresarial en el sector financiero. La inversión socialmente responsable. *Ecosostenible* (57), 4–16.

[180] Weber, O., & Feltmate, B. (2016). *Sustainable banking: Managing the social and environmental impact of financial institutions*. University of Toronto Press, Toronto, ON.

[181] www.jstor.org/stable/resrep24967.15. Accessed 20 March 2021.

[182] https://eur-lex.europa.eu/eli/reg/2019/2088/oj. Accessed 28 November 2020.

- The integration and consideration of sustainability risks and adverse sustainability affect their decision-making or investment advice processes; and
- The provision of sustainability-related information about financial products.

The disclosure obligations under the Disclosure Regulation apply to all financial market participants, including Alternative investment fund managers (AIFMs), Undertakings for Collective Investment in Transferable Securities (UCITS) applies to management organizations, investment firms, insurance and credit institutions supplying portfolio management, and to financial advisers giving investment and/or insurance advice.

In March 2020, the Technical Expert Group (TEG) on sustainable finance published its final report on EU position on these respect.[183] The report has recommendations relating to the EU classification overall design and extensive implementation guidance on how organizations and financial institutions can use and show against the classification. The report is. supplemented by a technical annex having[168]:

- Updated technical screening criteria for 70 climate change mitigation and 68 climate change adaptation activities, including standards for not doing any significant harm to other environmental goals.
- An updated method section to support the recommendations on the technical screening criteria.

In 2020, the EC published the list of members of the platform on sustainable finance.[184] The platform is an advisory body subject to the European Commission (EC)'s horizontal rules for expert groups and experts from the private and public sectors. This group of experts has these main tasks:

- Advise EC on the technical screening criteria for the EU Taxonomy, including on the usability of the requirements.

[183] https://ec.europa.eu/info/business-economy-euro/banking-and-finance/sustainable-finance/eu-taxonomy-sustainable-activities_en. Accessed 28 November 2020.

[184] https://ec.europa.eu/info/publications/sustainable-finance-platform_en. Accessed 38 November 2020.

- Advise EC on the Taxonomy Regulation review and cover other sustainability aims, including social goals and activities that significantly harm the environment. Monitor and report on capital flow toward sustainable investments.
- Advise the Commission on sustainable finance policy more broadly.

A strong ESG proposition correlates with higher equity returns.[185] ESG leaders are responding to the pressures. They are building concrete business cases that support the new behaviors. Financial institutions are doing that by making a climate-finance business to supply the organizations to either strengthen their resilience to long-term climate hazards or decarbonize their activities. Financial institutions must play a role in climate finance. It is the logical outcome of their commitments to the Paris Agreement, and it fulfills a critical part of their contract with society 5.0.[186] Building a climate-finance business requires four steps[187]:

- Think beyond the first-level impact.
- Shift lending from brown to green. Financial institutions will need to understand the effects of the energy transition in each sector that they serve.
- Tweak the operating model.
- Measure and correct.

Financial institutions can be second followers in many areas, but ESG must not be one of them. It will offer a substantial competitive advantage and a new business source or defense of an existing one for financial institutions that can supply a significant competitive advantage.[188]

AI can be used in conjunction with ESG to source company information and business activities to look for forward-looking indicators that

[185] www.mckinsey.com/industries/financial-services/our-insights/global-financialinstitutioning-annual-review. Accessed 1 December 2020.

[186] Potočan, V., Mulej, M., & Nedelko, Z. (2020). Society 5.0: Balancing of Industry 4.0, economic advancement and social problems. *Kybernetes*.

[187] www.mckinsey.com/industries/financial-services/our-insights/global-financialinstitutioning-annual-review. Accessed 1 December 2020.

[188] www.finextra.com/finextra-downloads/research/documents/174/finextra-future-of-esgtech-2020.pdf. Accessed 20 February 2021.

build a picture of the organization's sustainability and potential pitfalls or controversies.

This situation is from the regulatory point of view. From a practical point of view, Ernst & Young surveyed Swiss banks in 2020.[189]

- Most banks (55%) believe they can make an essential contribution to fighting climate change through their activities. This viewpoint is held by private banks (74%) and banks under foreign control (57%), and by institutions active in the asset management business.
- A considerable proportion of the banks surveyed (45%) remain skeptical and do not think that banks can make a valuable contribution to fighting climate change.
- Most banks (81%) are convinced that "sustainable investing" will be an enduring topic in the medium term and not just a fad.
- Most banks (70%) respond to the rising demand for sustainable investments and plan to ramp up their offering in this area in the future. Regional banks are an exception here, with the majority (55%) not having plans to expand their sustainable investment offering at present.
- Most banks (76%) say that while their customers are interested in sustainability, only in rare cases they think that they would sacrifice financial performance. This aspect might be typical in some countries and institutions.

ING[190]

Northvolt, a four-year-old start-up headquartered in Stockholm, Sweden, is building a giant production plant for lithium-ion battery cells in Skelleftea, northern Sweden. The gigafactory starts producing in 2021 and is widely expected to usher in a new era for Europe's automotive industry. Its batteries will play a key role in accelerating the adoption of electric vehicles.

Investors are on board. In July, Northolt raised USD 1.6 billion of debt from a consortium including ING, the European Investment Bank, Euler Hermes, BPI France, and Nexi. It raised a further USD 600 million in

[189] Ernst & Young. (2020). EY banking barometer 2020 Ey Report.

equity in September 2020 from investors including Goldman Sachs, Volkswagen, and Spotify. This capital is needed to cater for a growth market: ING forecasts that in a global fast-forward scenario, nearly three in every four cars could be electric by 2040.[191] ING decided early on to support the expansion of battery manufacturing capabilities in the EU. Northvolt's milestones are critical elements in the transition to a sustainable society.

Benefits and Challenges of Sustainability

A 2020 survey shows that customers are most likely to return to a brand for its quality. Sustainable business practices come a close second.[192] Sixty-eight percent of customers say they are motivated to be loyal to a brand by knowing that they share the same values.

While financial institutions have annual reports on their non-core business activities, such as programs that enhance employee welfare and philanthropic activities, there has been minimal reporting on the long- and short-term sustainability impact of their finances.[193] Financial institutions should report on this allocation within their portfolios.

Traditional banking can evolve into more ethical banking approaches when shifting their funds toward green investments. As a result, having robust reporting frameworks is essential for effective communication of ESG performance to diverse stakeholders and showing material climate-related financial disclosures.

Currently, materiality is the direct, mostly negative impact, of sustainability, environmental, social, and climate-related risks.[194] This situation

[190] https://new.ingwb.com/doyourthing/sectors/northvolt-the-battery-maker-accelerating-europes-sustainability-drive. Accessed 20 January 2021.

[191] www.transportenvironment.org/sites/te/files/publications/Briefing%20-%20How%20will%20electric%20vehicle%20transition%20impact%20EU%20jobs.pdf. Accessed 28 February 2021.

[192] https://DBR-274_WP_Transforming_the_digital_experience-ih6c46.pdf. Accessed 22 December 2020.

[193] Weber, O., & Feltmate, B. (2016). *Sustainable banking and finance: Managing the social and environmental impact of financial institutions*. University of Toronto Press, Toronto, ON.

[194] www.bankofengland.co.uk/speech/2015/breaking-the-tragedy-of-the-horizon-climate-change-and-financial-stability. Accessed 26 October 2020.

has some risks, particularly for the financial sector, with its indirect connections to the environment, society, and sustainable development. Following Carney, who mentioned transition risks as a significant risk for the financial services, there are indirect threats, such as reputation risks, litigation risks, and transition risks for the financial sector.[195] This situation addresses a topic that the industry has neglected for a long time. Although most financial risks and opportunities in banking come from their customers, borrowers, and investees' sustainability performance, the impact on investment and lending portfolios have not been reported. Therefore, there is a recommendation to a standard report of environmental, social, and climate-related risks and opportunities that financial institution portfolios are exposed to. AI can have risks from an ecological point of view. AI needs powerful computers, which require enormous energy consumption.[196] Encouraging the design of environmentally sustainable Al must be a priority if there is an intention to avoid worsening the environmental emergency, which is the most significant existential risk for the human species. Deploy AI by bringing it from the cloud to the edge, and the sensor node using embedded solutions can potentially answer this challenge. [197]

Conclusions

This chapter's central theme is that banking should move from traditional universal banks, selling all traditional products in pure banking, to innovative banking services. This move could create a myriad of new products and services. On the other hand, this should be the main target of any financial institution. The aim should be to add value to the customers. In so doing, they would ensure value for the shareholders and the employees.

[195] Spratt, S. (2015). Financing green transformations. In *The politics of green transformations* (pp. 171–187). Routledge, London, UK.

[196] Strubell, E., Ganesh, A., & McCallum, A. (2019). Energy and policy considerations for deep learning in NLP. arXiv preprint.

[197] Teerapittayanon, S., McDanel, B., & Kung, H. T. (2017, June). Distributed deep neural networks over the cloud, the edge and end devices. In *2017 IEEE 37th international conference on distributed computing systems (ICDCS)* (pp. 328–339). IEEE.

Banking 5.0 uses advanced solutions that enhance customer proximity, data availability, and banking processes. It is fundamentally changing the value creation of banking.[198]

The lessons learned out of all the experiences in the digital transformations suggested in this chapter are several. Some of them are:

- Consideration should go to the preconditions that enabled the successful launch and early growth of new business models in banking.
- It is essential to align the legal and regulatory framework with new policies promptly. Related to this point, it is the unchanging significance of capital adequacy for a financial institution.
- Relentless innovation was and will remain important.
- Digital finance is no longer a want but a need, as proved increasingly in the post-pandemic environment.

Fintech organizations will not be the great disrupters of traditional banking. The empirical evidence and academic studies tend toward relationships of cooperation rather than competition between the two parties.[199] Several financial institutions are looking for new banking and partnership models with fintech organizations to innovate every critical phase of their value network.[200] Some leading financial institutions have already set up solid partnerships with the top fintech organizations. Some of them have set up venture capital funds for their acquisition and benefitting from their developing solutions. They have increased innovation efforts and have even created good contests, named hackathons, to assure collaborations.[201] Financial institutions are now called upon to design digital infrastructure that improves customer engagement through distribution. The vision is to address them through a mix of internally driven innovation, joint ventures, and merger and acquisition activities.

[198] Eling, M., & Lehmann, M. (2018). The impact of digitization on the insurance value chain and the insurability of risks. *The Geneva Papers on Risk and Insurance-Issues and Practice, 43*(3), 359–396.

[199] Cappiello, A., & Cappiello, A. (2020). The digital (R)evolution of insurance business models. *American Journal of Economics and Business Administration, 12*(1), 1–13.

[200] Cappiello, A., & Cappiello, A. (2020). The digital (R)evolution of insurance business models. *American Journal of Economics and Business Administration, 12*(1), 1–13.

[201] https://vc4a.com/the-hatch/insurtech-hackathon/. Accessed 10 May 2020.

The development of fintech organizations and the creation of relevant, innovative products and services depend upon the formation and efficient functioning of a good ecosystem.[202] The ecosystem should include interrelated factors such as access to funding, regulations, solutions, demands, and capital, which are developing in parallel.[203] It seems unlikely that fintech organizations will cause a significant change or disruption to banking (today and in the future). The reason is that other organizations can copy the business model of fintech organizations. Financial institutions could easily buy small fintech organizations. Fintech organizations are focused more on cooperation than rivalry with traditional financial institutions. Regulations and lack of ability serve as entry barriers when fintech organizations want to expand their businesses.[204]

Banking 5.0 is not only AI and robotic process automation. It is big efforts in assuring sustainability. The financial institutions can play a key role in this respect.

[202] Eling, M., & Lehmann, M. (2018). The impact of digitalization on the insurance value chain and the insurability of risks. *The Geneva Papers on Risk and Insurance-Issues and Practice,* 43(3), 359–396.

[203] Nicoletti, B. (2017). *The future of FinTech. Integrating finance and solution in financial services.* Palgrave Macmillan, London, UK.

[204] Cappiello, A. (2020). The digital (R)evolution of insurance business models. *American Journal of Economics and Business Administration, 12*(1), 1–13.

CHAPTER 5

Artificial Intelligence in Support of Customer Proximity in Banking 5.0

A customer is the essential visitor on our premises, he is not dependent on us. We are dependent on him. He is not an interruption in our work. He is the purpose of it. He is not an outsider in our business. He is part of it. We are not doing him a favor by serving him. He is doing us a favor by giving us an opportunity to do so.

Mahatma Gandhi

Introduction

Financial institutions have several characteristics different from manufacturing organizations.[1] A one-to-one transfer of the principles of industry 5.0 from manufacturing to financial services is not suitable due to their differences.[2]

[1] Nicoletti, B. (1979, November–December). Aziende di servizio: Opportunità e problemi. *Sviluppo e Organizzazione, 10*(56), 19–32.

[2] Leyer, M., & Moormann, J. (2014). How lean are financial service financial institutions? Empirical evidence from a large-scale study in Germany. *International Journal of Operations & Production Management, 34*(11), 1366–1388, 6.

B. Nicoletti, *Banking 5.0*, Palgrave Studies in Financial Services Technology, https://doi.org/10.1007/978-3-030-75871-4_5

- Financial institutions offer information-processing services, which they collect, produce, and process.[3] These services are not tangible (even though employees process documents).
- Processing of financial services is independent of a specific location. Digital data can travel worldwide within seconds. The type of work is different from manufacturing, where typically, a tangible product is assembled in one or a few specific locations. Generic tasks for information-processing services range from support over processing transactions to primarily administrative work.[4]
- A core element of services is customers' direct involvement in the service process, including delivery, unlike in manufacturing industries.[5] Customers take part at specific points in time during the service process to use the services.[6]

In a banking 5.0 business model, it is necessary to dedicate special attention to customer proximity or relationships. Customers buy services that solve their pain points.[7] Online or mobile apps can deliver remotely real value once the first difficulty of using them is over.

When customers share data with financial institutions, financial institutions can use new opportunities to encourage a more secure behavior through education and positive reinforcements. Financial institutions can use customer data to supply rewards for security practices.[8]

[3] Davies, M. N. (1994). Bank-office process management in the financial services: A simulation approach using a model generator. *The Journal of the Operational Research Society, 45*(12), 1363–1373.

[4] Davies, M. N. (1994). Bank-office process management in the financial services: A simulation approach using a model generator. *The Journal of the Operational Research Society, 45*(12), 1363–1373.

[5] Corrêa, H. L., Ellram, L. M., Scavarda, A. J., & Cooper, M. C. (2007). An operations management view of the services and goods offering mix. *International Journal of Operations & Production Management, 27*(5), 444–463.

[6] Leyer, M., & Moormann, J. (2012). A method for matching customer integration with operational control of service processes. *Management Research Review, 35*(11), 1046–1069.

[7] iotinsobs.com/. Accessed 11 December 2019.

[8] www.naic.org/insurance_summit/documents/insurance_summit_2017_CIPR_16.pdf. Accessed 3 January 2020.

Availability of advanced solutions is a critical factor of success and competition. This factor is so relevant that, according to Gartner Group,[9] the financial institutions that will not expand and upgrade their technological systems in the coming years will decline and move to inevitable failure. The solutions that will help financial institutions to avoid these consequences is to innovate along the entire banking processes cycle, from managing marketing campaigns to account closing.

Banking initiatives should privilege customer-centricity in all aspects. All the contacts with customers should be thoroughly managed, integrated, and made consistently. Physical or virtual branches and customer proximity centers should have all the necessary analytics, tools, and services to make the customer journey unique and, thus improve sales. All the actions should include what McKinsey names "customer empathy."[10] Real empathy allows banking to respond to actual customer underlying needs, not superficial, stated interests. By doing this, it spurs breakthrough innovation.

In a Capgemini survey, financial institutions stated that improving customer experience (CX) is the key to launching AI-enabled initiatives.[11] However, a plain disconnect is emerging as some customer expectations are not yet being met. Half (49%) of customers rate their value from AI-enabled digital touchpoints as non-existent or less than expected. Customers are interested in getting a more "human" experience when interacting with AI-powered tools like chatbots, and 35% say that their current interactions lack the human touch.

Pandemic-driven changes in customer behaviors offer a unique opportunity for financial institutions to accelerate AI deployment. Customer interactions with AI are directly or indirectly distributed over several accesses throughout the financial services value network[12].

[9] www.gartner.com—Articles and research. Accessed 20 March 2020.

[10] www.mckinsey.it/idee/transforming-life-insurance-with-design-thinking. Accessed 10 April 2020.

[11] www.capgemini.com/wp-content/uploads/2020/11/Report-AI-in-CX-FS.pdf. Accessed 8 December 2020.

[12] www.capgemini.com/wp-content/uploads/2020/11/Report-AI-in-CX-FS.pdf. Accessed 8 December 2020.

- A majority (78%) of customers expect to use more touchless interactions through voice assistants, facial recognition, or apps. This percentage compares with just 61% pre-pandemic.
- Close to half (45%) of customers will increase their use of contactless payments post-pandemic.
- Pandemic is prompting a major behavioral shift by older customers as contactless payments adoption has grown by 37%in the 61–65-year age group and a 33% increase with those over 66.
- 47.73% of customers in another survey believe the change from physical to digital is here to stay.[13]

Value Proposition and Customer Proximity

Better customer proximity means not only supplying access to banking services via online or mobile. Customer proximity means[14]:

- Understanding the customer
- Assuring him/her a profitable customer journey
- Taking care of weaker parts of the society, such as the elders, unbanked, poor persons, handicapped, minorities, or the immigrants.

Contacts with the customers are essential. Specific methodologies can help. In architecture, Universal Design (UD) is "the design of products, environments, and communication to be usable by all people, to the greatest extent possible, without adaptation or specialized design."[15]

Ron Mace introduced the formal concept of UD.[16] Mace had polio as a child. He used a wheelchair to go around. He recognized in the

[13] Skinner, C. (2020). The Omniaccess Future. *Oracle Report*.

[14] Fasnacht, D. (2009). *Open Innovation in the financial services: Growing through openness, flexibility and customer integration*. Springer Science & Business Media, Cham, Switzerland.

[15] Fasnacht, D. (2016). History of universal design. Institute for Human Centered Design, Boston, MA.

[16] Schwab, C. (2015). *The innovator of universal design, Mr. Ron Mace explained differences between universal design and barrier free in 1989*. www.accessiblehealthhome.com/2015/10/09/the-father-of-universal-design-mr-ron-mace-explained-differences-between-universal-design-and-barrier-free-in-1989/. Accessed 20 January 2021.

1950s that the North American population was aging. He expected that persons who were no longer able to go up and down stairs or small bathrooms would have to move out of their now unusable homes and go into nursing facilities or the homes of relatives. Mace was sure that if architects designed homes to be "usable by everyone to the greatest extent possible" from the beginning, then more people could continue to stay at home when old.[17] The concept of Universal Design makes sense. It is possible to generalize universal design to the provision of banking services. It could become Universal Digital Access.[18]

As the USA progressed to ensure equal access to the built environment, disability rights advocates began raising awareness that telecommunication was not accessible to everybody. The Americans with Disabilities Act (ADA) was signed into law. USA Congress amended Section 508 of the Rehabilitation Act to include all communication and information solutions.[19] Phone lines, television shows, movies, the internet, information kiosks, and online banking must be accessible to everybody. This extension of UD principles from the physical environment to the virtual one is a significant step toward "universal" banking. Here universal banking is different from its meaning in the traditional banking world, where universal bank meant a bank offering all financial products.[20] This book is customer-centric, so universal means that all banking services should be accessible by anybody.

The nature of customer interactions has changed, thanks to the availability of innovative solutions. In the past and currently, financial institutions focus on pushing for new deals and contracts, with customers who passively are recruited and are not fully aware of what they are signing. This symptom is a characteristic of the so-called information

[17] Gaylord, V., Johnson, D. R., Lehr, C. A., Bremer, C. D., & Hasazi, S. (Eds.). (2004). *Impact: Feature issue on achieving secondary education and transition results for students with disabilities* (Vol. 16, no. 3). University of Minnesota, Institute on Community Integration, Minneapolis, MI.

[18] Digital-Access-20210118.pdf (nus.edu.sg). Accessed 9 February 2021.

[19] McLawhorn, L. (2001). Leveling the accessibility playing field: Section 508 of the Rehabilitation Act. *North Carolina Institute of Law and Solutions, 3*(6).

[20] Tilly, R. (1998). Universal banking in historical perspective. *Journal of Institutional and Theoretical Economics (JITE)/Zeitschrift für die gesamte Staatswissenschaft*, 7–32.

asymmetries.[21] Customers are taken care of by branches, help desks, other financial institutions, and financial consultants. They have been the leading players in a "sales heavy" model.[22] The market is moving in favor of a customer delight much more relevant. Financial institutions are getting aware of this trend. They are moving to a different relationship based on interactive proximity with the customers. Relations are developing toward "interactions," where customers become active and central players in an environment that is "customer-pulled."[23] A hybrid blend of digital and emotional connections offers a balanced approach to personalized proximity.[24]

The new goal of marketing is to create and increase the Customer engagement value (CEV).[25] In financial institutions, the value of keeping customers is essential. Retaining customers is even more relevant due to the diminishing number of physical contacts between customers and financial institutions. Developing and improving contractual relationships is critical. The focus changes from increasing the purchase intention to engaging customer loyalty and extending the customers' value, keeping them for years. In the past, financial institutions tried to get and keep customers based on price, trying to be the cheapest financial institution in the market. There is a focus on keeping an increased customer engagement value, which only partially depends on the services' attractive pricing.[26]

[21] Binks, M. R., Ennew, C. T., & Reed, G. V. (1992). Information asymmetries and the provision of finance to small firms. *International Small Business Journal, 11*(1), 35–46.

[22] web.bi.no/forskning/papers.nsf/0/b723c0570c4026eac12575b0004a329a/$FILE/2009-04-Jensen.pdf. Accessed 20 August 2016.

[23] Pereira, V. R., Kreye, M. E., & de Carvalho, M. M. (2019). Customer-pulled and provider-pushed pathways for product-service system. *Journal of Manufacturing Solutions Management*.

[24] worldinsurancereport.com/. Accessed 30 May 2020.

[25] Kumar, V., Rajan, B., Gupta, S., & Dalla Pozza, I. (2019). Customer engagement in service. *Journal of the Academy of Marketing Science, 47*(1), 138–160.

[26] Lee, S. K. (2018). A customer touch point management system for effective service communication. *Business Communication Research and Practice, 1* (1), 46–49. Shaw-Ching Liu, B., Petruzzi, N. C., & Sudharshan, D. (2007). A service effort allocation model for assessing customer lifetime value in service marketing. *Journal of Services Marketing, 21(1),* 24–35.

Customer Proximity Architecture

Interactions have a positive influence on the evolution of the customer engagement value factor.[27] Adding one interaction increases the chance of positive evolution of the CEV factor by 28.8%. In single interactions, telephone and direct communication supply the most significant contribution. For a series of interactions, a strategy based on combining the interaction accesses increases the chance of positive evolution of the CEV by 14.5%.[28]

It is essential to digitize and optimize customer journeys. This aspect includes improving access to information to drive customer insights, streamlining onboarding, enabling direct communications with customers, allowing self-service for credits and amendments, and so on. In the spirit of banking 5.0, financial institutions can extend the customer journey by being integrated or integrating added tools and services from other providers to deepen their capabilities and increase revenue streams.

Financial institutions must offer a broader portfolio of services to still being relevant to customers looking for customization. It is critical to have innovative portfolio management tools and to establish flexible product factories. These innovations are essential for the design of better products and their fast distribution.[29]

Customer Proximity in Banking 5.0

Financial institutions should help potential customers find their needs and the most suitable products/services to resolve their financial problems through a consultancy service, transparent, clear, and correct. It is challenging to assure total clarity without affecting the customer's sensitivity that might feel overstated. The customer could perceive the financial institution's advice as forced and intrusive, aimed at increasing the banking revenues, rather than to understand and resolve his/her problems. Other

[27] Westervoorde, P. M. (2020). *Using Customer Interactions to understand the Customer Engagement Value: A predictive study in the B2B insurance industry* (Master's thesis). University of Twente, Enschede, Netherlands.

[28] www2.deloitte.com/content/dam/Deloitte/nl/Documents/consumer-business/deloitte-nl-the-digital-transformation-of-customer-services.pdf. Accessed 22 November 2020.

[29] Digital transformation in insurance—EY. US. www.ey.com/Publication/vwLUAssets/Digital_transformation_in_insurance/$FILE/ey-digital-transformation-in-insurance.pdf. Accessed 30 May 2020.

customers, in possession of some banking knowledge, approach the financial institution, convinced to know everything. This type of customer creates some challenges for supplying helpful and correct advice similarly to the most confused and unprepared customers. The relationship between them and the financial institution often risks finding obstacles on controversy and misunderstandings.[30]

Financial institutions must always look for innovative solutions to propose to the customers. It is necessary to evolve and not to remain anchored to traditional banking services. Robust customer proximity not only directly contributes to the user experience but supplies access to customer information. This access is an absolute necessity in a world where ecosystems are essential.[31] Financial institutions can harness customer adoption of innovative solutions to create opportunities for better and more frequent customer interactions and improve efficiency through automation (such as trigger-based credits payments and apps).

An essential moment for customer proximity is at the time of collection. Banking 5.0 programs may drive innovation in back-office processes in the direction of automated collection management processes.

Benefits and Challenges of Customer Proximity

The development and technological progress are essential to introduce new and attractive products to the market and improve everyday work so that financial institutions can save time and resources. In the last decade, there has been a robust acceleration of technological changes. The penetration of the internet and social networks has grown significantly. For the customer, the benefits of these solutions are the speed and comfort of a transaction-notification process. They could avoid filling many papers and reduce transaction times.

Even with a lower rate of AI implementations than other sectors, financial institutions have realized significant benefits.[32] They have reduced their operations cost by 13% and have increased revenue per customer by

[30] Giudici, G. (2008). *Intermediazione Assicurativa e Mercato*. FrancoAngeli, Milano, Italy.

[31] www.mckinsey.com/industries/financial-services/our-insights/insurance-beyond-digital-the-rise-of-ecosystems-and-platforms. Accessed 10 January 2020.

[32] www.capgemini.com/wp-content/uploads/2020/11/Report-AI-in-CX-FS.pdf. Accessed 8 December 2020.

10% after deploying AI in customer-facing functions. AI has helped deliver improvements in customer delight. Financial institutions have greater customer engagement with brands from deploying customer AI. Around one in five organizations (25% for banks and 19% for insurers) have seen a 20–40% increase in customer engagement.

The deployment of AI to improve the overall customer experience (CX) has grown significantly in financial services in recent years.[33] Nine in ten (94%) organizations say that improving the customer journey is the critical goal behind launching new AI-enabled initiatives. Customers are becoming comfortable interacting with AI regularly. Just over half of customers (51%) have daily AI-enabled interactions (like talking to a chatbot) with financial institutions. This situation becomes even more important as most customers (78%) expect to increase touchless communications after the pandemic. Financial institutions have already perceived the positive impact on their bottom line of implementing AI in customer-facing functions, including reduced cost of operations (13%) and increased revenue per customer (10%).[34]

Customer Relationships Management

Customer relationship management (CRM) is the strategic process of selecting customers to profitably serve and shape the interactions between the organization and these customers.[35] The end goal is to optimize the current and future value of the customers for the organization. Better quality and affordable products and services can help organizations have loyal customers and simultaneously gain a competitive advantage for the organization.

To support customer proximity, a financial institution needs to set up a CRM application. It is a category of software that covers a broad set of applications. This software helps businesses manage customer data and customer interactions, access information, automate sales, marketing, and

[33] www.capgemini.com/wp-content/uploads/2020/11/Report-AI-in-CX-FS.pdf. Accessed 8 December 2020.

[34] AI boosting profits but not meeting customer expectations—report (finextra.com). Accessed 9 February 2021.

[35] Kumar, V., & Reinartz, W. (2012). Customer relationship management issues in the business-to-business context. In *Customer relationship management* (pp. 261–277). Springer, Berlin, Heidelberg, Germany.

customer support. Simultaneously, CRM can help in managing employee and partner relationships.[36] CRM covers the front end with the customer and the sales force. Typically, large financial institutions use CRM software. Some software products scale to a financial institution of any size, but small financial institutions are limited users of these solutions.

A CRM can help in several aspects of customer proximity[37]:

- Meeting the customer's needs involves creating a propensity scoring (that is, a dashboard to evaluate the banking services the customer uses). This solution allows offering to the customer services designed for his/her needs. A CRM helps with the more profitable customers by defining the best retention strategy.[38]
- Knowing and retrieving the customer's full potential, considering the possibility of a customer who could manage his/her accounts across several financial institutions thanks to open banking.
- Knowing and remediating a customer's riskiness by improving the portfolio's quality, supporting the launch of new products and services, and increasing banking productivity. This increase would be possible by using the information derived from a better understanding of the customer.

CRMs allow the users not only to find but keep the best customer relationships. A lack of customer profiles and prospects' databases determines a loss of a large amount of potential revenue. Seventy-five percent of organizations admit that this loss of income is taking place in their business. The potential revenue loss could be up to 50% for organizations working in finance or retail.[39]

[36] Nicoletti, B. (2016). Cloud Computing & Procurement. *ACM—International Conference Proceedings Series (ICPS)* & ACM Digital Library ISBN ACM ICPS to ICC.

[37] Coviello, A. (2008). *The impact of ICT in the insurance industry: The role of Customer Relationship Management*. www.itais.org/proceedings/itais2012/pdf/002.pdf. Accessed 22 March 2020.

[38] Lindgreen, A., & Antioco, M. (2005). Customer relationship management: The case of a European bank. *Marketing Intelligence & Planning*.

[39] Florez-Lopez, R., & Ramon-Jeronimo, J. M. (2009). Marketing segmentation through machine learning models. *Social Science Computer Review, 27*(1), 96–117.

Architecture of Customer Relationship Management

CRM is a concept that focuses on supporting customer relationships. To build long-lasting, profitable relationships with customers, CRM requires the management of "customer-related knowledge," which includes knowledge from, about, and for customers.[40]

The interactive approach made possible by CRM allows achieving a balance between corporate investments and customer needs' satisfaction to generate maximum customer delight and organizations returns.[41] This balance involves[42]:

- Following and continuously updating knowledge on customer needs, motivations, and behavior over the relationship's lifetime.
- Applying customer knowledge to continuously improve the performance through a process of learning from successes and failures.
- Integrating marketing, sales, and service activities affecting the customers to achieve their common goal.
- Implementing proper systems to support customer knowledge acquisition, sharing, and the measurement of CRM effectiveness.

There are three categories of CRM processes[43]:

- CRM delivery processes with direct customer contact to cover part of the customer processes (campaign management, sales management, service management, and complaint management).[44]

[40] Davenport, T. H., Harris, J. G., & Kohli, A. K. (2001). How do they know their customers so well? *MIT Sloan Management Review, 42*(2), 63–73.

Gebert, H., Geib, M., Kolbe, L. M., & Brenner, W. (2003). Knowledge-enabled customer relationship management—Integrating customer relationship management and knowledge management concepts. *Journal of Knowledge Management, 7*(5), 107–123.

[41] Shaw, R., & Reed, D. (1999). Measuring and valuing customer relationships: How to develop the measures that drive profitable CRM strategies. In *Business Intelligence*. London.

[42] Qian, F. (2007). A study on CRM and its customer segmentation outsourcing approach for small and medium businesses. In L. Xu, A. Tjoa, & S. Chaudhry (Eds.), *IFIP International Federation for Information Processing, 255, Research and Practical Issues of Enterprise Information Systems II, 2* (pp. 1387–1394). Springer, Boston, MA.

[43] Geib, M., Reichold, A., Kolbe, L., & Brenner, W. (2005, January). Architecture for customer relationship management approaches in financial services. In *Proceedings of the 38th Annual Hawaii International Conference on System Sciences* (240b-240b). IEEE.

[44] Shrivastava, M. (2017). *Learning Salesforce*. Packt Publishing, Einstein, UK.

- CRM support processes with direct customer contact that are not designed to cover part of the customer process and fulfill supporting functions within the CRM context (market research, loyalty management).
- CRM analysis processes combine and analyze customer knowledge collected in other CRM processes. The analysis results are the basis for the CRM delivery and support processes and the service innovation and service production processes to improve their effectiveness (dashboards, customer scoring, lead management, customer profiling, segmentation, feedback, and knowledge management).

Einstein

Salesforce is a global leader in CRM applications. It launched Einstein Analytics for Financial Services, a customizable analytics solution that supplies AI-augmented banking intelligence for wealth advisors, retail bankers, and managers.[45]

Einstein Analytics for Financial Services supplies AI-powered insights and recommendations specifically tailored to the customers. By bringing together data from financial services clouds and other data sources, users can instantly get actionable insights to grow their business sales and improve customer relationships.

Einstein Analytics for Financial Services functions include[46]:

- AI-powered predictive guidance and recommended actions, built directly inside day-to-day customer engagement.
- Pre-built industry-specific templates (such as customer financial goals, interactions, referrals, deposits, and fees) enable front-line wealth advisors and retail bankers to quickly use analytics.
- Quickly and easily build custom analytics apps and connections to external data sources to get a full view of their business sales to better understand their customers' financial goals and needs.
- Built-in compliance with regulations.

[45] www.salesforce.com/news/press-releases/2019/05/07/salesforce-announces-einstein-analytics-for-financial-services-ai-powered-insights-for-wealth-advisors-managers-and-retail-bankers/. Accessed 20 January 2021.

[46] Yu, J. (2019). *Getting started with Salesforce Einstein analytics: A Beginner's guide to building interactive dashboards*. Apress Media, Singapore.

Customer Relationship Management in Banking 5.0[47]

Implementing a CRM system provides a financial institution with a step to move toward one-to-one marketing. It is possible to use a model (called 6Cs) to define the process of implementing a CRM in banking[48]:

(1) Be close to the customer: to find and understand his/her needs and expectations.
(2) Have a clear vision on a plan for future activities, finding a development model.[49]
(3) Be consistent with the governance of the CRM activities to achieve the target goals and define the tools for checking the effectiveness, efficiency, and economics of the processes of active references.[50]
(4) Support continuous improvement: to define and continuously improve processes and procedures.
(5) Connect to the rest of the financial institution to define the CRM program's integrations with all the different areas of improvement of the customer relationships.
(6) Correct whatever errors are made in the customer relationships. Use them as an opportunity rather than a challenge.

The diffusion of CRMs in banking is progressing, even if not as fast as necessary. It is causing a discontinuity in the traditional culture of the financial institutions and their business models. Financial institutions need to take a practical customer focus, improve, and enrich customer service offerings, streamline production processes and administrative systems, and use the proximity networks in opportunities offered by the CRM.

[47] Geib, M., Reichold, A., Kolbe, L., & Brenner, W. (2005, January). Architecture for customer relationship management approaches in financial services. In *Proceedings of the 38th Annual Hawaii International Conference on System Sciences* (240b-240b). IEEE.

[48] Zineldin, M. (2005). Quality and customer relationship management (CRM) as competitive strategy in the Swedish banking industry. *The TQM magazine*.

[49] Productivity in handling requests through a better. www.coursehero.com/file/p1m96qe4/productivity-in-handling-requests-through-a-better-distribution-of-workloads/. Accessed 30 May 2020.

[50] Productivity in handling requests through a better. www.coursehero.com/file/p1m96qe4/productivity-in-handling-requests-through-a-better-distribution-of-workloads/. Accessed 30 May 2020.

In this perspective, investment in talents and employee training is a banking 5.0 top priority also to meet the challenges of a CRM best use while improving its effectiveness, efficiency, economics, and competitiveness. There are several guidelines for invest and run a CRM.[51] It is possible to envision three distinct types of CRM approaches that differ on the strategy, process, and system levels and the importance and use of customer knowledge[52]:

- CRM as Customer Delight Management considers an operational CRM system for improving customer service, online marketing, automating sales force, and so on.
- CRM as Customer Contact Management considers an analytical CRM system for building data warehouses, improving relationships, analyzing data, and so on.
- CRM as Customer Profitability Management considers a collaborative CRM system for building online communities, developing business-to-business customer exchanges, personalizing services, and so on.

The following paragraphs describe CRM at these three levels in the banking 5.0 approach.

Customer Delight Management

CRM as customer delight management aims at high customer satisfaction by offering customers a high quality of service and proximity.[53]

Customers expect imaginative, high-touch experiences with their advisors when needed. Banking must deliver modern experiences that are

[51] Coviello, A. (2008). *The impact of ICT in the insurance industry: The role of Customer Relationship Management*. www.cersi.it/itais2012/pdf/002.pdf. Accessed 20 March 2020.

[52] Geib, M., Reichold, A., Kolbe, L., & Brenner, W. (2005, January). Architecture for customer relationship management approaches in financial services. In *Proceedings of the 38th Annual Hawaii International Conference on System Sciences* (240b-240b). IEEE. Karimi, J., Somers, T. M., & Gupta, Y. P. (2001). Impact of information solutions management practices on customer service. *Journal of Management Information Systems, 17*(4), 125–158. Adebanjo, D. (2003). Classifying and selecting e-CRM applications: An analysis-based proposal. *Management Decision*.

[53] Geib, M., Reichold, A., Kolbe, L., & Brenner, W. (2005, January). Architecture for customer relationship management approaches in financial services. In *Proceedings of the 38th Annual Hawaii International Conference on System Sciences* (240b-240b). IEEE.

smart, personalized, and fast to differentiate their services. Financial institutions have always understood the importance of building best-in-class customer relationships. They often struggle to manually stitch together and correlate all their customer data from various applications to deliver them at scale. CRMs need to empower bankers. They can supply immediate, intelligent recommendations to meet customers' growing expectations for speed and personalization.

Artificial Intelligence (AI) fits this need since it can ingest and persist data in CRM while simultaneously serving low latency to large numbers of concurrent CRM users. In dealing with such large volumes of data in CRM, represented by all forms of transactions, a CRM needs to use AI to harness insights from a vast array of live inputs of the CRM.[54]

Combining AI, CRM software, and data storage like cloud solutions means that both AI and persons can analyze and harness more data than ever before. AI in CRM software can help automate time-consuming tasks, enhance personal insights, discovering hidden patterns in large volumes of data, or offer guidance to a junior sales representative.

Customer Contact Management

CRM as customer contact management aims to reduce costs by improved process efficiency and media-based communication accesses.[55]

Most of the financial products, such as credit, present a slight possibility of differentiation from competitors. The success or failure of retail and commercial financial institutions depends on its quality and effectiveness with their customers. Marketing campaigns can help. Launching a successful marketing campaign in a highly competitive market segment, such as retail banking, is challenging. Later campaigns in such market conditions are less and less effective, as customers, continually exposed to diverse types of advertisements, learn how to ignore them. CRMs can help by supporting personalized, direct marketing. Such an approach allows customizing the service characteristics per customer basis, thus increasing

[54] Damania, L. (2019). Use of Ai in customer relationship management. *Emerging Research, 59.*

[55] Geib, M., Reichold, A., Kolbe, L., & Brenner, W. (2005, January). Architecture for customer relationship management approaches in financial services. In *Proceedings of the 38th Annual Hawaii International Conference on System Sciences* (240b-240b). IEEE.

campaign efficiency and reducing costs.[56] Retail banks gather a large amount of information related to their customers' activity (in the form of customers' transaction data), making such personalization an exciting extension of mass campaigns.

It is possible to use classifications with random forests and deep neural networks for finding customers interested in banking services.[57] Such tools can extract significant patterns from customers' historical transfer and transactional data and predict, for instance, credit buying likelihood.

Customer Profitability Management

A CRM as customer profitability management should help in developing long-lasting, profitable relationships with customers. This goal is achieved by increasing customer loyalty and exploiting the potential of the customer base.[58]

Most businesses offer products or services to customers making sales one of the most critical banking development functions.[59] Finding leads and opportunities in CRM can use AI.[60] It is essential to use CRMs to get leads for cross-selling or up-selling. AI can be used to analyze an organization's historical sales data and current top factors of a lead to figure out whether the lead is evolving into an opportunity or not.[61] Factors

[56] Hossein Javaheri, S. (2008). *Response Modeling in Direct Marketing: A data mining-based approach for target selection* (Master Thesis). University of Lulea, Lulea, Sweden.

[57] Ładyżyński, P., Żbikowski, K., & Gawrysiak, P. (2019). Direct marketing campaigns in retail banking with the use of deep learning and random forests. *Expert Systems with Applications*, 134, 28–35.

[58] Geib, M., Reichold, A., Kolbe, L., & Brenner, W. (2005, January). Architecture for customer relationship management approaches in financial services. In *Proceedings of the 38th Annual Hawaii International Conference on System Sciences* (240b-240b). IEEE.

[59] Quan, X. I., & Sanderson, J. (2018). Understanding the artificial intelligence business ecosystem. *IEEE Engineering Management Review, 46*(4), 22–25.

[60] Yang, D. (2010, November). *Building brand equity through perfect customer relationship management* (pp. 329–332). IEEE.

[61] Salesforce. (2017). *Einstein Activity Capture*. c1.sfdcstatic.com/content/dam/web/en_us/www/documents/datasheets/salescloud-einstein-activitycapture.pdf. Accessed 20 January 2021.

and the data are displayed clearly to the user, making it easier to recognize the best leads and opportunities. Lead scoring with AI is interesting also for its improvements over time.[62]

Using AI for customer data analysis saves time and money by supplying a potential increase in margins.[63] Less time spent in lead qualification, data analysis, and customer activity tracking allows the operators to spend their time in more valuable actions, such as engaging on target opportunities and leads.[64]

AI allows for better management of data collected from the customers.[65] AI can analyze customer behavior at a deeper level than even expert users. This way, it allows operators to catch insights into the customer base and enables more personalized interactions, product placement, and marketing. This customization can increase customer loyalty and customer delight, thanks to the decrease in undesired messages, advertisement, and product placement.

Customer journey is the concept of a customer roaming the financial institution accesses, moving from page to page, in a path controlled by their clicks. AI can analyze this journey to create an optimal customer experience and supply an insight into best-performing accesses, messages, and events.[66]

CRMs in themselves cannot learn from customer's behavior, creating a substantial missed opportunity to gain all-important customer knowledge.[67] Limitations in information supply and interactivity cause a less personalized platform for the customer and a less effective organization

[62] Salesforce. (2017). *Einstein Lead Scoring*. c1.sfdcstatic.com/content/dam/web/en_us/www/documents/datasheets/salescloud-einstein-leadscoring.pdf. Accessed 20 January 2021.

[63] Quan, X. I., & Sanderson, J. (2018). Understanding the artificial intelligence business ecosystem. *IEEE Engineering Management Review, 46*(4), 22–25.

[64] Chagas, B. N. R., Viana, J., Reinhold, O., Lobato, F., Jacob Jr., Antonio F. L., et al. (2018, December). *Current Applications of Machine Learning Techniques in CRM: A Literature Review and Practical Implications* (pp. 452–458). IEEE.

[65] Salesforce. (2019). *Salesforce Einstein Basics*. railhead.salesforce.com/en/content/learn/modules/get_smart_einstein_feat. Accessed 20 January 2021.

[66] Yu, J. (2019). *Getting started with Salesforce Einstein analytics: A Beginner's guide to building interactive dashboards*. Apress Media, Singapore.

[67] Huang, Y., Chai, Y., Liu, Y., & Shen, J. (2019). Architecture of next-generation ecommerce platform. *Tsinghua Science and Solution, 24*(1), 18–29.

system. AI's ability to supply meaningful information at an increased pace allows for these limitations to be resolved.[68]

Benefits and Challenges of Customer Relationship Management

The combination of CRM with AI brings many benefits. The main goal of CRM software is to understand better customers' needs and offer them customized, user-friendly, and valuable products and services. From the beginning, CRM has used databases to achieve its goals more simply and then uses cloud storage for increased flexibility. The focus on CRMs has been collecting, storing, and supplying data at the request of users. In this way, organizations process the data extraction, analysis, and interpretation, which supply real value to the information and knowledge received. The challenge is an ever-increasing volume of data that organizations must handle; AI can support in this respect especially in extracting helpful information and actions from the data.

Despite recent legislation, such as the European GDPR, that aims to limit customer behavior profiling, analysis of buying patterns is one of the essential tools used in direct marketing. It helps incorporate temporal information in customer behavior analysis to estimate the best type of proposal directed to a specific customer and the most proper and timely moment when the customer should be contacted. Storing and processing in an intelligent way, all this data requires a combination of AI and CRM.

There are plenty of diversified solutions applicable to the diversity of automation needs in banking. This approach had a high rate of growth in recent years. It still suffers stiffness due to the legacy of traditional, inflexible ICT applications. The banking 5.0 uses of AI helps in overcoming this limitation.

[68] Salesforce (2019). *Icebreaker*. www.salesforce.com/customer-success-stories/icebreaker0/. Accessed 20 January 2021.

Conclusions

Banking 5.0 requires different customer proximity.[69] Innovative solutions present opportunities to satisfy customer expectations better.[70] Customer delight is undoubtedly increased by the possibility of supplying customized banking services and credits independently, anywhere, and at any time.[71] Customers want new ways of banking and managing risks, including immediate interactions. Customers wish to interact through various accesses when searching for and buying banking services. These customers' characteristics influence the online services' evolution, which changes the traditional "face-to-face" business model. The spread of information and websites can diminish the loyalty of the customers. The increasing lack of personal relationships, due to digital distribution, must move toward new banking interactions with customer proximity and continuous market analysis.

By integrating data from offline and online sources, financial institutions can understand how to approach their customers holistically and understand their expectations from initial inquiry to get banking services up to the use of their services.[72] Banking 5.0 compels each organization to restructure its proximity approach to build long-term customer relationships and to win more deals with a robust CRM in place.

Innovative solutions such as AI integrated with CRM can help to consider the customers' dynamic preferences. Higher customization of services with the market involves developing an integrated, customized

[69] Cappiello, A. (2020). The Digital (R) evolution of Insurance Business Models. *American Journal of Economics and Business Administration, 12*(1), 1 13.

[70] Larsson, A., & Broström, E. (2019). Banking customer retention: Financial institutions' perception of customer loyalty. *Marketing Intelligence & Planning*.

[71] Akroush, M. N., & Mahadin, B. K. (2019). An intervariable approach to customer satisfaction and loyalty in the internet service market. *Internet Research*. Demong, N. A. R., Othman, A. K., Yunus, N. H., & Amran, N. A. W. (2019). Service quality factors and customer satisfaction on life insurance services. *Journal of Islamic Management Studies, 2*(1), 22–31. Kaewsawad, S., & Li, Z. (2019, September). The effects of service quality of customer service on total customers' satisfaction in case of buying life insurance via the online channel. In *Proceedings of the IWEMB 2018: Second International Workshop on Entrepreneurship in Electronic and Mobile Business* (p. 119). BOD GmbH DE.

[72] Industry 5.0 and why there's a need for an effective CRM. blog.markgrowth.com/industry-4-0-and-why-theres-a-need-for-an-effective-crm-software-91963b865a73. Accessed 30 May 2020.

communication strategy, making it possible to better reach the customer to[73]:

- Understand customer needs and preferences.
- Evaluate customers' changing needs and predict them.
- Increase retention and up- and cross-selling.
- Monitor and oversee reputational dynamics that could otherwise escape control.

[73] Buttle, F., & Maklan, S. (2019). *Customer relationship management: Concepts and technologies*. Routledge, London, UK.

CHAPTER 6

Customer Partition in Banking 5.0

Marketing management is the art and science of choosing target markets and getting, keeping, and growing customers through creating, delivering, and communicating superior customer value.

Philip Kotler

Introduction

Banking 5.0 business model analyzes whether the digitization leads to a segmentation of the market into a cost competition or quality competition. Digitization increases the transparency in non-complex banking services. The digital distribution channel is direct. As a result, the segmentation can intensify. On one hand, there might be a fierce price competition with standardized products and high comparability. On the other extreme, the premium providers might generate an intensive quality competition.

The goal of digitization is to arrive at a market segment of one customer. In banking 5.0, the goal is that each service will be unique to its intended customer, designed, and deployed accordingly. To cater to the trend of one customer segment, financial institutions should have large, robotized advanced product "factories."

B. Nicoletti, *Banking 5.0*, Palgrave Studies in Financial Services Technology, https://doi.org/10.1007/978-3-030-75871-4_6

To develop a one-customer-oriented strategy, a financial institution must first understand who the target customer is. This scope requires answering some basic questions[1]:

- Who are the financial institution's most profitable customers? What makes them worthwhile?
- Why do they buy services from a financial institution and not from their competitors?
- Which percentage of the total population is represented by these customers? Is it possible to find more customers with the same profile?
- How can the financial institutions make these customers buy more from them?
- How will the financial institution manage the less profitable customers to reduce the costs they imply?

Customer Partition

Market segmentation involves the clustering of customers with similar needs and buying behavior into segments, each of which can be the target of a specific marketing program.[2] The concept is helpful to reconcile different customer needs with limited resources. It allows product and marketing proposals to suit distinct customer groups.[3] The theoretical basis for market segmentation comes from the economical pricing theory. This theory indicates that margins are maximized when prices that discriminate segments are set.[4]

Segmentations can be on these significant types of banking customers[5]:

[1] Matis, C., & Ilies, L. (2014). Customer relationship management in the insurance industry. *Procedia Economics and Finance, 15*(14), 1138–1145.

[2] Market Segmentation. A Tool for Improving Customer. https://jetems.scholarlinkresearch.com/articles/Marketpercent20Segmentation.pdf. Accessed 30 May 2020.

[3] Wind, Y. (1978, August). Issues and advances in segmentation research. *Journal of Marketing Research, 15*, 317–337.

[4] Frank, R.W., Massy, F., & Wind, Y. (1972). *Market segmentation*. Prentice-Hall, Upper Saddle River, NJ.

[5] Epetimehin, F. (2011). Market segmentation as a strategy for goal attainment in the insurance industry. SSRN 1749663.

- Risks-based.
- Life cycle.[6]
- Lifestyles and personality differences r.
- Social class-. The approaches to this segmentation are:

    (i) Geographic.
    (ii) Demographic.

The other segments that need special attention are:

(i) Students.
(ii) Gender.
(iii) Immigrants/Emigrants.

Millennials and Generation Z

An exciting segment, especially for banking 5.0, is about the so-called millennials. Millennials (or generation Y) are the generation between 1980 and 2000. Generation Z (Gen Z) is the demographic group succeeding millennials. These segments are highly active on the web, social media, and mobile phones. Generations Y and Z represent more than a quarter of the world population.[7] It is a significant but relevant challenge for financial institutions to gain these market segments. They are the customers of the future.

Banking 5.0 changes not only the banking services but also the relationship with the customers.[8] Today, the millennials want instant control of everything and look for more innovative products and services. Many millennials living in big cities do not own a car. These customers do not rely on their private sphere, as family or friends, to get information. Millennials prefer online reviews or social communities, like specialized forums and other online sites. Several factors and features play a unique

[6] Haas, R. W., & Berry, L. L. (1972). Systems selling of retail services. *Bankers' Monthly (USA)*, 276–283.

[7] How financial institutions can appeal to millennials in 2018 | Insurance. www.insurancebusinessmag.com/au/news/breaking-news/how-financialinstitutions-can-appeal-to-millennials-in-2018-86282.aspx. Accessed 20 April 2020.

[8] Nicoletti, B. (2016). *Digital insurance*. Palgrave-Macmillan, London, UK (translated in Chinese).

role in getting these segments, like quick transactions and transparency, convenience in shopping online, timesaving, cost-effective, high freebies as discount coupons.[9] With the radical diffusion of mobile phones and other mobile devices, millennials affect the old generation of customers' behavior. This effect is known as "equalizing."[10] Its consequence may be severe for a static industry like banking that has traditionally targeted a non-digital native market. The financial institutions that have shown a management mindset, a forward-looking attitude, and implemented digital solutions are still few.

This situation suits well to agile, digital-oriented innovators: like fintech organizations. A survey showed that Millennials and Gen Z had the most fintech accounts overall.[11] Gen Z saw a rise of 14% of inexperienced users (or a 27% increase), and millennials saw an increase of 8% (or a 17% increase). A substantial number of Baby Boomers (26%) rely on some sort of fintech account, contradicting the general opinion that digital tools are exclusively for younger people.

Segmentation with AI

The combination of big data, AI, and expert professionals supports a customer segmentation based on risk.[12] The model uses the banking domain knowledge to extract features from raw data via data mining. Such a system would use high, and low-level engineering approaches on transaction description to extract semantic items. All the extracted information will be linked to the banking domain knowledge, using developed APIs to create contextualized data. This contextualized data can be used to classify the transaction as either risky or not. Next, a subject-matter expert would analyze the input dataset and label each transaction to zero

[9] Deshpande, R. S. (2020). A study of adoption of artificial intelligence. In Banking Sector. *2. An empirical analysis on usage of e-transactions and mobile wallets among millennials and generation Z in* Mumbai, India, 61.

[10] www.mckinsey.it/idee/transforming-life-procurement-with-design-thinking. Accessed 30 May 2020.

[11] Krivkovich, A., White, O., Zac Townsend, Z., & Euart, J. (2020, December). How US customers' attitudes to fintech are shifting during the pandemic. *McKinsey Paper*.

[12] Zand, S. K. (2020). Towards intelligent risk-based customer segmentation in banking. arXiv preprint arXiv:2009.13929. Dean, J. (2014). *Big data, data mining, and machine learning: Value creation for business leaders and practitioners*. Wiley.

or one. Zero is not risky, and one shows a relationship with a risk activity. Subsequently, several machine learning algorithms can be used to evaluate the system's results and compare the proposed method's outcomes with the ones of a classic approach that is a combination of regular text cleaning and index searching. This method can classify more transactions compared to conventional methods. The system would allow the financial institutions to better understand their customers and their behavior by detecting risky activities, money laundering, transactions with sanctioned organizations and people, and, most importantly, finding the propensity to pay back loans.

Another approach is based on a Recency, frequency, and monetary value (RFM) model to compute the customers' value for the financial institution. Based on three distinct types of clustering algorithms, two other models can be applied to the data, which has customers' RFM values, to obtain customer segments.[13] In the first model, K-Means algorithms[14] have been used twice to separate customers into five attractive clusters based on their recency, frequency, and economic backgrounds. The second model is built by the synthesis of DBSCAN[15] and K-Means algorithm. First, DBSCAN supplies outliers/noise in the dataset. A second step, based on K-Means, uses these outliers/noise to separate them into two clusters according to their recency. As a result, this model supplies the most valuable customers for the financial institution.

Robo Advisors

Some AI technologies can help in segmenting the markets based on age or other characteristics. They can also help to interact with customers. One exciting solution is robotization. Software robots are particularly relevant, especially to younger generations. They accept to interact with a robot

[13] Aliyev, M., Ahmadov, E., Gadirli, H., Mammadova, A., & Alasgarov, E. (2020). Segmenting bank customers via RFM model and unsupervised machine learning. arXiv preprint arXiv:2008.08662.

[14] Raval, U. R., & Jani, C. (2016, May). Implementing & improvisation of K-means clustering algorithm. *International Journal of Computer Science and Mobile Computing, 5*(5), 191–203.

[15] Tran, T. N., Drab, K., & Daszykowski, M. (2013). Revised DBSCAN algorithm to cluster data with dense adjacent clusters. *Chemometrics and Intelligent Laboratory Systems, 120*, 92–96.

rather than with an operator. Robots can drastically reduce the costs of some transactions compared with the ones done by high-level and high-paid financial advisers.

The robo-advisors are one solution particularly relevant in this direction.[2] Robo-advisors are automated platforms that supply algorithm-driven financial and investment management advice.[16] They start from the information collected from customers, based on their status, goals, and plans. They use various technologies such as cognitive systems, machine learning, natural language processing, expert systems, and other AI algorithms. They can suggest (automatically or with a financial advisor's support) investment solutions personalized to the customer's expectations and needs. There are also "robo-for-advisors" in the case they support human advisors in helping customers with investment decisions.[17]

Robo-Advisor Architecture

Robo-advisors are different from existing online investment platforms or online brokerage for various conceptual aspects such as customer assessment, and portfolio management.[2] Robo-advisors' capabilities are[18]:

- Understanding customer needs and preferences, collecting customer information, assessing risk tolerance, and considering external situations.
- Proposing financial products, developing a financial plan, selecting capital allocation and portfolios.
- Implementing the proposal, opening accounts, transferring assets, procurement on the securities market.
- Monitoring and adjusting the financial products with periodically, or even continuous, performance reviews, dashboards and status alerts, market updates, and financial markets analysis.

[16] EBF position paper on AI in the banking industry. www.ebf.eu/wp-content/uploads/2020/03/EBF-AI-paper-_final-.pdf. Accessed 30 December 2020.

[17] Cuzzola, P. (2020). Roboadvice, artificial intelligence and responsibility: The regulatory framework between present scenarios and future perspectives. In *Economic and policy implications of artificial intelligence* (pp. 87–120). Springer, Cham, Switzerland.

[18] www.accenture.com/t20160509t220506__w__/us-en/_acnmedia/pdf-17/accenture-wealth-management-rise-of-robo-advice.pdf. Accessed 5 April 2020.

For customer portfolio management, robo-advisors can be classified: active or passive about portfolio management and dynamic or static about customer assessment.[19]

A robo-advisor is considered static if the investment strategy and portfolio construction approach is figured out after the first adjustment to a customer's profile. From that moment onwards, the robo-advisor only performs automated rebalancing if the portfolio composition differs from the best, for example, due to market developments. If the customer can change the overall strategy effectively during the relationship, the robo-advisor is classified as dynamic.[20]

There is a distinction between active and passive robo-advisors. Robo-advisors can do active management[21]:

- Collecting data and analyzing the markets continuously.
- Proposing (optional) shifts in asset allocation.
- Aiming at outperforming the market.

Robo-advisors can do passive management[22]:

- Acting on predefined parameters.
- Frequently restoring the predefined asset mix.
- Taking human emotion out of investment decisions.
- Aiming at long-term growth in analogy with the market.

A Deloitte survey found that in 2016[23]:

- Forty two percent of robo-advisors were with pure passive management.
- Twenty-five percent of robo-advisors were with pure active management.

[19] Jung, D., Dorner, V., Glaser, F., & Morana, S. (2018). Robo-advisory. *Business & Information Systems Engineering, 60*(1), 81–86.

[20] Digitalization and Automation of Financial Advisory. https://aisel.aisnet.org/cgi/viewcontent.cgi?article=1454&context=bise. Accessed 20 March 2021.

[21] Deloitte. (2016). Robo advisory in wealth management. *Deloitte Report*.

[22] Deloitte. (2016). Robo Advisory in Wealth Management. *Deloitte Report*.

[23] Deloitte. (2016). Robo advisory in wealth management. *Deloitte Report*.

- Nineteen percent of robo-advisors had both options available to the customer.

Robo-advisors supply more complex user interaction components (push notifications for market updates, opportunity/risk alerts, dashboards, and periodic portfolio reviews) and automated execution. Optionally, they can be allowed for self-directed, discretionary interventions by the customer.

Robo-advisor platform providers could have a Business-to-customers (B2C) or a Business-to-business (B2B) business model with a vastly different approach, costs, and target customers. In the B2C case, the onboarding procedure to get the customer (for example, fully or partially digital) should be considered an integral part of the use case.

Robo-advisors may be put in place through the combination of different technologies. The most important ones are[24]:

- Cognitive systems: tools to support cognitive tasks and decision-making.
- Task automation tools: interactive, iterative, and evidence-based systems.
- Machine learning: tools to support capabilities in learning. They can be:
  - Large-scale machine learning (for large-scale data sets).
  - Supervised learning and reinforcement learning (supporting a process of sequential and experience-driven decision-making).
  - Deep learning (algorithms based on neural networks).
- Natural language processing: understanding language by attributing meaning and purpose.
- Intelligent analytics/processing (predictive analysis and simulations, support for rule-based automatic actions, recommendation engines, and context-aware computing).
- Other technologies could be integrated with the robo-advisor platforms, such as user interface, data visualization, and operational support.

[24] Davenport, T. H. (2018). *The AI advantage: How to put the artificial intelligence revolution to work*. MIT Press. Cambridge, MA. www.ebf.eu/wp-content/uploads/2020/03/EBF-AI-paper-_final-.pdf. Accessed 20 November 2020.

Another robo-advisors classification distinguishes between fully automated robo-advisors and hybrid robo-advisors.[25] The first one uses an online platform, which transmits automated algorithm-based portfolio directly to the investor without human support. The second type is a hybrid platform, which uses traditional advisors to supply wealth management solutions. The latter model is a hybrid one which creates individual customized service and manages the portfolios with both computerized recommendations and financial analysts.

Robo-Advisors in Banking 5.0

Robo-advisors have the goal to transform the traditional, person-to-person advisory process into a digital, person-to-computer process.[26] Online questionnaires and self-reporting processes replace traditional investor profiling conducted during in-person interviews and bilateral interactions. Algorithm and automated processes quantify the customer's investment goals/purposes, risk affinity/aversion, and return/risk expectations. The assessment is not limited to risk profiling. It can include ethical and sector-specific preferences, for example, a preference for Islamic banking.

Robo Islamic Advisor[27]
Robo Islamic Advisor (RIA) is the world's first automated Islamic investment platform for customers. RIA aims to supply access to halal portfolio management for 2 billion Muslims worldwide.[28] The introduction of RIA is the world's first automated ethical investment platform.

[25] Phoon, K., & Koh, F. (2018). Robo-advisors and wealth management. *Journal of Alternative Investments, 20*(3), 79.

[26] Jung, D., Dorner, V., Glaser, F., & Morana, S. (2018). Robo-advisory. *Business & Information Systems Engineering, 60*(1), 81–86.

[27] Gazali, H. M., Jumadi, J., Ramlan, N. R., Abd Rahmat, N., Uzair, S. N. H. M., & Mohid, A. N. (2020). Application of Artificial Intelligence (AI) in Islamic investments. *Journal of Islamic Finance, 9*(2), 70–78. ISSN: 2289-2109 e-ISSN: 2289-2117.

[28] Friedberg, B. A. (2019). Wahed invest: A look at the new Islamic robo-advisor. www.investopedia.com/articles/personal-finance/112516/wahed-invest-peek-newislamicroboadvisor.asp#:~:text=Both%20access%20and%20investments%20are,risk%E2%80%94than%20their%20traditional%20competitors. Accessed 20 January 2021.

Wahed Invest (the investment organization) offers a lower minimum investment of USD 7,500 as a starter. The investment organization claims to be the first global Robo-Advisor, and their services are accessible for the lower socio-economic demography.[29] In the beginning, Wahed Invest was only available in the USA; it then expanded its banking to over 100 countries worldwide by 2017. Two months after launching the world's first Islamic Robo-Advisor, another organization known as the Kuala Lumpur-based Farringdon Group launched the Asia's first Shariah-compliant Robo-Advisor.[30] The online tool, called Algebra, will supply automated portfolio management advice, and will be opened to investors across all geographies with a minimum investment of USD 200 per month. In this regard, customers can choose funds from its Islamic Master Select Portfolio.[31] RIA is vital in Islamic investment, where it will help investors to perform investment on an Islamic platform.[32]

The customer portfolio management of robo-advisors differs from existing approaches. Customer portfolio management is defined as managing portfolios including one or more financial products, per mandates given by customers, on a discretionary customer-by-customer basis. Robo-advisory is normally based on products that require less active portfolio management, like Exchange-traded funds (ETFs).[33] Cost structures are often relatively simple and so easier to communicate. The strategic asset allocation is based on the risk profile of the customer. A quantitative model can define it.[34] The provisioning of the full service via an AI platform reduces staff and asset costs since many customers

[29] Fazmi, F. (2019). Role of robo-advisors in Islamic financial institutions. https://journal.wahedinvest.com/role-of-robo-advisors-in-islamic-financial-institutions/. Accessed 20 January 2021.

[30] Bank, D. I. (2017). Global Islamic finance report 2017. *Dubai Islamic Bank*. Dubai, UAE.

[31] Rahman, A. (2019). Opportunities and threats of Shariah-compliant robo advisory. The case of Wahed Invest.www.grin.com/document/540407. Accessed 20 January 2021.

[32] Gazali, H. M., Jumadi, J., Ramlan, N. R., Abd Rahmat, N., Uzair, S. N. H. M., & Mohid, A. N. (2020). Application of Artificial Intelligence (AI) in Islamic investments. *Journal of Islamic Finance, 9*(2), 70–78. ISSN: 2289-2109 e-ISSN: 2289-2117.

[33] Brenner, L., & Meyll, T. (2020). Robo-advisors: A substitute for human financial advice? *Journal of Behavioral and Experimental Finance, 25*, 100275.

[34] Digitalization and Automation of Financial Advisory. https://aisel.aisnet.org/cgi/viewcontent.cgi?article=1454&context=bise. Accessed 20 March 2021.

can be served simultaneously. These solutions' low complexity can for example support explaining to a wide range of customers the portfolio's management-related benefits of ETFs.

Currently, most financial institutions can use robo-advisors to augment and replace customer interactions over time. It is interesting to use analytics and intelligent machines to work even more in conjunction with banking specialists and advisors. This way will better address customers' needs for customized and proactive advice. Financial institutions will strengthen the provision of value-added services in an increasingly competitive industry.

In the front office, robo-advisors support financial data and account actions integration with AI-powered software agents. These agents can interact with customer chatting platforms using advanced language processing.[35]

There are three stages in the development of robo-advisors over time[36]:

- The first robo-advisory services were designed for retail investors. They were introduced in the USA after the financial crisis of 2008, also as an answer to the increasing distrust in the investment advisory banking.[37] The first idea of robo-advisory has been to disrupt banks' human advisory services by offering affordable investment advice to widen the customer base by including retail customers and making sound investment decisions, recommending an ETF-based portfolio of stocks and bonds.[38] Investment process by robo-advisors was quite simple at that time.[39] The measurement of risk preferences relied on a few questions. It was not enough to supply proper risk classification and hence to derive sound investment advice.

[35] OECD. (2017). *Solutions and innovation in the insurance sector*. OECD Publishing, Paris, France.

[36] Scholz, P. *Robo-advisory: Investing in the digital age*. Springer Nature, Cham, Switzerland.

[37] Becchi, S. M., Hamaloglu, U., Aggarwal, T., & Panchal, S. (2018). The evolution of Robo-advisors and Advisor 2.0 model: The future of investment management and financial advisory. *Ernst & Young Global Limited*.

[38] Nguyen, G. (2019). Competition between traditional banks and FinTech. Tampere *University of Applied Science*, Tampere, Finland.

[39] Tertilt, M., & Scholz, P. (2018). To advise, or not to advise—How robo-advisors evaluate the risk preferences of private investors. *The Journal of Wealth Management, 21*(2), 70–84.

- The robo-advisors became more complex over time, for example, by including more asset classes, active funds, tax optimization, and so on.
- Due to regulation and trust issues, such as moral hazards, investors are hesitant to use robo-advisors. To mitigate the distrust issue, hybrid models are applied where humans and robo-advisors are combined.[40]

The global robo-advisors' market is expected to grow at a compound annual growth rate of 53.4% translating into USD 97.03 billion by 2025.[41]

Responsive AI[42]:
Responsive AI is a start-up in Canada working on expanding worldwide. Its value proposition is to help advisors rapidly check and assess the customer's life through their financial data and then submitting the best options to take.[43] Responsive AI uses behavioral analytics to help wealth advisors make better and faster decisions. The platform generates prioritized actions that help the advisors focus on customizing their offerings with a framework that integrates several tools such as risk management, planning, and rebalancing.

Advisors want to service more mass affluent customers, while customers want more personalization, convenience, and responsiveness. Responsive AI helps to reduce the response time for an advisor to look at a customer case and produce a correct profile and actions that might be helpful for the customers while respecting the advisor's institution's fair policy. To make that possible, advisors should apply a person-centric AI.

[40] Scholz, P. *Robo-advisory: Investing in the digital age.* Springer Nature, Cham, Switzerland.

[41] Market Data Forecast. (2020). *Global robo advisory market research report.* Hyderabad, India. www.marketdataforecast.com/market-reports/robo-advisory-market. Accessed 20 January 2021.

[42] www.responsive.ai. Accessed 20 January 2021.

[43] https://wealth.insart.com/wp-content/uploads/2019/09/Research-and-Analysis-Responsive-AI.pdf. Accessed 20 September 2020.

In Canada, Responsive AI is working with around nine money transfer operators, which manages portfolios from USD 30 million to USD 4 billion. They are working with OP Financial, which is Finland's largest bank. Responsive AI takes hybrid wealth management and systems that aid decision-making, record decisions, and set up an integrated view of the customer's financial life.

Benefits and Challenges of Robo-Advisors

Robo-advisor capabilities benefit financial institutions. They allow expansion in wealth management while leaving agents to keep their focus on banking sales.[44] Thanks to cost savings by the automated customer profiling and the management of the customer lifecycle, robo-advisors can target the retail customer or non-professional's segments, regardless of the customer's actual wealth.[45] The costs of this type of service would be sufficiently low to support low-income customers. The charge is between 15 and 35 basis points of assets under management in case investment robo-advisors do the job.[46] For example, in comparison, in the UK, Santander's branch-based investment advice fees are 2.5% of assets invested, with a minimum GBP 500 and a maximum of GBP 150,000.[47]

Robo-advisors enable a great customer journey for customers that prefer digital interactions and the "do-it-yourself" approach. They offer contextualized products and experiences, supplying targeted financial advice and reducing the cost for customers.

With hybrid robo-advisors, personal interactions can bring benefits to a long-term relationship. Over time, with a human advisor, it is possible to develop trust and understanding between a customer and financial advisor/broker/agent. On the other side, robo-advisors can prepare a

[44] www.accenture.com/_acnmedia/PDF-2/Accenture-Wealth-Management-Rise-of-Robo-Advice.pdf. Accessed 30 May 2020.

[45] Jung, D., Dorner, V., Glaser, F., & Morana, S. (2018). Robo-advisory. *Business & Information Systems Engineering, 60*(1), 81–86.

[46] https://investorjunkie.com/robo-advisors/cost-comparison/. Accessed 5 April 2020.

[47] www.santanderbank.com/us/personal/banking/santander-select. Accessed 2 May 2020.

banking plan addressing multiple goals, including retirement, protection needs, and estate planning. Robo-advisors assure privacy, which some customers may feel more comfortable interacting with, given the sensitivity in discussing financial matters.

Robo-advisors can improve the customer experience through a wide range of choices in terms of services and customization capabilities based on better use of the data through advanced analytics, for example, through[48]:

- Offering contextualized, targeted products and experiences.
- Supplying better and consistent financial advice.
- Reducing costs for customers.
- And so on.

There are challenges with robo-advisors due to the need to respect regulations:

- The European Data Protection Framework (and Regulation [EU] 2016/679, of 27 April 2016, on the protection of natural persons about the processing of personal data and on free movement of such data—GDPR).
- Several European and national regulations on the financial market and wealth management (for example, MiFID II, Regulation 285/2013 of Banca d'Italia).
- CCPA— California Customer Privacy Act, in the USA.

To use natural language processing in customer front ends, legal requirements on customer information and consent must be adapted to fit this purpose.

With robo-advisors, there is a lack of transparency or knowledge by the customer about how their data is used. Comprehensive data privacy statements tend to produce information fatigue among customers quickly. The degree of details introduced by the GDPR and the "juridification" of its language to avoid the risk of penalties reduce clarity and understanding for the customer, thus going against the first purpose.[49]

[48] www.oecd.org/pensions/Solution-and-innovation-in-the-procurement-sector.pdf. Accessed 5 April 2020.

[49] www.ebf.eu/wp-content/uploads/2020/03/EBF-AI-paper-_final-.pdf. Accessed 20 November 2020.

Conclusions

This chapter explores the concept of customer partition of the banking market, its justification, and the banking 5.0 applications. It is critical to understand how the banking world works and the main processes and resources necessary for the customer partition to occur. Attention is placed on new ways to partition a market in transformation. This chapter underlines the relevance of the millennial and generation Z markets. To reach the goal of one-customer partitions, it is essential to use advanced automation tools, such as robo-advisors.

CHAPTER 7

Place or Accesses in Banking 5.0

Focus like a laser on the customer experience.
Jeff Bezos

Introduction

All organizations have limited control over their external environment, which has recently shown some drastic developments. They also connect to innovative solutions that should embrace the entire business model. It is interesting to examine two aspects of the distribution of banking services:

- To understand all the components that have significantly changed banking after years of technological stalemate.
- To analyze the levers on which financial institutions should rely on the distribution of their services-

B. Nicoletti, *Banking 5.0*, Palgrave Studies in Financial Services Technology, https://doi.org/10.1007/978-3-030-75871-4_7

Ubiquitous mobile phones, open-source software, remote working, pandemic, and cloud computing have reduced direct customer engagement.[1] Digital transformation has a significant impact on business distribution models. It is interesting to analyze the changes in channel management in this specific case. Compared with e-commerce, for banking customers, digital accesses' adoption and use are lagging, with many transactions performed over traditional media. These trends are changing after the pandemic. Digital adoption does not depend anymore on age. It is now standard across generations.[2] Extended pandemic lockdowns in 2020 forced a generalized learning and extensive use of digital accesses for day-to-day transactions. "Everyone is digital" is becoming a global slogan.[3] Customers are adopting online access as the preferred medium searching for banking services to advance their actual buying. In addition to pure traditional and digital customers, this behavior leads to a different customer group, the so-called search shoppers. They use one access for search and another one for purchase.[4]

Banking 5.0 and Distribution

Despite the growth of digital solutions and the increasing customer computer literacy level thanks to the diffusion of e-commerce, traditional banking accesses continue to dominate the distribution globally. The use of financial institution's branches was relatively have stable, from 60 to 70% of transactions in most markets. The distribution of banking services is the domain affected more by digital technologies and the so-called new normal after the pandemic. In Europe, while sales through e-commerce of non-financial sectors are rising at double-digit rates, the average proportion of direct online and mobile banking is only now growing. The expectation is that in 2026 88% of all retail financial institutions'

[1] Internet Trends Report. (2018). Kleiner Perkins. www.kleinerperkins.com/perspectives/internet-trends-report-2018/. Accessed 10 January 2020.

[2] Report. (2020). www.capgemini.com/de-de/wp-content/uploads/sites/5/2020/05/WorldInsuranceReport2020_Web.pdf. Accessed 30 May 2020.

[3] worldinsurancereport.com/. Accessed 30 May 2020.

[4] Mau, S., Cvijikj, I. P., & Wagner, J. (2018). Understanding the differences in customer portfolio characteristics and insurance consumption across distribution channels. *University of Lausanne* (pp. 56–58). Lausanne, Switzerland.

interactions will be mobile.[5] Some financial institutions in advanced economies are not yet pushing the opportunity to transact via the web. They prefer traditional accesses because they do not want to invest in advanced solutions, have legacy investments, and, especially, not lose contact with their customers.[6]

Digital solutions have substantial effects on all distribution processes: both on how products and services are delivered or supplied and, more generally, on how organizations interact with their customers. While in the past, customers relied exclusively on the branches of their financial institution for every need, today's customers are increasingly autonomous. They use media and various sources to search, learn from, and eventually use a specific banking service. Digitization has expanded the range of services available to customers in multiple accesses, including the web, email, live chat, mobile application, text messages, embedded banking, forums, and social.

This evolution toward a multi-touch and omniaccess distribution model is a phenomenon present in many markets. Thanks to the mobile, it is expanding to emerging countries.[7] Digital solutions supply many options for customers. For example, the transactions for payments, become more accessible and affordable, using a digital wallet.

Gartner surveyed several executives. It found that seventy-two percent of them focused on changing the business model. Seventy-two percent of them focused also on a change of channel.[8] This trend is not arriving at the closure of all financial institution branches but reducing their number.[9] Online transactions experienced explosive growth in several countries. This growth offers three distinct benefits:

[5] Wewege, L., Lee, J., & Thomsett, M. C. (2020). Disruptions and digital banking trends. *Journal of Applied Finance and Banking*, *10*(6), 15–56.

[6] www.assinews.it/07/2017/impatto-della-digitalizzazione-sulla-distribuzione-assicurativa-ancora-rivoluzione-tranquilla/660042393/. Accessed on 20 March 2020.

[7] Pegan, G., Vianelli, D., & de Luca, P. (2020). Online channels and the country of origin. In *International marketing strategy* (pp. 149–180). Springer, Cham, Switzerland.

[8] www.gartner.com/document/3995096?ref=TrackRecommendedEmail. Accessed 20 January 2020.

[9] Del Gaudio, B. L., Porzio, C., Sampagnaro, G., & Verdoliva, V. (2020). How do mobile, internet and ICT diffusion affect the banking industry? An empirical analysis. *European Management Journal*.

- Reduction of transaction costs.
- Capacity to supply services to customers any time (24*7).
- Access to any customer in the world by abolishing distance and physical barriers.[10]

The very nature of banking, and the resulting interrelation between supply and demand, ensure that the service distribution and delivery system represent one of the critical factors for the success of the financial institution's strategies. The interdependence between production, distribution, and consumption phases makes the distribution system fundamental in its characteristics, and qualification with the customer. [11]

Product differentiation can be implemented through a technological, relational, or organizational change that affects all the distribution system elements and changes the customer's use of the service.[12] Technological evolution becomes critical when changing banking services' distribution and operations processes and their innovation.[13] Online accesses make service differentiation and innovation possible.[14] More specifically, the changes introduced by the solutions may involve the product/service

[10] Kraemer, K., Gibbs, J., & Dedrick, J. (2002). *Impacts of globalization on e-commerce adoption and firm performance: A cross country investigation*. University of California, Center for Research on Information Solution Organization, Irvine, CA. Humphrey, J., Manshell, R., Pare, D., & Schmitz, H. (2003). *The reality of e-commerce with developing countries*. www.gapresearch.org/production/publications.html. Accessed 30 May 2020. United Nation Conference on Trade and Development. (2002). Ecommerce and development report. *United Nations, UNCTAD*. Yap, A., Das, J., Burbridge, J., & Cort, K. (2006). A composite-model for e-commerce diffusion: Integrating cultural and socio-economic dimensions to the dynamics of diffusion. *Journal of Global Information Management*, 14(3).

[11] Cappiello, A. (2020). The digital (r)evolution of insurance business models. *American Journal of Economics and Business Administration, 12*(1), 1–13.

[12] Nightingale, P. (2003). Innovation in financial services infrastructure. In L. V. Shavinina (Ed.), *The international handbook on innovation* (pp. 529–547). Elsevier Science Ltd., Oxford, UK. Pires, C. P., Sarkar, S., & Carvalho, L. (2008). Innovation in services – How different from manufacturing? *The Service Industries Journal*, *28*, 1339–1356.

[13] Coelho. F., Easingwood, C., & Coelho, A. (2003). Exploratory evidence of channel performance in single vs. multiple channel strategies. *International Journal of Retail & Distribution Management, 31*(11), 561–573.

[14] Coelho, F., & Easingwood, C. (2005). Determinants of multiple channel choice in financial services: An environmental uncertainty model. *Journal of Services Marketing, 19*(4), 199–211.

in the strict sense—with the introduction of new products—or the production and distribution process of the product/service. In the latter case, technological progress changes the traditional distribution system components and the relationships established between different processes.

Bypassing the direct link with branch staff implies more direct intervention and higher customer involvement in distributing many services.[15] In the banking sector (and in many other services), the distinction between product innovation and process innovation is not always cut and clear.[16] The final product and the distinct phases of its distribution system are often strictly related. The differentiation and modernization of the production and distribution processes significantly affect the service's qualitative and functional characteristics. The technological solutions innovate the distribution process and affect the innovation of the service itself.

Information and communication solutions are not only a tool for simplifying procedures and saving costs. They are factors of differentiation and innovation of the product/service and its distribution process critical to achieving sustainable competitive advantages.[17] The expansion of operational boundaries, financial innovation, and changing needs of the market leads to the emergence of suitable conditions for diversification and a specific specialization of the distribution systems.[18] This trend leads to a careful assessment of the composition and coordination of the entire distribution system related to the services offered and to the market segments served.

[15] Badoc, M. (1986). *Marketing pour le banque et l'assurance europeennes*. Les Editions d'Organization, Paris, France. Eiglier, P., & Langeard, E. (1987). *Servuction, le Marketing des Services*. McGraw Hill, Paris, France.

[16] Campanerut, M., & Nicoletti, B. (2010, December). Best practices for DFSS in the development of new services: Evidence from a multiple case study. *The Journal of American Business Review*, 16(1).

[17] Kabadayi, S. Loureiro, Y. K. & Carnevale, M. (2017). Customer value creation in multichannel systems: the interactive effect of integration quality and multichannel complexity. *Journal of Creating Value*, *3*(1), 1–18.

[18] Heinhuis D., & de Vries, E. J. (2009). Modeling customer behaviour in multichannel service distribution. *Enterprise Applications and Services in the Finance Industry*, *35*, 47–63.

Distribution Models Architecture

The value network deconstruction and reconstruction is based on a systematic approach to finding architectures for business models. This activity means finding value network elements and finding ways of integrating information in the network. It considers the possible creation of online or mobile markets. The classical scheme is as follows[19]:

- Value network deconstruction means changing the elements of the value network.
- Interaction patterns, which can be 1-to-1, 1-to-many, many-to-1, many-to-many.
- Value network reconstruction with the integration of information processing across several steps of the value network. Two sets of value network elements are considered in the interaction patterns in the earlier point.

Combining interaction patterns with value network integration support constructing innovative architectures for business models.

The *a priori* feasibility of implementing any business model's architecture depends very much upon the state-of-the-art of the solutions.[20] This statement holds true for the integration dimension, the realization of the single functions, and the support for interaction patterns. Any distribution model's commercial viability is a different matter altogether, which is a marketing model analysis domain.

Thanks to the internet[21]:

- Information and communication solutions enable a wide range of business models.
- Capability of the modern solutions is just one criterion in model selection.

[19] Timmers, P. (1998). Business models for electronic markets. *Electronic Markets*, *8*(2), 3–8.

[20] Oukharijane, J., Chaabâne, M. A., Said, I. B., Andonoff, E., & Bouaziz, R. (2020). *A hybrid approach based on reuse techniques for autonomic adaptation of business processes* (No. 4381). EasyChair.

[21] Teece, D. J. (2020). Fundamental issues in strategy: Time to reassess? *Strategic Management Review*, *1*(1), 103–144.

- Solutions in themselves do not supply guidelines for selecting a model in commercial terms.
- Guidance to solution development can come from the definition of new models.

It is possible to classify eleven online business models or generalizations of specific internet distribution models to possibly implement. Their characteristics in use are listed below.[22]

- E-shop. This characteristic is web marketing of a financial institution or a shop. In the first instance, the goal is to promote the financial institution and its products or services.
- E-procurement. This characteristic is digital tendering and procurement of products and services, including banking services.
- E-auction. Online auctions offer a digital implementation of the bidding mechanism used in traditional auctions.
- Digital mall. In its basic form, a digital mall consists of several e-shops, sometimes enhanced by a common umbrella, for example, a well-known brand or a physical or virtual ecosystem.[23]
- Third-party marketplace. This model is adopted when financial institutions are willing to leave the web marketing to a third party (as an add-on to their other accesses).[24]
- Community economy. Virtual communities' value comes from the members (customers or partners), who add their information onto an environment provided by the virtual community financial institution.[25] This economy is formed by financial institutions and organizations that place communities of people at the center of their business strategy.[26] These communities bring people together

[22] Timmers, P. (1998). Business models for electronic markets. *Electronic markets*, *8*(2), 3–8.

[23] Knowledge of The Problem Domain 3.1 Business Model. www.hec.unil.ch/aosterwa/PhD/3.pdf. Accessed 4 January 2021.

[24] What Is Third Party Marketplace | IGI Global. www.igi-global.com/dictionary/b2b-commerce-development-syria-sudan/30018. Accessed 4 January 2021.

[25] Om this case, some authors write about C2B: consumers are providing services to businesses. Kumari, P. (2020). MCQs with Question bank with Answer Key E-Commerce.

[26] Schmid, B. (2020). *Making transformative geographies: Lessons from Stuttgart's community economy* (p. 37). Transcript Verlag, Bielefeld, Germany.

around an idea derived from a passion, a common condition, a purpose, or a practice. Two things are essential in these communities: on one side, to create open accesses of conversation and constant exchange with users, to encourage a sort of co-creation and co-management of the business; on the other side, to aggregate people around a civic commitment, to promote concrete actions for critical social objectives, and to marry values felt by customers, such as sustainability.

- Value network service provider. These providers specialize in a specific function for the value network, such as digital payments. The intention is to make that one function their distinct competitive advantage. For example, banks have been positioning themselves for a long with traditional channels. They may find new opportunities using new online networks.
- Value-chain integrators. They focus on integrating multiple stages of the value network, with the potential to exploit the information flow between those steps as added value.
- Collaboration platforms. These platforms supply a set of applications and an information environment for collaboration between enterprises or with customers.

Over time, new models will come up.

Distribution Models in Banking 5.0

Direct banking is the sale of banking services without intermediation (banking branches or other financial institutions). Through the direct channel, financial institutions sell their products to their customers by telephone, internet, mail, or interactive television. Research by the consultancy Price Waterhouse Coopers showed that the average transaction carried out directly online by a financial institution can cost half when done over the telephone of over the branch network and one-tenth when conducted over the internet.[27] These cost reductions are significant for financial institutions to remain competitive in very price-sensitive markets. The real alternative is embedded banking with all its pros and cons.

[27] Page, Y. (2000). *E-commerce in insurance*. Informa. London, UK.

To upgrade communication methods and improve sales activities, financial institutions focus on mobile apps, websites, and official pages on the main social networks. They are trying to implement distribution methods and customer relationship management through chatbots and robo-advisors. Customers demand clarity and transparency in these accesses. A plus of digital access is the possibility for the customer to access more information online.

The benefits of direct banking for financial institutions are[28]:

- Possibility of spending the money they save on advertising their brand and attracting the customers directly.
- More flexibility in segmentation and pricing.
- Increased security and privacy in financial transactions.
- 100% ownership of the customer.
- Improvement in customer retention management and satisfaction (for example, thanks to faster services).
- Savings in cash and documents handling and storing.
- Increase in the financial institution's value.

The customers receive help from direct banking as well[29]:

- Attractive fees thanks to the lower operating costs.
- Instant service on a 24*7 basis.
- A faster route via internet or mobile.
- Direct access to information and access to a private reserved area. These accesses are fast and straightforward because they are available to the customers anytime, anywhere, and saves on managing and printing paper.
- The market structure can decide the success or failure of direct banking in a country to a substantial extent.

Direct banking can optimize its success possibilities when promoted in a country with a culture conducive to innovations (macroeconomic level).

[28] Tzanis, S. (2012). Direct insurance: The determinants of success. *Doctoral thesis, University of St. Gallen*, St. Gallen, Switzerland.

[29] Tzanis, S. (2012). Direct insurance: The determinants of success. *Doctoral thesis, University of St. Gallen*, St. Gallen, Switzerland.

Nations should have a banking market structure that helps develop direct banking (market level).

Swedbank

Swedbank is a Swedish banking institute that implemented an AI-based customer service assistant called Nina.[30] Swedbank is one of the largest financial institutions in the Nordic-Baltic region. Its primary target market is Sweden. It has a leading position in other countries such as Lithuania, Finland, and Latvia. Swedbank is present in China and USA markets.

Swedbank was founded in 1820 in Gothenburg and served as a traditional and classic savings bank only. In 2016, there were 4.5 million physical customer interactions (via phone or branch contact). Two million of these interactions were transactional, meaning that customers could have executed the request by themselves but preferred to engage with a Swedbank operator.[31] This situation shows that the customers are either not aware of the information available to them or that it is more comfortable to contact the bank.

Swedbank customer service staff was spending too much time looking up information. This search is done by asking each other or searching the intranet and internet, trying to find the customer's information. These interactions are not adding value to Swedbank and are a misuse of available resources. On the other side, Swedbank is concerned about new fintech competitors like Trustly or Tink. These pose a threat to Swedbank by supplying cheaper and user-friendly financial services for customers.[32]

Nina is a chatbot that serves as a virtual assistant and uses Artificial intelligence (AI).[33] Nina is accessible through the home page of Swedbank. The primary differentiation between Nina and a simple search engine is that, Nina prompts the user to ask more questions in response to a customer's question. This approach aims to let Nina understand the purpose of a user's inquiry in such a way to be able to supply the correct response. The intent is to present Nina as open and user-friendly as possible. Nina has an external and an internal layer. The external layer is visible for customers visiting the Swedbank website.

[30] Ates, M. (2017). Artificial intelligence in banking: A case study of the introduction of a virtual assistant into customer service.

[31] Kedbäck, M. (2016). Digital customer service manager at Swedbank. *Intelligent Assistance Conference (IAC)*, London, UK (Appendix C).

The inner layer is only accessible for Swedbank service staff. The purpose of having two layers is that if the customer is not happy with Nina's answer, s/he can opt to escalate the inquiry to a Swedbank support center. The service staff responding to the customer can access the internal layer, which has more specific information that might help respond to the customer inquiry.[34]

Thanks to Nina, the first-contact resolution rate is at 80%. Sixty-two percent of these are deflected, meaning that customers did not have to contact Swedbank at all to solve their problem. The other 18% are channeled, meaning that Swedbank chose to redirect the users to another channel, for example, their phone banking, branch, or online banking platform. Twenty percent of all interactions are categorized as attempted or unsolved inquires. Eighteen percent of those are abandoned, meaning that the user stopped interacting with Swedbank for an unknown reason.[35]

The main success of Nina depends on four factors.

1. Being customer-driven since it only includes information about topics that the customers ask about.
2. Accessible through the web browser of Swedbank and, especially the first-contact resolution, performs well and solves the customer's problems immediately.
3. Being a joint project between Swedbank, Nuance, and a cloud-based solution is very much user-friendly and changes can be implemented fast.[36]
4. Being staffed in such a way customers are directed to the proper information pipelines. The content management teams' main tasks are to monitor conversations, check if Nina's information is up to date, and assure that product owners, legal parties, and overall communication about Nina are handled appropriately.[37]

[32] Hernæs, C. (2015, March 5). Stockholm is leading the way for fintech in the Nordic region. hernaes.com/2015/03/05/stockholm-is-leading-theway-for-fintech-in-the-nordic-region/. Accessed 20 January 2021.

[33] Ates, M. (2017). Artificial intelligence in banking: A case study of the introduction of a virtual assistant into customer service.

[34] Kedbäck, M. (2016). Digital customer service manager at Swedbank. *Intelligent Assistance Conference (IAC)*. London, UK (Appendix C).

[35] Kedbäck, M. (2016). Digital customer service manager at Swedbank. *Intelligent Assistance Conference (IAC)*. London, UK (Appendix C).

Nina is expanding to the mobile channel as a dedicated virtual assistant. Forty percent of the customers use Swedbank's digital services only through the mobile channel. The goal is to create an intelligent virtual assistant, helping the customer throughout their whole customer journey. A banking service that could be addressed via Nina is a credit to the customers. A user could show the intent to buy, such as a new computer through the virtual assistant. Nina would start the loan process and guide the user through the necessary steps. The user could have the possibility to continue the loan process when at home in a omni access way.

Many studies tried to understand if and how customers differ over different accesses and which factors drive access selection.[38] The goal of these studies was to supply evidence on customer behavior within and across individual accesses.

Distribution accesses have different functional characteristics that depend directly on the type of service offered and the market segments' features.[39] The different nature of the needs expressed by the various customers' partitions, and the resulting specificity of the services offered, require unique delivery methods related to specific distribution accesses.[40]

The design of differentiated delivery systems depends on analyzing the features and competitive dynamics of the strategic banking areas in which

[36] Kedbäck, M. (2016). Digital customer service manager at Swedbank. *Intelligent Assistance Conference (IAC)*. London, UK (Appendix C).

[37] Kedbäck, M. (2016). Digital customer service manager at Swedbank. *Intelligent Assistance Conference (IAC)*. London, UK (Appendix C).

[38] Elliott, M. T., Fu, F. Q., & Speck, P. S. (2012). Information search and purchase patterns in a multichannel service industry. *Services Marketing Quarterly*, *33*(4), 292–310. Punj, G. (2011). Effect of customer beliefs on online purchase behavior: The influence of demographic characteristics and consumption values. *Journal of Interactive Marketing*, *25*(3), 134–144. Robertson, A., Soopramanien, D., & Fildes, R. (2007). Household solution acceptance: Heterogeneity in computer adoption. *AMCIS 2007 Proceedings*, 77. Montoya-Weiss, M. M., Voss, G. B., & Grewal, D. (2003). Determinants of online channel use and overall satisfaction with a relational, multichannel service provider. *Journal of the Academy of Marketing Science, 31*(4), 448–458.

[39] Normann, R. (2001). *Service management: Strategy and leadership in service business*. 3rd Edn. Wiley, Hoboken, NJ, ISBN-10: 0471494399, 256.

[40] Coelho, F., & Easingwood, C. (2008). An exploratory study into the drivers of channel change. *European Journal of Marketing, 42*(9/10), 1005–1022.

the institution runs. These banking areas depend on the following critical elements[41]:

- Customers' partitions.
- Needs they express (types of services).
- Satisfaction of these needs (production-distribution processes).

Banking services are between two extremes: simplicity and low unit added value, on the one hand, and high complexity, and significant added value, on the other end.[42]

The first category includes all services characterized by simple operations with the smallest customization content and easily standardizable. Examples are banking ordinary transactions, home banking, and so on. These transactions are in massive quantities. The demand for these services is characterized by price and comfort: the latter referring to the accessibility of the distribution point, easiness of use, and transaction execution speed. The financial institution must develop for the distribution of such services inexpensive distribution systems. Innovative solutions can help quite a bit in this direction.[43]

The complex, or specialist services, have opposite characteristics. They need a high degree of customization and bring high added value. An example is wealth management. Customers are sensitive to the quality of these services and often rely on personal relationships. These services require assistance and consultancy services before, during, and after the transaction. It is not easy to automatize the operations, as they impact proximity. The financial institution must have distribution and delivery systems that allow for unstructured and complex content service relationships. Financial institutions must supply high-quality accesses with substantial customization and operational flexibility in distributing these complex services. A distribution system is necessarily implying the right level of proximity with the customer, either based on persons or advanced robo-advisors.

[41] Cappiello, A. (2020). The digital (r)evolution of insurance business models. *American Journal of Economics and Business Administration, 12*(1), 1–13.

[42] Cappiello, A. (2018). *Solution and the insurance industry: Re-configuring the competitive landscape*. Palgrave Macmillan, Cham, Switzerland.

[43] Thornton J., & White L. 2001. Customer orientations and usage of financial distribution channels. *Journal of Services Marketing, 15*(3), 168–185.

The complexity of the distribution systems increases with the complexity of the services supplied and the customers' relationship. Complex distribution systems are used for assistance with higher specialist content and with a high value-added. Traditionally, this case takes place for wealth management with higher costs for both the customer and the financial institution. For these services, innovative solutions should improve the accesses' efficiency and effectiveness, not necessarily replacing them partially or entirely. The latter is happening instead with simple products, such as home banking.

It is possible to offer a service that has reached a specific degree of diffusion and simplification through automated procedures. In the case of lesser known, even if simple to use, products there is the need of direct contact with the customer. The products can be delivered through an access that allows for a specific number of interactive relationships to help promotional activities, service demonstrations, and excellent customer proximity. This situation takes place, for example, with wealth management products. For these products, the empathy and trust generated by the direct relationships between a consultant and the customer are essential. It is necessary the flexibility in the approach and assurance of professional responses. In this type of service, the creativity to define strategies and interventions to the events is critical.[44]

The increasing diversification of the services offered requires a corresponding specificity of the distribution systems. Specialization of the latter can be carried out within the same distribution access or through dedicated accesses. The selection of the distinct types of distributions is robustly influenced by the financial institution's service policies, the features of the segments served, and the current distribution structure. This structure creates constraints. It conditions the strategic choices on the rationalization and restructuring of the entire distribution system, including the enlargement of the distribution types.

In the past, the promotion of banking services took place through billboards, television commercials, newspaper advertising, and other media.[45] The new promotion accesses are sponsoring, technical articles, and social networks (such as Facebook and LinkedIn). Some communication accesses are most proper for a particular type of customer. For example,

[44] Magnani, N. (2020). *Robot*. Utet, Milano, Italy

[45] tesi.supsi.ch/2609/. Accessed 11 December 2019.

Facebook is suitable for individuals. For banking contacts with organizations, it is better to access LinkedIn because it is a professional social network.

Distribution Models Challenges and Benefits

The adoption of a distribution system is characterized by higher specialization, efficiency, effectiveness, and economics. The higher specificity of the access is apt to satisfying the target market's needs more appropriately and perfecting the customer relationship. Innovation allows for the activation of new distribution systems and accesses for specific combinations of services offered/customer segments served. These distribution accesses are an innovation in the distribution systems that, in the past, related to physical accesses.[46] The automation and outsourcing of some production-distribution processes and easily standardized services bring an improvement in the financial institution system's operational efficiency, effectiveness, and economics.

Banking 5.0 unlocks new competitive and marketing opportunities. It allows for remote interaction with the user. The automation, if not used interactively, contributes to a progressive decustomization of the institution–customer relationships. This situation is due to the intangible nature of the banking service. It can be easily evaluated in its qualitative aspects at the time of use. The components of the service distribution system have a significant impact on the quality perceived. This impact results with the combination of different elements such as ease of access and convenience of the interaction, time frames, reduction of errors, transparency, the cost-effectiveness of the relationship, professionalism, and courtesy of the intermediaries.[47] Innovation offers the opportunity to improve many

[46] Stepanek, L., & Roman, P. (2017). Urban insurance industry ideas of the second millennium. *Ecoforum, 6*, 1(10).

[47] Normann, R. (2001). *Service management: Strategy and leadership in service business*. 3rd edn., Wiley, Hoboken, NJ, ISBN-10: 0471494399. Kotler, P. (2001). *A framework for marketing management*. Prentice Hall, Upper Saddle River, NJ. Donnelly, J. Berry, L. L., & Thompson, T. W. (1985). *Marketing financial services: A strategic vision*. Dow Jones Irwin, New York, NY.

of these aspects. It can increase the frequency of customer interactions, offering the possibility to enhance customer loyalty and cross-selling.[48]

Due to the expansion of digital accesses and the customer's economic and cultural evolution, the fragmentation of contact points reduces customer loyalty. It makes it more challenging to set up a lasting relationship. The decustomization of the transactions leads to an evaluation of the service's quality on technical and economic considerations and less on personal/emotional factors.[49]

Another aspect to consider is the increasing competition between financial institutions, especially with new entrants such as fintech organizations. The possible overlapping of areas of expertise is made possible by the growing spread of solution knowledge.

The financial institution should manage the technological variable not only from a purely productive perspective (to streamline procedures and reduce operating costs) but as a marketing tool to improve its brand. The loss of direct contact with customers is a negative factor. It is necessary to balance the need for a personalized relationship with the customers through automation benefits. A marked standardization of elementary services, associated with the banking customer link's higher specialization, can obtain such balance. It is critical to adopt a personalized approach to the customer according to the logic of mass customization and innovative solutions.[50] Through a more precise identification of diverse needs, higher customization is possible.

It is necessary to renew and innovate the relationship with customers to cover as much as possible their expectations.[51] Customers expect to communicate and be involved with the financial institution any time, wherever they want, and with any device. They accept to use innovative

[48] Accenture. (2017). The future of insurance distribution. New models for a digital customer. www.accenture.com/_acnmedia/pdf-38/accenture-reimagine-procurement-pov-final.pdf. Accessed 21 March 2020.

[49] Reicheld, F. F. (1996). *The loyalty effect*. Harvard Business School Press, Boston, MA. Schwarz, G., Naujoks, H., Goossens, C., Whelan, D., Schwedel, A., & Singh H. (2014). Customer loyalty and the digital transformation in P&C and life insurance. www.bain.com/insights/customer-loyalty-and-the-digical-transformation-in-p-and-c-and-life-procurement/. Accessed 20 March 2020.

[50] Bardakci, A., & Whitelock, J. (2003). Mass-customization in marketing: The customer perspective. *Journal of Customer Marketing*.

[51] Hänninen, N., & Karjaluoto, H. (2017). The effect of marketing communication on business relationship loyalty. *Marketing Intelligence & Planning*.

services if they are easy to use, more interactive, and bring improvements in interfacing. In support of the modification in the distribution, financial institutions can offer a digital experience omniaccess[52] and advanced customization of their products and services.[53] In the past, customers would choose an access (mobile phone, branch, and so on) and stick to it until finishing their transaction. Now, these paths are becoming more complex and will become even more in the future. The new customer journeys include several accesses at a time (branch, personal computers, social media, mobile phones, and so on). Each access forms a hub making the multiaccess essential and an opportunity that financial institutions must carefully consider.[54]

Completing a transaction is not necessarily done in the same access where customers started to search for information. Marketers call it the "ROPO effect."[55] It is an acronym that expresses the behavior of those who, before shopping, search for information online but then buy offline.[56]

Customer Proximity Center

Customer proximity and experience are critical in the strategy of organizations and hence in banking 5.0.[57] A survey shows that 66% of managers chose customer relationships as the third most crucial source of sustained

[52] An omniaccess strategy enables customers to use channels seamlessly and interchangeably and experience the channels uniquely. Mirsch, T., Lehrer, C., & Jung, R. (2016). Channel integration towards omnichannel management: A literature review. 2016. *20th Pacific Asia Conference on Information Systems (PACIS)* 2016. Chiayi, Taiwan.

[53] Insurance Europe. (n.d.). *Digitalisation. The benefits of digitalization*. www.insuranceeurope.eu/digitalisation. Accessed 20 January 2020.

[54] Barwitz, N. (2020). The relevance of interaction choice: Customer preferences and willingness to pay. *Journal of Retailing and Customer Services*, *53*, 101953.

[55] www.assinews.it/07/2017/impatto-della-digitalizzazione-sulla-distribuzione-assicurativa-ancora-rivoluzione-tranquilla/660042393/. Accessed on 20 March 2020.

[56] repository.upb.edu.co/bitstream/handle/20.500.11912/4507/Omnichannel%20Shopping%20Patterns.pdf?sequence=1&isAllowed=y. Accessed 28 April 2020.

[57] Sheth, J. N., Parvatiyar, A., & Sinha, M. (2015). The conceptual foundations of relationship marketing: Review and synthesis. *Journal of Economic Sociology=Ekonomicheskaya sotsiologiya*, *16*(2), 119–149. Kohlbacher, F., & Herstatt, C. (2010). *The silver market phenomenon: Marketing and innovation in the aging society*. Springer Science & Business Media.

economic value for the organization,[58] One of the way organizations use to relate with customers is the Customer proximity center (CPC), or contact center,[59] or voice operation center.[60] CPCs are changing over time due to several factors, such as strategy and digital transformation.[61]

Financial institutions pay attention to the ways products and services are delivered and on the customer journey to gain competitive advantages.[62] A CPC is typically an operational center that interacts with the customers in many ways, from issue resolutions, user guidance, administrative support, billing clarifications, provisioning, up to technical support, and more. CPCs are globally one million.[63] They are a profitable business. In some countries, the labor market cannot meet the demand for CPC agents, often called customer service representatives or associates, or operators. This industry is continuously changing. Information and communication technologies (ICT) have drastically improved operations, helping cut costs, and more.[64]

[58] IBM. (2013). *IBM BusinessConnect 2013: Realize the art of the possible*, July 6–9, Bucharest, Romania.

[59] Koole, G., & Mandelbaum, A. (2002). Queueing models of CPCs: An introduction. *Annals of Operations Research, 113*(1–4), 41–59.

[60] Jack, E. P., Bedics, T. A., & McCary, C. E. (2006). Operational challenges in the CPC industry: A case study and resource-based framework. *Managing Service Quality, 16*(5), 477–500.

[61] Heskett, J. L. (1987). Lessons in the service sector. *Harvard Business Review, 65*(2), 118–126. Haynes, R. M., & DuVall, P. K. (1992). Service quality management: A process-control approach. *International Journal of Service Industry Management, 3*(1), 14.

[62] Johnston, R. (1994). Operations: From factory to service management. *International Journal of Service Industry Management, 5*(5), 49–63.

[63] Aksin, O. Z., Armony, M., & Mehrotra, V. (2007). The modern CPC: A multidisciplinary perspective on operations management research. *Production and Operations Management, 16*(6), 665–688.

[64] Aksin, O. Z., Armony, M., & Mehrotra, V. (2007). The modern CPC: A multidisciplinary perspective on operations management research. *Production and Operations Management, 16*(6), 665–688.

CPCs today are multiaccess communication centers that supply several types of services using various media and devices.[65] Outsourcing operations is a significant trend.[66] Most organizations have outsourced their CPCs to external contractors, often offshoring the services. Other organizations decided to keep the CPCs in house or outsource only part of the services ("co-sourced"). An example of a growing service provided by CPC is support to help for the access by the customer to online banking.[67] Organizations have redefined the role of their CPCs. They are often their only direct point of proximity with the customers.[68]

CPCs can be categorized as inbound, receiving the calls and outbound, making the calls, and mixed[69]:

- Inbound services manage incoming requests, such as information about the organization's products and services, technical assistance (help desk), counseling, complaints handling, and so on.
- The organizations use outbound services (outgoing) to reach out to their existing or potential customers for direct sales by phone, perform surveys on the degree of customer delight, marketing campaigns, debt collection, completing the sales process, and so on.

There is an essential aspect of the evolution over time of the CPCs. CPCs moved from managing the non-quality (of the products or of the organization's services) to adding value to the product or service and creating value for the customers and the organization. It is a significant evolution (or a revolution) since it is consistent with the management shift in

[65] Jack, E. P., Bedics, T. A., & McCary, C. E. (2006) Operational challenges in the CPC industry: A case study and resource-based framework. *Managing Service Quality, 16*(5), 477–500.

[66] Ren, Z. J., & Yong-Pin, Zhou. (2008). CPC outsourcing: Coordinating staffing level and service quality. *Management Science, 54*(2), 369–383.

[67] Aksin, O. Z., de Véricourt, F., & Karaesmen, F. (2008). CPC outsourcing contract analysis and choice. *Management Science, 54*(2), 354–368.

[68] Aksin, O. Z., Armony, M., & Mehrotra, V. (2007). The modern CPC: A multidisciplinary perspective on operations management research. *Production and Operations Management, 16*(6), 665–688.

[69] Aksin, O. Z., Armony, M., & Mehrotra, V. (2007). The modern CPC: A multidisciplinary perspective on operations management research. *Production and Operations Management, 16*(6), 665–688. Koole, G., & Mandelbaum, A. (2002). Queueing models of CPCs: An introduction. *Annals of Operations Research, 113*(1–4), 41–59.

thinking of the financial institution as a service provider and as a value-adding to the customer. The customer journey, including the CPC, has become central to their strategy.

Gronroos presented two dimensions to the service: the technical aspect—what service provides, defined as the process's outcome—and the functional aspect—how the service is delivered, the process quality dimension.[70] Gronroos introduced the concept of corporate image and its impact on customer perceptions.[71] Lehtinen and Lehtinen added other dimensions: physical quality (product and material support), interactive quality (the interaction with the customer), and corporate quality (how customers perceive the organization).[72] A further contribution was the inclusion of the corporate brand and social responsibility dimensions.[73]

A certain number of authors considered the possible evolution of the CPCs. Anton wrote that customers want improved access to their vendors.[74] Anton reviewed how organizations responded to this requirement. He looked at the past, present, and future information needs of the customers and how they have been met. He forecasted the future technological developments which will change the type of interactions and the information availability.

Customer Proximity Center Architecture

The relevant processes in a CPC are service, complaince, campaign, sales management. The CPC evolves for many reasons. There are several trends in CPC management[75]:

[70] Gronroos, C. (1982). *Strategic management and marketing in the service sector.* Chartwell-Bratt, London, UK. Gronroos, C. (2001). The perceived service quality concept – a mistake? *Managing Service Quality, 11*(3), 150.

[71] Gronroos, C. (2001). The perceived service quality concept – a mistake? *Managing Service Quality, 11*(3), 150.

[72] Lehtinen, U., & Lehtinen, J. R. (1991). Two approaches to service quality dimensions. *Service Industries Journal, 11*(3), 287–303.

[73] Kang, G. D., & James, J. (2004). Service quality dimensions: An examination of Gronroos's service quality model. *Managing Service Quality, 14*(4), 266.

[74] Anton, J. (2000). The past, present & future of customer access centers. *International Journal of Service Industry Management, 11*(2): 120–130.

[75] Williams, G. (2003). CPC operations: Profiting from teleservices. *Consulting to Management, 14*(2), 57–58.

- Increase in the scale and scope of the CPC operations. Customers' expectations for quality service from the CPCs are higher than in the past. In today's marketplace, relationships, quality, convenience, speed, precision, and value, are critical competitive advantages.
- Diffusion of multichannel communication centers where several new accesses supply a wide variety of services to customers. For example, phones, internet, emails, chatbots, embedded banking, and social networks are all used to maximize opportunities for customer contacts.
- Outsourcing of CPC operations to low-cost countries. Advanced telecommunications systems have enabled organizations (for example, financial services) to outsource their CPCs to nearshore or offshore locations (for example, India, East Asia, East Europe, or North African countries).
- Automation is changing and powering more CPCs. Chatbots represent an exciting approach to interact with customers. A chatbot, short for chatterbot, is a computer program that simulates a person's conversation through voice commands or text chats, or both.[76] A chatbot is an Artificial intelligence (AI) feature embedded and used through any messaging applications. Young persons prefer to send a message rather than making a call.[77] For this reason, app messaging has become the leading platform for chatbots.

AI can help in customer proximity with[78]:

- Servicing persona.
- Dynamic customer routing (channel, agent).
- Real-time recommendation engine.
- Agent review and training.

[76] www.investopedia.com/terms/c/chatbot.asp. Accessed 20 April 2020.

[77] Ade, M. (2018, May). *Il suo nome è bot, chatbot*. www.axa.ch/it/ueber-axa/blog/trend/chatbot-digital-ux-cx-axa-chatbot.html. Accessed 15 December 2020.

[78] https://www.mckinsey.com/industries/financial-services/our-insights/ai-powered-decision-making-for-the-bank-of-the-future?cid=other-eml-alt-mip-mck&hdpid=b28e9a1e-b64b-4be4-b5d3-10470b96c23c&hctky=9204549&hlkid=cac4d2e1c59944c08c8f684d35c897e0#. Accessed 22 March 2021.

Customer Proximity Center in Banking 5.0

The relevant functions in banking 5.0 in a customer proximity center are[79]:

- An excellent customer journey (CX) is a top priority. It is essential to attract new customers and retain the current ones.
- Innovative solutions to supply a seamless service and journey to their customers. The growing use of AI or AI-powered chatbots transforms customer service by supplying 24*7 customer support and increasing customer engagement.
- Through the solutions available to enable omniaccess, the integrated and coordinated management of all CPCs' interactions with the customer in a multi-media interaction.
- Measurement and monitoring of the quality of products/services.

It is interesting to refer to two models to analyze the changes in the CPCs. Chandler described corporate strategy as defining long-term goals and aims, adopting courses of action, and related allocation of resources needed to achieve the goals. He defined structure as the instrument of the organization through which strategy is managed. Changes in an organization's approach led to new management, operational, and administrative problems. In turn, they need a new or remodeled structure for the successful implementation of the new strategy. Chandler's thesis argued that new organizational forms are a derivative of strategy.[80]

Leavitt brought an innovative approach to looking at organizations. Every organization includes four interactive components: People, Task, Structure, and Solutions.[81] The interactions between these four components are the basis of the success of an organization. The graph showing the relationships between these four components resembles a diamond. For this reason, the model is called Leavitt's diamond. Leavitt emphasized that any change in one of these elements directly affects all the other parts.

[79] Importance of Artificial Intelligence in Customer Service. www.countants.com/blogs/importance-of-artificial-intelligence-in-customer-service/. Accessed 4 January 2021.

[80] Chandler Jr., A. D. (1962). *Strategy and structure: Chapters in the history of the American industrial enterprise*. MIT Press, Cambridge, MA.

[81] Leavitt, H. J., & Whisler, T. L. (1958). Management in the 1980's. *Harvard Business Review, 36*, 41–48.

They need to transform to accommodate the changes. Leavitt's diamond is an integrated approach. It is widely used for managing organizational change.

This chapter considers a model shown in Fig. 7.1, based on the Chandler and Leavitt models' combinations. This model replaces the "Tasks" in the Leavitt model with "Processes," "Solutions" with "Platforms," and "People" with "Persons/Applications," since it seems more proper.

Based on this model, the evolution of the CPC is summarized in Table 7.1, it is necessary to consider that:

- The column of the years is purely indicative of the year of the introduction of the model.
- New CPC models have been added over time. The previous models continues to exist.
- The model underlines the main characteristics. It might be useful to consider added features in specific cases.

It is interesting to analyze each of the Chandler/Leavitt model components and how they interact with each other.

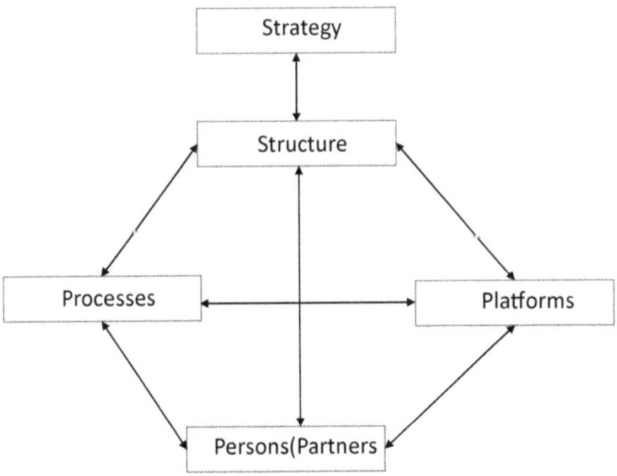

Fig. 7.1 Modified Chandler-Leavitt model

Table 7.1 Evolution of the call center

Years	*Denomination*	*Description*	*Strategy*	*Structure*	*People*	*Technology*	*Assessment*
1960	Call Center	The aim was to provide the customers the idea that they could "call" somebody to describe the issues and get advices on how to resolve them. It was born as a branch of the Claim Office	Claims avoding. Resisting	Operations	Low skilled	Telephone	Call volumes Talk timeHolding time
1970	Contact Center	This name shows one important aspect of the call center: the fact that it is the contact point between the organization and the customers. This name emphasized the way the organization "saw" the call center as the border of the organization.	Product centric. Passive	Operations	Medium skilled	PABX	Call waitingNumber of contactsAverage duration of the call
1980	Customer Services	This denomination introduced the concept of service. It was still very much an internal view of the relationships and a passive way versus the customer;	Service centric. Passive	Operations	Professional	ACD—Automatic Call Distribution	Customer DedicationClaim resolution
1990	Customer Support Center	The idea here is that the customer should be supported in their activities.	Sale centric. Passive-Active	Sales	Supportive and caring people	IVR—Interactive Voice Response	First call resolutionAverage duration of the callqueu durationHang-ups

Years	Denomination	Description	Strategy	Structure	People	Technology	Assessment
2000	Service To Sale	The idea is to use the contact to service but also to sell more services and products. At the same time perform also campaign	Marketing centric. Active-Passive	MarketingOffshoring	Sales persons	CTI—Computer Telephony IntegrationCampaign ManagerCall recording	Customer SatisfactionAbility to up-sale/cross-sale
2010	Customer Relationships (CR)	This expression underlines the fact that the call center is a point of relationships with the customer. It is one of the most important points to do Customer Relationships Management. It must be the place to add value to the customers and to the organization.	Customer Centric. Active	Outsourced or Cosourced	Relationships persons	UCC—Unified Communication and Collaboration (voice-over-IP, email, Chat, fax)	Customer experience in the IVRs, queues and with agents (through surveys at the end of the call)Customer Retention
2020	Virtual Call Point (CRP)	More and more CR are becoming distributed, thanks to the technology more and more available	Network Centric. Proactive	AutomaticTeleworkSelf Service	Technical, Coach	AutomationIVR, queue and speech analytics Social NetworksGeo-location	Value for the customer per call

Persons

The persons or the chatbots are the operators of the CPCs. Since chatbots are more used, it is essential to dedicate particular attention to them. The chatbot's ability to present all information and details is central to assessing the service's competence and quality. The feeling of the chatbots' ability to connect with the customer and express empathy is essential. To replicate these characteristics in a chatbot requires careful design, implementation, and continuous update. Machine learning and natural language processing can help.

Another critical factor is the chatbot's ability to follow up. Many customers feel that it is essential to not end the interaction after a call since the remediation might not be complete. The relationship with the customers is at the heart of any strategy for chatbots. Innovative solutions based on ICT and AI are a great support for their development (see the column on platforms in Table 7.1). Using qualified and "professional-like" chatbots, with distinct operator professional capabilities are strategies which can transform problems into competitive advantages. Chatbots in this activity can reduce costs and variations, improving service quality.

The activities and the capabilities are essential. These capabilities in the case of chatbots include both the management capabilities (the ability to interact with persons and relationships) and the technical and professional capabilities (the ability to supply clear answers to the customer) for all applications involved in the practical operations of a CPC. Hence, training is a critical tool for building and keeping these virtual operators updated with machine learning.

Processes

Processes consist of two aspects: how things are done; and what they need to achieve. It is critical to focus more on the processes' qualitative elements than the actual tasks and goals. When looking at the activities in the operations, one should consider their relevance and their benefits. When examining processes, it is critical to evaluate the yield and productivity in the interactions with the customers using chatbots (Fig. 7.2).

Structure

Leavitt's diamond patterns or structural component of Leavitt's diamond include the hierarchical structure and the relationships, communication, and coordination between different management and operational levels,

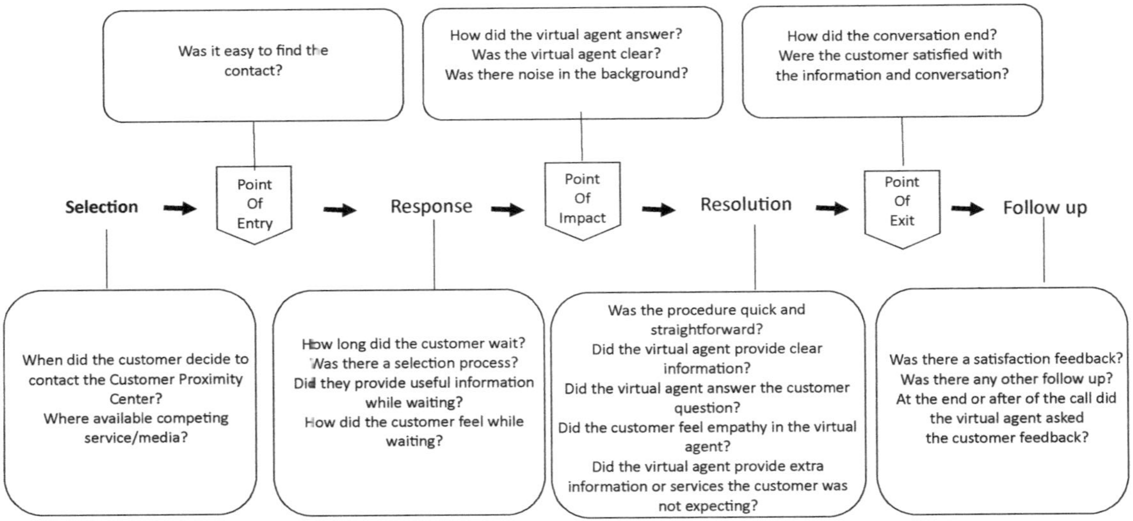

Fig. 7.2 Interaction with the customer in the proximity center (Adapted by the Author from Bicheno, J., & Catherwood, P. (2005). *Six sigma and the quality toolbox* (rev. ed.). Picsie Books, Buckingham, UK)

sections, and virtual persons in the organizations. These aspects include how the flow of authority and responsibility runs inside the organization. The structure needs to be changed when transforming strategy or/and any other Leavitt diamond component.

Platforms

Platforms or solutions are the components that support or help to implement the activities in the processes. Computers, networks, telephone equipment, Interactive voice response unit (IVR), chatbots, software applications, and other means are all parts of the platform. Like all the other components of the Leavitt diamond, platforms need to change when any other element is modified.[82] The most significant development in the customer relationships will be in the solutions to reduce the need for a traditional CPC and allow the customer to do self-service or self-assisted service through chatbots.

Small and large financial institutions are scaling up their customer services (while keeping their costs down) through the deployment of intelligent chatbots. The 2019 Chatbot report forecasts that the AI use in banking customer service will automate 90% by 2022 of customer interactions using chatbots.[83] Sixty percent of online customers do not want to wait more than 60 seconds to respond to their queries. Chatbots are drastically reducing customer wait times and assuring a quicker resolution of their questions, thus improving customer loyalty. Chatbots with Natural language processing (NLP) capabilities can resolve customer complaints through faster responses, thus improving customer delight.

The cost savings from banks' chatbot usage alone is expected to reach USD 7.30 billion worldwide by 2023, up from an estimated USD 209 million in 2019, according to a February 2019 report from Juniper Research.[84] Chatbot integration in mobile banking apps is expected to make up 79% of chat-driven customer interactions in 2023. Increased

[82] Leavitt's Diamond: An interactive approach to change. www.brighthubpm.com/change-management/122495-a-look-at-the-components-of-leavitts-diamond/. Accessed 30 May 2020.

[83] Chatbot Report. (2019). Global trends and analysis | by Brain [Brn.Ai] Code for Equity | *Chatbots Magazine*.

[84] www.emarketer.com/content/seven-charts-the-state-of-digital-banking-in-2020. Accessed 4 January 2021.

customer preference for app-based banking contributes to this, according to this research organization.

Beyond the use of chatbots and self-service platforms, AI-driven automation can transform the customer journey by customizing product offerings personalized to customer's individual needs.[85] Using the customer-level profile, transaction, and servicing log data, a multi-task neural network can be trained to predict if a customer will call the financial institution for any customer service request in the following few days. In the Interactive voice response (IVR) system, a personalized voice prompt can recommend relevant digital services based on the model prediction and redirect the customer to digital services through an SMS with a website to a chatbot.

Chatbot Architecture

Chatbots support standardized customer interactions. It can supply computer-generated advice about the type of banking services customers can buy or the services he/she is using.[86] An example of a chatbot is the virtual assistant Kate, launched by Geico in the USA.[87] It responds to questions from customers about banking policies and payments.

Chatbots can help customers deal quickly and on a 24*7 basis with specific standard chores such as banking transactions, obtaining documents, filing defaults, or having simple questions answered. Chatbots simulate conversation with persons. They can help to supply personalized product offers based on the history of interactions.[88] These points of contact help collect relevant information about customers to enrich the database storing these services.

[85] Zhang, X., Agarwal, S., Choy, R., Wong, K. J., Lim, L., Lee, Y. Y., & Lu, J. J. (2020, July). Personalized digital customer services for consumer banking call centre using neural networks. In *2020 International Joint Conference on Neural Networks (IJCNN)* (pp. 1–7). IEEE.

[86] Albrecher, H., Bommier, A., Filipović, D., Koch-Medina, P., Loisel, S., & Schmeiser, H. (2019). Insurance: Models, digitization, and data science. *European Actuarial Journal*, *9*(2), 349–360.

[87] Nordman, E., Director, C. I. P. R., DeFrain, K., Hall, S. N., Karapiperis, D., & Obersteadt, A. (2017). How artificial intelligence is changing the insurance industry. *CIPR Newsletter*, 2.

[88] Hong, S. J., & Weiss, S. M. (2001). Advances in predictive models for data mining. *Pattern Recognition Letters*, *22*(1), 55–61.

Usually, customers are willing to prove the chatbots. They tend to use them, especially in case of straightforward requests, not for critical issues. Other customers are eager to consider this solution when it will mature further. Chatbots are secure, easy to use, and efficient. They are an excellent source to have instant information at any time. The lack of personal contact is the only negative side.

Chatbots in Banking 5.0

There are many use cases for chatbots or smart assistants in banking[89]:

1. It is possible to pay bills, monitor money transfers, and set up or cancel payments if needed. Chatbots can help users charge up their prepaid cards or pay off their bills.
2. Chatbots can supply the balances for accounts. AI assistants can supply debit estimates and alert users if debits are in danger of falling below or above certain thresholds.
3. Users can ask about their accounts, such as card loyalty points, recurring payments, and expense and transfer limits.
4. Chatbots can answer different non-complex questions about banking services or customer accounts.
5. Answers to user questions can vary depending on their location, such as in a request about the nearest ATM.
6. Chatbots can be programmed to send reminders. They can send important notifications, like banking news and changes in credit scores or financial market information.
7. Banking chatbots can help customers with problems that may be non-complex but are critical.
8. Customers can ask chatbots to supply an overview of their transactions and get a periodical dashboard on spending, supporting better management of their finances. Chatbots can send alerts whenever a charge, deposit, or refund occurs in the account.
9. Chatbots can help customers go through applying for loans, new or replacement cards, or loyalty programs.
10. They can provide help in cases of suspicious activity.

[89] Bika, N. (2020). Potential use cases of chatbots in banking: 12 examples. https://acquire.io/blog/use-cases-chatbots-banking/#:~:text=Banks%20percent20like%20percent20ATB%20percent20Financial%20percent20and,question%20percent20variations%20percent20by%20percent20mid%20percent2D2019. Accessed 20 January 2021.

11. Chatbots can supply a range of valuable insights for customers, like their spending habits, an overview of recurring charges for the year, and payments on specific months or specific locations. Due to the increasing customization, chatbots can support customers as omnipresent advisors and influence their financial behavior.[90] By knowing the exact spending and consumption behavior of the customer, chatbots can warn of bad or risky decisions and, if necessary, suggest better solutions.
12. Chatbots can be deployed on a financial institution's website, usually within online banking, but potentially on browsing pages, too.

Citizens Bank[91]

Citizens Bank, with USD 177 billion in total assets, is the 17th largest bank in the USA. It has about 1,000 branches distributed in 11 states (in the Northeast and Midwest) offering federal student loans and indirect auto lending businesses and has a direct bank, Citizens Access, launched in 2018.

CXO is a position at Citizens as the Chief Experience Officer. Citizen Bank needed to "elevate how we thought about the experience, particularly digital experience design powered by analytics."[92] The bank has used data analytics extensively in marketing and for creating its digital experience. It wanted to create an enterprise experience organization for both the retail and commercial businesses.

The digital transaction has increased over time. It experienced a significant bump once the pandemic crisis took full effect. Simultaneously, the bank's extensive branch network overnight went from gradually declining traffic to a significant decrease during the pandemic, with only a partial return afterward.

Citizens Bank launched its first customer-facing chatbot during the pandemic. The bot is driven by AI but is text-based since it was easier to implement quickly. Thanks to this architecture, the chatbot has stop/start capability. It enables customers to step away to deal with a child or other situation and come back to where they left off.

[90] King, B. (2018). *Bank 4.0: Banking Everywhere Never at a Bank*, Marshall Cavendish Business, Singapore.

> The chatbot helps the financial institution send routine questions out of the contact center. Digital accesses supply a better experience and let the bank invest in customer journey to incur the costs of persons answering the phone for simple questions. A key chatbot feature is being omniaccess. It can effortlessly hand off to a live agent or a branch staffer when a more in-depth discussion is needed.

Chatbots can process customer complaints. The UK Financial Conduct Authority defines a complaint as "*any oral or written expression of dissatisfaction, whether justified or not, from, or on behalf of, a person about the provision of, or failure to provide, a financial service or a redress determination, which alleges that the complainant has suffered (or may suffer) financial loss, material distress or material inconvenience.*"[93] This definition leads to large volumes of calls to CPCs.

Financial institutions must resolve those claims in compliance with regulatory requirements. Customers not satisfied with the responses supplied to their complaints can appeal to regulatory authorities. Given the volumes of data, AI can help prevent complaints and enhance complaint handling and replying, reducing complaints raised by customers and partners. To process the protests, the offices of financial institutions can use machine learning and big data solution. Some financial institutions use natural language processing to automatically manage and classify large volumes of unstructured text documents. These solutions classify hundreds of thousands of queries into types. Some financial institutions are exploring voice analytics and computer vision to manage customer complaints in real time. This innovation would not only accelerate the resolution process. It would improve the customer journey and delight.

Benefits and Challenges of Chatbots

AI solutions (such as natural language processing) help financial institutions classify large volumes of unstructured text documents automatically

[91] thefinancialbrand.com/98116/citizens-bank-cx-on-covid-retail-banking-digital-branch-chatbot/thefinancialbrand.com/98116/citizens-bank-cx-on-covid-retail-banking-digital-branch-chatbot/. Accessed 20 January 2021.

[92] thefinancialbrand.com/98116/citizens-bank-cx-on-covid-retail-banking-digital-branch-chatbot/. Accessed 30 March 2021.

[93] www.liquisearch.com/history_of_banking. Accessed 8 September 2020.

and categorize hundreds of thousands of queries into classes. AI ensures they are routed to the right team for resolution. In this way, financial institutions can ensure consistency in responses to the same type of queries or complaints and make the auditability of the process easier than with traditional manual classification processes.

The public likes using chatbots for banking. A 2018 survey shows that: 44% of people surveyed would prefer to communicate with a chatbot than a person, assuming it can answer questions as reliably.[94] Research suggests that 61% of people think a chatbots can supply faster service than a person when performing repetitive tasks.[95]

Chatbots used by banks and financial institutions can:

- Improve customer service.
- Personalize customer journey. Sixty-three percent of customers expect personalized service.[96]
- Reduce waiting times either at the branch or in the phone lines of financial institutions.
- Decrease costs. Chatbots can deliver cost savings of over USD 8 billion per year by 2022 in the banking and healthcare sectors.[97] Traditional financial institutions could cut 22% in costs by 2030, that is USD 1 trillion in projected cost savings, using AI.[98]
- Help employees improve their jobs. Sixty-four percent of agents supported by AI chatbots can focus on solving complex problems instead of getting hung up on replying to basic queries, compared to 50% of agents without this support.[99]
- Build a better picture of customer needs.

[94] acquire.io/blog/use-cases-chatbots-banking/. Accessed 28 November 2020.

[95] Lui, A., & Lamb, G. (2018). Artificial intelligence and augmented intelligence collaboration: Regaining trust and confidence in the financial sector. *Information and Communications Solution Law*. ISSN 1360-0834.

[96] www.retailcustomerexperience.com/news/customers-expect-personalization-reveals-report/. Accessed 4 January 2021.

[97] www.juniperresearch.com/new-trending/analystxpress/july-2017/chatbot-conversations-to-deliver-8bn-cost-saving. Accessed 4 January 2021.

[98] thefinancialbrand.com/72653/artificial-intelligence-trends-banking-industry/. Accessed 4 January 2021.

[99] www.salesforce.com/blog/2019/08/chatbot-statistics.html. Accessed 4 January 2021.

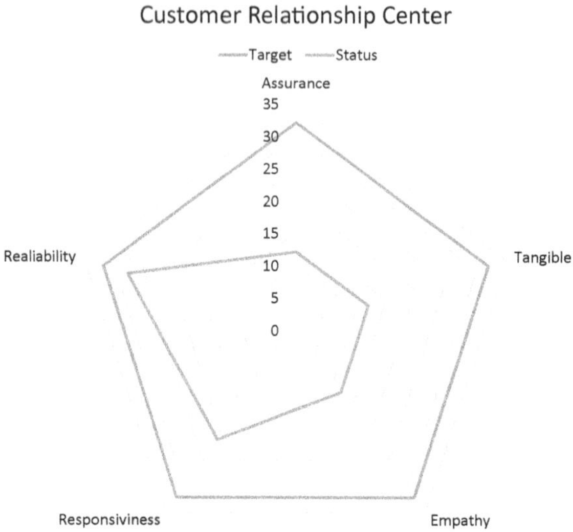

Fig. 7.3 Example of RATER assessment

Benefits and Challenges of a Customer Proximity Center

A critical aspect of the evolution of the CPCs is their assessment needs to change. This aspect is considering that strategy changes over time and among organizations.

The CPC is a service, which can be represented in a workflow (see a simplified workflow in Fig. 7.2). Before examining the CPC quality, it is interesting to see how the quality of service has changed over time.

Drucker wrote: "If you can't measure it, you can't manage it." Hence the importance of the diagnostic tools to assess and monitor the quality of the service over time.[100] Shostack argued that it is impossible to ensure quality and uniformity in services without a detailed design. She developed a blueprint to find the processes involved in delivering a service.[101]

[100] Oliver, R. L., & Rust, R T. (1997). Customer delight: Foundations, findings, and managerial insight. *Journal of Retailing, 73*(3), 311–336. Ghobadian, A., Speller, S., & Jones, M. (1994). Service quality. Concepts and models. *International Journal of Quality and Reliability Management, 11*(9), 43.

[101] Shostack, G. L. (1984). Designing services that deliver. *Harvard Business Review, 62*(1), 133–139.

By visually seeing the steps involved in the service delivery, an organization can find the timeframe, the costs involved, and the possible weak points.[102]

A general measurement of the quality of the services is along several dimensions.[103] The configuration and the quality of a CPC depend on the strategy of the organization.[104] A diagnosis framework stems from SERVQUAL's five dimensions of quality.[105] Parasuraman et al. developed the service quality model to find the gaps on the service provider's side that cause discrepancies between the customer's expectations and perceptions.[106] This discrepancy has a direct impact on the quality of the service.[107]

Johnston developed a framework to assess the service quality from the customer's perspective.[108] The customer proximity operations outline the steps and activities in the service delivery and highlight the threats to achieving an excellent customer journey.[109] Carlzon defined "moments of truth" as when a customer assesses the perceived quality during the service delivery.[110] This model seeks to find the elements that create

[102] Shostack, G. L. (1984). Designing services that deliver. *Harvard Business Review, 62*(1), 133–139.

[103] Parasuraman, A., Zeithaml, V. A., & Berry, L. L. (1985). A conceptual model of service quality and its implications for future research. *Journal of Marketing, 49*, 41–50. Bicheno, J., & Catherwood, P. (2005). *Service quality concepts. Six sigma and the quality toolbox* (pp. 132–150). PICSIE Books, Buckingham, UK.

[104] Nicoletti, B. (2015, March). Optimizing Innovation with the Lean and digitize innovation process. *TIM Review*.

[105] Parasuraman, A., Zeithaml, V. A., & Berry, L. L. (1985). A conceptual model of service quality and its implications for future research. *Journal of Marketing, 49*(4), 41–50.

[106] Parasuraman, A., Zeithaml, V. A., & Berry, L. L. (1985). A conceptual model of service quality and its implications for future research. *Journal of Marketing, 49*(4), 41–50.

[107] Nicoletti, B. (1987), *La gestione della qualità* (pp. 1–229). FrancoAngeli, Milano.

[108] Johnston, R. (1995). The determinants of service quality: Satisfiers and dissatisfiers. *International Journal of Service Industry Management, 6*(5), 53. Bicheno, J., & Catherwood, P. (2005). *Service quality concepts. Six sigma and the quality toolbox* (pp. 132–150). PICSIE Books, Buckingham.

[109] Bicheno, J., & Catherwood, P. (2005). *Service quality concepts. Six sigma and the quality toolbox* (pp. 132–150). PICSIE Books, Buckingham.

[110] Carlzon, J. (1987). Putting the customer first: The key to service strategy. *McKinsey Quarterly* (3), 38–51.

the customer's perception, even if it does not supply practical means for improving the service quality.[111]

High service quality results in better organizational performance and so higher margins[112] even during economic downturns or pandemic.[113] Given the nature of services, there is no straightforward way to assess or measure the service quality per se. Quality is a multidimensional concept for Parasuraman et al.[114] Service quality is the difference between the customers' expectations and their perceptions after the service.[115] The service quality work and SERVQUAL scale, developed by Parasuraman and his team, has some limitations as a helpful tool to measure service quality issues. A refined model considers only five of them with the acronym of RATER: Reliability, Assurance, Tangibles, Empathy, and Responsiveness (see an example in Fig. 7.3).[116] The interpretation of the RATER dimensions in the case of a chatbot could be:

- Reliability. This dimension is based on the differences between responses to the calls.
- Assurance. This dimension assesses the chatbots' ability to answer the customer questions or solve their problems and their competencies to supply trust, confidence, and security.[117]

[111] Ghobadian, A., Speller, S., & Jones, M. (1994). Service quality. Concepts and models. *International Journal of Quality and Reliability Management, 11*(9), 43.

[112] Parasuraman, A., Berry, L. L., & Zeithaml, V. A. (1991). Perceived service quality as a customer-based performance measure: An empirical examination of organizational barriers using an extended service quality model. *Human Resource Management, 30*(3), 335–364.

[113] Fornell, C., Rust, R. T., & Dekimpe, M. G. (2010). The effect of customer satisfaction on customer spending growth. *Journal of Marketing Research* (JMR), *47*(1), 28–35.

[114] Parasuraman, A., Zeithaml, V. A., & Berry, L. L. (1985). A conceptual model of service quality and its implications for future research. *Journal of Marketing, 49*(4), 41–50.

[115] Parasuraman, A., Zeithaml, V. A., & Berry, L. L. (1988). SERVQUAL: A multiple-item scale for measuring customer perceptions of service quality. *Journal of Retailing, 64*(1), 12–40.

[116] Bicheno, J., & Catherwood, P. (2005). *Service quality concepts. Six sigma and the quality toolbox* (pp. 132–150). PICSIE Books, Buckingham, UK.

[117] Bicheno, J., & Catherwood, P. (2005). *Service quality concepts. Six sigma and the quality toolbox* (pp. 132–150). PICSIE Books, Buckingham, UK.

- Tangibles. This dimension includes the technical aspects of the CPC service: the quality of the media used in the CPC, the clarity and speed of the chatbot's voice or the chatbot's response, and so on.
- Empathy. This dimension measures the ways the chatbot is programmed to engage with the customer.
- Responsiveness. This dimension assesses the virtual agents' response to a particular request (for example, details on the payment due) and their ability to follow-up.

Service quality in CPC operations is not easy to assess. Koole and Mandelbaum presented a simplified model suggesting measuring service quality in CPCs along two dimensions: qualitative aspects—the psychological size, often prioritized in marketing and social sciences—and quantitative issues—analytical approach, relating to the operational capabilities.[118] Performance measurement systems for CPC chatbots often use this model. The appraisal of operations takes place on both the quantitative dimensions—number of calls, call duration, and so on—and qualitative ones—adherence to policies, content, follow-up on customers, and so on.[119] Organizations often prefer to measure critical performance only on quantitative measures, like the waiting time or call duration.

- Most customers will not complain, but they will either change the banking services provider or complain with other customers.[120]
- Most dissatisfied customers will call back, with operational consequences, such as CPC overloading.[121]

Many financial institutions publish annual reports on the service, quality, and customer requests received and solved.[122] They somehow draw a

[118] Koole, G., & Mandelbaum, A. (2002). Queueing models of CPCs: An introduction. *Annals of Operations Research, 113*(1–4), 41–59.

[119] Aksin, O. Z., Armony, M., & Mehrotra, V. (2007). The modern CPC: A multidisciplinary perspective on operations management research. *Production and Operations Management, 16*(6), 665–688.

[120] Mitchell, V. W. (1993). Handling customer complaint information: Why and how? *Management Decision.*

[121] De Véricourt, F., & Zhou, Y. P. (2005). Managing response time in a call-routing problem with service failure. *Operations Research, 53*(6), 968–981.

[122] www.unicredit.it/it/info/normativa-mifid.html. Accessed 20 February 2021.

link between these numbers and their customers' satisfaction. Even if the handling of questions is crucial since, for example, complaining customers show stronger brand loyalty, service quality, and customer delight have more complex dimensions.[123]

The assessment of the quality of a CPC supporting banking is related to the organization's strategy (see Table 7.1).

The last column in Table 7.1 shows how to assess quality in a CPC according to the banking strategy.

There are several tools developed to help in automating the CPCs. One of the most effective tools is Operational data analytics (ODA).[124] Data analytics is the discovery and communication of meaningful patterns in the data and the organization's information.[125] Data analytics can be applied in areas rich with stored or accessible data, as possible with chatbots. Data analytics works on the simultaneous application of statistics, computer programming, and AI systems to analyze why, what, when, where, who performs and makes decisions on the best way to go ahead. Data analytics tends to be more productive by visualizing the data to communicate insights. Organizations may apply analytics to banking data to describe, forecast, and make decisions to improve a CPC's banking performance.

ODA is particularly crucial in supporting improving chatbots. ODA analytics should be done as much as possible in real or near real time to help operational banking processes. By way of contrast, investigative analytics is done according to the timing requested by research, not the speed of operational banking processes.

The goal of ODA is to implement the cycle:

- Banking automation.
- Sensors on chatbots to get actual data in real time.

[123] Fornell, C., & Wernerfelt, B. (1987). Defensive marketing strategy by customer complaint management: A theoretical analysis, *Journal of Marketing Research* (JMR), *24*(4), 337.

[124] Banerjee, A., Bandyopadhyay, T., & Acharya, P. (2013). Data analytics: Hyped up aspirations or true potential? *Vikalpa*, *38*(4), 1–12.

[125] LaValle, S., Lesser, E., Shockley, R., Hopkins, M. S., & Kruschwitz, N. (2011). Big data, analytics and the path from insights to value. *MIT Sloan Management Review*, *52*(2), 21–31. Davenport, T. H., & Kim, J. H. (2013). *Keeping up with the quants: Your guide to understanding and using analytics*. Harvard Business Press, Brighton, MA.

- Analytics to suggest (or take) actions to improve.

Voice analytics is becoming more feasible and accessible.[126] It is a powerful way to help measure quality also with chatbots. The way it could work is[127]:

1. Full end-to-end call analytics. Innovative solutions should reveal the quality and performance of each segment of the customer journey with the CPC.
2. Measures reveal specific performance based on success and failure in the chatbots.
3. Automatic measures of caller experience.
4. Analysis of First call resolution (FCR) by task.
5. Measurement of Key performance indicators (KPIs) by comparing the call flow design with actual caller behavior.
6. Focus operators on meeting banking goals, whether they are cost savings, customer journey improvements, improving training and competencies routing, or increasing revenues.
7. Link design decisions to operational costs.

A Global Bank[128]

For one large bank, the pandemic accelerated efforts to bring together customer service data from both online and offline interactions (for example, at physical branches) to supply more prompt and targeted service to corporate customers during the pandemic, particularly about government grants offered to address strained organizations. The bank launched an AI-powered chatbot to respond to customer queries. ODA analytics were done as much as possible in real or near real time to help operational banking processes. By way of contrast, investigative analytics is done according to the timing requested by research, not the speed of operational banking processes. The impact was such a strong driver for the

[126] Imran, A., Pandharipande, M., & Kopparapu, S. K. (2013). SpeakRite: Monitoring speaking rate in real time on a mobile phone. *International Journal of Mobile Human Computer Interaction (IJMHCI)*, *5*(1), 62–69.

[127] Nicoletti, B. (1979). Maintenance strategies. *Terotechnica* (pp. 1–11). Amsterdam, Netherlands.

bank management and ICT department to see what is possible with AI that at once it was clear to use more of it.

Conclusions

This chapter covers the resources used for banking proximity. It included the strategies, the types of customers, and the relationships, partnerships and collaborations, costs, investments, and revenues. The chapter does not intentionally cover another component of the business model canvas, related to the partnership with intermediaries. Another chapter considers the convergence of this component with banking 5.0.

This chapter analyzes the impact of solutions on traditional banking processes. Needs for new digital solutions are challenging the legacy systems. Modern solutions offer options for innovative services distribution. Digitization has a profound impact on all phases of the value network of the processes. It supplies benefits by reducing asymmetric information, properly combining the correct pricing, responsive risk management, proper credit scoring, improved customer management, and fast and reliable distribution systems.

This chapter underlines that there should be a close connection between the assessment of the quality of a customer proximity center (CPC) and the financial institutions' strategy. The strategy of the organizations changes over time, and it should include the CPCs. Therefore, the parameters used to assess the quality, effectiveness, efficiency, and economics have changed. Now all these parameters should refer to the chatbots used.

This chapter presents a model of the CPC evolution and has introduced some parameters used to assess the chatbots' quality. The different models in the development of the CPCs have profound consequences on the management of all the CPC's components as listed in Chandler and Leavitt's works.

[128] www.mckinsey.com/business-functions/mckinsey-analytics/our-insights/global-survey-the-state-of-ai-in-2020?cid=podcast-eml-alt-mip-mck&hdpid=edff6cd6-3b1f-4ffc-b0f7-. Accessed 20 January 2021. e73691cf1abe&hctky=9204549&hlkid=8888947fdfc344bfa38308d54a015fea-. Accessed 30 November 2020.

The future will see some fundamental changes in the relationships with the customer. The proximity center needs to become simple, predictive, proactive, responsive.[129] One of the main drivers will be the solution: to better support the CPCs and self-help aids in the products and services. There will be more attention to improve the reliability, robustness, usability, and support to the customer journey on products and services use. CPCs will move more to the cloud.[130] The result will be an increasing importance of the CPCs. On the other side, the increased use of mobile devices will simplify the connection with the CPCs and require substantial changes in the design and deployment of banking services.[131] These aspects will significantly influence the quality of the services provided to the customers and their assessments.

CRMs and CPCs will become more central in improving customer journeys. The models suggested in this chapter help select the best strategy and implementation of better customer access to banking in connection with the organization's strategy.

[129] www.mckinsey.com/business-functions/operations/our-insights/simple-predictive-proactive-responsive-the-future-of-customer-operations?cid=other-eml-alt-mip-mck&hdpid=ddb516fb-0e40-4783-96ce-a85731773d86&hctky=2743882&hlkid=4165755c107c4fdd8fb0fe4ad26612a5. Accessed 28 February 2021.

[130] Nicoletti, B. (2013). *Cloud computing and financial services*. Palgrave Macmillan, London, UK.

[131] Nicoletti, B. (2014). *Mobile banking: Evolution or revolution*. Palgrave Macmillan, London, UK.

CHAPTER 8

Platforms for Banking 5.0

It almost seems impossible until is done.
Nelson Mandela

Introduction

An increasing number of financial institutions consider investing in digitation as a priority, considering that the sector has lagged with respect to other industries in adopting digital technologies due to regulations, cultural resistances, and legacy assets involved.[1] Many traditional financial institutions are now working on upgrading their digital capabilities, on improving customer engagement, and collect data for managing new and old risks. In some cases, financial institutions have increased spending on research and development to foster in-house innovation. In other cases, they have innovated thanks to external solutions and partners.

A platform is a group of technologies used as a base upon which it is possible to develop other applications, processes, or technologies. In this chapter, the term platform shows any information and communication system or automation support. In this sense, the support from the platforms has increased over time (Fig. 8.1).

[1] Watson, W. T. (2017). New horizon: How diverse growth strategies can advance digitisation in the insurance industry. www.mergermarket.com/info/new-horizons-how-diverse-growth-strategies-can-advance-digitalisation-insurance-industry. Accessed 30 May 2020.

B. Nicoletti, *Banking 5.0*, Palgrave Studies in Financial Services Technology, https://doi.org/10.1007/978-3-030-75871-4_8

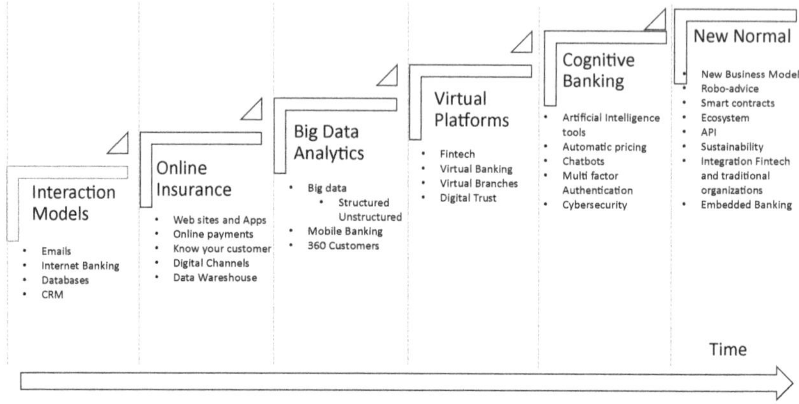

Fig. 8.1 Digital banking transformation

It is interesting to analyze the developments in the platforms relevant to banking 5.0. This chapter refers to them as the seven Cs[2]:

- Cloud computing.
- Communication increasingly mobile.
- Cognition is the improvement of the knowledge of the organizations also through big data analytics.
- Cyber security to assure protection from unauthorized accesses and data privacy.
- Collaboration, through the so-called social networks.
- Cooperation with external partner organizations
- Costs to be increasingly reduced due to the challenging economic and competitive situations.

Each of these trends is a robust change agent in the banking processes:

- Cloud computing uses computing resources, accessed through networks and payments for services supplied and charged based on usage. The impacts on banking are significant since they open new

[2] This classification is related but not the same as the model of the 8 Cs presented in Chapter 2.

horizons for marketing activities and access/flexibility to computing resources.

- Communication pushes toward interactions anywhere, anytime, and on any device.
- Big data analytics tools, supports the analysis of the banking processes. This analysis is much easier than in the past, thanks to the increasing availability of many data, information, and documentation.
- Cyber security is the practice of protecting computers, servers, applications, mobile devices, digital systems, networks, and data from malicious attacks or unauthorized accesses.[3]
- New collaboration tools can develop integration along with the value network.
- Need to be lean pushes the use of external organizations, for including banking in an ecosystem. In this case, the difficulty is to select and continuously evaluate the partners.
- Reduction of costs is pressing in these times of deep and prolonged crisis and intense local and global competition.

This chapter examines the most relevant of these platforms to analyze their uses in support of banking 5.0.[4] This chapter starts with architectural considerations related to digital banking, which can be considered the foundation for banking 5.0. These platforms are classified, considering the model in Fig. 8.2.

The opportunity for financial institutions to use better platforms is significant.[5] These solutions can supply information and insights to support strategic decision-making, marketing, sale, and operational processeswhen appropriately used. They can help with the precise tracking and reporting of revenues, costs, and risks. It is possible to automate many transactional tasks.

[3] www.kaspersky.com/resource-center/definitions/what-is-cyber-security. Accessed 31 May 2019.

[4] Lu, Y. (2017). Industry 5.0: A survey on technologies, applications and open research issues. *Journal of Industrial Information Integration*, *6*, 1–10.

[5] www.assets.kpmg/content/dam/kpmg/pdf/2012/07/the-power-of-insurance-a-global-survey-of-insurance-functions.pdf. Accessed 13 May 2019.

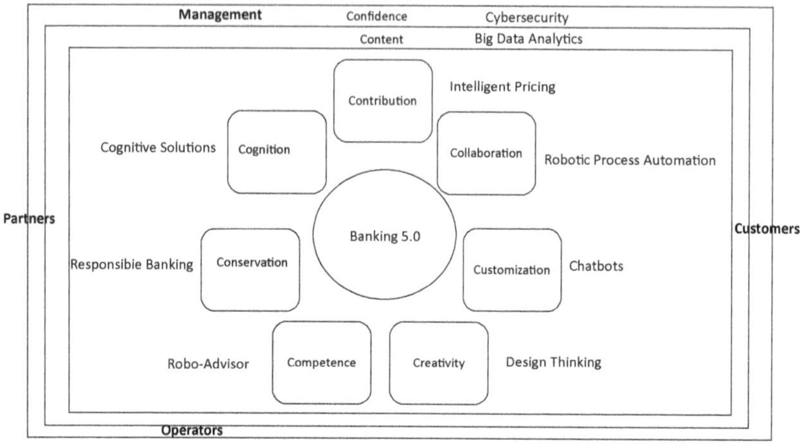

Fig. 8.2 Banking 5.0

The digitization of banking processes has several benefits.[6] The banking institutions can focus on their strategic tasks and contribute to the organization's performance. Apart from the overall increase in organization performance, digitization supports administrative tasks and complex decision-making processes. Digitization is the basis for setting up new business models, services, and products. Digitizing banking processes comes with challenges from the current procedures and processes. The financial institutions must overcome these difficulties to fully use the improved characteristics of banking 5.0 as an asset.[7]

Each financial institution must give more of its capital budget into investments to support banking 5.0. An essential question is on the amount that should be invested and in which solution. No rule-fits-all exists. Specificity is constantly modifying and changing the outcomes of financial institution actions. Fifty percent of surveyed financial institutions

[6] Härting, R. C., Reichstein, C., & Sochacki, R. (2019). Potential benefits of digital business models and its processes in the financial and insurance industry. In *Intelligent decision technologies 2019* (pp. 205–216). Springer, Singapore.

[7] Bienhaus, F., & Haddud, A. (2018). Procurement 4.0: Factors influencing the digitization of procurement and supply chains. *Business Process Management Journal*, *24*(4), 965–984.

said they are focusing on cloud computing, Artificial intelligence (AI), Application programming interfaces (APIs), and Mobile.[8]

Platforms

A classification of the platforms considers three different attributes relative to the physical automation level, the type of the interfaces, and the decisional processesinvolved.[9]

- On the level of automation, the platforms can be manual, partially automated, or completely automated.
- On the type of interfaces and capability of an object or an asset to collect and send data, there might be non-connected objects with data collected manually or reading a barcode or a QR.
- On the decisional processes, traditionally, the decisions were taken in a centralized way, sometimes with ICT applications' support. In banking 5.0, the decisional activities should be mostly decentralized, with the assets self-configuring, in typical situations, without external agents' interventions, or completely automated. In the latter case, the platforms can evaluate the context and make proper decisions in an automated way thanks to AI.

Architecture for the Platforms

The Application programming interfaces (API) are the base for an architectural concept connected with platforms. At an elementary level, an application programming interface, or API, is "a way for two computer applications to talk to each other over a network using a common language that they both understand."[10] APIs are "electrical sockets that have predictable patterns of openings."[11] Other applications that match

[8] www.thefinanser.com/wp-content/uploads/2020/12/The_Omniaccess_Future.pdf. Accessed 4 January 2021.

[9] Tappia, E., & Moretti, E. (2019). La Ricerca dell'Osservatorio Contract Logistics Gino Marchet. *Euromerci, 4–5*, 34–37.

[10] Jacobson, D., Brail, G. & Woods, D. (2012) *APIs: A strategy guide—Creating channels with application programming interfaces*. O'Reilly, Sebastopol, CA.

[11] www.programmableweb.com/news/what-api-exactly/analysis/2015/12/03. Accessed 24 October 2020.

those patterns can plug in and use the data in other applications in the same way electrical devices use electricity. Organizations can use APIs internally to integrate diverse applications.[12] This way of sharing data can make it easier for teams to collaborate and access information when and how they need them, helping to interconnect services and banking processes intra- and inter-organizations. They allow to improve employee productivity and potentially create better omniaccess experiences for customers.[13] External APIs can further integrate with partners and allow third parties to exchange data, and lead to cross-selling and up-selling opportunities.

APIs can either be internal or external APIs. Internal APIs are used to ease intra-organization integration and operational efficiency. External APIs can be customized. They are designed specifically for partners who want to interface directly with their vendors or customers to access data or applications. These private APIs are already used by financial institutions and supply incredible value to organizations.

On the other side, external or open APIs are accessible by anyone and available to use with "little or no contractual arrangement" once agreed to the terms and conditions mandated by the API providers.[14] This situation allows organizations that supply open APIs to create digital economies or banking platforms. Therefore, communities of innovators can develop API-consuming applications and pay a fee for using the APIs. This kind of monetization of APIs is an essential part of the API economy.

[12] Zachariadis, M., & Ozcan, P. (2017). The API economy and digital transformation in financial services: The case of open banking. *SWIFT Institute*.

[13] Nijim, S., & Pagano, B. (2014). *APIs for dummies*. Apigee Special Edition. St Hoboken: John Wiley & Sons, Hoboken, NJ.

[14] Jacobson, D., Brail, G., & Woods, D. (2012) *APIs: A strategy guide—Creating channels with application programming interfaces*, O'Reilly, Sebastopol, CA.

Mattereum[15]
Mattereum is an innovative blockchain-based business. It highlights how banking is critical. This venture uses blockchain solutions. It is an unchangeable, high fidelity record, or digital twin, of real-world entities and concepts.

A digital twin is an abstract idea connected with governance, ownership, and legal obligations.[16] An investor can fractionally own a USD 9M Stradivarius violin on Mattereum's platform. The platform autonomously handles voting rights, transfers of ownership, and dispute resolution. Once again, because this model is autonomous and new, there are heightened customer feelings.

Platforms in Banking 5.0

Banking 5.0 platforms are a digital and automatic integrated way to manage banking. Organizations implement some forms of digital banking on the cloud. Their benefits are a more extensive choice of customers and partners.

APIs in banking 5.0 are based on the Bank-as-a-Service (BaaS) concept.[17]

- BaaS is a concept that can disrupt the delivery of financial products.
- BaaS providers are an intermediary between financial institutions and fintech organizations that offer financial products and services to end-users.[18]
- With an infrastructure built on Application programming interfaces (APIs), BaaS is the gateway for financial data to stream back and forth between users and financial institutions.

[15] www.mattereum.com. Accessed 11 January 2021.

[16] Kim, H., & Mehar, M. (2019). Blockchain in commercial insurance: Achieving and learning towards insurance that keeps pace in a digitally transformed business landscape. *SSRN. 3423382.*

[17] www.fintechtris.com/blog/banking-as-a-service. Accessed 28 November 2020.

[18] FinTech Focus: What is Banking-as-a-Service (BaaS)? www.medium.com/fintechtris/fintech-focus-what-is-banking-as-a-service-baas-2627e9a73377. Accessed 18 January 2021.

- BaaS is an ecosystem with multiple components and leaders, which changes globally due to regulatory frameworks for data access.[19]
- As BaaS continues to develop more profound financial offerings, the playing field will widen for all organizations to effortlessly deliver banking services.[20]

2019 has been an important year for Banking-as-a-Service (BaaS). This growing sector within the fintech organizations helped to create the neobank movement. BaaS is about digital-based banking structures that create and deliver financial services through data sharing, optimized process management systems, and technical innovation.[21]

Fintech organizations use Banking-as-a-Service (which influenced Open Banking in the EU) to offer banking outreach.[22] to underserved market segments, such as the unbanked and underbanked, small, and medium-sized business owners, and immigrants.[23]

By connecting with APIs to supply to their own customers more services, it is possible to implement a "composable bank."[24]

NEC Payment B.S.C.

NEC Payments B.S.C(c) is a digital banking and payment technology company based in Bahrain's Kingdom and licensed and regulated by the Central Bank of Bahrain as an Ancillary Services Provider: Card Processor

[19] FinTech Focus: What is Banking-as-a-Service (BaaS)? www.medium.com/fintechtris/fintech-focus-what-is-banking-as-a-service-baas-2627e9a73377. Accessed 18 January 2021.

[20] Galarza, O. U. (2020). Double movement, embeddedness and the transformation of the financial system. In *Karl Polanyi and twenty-first-century capitalism*. Manchester University Press.

[21] FinTech Focus: What is Banking-as-a-Service (BaaS)? www.medium.com/fintechtris/fintech-focus-what-is-banking-as-a-service-baas-2627e9a73377. Accessed 20 January 2021.

[22] Demirguc-Kunt, A. (2007). Reaching out: Access to and use of banking services across countries. *Journal of Financial Economics, 85*(1), 234–266.

[23] FinTech Focus: What is Banking-as-a-Service (BaaS)? www.medium.com/fintechtris/fintech-focus-what-is-banking-as-a-service-baas-2627e9a73377. Accessed 20 January 2020.

[24] Chang, R. N., Bhaskaran, K., Dey, P., Hsu, H., Takeda, S., & Hama, T. (2020, October). Realizing a composable enterprise microservices fabric with AI-accelerated material discovery API services. In *2020 IEEE 13th International Conference on Cloud Computing (CLOUD)* (pp. 313–320). IEEE.

and Payment Services Provider.[25] The company provides innovative financial technology solutions to power high-performance, flexible, and secure digital banking, payment processing, compliance, and financial control systems. These services may be securely deployed on the cloud, on-premises, and into hybrid environments to supply flexibility, scalability, redundancy, and drive rapid growth.

NEC Payments' Banking-as-a-Service enables fintech start-ups, co-branders, and distributors to develop innovative digital financial services products for multiple business and consumer use cases by supplying access to vertically integrated digital banking and transaction processing technologies.

Benefits and Challenges of Banking 5.0 Platforms

Innovative platforms in banking 5.0 bring a series of benefits, such as flexibility and cost saving. Banking 5.0 is much more than just a new solution or a cost-saving model. It can change the culture of the organization, products, processes, organizations, and business models.[26]

Digital banking leads to lower costs, increased quality, improved delivery, short cycle times, and reduced total cost of ownership and convenience. When using banking 5.0 platforms, the primary sources of increase in the margins came from reducing costs (automated marketing processing, more cost-effective offers, and similar).[27] Now, more margins are coming out of better services. The challenges connected with banking 5.0 are the needs of:

- Customer-centricity.
- Cultural changes.
- Availability of the applications, platforms, networks, and infrastructure.

[25] www.necpayments.com/nec-payments-wins-cfis-award-as-the-best-digital-banking-technology-innovator-in-the-middle-east-2021/. Accessed 20 March 2021.

[26] Nicoletti, B. (2012). *Lean and digitize: An integrated approach to process improvement*. Gower Publishing, Farnham, UK. ISBN-10: 1409441946.

[27] Timmers, P. (1998, September). Business models for electronic markets. *CommerceNet Research Report*.

- Security, privacy, and trust issues.
- Reliability.
- Governance of the processes.
- Talents and training.

ABN Amro[28]

ABN Amro launched an interesting API called Tikkie. It implements the approach of embedded banking. Two examples of API products are part of its "Tikkie" payments offering. Tikkie Payment Requests is used by service providers, both B2C and B2B, to request payments. Web shops can use Tikkie Fast Checkout to enable customers to check out easily in just a few seconds.

ABN Amro decided to monetize the Tikkie APIs on a per-API-call basis. Only API calls that result in a successful payment are charged for. Tikkie has over 4 million users.

Artificial Intelligence

Artificial Intelligence (AI), also called augmented intelligence, is computers' ability to solve complex problems, react like persons, and show intelligent behaviors.[29] A definition of AI is "the scientific study of the computational principles behind thought and intelligent behavior."[30] Gartner supplies an interesting definition: "AI applies advanced analysis and logic-based techniques, including machine learning, to interpret events, support, and automate decisions, and to take actions."[31]

There are at least four different ways of understanding AI. These approaches are[32]:

[28] Choose the Right API Monetization and Pricing Model (www.gartner.com). Accessed 11 January 2021.

[29] Burgess, A. (2017). *The executive guide to artificial intelligence: How to find and implement applications for AI in your organization*. Springer, Cham, Switzerland.

[30] Skilton, M., & Hovsepian, F. (2017). *The 4th industrial revolution: Responding to the impact of artificial intelligence on bussiness*. Springer. Cham, Switzerland.

[31] www.gartner.com/document/3996413?ref=gfeed. Accessed 10 February 2021.

[32] www.just.edu.jo/~najadat/Artificialpercent20Intelligence/Chapter_1.ppt. Accessed 28 November 2020

- Think like a person. The Turing test approach is a criterion based on the ability to discriminate whether the answer to a question is from a person or a program.
- Act like a person. Simulation approach
- Reason. Logical approach
- Rationally acting. Rational agents' approach.

Some academicians aim to solve the ultimate problem: creating. Artificial general intelligence (AGI). AGI should be able to handle any problem, situation, and thought process like a person can (so-called strong AI). The majority of those who are talking about AI in organizations are not talking about AGI[33] or solving these fundamental questions of intelligence. They are looking at applying subsets of AI to problem areas (in the so-called weak AI).

AI is one of the engines of the fifth industrial revolution together with robots. It is interesting to analyze the consequences. With AI, computers can learn, plan, recognize, and solve problems by themselves. AI has three characteristics[34]:

- AI works intentionality. AI algorithms use real-time data and combine various information from various sources in such a way to be able to do complex and fast analysis and make better decisions.
- Currently, Machine learning (ML) and big data analytics technologies power many AI solutions. By using these two technologies, AI can collect data and search for potential rules and patterns. In this way, it is possible to identify the rules and apply them to specific issues with the ML software being trained with the relevant data for a particular problem.
- AI runs in an adaptable way. AI can learn and help to make decisions.

Many AI applications cannot "read inside" (from the Latin words *intus legere*) the reality or develop an autonomous form of consciousness, an

[33] Artificial general intelligence is the hypothetical intelligence of a machine that can understand or learn any intellectual task that a human being can. It is a primary goal of some artificial intelligence research and a common topic in science fiction and futures studies, also creating some concerns.

[34] www.europarl.europa.eu/RegData/etudes/STUD/2020/641547/EPRS_STU(2020)641547_EN.pdf. Accessed 28 November 2020.

appreciation of the context in which they run, or a vision of the environment in which they are. AI is not a single solution but a family of technologies ranging from knowledge representation to automatic reasoning that underlies planning and decision support, feeling and machine learning.

AI developments have mostly taken place in machine learning. Machine learning allows the processing of vast quantities of data and forms of learning based on repeated exposure to empirical conditions combined with the definition of complex learning algorithms. It is possible to train the program to recognize images, interpret language, spot risks, find patterns and trends that are often difficult for a person to find, and thereby increasing the operator's interpretation of reality. In its current form, an ML application is dependent on the availability of significant data sets, with structured and unstructured data.

AI potential increases the more developed the technological and personal ecosystem in which it is developed and implemented. It is not possible to consider AI without considering complementary technologies. AI strongly depends on High-performance computing (HPC) on fixed and mobile broadband technologies, in nano solutions, new hardware, software architects, and especially of big data analytics.[35]Successful AI implementation depends on sufficient and reliable data.[36]

The financial institutions using AI can[37]:

- Synthesize information (using AI to convert data into information and then into knowledge),
- Learn (using AI to understand relationships between knowledge and apply the learning to banking).
- Deliver insights at scale (using AI to support decisions and automation).

Two of the leading drivers for AI adoption are delivering a better customer journey and helping employees to get better at their jobs. The

[35] www.ec.europa.eu/digital-single-market/en/high-performance-computing. Accessed 28 November 2020.

[36] Hassani, H., Huang, X., & Silva, E. (2018). Digitalization and big data mining in banking. *Big Data and Cognitive Computing*, *2*(3), 18.

[37] www.idc.com/events/archivedevents Accessed 12 February 2021.

more interesting use cases for AI are automated customer service agents, sales process recommendation and automation, automated threat intelligence and prevention, and ICT automation. These four use cases overed a third of all AI spending in 2021.[38]

AI investment is growing fast, and AI already has a significant banking impact. Global spending on AI is forecast to double over the next few years, growing from $50.1 billion in 2020 to more than $110 billion in 2024.[39] These numbers compared with the estimation that USD 50 billion were invested in AI start-ups between 2011 and mid-2018.[40] Of this amount, internal corporate investment represented about 70%, investment in AI start-ups some 20%, and AI acquisitions stood for some 10%.[41] Bigtech organizations made three-quarters of these investments.[42]

Artificial Intelligence Architecture

AI can process vast volumes of data faster and better than the ability of persons.[43] It includes algorithms that enable machines to show "intelligent" competencies. Machine learning proves the potential capabilities of AI. This tool can extract patterns and rules from a series of observations.[44]

AI solutions have three characteristics:

- AI and machine learning work together with data analytics.

[38] www.idc.com/events/archivedevents. Accessed 12 January 2021.

[39] Worldwide Artificial Intelligence Spending Guide (www.idc.com). Accessed 12 February 2021.

[40] Peña-López, I. (2019). Artificial intelligence in society. www.ictlogy.net/bibliography/reports/projects.php?idp=3874&lang=ca. Accessed 20 January 2021.

[41] Dilda, V. (2017, October). *AI: Perspectives and opportunities*. Presentation at AI: Intelligent machines, smart policies conference, Paris, France.

[42] OECD Library. www.oecd-ilibrary.org/sites/3abc27f1-en/index.html?itemId=/content/component/3abc27f1-en. Accessed 20 January 2021.

[43] Allianz Global Corporate & Specialty. (2018). The rise of artificial intelligence: Future outlook and emerging risks. www.agcs.allianz.com/news-and-insights/reports/the-rise-of-artificial-intelligence.html. Accessed 12 December 2019.

[44] Cambosu, D. (2018, June). Intelligenza artificiale, perché è sempre più importante per l'insurance. www.insuranceup.it/it/business/intelligenza-artificiale-perche-e-sempre-piuimportante-per-l-insurance_1925.htm. Accessed 30 March 2020.

Intelligence	Ability
Mechanical	Automatically perform routine, repeated, and simple tasks.
Analytical	Process information for problem-solving and learn from it
Intuitive	Resolve with their abilities the kinds of problems that confront the daily life, such as on the job or at home.
Creative	Think creatively and adjust effectively to new situations
Empathetic	Recognize and understand other peoples' emotions, respond appropriately emotionally, and influence others' emotions

Fig. 8.3 Types of intelligence

- AI can support complex processing, predictions, and decision-making.
- AI can adapt. AI can learn and make simple decisions.

The Five Waves of Artificial Intelligence
It is possible to distinguish AI development in five waves based on each phase's characteristics' intelligence types. There are five types of intelligence potentially implementable in AI. Their developmental sequence is mechanical, analytical, intuitive, creative, and empathetic (Fig. 8.3).[45] The five intelligences may be both ordinal and parallel: They are ordinal since some human intelligences are more difficult to implement in AI. It takes longer to implement the corresponding AI applications. They may go in parallel because once AI has reached a certain intelligence level, all lower AIs can continue supplying their services.[46] The following section discusses the five AIs, highlighting their characteristics, their relevance to both people and machines, and their applications,

Each AI can deliver its unique benefit: mechanical AI is best for standardization, analytical AI is good for personalization, Intuitive AI is for intuition, creative AI is for innovating, and empathetic AI is ideal for relationships (Fig. 8.4).[47]

[45] Huang, M. H., & Rust, R. T. (2018). Artificial intelligence in service. *Journal of Service Research*, *21*(2), 155–172.

Huang, M. H., & Rust, R. T. (2020). A strategic framework for artificial intelligence in marketing. *Journal of the Academy of Marketing Science*, 1–21.

[46] Artificial Intelligence in Service—Ming-Hui Huang. www.journals.sagepub.com/doi/full/10.1177/1094670517752459. Accessed 20 January 2021.

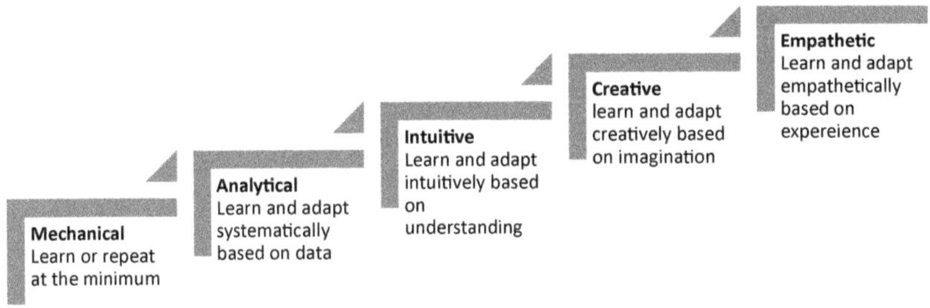

Fig. 8.4 Five AI generations

Mechanical or Simple Intelligence

Mechanical intelligence refers to the ability to perform routine, repeated, and simple tasks automatically. It may appear not particularly smart, but it can help in many tasks. Mechanical AI has limited learning and adaptive ability. Most of the current robots are one of its typical applications. Service robots can perform physical tasks, run autonomously without needing instruction, and are directed by computers without help from operators.[48] Service robots are rule-based. They rely on *a priori* instructions and continuous sensor perception to check and react to the physical and temporal variability in the environment in which they operate.[49] Service robots sense, but they do not understand the environment and cannot adapt automatically. Their knowledge is updated in a specific way thanks to the repetitive nature of their activities.[50] More advanced versions include automatic updating functions.[51] Most robots

[47] Huang, M. H., & Rust, R. T. (2017). Solution-driven service strategy. *Journal of the Academy of Marketing Science, 45*(6), 906–924.

[48] Colby, C. L., Mithas, S., & Parasuraman, A. (2016). Service robots: How ready are consumers to adopt and what drives acceptance? In *The 2016 Frontiers in Service Conference*. Bergen, Norway.

[49] Artificial Intelligence in Service—Ming-Hui Huang. www.journals.sagepub.com/doi/full/10.1177/1094670517752459. Accessed 20 January 2021.

[50] Engelberger, J. F. (1989), *Robotics in service* (pp. 108–109). The MIT Press, Cambridge, MA.

[51] Kim, M. (2007), Challenges on the development of robotic intelligence. In *16th IEEE International Conference on Robot & Human Interactive Communication*, Jeju, Korea.

have limited intelligence, only sufficient to perform the planned tasks.[52] Mechanical AI has a relative advantage over persons in being strongly consistent, tireless, and available potentially anytime. Their applications do no need to learn. External operators can do and change applications. It relies on simple observations to act and react repetitively. Examples are virtual chatbots, which turn customer service into self-service.[53]

Mechanical AI supplies standardization benefits thanks to its consistency.[54] This characteristic is important in marketing. Examples are collaborative robots (cobots), which help with packaging,[55] drones distributing physical products, self-service robots delivering services, and service robots automating the front line's social presence.[56] All these applications aim to generate standardized, consistent, and reliable outputs.[57]

[52] Kim, M. (2007), Challenges on the development of robotic intelligence. In *16th IEEE International Conference on Robot & Human Interactive Communication*, Jeju, Korea.

[53] Sawhney, M. (2016, September). Putting products into services. *Harvard Business Review*, 82–89.

[54] A strategic framework for artificial intelligence in marketing. www.link.springer.com/content/pdf/10.1007/s11747-020-00749-9.pdf. Accessed 20 January 2021.

[55] Colgate, E., Wannasuphoprasit, W., & Peshkin, M. (1996). Cobots: Robots for collaboration with human operators. In *Proceedings of the ASME Dynamic Systems and Control Division* (Vol. 58, pp. 433–439), New York, NY.

[56] Mende, M., Scott, M. L., van Doorn, J., Grewal, D., & Shanks, I. (2019). Service robots rising: How humanoid robots influence service experiences and elicit compensatory consumer responses. *Journal of Marketing Research, 56*(4), 535–556.

van Doorn, J., Mende, M., Noble, S., Hulland, J., Ostrom, A., Grewal, D., & Petersen, A. (2017). Domo arigato Mr. Roboto: Emergence of automated social presence in organizational frontlines and customers' service experiences. *Journal of Service Research, 20*(1), 43–58.

[57] A strategic framework for artificial intelligence in marketing. www.link.springer.com/content/pdf/10.1007/s11747-020-00749-9.pdf. Accessed 20 January 2021.

Analytical or Thinking Intelligence

Analytical intelligence is the ability to process information for problem-solving and learn from it.[58] This intelligence is present in information processing, logical reasoning, and mathematical competencies.[59] Training, ability, and specialization in cognitive thinking supply these skills. Machine learning and data analytics are the major analytical AI applications in banking. Their intelligence limitation occurs because they do not have conscious states, no mind, and no subjective awareness.[60] This intelligence can perform complex, systematic, consistent, and predictable tasks. Their performance is important, for example, for those applications that are data- and information-intensive. Their systematic nature makes them suitable for mass customizations based on big data from customers, with collaborative personalization being one example. An example is IBM's Watson, which helps, for example, H&R Block for tax preparation.[61]

Analytical AI supplies personalization benefits due to its ability to recognize patterns from data (for example, text mining, speech recognition, or visual recognition). Any marketing function and activity that can receive help from personalized outcomes should consider analytical AI. The most common applications in marketing are various personalized recommendation systems,[62] such as cross-selling recommendations.

[58] Sternberg, R. J. (2005). The theory of successful intelligence. *Interamerican Journal of Psychology, 39*(2), 189–202.

Sternberg, R. J. (1984). Toward a triarchic theory of human intelligence. *Behavior and Brain Sciences, 7*(2), 269–315.

[59] Sternberg, R. J. (1999). The theory of successful intelligence. *Review of General Psychology, 3*(4), 292–316.

[60] Azarian, B. (2016). A neuroscientist explains why artificially intelligent robots will never have consciousness like humans. *Raw Story, March.* www.rawstory.com/2016/03/aneuroscientistexplainswhyartificiallyintelligentrobotswillneverhaveconsciousnesslikehumans/]. Accessed 20 January 2021.

[61] Davenport, T. H., & Kirby, J. (2015, June). Beyond automation. *Harvard Business Review*, 59–65.

[62] Chung, T. S., Rust, R. T., & Wedel, M. (2009). My mobile music: An adaptive personalization system for digital audio players. *Marketing Science, 28*(1), 52–68.

Chung, T. S., Wedel, M., & Rust, R. T. (2016). Adaptive personalization using social networks. *Journal of the Academy of Marketing Science, 44*(1), 66–87.

Intuitive or Practical Intelligence

Intuitive intelligence is often referred to as implicit knowledge or learning. It relates to experiences got in the past and either forgot or did not realized as learned.[63] Intuitive intelligence is energetic sensitivity, referring to the nervous system's ability to detect and respond to environmental signals such as electromagnetic fields.

Intuitive intelligence involves individuals applying their abilities to the types of problems that confront them daily, such as on the job or at home.[64] Intuitive intelligence involves applying intelligence components to experience to: (a) adapt, (b) shape, and (c) select environments. Adaptation is involved when one changes oneself to suit the environment. Shaping is involved in changing the environment to suit oneself. Selection is involved when one decides to seek out another domain that is a better match to one's needs, abilities, and desires. People differ in their balance of adaptation, shaping, choice, and the competencies they balance among the possible courses of action.

One application of intuitive intelligence AI is to find threats and opportunities without being told what to look for, just as human intuition allows persons to make decisions in the absence of exact information.[65] The financial market and institutions have used this type of AI to detect new cyber crime offenses, including money laundering, fraud, and piracy. Suspicious activity usually hides among thousands of transactions. Innovative algorithms can find the most influential parameters and present them to analysts. It is then up to the latter to analyze the unusual data and decide whether it is an offense or it is a false-positive. By discovering these relationships, the program can alert financial institutions to previously invisible attacks or trends.

Intuitive intelligence in banking finds applications in robo-advisors.

Creative or Cognitive Intelligence

Creative intelligence is the ability to think creatively and adjust effectively to new situations. It can be considered wisdom based on rounded and

[63] McCraty, R., & Zayas, M. (2014). Intuitive intelligence, self-regulation, and lifting consciousness. *Global Advances in Health and Medicine, 3*(2), 56–65.

[64] Sternberg, R. J. (1999). The theory of successful intelligence. *Review of General Psychology, 3*(4), 292–316.

[65] Graziano, M., & Leone, G. (2019). *Artificial intuition.* Master Degree Thesis, Politecnico di Torino, Torino, Italy.

experience-based thinking.[66] Creative intelligence includes hard thinking professional skills. These skills require insights and creative problem-solving. Understanding may be considered as the key defining characteristic of creative AI that distinguishes it from the previous AI types. Creative AI is built to emulate a wide range of person cognition and learn similarly to a person child (much faster due to its computing power and connectivity and consistent and continuous actions). Tasks that are complex, creative, chaotic, rounded, empirical, and contextual require creative intelligence. The complex yet distinct nature of the jobs makes them rely on creativity for successful service delivery.

Creative intelligence in banking should be able to design new products and services that would please a particular segment of customers. An application that is moving in the direction of creative intelligence is GPT-3 (Generative Pre-Trained Transformer, created by OpenAI). It is a deep learning model that emulates human-like text.[67]

Empathetic or Feeling Intelligence

Empathetic intelligence is the ability to recognize and understand other peoples' emotions, respond appropriately emotionally, and influence others' feelings.[68] Specific skill examples include communication, relationship building, leadership, advocating and negotiating, work–life balance,[69] social teamwork, cultural diversity, and charisma. Empathetically skilled professionals work in jobs that require people skills such as politicians and negotiators and feeling jobs such as psychologists.

Empathetic AI describes an application that can feel or at least behave as though it has feelings idiosyncratic. It is possible to define empathetic computing as computing that relates to, arises from, or influences

[66] Sternberg, R. J. (1984). Toward a triarchic theory of human intelligence. *Behavior and Brain Sciences, 7*(2), 269–315.

Sternberg, R. J. (1999). The theory of successful intelligence. *Review of General Psychology, 3*(4), 292–316.

Sternberg, R. J. (2005). The theory of successful intelligence. *Interamerican Journal of Psychology,39*(2), 189–202.

[67] All, I. U. (2019). The future of banking. M4_v0.7.pdf (www.mudano.com). Accessed 20 January 2021.

[68] Goleman, D. (1996). *Emotional intelligence: Why it can matter more than IQ*. Bloomsbury Publishing, London, UK.

[69] Caprino, K. (2012, April). What you do not know will hurt you: The top 8 skills professionals need to master. *Forbes*.

emotions.[70] The essential role of emotion in both person cognition and perception is proved by neurological studies. These studies show that empathetic AI applications should supply better performance in helping persons and enhance their capabilities to make decisions. The defining characteristic of empathetic AI is "experience," the ability to experience things. It is challenging to think about how machines can be programmed to experience emotions as persons do. Very simple examples are chatbots, which communicate with customers and learn from them out of their reactions. Sophia's robots interact with customers as if employees do, but to be fair non as a human analyst could do.[71]

Empathetic AI should supply relational benefits (that is, personalized relationships), thanks to its capability to consider and respond to emotions. This feature is important for any marketing functions or activities that require interaction and communication, with the goal of relational benefits (for example, when customer lifetime value is high). In these cases, it is essential to consider empathetic AI.[72] One example is customer proximity. A broad range of marketing functions involves feelings, for example, customer delight, customer complaints, customer moods, and emotions in advertising, and so on., and could make use of empathetic AI.

Applications of empathetic intelligence are still to come.

What could come after empathetic intelligence? One of the human intelligence characteristics is its flexibility to move from one type of intelligence to another one. In the future, AGI will move in this direction.

[70] Picard, R. W. (2000). *Affective computing*. MIT Press, Cambridge, MA.

[71] Xiao, L., & Ding, M. (2014). Just the faces: Exploring the effects of facial features in print advertising. *Marketing Science*, *33*(3), 338–352.

Rafaeli, A., Altman, D., Gremler, D. D., Huang, M.-H., Grewal, D., Iyer, B., Parasuraman, A., & de Ruyter, K. (2017). The future of frontline research: Invited commentaries. *Journal of Service Research*, *20*(1), 91–99.

[72] A strategic framework for artificial intelligence in marketing. www.link.springer.com/content/pdf/10.1007/s11747-020-00749-9.pdf. Accessed 20 January 2021.

Table 8.1 State of AI in financial services

	Payments	*Banking*	*Capital markets*	*Investment Mgmt*	*Insurance*
Front office	Decisioning and personalization engine				
	Natural language processing				
	Authentication and biometrics				
	Chatbot				
	predictive analysis				
		Attrition analysis			Attrition analysis
Middle office			Monitoring		
	Antifraud and risk		KYC/AML		
	Complex legal and compliance workflows				
Back office		Customer service and text analysis			
	AI-enabled search				
		Credit underwriting	Alternative data in trading and asset management	Robo advisors	Risk underwriting
	Smart contracts infrastructure				
	Asset management				
	More mature		Less mature		

Artificial Intelligence in Banking 5.0

Banks are exploring AI applications to replace activities that are costly, arduous, and repetitive.[73] The focus is on several fields. Attractive sectors are operational risk management like fraud detection, improved Know your customer (KYC), and opportunities for cost reduction and service improvement like chatbots or robo-advisors (Table 8.1).

Potential AI applications in banking are into three broad categories, crossed with the customer journey and operational efficiency (Fig. 8.5)[74]:

[73] Messina, E., Erlwein-Sayer, C., & Mitra, G. (2021). AI, machine learning and sentiment analysis applied to financial markets and consumer markets.

[74] Author Elaboration on Financial Stability Board, F. S. B. (2017). Artificial intelligence and machine learning in financial services. *Market developments and financial stability implications*.

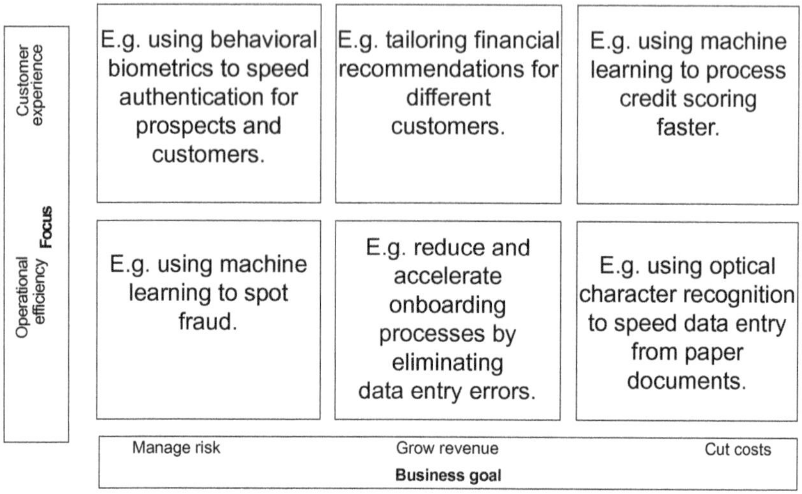

Fig. 8.5 Artificial intelligence in banking

- Manage Risks

    1. Risk management. A natural area of application of AI is automated credit scoring.[75] Financial institutions tend to rely on past data to assess and price risks. Much of these data are relevant for implementing an AI approach to credit scoring based on documents in an unstructured form. They are emails, handwritten documents, or pictures. To exploit this data, it is necessary to have them in a digital format. This operation typically involves scanning and using image processing or natural language processing capabilities.
    2. Pricing Optimization.

Cambosu, D. (2018, June 22). Intelligenza artificiale, perché è sempre più importante per l'insurance. www.insuranceup.it/it/business/intelligenza-artificiale-perche-e-sempre-piuimportante. Accessed 20 January 2021.

[75] Albrecher, H., Bommier, A., Filipović, D., Koch-Medina, P., Loisel, S., & Schmeiser, H. (2019). Insurance: Models, digitization, and data science. *European Actuarial Journal*, *9*(2), 349–360.

3. In the middle office, AI can ease risk management and regulatory oversight processes. AI is helping portfolio managers to invest more efficiently and accurately.
4. KYC processes to verify the identity of customers.

- Grow Revenue

  1. Customer delight and journey analysis.
  2. Customer reporting analytics.
  3. Customer loyalty or retainment analysis.
  4. Customized graphical user interfaces (GUI).
  5. Chatbots digital assistants interact with customers by text or voice. They aim to address their requests without the involvement of a banking operator.
  6. Customer portfolio management.
  7. Promotion customization.
  8. Cross- and up-selling suggestions.

- Save Costs

  1. Visualization from legal documents or annual reports and extracting essential clauses.
  2. Back-office applications.
  3. (Account or ATM) Replenishment optimization.
  4. Regulatory compliance.
  5. Real-time identification and prevention of fraud in online banking.[76] Fraud and risks are connected. In many cases, one integrated team manages them.

Some existing financial solution tools evolve as proper AI solutions do over time. Good examples include robo-advisors that enable full automation in certain asset management services and online financial planning tools that help customers make more informed consumption and saving decisions.

[76] Mai, H. (2018). Card fraud in Germany: Few incidents, but high costs. *Deutsche Bank Research. Talking Point.*

Financial institutions are still experimenting with AI technologies rather than fully implementing them in their processes, with few exceptions. Customer- and operations-focused AI solutions seem to be undergoing more intensive explorations and implementations than others[77]: Figure 8.3 for more information.

Deutsche Bank[78]

Using AI and machine learning tools, it is possible to quantify geopolitical risk and predict its effect on financial markets. For example, Deutsche Bank's Alpha-Dig platform infers context from news media, social media, and other natural language articles. It then builds a picture of a country's political risk profile.

Alpha-Dig uses algorithms to mine global financial news as a proxy for how much media pay attention toward certain countries' risks. The process uses natural language processing and machine learning tools to collect context in news articles and ensure that positive and negative indicators are extracted. As a second step, Alpha-Dig overlays learnings from Wikipedia, whose reports are in majority correct and easily readable by machines. To adjust for potential biases, the platform uses readership data to see what topics are trending. Once data from the mainstream financial news is enhanced with learnings from Wikipedia, Alpha-Dig can create a picture that shows how political issues have become significant over time. Among other statistical methods, Alpha-Dig can calculate Z-scores, which looks at the average amount of daily geopolitical news for a topic appeared in the recent past and see what proportion of all geopolitical information is used on that topic. If a particular political event is receiving greater attention than two standard deviations more than usual, it is labeled an "outlier" event. Alpha-Dig supplies a goal measure that can aid investors in what are notoriously tricky times, thanks to AI advancements.

According to the World Banking Report 2017, for financial institutions, AI is essential to the extent of 69% of banking activities. Eighty

[77] Kaya, O., Schildbach, J., AG, D. B., & Schneider, S. (2019). Artificial intelligence in banking. *Artificial intelligence.*

[78] Kaya, O., Schildbach, J., AG, D. B., & Schneider, S. (2019, January). Deutsche Bank Research. *Konzept*, 34–39.

percent of respondents showed that they are already investing in this solution or plan to do so in the following three years.[79]

One of the areas essential for banking 5.0 is the customization of the interaction with customers, including the customization of service offerings.[80] Traditionally financial institutions have been strong at selling banking but not necessarily in continuing customer relationships after the first contact. This approach must change since customers have experience with other product and service providers and expect similar experiences from AI. Cultivating customer relations and customer ownership will be an essential field on which traditional financial institutions and start-ups will fight to gain access to and keep profitable banking. Next to technical credit scoring competencies, superior products and services will be the critical success factors.[81]

Softwares can make decisions on loans. It can take into consideration several selected data about a borrower, rather than just a credit score and a background check.[82] Robo-advisors create personalized investment portfolios, replacing the need for stockbrokers and financial advisors.[83] These advances are designed to take subjective opinions out of investing, undertake decisions based on detailed considerations, and make these choices quickly.

A typical example of this functionality is used in stock exchanges, where high-frequency trading by machines has replaced much of personal

[79] Kumaresan, A., Saurav, S., & Raghunanda, K. (2017). *Top 10 trends in property & casualty insurance 2018*. www.capgemini.com/wpcontent/uploads/2017/12/property-and-casuality-insurance-trends_2018.pdf. Accessed 19 January 2020.

[80] Albrecher, H., Bommier, A., Filipović, D., Koch-Medina, P., Loisel, S., & Schmeiser, H. (2019). Insurance: Models, digitization, and data science. *European Actuarial Jssournal*, *9*(2), 349–360.

[81] McKinsey. (2017). Digital disruption in insurance: Cutting through the noise. www.mckinsey.com/~/media/mckinsey/industries/financialpercent20services/ourpercent20insights/timepercent20forpercent20insurancepercent20financialinstitutionspercent20topercent20facepercent20digitalpercent20reality/digital-disruption-in-insurance.ashx. Accessed 30 May 2020.

[82] Nathaniel Popper, Stocks and Bots, *New York Times Magazine*, February 28, 2016.

[83] Nathaniel Popper, Stocks and Bots, *New York Times Magazine*, February 28, 2016.

decision-making.[84] People send buy and sell orders. Computers match them in fractions of seconds without personal intervention. Applications can spot trading inefficiencies or market differentials on a tiny scale and execute trades that can gain money according to investor instructions.[85] There are some advanced computers under development (quantum computers) which will shorten in a dramatic way the running times of these AI applications.[86] Algorithmic trading has grown dramatically. It now accounts for most trades put through exchanges globally.[87] In 2017, JPMorgan estimated that just 10% of trading volume in stocks was "regular stock picking."[88] Increased computing capabilities enable "high-frequency trading" where millions of orders are transmitted every day, and many markets are analyzed simultaneously. AI allows more factors to be considered.

Fraud detection is another use of AI in financial systems. It is sometimes difficult to spot fraudulent activities in large organizations. AI can find abnormalities, outliers, or deviations requiring more investigation. In this way, they help operators find problems early in the cycle before they reach dangerous levels.[89]

Despite slow adoption, financial services and products increasingly look to AI to improve their banking operations and customer journeys using chatbots, fraud and risk detection features. A report from IHS Markitshows that AI's banking value of AI in global banking is expected

[84] How artificial intelligence is transforming the world. www.brookings.edu/research/how-artificial-intelligence-is-transforming-the-world/. How artificial intelligence is transforming the world. www.brookings.edu/research/how-artificial-intelligence-is-transforming-the-world/. Accessed 20 January 2021.

[85] Lewis, M. (2015). *Flash boys: A wall street Revolt*. Norton, New York. NY.

[86] Metz, C. (2017, November). In Quantum Computing Race, Yale Professors Battle Tech Giants, *New York Times*, B3.

Metz, C. (2017, November). In Quantum Computing Race, Yale Professors Battle Tech Giants, *New York Times*, B3.

[87] OECD Library www.oecd-ilibrary.org/sites/79edf9d8-en/index.html?itemId=/content/component/79edf9d8-en. Accessed 20 January 2021.

[88] Cheng, E. (2017), Just 10% of trading is regular stock picking, JPMorgan estimates. www.cnbc.com/2017/06/13/death-of-the-human-investor-just-10-percent-of-tradingis-regular-stock-picking-jpmorgan-estimates.html. Accessed 28 January 2021.

[89] Executive Office of the President. (2016. December). *Artificial intelligence, automation, and the economy*, 27–28.

to reach USD 300 billion by 2030.[90] North America could become the largest market for AI in banking between 2019 and 2023, reaching USD 79 billion. Asia–Pacific, Europe, and other global regions will roll out more AI solutions in the banking sector between 2024 and 2030.[91] The market for AI is vast.

Large financial institutions such as JPMorgan, Citibank, State Farm, and Liberty Mutual are rapidly deploying AI in the financial sector.[92] The same is true for start-ups. Financial service organizations are combining different Machine learning (ML) practices. For example, French start-up QuantCube Solutions analyzes several billion data points collected from over 40 countries.[93] It uses language processing, deep learning, graph theory, and more, to develop AI solutions for financial corporates' decision-making.

Ant Financial

In the People's Republic of China, Ant Financialhas based its loan success on e-commerce and AI.[94] It uses algorithms to process the vast amount of transaction data generated by small businesses on its platform. This situation has allowed Ant to lend more than USD 13.4 billion to 3 million small businesses. Ant's algorithms automatically analyze transaction data on all borrowers and all their behavioral data in real time. It can process loans as small as several hundred Yuan Renminbi (around USD 50) in a few minutes. Every action which is taken on Alibaba's platform—transaction, communication between seller and buyer, or connection with other services—affects a business's credit score. Simultaneously, the algorithms that calculate the scores themselves evolve, improving decision-making quality with each iteration. The micro-lending operation has a default rate of about 1%, compared to the World Bank's 2016 estimate of an average of 4% worldwide.

[90] www.news.ihsmarkit.com/prviewer/release_only/slug/solution-global-business-value-artificial-intelligence-banking-reach-300-billion-203. Accessed 20 January 2021.

[91] www.emarketer.com/content/seven-charts-the-state-of-digital-banking-in-2020. Accessed 20 October 2020.

[92] Cooperman, E. S. (2018). Corporations to the rescue: A new stakeholder paradigm? An overview for US corporations & financial institutions. *International Review of Accounting, Banking & Finance, 10.*

[93] Bajulaiye, O., Fenwick, M., Skultetyova, I., & Vermeulen, E. P. (2020). Digital transformation in the hedge fund and private equity industry. *Lex Research Topics in Corporate Law & Economics Working Paper.*

[94] Zeng, M. (2018, September–October). Alibaba and the future of business. *Harvard Business Review.*

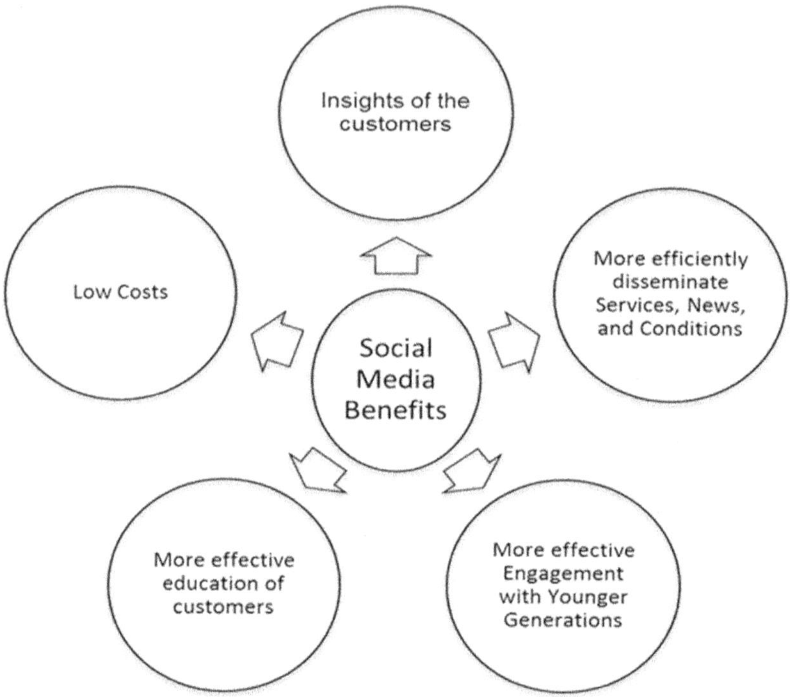

Fig. 8.6 Social media benefits

An exciting development is the use of sentiment analysis on social media platforms (Fig. 8.6). Organizations such as Seeking Alpha and StockTwits focus on the stock market, enabling users to connect and consult with professionals to grow their investment. Decision-making processescan integrate the data produced on these platforms.[95] AI helps enable online and mobile banking by authenticating users via fingerprint or facial recognition captured by mobile phones. Alternatively, banks use voice recognition as a password to customer service rather than numerical passcodes (Fig. 8.6).[96]

[95] Sohangir, S. et al. (2018). Big data: Deep learning for financial sentiment analysis. *Journal of Big Data*, *5*(1).

In the middle office, AI can ease risk management and regulatory oversight processes. AI is helping portfolio managers to invest more efficiently and accurately. In back-office, AI broadens data sources to assess credit risks.

CaixaBank[97]

CaixaBank developed an ML-based system to estimate the best product offer for each customer based on their sociodemographic and financial profile, browsing behavior, and payment methods. The bank uses this engine to personalize both the outbound marketing and its customers' browsing experience across different platforms.

CaixaBank has used a quantum computing framework that combines quantum and conventional computing in distinct phases of the calculation process to classify credit risk profiles. This approach helped to improve risk scenario simulations and augment machine learning capabilities.

CaixaBank has merged its 17 data marts into one, which holds over 1,200 terabytes of information and can handle over 12,000 transactions per second during peak hours. This situation enables an advanced analytics and business intelligence application to extract value from the data and supply the agility needed to drive future digitalization. Consolidation of data will be critical as innovative solutions will continue to act as the main competitive differentiator for financial institutions in a crowded marketplace.

Benefits and Challenges of Artificial Intelligence

Deploying AI in the financial sector has many significant benefits. These include improving the customer journey, finding rapidly smart investment opportunities, and granting customers more credit with better conditions. However, it raises social and legal questions related to ensuring accuracy and preventing discrimination and the broader impact of automation on jobs.

[96] Sokolin, L., & Low, M. (2018). *Machine intelligence and augmented finance: How artificial intelligence creates $1 trillion dollar of change in the front, middle and back-office*. Autonomous Research LLP, London, UK.

[97] www.finextra-future-of-core-banking-2020.pdf. Accessed 4 January 2021.

AI can bring several improvements to banking. Among others:

- Operating and staff costs and expenses reduction: The digitization of the entire banking management process leads to improving the process's efficiency with customer delight. It allows reducing the financial institution's operating costs: process automation and use of collaborative digital tools. One of the main goals of AI solutions is to improve efficiency. However, AI's foremost opportunity is to adopt an even more robust customer-centric approach, ensuring that customers are empowered through innovative products and services stemming from the AI solutions. In the banking sector, this has many opportunities.[98]
- Better customer journeys: The continually evolving data-driven approach can be applied to improve many processes that might typically rely on intuition or limited or incomplete information. In compliance with data protection regulation and data usage requirements, AI-supported automated services will bring a wide range of choices in terms of services offered. Customization capabilities are driven by better use of data through advanced analytics, for example[99]:
  - Offering contextualized, personalized products and experiences.
  - Making more accurate creditworthiness assessments.
  - Supplying better financial advice.
  - Reducing costs for customers. and
  - Better protecting customers from fraud.
- Democratization of financial services: Thanks to the lower complexity and costs associated with some assistance, AI makes easier access to financial services. For example, robo-advisor's main contribution will be bringing portfolio investment to customer groups who previously had no access to it for its costs.
- Gains in term of efficiency and robustness in banking processes: These solutions can improve the focus of resources and sales on the

[98] EBF position paper on AI in the banking industry. www.ebf.eu/wp-content/uploads/2020/03/EBF-AI-paper-_final-.pdf. Accessed 20 January 2021.

[99] Mohanty, S., Jagadeesh, M., & Srivatsa, H. (2013). *Big data imperatives: Enterprise 'Big Data' warehouse, 'I'mplementations and analytics*. Apress, New York, NY.

right customers at the right time, use better/more complex products with lower costs, and so on.

- New banking opportunities: The potential of big data analytics and AI allows financial institutions to improve customer services, raise efficiency, and create new customer proposals in the traditional banking segments and new fields of activity beyond banking.
- Better risk management: Data analytics contributes to an understanding of financial institutions' activities, more effective risk management, and improved monitoring of compliance. AI could help prevent systemic risks. AI and the underlying technologies must be part of "responsible innovation" processes as they could disrupt the stability and security of the financial system. AI also has the potential to be used to detect better and manage systemic risks.
- AI can provide financial institutions better control and raise the transparency of all data they hold, including solutions for data ranking or cartographies regardless of source: database, transactions, emails, excel files, and so on. This possibility supports compliance with the conduct of banking rules, such as MiFID II, short-selling, and so on.
- Anti-money laundering (AML)/Financial crimes (FC)/Fraud are complex continuous challenges. Segmentation is a source of better AML/FC outcomes. AI may transform the current segmentation step process, reduce the burden, and increase the controls.[100]

AI has many challenges. It is possible to classify challenges according to a taxonomy in different fields, which can be named with the initials of the character of the word CAMELS. The chapter provides a taxonomy through the lens of CAMELS which stands for C (Capital), A(Asset), M(Management), E(Earnings), L(Liquidity), and S(Sensitivity).[101]

Data privacy and data availability remain potential challenges for financial institutions. AI's infrastructural problems are vast. They should be considered when, for example, a financial institution is deciding on implementing an AI solution into their banking or platform solutions. These

[100] Han, J., Huang, Y., Liu, S., & Towey, K. (2020). Artificial intelligence for anti-money laundering: A review and extension. *Digital Finance*, *2*(3), 211–239.

[101] Joneidy, S., & Ayadurai, C. (2021). Artificial intelligence and bank soundness: Between the devil and the deep blue sea—Part 2. *Chapters*.

problems include areas related to software, personnel, storage, and security. Starting with software and algorithms, a financial institution must fine-tune the AI solutions for their use. This situation can be problematic. Understanding AI is not simple. AI into the organization's structure might have also detrimental consequences rather than potential positive results, if not properly managed.[102]

Storing all the data necessary for AI might prove problematic. Many organizations use cloud storage.

Understanding personal intelligence has proven difficult, which means AI is no different. AI can be unpredictable when it could make decisions that seem correct to it but are considered flawed by persons. Trust is considered the most important feature of AI.[103] In surveys, many participants state that they are not at all ready to use AI. Mistrust is connected to resistance to change, which is a crucial matter of controversy in general.

There are other AI challenges, particularly those relating to the interactions of AI systems with persons and other AI systems. AI can generate risks in social and environmental terms. Regarding social risks, organizations may replace their workers with Al systems.[104] In this way, the danger of the progressive loss of skills (de-skilling) depends on the excessive reliance on so-called "intelligent" machines.[105]

To help overcome all these challenges, AI must have[106]:

1. Person supervision to guarantee respect for fundamental rights and the well-being of the user.
2. Robustness, security, reliability of the algorithms, and sealing of the control systems in hypothetical illegal operations.

[102] Kiruthika, J., & Khaddaj, S. (2017, October). Impact and challenges of using of virtual reality & artificial intelligence in businesses. In *2017 16th International Symposium on Distributed Computing and Applications to Business, Engineering and Science (DCABES)* (pp. 165–168). IEEE.

[103] Lazanyi, K. (2018, September). Readiness for artificial intelligence. In *2018 IEEE 16th International Symposium on Intelligent Systems and Informatics (SISY)* (000235–000238). IEEE.

[104] Acemoglu, D., & Restrepo, P. (2019). Automation and new tasks: How solution displaces and reinstates labor. *Journal of Economic Perspectives*, *33*(2), 3–30.

[105] Hawkins, J., & Blakeslee, S. (2004). *On intelligence*. Palgrave Macmillan, London, UK.

[106] www.nist.gov/topics/artificial-intelligence. Accessed 19 October 2020.

3. Privacy, data control, and management.
4. Diversity, fairness, absence of discrimination: AI systems should consider different and distinct person competencies, and abilities while ensuring free access to these tools for all; with the proper security.
5. Social and environmental well-being. This aspect requires considering the impact on the environment and the social order, promoting AI only where its use can guarantee sustainable development; It is necessary to follow the principle of solution-neutrality.[107]
6. Responsibility, i.e., continuous verification of systems, both internally and externally.

There are three significant areas of critical importance to achieving a human-centric AI (1) Privacy and data ownership. (2) transparency, and explainability, and (3) fairness.[108] Although not ethical values in themselves, the concepts of transparency and explainability are critical AI challenges. Transparency is a mechanism to ensure the necessary information to make an informed choice.[109] The High-Level Expert Group on AI defines explainability as "*the ability to explain both the technical processes of an AI system and the related person decisions (for example, application areas of a system). Technical explainability requires that the decisions made by an AI system can be understood and traced by persons*."[110] AI should not increase explainability requirements per se. Several solutions can in practice ensure meaningful transparency and explainability: execution and

[107] Turilli, M., Vaccaro, A., & Taddeo, M. (2012). Internet neutrality: Ethical issues in the internet environment. *Philosophy & Solutions*, *25*(2), 133–151.

[108] Lepri, B., Oliver, N., & Pentland, A. (2021). Ethical machines: The human-centric use of artificial intelligence. *Science*, 102249.

[109] Another example, in the field of customer segmentation, is the possibility to increase the probability of being ranked as a high-income person by using an iOS device. According to the paper on the rise of fintech organizations—credit scoring using digital footprints, published by the National Bureau of Economic Research in July 2018, the difference in default rates between customers using iOS and Android is equivalent to the difference in default rates between a median credit score and the 80th percentile of the credit score. Bertrand & Kamenica (2017) document that owning an iOS device is one of the best predictors for being in the top quartile of the income distribution, obtaining the best results in each case.

[110] Independent High-Level Expert Group on Artificial Intelligence established by the European Commission, *Ethics Guidelines for Trustworthy AI*, 8 April 2019, 18.

documentation of the learning phase, tests, and simulations; implementation of back-testing procedures; alerts in case of unexpected outcomes, and so on.

Components of Artificial Intelligence

AI has several components. It is useful for banking 5.0 to analyze the most important of them.

A classification of AI components is the following[111]:

- Probabilistic reasoning

  Machine Learning. It is a set of algorithms used to make a system artificially intelligent, enabling it to recognize patterns from large datasets and apply past findings to new data. Machine learning can be divided into three categories[112]:
    - supervised learning,
    - unsupervised learning, and
    - reinforcement learning.

  Most current applications of machine learning involve supervised learning algorithms.[113]
    - Neural Networks. It is a type of algorithms that can also be considered a subfield of machine learning. It characterizes by using several layers of neural networks (algorithms that mimic a human brain) and requiring intense supervised or unsupervised learning.
    - Predictive Analytics. It combines data, statistical algorithms, and machine learning tools to find the likelihood of future outcomes based on historical data and improve the predictions' confiability.

- Computational logic.

[111] Krishnamoorthy, C. S., & Rajeev, S. (2018). *Artificial intelligence and expert systems for engineers*. CRC Press, Boca Raton, FL.

[112] When Should You Learn Machine Learning using C++? www.medium.com/ml2b/when-should-you-learn-machine-learning-using-c-6edd719f95ff.

[113] Richman, R. (2018, July). AI in actuarial science. *SSRN*. www.ssrn.com/abstract=3218082. Accessed 30 May 2020.

- Rule-Based Reasoning. It is a set of algorithms used to store and manipulate knowledge and interpret helpful information.
- Expert systems. It uses rules as knowledge representation. These rules are coded into the system in the form of if-then-else statements.[114] The main idea is to capture a human expert's knowledge in a specialized domain and embody it within a computer application. They are similar to rule-based reasoning.
- Constraint-Based Reasoning
- Automated Reasoning—This subfield focuses on logical deduction. It defines problem domains by facts, and rules and reasoning are applied to derive new rules and facts. It is possible to use automated reasoning systems to build theorem provers or obtain solutions that fit a set of constraints.

- Smart Interfaces

  - Natural Language
    - Natural Language Processing (NLP) and generation. This subfield is concerned with the interactions between computers and human (natural) languages. It aims for machines to read and understand human language. A sufficiently robust natural language processing system would enable the acquisition of knowledge directly from human-written sources. Some applications of NLP include information retrieval and question answering.
    - Natural Language Understanding (Sentimental Analysis, Conversational AI bots).
    - Automatic Translation
    - Text analytics (including grammar and style corrections).
    - GPT-3 (Generative Pre-Trained Transformer, created by OpenAI). It is a deep learning model that emulates the writing of human-like text.[115]
  - Chatbots

[114] AI in software testing: Rule-based testing vs. learning. www.tricentis.com/artificial-intelligence-software-testing/ai-approaches-rule-based-testing-vs-learning/. Accessed 20 January 2021.

[115] All, I. U. (2019). The future of banking. M4_v0.7.pdf (www.mudano.com). Accessed 20 January 2021.

- Computer Vision. It is the capability in support of a machine to see and visually sense the environment around it. Computer vision is concerned with the automatic extraction, analysis, and understanding of helpful information from a single image or a sequence of images.

- Smart Process Automation
    - Cognitive Technologies. These solutions mimic the functions of the person's brain through various means. Different from artificial general intelligence, cognitive solutions have specific goals. It includes cognitive search. This latter application collects, analyzes, and supplies meanings to distinct types of data, like person cognition to make decisions in complex situations.
    - Robotic Process Automation. Use of software robots to automate processes.
    - Robotics Motion and Manipulation. This subfield relates to control systems that let machines manage physical tasks like movement while sensing and adjusting to environment's change.

- Other Fields
    - Knowledge Representation. This field relates to the ability to represent abstract concepts about the world and the relationships between them. The idea is to convey information about the world in a form that a computer system can use to solve complex tasks such as deriving new relations between concepts or question answering.
    - These fields include planning and creativity, artificial general intelligence, and so on.

Machine Learning

Machine learning (ML) is an application of AI. It allows software applications to learn from experience without being explicitly programmed, and it is useful in predicting analysis.[116] Machine learning applications are not

[116] Choi, R. Y., Coyner, A. S., Kalpathy-Cramer, J., Chiang, M. F., & Campbell, J. P. (2020). Introduction to machine learning, neural networks, and deep learning. *Translational Vision Science & Solution*, *9*(2), 14–14.

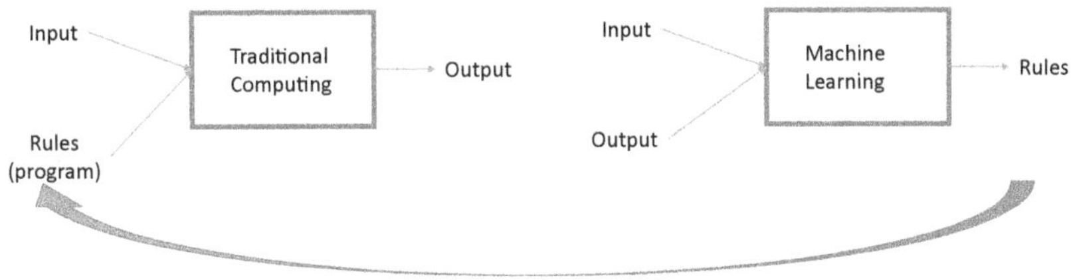

Fig. 8.7 Machine learning vs. traditional computing

programmed. They are trained, similarly to what happens in humans. This solution's basic principle is to build algorithms that can access data, find patterns, and use advanced statistical tools to predict the results and help make decisions in several areas (Fig. 8.7).

Machine learning enables computer programs automatically to improve their performance at some tasks through experience.[117] This solution connects with pattern recognition and statistical inference. Research on machine learning has focused on classification, developing models from a set of previously classified examples that can correctly categorize new cases from a similar population. Many banking problems fall under this category. Banking professionals need to assign a class label to an object, or a situation based on the specific values of a set of parameters so that the machine can learn. A typical example is credit scoring.

Machine Learning Architecture

Machine learning (ML) solutions include inductive-learning algorithms such as decision-tree induction and rule induction, instance-based learning, genetic algorithms, and Bayesian-learning algorithms.[118] Inductive learning is the most used in real-world application domains. Inductive-learning tools are fast compared to other applications and are

[117] Pham, D. T. & Afify, A. A. (2005). Machine-learning techniques and their applications in manufacturing. *Proceedings of the Institution of Mechanical Engineers, Part B: Journal of Engineering Manufacture, 219*(5), 395–412.

[118] Pham, D. T. & Afify, A. A. (2005). Machine-learning techniques and their applications in manufacturing. *Proceedings of the Institution of Mechanical Engineers, Part B: Journal of Engineering Manufacture, 219*(5), 395–412.

simple.[119] Inductive learning allows generating models easy to understand. This situation is critical to supply transparency to the solutions using AI.

Classification of machine learning applications is the following one:

- Shallow learning is based on the learning of data without using networking or relational details of the data.[120] The lack of links between the old and new data causes shallow learning programs to learn irrelevant details that can harm the systems or increase their size unnecessarily. The shallow learning methods are faster as compared to the deep learning methods. Machine learning methods of this type prove to be highly effective in various areas of cyber security.[121]
- Deep learning methods are an advanced version of machine learning methods.[122] Deep learning, as the name implies, is a precise method of learning. It ensures that only relevant information is extracted and used for system development and improvement.[123] These methods are time-consuming as they include various processes before learning is performed. These methods require more carefulness and ability of the developers.[124]

Each one of these categories can be of two types:

[119] Michalski, R. S. (1983). A theory and method of inductive learning. In *Machine learning* (pp. 83–134). Springer, Berlin/Heidelberg, Germany.

[120] Zhang, C., &Ma, Y. (2012). *Ensemble machine learning: Methods and applications*. Springer Science & Business Media, Cham. Switzerland.

[121] Brynjolfsson, E., & Mcafee, A. (2017). The business of artificial intelligence. *Harvard Business Review,* 1–20.

[122] Liermann, V., Li, S., & Schaudinnus, N. (2019). Deep learning: An introduction. In *The impact of digital transformation and FinTech on the finance professional* (pp. 305–340). Palgrave Macmillan, Cham, Switzerland.

[123] Apruzzese, G., Colajanni, M., Ferretti, L., Guido, A., & Marchetti, M. (2018). On the effectiveness of machine and deep learning for cyber security, in *2018 10th International Conference on Cyber Conflict (CyCon).*

[124] Goodfellow, T., Bengio, Y. & Courville, A. (2016). *Deep learning*. MIT Prsess, Cambridge, MA.

Yahya, O. H., Alrikabi, H., Aljazaery, I. A., & Engineering, B. (2020). Reducing the data rate in internet of things applications by using wireless sensor network. *International Journal of Interactive Mobile Technology, 16*(3), 107–116.

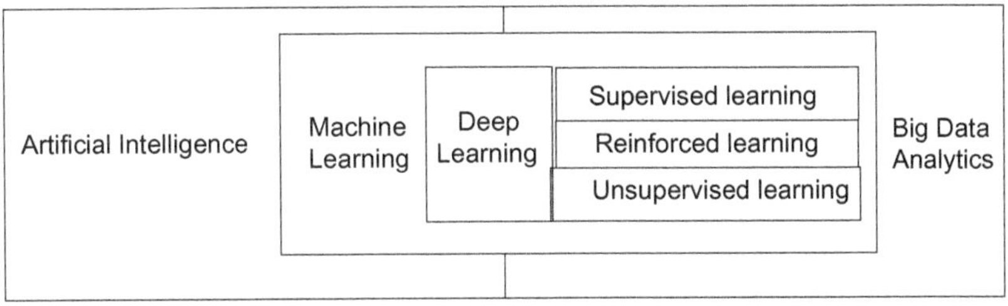

Fig. 8.8 AI, ML, and big data analytics

- Supervised algorithms require data professionals with machine learning skills to supply inputs and outputs. The data professionals should decide the variables, features, and models which should analyze. Once is completed all the settings; the algorithm will apply the learnings to new data.
- Unsupervised algorithms do not need the intervention of data professionals. They are applied in complex processing tasks. They use. deep learning to review data and arrive at rules.

Figure 8.9 shows a classification of machine learning solutions. Figure 8.8 shows some of these classifications and their relationships with other technologies graphically.[125]

Machine Learning in Banking 5.0

It is significant that machine learning uses the word "training" instead of "programming" when developing computer programs to perform thinking fast tasks. Machine learning "trains" an extensive statistical model designed to guess solutions to particular problems. This method requires substantial amounts of data and massive amounts of computing power to invert the matrices needed to "train" the computer model. With this new way of "programming" computers, virtual robots can perform and mimic humans in many mental tasks, like photo recognition, handwriting recognition, or language translation.

[125] Difference Between Machine Learning and Deep Learning. www.iamwire.com/2017/11/difference-between-machine-learning-and-deep-learning. Accessed 4 January 2021.

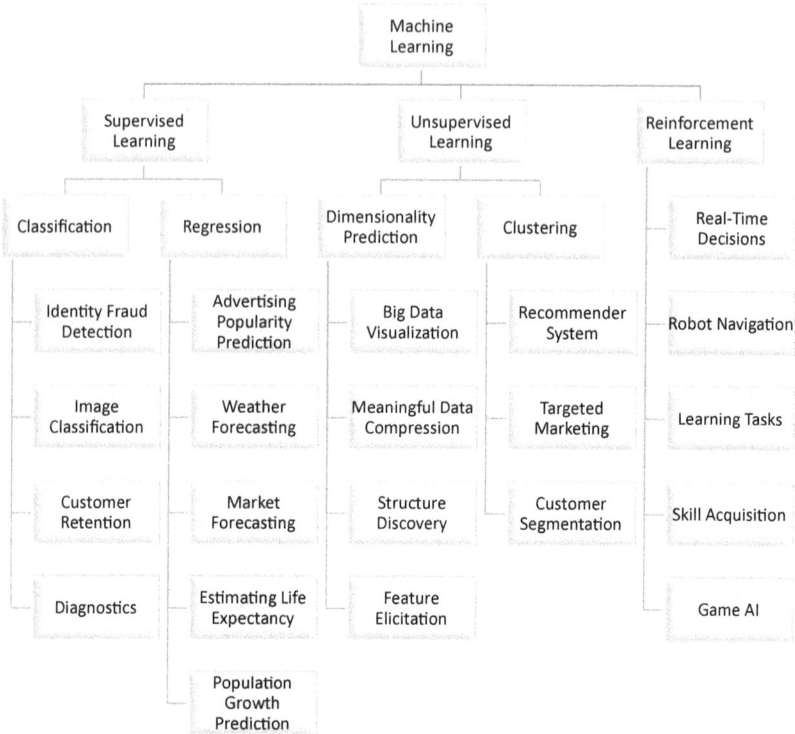

Fig. 8.9 Classification of machine learning

Many of the new mental abilities gained by computers with ML are helpful in office and service jobs. Many new service-sector tasks are more automatable now than previously with traditional ICT, which is one reason machine learning is more than simply better ICT.

Financial institutions have begun exploring and using ML in many ways to serve their customers better and meet increasingly demanding regulatory requirements.[126] Programs like smart business analytics show that machine learning can enable financial institutions to improve their

[126] Wall, L. D. (2018). Some financial regulatory implications of artificial intelligence. *Journal of Economics and Business*, *100*, 55–63.

decision-making power and get improved efficiency.[127] The machine learning methods can develop cyber security systems that can keep the data storage and process secure for financial institutions.

The principal areas in which ML (Machine Learning) can help are:

- Credit risk.
- Strategies for investing and order execution.
- Anti-money laundering.
- Know your customer.
- Cyber security.

ML can help in measuring credit risks. A financial institution that could find customers currently paying higher credit risk prices than is justified could gain profitable market share by offering similar customers lower price loans. Similarly, a financial institution that could find customers undercharged for credit risk could reduce their losses by charging them more or denying their loan requests.

Another use of ML is to develop strategies for investing and order execution.[128] Traditional electronic trading programs are designed to follow specific rules in certain market conditions. They must be reprogrammed when they meet new scenarios. This solution implies interruption. On the other hand, ML is dynamic: it can adapt to changing market conditions,[129] For example, by observing an investment, AI can evaluate how external factors can determine the success or the investment's failure. AI tracks stocks, exchange rate values, and a country's economy. It can predict and inform forthcoming threats.[130] ML is not entirely

[127] Injadat, M., Moubayed, A., Nassif, A. B., & Shami, A. (2021). Machine learning towards intelligent systems: Applications, challenges, and opportunities. *Artificial Intelligence Review*, 1–50.

[128] Huang, B., Huan, Y., Xu, L. D., Zheng, L., & Zou, Z. (2019). Automated trading systems statistical and machine learning methods and hardware implementation: A survey. *Enterprise Information Systems*, *13*(1), 132–144.

[129] www.investmentexecutive.com/newspaper_/building-your-business-newspaper/how-banks-are-harnessing-artificial-intelligence/. Accessed 25 February 2021.

[130] Christodoulou, P., Zinonos, Z., Carayannis, E. G., Chatzichristofis, S. A., & Christodoulou, K. (2021). Known unknowns in an era of technological and viral disruptions—Implications for theory, policy, and practice. et/11728/11735 Downloaded from HEPHAESTUS Repository, Neapolis University, Paphos, Cyprus.

autonomous. As with other AI platforms, humans should be able to overrule ML's investment decisions when necessary. Before that happens, ML must be able to explain its recommendations to a human supervisor. This feature is essential for an AI platform.

These machine learning tools not only can manage extensive databases and order the sequence of decisions. They often show better prediction accuracy than the traditional prediction methods. For example, JPMorgan uses ML to execute trades for its customers in equity markets.[131]

ML is coming to play an increasingly significant role in financial services. The market size for machine learning in 2016 was USD 61,34 million. It grows to USD 3.75 billion by 2021, with a CAGR of 43.7% from 2016 to 2021.[132]

Benefits and Challenges of Machine Learning

The application of deep learning tools might significantly improve lending decisions. An ML algorithm was able to accurately predict 88.41% of financial institution customers' online banking adoption profile, 70.11% of the type of digital use of online banking, 70.01% of the variety of digital use of mobile banking, 85% of debit (credit) card adoption, and 76.14% of non-financial institution payment instruments adoption.[133] The standard ordered logit and simple logit models were able to accurately predict 79.27% of financial institution customers' online banking adoption, 55.01% of the variety of digital use of online banking, 59.57% of the type of digital use of mobile banking, 84.23% of debt (credit) card adoption, and 73.46% of non-financial institution payment methods adoption.

Lack of transparency in the ML models is a potential challenge. On the other side, AI can help supervisors find potential violations and help regulators better predict the impact of regulation changes.[134] A lending algorithm could be found in violation of this prohibition even

[131] www.ft.com/content/16b8ffb6-7161-11e7-aca6-c6bd07df1a3c. Accessed 20 January 2021.

[132] www.marketsandmarkets.com. Accessed 10 October 2020.

[133] Valverde, S. C., & Fernández, F. R. (2020). Financial digitalization: Banks, Fintech, Bigtech, and consumers. *Journal of Financial Management, Markets and Institutions*, *8*(01), 2040001.

[134] Wall, L. D. (2018). Some financial regulatory implications of artificial intelligence. *Journal of Economics and Business*, *100*, 55–63.

if the algorithm does not directly use any of the prohibited categories but uses data that may be highly correlated with protected classes, such as grammatical errors in the lending applications.[135] The lack of transparency could become an even more difficult problem in the European Union (EU). The General Data Protection Regulation gives EU citizens the right to receive explanations for decisions based solely on automated processing.[136] Various efforts are underway to mitigate the lack of transparency and make ML results more transparent.[137]

ML for lending raises other potential problems. The data used to train the machine learning algorithm may not represent the range of customers that will apply for the loans. In this situation, these methods can lead to a significant error rate. Another problem is that as people learn how the model works, the higher risk borrowers can mimic lower risk borrowers' behavior before applying for a loan.

One concern on the increased use of machine learning in investment advising and trading is that the application of ML could ease more trading errors. A deeper problem is that it could lead to excess volatility or increase pro-cyclicality due to herding.[138] The concern is that the underlying algorithms could be too sensitive to price moves or that the algorithms may produce highly correlated recommendations.

Cognitive Solutions

Cognitive solutions can perform and augment actions to help people carry out tasks and decisions that need personal intelligence to solve, such as planning, reasoning from partial or uncertain information, and learning. These technologies can increase effectiveness and reduce person involvement by bringing new insights and working modes.

[135] Petrasic, K., Saul, B., Greig, J., & Bornfreund, M. (2017), Algorithms and bias: What lenders need to know, white and case. www.whitecase.com/publications/insight/algorithms-and-bias-what-lenders-needknow. Accessed 20 January 2020.

[136] Goodman, B., & Flaxman, S. (2017). European Union regulations on algorithmic decision-making and a right to explanation. *AI Magazine*, *38*(3), 50–57.

[137] Wall, L. D. (2018). Some financial regulatory implications of artificial intelligence. *Journal of Economics and Business*, *100*, 55–63.

[138] Carney, M. (2017, January). The promise of Fintech—Something new under the sun. In *Speech at Deutsche Bundesbank G20 Conference, by Bank of England Governor Mark Carney, January 25th.*

Although AI solutions and cognitive computing seem similar, there are two main differences between them. One is that cognitive computing does not try to mimic personal thought processes. A sound cognitive computing application is the best possible algorithms for solving a given problem. Another is that cognitive computing technologies only help persons make decisions, but the application itself does not make decisions alone.

Applying cognitive solutions is still in the early stage. Early adopters achieved exciting benefits. Consequently, more organizations are starting to realize the importance of cognitive solutions. Cognitive solutions have been used in different organization areas, such as product recommendations, pricing optimization, and fraud detection. The global cognitive solution market is expected to grow at a Compound annual growth rate (CAGR) of 34.2% and is estimated to reach USD 36 billion by 2023.[139]

Cognitive Solution Architecture

The Cognitive Computing Consortium has recommended four features for cognitive solutions.[140] Cognitive solutions should:

- Mimic the brain's ability to learn and adapt from the environment, which needs a connected system that can understand goals and collect data dynamically.
- Interact all the elements available and use natural language processing and deep learning to understand inputs and then supply relevant solutions.
- Be iterative and stateful. Cognitive systems need to store earlier interaction records and return the relevant information for the specific application in a short time. This solution requires high data governance and assurance that the system is always provided with updated and reliable data.
- Understand, find, and extract contextual elements such as meaning, time, location, user's profile, process, task, and goals.

[139] www.globenewswire.com/news-release/2020/06/11/2047035/0/en/The-Global-Cognitive-Computing-Market-is-expected-to-grow-from-USD-7-902-89-Million-in-2019-to-USD-13-942-38-Million-by-the-end-of-2025-at-a-Compound-Annual-Growth-Rate-CAGR-of-9-9.html. Accessed 20 January 2021.

[140] www.cognitivecomputingconsortium.com/. Accessed 28 November 2020.

Figure 8.10 shows the process of cognitive solutions.

It is possible to group the characteristics of cognitive solutions into five "Ps" categories[141]:

- Perceive: Understand the environment around the applications and inputs coming from sensors. Perception-related cognitive solutions include: image and object recognition and classification, natural language processing and generation, unstructured text and information processing, robotic sensors, and Internet of things (IoT) signal processing, and other forms of perceptual computing.
- Predict: Understand patterns in such a way as to be able to predict what will happen next and learn from different iterations to improve the overall performance of the system.
- Plan: Use what learned and perceived to make decisions and plan the next steps. Planning focused cognitive solutions include decision-making models and methods that try to mimic how persons make decisions.
- Perform: Implement the solutions found using virtual robots.
- Peek: Monitor the results and continuously improve.

Cognitive search delivers contextually aware information relevant to the user's information quest by understanding the user's intent and the patterns and relationships within the aggregated data.[142]

Big Data's 9Vs characteristics: (Veracity, Variety, Velocity, Volume, Validity, Variability, Volatility, Visualization, and Value) present significant opportunities for rich insights. Traditional methods have difficulty in getting such insights. Organizations suffer from slow and ineffective decisions resulting from limited insights due to massive dark data of diverse formats trapped in the data silos.

Cognitive search enables knowledge discovery that is highly relevant to customers' intent.[143] It does this by deriving conceptual insights from contextual data. It recognizes patterns and relationships within any type of

[141] Walch, K. (2019, December). Why cognitive solution may be a better term than artificial intelligence. *Forbes*.

[142] www.microfocus.com/en-us/what-is/cognitive-search. Accessed 24 October 2020.

[143] What Is Cognitive Search? | Micro Focus. www.microfocus.com/en-us/what-is/cognitive-search. Accessed 20 January 2021.

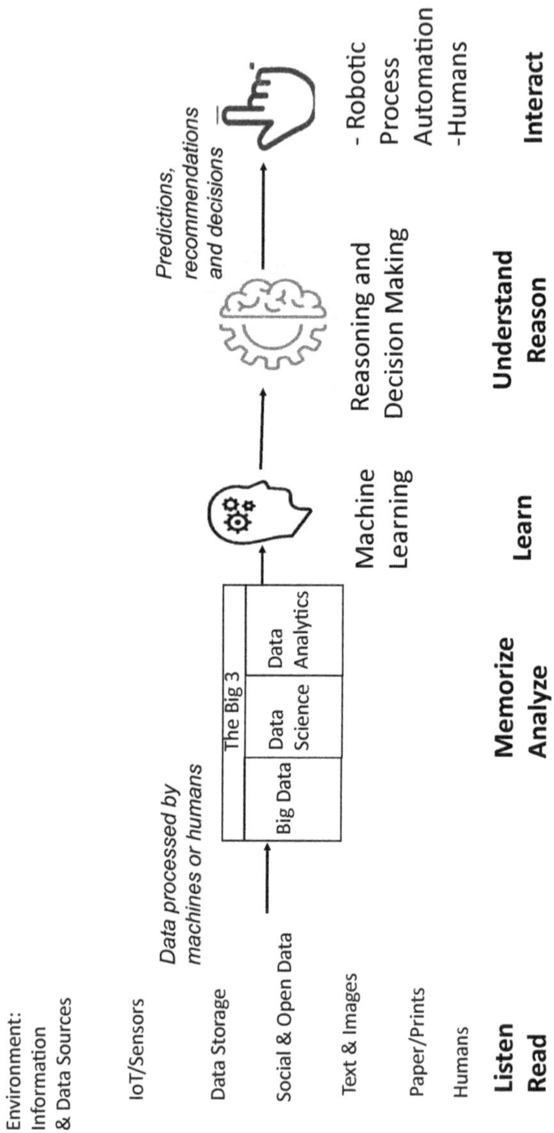

Fig. 8.10 Cognitive solutions

information—structured or unstructured, written or spoken. Like Natural language processing (NLP), this ability to understand data can automate manual operations. This tool can extract meaning and perform proper actions in real time. Unlike NLP, which focuses solely on linguistics, cognitive search follows a language-independent, statistical approach to understanding hidden patterns in the data. Cognitive search can access diverse data types (text, video, image, and audio) and sources (outside and inside the institution). The underlying content analytics solution is based upon machine learning, continuously learning, and adapting as more data becomes available to achieve the best possible precision.

Cognitive Solutions in Banking 5.0

Some goals of the applications of cognitive solutions in banking are[144]:

- Replace the operators in complex repetitive banking tasks.
- Supply integrated support in the acquisition of new customers.
- Automatically create new business models, evaluate customers, and set prices:
- Manage emergencies or disasters due to difficulties in banking from a specific event or territory.
- Integrate with the robots to implement automated and integrated solutions to support the banking processes using Robotic process automation (RPA).[145]

The possibility to use cognitive banking from mobile phones and tablets can further help its use[146]:

[144] Laudon, K. C., & Laudon, J. P. (2015). *Management information systems*. Pearson. Upper Saddle River, NJ.

[145] Madakam, S. Holmukhe, R. M. & Jaiswal, D. K. (2019). The future digital work force: Robotic process automation (RPA). *JISTEM-Journal of Information Systems and Solution Management*, *16*.

Syed, R., Suriadi, S., Adams, M., Bandara, W., Leemans, S. J., Ouyang, C., & Reijers, H. A. (2020). Robotic process automation: Contemporary themes and challenges. *Computers in Industry*, *115*, 103162.

[146] Balasubramanian, R., Libarikian, A., & McElhaney, D. (2018). Insurance 2030—The impact of AI on the future of insurance. *McKinsey & Financial Institution.*

- Allow navigating through multiple accesses and banking applications.
- Recommend related products in the best possible way to the demands by adding transparency to the operator work.
- Recommend actions on selecting banking services from catalogs.
- Allow interacting in natural language for improved user experience.

Some financial institutions are applying cognitive tools and using these solutions for product recommendations, pricing optimization, fraud detection, and so on. Some financial institutions are developing conversational AI platforms for automated customer service and sales support.

An investigation of over one hundred organizations, which were using cognitive solutions, showed that these applications are usually applied in three areas which are product, process, and insight.[147]

1. Embedding cognitive solutions into organizations' products and services. The application of this action can increase the organization's efficiency and create more value.
2. Enabling internal processesautomation with cognitive solutions. Operators' work can improve by applying cognitive solutions. These solutions can replace some repetitive jobs for high-level subject-matter experts.
3. Learning from the information. Cognitive solutions can create insights from large and complex data sets to make high-quality forecasts from operational data. With natural language processing tools, persons can analyze large unstructured textual information.

Cognitive analytics[148] extends the scope of the analyzes to include "implicit knowledge" and perspectives that may be represented by lexicons, taxonomics, models, or rules-based computations tailored to the

[147] Schatsky, D., Muraskin, C., & Gurumurthy, R. (2015). Cognitive technologies: The real opportunities for business. *Deloitte Review*, *16*, 115–129.

[148] Gudivada, V. N., Irfan, M. T., Fathi, E., & Rao, D. L. (2016). Cognitive analytics: Going beyond big data analytics and machine learning. In *Handbook of statistics* (Vol. 35, pp. 169–205). Elsevier, Amsterdam, Netherlands.

areas of interest represented by the data in a knowledge management system.[149]

Cognitive analytics can help to recommend a financial institution using (un)structured data (semantic analytics), speech processing (context-sensitive dialogue).[150] Use cases are:

- Next-best action (machine learning).
- Automatic advisor support/augmented 360° customer perspective.
- AI-based advisory services and interested-party management.

Bbva

BBVA Compass bank is one of the typical examples of applications of cognitive tools. Using a social media sentiment monitoring technique, the bank can track and check customers' comments about the financial institution and its competitors to make adaptable strategies to supply better customer service and make better market plan.

BBVA Compass Financial Tools available to customers on mobiles include[151]:

- Budgets: A chart shows customers' monthly budgets. Budget categories change color from green to yellow and red if the customer exceeds set spending limits.
- Spending: Customers can see the percentages of their spending in each transaction category. If they tap on a section, they will see how much they spent in each category.
- Accounts: Allows customers to link and manage their external financial reports to view their full economic life in one place easily.

[149] Gudivada, V. N., Irfan, M. T., Fathi, E., & Rao, D. L. (2016). Cognitive analytics: Going beyond big data analytics and machine learning. In *Handbook of statistics* (Vol. 35, pp. 169–205). Elsevier, Amsterdam, Netherlands.

[150] Pertlweiser, M. (2016, September). *For the banking of the future—Deutsche Bank's digital factory*. Deutsche Bank Private, Wealth and Commercial Client. Frankfurt, Germany.

[151] www.bbva.com/en/bbva-compass-financial-tools-success-via-aggregation/. Accessed 24 October 2020.

Benefits and Challenges of Cognitive Solutions

Cognitive solutions enhance competitive advantages and supply benefits from an economic point of view. So attractive are these solutions in banking 5.0: that people start talking about cognitive banking.[152] It is another step in the banking 5.0 transformation (Fig. 8.10).

The benefits associated with cognitive banking are several[153]:

- Increasing workforce productivity and reduction of the need for their education and training.
- Logging on to a more abundant and significant set of data.
- Allowing the organization to discover hidden information.
- Automating repetitive tasks.
- Improving credit scoring timings and their accuracy.
- Increasing efficiency in supplying customized information suited to circumstances.

Apart from major financial institutions, many new financial institutions realize the benefits that cognitive solutions can bring. They are investing in them to improve and develop better services and gain competitive advantages.[154]

According to IBM's report,[155] the early adopters believe cognitive capabilities play a critical role in their business growth. Sixty-five percent of early adopters view that these solutions are crucial to their organization's strategy and success. Fifty-eight percent say cognitive solutions are an essential element of their organization's digital transformation. About half of early adopters have already gained competitive advantages and achieved excellent value. According to the early feedbacks, applying

[152] Schoenherr, T. (2018). System capability and solution. *CPSM Study Guide*, 3rd.

[153] www.mckinsey.com/featured-insights/future-of-work#. Accessed 28 November 2020.

[154] www2.deloitte.com/content/dam/Deloitte/pt/Documents/tech-trends/TechTrends2020.pdf. Accessed 24 October 2020.

[155] www.globenewswire.com/news-release/2020/06/11/2047035/0/en/The-Global-Cognitive-Computing-Market-is-expected-to-grow-from-USD-7-902-89-Million-in-2019-to-USD-13-942-38-Million-by-the-end-of-2025-at-a-Compound-Annual-Growth-Rate-CAGR-of-9-9.html. Accessed 20 January 2021.

cognitive solutions brought competitive benefits and success to their organization. Half of them believe cognitive solutions will be a "must-have" to remain competitive in the next few years.[156]

Cognitive solutions have some limitations and challenges. The potential risks are insufficient skills, high solution costs, and security concerns. According to IBM's Cognitive Benefit Global Market Report, the challenges in applying cognitive solutions are several: 46% of early adopters lack a strategic approach to cognitive solutions and struggle to define a roadmap to implement cognitive solutions.[157] Only 7% shows that they have a comprehensive, financial institution-wide strategy. There are 41% early adopters to have developed a broader strategy. Forty percent of early adopters are taking a more tactical approach based on specific projects.

Person interventions in the application of these solutions are essential for risk analysis and final decision-making. Cognitive systems need a careful training data process and need highly customized or innovative applications (Fig. 8.11). These applications may cause unpredictable costs and timelines. Another challenge is security and privacy. Access to data is easy and vulnerable for organizations, so data security is an essential aspect to consider.

The application of cognitive solutions challenges employees and operations. Organizations that implement cognitive solutions need to redesign the tasks, management practices, and goals because some of these technologies can eliminate or change the jobs done by their employees.

Natural Language Processing

Natural language processing (NLP) is a branch of AI that helps computers understand, interpret, and manipulate languages. It allows turning speech, text, and customer service queries into structured and searchable data.

[156] www.globenewswire.com/news-release/2020/06/11/2047035/0/en/The-Global-Cognitive-Computing-Market-is-expected-to-grow-from-USD-7-902-89-Million-in-2019-to-USD-13-942-38-Million-by-the-end-of-2025-at-a-Compound-Annual-Growth-Rate-CAGR-of-9-9.html. Accessed 20 January 2021.

[157] www.ibm.com/watson/advantage-reports/market-report.html. Accessed 3 October 2020.

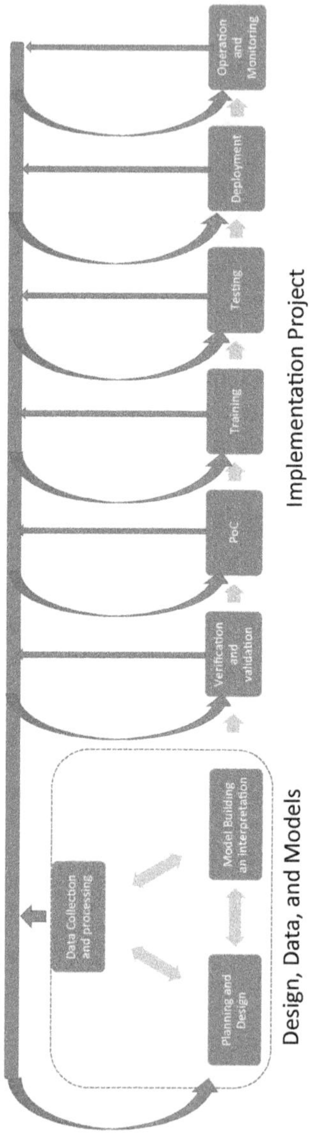

Fig. 8.11 Cognitive solution life cycle (Elaboration of the author on the AIGO framework)

Voice interaction with computers is one of the most exciting developments connected with banking 5.0 since it dramatically improves the robot–person collaboration and makes it more natural.[158]

A subfield of NLP called natural language understanding (NLU) is an exciting development.[159] NLU has interesting potential in cognitive applications.[160] It is much more than language processing and interpretation. It generates its well-formed personal language. The road of transforming NLP to NLU supplies insights and implications for organizations and customers.

Natural Language Processing Architecture

As the text and voice-based data vary broadly, natural language processing needs to apply many different technologies to interpret individual languages. These technologies include statistical-based machine learning methods and rule-based algorithmic approaches. These solutions break down language into several parts and try to understand the connections between these parts. Once they completed this step, they find out when these parts combine and how to understand meanings. This process usually combines with text analytics to count and categorize words and extract meanings from a large amount of content.

Natural Language Processing in Banking 5.0

Financial institutions can apply natural language tools to any function that processes large volumes of text or speech data. There are several applications of this type in compliance, risk management, or transaction execution.

Natural language processing (NLP) supports document processing, analysis, and customer service activities. Potential applications include[161]:

[158] Wang, L., Gao, R., Váncza, J., Krüger, J., Wang, X. V., Makris, S., & Chryssolouris, G. (2019). Symbiotic human–robot collaborative assembly. *CIRP Annals, 68*(2), 701–726.

[159] Singh, A., Ramasubramanian, K., & Shivam, S. (2019). *Building an enterprise chatbot: Work with protected enterprise data using open-source frameworks*. Apress, New York, NY.

[160] Rajurkar, T., Kadam, A., Ingle, P., Yadav, S., & Pradhan, M. (2020, July). Open banking using voice enabled personal assistants. *International Journal for Research, 8*(7).

[161] www.towardsdatascience.com/natural-language-processing-in-banking-current-uses-7fbbaee837de. Accessed 28 November 2020.

- Intelligent document search: finding relevant information in large volumes of original or scanned documents.
- Investment analysis: automating the routine analysis of earnings reports and news so that analysts can focus on alpha generation.[162]
- Customer service and insights: deploying chatbots to answer customer queries and understand customer needs.

The application of these solutions takes place in these ways[163]:

- Natural language processing can help to harness the valuable data from emails, social media, e-commerce, and browsing behaviors to do keyword matching and find the meaning of a word in a sentence.
- For assuring customer delight, many financial institutions analyze customer call recordings and design chatbots to respond and solve problems for the customers. Another use case is answering requests and questions received by persons in a natural language. An example of an application of NLP is the automatic analysis of emails and their routing to a suitable department in the financial institution.
- Monitoring reputation is essential for a financial institution to assure customer trust. Using natural language processing by applying sentiment analysis and co-reference[164] resolution, organizations can search in the internet about customer reviews of their brand and services.

Benefits and Challenges of Natural Language Processing

Natural language processing can automate routine document analysis, research, and customer service.[165] Cost savings are just one part of the potential benefits. By analyzing text and speech data in copious quantities faster and extracting more actionable insights on customers and the market, financial institutions can serve customers better and take corrective actions. The potential for a larger market share and income are the real difference makers.

[162] www.investopedia.com/terms/a/alpha.asp. Accessed 28 November 2020.

[163] www.marketingaiinstitute.com/blog/ai-in-advertising. Accessed 24 October 2020.

[164] www.thefreedictionary.com/coreference. Accessed 28 November 2020.

[165] www.towardsdatascience.com/natural-language-processing-in-banking-current-uses-7fbbaee837de. Accessed 28 November 2020.

Neural Networks
An Artificial neural network (ANN) is a machine learning algorithm mimicking a biological neural network.[8,9,21] An ANN has nodes that communicate with other nodes via connections. Connections between nodes in an ANN are weighted based upon their ability to supply the desired outcome1.

Neural Network Architecture
There are many types of neural networks:

The most used network topologies are the following[166]:

- Layered.
- Completely connected.

Networks of the first category have neurons subdivided into layers.[167] If the connections are only in one direction (that is, each neuron receives inputs from the earlier layer and sends output to the following layer), they are called feedforward networks. Otherwise, if 'loops' are allowed, the network is called a recurrent network. Completely connected networks, on the other hand, have neurons that are all connected.

Neural Network in Banking 5.0
There are several applications of neural networks in financial products and services.[168] One of the central banking areas that has been affected by neural networks is trading and financial forecasting. Neural networks

[166] Angelini, E., di Tollo, G., & Roli, A. (2008). A neural network approach for credit risk evaluation. *The Quarterly Review of Economics and Finance*, *48*(4), 733–755.

[167] Angelini, E., di Tollo, G., & Roli, A. (2008). A neural network approach for credit risk evaluation. *The Quarterly Review of Economics and Finance*, *48*(4), 733–755.

[168] Smith, K. A., & Gupta, J. N. (2000). Neural networks in business: Techniques and applications for the operations researcher. *Computers & Operations Research*, *27*(11–12), 1023–1044.

have been applied very successfully to problems like derivative securities pricing and hedging,[169] futures price forecasting,[170] exchange rate forecasting,[171] and stock performance and selection prediction.[172]

Neural networks can improve many areas of financial services. For many years, financial institutions have used credit scoring methods and tools to find which loan applicants they should finance. Traditionally, statistical tools have driven this type of software. Neural networks can be the underlying infrastructure driving the decision-making.[173] Hecht-Nielson Co. has developed a credit scoring system that increased profitability by 27% by correctly finding acceptable credit risks and low credit risks.[174] Neural networks have been successful in learning to predict corporate bankruptcy. The Basel Committee on Banking Supervision proposes a capital adequacy framework that allows banks to compute their banking books' capital requirements using internal assessments of key risk drivers.[175]

[169] Hutchinson, J. M., Lo, A. W., & Poggio, T. (1994). A non-parametric approach to pricing and hedging derivative securities via learning networks. *The Journal of Finance*, XLIX, 851–889.

[170] Grudnitski, G., & Osburn, L. (1993). Forecasting S&P and gold futures prices: An application of neural networks. *The Journal of Futures Markets, 13*, 631–643.

[171] Leung, M. T., Chen, A. S., & Daouk, H. (2000). Forecasting exchange rates using general regression neural networks. *Computers and Operations Research, 27*(11–12), 1093–1110.

[172] Barr, D. S., & Mani, G. (1994). Using neural nets to manage investments. *AI Expert, 9*, 6–21.

Ryzanowski, L., Galler, M., & Wright, D. W. (1993). Using artificial neural networks to pick stocks. *Financial Analysts Journal, 49*, 21–27.

Motiwalla, M., & Wahab, M. (2000). Predictable variation and profitable trading of U.S. equities: A trading simulation using neural networks. *Computers and Operations Research*, 27(11–12), 1111–1129.

Swales, G. S., & Yoon, Y. (1992). Applying artificial neural networks to investment analysis. *Financial Analysts Journal, 48*, 78–80.

[173] Jensen, H. L. (1992). Using neural networks for credit scoring. *Managerial Finance*, 15–26.

West, D. (2000). Neural network credit scoring models. *Computers and Operations Research, 27*(11–12), 1131–1152.

[174] Harston, C. T. (1990). Business with neural networks. In Maren, A., Harston, C., Pap, R. (Eds.), *Handbook of neural computing applications*. Academic Press, Fribourg, Switzerland.

[175] Angelini, E., di Tollo, G., & Roli, A. (2008). A neural network approach for credit risk evaluation. *The Quarterly Review of Economics and Finance, 48*(4), 733–755.

It is necessary to have systems to assess credit risk. Neural network solutions are promising.[176] It is possible to use two neural architectures to classify borrowers into two distinct classes: *in bonis* and default.[177] The system needs to be trained and tested on data specific to the application examined. One of the methods developed is based on a classical feedforward neural network, while the other with a unique purpose architecture. In both cases, results show that the approach is highly effective and leads to a system able to classify the inputs with a low error rate, provided that careful data analysis, data pre-processing, and training are performed.

Financial fraud detection is another important application area of neural networks in financial services. Visa International has an operational fraud detection systembased upon a neural network and runs in five Canadian and ten USA financial institutions.[178] Comparing legitimate card use with known fraud cases can train the neural network to detect fraudulent activity. The system saved Visa International an estimated USD 40 million within its first six months of operation.[179] Neural networks have been used in the validation of financial institution signatures,[180] finding forgeries significantly better than human experts.

Another example of an application of neural networks in banking is future-exposure modeling. This situation is the leading block in current valuation-adjustment models; portfolio valuation, and risk determination. Calculations must be fast and correct. Traditional approaches do not meet these goals simultaneously. A successful neural-network approach can[181]:

- Perform portfolio evaluation and risk calculations.
- Train the neural networks.
- Use differential regularization to optimize accuracy for both pricing and risks while achieving fast training.

[176] A neural network approach for credit risk evaluation. www.sciencedirect.com/science/article/pii/S1062976907000762. Accessed 20 January 2021.

[177] Angelini, E., di Tollo, G., & Roli, A. (2008). A neural network approach for credit risk evaluation. *The Quarterly Review of Economics and Finance*, *48*(4), 733–755.

[178] Goonatilake, S., Treleaven, P. (1005). *Intelligent systems for finance and business*. John Wiley & Sons, Chichester, UK.

[179] Holder, V. (1995, February). War on suspicious payments. *Financial Times*.

[180] Francett, B. (1989). Neural nets arrive. *Computer Decisions*, 58–62.

[181] Angelini, E., di Tollo, G., & Roli, A. (2008). A neural network approach for credit risk evaluation. *The Quarterly Review of Economics and Finance*, *48*(4), 733–755.

Neural networks can help in wealth creation. Neural networks have been used to model the relationships between corporate strategy, short-run financial health, and an organization's performance.[182] This situation is a promising new area of application.

Benefits and Challenges of Neural Networks

The neural network data analysis adds accuracy, processing speed, fault tolerance, latency, performance, volume, and scalability.[183] It is creating analytics from the available data aids in prioritizing information and supply its business value, Neural networks in turn, help in combating fighting and mitigate potential risks.

Neural networks' popularity lies in information processing characteristics of learning power, high parallelism, fault tolerance, nonlinearity, noise tolerance, and generalization capabilities. The critical issues for developing neural network solutions are data analyzing and processing.[184]

Rule-Based Reasoning or Expert Systems[185]

Rule-based reasoning or expert systems are a particular type of reasoning which uses "if–then-else" rule statements. Rules are simple patterns. An inference engine searches for ways in the rules that match patterns in the data. The "if" means "when the condition is true," the "then" means "take action A," and the "else" means "when the condition is not true take action B."[186]

[182] St. John, C. H., Balakrishnan, N., Fiet, J. O. (2000). Modeling the relationship between corporate strategy and wealth creation using neural networks. *Computers and Operations Research*, *27*(11–12), 1077–1092.

[183] Abiodun, O. I., Jantan, A., Omolara, A. E., Dada, K. V., Mohamed, N. A., & Arshad, H. (2018). State-of-the-art in artificial neural network applications: A survey. *Heliyon*, *4*(11), e00938.

[184] Fletcher, D., & Goss, E. (1993). Forecasting with neural networks: An application using bankruptcy data. *Information & Management, 24*, 159–167.

Udo, G. (1993). Neural network performance on the bankruptcy classification problem. *Computers & Industrial Engineering*, *25*, 377–380.

Wilson, R., & Sharda, R. (1997), Business failure prediction using neural networks. In *Encyclopedia of computer science and solution* (Vol. 37, no. 22, pp. 193–204). Marcel Dekker, New York, NY.

[185] www.igi-global.com/dictionary/rule-based-reasoning/47486. Accessed 18 November 2020.

[186] www.tele9752.wikia.org/wiki/XxUH. Accessed 18 November 2020.

Rules can be forward-chaining, known as data-driven reasoning, because they start with data or facts and look for rules that can help reach that goal until a conclusion is reached. Rules can be backward-chaining, known as goal-driven reasoning since they start with a goal and look for rules which can help in reaching that goal until a conclusion is reached.[187] Expert systems are old solutions of AI mainly used in the past. There are several applications in banking.[188]

Computer Vision

Computer vision is the field of study on how computer applications read and understand digital images and videos.[189] Computer vision covers all tasks performed by biological vision and brain systems. This capability includes seeing or sensing a visual stimulus, working to understanding what is seen, and getting complex information into a form that other processes can use.[190] This interdisciplinary field simulates and automates a person's vision systems using sensors, computers, and machine learning techniques.

Many examples of computer vision can be applied to any area where a computer needs to "see" its surroundings. Examples of computer vision are facial recognition for security reasons.

Big Data Analytics

It is a complex process to examine large and varied data sets or perform big data analytics to uncover relevant information such as market trends, hidden patterns, customer preferences, and other aspects. All this information helps in making better decisions. Big data analytics allows to analyze a large amount of data, gather them from various sources, and get answers from it instantly.[191]

[187] What is rule-based reasoning. www.synotix.home.xs4all.nl/robbieng/docs/inference engine.doc. Accessed 20 January 2021.

[188] Chorafas, D. N., Steinmann, H., & Steinman, H. (2016). *Expert systems in banking: A guide for senior managers*. Springer, Cham, Switzerland.

[189] www.deepai.org/machine-learning-glossary-and-terms/computer-vision. Accessed 8 January 2021.

[190] Computer Vision Definition. www.deepai.org/machine-learning-glossary-and-terms/computer-vision. Accessed 20 January 2021.

[191] Madhavan, A. N. (2016). Exchange-traded funds and the new dynamics of investing. Oxford University Press, New York, NY.

Big data analytics is an advanced solution. It is getting more important in financial services. Most financial institutions have a large amount of valuable data. It is essential to understand the potential value of these data. It is necessary to harness these data and find new opportunities for the organization.

Specialized analytics systems and computing systems drive big data analytics. Thanks to them, financial institutions can gain many benefits, such as making smarter banking moves, improving marketing and operations, offering better customer service, and achieving higher margins and competitive benefits.

Big data analytics usually include data from internal and external sources, such as internet data, social media data, web server logs, survey responses, and customers' data offered by third-party information services providers. Subject-matter experts can analyze these data by using big data analytics tools to predict and simulate the situation to help organizations to make better decisions.

According to a 2019 IDC publication, the total volume of digital data will increase substantially.[192] More than a quarter of the digital data are transmitted in real time. Among these data, more than 95% is generated by connected objects.

Big Data Analytics Architecture

Big data analytics may require the processing of vast amounts of data.[193] Big data analytics can serve as a basis for defining strategy and assessing different customers' risks for several categories.[194] Master data is gathered, cleaned, and stored.[195] Reliable master data is crucial for several applications.[196] In short, big data analytics is a powerful tool that makes

[192] www.idc.com/getdoc.jsp?containerId=TEA003093&pageNumber=0&pageSize=10. Accessed 21 March 2020.

[193] McAfee, A., Brynjolfsson, E., Davenport, T. H., Patil, D. J., & Barton, D. (2012). Big data: The management revolution. *Harvard Business Review, 90*(10), 60–68.

[194] Capgemini. (2018). Digital insurance Research 2018: Uncovering the solutions that bring you forward. www.capgemini.com/nl-nl/wp-content/uploads/sites/7/2018/10/CapgeminiDigital-insurance-Research-2018_web-version1.pdf. Accessed 24 July 2019.

[195] Berson, A., & Dubov, L. (2007). Master data management and customer data integration for a global enterprise: McGraw-Hill, Inc. Accessed 24 July 2019.

[196] Capgemini. (2018). Digital insurance Research 2018: Uncovering the solutions that bring you forward. www.capgemini.com/nl-nl/wp-content/uploads/sites/7/2018/10/CapgeminiDigital-insurance-Research-2018_web-version1.pdf. Accessed 24 July 2019.

things easier in various fields. Using big data analytics, financial institutions can deal with the data more smartly and supply more new opportunities to exploit.

Big data analytics is characterized by the so-called nine "V"[197]:

- Volume: there should be a (relatively) high amount of data.
- Variety: there should be data of all types.
- Velocity or speed: at which data are generated and the speed they move in the value network.
- Veracity is the accuracy or reliability of the information and decisions arising from there.
- Value: the data should be able to add value,
- Validity means that the data is correct and correct for the intended use.
- Variability: The data flow may be highly inconsistent. It might have periodic peaks, daily, seasonal, and event-triggered peak data loads.[198] These variations can be challenging to manage, especially with unstructured data involved.
- Volatility is based on the retention period. Once the retention period expires, data are usually destroyed.
- Visualization means complex graphs that can include several variables of data while understandable and readable.

Integrated analytics (IA) can analyze many data by applying multidimensional layers and statistical analysis criteria.[199] These analyzes allow moving from primary data to information and information to knowledge through combination processes, statistical inference,[200] and multivariate

[197]Oweis, N. E., Owais, S. S., George, W., Suliman, M. G., & Snášel, V. (2015). A survey on big data, mining:(tools, techniques, applications and notable uses). In *Intelligent data analysis and applications* (pp. 109–119). Springer, Cham, Switzerland.

[198]Extract Five Categories CPIVW from the 9V's. www.thesai.org/Downloads/Volume 7No3/Paper_37-Extract_Five_Categories_CPIVW.pdf. Accessed 20 January 2021.

[199]Chen, Q., Hsu, M., & Liu, R. (2009, August). Extend UDF solution for integrated analytics. In *International Conference on Data Warehousing and Knowledge Discovery* (pp. 256–270). Springer, Berlin/Heidelberg, Germany.

[200]Casella, G., & Berger, R. L. (2002). *Statistical inference* (Vol. 2). Duxbury, Pacific Grove, CA.

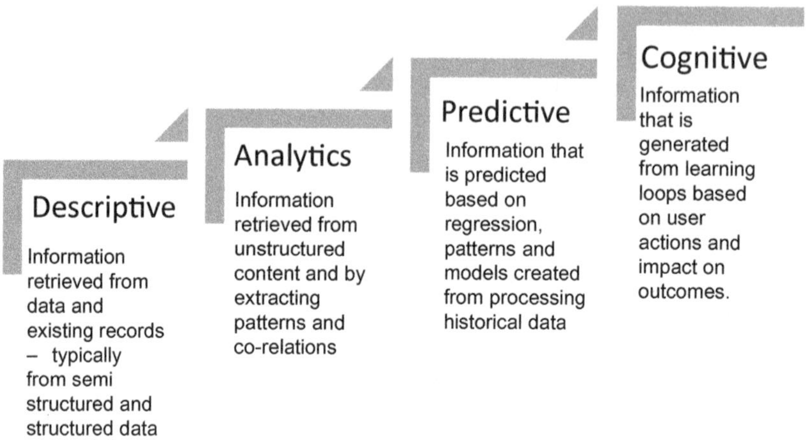

Fig. 8.12 Types of big data analytics

analysis.[201] The applications of integrated analytics can support diverse types of functionality (Fig. 8.12).[202]

- Descriptive analytics can, for example, contextualize the behavior of the customers, grouping them into homogeneous classes ("what happened").
- Predictive analytics can predict the customers' future behavior based on their past behavior and the specific context as shown by the descriptive algorithms ("what could happen").
- Prescriptive analytics, or decision-making, allows relating all the components of a decision to predict the outcome and support the operators' decision-making ("what should happen").
- Cognitive analytics allow an understanding of the root causes connected with the data ("why it happened").

[201] Var, I. (1998). Multivariate data analysis. *Vectors, 8*(2), 125–136.

[202] www.digital4.biz/insurance/ufficio-acquisti-digitale-cose-quali-benefici-del-insurance-4-0/. Accessed 9 March 2019.

The analytics are models for data analysis. They are valuable in areas rich in data. This situation is increasingly standard due to the use of pervasive information systems for banking. This analysis can be the production of:

- Statistics.
- Reports; or
- Executive dashboards.

These outputs allow the organization to get better management transparency.

Applications of Big Data Analytics in Banking 5.0

The massive volumes of data generated in the last decades have shifted financial institutions' attention to data governance and management. Their focus is on those vast, diverse, and complex data that can be extracted from various sources, such as documents, videos, photos, chats, emails, social networks, and so on.[203] This data is unstructured. It has considerable value for financial institutions. They are different from structured data, stored in a fixed format in a field within a record or a file[204] as a spreadsheet or a database, it is much more difficult for a financial institution to extract information from unstructured data.[205] Organizations should not miss this opportunity to get competitive advantages. Those financial institutions that are willing to use big data analytics should look to all the tools available. Non-relational databases can manage unstructured data.[206] This solution deploys advanced and complex technologies able to manage massive quantities of unstructured data. D3.js is an example of these solutions.[207] It is indicative of the relevance of data

[203] Big Data Analytics—The Future of FinTech: Integrating. www.ebrary.net/79679/business_finance/data_analytics. Accessed 20 May 2020.

[204] www.webopedia.com/TERM/S/structured_data.html. Accessed 20 August 2016.

[205] Big Data Analytics. The Future of FinTech: Integrating. www.ebrary.net/79679/business_finance/data_analytics. Accessed 3 April 3030.

[206] Wu, X., Zhu, X., Wu, G. Q., & Ding, W. (2013). Data mining with big data. *IEEE Transactions on Knowledge and Data Engineering*, *26*(1), 97–107.

Big Data Analytics. The Future of FinTech: Integrating. www.ebrary.net/79679/business_finance/data_analytics. Accessed 20 March 2020.

[207] www.d3js.org/. Accessed 2 May 2020.

design in documents and supports the internet of data.[208] The suggested approach for financial institutions is a hybrid one.[209] The suggestion is to combine relational and non-relational databases.[210] The goal would be pushing the paradigm to the limit while using big data analytics with innovative solutions.

Financial institutions should make increasing and more intensive use of data to significantly improve their products and services.[211] This can have positive effects on productivity growth and inclusion. Although with different intensities across banking lines and financial institutions, the use, collection, and analysis of data is becoming an integral part of the banking models of the most digitized organizations.

Data analysis can allow financial institutions to extract more of the customers' assets through pricing and, increase their potential profitability. The expectation is that data analytics benefits will increase exponentially with the amount of information connected with a specific customer. This effect is due to economies of scope: the more differentiated the stories the big data holds, the more insights it provides.

The value creation process can be described as a value cycle involving several interconnected phases[212]:

1. Data origination: this phase generates digital data from online activities such as transactions, operations, or communication.
2. Data collection leads to big data analytics: Data collection processes increases volumes of digital data stored by private and public entities.
3. Data analytics: Processing, interpretation, and analysis of the data can generate economic value.

[208] Fan, W., Chen, Z., Xiong, Z., & Chen, H. (2012). The internet of data: A new idea to extend the IOT in the digital world. *Frontiers of Computer Science*, *6*(6), 660–667.

[209] Bharal, P., & Halfon, A. (2013), Making sense of big data in insurance. www.marklogic.com/resources/making-sense-of-big-data-in-insurance/resource_download/whitepapers/. Accessed 5 August 2016.

[210] Big Data Analytics. The Future of FinTech: Integrating. www.ebrary.net/79679/business_finance/data_analytics. Accessed 30 April 2020.

[211] OECD. (2018). Digitalization, business models and value creation. In *Tax challenges arising from.*

Digitalisation. Interim Report 2018: Inclusive Framework on BEPS, OECD Publishing, Paris, France.

[212] OECD. (2015). *OECD science, solutions and industry scoreboard 2015: Innovation for growth and society*. OECD Publishing, Paris, France.

4. Knowledge base: The knowledge accumulated through analytical activities is the basis for the economic value generated throughout the process.
5. Data-driven decision-making: Knowledge gained through the previous phases, such as through data analytics, can be used to inform decision-making and generates economic value.

Advanced analytics is the autonomous or semi-autonomous analysis of information through complex tools to understand the data more in-depth.[213] Advanced analytics is different from a traditional analysis since it goes beyond the historical data. The method collects and analyzes data in real time and can perform predictive analysis of future risks. The data analysis allows improving risk assessment as predictive models are developed. Using them, financial institutions can compute the probability of defaults.[214] Consequently, they can enhance the determination of the pricing of credit products.[215]

The most use cases of big data analytics in banking are[216]:

- Customer insights,
- Customer experience and journey,
- Risk management.
- Fraud detection,
- Automation: and more innovative jobs; and
- Finance support.

[213] Johansson, S., & Vogelgesang, U. (2016). Automating the insurance industry. *The McKinsey Quarterly*.

[214] de Campos Souza, P. V., & Torres, L. C. B. (2020). Extreme wavelet fast learning machine for evaluation of the default profile on financial transactions. *Computational Economics*, 1–23.

[215] Generali. (2018, February). *Le assicurazioni tutto connesso*. www.generali.com/it/info/discoveringgenerali/all/2018/A-fully-connected-insurance. Accessed 31 March 2020.

[216] Senousy, Y. M. B., Mohamed, N. E. K., & Riad, A. E. D. M. (2018, December). Recent trends in big data analytics towards more enhanced insurance business models. (IJCSIS) *International Journal of Computer Science and Information Security, 16*(12).

Ravi, V., & Kamaruddin, S. (2017, December). Big data analytics enabled smart financial services: Opportunities and challenges. In *International Conference on Big Data Analytics* (pp. 15–39). Springer, Cham, Switzerland.

Financial institutions have three main imperatives[217]:

- Profitable growth delivered through valuable customer acquisition and retention, cross-selling, and up-selling.
- Risk managed through excellent credit scoring, capital efficiency, and operational risk management. For this component, strict cooperation between risk, sales, and finance departments are essential.
- Operational efficiency achieved through cost reduction, credit management, and productive strategies. The support of resources is essential for this component.

Big data analytics can help to obtain all these three imperatives.[218] According to a PriceWaterhouseCoopers survey, more than 30% of the banking's senior management lacks the competencies to make the most of this added information and capabilities.[219]

Financial institutions need to think about the implication that bigtech organizations such as Google and Amazon may have for their business. These big players have access to millions of customers' data. They have the right competencies and tools to analyze those data. They might target tailored products offered at low-risk customers. This competition could be very unpleasant for financial institutions, and it is happening in some parts of the world.

The financial institutions with predictive analytics capabilities can collect raw data from customer interactions and behavior and use the data to discover critical issues, and target offers based on customer data. Predictive analytics capabilities can allow financial institutions relevancy in communication and personalized customer service while engaging with customers throughout the proximity cycle. The strategy enables driving

[217] Big Data Analytics. The Future of FinTech: Integrating. www.ebrary.net/79679/business_finance/data_analytics. Accessed 20 March 2020.

[218] Boobier, T. (2018). *Advanced analytics and AI: Impact, implementation, and the future of work*. John Wiley & Sons, Hoboken, NJ.

[219] www.pwc.com/mu/pwc-22nd-annual-global-ceo-survey-mu.pdf. Accessed 2 May 2020.

growth and improving cross-selling rates by exploiting the customer insight in promotions and campaigns.[220]

Personalized customer insights help target marketing actions precisely. The Next best offer (NBO), among many other marketing analytics, allows this opportunity to financial institutions.[221] Recommendation models, including the NBO model, drive customer-oriented marketing communications by allowing personalized communication and recommendations for customers in multiple accesses.[222] For example, product, transaction, inquiries, and web data can be analyzed in real time to predict the needs and propose the next best offer for the customers.[223] In this way, NBO allows financial institutions to shift from a product-centric view to a customer-centric focus.[224]

To analyze big data analytics in large financial institutions, the researchers interviewed more than 50 enterprises and figure out how they use big data analytics and gain value from it.[225] Usually, banking uses big data analytics in three ways.

- Big data analytics solutions can find more effective and efficient ways of doing banking. The financial institutions can extract and monetize their abundant amounts of data, getting significant cost benefits.[226]

[220] Teerlink, M., & Haydock, M. (2012). Customer analytics pays off: Driving topline growth by bringing science to the art of marketing. IBM Global Business Services. *IBM Institute for Business Value.*

Woodcock, N., & Stone, M. (2012). Simple strategies to win and keep customers profitably. *Journal of Database Marketing & Customer Strategy Management, 19*(4), 275–285. www.doi.org/1010.1057/dbm.2012.25.

[221] Goldenberg, B. (2017). Make your customer engagement a closed loop. Customer Relationship Management: *CRM*, 21(10), 6(2), 4.

[222] Deloitte MCS Limited. (2013). Next Best Action driving customer value through a rich and relevant multichannel experience in Financial Services. *Deloitte Analytics.*

[223] Woodcock, N., & Stone, M. (2012). Simple strategies to win and keep customers profitably. *Journal of Database Marketing & Customer Strategy Management, 19*(4), 275–285.

[224] Deloitte MCS Limited. (2013). Next Best Action driving customer value through a rich and relevant multichannel experience in Financial Services. *Deloitte Analytics.*

[225] Amakobe, M. (2015). The impact of big data analytics on the banking industry. *Colorado Technical University, 4.*

[226] Najjar, M. S., & Kettinger, W. J. (2013). Data monetization: Lessons from a Retailer's Journey. *MIS Quarterly Executive, 12*(4).

- By using these solutions and analyzing new sources of data, financial institutions can instantly analyze information and make better decisions based on the data captured, and the lessons learned.
- These solutions measure customer needs and satisfaction. Due to understanding what customers want, organizations can change and innovate services to fit customers' needs.

Santander[227]

Santander made efforts to help customers understand their financial health and find which products and services might help them achieve their financial goals. The Santander data science team is continually improving and using machine learning algorithms, working with the global data science community. They aim to ensure correct identification of new ways to solve most usual challenges, binary classification problems such as: is a customer satisfied? Will a customer buy this product? Can a customer pay his/her loan? Santander implemented a system to help find which customers will make a specific transaction in the future, irrespective of the amount of money transacted.

Benefits and Challenges of Big Data Analytics

Big data analytics' real value is finding the best use of these data: the so-called data monetization.[228] For this reason, in this book, the expression used is big data analytics. There is a vigorous power coming from analyzing structured and unstructured data, such as social media posts, videos, photos, email, social networks, chats, sounds, and so on. There are more accesses for data collection via cloud computing.[229] Thanks to the tools of big data analytics, these large numbers and complex data can be transformed into knowledge and value. Financial institutions can make better decisions.

[227] www.github.com/abhiyu/Santander-Customer-Transaction-Prediction. Accessed 18 January 2021.

[228] Thomas, R., & McSharry, P. (2015). *Big data revolution: What farmers, doctors and insurance agents teach us about discovering big data patterns*. John Wiley & Sons, Hoboken, NJ.

[229] Nicoletti, B. (2013), *Cloud computing & financial services*. Palgrave-MacMillan, London, UK (translated in Chinese).

Based on customer data, financial institutions can revisit their portfolios with a keen eye on products that accommodate customers' current needs and high demand for new financial services. Meaningful data processed with AI tools can help financial institutions map the customer journey to enhance offerings and promotional timing. A hybrid blend of digital and emotional connections offers a balanced approach to personalized engagement.

Financial institutions are focusing increasingly on big data analytics and AI to detect fraud cases and analyze web content to gain new customers. Big data analytics allows a micro-segmentation of risks.[230]

On the challenging side, big data analytics' use has some challenges.[231] There might be problems with customer privacy. The data are collected with potentially invasive tools.[232] There is the risk of an increase in the market position against anti-competitive regulations. The information from the customers and the innovative solutions can create barriers for the entry of new competitors. Traditional financial institutions could receive benefits from such restrictions. These restrictions could penalize the financial institutions that cannot compete in collecting and using the data. There are possibilities of anti-competitive consequences on big data analytics. On the other side, financial institutions not using these solutions would find it difficult to implement marketing strategies based on the customers' data available with these innovative solutions.[233]

Conclusions

This chapter considers the leading platforms that support banking 5.0. The list is not exhaustive, and it is dynamic. There will be the introduction of innovative solutions over time. The greatest successes come with a combination of more than one solution. The examples are several.

[230] Eling, M., & Lehmann, M. (2018). The impact of digitization on the insurance value chain and the insurability of risks. *The Geneva Papers on Risk and Insurance-Issues and Practice, 43*, 359–396.

[231] www.corrierecomunicazioni.it/digital/42773_come-cambiano-le-assicurazioni-ai-tempi-dei-big-data.htm. Accessed 30 July 2016.

[232] Big Data Analytics. The Future of FinTech: Integrating. www.ebrary.net/79679/business_finance/data_analytics. Accessed 30 May 2020.

[233] Big Data Analytics. The Future of FinTech: Integrating. www.ebrary.net/79679/business_finance/data_analytics. Accessed 20 March 2020.

Think about the mobile phone. It is a combination of a telephone with a computer. This rule applies to banking 5.0. Thanks to the combination of ICT with AI technologies, banking 5.0 can bring significant benefits but also challenges, such as cyber security.

Banking 5.0 integrates the analog and digital worlds with innovative solutions that enhance customer interaction, data availability, and banking processes.[234] The new platforms are in the fields of data acquisition and analysis (AI, big data analytics), data storage and processing (blockchain solutions, cloud computing), and communication (natural language processing, machine vision, and so on).

Platform solutions are robust tools that open many possibilities for banking. The traditional banking model suffers from various problems, fraud, expensive credit, complex procedures, and lack of data about for instance new prospects. This situation leads to unsuitable offers, costly unnecessary procedures, and delays in credit issuance. This latter point is particularly damaging for the financial institutions' brands.

The different use cases reported in this chapter underline the possibility of banking 5.0 of significant procedure improvements (automation, coupled with AI, new types of contracts, and robotic process automation). Adopting these solutions enables record-keeping, real-time tracking, data-driven banking, simplification of interactions between several parties, KYC optimization, speeding processes, easing audit, and improved credit scoring.

There is interest from big financial institutions to invest in platform solutions. Market competitors are pushing to make the solutions better, work with start-ups, evolve, and be up to date. Some financial institutions can obtain significant cost cuts. Bearing in mind the competitive market, these financial institutions can reduce costs to decrease their prices. Banking ecosystems are getting stronger, involving more financial institutions worldwide as well, with platform solutions consortiums. They will reinforce the different sector actors' relationship (financial institutions, e-commerce operators, insurance organizations, other services, intermediaries). It has a potential impact on the market by changing the working paradigms and setting up collaborative ecosystems. Platform solutions can transform the whole value network of banking.

[234] Eling, M., & Lehmann, M. (2018). The impact of digitalization on the insurance value chain and the insurability of risks. *The Geneva Papers on Risk and Insurance-Issues and Practice*, *43*(3), 359–396.

The adoption of these platforms requires further automation and integration. Persons and assets are more connected. Is society ready to shift and supply personal information to financial institutions? Data sharing is a focal and sour point. PSD2 and open banking help, but it is necessary for the customers to collaborate.

The shift to the platforms presented is challenging in big, well-established financial institutions. It will require significant adjustments and reorganization within the financial institutions themselves and even the regulatory organizations.

CHAPTER 9

Processes in Banking 5.0

If you can't describe what you are doing as a process, you do not know what you're doing.

W. Edwards Deming

Introduction

The global recession has hit and is hitting hard. It affects all the main functions of the organizations in every sector. Under this scenario, banking management should consider four main priorities:

- Attention to the effectiveness, efficiency, and economics of the banking processes.
- Willingness to invest in improving the competencies and capabilities of the staff working along with all banking processes.
- Ability to analyze and better manage the available data.
- Ability to strengthen and improve collaboration and partnerships using the AI and robot process optimization.

B. Nicoletti, *Banking 5.0*, Palgrave Studies in Financial Services Technology, https://doi.org/10.1007/978-3-030-75871-4_9

In transforming processes for banking 5.0, it is critical to consider the following principle[1]:

- Modeling: The focus is on making processes adaptive, flexible, and easily configurable so they could evolve quickly rather than being rigidly defined.
- Infrastructural logic: The emphasis is on an infrastructure's capability to accommodate continuous change requests rather than a pre-mapped infrastructure.
- Agential logic: Actors should be able to make decisions in ambiguous situations being effectively supported. The emphasis is on swift reactions and responses in engaging with unexpected challenges or opportunities.

The processes of financial institutions in banking 5.0 should be data-driven and real-time. Data are based on the information on customer and environmental needs and conditions. It is critical for financial institutions to have adequate processes and tools to collect, secure, manage, and analyze them to take strategic actions. This transformation requires a structured approach to measuring the value created, systematically checking those measurements, and rigorously use an improvement method. Banking 5.0 products and services require a constant process of monitoring and fine-tuning.

Basic Banking Processes

The financial institutions' processes in banking 5.0 should be able to sense, understand, and act in real-time on value creation actions. The ability to work on real-time data supports the management of the customers.

The more a financial institution promises its customers, the more robust, resilient, and consistent its processes must be in such a way to keep the promises in any circumstances. Prevention and mitigation require concrete actions to show alerts or messages on a digital front end. If necessary, the financial institutions should be ready to change and adapt.

[1] Baiyere, A., Salmela, H., & Tapanainen, T. (2020). Digital transformation and the new logics of business process management. *European Journal of Information Systems*, 1–22.

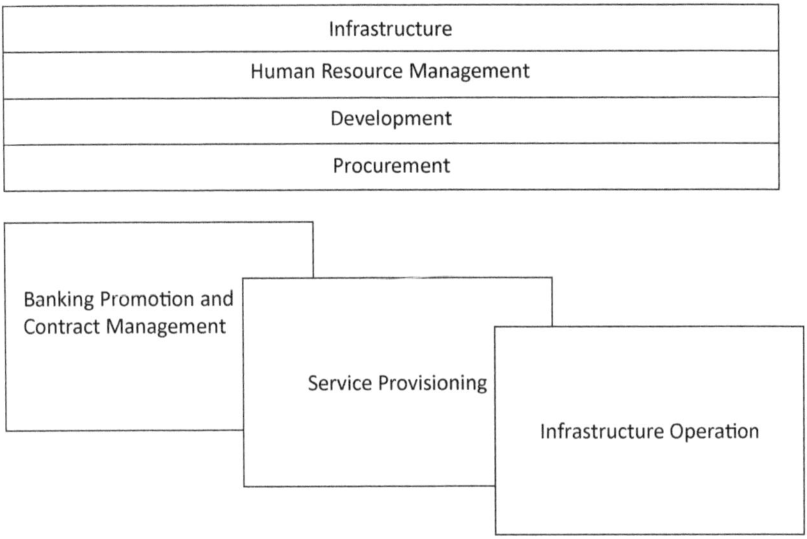

Fig. 9.1 The banking value network (*Source* Stabell, C., & Fjeldstad, Ø. (1998). *Configuring value for competitive advantage: On chains, shops, and networks*. John Wiley & Sons, Hoboken, NJ)

Banking, in the value network model considered in this book, has the following primary processes (Fig. 9.1)[2]:

- Banking promotion and contract management: Activities associated with inviting prospects to join the banking activity, choice of users that can join, and onboarding, management, and termination of contracts governing service provisioning and charging.
- Service provisioning: Activities associated with setting up, keeping, and stopping links with customers and charging for value provided.
- Network and infrastructure operations: Activities associated with keeping and running the banking physical and information infrastructure. These activities need to keep the network in alert status, ready to service user requests.

[2] Stabell, C., & Fjeldstad, Ø. (1998). *Configuring value for competitive advantage: On Chains, shops, and networks*. John Wiley & Sons, Hoboken, NJ.

Banking has four support activities[3]:

- Procurement: Activities associated with procuring inputs or services used in the financial institution's value network.
- Human resource management: Activities associated with recruiting, hiring, training, human capital development, and compensation of all types of personnel.
- Development: Activities broadly grouped into efforts to improve the product(s) and process(es), from basic research and service design to media research.
- Institution infrastructure: Activities including general management, planning, finance, accounting, ICT, legal, government affairs, and quality management.

This chapter also considers network promotion and development, while other chapters consider the other processes in banking 5.0.

Development Process

A financial institution to continue to exist, must innovate its services. For the banking organizations that cover various dimensions, normative environments, and countries, product development expresses the financial institution's strategy, the proposal of value, and the competitiveness position. It deals with a creative and interdisciplinary activity that turns an opportunity of market and solutioning ability into products that respond to the customers' demands. Simultaneously, these products should add value to the financial institution.

Innovation can be in the services or the processes.[4] Innovation can be classified based on whether it is incremental or radical,[5] or modular or

[3] Porter, M. (1985). *Competitive advantage creating and sustaining superior performance*. The Free Press, New York, NY.

[4] Tushman, M., & Nadler, D. (1986). Organizing for innovation. *California Management Review, 28*(3), 74–92.

[5] Ettlie, J. E., Bridges, W. P., & O'Keefe, R. D. (1984). Organization strategy and structural differences for radical versus incremental innovation. *Management Science, 30*, 682–695.

architectural.[6] The innovation work has at its base the ability to connect the strategy and tactics associated with developing a system of innovation from a macro-perspective, with effectively transitioning ideas into products, processes, organization, or business models.

Financial institutions need to specify their product development strategies (low-cost leadership, cost focus, niche market leadership, quality market leadership), reacting quickly to market changes.[7]

The most effective financial institutions can complete most product development efforts quickly, from idea generation to the launch of the products.[8] Financial institutions should aim to become more agile.

Digital Marketing

In banking, marketing has a crucial role in satisfying the demand because the banking services are intangible, and they exist only in the form of promises.[9] To sell a promise requires trust and the definition of four core components (marketing mix): product, price, place (distribution), and promotion[10]:

- The first product for financial institutions is banking. Other products could be offered: investments, services, insurance, and so on. Most financial institutions do not sell single products, and very seldom they now go to the model of the universal banks supposed to sell all the types of banking services.[11]

[6] Henderson, R. M., & Clark, K. B. (1990). Architectural innovation: The reconfiguration of existing product technologies and the failure of established firms. *Administrative Science Quarterly, 35*(1), 1990.

[7] Porter, M. E. (1990). New global strategies for competitive advantage. *Planning Review*.

[8] www.rgare.com/docs/default-source/newsletters-articles/understanding-product-development-overview.pdf?sfvrsn=d29da788_0. Accessed 30 May 2020.

[9] Zekaj, B. (2016). Marketing in insurance industry, marketing functions in insurance industry. *European Journal of Multidisciplinary Studies, 1*(5), 33–39.

[10] Borden, N. H. (1965). The concept of the marketing mix. In G. Schwartz (Ed.), *Science in marketing* (pp. 386–397). John Wiley & Sons, Hoboken, NJ.

[11] A review of marketing mix: 4Ps or more? pdf.123doc.net/document/1151536-a-review-of-marketing-mix-4ps-or-more-pdf.htm. Accessed 5 May 2020.

- The traditional critical component in the banking market is the price of the financial institution's services.
- Place or distribution of banking services can be either through branches or online, indirect, or direct.
- Promotion is a communication process between providers and customers to create a definite belief in the buyers for the financial institution's services. Advertising should be a continuous process of communication to current and potential customers. According to Kotler, promotion includes all the marketing system tools, whose task is to communicate with potential buyers.[12] Organizations and services are essential, but if the organization does not have adequate communication with customers, it will miss success.[13]

There are other relevant aspects apart from these four Ps. They are described in specialized books.[14]

AI is influencing marketing in banking 5.0 in many ways.[15] At the core, Artificial intelligence (AI) is enabling the personalization of customer experiences. Developments in Machine learning (ML), coupled with the massive quantities of data generated, increasingly supports advertisers targeting their campaigns. They can deliver personalized and dynamic ads to customers at an unprecedented scale.[16] They can find a customer's preferences or a life event that triggers a banking need.[17] Personalized advertising increases sales and the return on investment of marketing campaigns.

[12] Zekaj, B. (2016). Marketing in insurance industry, marketing functions in insurance industry. *European Journal of Multidisciplinary Studies, 1*(5), 33–39.

[13] Zekaj, B. (2016). Marketing in insurance industry, marketing functions in insurance industry. *European Journal of Multidisciplinary Studies, 1*(5), 33–39.

[14] Goi, C. L. (2009). A review of marketing mix: 4Ps or more? *International Journal of Marketing Studies, 1*(1), 2; Möller, K. (2006). The marketing mix revisited: Towards the 21st century marketing by E. Constantinides. *Journal of Marketing Management*, *22*(3), 439–450.

Fakeideas. (2008). Revision: Reviewing the marketing mix. fakeideas.co.uk/2008/03/07/revision-reviewing-the-marketing-mix. Accessed 30 March 2020.

[15] OECD Library. www.oecd-ilibrary.org/sites/79edf9d8-en/index.html?itemId=/content/component/79edf9d8-en. Accessed 20 January 2021.

[16] Chow, M. (2017). AI and machine learning get us one step closer to relevance at scale, *Google*.

[17] Hinds, J., & Joinson, A. N. (2018). What demographic attributes do our digital footprints reveal? A systematic review. *PloS one*, *13*(11), e0207112.

The following is a non-exhaustive list that outlines some developments in AI that could have an exciting impact on marketing practices:

One of the major subfields of AI that increases ads' customization and marketing messages is Natural language processing (NLP). It enables tailoring marketing campaigns based on linguistic contexts such as social media, emails, chats, customer service interactions, and product reviews. Through NLP, computers learn words and find patterns of words in everyday human language. They improve their accuracy as they go. NLP can enhance the quality of online search results. It can match the customer's expectations, and the ads presented. In this way, it is possible to increase advertising effectiveness and efficiency.

AI's marketing impact goes beyond NLP models to analyze "unstructured data." Online recommendation algorithms vastly beat simple sets of guidelines or historical ratings from users, thanks to AI. Instead, AI can extract from a wide range of data customized recommendations.[18]

In online advertising, Click-through rate (CTR) (the number of people who click on an ad divided by the number who have been exposed to the ad) is an essential metric for assessing ad performance. Based on ML algorithms, click prediction systems can perfect the impact of sponsored ads and online marketing campaigns. It is possible to use reinforced learning algorithms to select the advertisements that incorporate the characteristics that would maximize CTR in the targeted population.[19]

AI can support marketing on many respects[20]:

- Hyperpersonalized offer.
- Customer retargeting.
- Propensity to buy scoring.
- Access mapping.

[18] Plummer, L. (2017, August). This is how Netflix's top-secret recommendation system works. *Wired*, 22.

[19] Hong Tay, P. (2017, August). Using machine learning to boost click through rate for your ads. www.linkedin.com/pulse/using-machine-learning-boost-click-through-rate-your-ads-tay/. Accessed 204 January 2021.

[20] www.mckinsey.com/industries/financial-services/our-insights/ai-powered-decision-making-for-the-bank-of-the-future?cid=other-eml-alt-mip-mck&hdpid=b28e9a1e-b64b-4be4-b5d3-10470b96c23c&hctky=9204549&hlkid=cac4d2e1c59944c08c8f684d35c897e0. Accessed 22 March 2021.

Onboarding Process

Customer onboarding is the process a financial institution undertakes when bringing a new customer on board.[21] Onboarding new customers involve gathering relevant information on the customer and conducting identity checks to comply with Know your customer (KYC) regulations. Only when the financial institution has all the necessary documentation on the customer s/he can open an account or begin a relationship with the financial institution. The critical challenge of customer onboarding for banking is the base for supplying an excellent customer journey while meeting compliance requirements and be efficient.

Traditionally, the customer onboarding process for banking involves multiple forms, paper files, manual compliance checks, and in-person identification checks. This process is obsolete, time-consuming, and normally represents a poor user experience. Meeting compliance and legal regulations are often the most time-consuming stage due to the vast number of documents and data that need to be collected and analyzed.[22] Many financial institutions have recently introduced innovative solutions to significantly modernize and perfect their customer onboarding process, improving efficiencies, and creating a superior customer journey.

McKinsey asked customers to assess different characteristics of the end-to-end experience on banking, including the onboarding, the ease of identifying the right services, and staff's knowledge and professionalism.[23] The survey found that only a small number of characteristics (typically three to five out of 15) had a material impact and represented the bulk of overall satisfaction.[24] For example, when analyzing the customer's features onboarding journey, McKinsey found that transparency of price and fees, ease of communication with the financial institution, and ability to track the onboarding process status accounted for 42% of the overall satisfaction. This finding suggests that financial

[21] https://www.duedil.com/blogs/a-guide-to-customer-onboarding-for-banking#:~:text=What%20is%20client%20onboarding%20in,to%20comply%20with%20KYC%20regulations. Accessed 4 December 2020.

[22] A guide to customer onboarding for banking. www.duedil.com/blogs/a-guide-to-customer-onboarding-for-banking. Accessed 20 January 2021.

[23] Dias, J., Ionutiu, O., Lhuer, X., & Ouwerkerk, J. V. (2016). The four pillars of distinctive customer journeys. *McKinsey Paper.*

[24] A guide to customer onboarding for banking. www.duedil.com/blogs/a-guide-to-customer-onboarding-for-banking. Accessed 20 January 2020.

institutions should concentrate on those actions that make the most difference to customer delight.

The application of AI in risk management in the onboarding process can build interactive and personalized platforms and augmented reality interfaces for the customer.[25] Robotic process automation can increase the productivity of the onboarding process.

Other Processes

Apart from the processes examined until this point, in banking 5.0, several other processes need to be considered and other chapters consider them in details.

- Customer relationship management. Banking 5.0 helps deliver superior customer service levels while maximizing per customer profitability. For example, banking 5.0 customer proximity centers solutions vastly increase first-contact resolution rates.
- Risk, fraud, and compliance. Banking 5.0 solutions can help financial institutions gain the agility needed to comply with regulations, mitigate risk, and stop fraud. Advanced analytics help detects early signs of fraud or excessive portfolio risks. Banking 5.0 must generate comprehensive audit trails and supports specialized compliance reporting.

Design Thinking

Design thinking (DT) is a method that can be used to introduce, implement, and improve banking 5.0 processes. It uses a customer-centric approach that helps discover nuanced, even implicit, customer needs at the start of the innovation process. It takes into consideration feasibility, including the available solutions and their viability.[26]

[25] Dzhaparov, P. (2020). Application of blockchain and artificial intelligence in bank risk management. *Икономика и управление, 17*(1), 43–57.

[26] Gruber, M., de Leon, N., George, G., & Thompson, P. (2015). Managing by design. *Academy of Management Journal, 58*, 1–7. UK Design Council. (2007). The value of design factfinder report, *Design Council*.

The critical differences between design thinking and traditional banking thinking are in three categories[27]:

- Design thinking shifts the focus in the direction of the customer. An empathy exercise achieves this, trying better understanding customer needs and behaviors from their own perspective. It is important not to rely necessarily on what the customer says but on what the customer does. In this way, it is possible to get more relevant insights than just confirm problems.
- A characteristic of design thinking is creating a stimulating atmosphere that promotes innovative ideas and encourages the participation and experimentation of the entire team.
- Design thinking does not require expert persons. It requires only a team with different profiles and diverse ways of thinking. The method promotes collaboration and the generation of innovative ideas, thus reducing the risk of relying on unique opinions.

Implementing design thinking is not enough to set up an innovation lab and apply design thinking within an organization. Many organizations struggle to make it part of their day-to-day culture and processes.[28]

Design Thinking Method

The design thinking process has five stages[29]:

- Empathize requires understanding the end-user's problems and needs.
- Define involves reviewing all the information gathered to define the problem to be solved and start setting goals.

[27] Various. (2015). Spotlight on the evolution of design thinking. *Harvard Business Review*, 56–85.

[28] Liebau, D. (2016). *Design thinking in financial services*. Lightbulb Capital, Singapore.

[29] Siota, J., Klueter, T., Wyman, O., Staib, D., Taylor, S., & Ania, I. (2017). Design thinking the new DNA of the financial sector—"How banks can boost their growth through design thinking in an era of de-banking". *IESE Business School*.

- Ideate requires thinking of new ways to solve the banking core's problems. It involves generating ideas to produce innovative solutions.
- Prototype is essential to produce cost-effective and simple prototypes that generate feedback from potential end-users or financial institution staff.
- Test aims to get feedback from the end-users. This stage is related to the Empathize stage since the aim is to understand what the customer thinks about the service, and why he/she feels that way.[30]

After those design stages in a banking 5.0 project, it is necessary to add the "Deploy" step, moving to implementation, "Monitor," and "Continuously improve" steps.

Design Thinking in Banking 5.0

It is possible to apply design thinking to any process and in any type of industry. Financial institutions have improved thanks to the application of design thinking in several cases.[31] The drivers of shifting to customer focus and banking 5.0 transformation have contributed to design thinking. In a certain number of cases, early adopter financial institutions have started to use design thinking as a unique differentiator in how their services are designed, sold, and deployed.

Using the design thinking approach, a study explored the customer-centric challenges faced by seven Hungarian financial institutions.[32] The research aimed to get more in-depth insights into the customers' needs, find the problems, evaluate the challenges, and ideate solutions. The

[30] Nash, K. (2015). CIO voices: Bank of America's Cathy Bessant says 'no' to innovation labs. *CIO Journal, The Wall Street Journal.*

[31] Thomas, R., & McSharry, P. (2015). *Big data revolution: What farmers, doctors and insurance agents teach us about discovering big data patterns.* John Wiley & Sons, Hoboken, NJ.

[32] Feher, P., & Varga, K. (2017, July 18–21). Using design thinking to find banking digitization opportunities: Snapshot of the Hungarian banking system. *The 30th Bled eConference*, Bled, Slovenia.

authors changed the standard design thinking approach and developed a "One Week Sprint" method. It consisted of the following steps[33]:

1. Preparation: problem mapping based on stories
2. Discovery: learning from experts
3. Interpretation: documentation of experiences such as stories, post-it notes, visual reminders to find the need, and problems needed to be solved
4. Ideation: brainstorming of ideas
5. Experimentation: presenting the ideas through a storyboard or one-page business model canvas and get feedbacks
6. Evolution: pitching the concept, risk analysis, tracking progresses, and learnings.

This study pointed out problems in the financial institution branches' role, online and mobile phone services, products and services, and several digital solutions were ideated. Young customers viewed the branch as an annoyance, and when customers need to appear personally, the waiting time was long and dull. During the ideation phase, the group produced ideas such as supplying tablet games to know customer intentions while waiting, supplying multi-functionality in mobile banking services such as augmented reality, and envisioning an online dashboard with important personal data readily available.

Gartner surveyed experienced leaders. One of the takeaways was 83% of them used design thinking methods to understand customers better when deciding how to change products and services.[34]

[33] Feher, P., & Varga, K. (2017, July 18–21). Using design thinking to find banking digitization opportunities: Snapshot of the Hungarian banking system. *The 30th Bled eConference*, Bled, Slovenia.

[34] www.gartner.com/document/3995096?ref=TrackRecommendedEmail. Accessed 30 January 2021.

National Australian Bank
The National Australian Bank (NAB) partnered with the consulting group Oliver Wyman to supply customer-centric solutions for their Small and medium enterprise (SMEs) customers.[35] Using the design thinking method, NAB used the "day in the life of" tool to find out how customers experienced the lending process. The conclusion was that the process was complex, time-consuming, and unsecured. Customers preferred mobile services. The ideation process led to an online application called the NAB Quickbiz Loan. This app consisted only of three steps. It relates to a cash-flow credit model that allowed SMEs to get up to USD 50,000 in business loans, with a decision-making time of 60 seconds and three days for the fund disbursements.

Deutsche Bank
The design thinking transformation at Deutsche Bank went in three phases: Learning (P1), Adapting (P2), and Diffusing (P3).[36] Once the ICT community started seeing this design thinking team's results, the design thinking adaptation went ahead step by step. This effort led to completing the first prototype in less than one year and the second prototype in less than 18 months (about one and a half years). Five years saw the completion of eight customer-centric projects. After this "subversion" was considered adequate, design thinking became part of the organization with the hiring of a Vice President for Design Thinking.[37]

[35] Oliver Wyman, & IESE. (2017). *Design thinking: The new DNA of the financial sector*: media.iese.edu/research/pdfs/ST-0441-E.pdf. Accessed 20 January 2021.

[36] Vetterli, C., Uebernickel, F., & Brenner, W., & Petrie, C. (2016). How Deutsche Bank's IT division used design thinking to achieve customer proximity. *MIS Quarterly Executive, 15*(1), 37–53.

[37] Vetterli, C., Uebernickel, F., & Brenner, W., & Petrie, C. (2016). How Deutsche Bank's IT division used design thinking to achieve customer proximity. *MIS Quarterly Executive, 15*(1), 37–53.

OCBC

OCBC Bank is an example of an institution that successfully implemented design thinking principles. A diversified team within OCBC Bank developed the first product concept based on customers' insights through design thinking principles. Once this product concept was ready, the team had a co-creation workshop with a front-line employee. During the session, co-creators were confirming the development outputs and redefining a new product communication concept.

The team prototyped communication ideas with the help of front-line employees. The team used simple materials and stationery. By involving employees in the process, the team could not only design what would work for them in an advisory meeting. They learned how to explain the product in a simple and convincing way.[38] After the process, OCBC Bank increased sales of its new investment product by 150% and increased its customers' trust belief.

In producing solutions, OCBC used customer insight, co-creation, community engagement, stakeholder involvement, and prototyping. For example, OCBC Bank developed a family and kid-friendly bank policy called OCBC Full-Service Sunday Banking using design thinking. The bank used the diary research tool to produce an "outside-in" perspective, focus group discussions, moment mapping for prototype and testing, and learning labs for learning.[39]

There are common patterns in the adoption of design thinking in banking:

- The framework and processes of traditional design thinking typically influences the first adoption.[40]
- The tendency is to localize the design thinking process to suit the financial institution's method and type of customers' engagement they are involved in.

[38] Kang, J. (2012). Design thinking. *EFMA Journal*.

[39] Wah, K. Y. (2013). *OCBC Bank service excellence in banking: Delivering a differentiated customer experience*. Presentation at Dubai's Share Best Practice Conference & Exhibition. www.dqg.org/wp-content/uploads/SBP2013_Presentation03_KuYuenWah.pdf. Accessed 20 January 2021.

[40] Brown, T. (2008, June). Design thinking. *Harvard Business Review*, 84–92.

- The first use of design thinking projects is on retail/mass customer segment rather than corporate or High net worth (HNW) customers since retail customers are more comfortable engaging. Later, design thinking applications are on corporate or HNW customers. These customers are typically harder to engage in showing the value of design thinking.

Benefits and Challenges of Design Thinking

There is a link between design thinking and organizational performance.[41] According to the Design Management Institute's Design Value Index, "design-led organizations have maintained a significant stock market advantage, outperforming the Standard & Poor (S&P) stock index by an extraordinary 211 percent" from 2005 to 2015.[42]

The challenges with design thinking are at three levels: leadership, team, and individual. There is normally a lack of resources at the leadership level to carry out the complete design thinking processes and unrealistic expectations about generated outputs; plus, the detail level tends to be too low. There might be a loss of focus on the team during the process, time constraints, and other specific management issues. At the individual level, the team leaders are sometimes weak facilitators, and there might be issues with some participants.

To tackle these challenges, financial institutions should redefine their execution to adopt agile principles.[43] This adoption requires a cultural change.

Bank of America
An example of a successful buy-in from the leadership level is the case of Bank of America's chief solution officer, who explained her approach to innovation at an organizational level that increasingly viewed the bank as a fintech player.

[41] Moultrie, J., & Livesey, F. (2014). Measuring design investment in firms: Conceptual foundations and exploratory UK survey. *Research Policy, 43,* 570–587.

[42] (2016). Design value index, *Design Management Institute.*

[43] Christopher, L., & de Vries, M. (2020). Selecting a scaled agile approach for a Fin-Tech company. *The South African Journal of Industrial Engineering, 31*(3), 196–208.

It is more powerful to capture innovation from 10,000 people than to put ten people in a lab.[44] With the business model's alignment and the C-suite buy-in Bank of America undertook a user-centered redesign of its process for onboarding. Thanks to this digital transformation, the number of online banking onboardings rose by 45%.[45]

Lean and Digitize Banking 5.0

Innovation is crucial to the success of any banking process. Many organizations spend most of their efforts on improving operations, finance, and marketing and not enhancing innovation. Lean innovation is the systematic interpretation of lean thinking principles on innovation in its different forms. This section focuses on the lean processes for innovation, describes their activities, and proves how to use and benefit from combining the lean six sigma method with digitization. The result is a potent lean and digitize innovation method for improving processes.[46] The method aims to add value to customers, improve effectiveness, cut waste, minimize operating costs, and reduce time-to-market by redesigning the innovation processes and automation.

Lean and digitize innovation is based on a method introduce by the Author called Lean and Digitize (Fig. 9.2).[47]

To be successful, lean and digitize innovation must adopt the approach described as the 7 Ds: define, discover, design, develop, digitize, deploy, and diffuse. It is essential to apply this method and its tools in a strong partnership between the organization's sectors quality assurance and support departments (such as ICT, finance, or operations).[48] Stakeholders need to work in setting up and staffing the improvement project team. Even more important, the organizations must consider the first application of the lean and digitize innovation process as the start of an

[44] Nash, K. (2015). Bank of America's Cathy Bessant says 'no' to innovation labs, *CIO Voices*:

[45] Ross, J. (2014). The business value of user experience, *Infragistics*.

[46] Nicoletti, B. (2016). *The method of lean and digitize*. Gower Press, Farnham, UK.

[47] Nicoletti, B. (2012). *The method of lean and digitize*. Gower Press, Farnham, UK.

[48] Nicoletti, B. (2012). *The method of lean and digitize*. Gower Press, Farnham, UK.

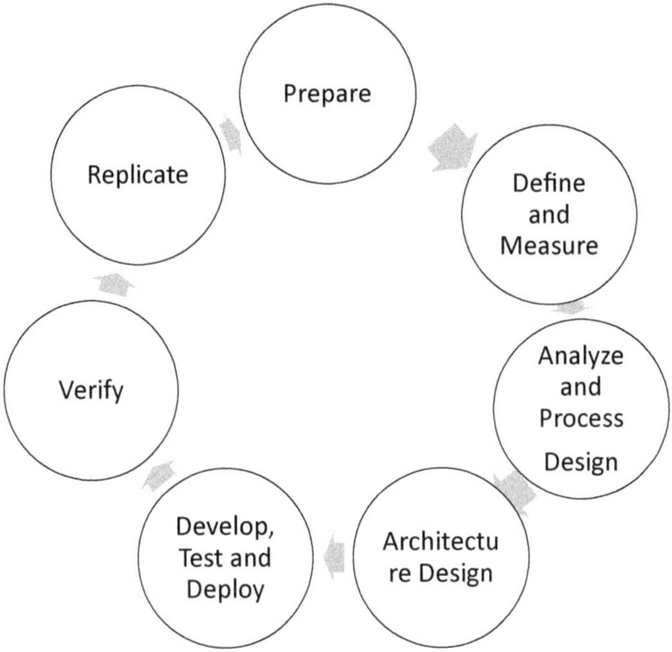

Fig. 9.2 Lean and digitize method

iterative cycle that generates continuous improvement and leads the organizations' culture toward lean thinking.[49] Process improvement should be a substantial part of the organizational culture.

The lean and digitize innovation process can be divided into seven stages and 30 steps, as described below, and illustrated in Fig. 9.3.[50] At the end of each stage there are tollgates, when the innovation steering committee controls the advancement of the project.

[49] Womack, J. P., & Jones, D. T. (2003). *Banish waste and create wealth in your corporation*. Free Press, New York, NY.

[50] Nicoletti, B. (2015, March). Optimizing innovation with the lean & digitize innovation process. *TIM Review*.

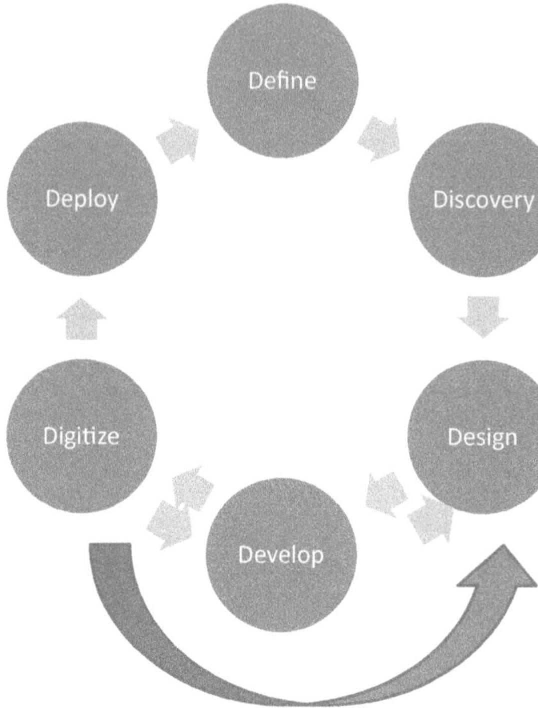

Fig. 9.3 The lean and digitize innovation process and its seven stages, or the "7 Ds"

Stage 1: Define

Before implementing an idea, it is essential to think about how to redesign banking to add value to the customer and the financial institution by making offerings and processes better, faster, cheaper, or more convenient.

In this stage, the institution needs to set the ground for innovation and define the environment.

1. Context: find the needs or the requests of the customers, shareholders, and employees; the challenge of competitors and the respect for compliance (for example, legislation and regulations).

2. Culture: detect the organization's culture, the community, and the nation at the base of the organization.
3. Vision: define how to improve effectiveness, efficiency, economy, ethics, and quality of innovation.
4. Strategy: define the achievable goals and content of the innovation.
5. Kick-off: launch the project during a special meeting and inform all the stakeholders.
6. Governance: define how to manage the project and set up the project team.
7. Voice of the Customer: listen to the Voice of the customers (VoC) associated with the potential innovation and verify if the innovation is consistent with the VoC.

Stage 2: Discover

The following stage is the discovery of innovative ideas for potential development into a process, product, organization, or business model innovation in this stage.

The critical question in any digital transformation strategy is how it can create new value for the customers and the organization. It is necessary to translate that challenge into clear project goals.

A traditional success metric for new projects is Return on investment (ROI). ROI does not help understand what value a project adds for customers, at least not directly. To compute a ROI, it is necessary to estimate both investments and returns, which at this stage are not yet available. It is essential to find metrics that are more linked to the specific improvements connected with the innovation.

Progressing along the innovation process, it is possible to test and refine assumptions. It is possible to get new insights and which value they can bring. More in the project, it is possible to arrive at the calculation of a ROI.

8. Invention: the creation of something new through an organization's creative process
9. Choice: finding and evaluating an innovation potentially to develop or adopt
10. Metrics: translate the innovation and the VoC into Critical to quality (CtQ) factors.

11. As-Is: map the existing situation in terms of products, processes, organization, or business model.

Stage 3: Design
This stage is for defining the framework and the sequence of activities.

12. Lean: define how to innovate with the support of the project team in workshops and meetings
13. Kaizen Plan: define improving intervention plan.
14. Architecture Design: define the rules, policies, and process structure of the potential innovations.

Stage 4: Develop
This stage is for developing an idea into a usable innovation. Team members should think about competition not as a marketplace where similar players offer rival products and services but as what strategists call an arena. The customer needs define an arena. It is a notion introduced by Levitt, who recommended that financial institutions see themselves as competing players.[51]

15. Build: construct the chosen solutions.
16. Package: surround the core solution with complementary products and services in such a way to form a solution that can be effectively used for the initiative by the target adopters.
17. Configure: decide which solution features will be used, whether they will be used As-Is or with adaptations, how the solution will integrate with other solutions the organization already have in place, how related organizational elements (for example, structures, processes) will change, and how the organization will absorb and make use of the solution.
18. Change management: manage the changes.

Stage 5: Digitize
This stage includes the application of digitization and automation at the highest possible level. It is essential in this stage to test the assumptions. It is possible to use an assumption checkpoint table. To create one, it is

[51] Levitt, T. (1960, July–August). Marketing Myopia. *Harvard Business Review*, 45–56.

necessary to write down the following few milestones that the innovation project will go through, which assumptions need to be tested at each, and if possible, how much that test will cost. In this way, it is possible to evaluate if the innovation is worth the costs.

19. Implement: implement the digitized application.
20. Test: the project team and the users should conduct unit tests, system tests, integration tests, regression tests, and user acceptance tests

Stage 6: Deploy
This stage includes the implementation of the innovation and of some auxiliary activities.

21. Deploy: implement the chosen solution.
22. Document: produce and issue the documents related to the innovation.
23. Verify: control the improvements.
24. Evaluate internal and external benefits: assess the benefits, external (that is, take notice of customers, shareholders, and employee satisfaction) and internal (that is, assess the profitability, market share, and internal improvements related to the new process).
25. Lessons Learned: learn from the initiative.
26. Celebrate: acknowledge the team's work.

Stage 7: Diffusion
In this stage, it is necessary to assemble and arrange the resources needed to (i) persuade and enable the organization and the individuals to adopt and use the innovation, and (ii) diffuse or spread it across a set of potential users.

27. Assimilate: when individuals and other units absorb the innovation into their daily routines and the financial institutions' work-life.
28. Appropriation: involves tasks such as managing intellectual property and the ecosystem of complementary products and services so that margins are optimized, considering partners, customers, and imitators.

29. Transform: change the solution and organization to take advantage of the new opportunities brought about by the innovation. Transformations can happen at the market and societal levels.
30. Replicate: extend the solution to other departments in the institution or to other organizations in the group.

Stage 3, 4, and 5 should be done with an agile approach, doing several cycles, or "springs" in the agile terminology.[52] It is possible to use many tools in support of the process described. They can come from the tools used in Lean, Six Sigma, Agile management, and digitization.

One of the best tools for process design is Quality Function Deployment (QFD), commonly known as the House of Quality. It finds the potential customer value of the innovation based on the customers' (be they internal or external) needs and an innovation's (usually a product) quality characteristic.

Another essential tool is prototyping, which is both a culture and a language.[53] It is possible to prototype everything: a new product or service, a process, even an organization or a business model. What counts is moving the ball forward, achieving at least some parts of a goal.

There are several practices connected with the agile approach. They enable the team to work together to decide goals because of the iterative development method, the focus on cutting waste from lean manufacturing; and the daily scrum update meetings from product development. These processes enable the innovation team to adapt to changing needs, reduce the project risk, increase the transparency of team progresses, involve stakeholders and the staff from the beginning of projects, and speed up the creation of value that the team contribute to the business.

Auckland Savings Bank (ASB)

Facing the pressure of fintech disruptors, ASB New Zealand decided to improve its customers' user experience through agile principles.[54] The bank used video chats to interact directly with customers over mobile

[52] Margaria, T., & Steffen, B. (2010). Simplicity as a driver for agile innovation. *Computer, 43*(6), 90–92.

[53] Kelley, T. (2001). Prototyping is the shorthand of innovation. *Design Management Journal* (Former Series), *12*(3), 35–42.

[54] www.oliverwyman.com/content/dam/oliver-wyman/v2/publications/2017/apr/Design_Thinking.pdf. Accessed 4 March 2021.

devices, reducing the need for visits to a physical branch. Detractors may argue that in-the-in-person interactions still form an essential part of day-to-day operations. However, branchless banking's rapid growth in both traditional and emerging markets should sound the alarm for everybody.

Conclusions

This chapter reviews the transformation of processes in support of banking 5.0. The chapter does not cover all the banking processes but those critical in helping banking 5.0.

Innovation in banking can take many forms. Often, but not always, a new solution helps. It is critical improving processes. The answers will be a combination of methods and platforms. It is essential to select the solution/(s), which suits the organization's needs. It is critical not to forget that the financial institution that hesitates to innovate processes has lost. This statement is true in organizations and personal life.

Design thinking and lean and digitize innovation are methods that can significantly improve banking 5.0. Organizations must digitally transform using design thinking and a lean and digitize[55] approach to all processes. Innovative solutions allow the organization to have an integrated view. This approach eases decisions that affect the entire value network. Innovative solutions allow financial institutions to improve in smooth ways processes. The goal is to improve customer delight and increase productivity and customer ease of use.

[55] Nicoletti, B. (2012). *Lean & digitize: An integrated approach to process improvement*. Gower Publishing, Farnham, UK. ISBN-10: 1409441946.

CHAPTER 10

Persons in Banking 5.0

Great things in business are never done by one person. They are done by a team of people.

Steve Jobs

Introduction

Job roles in banking will evolve and integrate multiple skills into one. Profiles such as quality assurance will merge into banking operators and become one job. This situation will require employees training in various and diverse job roles. Additionally, banking 5.0 will enable day-to-day products to respond to the customers' needs through edge intelligence.[1] With traditional banking, it was possible to collect usage data, track usage patterns, and send them to the observer. There was limited actionable intelligence built into the process. Supported by new business models, banking 5.0 products can perfect their performance and deliver maximum efficiency throughout the product's lifetime.

In a banking 5.0 transformation, the determining factor is the person, both human or virtual. To further extend and deepen innovation and

[1] Zhou, Z., Chen, X., Li, E., Zeng, L., Luo, K., & Zhang, J. (2019). Edge intelligence: Paving the last mile of artificial intelligence with edge computing. *Proceedings of the IEEE, 107*(8), 1738–1762.

B. Nicoletti, *Banking 5.0*, Palgrave Studies in Financial Services Technology, https://doi.org/10.1007/978-3-030-75871-4_10

adopt advanced solutions, the persons' role appears as decisive. E-competencies are essential.[2] Banking 5.0 requires critical resources for the innovative approach in the organization's value propositions/to customers. This chapter frames the banking sector's various categories to understand the talents necessary for banking 5.0. The chapter also examines virtual persons, the robots. Banking 5.0 requires new types of collaborations between humans and robots.

There is a concern that the banking 5.0 transformation will lead to a reduction in employment. OECD has estimated that robots will bring a decrease of 14% of the workforce.[3] Still, in Germany, employment levels have been strong, despite the industry 4.0 initiative, based on the number of those employed and the volume of working hours.[4] Indeed, many persons (around 31%) will need to change their jobs significantly.

Persons are a challenge but a significant important opportunity. In launching a banking 5.0 initiative, financial institutions should be ready to build up the required capacities and competencies to support the organization's vision and mission from a more strategic and innovative perspective. The new role of banking 5.0 is to be a vital network node within its ecosystems, and influence value-adding services. This approach requires rethinking the tasks, functions, and responsibilities of all banking stakeholders. It is necessary to set up cross-functional interdisciplinary roles to speed up transactions and processes to stay at the forefront of innovative solutions. These new roles need to drive organizational successes in the most efficient, effective, and economical ways based on sustainable and diversified profitability.[5]

Banking 5.0 needs persons properly prepared, formed, and trained in banking 5.0 processes and solutions. This situation is a challenge since most current employees in the organizations and their partners started

[2] Dobozy, E., & Ifenthaler, D. (2014, May). Initial teacher education by open and distance modes: A snapshot of e-competency experiences in Australia. *eLearning Papers: Digital Literacies & eCompetencies, 38*, 57–67.

[3] OECD Employment Outlook 2019: oe.cd/il/2zn. Accessed 10 January 2021.

[4] Eichhorst, W., Hinte, H., Rinne, U., & Tobsch, V. (2017). How big is the gig? Assessing the preliminary evidence on the effects of digitalization on the labor market. *Management Revue, 28*(3), 298–318; OECD (2018). Income statement and balance sheet. stats.oecd.org/. Accessed 20 January 2020.

[5] Bienhaus, F., & Haddud, A. (2018). Procurement 4.0: Factors influencing the digitization of procurement and supply chains. *Business Process Management Journal, 24*(4), 965–984.

working when industry 5.0 does not even exist as a concept. Banking 5.0 is an opportunity to revitalize the interests of the persons and supply opportunities for talents. For this reason, this chapter focuses on the training for banking 5.0: education 5.0.

Financial institutions compete for talents. Start-ups attract them more. Financial institutions must prioritize recruiting a workforce that considers the world's demographics. The persons will be diverse across education and experience, personalities, cultural needs, and preferences. The inclusion of all those differences can generate new learnings and ideas for improving banking results. Talents are more mobile than ever. Millennials and Generation-Z[6] expect to work in corporate cultures that supply good opportunities to move in the organization and work collaboratively for projects that inspire and provide challenges.[7]

Some research offers insights into the current on-going practices in the banking institutions undergoing a business transformation.[8] As innovative solutions become more ubiquitous, an algorithm cannot reduce some critical skills and capabilities. Differentiated person skills such as creativity, innovation, critical thinking, complex problem-solving, and emotional intelligence will be increasingly important. Human resources management (HRM) should lead by defining technical and person-centered capabilities fit for banking 5.0. Financial institutions' HRM function should be aware of the digital banking transformation's impact on the persons and organization perspective and transform the HRM practices and initiatives.

DBS[9]

DBS, the Singapore-based bank, has rewired for the digital era. Its digital transformation efforts are one of the most comprehensive for

[6] Gen Y, or Millennials, were born between 1980 and 1994. Gen Z is the newest generation to be named and was born between 1995 and 2015. Shatto, B., & Erwin, K. (2017). Teaching millennials and generation Z: bridging the generational divide. *Creative nursing, 23*(1), 24–28.

[7] Singh, A. P., & Dangmei, J. (2016). Understanding the generation Z: The future workforce. *South-Asian Journal of Multidisciplinary Studies, 3*(3), 1–5.

[8] Latif, K. A., Mahmood, N. H. N., & Ali, N. R. M. (2019). Exploring the changing human resource management role in the context of digital banking transformation. *Open International Journal of Informatics (OIJI), 7*(2), 1–13.

a financial institution. Euromoney selected DBS Bank as the "world's best digital bank," It has executed its digital business strategy and relentlessly taken steps in developing its digital capabilities by overhauling all elements in the structure, processes, platforms, and persons.[10] DBS invested heavily in solutions as a competitive enabler and successfully undertook radical digital innovations. Based on the DBS success story, there are few critical thrusts of the DBS digital transformation strategy: strategic focus on grooming the leadership for digital transformation, developing agile and scalable digital operations, designing new digitally enabled customer journeys, and incubating and accelerating emerging digital innovations. Its first design thinking project was DBS Home Connect in 2013.[11] Fueled by a leadership passionate and severe about using design thinking, DBS transformed its solution infrastructure to accommodate big data analytics, AI, and biometrics.[12] DBS Home Connect resulted from several customer consultations and creativity that led to a mobile phone app that allows for instance users to compute mortgage payments for home buys and check information on earlier transactions, including rental information.[13]

At the core of the DBS's transformation is the Human Resource (HR) function's instrumental role in fostering reinvention in the organization. DBS used resources and tools such as empirical learning through programmers called hackathons to crowdsource innovative ideas and develop digital leaders and evangelists among its employees. The forward-thinking HR leaders in DBS moved outside of the HR

[9] Sia, S. K., Soh, C., & Weill, P. (2016). How DBS Bank pursued a digital business strategy. *MIS Quarterly Executive, 15*(2).

[10] Sia, K. S., Soh, C., & Weill, P. (2016). How DBS Bank pursued a digital business strategy. *MIS Quarterly Executive, 15*(2), 105–121; Latif, K. A., Mahmood, N. H. N., & Ali, N. R. M. (2019). Exploring the changing human resource management role in the context of digital banking transformation. *Open International Journal of Informatics (OIJI), 7*(2), 1–13.

[11] Groenfeldt, T. (2018, April 15). Going digital in banking—DBS, Citi, BBVA, ING lead the way. *Forbes*. www.forbes.com/sites/tomgroenfeldt/2018/04/15/going-digital-inbanking-dbs-citi-bbva-ing-lead-the-way/#3e3a8d605877.

[12] DBS Bank. (2016). How DBS Bank is using human centered design principles to create an exceptional customer experience.

[13] Tan, M. (2013, October). DBS launches mobile phone. *The Straits Times*. www.straitstimes.com/business/dbs-launches-mobile phone-mortgage-app. Accessed 20 January 2021.

silo and used design thinking in re-imagining the way HR functions delivered their services and practices.[14] Bold changes were made in the HR function, specifically artificial intelligence and leveraging data, to gain a competitive advantage in the talent domain. According to Euromoney, DBS' difference in leading digital disruption is to embeds digital innovation into everything the bank does, with a concrete positive impact on the margins.[15]

New Working Models

Innovative solutions create new markets and jobs. Many traditional jobs are in extinction. There is a long-term trend toward improving the use of talents.[16] Potential strategies are:

- Organizations choose to reduce employment. Those selected to remain are enrolled in various training schemes to develop skills to increase labor productivity, thus increasing capital and labor investment by complementing each other and increasing workers' skills and welfare.
- Organizations tend to replace the workforce with capital whenever it is possible and makes sense. Organizations move to robots and computers to perform their tasks more efficiently. In this new scenario, it is essential to assure human–technology collaboration.

Both trends will play an essential role in the global labor market.[17]

[14] Chia, A. J. H., & Lee, J. J. (2019). Banking outside-in: How design thinking is changing the banking industry? *IASDR 2019*.

[15] Euromoney. (2019). Euromoney names the world's best banks in its 2019 Awards for Excellence. www.euromoney.com/research-and-awards/surveys-and-awards/awards-for-excellence/2019. Accessed 30 August 2020.

[16] Ungureanu, A. V. (2020). The transition from industry 4.0 to industry 5.0. The 4Cs of the global economic change. *LUMEN Proceedings, 13*, 70–81.

[17] Kaji, J., Hurley, B., Gangopadhyay, S., Bhat, R., & Khan, A. (2019). Leading the social enterprise: Reinvent with a human focus. Deloitte Global Human Capital Trends. *Deloitte Insights*.

Remote Working

Banking 5.0 requires more remote or smart working. This way of working is becoming the new normal, at least in banking and other businesses, after the pandemic. There could be similar events in the future: another pandemic, a financial crisis, or a significant disruption. Financial institutions need to be prepared and agile enough to manage disruptions in the short- and long-term future.

The McKinsey Global Institute (MGI) estimates that more than 20% of the global workforce (most of them in high-skilled jobs in sectors such as finance, insurance, and ICT) could work most of its time away from the office, being just as effective.[18]

Many financial institutions are handling the remote working well. Some areas are more challenging than others:

- Person management.
- Overloaded customer proximity centers due to the increased activities connected with customers' interactions, increasingly working with financial institutions online, via the phone, or messages.[19]
- Office areas like sales, marketing, and distribution which had more face-to-face interactions with customers traditionally They must now adapt to mediation of technological media.[20]
- Settlement and billing (mostly due to access to systems and complexity) and billing disputes.
- Compliance assessments and audit:
- Integrated management of outsourced processes.
- Physical security.

The challenges are not so much connectivity or gaps in the solutions. They are about person management skills, and processes. Many financial institutions are managing well with moving to remote connectivity. Others have not been able to work at the correct level for several network problems.

[18]Trends for the next normal | McKinsey. Accessed 20 January 2021.

[19]The future comes early—KPMG Global. home.kpmg/xx/en/home/insights/2020/04/insurance-workforce-transformation-through-covid-19.html. Accessed 12 June 2020.

[20]The future comes early—KPMG Global. home.kpmg/xx/en/home/insights/2020/04/insurance-workforce-transformation-through-covid-19.html. Accessed 12 June 2020.

The more in-depth challenge is to manage the remote workforce to achieve proper ability in the right areas. This challenge has already shown itself in the vast surge in inquiries and claims for health cover that many financial institutions have experienced during the pandemic. This situation is in contrast with other areas, which have declined. Financial institutions need the flexibility to respond and react quickly. They need a liquid workforce in which resources are more flexible.

Remote working requires the creation of a new model, especially for banking services distribution. The model must bring the flexibility and functionality that organizations need to work in a highly uncertain environment. It is something that many financial institutions need to learn quickly. Often, banking organizations are traditional, with a high emphasis on in-person presence.

There are several challenges in this new working model. Remote working struggles to replicate some of the benefits of face-to-face interactions. Many customers reported that creativity and spontaneity, the brainstorming of ideas that occur when a group of persons comes together to discuss a problem, or a need is not easy to reproduce virtually. The water fountain effect disappears, where persons informally meet and talk. In some cases, social networks or groupware can help. Still, persons refrain from putting in writing some observations or information.

Remote management is the most challenging part with a remote workforce. Organizations must make efforts to support managers on how they need to help their staff. Managing a team where most or all the persons are working remotely is challenging. It is necessary to ensure that persons feel motivated and supported. It is essential to help them perform at their creative best. looking after individuals' mental and emotional well-being, setting goals, and evaluating performance. There is no real roadmap for this on the scale that banking 5.0 requires. Targets and performance measures are tough to set. Pay and reward decisions will be drastically different in this unique environment.

It is critical to set up a correct framework for running a remote workforce. A more flexible and remote workforce can lead in the longer term to consider other aspects of the compensation. In the future, the overall organization-wide distribution of time spent in the office against time working remotely should be around 30–70%. Some staff may come into the office one or two times a week or a month, if ever.

Security is critical in the case of remote working. Hackers have taken the opportunity to exploit the pandemic. Persons working from home do not have access to the protective infrastructure that they would have at work. As a result, there has been an increase in phishing, fraud, and ransomware attacks. This situation requires an enhanced cyber security infrastructure and awareness.

Working remotely raises several challenging compliance issues which need to be managed. Data security becomes a critical concern, with a need to ensure that staff only use approved communication, documentation, and data transfer methods. Compliance with regulated or banking-critical processes stays vital. Management must ensure that the necessary online approval processes are in place. They should consider if it is needed to introduce any new actions or rules for full compliance.

Person Contribution to Banking 5.0

Persons in the organization must contribute to banking 5.0 at two levels:

- Persons are the base of organizational procedures and processes. They must be fully involved in the transformation into banking 5.0. Persons are affected by this transformation for the changes in the working processes. The results of a survey[21] show that employees are partly undecided based on the micro-level perspective, which technologies can use banking 5.0 and how it will affect their work habits. On the macro-level perspective, the employees understand and highlight the importance of banking 5.0 transformation as a success factor for the organization's future or even survival.
- At the management level, the banking 5.0 transformation and increasing global connectivity with cross-functional teams push the management to set up a working environment that can free the potential for creativity and innovation. Managers need to find the bottlenecks and challenges at the macro-level perspective and define proper actions to resolve them.

Some leaders need to work hard to match the desired agility and expectations and the essential information and communication security on a

[21] Bienhaus, F., & Haddud, A. (2018). Procurement 4.0: Factors influencing the digitization of procurement and supply chains. *Business Process Management Journal, 24*(4), 965–984.

banking 5.0 roadmap.[22] Some organizations have already introduced a new profile, called Chief digital officer (CDO), to support banking 5.0,[23] The CDO's job is to overcome the lack of agility, banking focus, and inflexible nature of some of the current staff, processes, and systems. The managers need to lead from the front and collaborate more closely with the concerned team, managers, and executives. There is a need for support from the top management to redefine everybody in their roles.

New Competencies

In connection with banking 5.0, there is a need to:

- Review the current competencies.
- Introduce new competencies, especially e-competencies.

Some examples of new competencies are commented in the following pages (Fig. 10.1).

Leadership in Banking

The role of banking executives and managers is essential in banking 5.0. They should:

- Define the priorities for their organization.
- Sell the solutions to the decision-takers.
- Plan and check actions.
- Implement pilots and proofs of concept.
- Understand the lessons learned and implement them in normal banking operations.

[22] Sharma, A. (2020). Industry 5.0—An opportunity to revivify the IT function. https://cio.economictimes.indiatimes.com/news/corporate-news/industry-4-0-an-opportunity-to-revivify-the-it-function/73078237. Accessed 28 January 2020.

[23] Horlacher, A., & Hess, T. (2016, January). What does a Chief Digital Officer do? Managerial tasks and roles of a new C-level position in the context of digital transformation. In *2016 49th Hawaii International Conference on System Sciences (HICSS)*, 126–5135. IEEE.

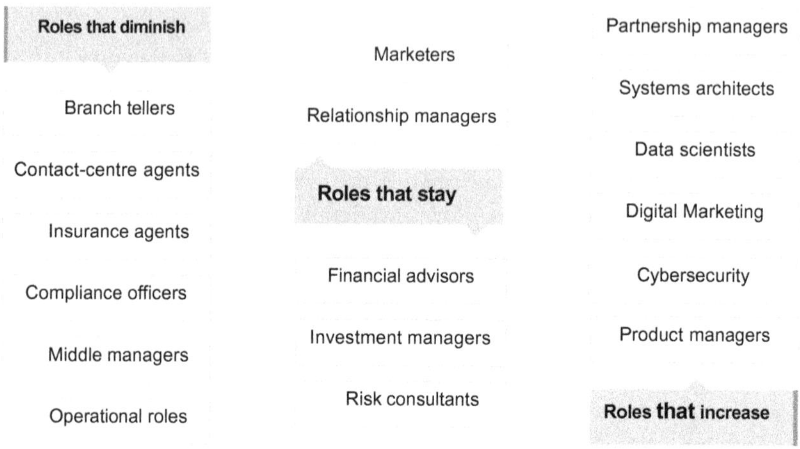

Fig. 10.1 New roles in insurance 4.0

New Competencies in Banking 5.0

Addressing the new challenges in banking 5.0 require models, processes, and platforms. Persons are essential. The following section covers a certain number of new and critical roles. For the search of these talents, it is necessary to use non-traditional sources. Academic partnership programs and research centers can help. It is necessary to explore new channels, such as social networks, social media, and top-performing employees. Only if banking personnel have e-competence can an organization fully benefit from the opportunities provided through digitization and automation (Fig. 10.2).[24]

Risk Scorer

The role of the risk scorers should consider the threats in the environment. It is necessary to:

[24] Competence is a demonstrated ability to apply knowledge, skills, and attitudes for achieving successful results. The European e-Competence Model (e-CF) provides a reference of 40 competencies as required and applied at the digital transformation workplace, using a common language for competencies, skills, and capability levels. More in www.ecompetencies.eu/wp-content/uploads/2014/02/European-e-Competence-Model-3.0_CEN_CWA_16234-1_2014.pdf. Accessed 30 May 2020.

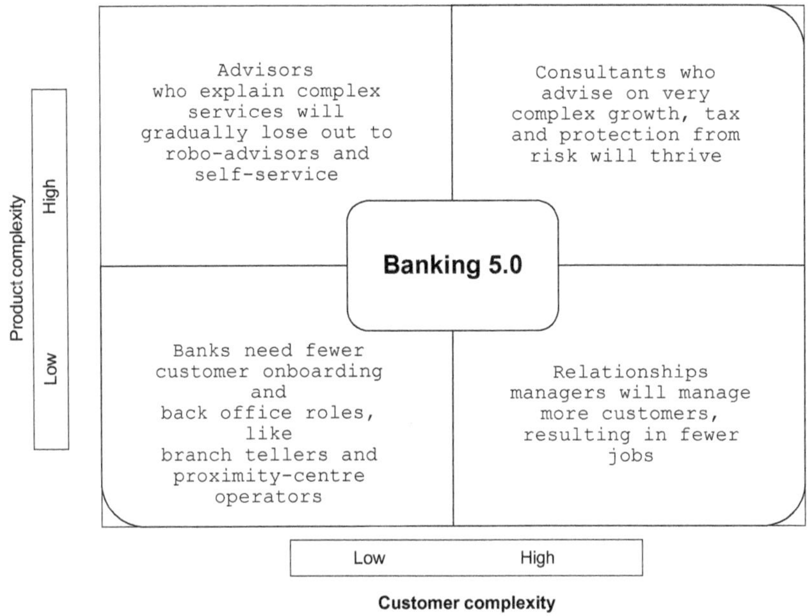

Fig. 10.2 Customer Facing Jobs in Banking 5.0

- Promote the organization's needs for risk management and resilience in banking.
- Conduct a careful assessment of banking risks connected with commercial strategies.
- Analyze and assess risks (old and new).
- Inquire about the prospects and their assets to evaluate the chances of new customers creating issues.
- Be aware of a series of contractual strategies and tactics applicable when the organization defines and negotiates contracts to avoid or mitigate risks.
- Take account on regulations on personal data.

To address in an effective, efficient, and economical way risk management, the risk scorers should have the following competencies[25]:

- Knowledge of banking processes and market characteristics.
- Knowledge of the risks methods, management tools, and techniques.
- E-competencies.
- Attention to the details.
- Analytical and open mind.
- Goal approach.

Machine Learning Engineer

It does not exist a general role for Artificial intelligence (AI) implementations. There are distinct roles, for example, machine learning engineers. They are mostly responsible for building and managing platforms for machine learning projects. They are highly sought after and command a high annual wage.[26] The role of a machine learning engineer is at the base of AI projects. It is suitable for those who come from a background in applied research and data science. It is necessary to program and prove a thorough understanding of multiple programming languages and readiness to learn new ones.

Machine learning engineers should apply predictive models and leverage natural language processing when working with big data analytics. The experience with agile development practices and familiarity with leading software helps Integrated development environment (IDE) tools like Eclipse and IntelliJ are also useful.[27]

Most jobs require candidates with experience in machine learning, deep learning, neural networks, and cloud applications. Significant is the presence of solid computer programming, mathematical, and analytical skills.

[25] www.cii.co.uk/media/1921347/c13j_8582_job_role_and_competency_framework_v2.pdf. Accessed 20 May 2020.

[26] www.springboard.com/blog/5-careers-in-artificial-intelligence/. Accessed 20 January 2021.

[27] Yang, Z., & Jiang, M. (2007). Using Eclipse as a tool-integration platform for software development. *IEEE Software, 24*(2), 87–89.

Data Scientist

The data scientist profile is relevant for data analysis, management, and mining. Data scientists need in-depth domain knowledge and a broad set of analytical competencies.[28] Data scientists are highly trained computer scientists. They are innovators able to find new perspectives on general trends out of the available data.[29] A data scientist analyzes data from several and diverse sources.[30] S/he examines the different tasks to reach a general understanding of the aspects that enable a financial institution to develop competitive advantages.

Process Architect

The process architects design future state processes ("To-Be") supported by banking 5.0. The processes are associated with several solution-related factors to banking 5.0, like robotic processing automation, AI, sustainability, and person–robot collaborations. The process architects define new processes, either long term or short term, centralized, or decentralized processes and systems.[31] They need to understand the current system flow, find the system components gaps, task handling, time needs, and cost reductions, along with systems effectiveness, efficiency, and economics. S/he and business analysts handle processes redesign in a digital transformation.

Technologist

Technologists develop solutions that translate banking logic into digital and automation platforms. Usually, a technologist is an engineer who

[28] Waller, M. A., & Fawcett, S. E. (2013). Data science, predictive analytics, and big data: a revolution that will transform supply chain design and management. *Journal of Business Logistics, 34*(2), 77–84.

[29] Molino, J. L., & Sedkaoui, S. (2016). *Big data, open data and data development*. ISTE Ltd. and Wiley, Hoboken, NJ.

[30] Big data, open data and data development—Slidelegend.Com. slidelegend.com/big-data-open-data-and-data-development_59b99b031723dde15b68a08e.html. Accessed 20 May 2020.

[31] Cho, E. S., Cha, J. E., & Yang, Y. J. (2004, May). Marmi-Re: a method and tools for legacy system modernization. In *International conference on software engineering research and applications* (pp. 42–57). Springer, Berlin/Heidelberg, Germany; The future digital work force: Robotic process automation. www.scielo.br/scielo.php?script=sci_arttext&pid=S1807-17752019000100300. Accessed 10 October 2020.

specializes in a specific technology or who uses a key solution in a particular field.[32] A banking 5.0 initiative usually includes a team of dedicated architects, designers, and developers (possibly in a low-cost location) to activate the program and test the applications. The technical competencies needed for banking 5.0 tools need open-minded solution experts in several areas of digital and automation.

Banking in Team

The correct approach in banking 5.0 is to consider the Ps: processes, platforms, persons, partnerships, and protection. Lately, there is much talk of teamwork in banking due to the increasing importance and complexity of the value network and remote working. Collaboration is now increasingly appreciated and valued. The current banking model will change in a future perspective about functions, responsibilities, and stakeholders. These changes are pushed by teamwork to increase digitization and opportunities, supported by ecosystems and other trends outlined in this book.[33]

Persons and Organization

Banking 5.0 is teamwork within the organization and the banking ecosystem. For example, it is critical to have in the project team members and subject-matter experts of distinct banking services and processes in a project. They would be members of the project, full or part-time, based on the project's size. For organizations that are stakeholders of the project, it is interesting to work within the group to achieve synergies in the standard policies. In the case of organizations that are not part of the same group, the organization can team up with other organizations in the same ecosystem.

The benefits of teamwork can be significant from the standpoint of effectiveness, efficiency, and economy. The most important benefits are

[32] Pramanik, H. S., Kirtania, M., & Pani, A. K. (2019). Essence of digital transformation—Manifestations at large financial institutions from North America. *Future Generation Computer Systems, 95*, 323–343.

[33] Sengupta, S. (2013). 10 trends in supply chain management. *Supply Chain Management Review, 17*(4), 34–39.

the increase in the banking organization's effectiveness: especially in unexpected situations, in response times, and the customers' delight.

Old style managers believe that teams of persons need to be physically present together for proper functioning. The pandemic shows that teams can be set up and engaged in diverse ways and still be very productive. Pandemic is pushing to adopt smaller, leaner, and significantly more effective teams. These teams break down large functions into small working groups that can self-organize, connect highly effectively, and react quickly to changing needs. The difficulty is a change of culture since teamwork has not been very much present in financial institutions.

Processes

In banking, teamwork is effective in supporting, for instance, banking marketing. In this case, the participation of many persons with diverse experiences can provide an effective support.

Platforms

The support that the Information and communication technologies (ICT) can supply for teamwork is growing and improves over time. For banking 5.0, it is helpful that the ICT platforms include three essential aspects of the collaboration:

- Communication is the backbone of teamwork. A banking platform supporting teams uses various media, such as chats, emails, video, and audio conference calls, at several levels of participation.
- Coordination is based on rules, explicit or implicit, to enable distinct team members to run in cooperation. Typical tools used in a banking 5.0 team are group calendars, teaming applications, and automatic software packages for planning and document sharing.
- Cooperation implies the sharing of a context that varies with the characteristics of the working team's initiatives.

In the past, the platforms for teamwork were proprietary. Today many commercial solutions are available. They are called groupware.[34] They are methods and tools that enable users with networked workstations to:

- Communicate in several ways with exchanges of messages (emails, chats, and similar), voice calls, and videos.
- Allow Condivision of multimedia documents (text, data, video, images, and sounds).
- Co-work on the same application programs, whether it is a simple spreadsheet, or a complex application, with different team members.
- Get Consensus on decisions at several stages of the process, using tools that ease discussion and idea generation, such as online brainstorming sessions.

Intra-organization and inter-organization can exploit cloud computing solutions. It allows the organization to use cloud computing to interact effectively, efficiently, economically, and in total transparency with all the team members and partners. AI can help a lot in teamwork, especially in computer vision, natural language processing, and translation.

Protection or Security

In teamwork, attention must be paid to data security and confidentiality, the protection and tracking of information, and data transparency for all partners and customers. It is critical to control access to the teamwork, tools, and data sharing to avoid data breaches with competitors or hackers.

Education 5.0

Regarding banking 5.0, the persons are the capital asset.[35] Persons do not come with embedded knowledge. Banking know-how may be essential, but for many types of banking services, for example, financial advisors or

[34] Kadir, B. A., & Broberg, O. (2020). Human well-being and system performance in the transition to industry 5.0. *International Journal of Industrial Ergonomics, 76*, 102,936.

[35] Baldwin, R., & Forslid, R. (2020). *Globotics and development: When manufacturing is jobless and services are tradable* (No. w26731). National Bureau of Economic Research.

project management, the technology is a sideshow. The skills and experiences of the persons, the service providers, are the real limitation. Joining service value networks require a significant push. Accumulation of human capital may take longer compared to the expansion of physical capital.

Banking 5.0 is associated with the support of AI, robotic process automation, and sustainability. The approach suggested in this chapter for education 5.0 is holistic and integrated.

Education 5.0 requires three steps to lead to banking 5.0[36]:

- Develop education and training programs. Education 5.0 must be an integrated process. It starts to create awareness and sensitivity from the top management downward. This approach must be consistent with the financial institution's strategy and, in general, with its policy.[37]
- Redesign how persons work and interact. The organization should redesign the work experience of the persons within the organization and the critical intermediaries.
- Attract new talents from the labor market. The innovative ways of working (new roles, new competencies, new relationships and partnerships, new tools, and so on) can be challenging to be accepted and integrated within their work by some persons in the organization.

Some aspects that characterize industry 5.0, and hence banking 5.0, are[38]:

[36] This section follows the guidelines introduced and pioneered by Prof. Marco Perona and presented in www.digital4.biz/insurance/strategie/insurance-4-0-la-check-list-lufficio-acquisti-digitale/. Accessed 9 March 2019.

[37] In 2006, the European Parliament proposed the first definition of Digital Competence in the Recommendation of the European Parliament and the Council of December. It includes eight critical competencies for lifelong learning. Digital competence is used with confidence and critical Information society technologies (IST) for work, leisure, and communication. Its bases are the primary competencies in ICT (Information and Communication Technologies): the use of computers to retrieve, assess, store, produce, present, and exchange information and communicate and participate in collaborative networks via the internet.

[38] Kayikci, Y. (2018). Sustainability impact of digitization in logistics. *Procedia Manufacturing, 21*, 782–789.

- Cooperation. Innovative solutions enable the creation of virtual teams through which organizations exchange ideas, data, information, and documents.
- Connectivity. Banking 5.0 should enable horizontal and vertical integration in the value network and ensures information transparency in all network links.
- Adaptiveness. The system of connected digital and automation resources must be flexible. It must be able to respond to changes in the environment (requests, customers, users, partners, and so on).
- Integration. In the digital world, the banking systems combination involves connecting different software applications, machinery automation, physically or functionally, to coordinate the banking flows. There should be an integration between humans and machines.
- Autonomous. Smart objects, physical or virtual, should be independent but able to communicate and support decisions-making with ICT and AI applications.
- Cognition. Application of devices and systems for the automation of tasks requires personal competencies, knowledge, perception, and cognitive competencies (planning, reasoning, and learning).

Banking 5.0 launched at the organization level requires a significant effort and rethinking of education and training. Underlying banking 5.0, there are the 12 Ps of the business model canvas. Among them, processes, platforms, persons, and partnerships require special attention. Persons are essential to architect, design, develop, check, and control innovative solutions. Hence the education and training of persons on the banking 5.0 vision and characteristics involve many persons. It is critical developing their e-competencies.[39]

Education 5.0 must relate the persons to the other three relevant Ps: Processes, Platforms, and Partnerships. Some persons believe that banking 5.0 is only automation and digitization. It is critical to review the processes and partnerships and re-engineer them in the direction of the banking 5.0 robust organization goals.

[39] Arballo, N. C., Núñez, M. E. C., & Tapia, B. R. (2019). Technological competencies: A systematic review of the literature in 22 years of study. *International Journal of Emerging Technologies in Learning, 14*(4), 4–30.

A McKinsey survey reported that more than 40% of the current workforce would need to be either replaced or fundamentally retrained to make up for their organizations' skills gaps in a banking 5.0 organization.[40] Only 15% of respondents say their organizations plan to pursue a talent-strategy transformation in the next two years, even though the talent challenge still is important.

Attention should go in education and training in small- and medium-sized financial institutions through practical research and tailor-made knowledge transfer. The items to consider are several, such as automation, process banking 5.0 transformation, both accompanied by the business model transformation.

The education and the application of banking 5.0 require a team effort. It is critical to promote training on improving teamwork and making it more effective, efficient, and value-adding. Education 5.0 must be at all levels and roles of the organization. It should not be limited to persons working on automation and ICT. On the contrary, it is necessary to develop e-competencies in all areas. Banking professionals, management, staff, strategy, marketing, operations, sales, and administration should be involved in education 5.0.

It helps start with an activity of "train the trainers"[41] that is training other trainers or at least the key users throughout the organization. The number of persons involved in the organization in a banking 5.0 transformation could be remarkably high. Training trainers in the organization can help reduce costs and foster the creation of "evangelists" who spread best practices across the organization.

Ideally, training for banking 5.0 should start in schools and universities. It is also essential to train the staff already employed to convert and provide active support to the initiative. Banking 5.0 requires new competencies and capabilities. Persons in the organization should be involved well before starting a banking 5.0 initiative.

The ideal location for training 4.0 is in or near the organization's premises. Training on the job with frequent applications and interactions is essential. Training limited to the classroom would not achieve

[40] Dhasarathy, A., Frazier, R., Khan, N., & Steagall, K. (2021, March). Seven lessons on how technology transformations can deliver value. *McKinsey Digital*.

[41] Pearce, J., Mann, M. K., Jones, C., van Buschbach, S., Olff, M., & Bisson, J. I. (2012). The most effective way of delivering a Train-the-Trainers program: a systematic review. *Journal of Continuing Education in the Health Professions, 32*(3), 215–226.

the purpose of the transformation: the organization would be unable to prototype and do proofs of the concept of banking 5.0. In that case, the organization can use training as the playground for the first small implementations of banking 5.0 and succeed. It would be possible to strengthen the participants in the importance and viability of banking 5.0.

Apart from classroom training and on the job, it helps include visits to other organizations that have successfully implemented banking 5.0. A visit to research centers would be helpful to expand the network of relationships.

Robotic Process Automation

The use of virtual robots is exciting.[42] They are agents or programs with a proper level of AI. Virtual robots can replicate some person's actions. As an example, software robots can carry out data entry tasks or interact with a system's user interface as would operators do. Robotic process automation (RPA) studies and applies these types of operations. By using a machine learning algorithm, over time, RPA can improve.[43]

Robotic Process Automation Architecture

RPA uses AI and robots (based on software or in a few cases physical) to automate simple and repetitive tasks.[44] RPA supports several standardized and rule-based tasks and processes.[45] The term robot in RPA refers to "software programs that mimic person actions."[46] The term automation in RPA is related to a "solution that deals with the application of

[42] Perona, M. (2019). Procurement 4.0, the check list for purchasing digital. www.digital4.biz/insurance/ufficio-acquisti-digitale-cose-quali-benefici-del-insurance-4-0/. Accessed 9 March 2019.

[43] Mohri, M., Rostamizadeh, A., & Talwalkar, A. (2018). *Foundations of machine learning*. MIT Press, Cambridge, MA.

[44] Anagnoste, S. (2017, July). Robotic automation process—Next major revolution in back-office operations improvement. *Proceedings of the International Conference on Business Excellence, 11*(1), 676–686. De Gruyter Open, Berlin, Germany

[45] Lacity, M., & Willcocks, L. (2015). What knowledge workers stand to gain from automation. *Harvard Business Review*.

[46] Tripathi, A. M. (2018). *Learning robotic process automation*. Packt, Birmingham, UK.

machines and computers to the production of products and services."[47] RPA applies specific solutions and methods to use a computer as a virtual Full-time equivalent (FTE) person.

RPA processes tasks in the same way that a person processes transaction. There are differences between RPA and traditional automation processes.[48] RPA can take over some parts of the operations, while traditional methods use instructions based on program codes.[49] RPA is flexible. It can deal with dynamic and fast-changing environments. An example in this direction was the use of RPA to support some activities required by the sudden pandemic outbreak.

The past years saw a substantial increase in robotic process automation in back-offices and shared service operations.[50] Examples of such uses are data transfer from multiple input sources, like emails and spreadsheets, to Enterprise resource planning (ERP) and Customer relationship management (CRM) systems.[51] Thanks to RPA, organizations can free time of their expert professionals.

An RPA has several components.[52]

- The development studio configures and trains the robots. This activity requires setting up codes with instructions and some decision-making logic. The development studio consists of two components: the recorder, which handles the configuration of the robot, and the plugin/extension, which simplifies the development and interfacing of the robot.
- The control center aims to control and check the different operations of the robot.[53]
- The bot runner is the component that performs the activities in the processes involved.

[47] Tripathi, A. M. (2018). *Learning robotic process automation*. Packt, Birmingham, UK.

[48] Tripathi, A. M. (2018). *Learning robotic process automation*. Packt, Birmingham, UK.

[49] Sutherland, C. (2013, October). Framing a constitution for robotistan. *Hfs Research*.

[50] Willcocks, L., & Lacity, M. (2016). *Service automation, robots and the future of work*. SB Publishing, Stratford, CT.

[51] Lacity, M. C., & Willcocks, L. P. (2016). A new approach to automating services. *MIT Sloan Management Review, 58*(1), 41.

[52] Tripathi, A. M. (2018). *Learning robotic process automation*. Packt, Birmingham, UK.

[53] Tripathi, A. M. (2018). *Learning robotic process automation*. Packt, Birmingham, UK.

The global robotic process automation market size was valued at $1,636 million in 2019 and the forecast is at $19,534 million by 2027, growing at a Compound annual growth rate (CAGR) of 36.4% from 2020 to 2027.[54]

Ladenburg[55]
Ladenburg Thalmann Financial Services Inc. is a publicly traded diversified financial institution based in Miami, Florida. They launched $ymbil[SM], a self-service investment platform that matched Ladenburg affiliated advisors' customers to a diversified portfolio consistent with their risk tolerance. With a minimum investment of USD 500, $ymbil[SM] allows customers to fund their accounts and start investing in a brief time. $ymbil[SM] uses a proprietary scoring method to recommend portfolios in multiple risk categories. The portfolios use globally diversified asset allocations and tactical decisions to capitalize on market conditions and unique investment opportunities.

Human–Machine Collaboration[56]
The diffusion of technologies such as AI and virtual reality are opening new scenarios. They will change work. There will be mixed teams composed of persons and smart technologies. In this way, it is possible to combine personal experience with AI. Forty-three percent of Italian manufacturing Subject matter experts (SMEs) share this opinion. They have already adopted or intend to introduce innovative solutions/processes, including ICT security, cloud computing, collaborative robotics, and the Internet of things.[57]

When combined with human ingenuity and creativity, AI allows both humans and financial institutions to achieve much more. Accenture calls it "applied intelligence." Financial institutions gain the ability to solve

[54] www.alliedmarketresearch.com/robotic-process-automation-market. Accessed 20 February 2021.

[55] www.businesswire.com/news/home/20160321005351/en/Ladenburg-Thalmann-Launches-ymbil---Robo-Advisor-Platform. Accessed 20 August 2016.

[56] https://home.kpmg/xx/en/home/insights/2020/04/insurance-workforce-transformation-through-covid-19.html. Accessed 30 May 2020.

[57] www.mecspe.com/en/comunicati-stampa-en/osservatorio-mecspe-focus-nazionale/. Accessed 5 August 2019.

complex challenges, develop new products and services, and break into or create new markets.[58]

Robots will become cobots increasingly. Cobot combines two words COllaborative and roBOT. Cobots combine operational and integrative flexibility capable of interacting securely with the work environment and with the operators with whom they share their work. Cobots are power tools that add power to the operators in terms of speed, accuracy, and precision with a human touch. Financial institutions are interested in virtual or software cobots. Some uses of these cobots are:

- Automatic preparation and sending of documentation requests.
- Use of smart contracts and support the drafting of the agreements. These solutions are computer protocols that ease, verify, enforce, negotiate, or execute a contract.
- Automated performance management and monitoring. Fraud detection. Automated customer assessments.
- Production of automatic dashboards and automated indications of the improvement actions.
- Production of customized services.

Machine learning systems almost never replace the entire job, process, or business model. Most often, they complement human operators' activities.[59] The essence of "person augmentation" is in concepts such as augmented intelligence,[60] or "person-AI symbiosis."[61] In this way, AI systems amplify intellective, cognitive, and if necessary personal sensitive capabilities rather than replace them. The most valuable competency that humans contribute to AI-powered decision-making is a critical judgment and creativity.

[58] www.accenture.com/_acnmedia/PDF-77/Accenture-Workforce-Banking-Survey-Report. Accessed 28 November 2020.

[59] Brynjolfsson, E., & McAfee, A. (2017). The business of artificial intelligence. *Harvard Business Review*, 1–20.

[60] Zheng, N. N., Liu, Z. Y., Ren, P. J., Ma, Y. Q., Chen, S. T., Yu, S. Y., & Wang, F. Y. (2017). Hybrid-augmented intelligence: Collaboration and cognition. *Frontiers of Information Solution & Electronic Engineering, 18*(2), 153–179.

[61] Jarrahi, M. H. (2018). Artificial intelligence and the future of work: Human-AI symbiosis in organizational decision making. *Business Horizons, 61*(4), 577–586.

AI systems will push this approach further, causing workers' interactions with corporate actions and processes to become more abstract.[62] The new role is to oversee, analyze, and ease interactions between AI operators with customers, using a unique combination of soft and complex competencies.

Some AI tools, for example, deep learning systems, can make errors and can be fooled.[63] Such fundamental limitations of AI systems push AI's vision to augment persons' intelligence rather than working autonomously in most organizational processes. Decision responsibility eventually lies with persons, and their active participation ensures the accountability of decisions taken.[64] To avoid the pitfalls of cognitive complacency, human contributors need to understand how their technological partners develop inferences. They need a decision support system in the form of an "intelligent interface layer" that eases interactions with the intelligent machine.[65] An intelligent interface sets in motion a process of mutual learning.[66]

Human–robot collaboration (HRC) can be characterized by several aspects of different research fields, from robotics to personal factors. The direct human–robot interaction describes banking 5.0.[67] Some authors have found eight HRC latent dimensions (autonomy, information exchange, team organization, adaptivity and training tasks, person factors, ethics, and cyber security). For each dimension, an evaluation method can be described arriving at an HRC framework.[68] Within this framework,

[62] Zuboff, S. (1985). Automate/informate: The two faces of intelligent solutions. *Organizational Dynamics, 14*(2), 5–18.

[63] Rouse, W. B., & Spohrer, J. C. (2018). Automating versus augmenting intelligence. *Journal of Enterprise Transformation*, 1–21.

[64] Lupton, D., & Jutel, A. (2015). 'It's like having a physician in your pocket!'A critical analysis of self-diagnosis mobile phone apps. *Social Science & Medicine, 133*, 128–135.

[65] Jarrahi, M. H. (2019). In the age of the smart artificial intelligence: AI's dual capacities for automating and informating work. *Business Information Review, 36*(4), 178–187.

[66] Rouse, W. B., & Spohrer, J. C. (2018). Automating versus augmenting intelligence. *Journal of Enterprise Transformation*, 1–21.

[67] Bauer, M. (2020). Preise kalkulieren mit KI-gestützter Onlineplattform BAM GmbH, Weiden, Germany.

[68] Gervasi, R., Mastrogiaconno, L., & Franceschini, F. (2020). A conceptual framework to evaluate human–robot collaboration. *International Journal of Advanced Manufacturing Solution.*

different collaborative applications can be evaluated and compared on the various dimensions that characterize HRC.

Robotic Process Automation in Banking 5.0

The financial sector is one of the important markets for the implementation of RPA.[69] The expectation is that this sector will grow to 34% of the global RPA market by 2022. Increased diffusion of internet-connected devices has changed the financial industry's conventional operations. making applications more intelligent. The demand for smart solutions in this sector is rising, as financial institutions seek new ways to increase their customer delight and cater to the large customer base with fast services.[70] The main reason for using RPA in financial and accounting processes is the need to manage the growing volume of transactions and cope with moving from physical branches to online.[71] Implementing the RPA platform improves accuracy.[72] An RPA supplies the best efficiency and accuracy in financial and external reporting, and general accounting.[73] Using RPA, AI offers many possibilities for the automation of manual and standardized processes in all categories, for example, for risk management.[74]

There are several areas of application of software robots in support of banking.[75] By combining AI, machine learning, and advanced RPA systems, financial institutions can handle customers' inquiries and applications far more quickly and accurately. Innovative email management

[69] www.juniperresearch.com/press/press-releases/robotic-process-automation-revenues-in-banking. Accessed 25 September 2020.

[70] www.alliedmarketresearch.com/robotic-process-automation-market. Accessed 20 February 2021.

[71] Aberdeen Group. (2017). The financial close: Automation, efficiency and the emergence of RPA. Waltham, MA.

[72] Aberdeen Group. (2017). The financial close: Automation, efficiency and the emergence of RPA. Waltham, Ma.

[73] https://insightsbenelux.com/publications/%2314_werkplaats_(ochtend)_EY_Finance_Robotics.pdf. Accessed 25 September 2020.

[74] Dzhaparov, P. (2020). Application of blockchain and artificial intelligence in bank risk management. *Икономика и управление*, *17*(1), 43–57.

[75] www.scriptieprijs.be/sites/default/files/thesis/2019-09/MBA_Valgaeren_H_Final_Report1819.pdf. Accessed 25 September 2020.

systems can filter and redirect incoming emails. In this way, it is possible to automate the responses to common inquiries and complaints. Automated call-center and web-chat services significantly improve the quality of customer services.[76]

RPA solutions help to minimize growing compliance risks. Some examples are tracking risk limit breaches, risk data quality assessments, and reporting documents preparation. The financial institution can quickly and effectively discover various regulatory information from multiple public sources.[77] Virtual robots can automate the larger part of these manual activities. RPAs bring benefits in terms of compliance risk. They can coordinate between risk management teams and those engaged in compliance with regulations, avoiding fines and reputational damages, supplying comprehensive and correct information for auditors.

Estimates vary, but adoption of RPA solutions currently sits at about 25% of financial institutions. Gartner estimates this will rise to 85% by 2022.[78]

Benefits and Challenges of Robotic Process Automation

Financial institutions typically choose cloud-based RPA solutions to improve performance in several ways, such as cost savings and usage-based billing, business agility and focus, and many others.[79] RPA improves accuracy across financial institutions. Simultaneously, it delivers profitability. By applying RPA, the financial institution can[80]:

[76] https://insuranceblog.accenture.com/intelligent-automation-gives-financial institutions-a-big-opportunity-to-boost-the-quality-of-their-customer-service. Accessed 24 December 2019.

[77] Kofax. (2018). *Forecasting your future: How financial institutions are improving operations*. https://badr.blog/wp-content/uploads/2018/09/kofax-kapow-how-financial-instit utions-are-improving-operations-with-rpa-ebook.pdf. Accessed 20 January 2021; Dzhaparov, P. (2020). Application of blockchain and artificial intelligence in bank risk management. *Иkономиka и управление, 17*(1), 43–57.

[78] www.finextra.com/sibos-2020-report---digital-transformation-accelerated.pdf. Accessed 10 December 2020.

[79] www.alliedmarketresearch.com/robotic-process-automation-market. Accessed 20 February 2021.

[80] Burgess, A. (2017). *The executive guide to artificial intelligence: How to find and implement applications for AI in your organization*. Springer, Berlin/Heidelberg, Germany.

- Increase speed, productivity, and controls.
- Assure better accuracy and reduction of labor costs.
- Be scalable.
- Deliver business intelligence and accelerate banking 5.0 transformation. The development of an application in RPA takes a fraction of the time and costs compared to traditional ICT solutions and less for its maintenance.
- Keep working at 100% capacity 24*7. It can execute tasks in many environments and across many applications.

A British financial institution has implemented RPA in its financial and accounting processes.[81] Before the implementation of RPA, every single transaction had a transaction time of 30 minutes. By implementing RPA, the financial institution's transaction time was 10 minutes per transaction. The return of investment was 80% within six months. RPAs can reduce costs from 30 to 80%.[82] The automation of accounting-related processes like payments and transactions leads to more efficient and precise statements and reports. With intelligent automation solutions, it is possible to reduce data handling times by 40% and cut its processing costs by 80%.[83] The substantial improvement in processing accuracy enables the financial institution to improve the times the staff spent addressing customer needs by 43%.

The most significant benefits that the RPA application brings in risk management automation: time savings, reduced need for manual interventions, fewer errors, compliance costs reduction, risk reports generation in (almost) real-time, better control over processes, keeping the operational flexibility necessary, and improving system effectiveness.[84] Automated models allow risk teams to test a large amount of output data by

[81] www.capgemini.com/consulting-de/wp-content/uploads/sites/32/2017/08/robotic-process-automation-study.pdf. Accessed 20 November 2020.

[82] www.mckinsey.com/business-functions/operations/our-insights/operations-management-reshaped-by-robotic-automation. Accessed 20 January 2021.

[83] https://insuranceblog.accenture.com/intelligent-automation-gives-financial-institutions-a-big-opportunity-to-boost-the-quality-of-their-customer-service. Accessed 10 April 2020.

[84] https://insightsbenelux.com/publications/%2314_werkplaats_(ochtend)_EY_Finance_Robotics.pdf. Accessed 25 September 2020.

parallel simulations, choose the correct ones, and use the time saved to solve other banking problems.[85]

The implementation of RPA leads to a lower workload and reduces the employees' overall stress level. The introduction of RPA can lead to an increase in the quality of accounting methods within an organization.[86] Benefits, challenges, and the implementation of RPA may be different in other countries due to differences in culture and regulations.

RPA also presents a lot of challenges, risks, and potential errors.[87] It is essential to start implementing RPA in low-value tasks and only use it for complex tasks when the organization is RPA-mature.

Research has investigated the impact of RPA on employees.[88] A study done in London, UK,[89] ended up having contrasting results with a study done in several Asian countries.[90] Lacity and Willcocks mention that employees were happy with introducing virtual robots as they saw them as an opportunity to get new challenges and more responsibilities.[91] This finding is partially supported by a study that states that using RPA brings a change in skills and profiles that will lead to new and more complex jobs.[92] Another research mentions that the robots' introduction demotivated employees because they had difficulties with internal process

[85] BCG. (2019). *Global Risk 2019: Creating a More Digital, Resilient Bank*. www.bcg.com/publications/2019/global-risk-creating-digital-resilient-bank.aspx. Accessed 20 January 2021.

[86] Kloviene, L., & Gimzauskiene, E. (2015). The effect of information solution on accounting system's conformity with business environment: A case study in banking sector company. *Journal of Economics and Finance, 32*, 1707–1712.

[87] https://insightsbenelux.com/publications/%2314_werkplaats_(ochtend)_EY_Finance_Robotics.pdf. Accessed 25 September 2020.

[88] Meena, M. M. R., & Parimalarani, G. (2020, January). Impact of digital transformation on employment in banking sector. *International Journal of Scientific & Solutions Research, 9*(1).

[89] Lacity, C. M., & Willcocks, P. L. (2016). A new approach to automating services. *MIT Sloan Management Review*.

[90] Fernandez, D., & Aman, A. (2018). Impacts of robotic process automation of global accounting services. *Asian Journal of Accounting and Governance, 9*, 123–131.

[91] Lacity, C. M., & Willcocks, P. L. (2016). A new approach to automating services. *MIT Sloan Management Review*.

[92] Perez, C., & Martin, F. (2018). *Digitalisation and artificial intelligence: The new face of the retail banking sector—Evidence from France and Spain*. Federal Reserve Bank of St. Louis, St. Louis, MO.

changes.[93] The implementation of RPA significantly impacts the current jobs in a banking institution since RPA requires a change in current employees' skills and profiles. As the number of employees within the banking sector is already decreasing, the introduction of robots seems to be another reason employees fear losing their jobs.

Disadvantages and criticalities with RPA fall into three categories: special regulations, the costs of setting up a program, and the risk of third-party litigations.

Another challenge implies that there are no clear regulations about what a robot may or may not do and that the current laws differ among countries.[94] Some customers fear accuracy and reliability issues as they may think that robots are taking over all person tasks and it might be easy to hack robots.[95]

Financial institutions need to consider that RPA is not made to take over all the organization's tasks.[96] According to Ernst & Young, in general, the best combination would be 70–80% of automation and a personal workforce of 20–30%.

Financial institutions using RPA need to follow robot regulations. Financial institutions will incur costs to set up a robotic program. Apart from the purchase or leasing cost, financial institutions need to consider maintenance and compliance costs and create internal rules governing their use.

[93] Fernandez, D., & Aman, A. (2018). Impacts of robotic process automation of global accounting services. *Asian Journal of Accounting and Governance, 9*, 123–131.

[94] Anagnoste, S. (2017, July). Robotic automation process—The next major revolution in terms of back-office operations improvement. *Proceedings of the International Conference on Business Excellence, 11*(1), 676–686. Sciendo.

[95] Mehta, N., Agashe, A., & Detroja, P. (2017). *Swipe to unlock: The non-coder's guide to solutions and the business strategy behind it*. CreateSpace Independent Publishing Platform, Scotts Valley, CA.

[96] https://insightsbenelux.com/publications/%2314_werkplaats_(ochtend)_EY_Finance_Robotics.pdf. Accessed 25 September 2020.

HSBC

HSBC rolled out RPA solutions across all its China operations supporting commercial and retail bank products, KYC, onboarding, and other functions.[97] The digital operations center in China supports internal businesses in Japan, Malaysia, and other regions. The bank includes analytics to its RPA suite, adding another layer of intelligence, with tools like Optical character recognition (OCR) and indexing or categorizing data. These features support AI functions, such as voice-to-text conversions or analyzing text to understand a conversation's tone. The banking goal is to apply it to all its call centers.

Conclusions

This chapter studies the impact of banking 5.0 on persons. The results described in this chapter would be interesting for financial institutions who doubt whether to implement banking 5.0 in their internal processes. Banking 5.0 yields many benefits and opportunities but still poses challenges. The current positive balance between benefits and challenges will improve over time.

New profiles, education, and training are essential for banking 5.0. It is necessary to address them holistically, consider all aspects, and address them in a consistent and integrated framework.

Five essential competencies are essential in implementing banking 5.0 in the organization:

- Take care of the talents with new profiles and re-training the existing workforce.
- Manage innovation in human–digital–automation collaboration.
- Manage digital value networks and ecosystems.
- Implement a lean and digitize approach.[98]

[97] HSBC plans self-learning RPA expansion—DigFin (digfingroup.com). Accessed 4 January 2021.

[98] Elg, M., Gremyr, I., Hellström, A., & Witell, L. (2011). The role of quality managers in contemporary organizations. *Total Quality Management & Business Excellence, 22*(8), 795–806.

- Assure core competencies in safety and cyber security both in the ICT and Operations technologies (OT) domains.[99]

Specific surveys on industry 5.0 are not available. It is interesting to examine the study of the Osservatorio del Politecnico di Milano (Italy). They surveyed the profiles of some Italian organizations in their knowledge of competencies in terms of industry 4.0.[100] Half of the organizations knew about industry 4.0 or claimed to have assessed their competencies for industry 4.0. This news is positive. It is in a context where another 25% say they want to implement it soon. The survey revealed that the training was for persons engaged in operations, employees, and profiles directly involved in digitization and automation systems. The sensitivity in the training courses does not stop at the operational floor. Instead, managers and entrepreneurs should be involved in the roadmap to e-competencies. The survey was helpful in deciding some essential aspects of a digital transformation. The training of internal staff (24%) or external acquisition (11%) of the competencies needed are the two feedbacks from organizations engaged in a digital transformation. The survey creates some concerns of the marginal role of the HR function in the transformation education. Only 12% of the sample involved HR in guiding and directing the training roadmap to the industry 4.0 transformation. For 70% of the survey participants, HR either was not involved or only in a marginal way.

The implementation of RPA brings a lot of benefits for the organizations.[35] The financial and accounting processes, which are manual, repetitive tasks, can be done using RPA fast and at a constant level of quality. Employees enjoy a lower workload and can focus on more complex jobs, increasing employee and customer delight. Since the banking sector focuses on being innovative, it will get a competitive position in the global market. Financial institutions need to consider that there are several challenges and risks linked to the introduction of RPA. Financial institutions need to follow strict regulations that can differ

[99] Hickson, D. J., Pugh, D. S., & Pheysey, D. C. (1969). Operations solution organization structure: An empirical reappraisal. *Administrative Science Quarterly*, 378–397.

[100] www.industry4business.it/osservatori/osservatorio-industria-4-0-industrial-iot-analytics-e-cloud-manufacturing-spingono-il-mercato-a-24-mld-con-un-30/. Accessed 25 May 2019.

between countries. Using robots will cause not only jobs but ability losses. RPA is not the only solution available. Financial institutions need to consider the presence of alternative solutions, such as machine learning and AI.

CHAPTER 11

Partnerships in Banking 5.0

None of us including me ever do great things. But we can all do small things with great love and together we can do something wonderful.
Mother Teresa

Introduction

This book does not use the term vendor, intermediaries, agents, and similar but partners. There are several reasons for using this term. The first reason is that the partners can be of vastly diverse types: distributors of products, services, and systems, custodians, payment providers, partners external or from the same group of the financial institutions or even from the same organization or academic research institutions, consultants, and so on. The reason to use the word partner is that all these mentioned external parties are real partners. A partner is a person, natural or legal, with which the organization works together in activities in which sales and operations require the participation of more than one person and more than one competency. A partner is an ally. If the delivery is unsuccessful, both the partners and the customers suffer in their reputation, if not directly from a financial point of view. In banking 5.0, the partners play an essential role in the value network because of their relevance and close

B. Nicoletti, *Banking 5.0*, Palgrave Studies in Financial Services Technology, https://doi.org/10.1007/978-3-030-75871-4_11

interconnections. For a financial institution to realize the digital transformation's potential value, it must include partners in their transformation to banking 5.0.[1]

Coordinating partnerships that are best-in-class to deliver an engaging banking offering might be challenging. It can bring many benefits. Such an alliance can move quickly (as opposed to building internal capabilities from scratch) and allow opportunities to test and learn to improve the program. The key to successfully managing these new partnerships is to hold partners to the banking brand's standards.

Banking 5.0 reflects an increasing emphasis on the importance of partners. The activities that banking 5.0 organizations must implement are quite different from the past. Banking 5.0 requires partner developments, partner design engagements, use of full-service providers, selection of total cost partners, long-term partner relationships, strategic cost management, enterprise resource planning, integrated internet connections, and shared databases and systems as ways of creating new value within the value network.[2]

The embedding of banking in the partners' transactions enables organizations to capture the benefits from exchanging information. The use of Information and communication technologies (ICT) is an essential foundation for integration with partners in a banking 5.0 perspective.[3]

Outsourcing helps the organization to achieve higher levels of value creation for the end customer.[4] Drivers of outsourcing come from organizational initiatives, improvement focus, financial and cost goals, growth goals, a search for flexibility, or the need for critical resources not available internally. Financial institutions increasingly outsource a wide range of core and non-core essential organizational processes. These processes

[1] iotinsobs.com/. Accessed 11 December 2019.

[2] Rodrigues, M., Sousa, B., & da Costa, J. B. (2019). The improvement of the supply chain channel based on digital transformation: An exploratory study in the sustainable industry 5.0 *4th Regional Helix-Book of Abstracts* Parallel Session 4, Porto, Portugal.

[3] Vanpoucke, E., Vereecke, A., & Muylle, S. (2017). Leveraging the impact of supply chain integration through information solution. *International Journal of Production Management*, *37*(4), 510–530.

[4] Ghodeswar, B., & Vaidyanathan, J. (2008). Business process outsourcing: An approach to gain access to world-class capabilities. *Business Process Management Journal*, *14*(1), 23–38.

cover a broad spectrum of sectors and operations, enabling host organizations to world-class capabilities. In the past, financial institutions have outsourced functions such as a part of credit scoring or collection. To be successful, banking 5.0 requires the banking managers to professionally check whichever part of the banking value network should go to the partners.[5]

Uber[6]

Uber is a brokerage platform for driving services that use embedded banking to pay its drivers.[7] The company has pursued an extraordinarily rapid growth strategy over the past few years. In such a strategy, it had problems finding enough drivers with bank accounts in certain regions. Uber decided to issue its digital debit card to new drivers. In this way, a bank account was no longer a hiring requirement supporting the company's fast growth. The driver's compensations are now fully automatically transferred to the cards up to three times a day. The drivers are paid directly depending on the workload and no longer must wait for their monthly salary or, if they need a loan, they can take it out until the next payout. Banking takes place with full automation, digitized in a very user-oriented way.[8]

Banking 5.0 and Partnerships

The financial institutions must consider the increasing importance given to partners and the relationships with them. To achieve this, some organizations have tried to get a higher degree of flexibility with their partners through increased transparency into their banking flows and administrative aspects and vice versa. There are three different fields for redefining innovation with the partners: the simplification and digitization at the

[5] Hood, J., & Stein, W. (2003). Outsourcing of insurance claims: A UK case study. *The Geneva Papers on Risk and Insurance-Issues and Practice*, *28*(3), 510–520.

[6] Hastenteufel, P. D. J., & Hagmann, U. (2020). IUBH discussion papers. *Business & Management, 5*.

[7] Uber. (NA). *Using your debit card with instant pay*. www.uber.com/us/en/drive/basics/how-payments-work/. Accessed on 20 February 2021.

[8] King, B. (2018). *Bank 4.0: Banking everywhere never at a bank*. Marshall Cavendish Business, Singapore.

level of transactions, the assignment of benefits, and the degree of contribution by and from the partners.[9]

A McKinsey survey reports changes to the organizations' procurement strategies,[10] Forty-seven percent are relying more on partners to supplement internal capabilities.

Organizations should promote the sustainability of banking 5.0 ecosystems. The value of this innovation often revolves around the initiative of an organization that has chosen to innovate. Change does not only perfect the relationships between partners and customers. It eases the continuity of the partnerships. If large organizations expand the value network members' perspective, the benefits are risk-sharing in exchange for more reliable revenues and more stable supplies.

Ecosystems

This section examines the rise of ecosystems and the implications for financial institutions, especially from a distribution perspective. An ecosystem is "an interconnected set of services (or products) that allows users to satisfy a variety of needs in one seamless experience."[11] Ecosystems live around customer needs. They are different from simple partnerships across industry boundaries to bring together digitally accessible services or products. An ecosystem can supply customers with an innovative end-to-end experience. Ecosystems will generate USD 60 trillion in revenue by 2025.[12] This revenue will be 30% of global sales in that year.[13] A July 2018 survey by DXC Solution found that 22% of European financial institutions said they were already part of an ecosystem that

[9] Wuttke, D. A., Blome, C., Foerstl, K., & Henke, M. (2013). Managing the innovation adoption of supply chain finance-Empirical evidence from six European case studies. *Journal of Business Logistics, 34*(2), 148–166.

[10] Dhasarathy, A., Frazier, R., Khan, N., & Steagall, K. (2021, March). Seven lessons on how technology transformations can deliver value. *McKinsey Digital.*

[11] www.mckinsey.com/~/media/mckinsey/industries/financial-services/our-insights/winning-in-a-world-of-ecosystems-vf.pdf. Accessed 20 May 2020.

[12] www.mckinsey.com/~/media/mckinsey/industries/financial-services/our-insights/how-banks-can-use-ecosystems-to-win-in-the-sme-market-vf.ashx. Accessed 15 November 2020.

[13] www.mckinsey.com/~/media/mckinsey/industries/financial-services/our-insights/winning-in-a-world-of-ecosystems-vf.pdf. Accessed 20 May 2020.

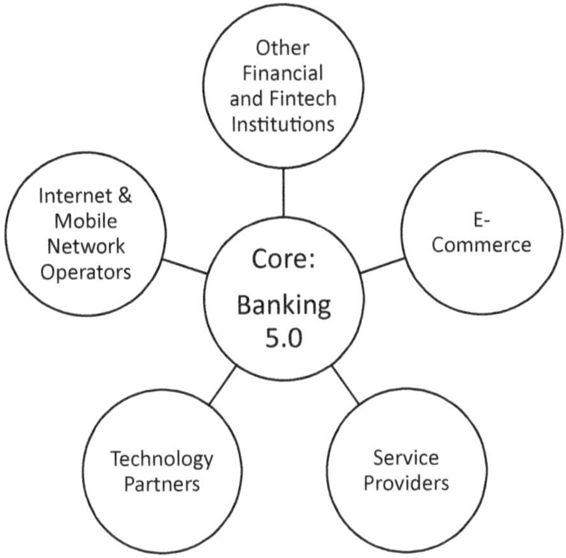

Fig. 11.1 Banking 5.0 ecosystem

could supply added services. Another 46% said that becoming part of an ecosystem would be a high priority[14] (Fig. 11.1).

Financial institutions are not alone. It is time for financial institutions to embrace open ecosystems. They need to collaborate with mature fintech organizations and third-party specialists to develop innovative solutions and enable quick market successes.[15]

Society's growing reliance on digital technologies is reshaping customer expectations. It is also redefining boundaries across industries. Financial institutions cannot avoid this occurrence: as traditional borders disappear. Platforms and ecosystems will influence the future of banking[16]

[14] DXC Solution. (2019, July). *Advancing digital insurance: A survey on the digital maturity of the European insurance industry*, DXC solution. Accessed 10 May 2020.

[15] worldinsurancereport.com/. Accessed 30 May 2020.

[16] www.mckinsey.com/industries/financial-services/our-insights/insurance-beyond-digital-the-rise-of-ecosystems-and-platforms. Accessed 10 January 2020.

and ecosystems.[17] The most successful organizations in the digital era, including Alibaba, Amazon, and Facebook, were all designed on platform business models. Their bases are ecosystems. An ecosystem is an interconnected set of services that allows users to fulfill several of their needs in one integrated experience.[18] Customer ecosystems currently emerging worldwide tend to concentrate on needs such as travel, healthcare, or housing. Business-to-Business (B2B) ecosystems revolve around a specific decision-maker, for example, marketing and sales, operations, procurement, or finance professionals.[19] Ecosystems are an opportunity for financial institutions to sell more services integrated or embedded into other products or services.

There are two ways for a financial institution to get involved in an ecosystem: orchestration and participation.[20] Orchestration means assembling diverse services into a transparent customer journey. Some financial institutions, such as Chinese Ping An, arrange their ecosystems using their subsidiaries.[21] Their common name is "builders." Others create partnerships to integrate non-banking services into the financial institution's domain to ensure scalability. Other financial institutions take part in ecosystems orchestrated by other players. Their goal is often to gain access to the ecosystem for lead generation.[22]

There is the need of different transformation management to benefit from banking 5.0 and reduce the risks related to this innovation.[23]

[17] Komninos, N. (2019). *Smart cities and connected intelligence: Platforms, ecosystems and network effects*. Google Books.

[18] Global Banking Practice The ecosystem playbook: Winning in. www.mckinsey.com/~/media/mckinsey/industries/financial-services/our-insights/winning-in-a-world-of-ecosystems-vf.ashx. Accessed 22 June 2020.

[19] www.mckinsey.com/industries/financial-services/our-insights/insurance-beyond-digital-the-rise-of-ecosystems-and-platforms. Accessed on 10 May 2020.

[20] Catlin, T., Lorenz, J. T., Nandan, J., Sharma, S., & Waschto, A. (2020). Insurance beyond digital: The rise of ecosystems and platforms. www.mckinsey.com/industries/financial-services/our-insights/insurance-beyond-digital-the-rise-of-ecosystems-and-platforms. Accessed 21 March 2020.

[21] www.the-digital-financialinstitution.com/china-in-depth-ecosystems-in-china/. Accessed 15 June 2020.

[22] www.the-digital-financialinstitution.com/insurance-beyond-digital-the-rise-of-ecosystems-and-platforms/. Accessed 10 January 2010.

[23] www.mckinsey.com/industries/financial-services/our-insights/insurance-beyond-digital-the-rise-of-ecosystems-and-platforms. Accessed 11 January 2020.

The options include offering innovative mixed solutions in banking and services with partners from other industries.[24] An ecosystem allows financial institutions to implement the strategy of contextual or embedded banking where a banking transaction becomes a component of other services and products offerings.[25] The banking transaction might even become "invisible" to the customer, being part of other types of transactions. This strategy is possible through the use of smart assistants, which are now installed as standards in e-commerce. Financial institutions could enhance how they manage their risks by exploiting information from other industries. Financial institutions could draw on their analytics ability to offer proprietary data, analytics solutions, and risk management to third parties.

All players must find and prioritize the specific ecosystems in which they can and want to play. Moving to an ecosystem requires the banking 5.0 institutions to become increasingly a complex network coordinator (Fig. 11.2).[26]

Due to their solutions, robust organizational needs, ecosystem, and platform business models are not easy to build up and scale.[27] If successful, ecosystems enable new growth sources, help attract and keep customers. Financial institutions could receive help from robust economies of scale and growth through resources that they do not necessarily need to have themselves.

Ping An[28]
Ping An is an example of a Chinese ecosystem orchestrator in banking. The financial institution does not only sell banking services, offering

[24] Bouwman, H., de Vos, H., & Haaker, T. (Eds.). (2008). *Mobile service innovation and business models*. Springer Science & Business Media, Berlin/Heidelberg, Germany.

[25] Dieter, M., & Tkacz, N. (2020). The patterning of finance/security: A designerly walkthrough of challenger banking apps. *Computational Culture* (7).

[26] Chang, H. H., Chou, P. B., & Ramakrishnan, S. (2009, October). An ecosystem approach for healthcare services cloud. In *2009 IEEE international conference on e-business engineering*, 608–612. IEEE.

[27] Catlin, T., Lorenz, J. T., Nandan, J., Sharma, S., & Waschto, A. (2020). Insurance beyond digital: The rise of ecosystems and platforms. www.mckinsey.com/industries/financial-services/our-insights/insurance-beyond-digital-the-rise-of-ecosystems-and-platforms. Accessed 21 March 2020.

its customers an ecosystem of services such as Ping An Good Doctor, PingAnfang, and Autohome to address their health, housing, and mobility needs more completely. By stocking the ecosystem with its subsidiaries, this approach generates cross-selling among its customers and increases-customer loyalty. Ping An's online car-procurement platform, Autohome, has 30 million unique visitors each day. It generates one-third of customer leads for the financial institution's Property and Casualty (P&C) and financial services businesses. Most the Ping An companies financial transactions are embedded in other types of commercial transactions.[29]

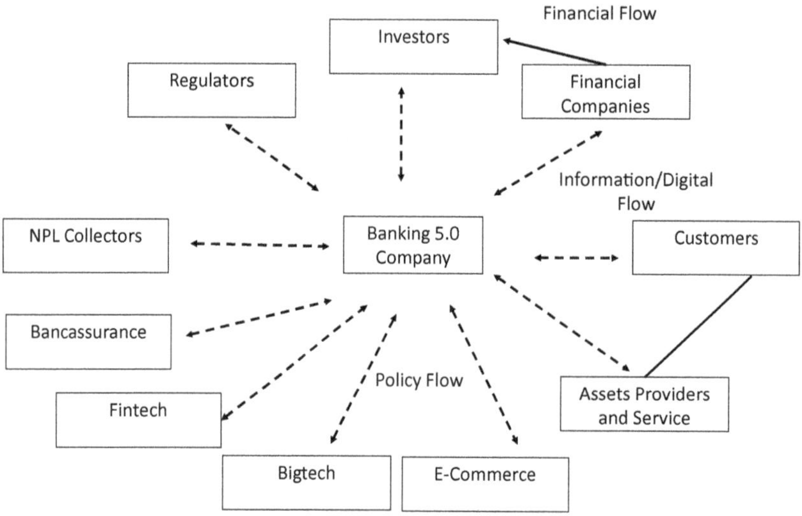

Fig. 11.2 Ecosystem coordination

[28] Catlin, T., Lorenz, J. T., Nandan, J., Sharma, S., & Waschto, A. (2020). Insurance beyond digital: The rise of ecosystems and platforms. www.mckinsey.com/industries/financial-services/our-insights/insurance-beyond-digital-the-rise-of-ecosystems-and-platforms. Accessed 21 March 2020.

[29] Form 20-F, United States Securities and Exchange Commission, April 12, 2019, ir.autohome.com.cn. Accessed 20 January 2021.

Intermediaries for Banking

Traditionally banking has been taken as an activity completely separated from the ordinary business of the persons or organizations. The ideal would be that during a business operation, if necessary, there would be a banking transaction to support that operation, and then the business activity would continue fast. A typical example is trade finance. Trade finance can be a separate activity from trade, but it can become a key component of the trade activity. This consideration applies to businesses, but it applies to ordinary people. As it happens with buying a good, there could be an integrated offer to get a loan or pay in installments. This approach is consumer finance. PayPal has done it with customers with enormous success. In this way, unbanked persons or organizations can become delighted customers and do "banking," out of the financial institution's virtual branches. In this respect, artificial intelligence can help quite a bit.

Pitney Bowes[30]

Founded in 1920, US-based Pitney Bowes is known mostly for postage meters, mailing equipment, and services. This traditional, vertically integrated organization handled end-to-end production of its meters, associated services, and add-ons. Post-2008 recession, Pitney Bowes executives decided to embrace a digital transformation strategy using mobile, data, Internet of Things (IoT), and other emerging technologies. The organization aimed to become a platform-based business to build a digital footprint, accelerate speed to market, and expand its customer base and innovation opportunities through a broader ecosystem.

The organization partnered with Google Cloud to build an API-driven platform that allows third-party developers to use Pitney Bowes' data to innovate new products.[31] Pitney Bowes' transformative platform model enables the organization to use modem solutions to deliver e-commerce and shipping solutions, set up extensive partnerships, improve the customer journeys, and perfect its operations. In Q4 2017, Pitney Bowes grew its revenue for the first time in a decade.

[30] www.capgemini.com/news/world-retail-banking-report-2020/-. Accessed 20 November 2020.

Conclusions

Porter states that the source of competitive advantage is the skillful management of connections in the value network.[32] It is possible to generalize the statement to an ecosystem. Other authors add that the complexity of offers increases with the complexity of the partnerships necessary to deliver these offers.[33] As a result, strategic activities should be oriented to reconfiguration roles and relationships between partners to supply new value forms for the customer. The purpose of banking 5.0 needs to change the traditional approach.

Financial institutions' operations are increasingly a network in which the different paths allow advanced customization of the product. The goal of banking 5.0 is not merely delivering services but to add value to customers and the organization. In this new vision, financial institutions need to work as a coordinator of a network of partners in an ecosystem. This ecosystem must work as one team. The assessment of the partners becomes an essential aspect. The relationships with the partners should be of mutual value. Reviews should ensure the continuous improvement or, at the extreme, the fixing or closing of the partnerships.

[31] Alfresco. (2018, June). Customer insights: How Pitney Bowes is reinventing its business with platform thinking and digital technologies. www.aifresco.com/biogs/power-platfarm/customer-insights-how-pitney-bowes-reinventing-its-business-ptatform-thinking. Accessed 8 January 2020.

[32] Porter, M. E., & Heppelmann, J. E. (2014). How smart, connected products are transforming competition. *Harvard Business Review*, *92*(11), 64–88.

[33] Normann, R., & Ramirez, R. (1993). From value chain to value constellation: Designing interactive strategy. *Harvard Business Review*, *71*(4), 65–77.

CHAPTER 12

Artificial Intelligence and Pricing in Banking 5.0

some people always know the price, but not the value.
Oscar Wilde

Introduction

This chapter deals with another component of the business model canvas: pricing. It is about critical processes and activities, including various aspects and elements that should support a proper risk analysis.

A Gartner survey found that 65% of respondents expect their financial institutions' use solutions to support revenue growth rather than cost reduction.[1] Twenty-five percent of respondents say that increased revenue from new customers will be the primary outcome of innovations in the next few years.[2] Roughly one-fifth of respondents expect innovative solutions to increase engagement with current customers (21%) or increase

[1] www.mckinsey.com/business-functions/mckinsey-digital/our-insights/managing-the-fallout-from-solution-transformations?cid=other-eml-alt-mip-mck&hlkid=bf4d7318cabc44d99ce3ad00689ae9fc&hctky=2743882&hdpid=eac0bc3c-8635-4f36-a0ed-4322b51bbc6a. Accessed 9 March 2020.

[2] Managing the fallout from solutions transformations. www.mckinsey.com/~/media/McKinsey/Business%20Functions/McKinsey%20Digital/Our%20Insights/Managing%20the%20fallout%20from%20solutions%20transformations/Managing-the-fallout-from-solutions-transformations.pdf?shouldIndex=false. Accessed 20 January 2021.

B. Nicoletti, *Banking 5.0*, Palgrave Studies in Financial Services Technology, https://doi.org/10.1007/978-3-030-75871-4_12

revenue from new products or business models (19%). Another 21% of respondents believe that reduced costs through automation and digitization will be the outcome of their financial institutions' use of innovative solutions.

One of the significant benefits of banking 5.0 is the increase in the financial institutions' ability to forecast risks and customer demand with higher precision than ever before, transforming financial institutions' value proposition from reactive actors to preventive advisors[3] lowering prices and selecting their targets.

Revenue in Banking

Based on their sources, financial institutions' revenues can be classified into two macro areas: net interest income and non-interest income. The sum of those two areas supplies the total revenue, which, on average, traditionally is composed of 56% by net interest income and of 44% by non-interest income.[4]

Interest income refers to revenues arising from lending activity. In this case, financial institutions use the resources collected from direct fundraising to grant loans and exploit the net interests' difference. Non-interest income refers to commissions and fees for banking services. Most of them arise from indirect fundraising and commissions on assets under management. As in its long history, lending is the primary banking activity despite the problems that banking is facing about non-performing loans, even if services are becoming more critical.[5]

Financial institutions offer distinct types of credit according to the scope of the loan. They are customer loans, repair loans, current account overdraft, mortgages, trade finance, and credit cards. It is possible to distinguish between two primary forms of credit: unsecured and secured. The first type is typical of credit cards and small unsecured loans. Secured credits require collaterals such as mortgage loans and personal contract plan credit agreements.

[3] Bouyon, S. (2018). Cost and value in banks: A model fit for the digital era? *ECRI Research Report*, 20 April 2018.

[4] Finocchiaro, M. (2018). *Blockchain disruption: A focus on the banking system.* Master Thesis, Luiss University, Rome, Italy.

[5] Blockchain disruption: A focus on the banking system. tesi.luiss.it/23311/1/682731_Finocchiaro_Maurizio_Blockchain%20disruption_a%20focus%20on%20the%20banking%20system_MF%20.pdf. Accessed 20 January 2021.

Regarding the non-interest income, financial institutions in the aftermath of the credit crisis have been focusing on this segment to exploit diverse sources of income and offset the decreasing revenues of lending due to low-interest rates and non-performing loans. Non-interest income refers to revenues derived mostly from fees and other activities outside the core activity of lending. Payment services, gains and losses from the sale of loans and securities, cards' fees, annual fees, and many other services generate fees.[6] Wealth management, the sale of insurance products, financial planning services, annuities, brokerage services, and the perspective of other services have a great impact on generating fees.

Pricing 5.0

Credit scoring is the process of reviewing and selecting risks that a financial institution might cover, under which terms and assignment of expected costs and levels of riskiness.[7] It is the base for pricing and credit policy. A financial institution will evaluate a potential customer's risks based on a certain number of actuarial factors. The target of such a credit scoring process is to supply a price based on its risk.[8]

Credit scoring staff have a critical role in data selection, setting goals according to the financial institution policy, and managing ethical and reputational risks.[9] AI-powered pricing solutions can enable financial institutions to improve their margins and get market share with dynamic and customized pricing models. This approach embeds all the pricing process steps into a single solution, automating the model building. AI must justify their recommendations rather than working as black boxes, giving users control over the models.[10]

[6] Blockchain disruption: A focus on the banking system. tesi.luiss.it/23311/1/682731_Finocchiaro_Maurizio_Blockchain%20disruption_a%20focus%20on%20the%20banking%20system_MF%20.pdf.

[7] Treacy, W. F., & Carey, M. (2000). Credit risk rating systems at large US banks. *Journal of Banking & Finance*, *24*(1–2), 167–201.

[8] Siddiqi, N. (2012). *Credit risk scorecards: Developing and implementing intelligent credit scoring* (Vol. 3). Wiley, Hoboken, NJ.

[9] Albrecher, H., Bommier, A., Filipović, D., Koch-Medina, P., Loisel, S., & Schmeiser, H. (2019). Insurance: Models, digitization, and data science. *European Actuarial Journal*, *9*(2), 349–360.

[10] Corea, F. (2019). *Applied artificial intelligence: Where AI can be used in business*. Springer International Publishing, Cham, Switzerland.

Pricing Architecture

Pricing activities correctly is essential for financial institutions. These activities are based on credit scoring: assessing the wealth and the assets or the persons. Based on that risk assessment, the financial institution will decide whether to supply credit. If the customer application is provisionally accepted, the following step is pricing of the credit and its conditions.[11]

The risk management process is a crucial aspect to consider in banking 5.0. Risk in financial terms is the chance that an outcome or investment's actual gains will differ from an expected outcome or return.[12] Risk includes the possibility of losing part or all of the original credit. Common types of threats in banking are fraud, costs, and customer quality.[13] The financial institution approves the prices and should consider the standards used to decide the customer's acceptance. These standards should be reasonable and not discriminatory. Regulatory norms are an essential factor in this process.[14]

When one considers a level of banking risk, there is a paradox. The hope is that a non re-payment incident never occurs, but the riskiness justifies prices. A credit scoring process aims to supply a price for the banking services based on their risk.[15]

Pricing management includes several critical activities. These actions supply a structured and effective way to address the issues of risk management. These actions are essential since prevention is always better than cure.

[11] Siddiqi, N. (2012). *Credit risk scorecards: Developing and implementing intelligent credit scoring* (Vol. 3). Wiley, Hoboken, NJ.

[12] www.investopedia.com/terms/r/risk.asp#:~:text=Risk-is-defined-in-financial,all-of-an-original-investment.&text=In-finance,-standard-deviation-is-a-common-metric-associated-with risk. Accessed 3 December 2020.

[13] Trkman, P., & McCormack, K. (2009). Supply chain risk in turbulent environments—A conceptual model for managing supply chain network risk. *International Journal of Production Economics*, *119*(2), 247–258.

[14] Ogus, A. I. (2004). *Regulation: Legal form and economic theory*. Bloomsbury Publishing, London, UK.

[15] Remains, A., & Sironi, A. (2011). The financial crisis and Basel 3: Origins, aims and structure of the new regulatory framework (No. 1). *Carefin Working Paper*.

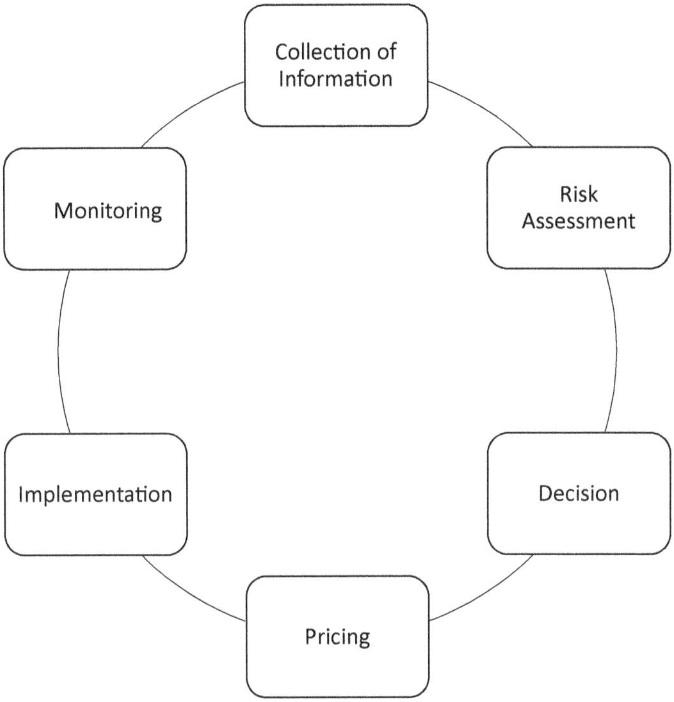

Fig. 12.1 Phases of risk scoring

The credit scoring activity has two main components: risk assessment and pricing.[16] The traditional credit scoring process is well defined. It includes several phases, listed in the following pages (Fig. 12.1).

Information Collection
The credit scoring process begins with the receipt of a credit request. The first activity in the process is the collection of all the information necessary to assess assets or persons' risks in the credit request. There might be a need for the credit scoring office to request additional documentation on respect to the standard one, such as surveys and reports.

[16] Araujo, M. (2017, November). *What is insurance credit scoring?* www.thebalance.com/what-is-insurancecreditscoring-2645778. Accessed 25 December 2019.

Risk Analysis

Risk analysis is the process of finding all potential events that can create problems.[17] The lenders, using an automated credit scoring system, enter a borrower's application information into the system.[18] in the USA and other countries, credit reporting agencies supply other information on the applicant. A customer reporting agency is a private or government organization that collects and supplies information about the individuals' creditworthiness. Its job consists of collecting debtors' data and not assigning a credit score. Customer reporting agencies sell the collected data to the credit bureau, which then generate a credit report. Credit bureau helps lenders reducing information asymmetry, supplying a better understanding of customers' solvability. On the other side, credit bureau creates asymmetry on the borrowers' side since, the latter usually do not know their scores.

Credit Rating

Credit rating or scoring refers to finding the probability of a risk, the potential impact that may have on the processes, and how to try to forecast its happening.[19] This evaluation is not an easy task, considering that banking is a complex system applied to various sectors.

Two components are based on the probabilities of occurrence of the risk: the likelihood that the risk occurs (measurement based on experiences or the presence of factors that may affect the possibility) and the severity of the potential loss (economic impact). Risk predictability is essential.[20] It is the probability that the financial institution could expect a default in the future. For this evaluation, the credit scorer must consider criteria such as age, gender, assets owned, business plans, and others.[21]

[17] Hallikas, J., Karvonen, I., Pulkkinen, U., Virolainen, V. M., & Tuominen, M. (2004). Risk management processes in vendor networks. *International Journal of Production Economics*, *90*(1), 47–58.

[18] www.stlouisfed.org/publications/bridges/winter-1998/what-are-credit-scoring-and-automated-underwriting. Accessed 20 January 2020.

[19] Baird, I. S., & Thomas, H. (1985). Toward a contingency model of strategic risk-taking. *Academy of Management Review*, *10*(2), 230–243.

[20] Kitchens, F. (s.d). Financial implications of artificial neural networks in automobile insurance credit scoring. *International Journal of Electronic Finance*, *3*, 311–319.

[21] California Insurance CE. (n.d.). *Insurance credit scoring*. www.ceclass.com/164.pdf. Accessed 30 March 2020. Accessed 30 April 2020.

Automated underwriting systems assess the riskiness of the credit based on a critical evaluation. The analysis can be informal, using an iterative or intuitive process. The automated underwriting system weighs all this information to decide the likelihood that this credit will be repaid as agreed, based on how similar loans with comparable borrowers' asset and loan characteristics have performed in the past.

Artificial intelligence (AI) can help, especially in the credit scoring and pricing process.[22]

Decision

Depending on the risk assessment, the credit scorer decides whether to accept the proposal totally or partially, or reject it. Financial institutions agree to supply credits that have various levels of risk. The acceptance takes place under other conditions, for example, by applying higher pricing, applying exclusions, or getting collaterals. Financial institutions, according to customers' credit scores, decide whether to grant a loan or not. The credit score is the basis to determine the largest amount the financial institution is willing to lend.

Pricing

If the credit proposal is accepted, the following step is to decide the pricing or interest that the borrower will have to pay to get the credit. Traditionally, the financial institution performs a risk classification, which means that persons with a similar risk level are assigned to the same category and get similar pricing. Customers with a considerable risk must pay higher pricing than those with a lower probability of being involved in a default.[23] This step aims to define pricing for the customer equal to his/her level of risk.[24] In calculating prices, the financial institution must

[22] Thomas, L., Crook, J., & Edelman, D. (2017). *Credit scoring and its applications.* Society for Industrial and Applied Mathematics, Philadelphia, PA. Ghodselahi, A., & Amirmadhi, A. (2011). Application of artificial intelligence techniques for credit risk evaluation. *International Journal of Modeling and Optimization*, *1*(3), 243.

[23] Manulife Insurance. (n.d.). *What you need to know about insurance credit scoring.* manulife.ca/wps/wcm/connect/3ef82954-404f-4cce-bebd-0813142c3848/ins_under_whatyouneed.pdf?MOD=AJPERES&CACHEID=3ef82954-404f-4cce-bebd-0813142c3848. Accessed 20 March 2020.

[24] The Institutes. Risk & Insurance knowledge group. (n.d.). *Credit scoring.* The Institutes. Risk & Insurance knowledge group: www.theinstitutes.org/Comet/programs/ins24/assets/pdf/INS24.pdf. Accessed 22 March 2020.

ensure that it has the financial ability to cover current and future costs and generate margins.[25]

Implementation
Completed the analysis, the next step is the release of the credit and the registration of the customer and/or the asset information into the system for recording the credit. The registration is necessary for the accounting processes, monitoring, and performing statistics.

Monitoring of Risks and Lessons Learned
Like most competencies, effective risk management improves with experience and practice. It is critical to check the trend of the risks. Periodically, it is necessary to review what happened or is expected to come. Monitoring and measurement are not a one-time task but a structured process. When the credit is released, the credit scorer checks the risk exposure to ensure that the results are satisfactory. The monitoring is carried out at contract renewal or its extensions, usually every year and/or if there is a notice of a default or some macroeconomic event. If the customer has had several defaults during the earlier period, the financial institution can increase the prices or refuse to renew the line of credit. This decision-making is either regulated or checked by the regulators to prevent abuses by the financial institutions and avoid usury.[26]

The process presented is general. In practice, for each financial institution, it is possible to measure a risk management maturity as represented in Table 12.1.

Pricing in Banking 5.0

Credit scoring and pricing are not new and were among the first application of statistical modeling in the financial sector.[27] To measure the customers' solvency, financial institutions rely on gathering transactional data, statistical analysis, and AI to better estimate a customer's credit risk.

[25] Parodi, P. (2016, October). General insurance pricing. www.cii.co.uk/knowledge/resources/articles/basic-concepts-and-techniques-of the-pricing-process/43681. Accessed 22 March 2020.

[26] California Insurance CE. (n.d.). *Insurance credit scoring*. www.ceclass.com/164.pdf. Accessed 20 March 2020.

[27] Thomas, L. C. (2009). *Consumer credit models: Pricing, profit and portfolios: pricing, profit and portfolios*. OUP Oxford, UK.

Table 12.1 Risk management maturity levels

Maturity level	*Description*
Informal and unstructured	Nonexistent or very weak function with no structured approach for risk management practices. Risk management may be at an initial stage (conceptual) and mostly not supported by a formal framework or dedicated resources
Developing	Initiated but function not fully developed. The elements of risk management are defined (in form) but not yet implemented through a formal established process and structure
Implementing	Present but still fragmented. A risk management approach is implemented and most tools and techniques are effectively functional; additional work is required to ensure overall integration of risk management practices within the activities of the bank
Optimized	Risk management is mature and has been embedded in the operations of the central bank. All elements of the framework are consistently applied and continuously evolving with the profile of the bank

Source IMF Staff—"Maturity Progression of Risk Management Practices at a Central Bank – Assessment Guidance"

To set up the credit score, a machine-based system can support the credit granting.[28] Its output task is to find a credit score for a given set of goals based on the AI model that defines solvency. It does so by using machine-based inputs such as historical data on people's profiles and whether they repaid loans and human-based inputs, such as a set of rules. With these two sets of information, the system evaluates whether people will repay their loans. It then automatically abstracts these feelings into models.

AI solutions enable correct scoring and allow improved access to the credit by reducing the risks, false positives, and false negatives. This situation will help financial institutions to find the most suitable debt plan for each of their customers. It ensures financial institutions effectively manage credit risks, which is essential for financial stability. This evaluation is vital as there exist several supervisory controls.

Financial institutions usually collect documentation at the credit scoring time. Reliance only on these documents does not supply a correct and detailed customer's opinion. Thanks to digitization, it is possible to

[28] A first look at the OECD's Framework for the Classification of AI Systems, designed to give policymakers clarity—OECD.AI. Accessed 12 December 2020.

collect data through different accesses, such as social media and chatbots.[29] The risks can be analyzed using complex algorithms, such as AI or machine learning. AI can give meaning to many data collected in real-time via transactions and online platforms. It allows financial institutions to have a more precise and faster risk assessment and pricing.[30] This solvency assessment is often subject to strict requirements such as those imposed in the European Banking Authority (EBA)'s "Guidelines on creditworthiness assessment"[31] under the Mortgage credit directive (MCD).[32] In the USA, the Fair Credit Reporting Act (1970) and the Equal Credit Opportunity Act (1974) imply that the processes and the outputs of any algorithm must be explainable, or for example, Equifax, a credit reporting agency, and SAS, a data analysis organization, have created an interpretable credit scoring tool based on deep learning.[33] These technical standards have the goal to ensure consistency in the model's outputs and comparability of risk-weighted exposures. Deep learning or unsupervised learning is challenging to use for this purpose. The difficulty to explain results from many credit scoring algorithms based on AI is an issue. AI-based risk models require more changes than earlier models due to a faster validation feedback loop. Today's approval processes on the supervisory side often take too long and delay shorter model cycles. To make use of the significant benefits of AI-based models, such as dynamic adaptation to

[29] Kostelník, P., Isakovic, I., Muroň, M., Dařena, F., & Procházka, D. (2019). Chatbots for enterprises: Outlook. *Acta Universitatis Agriculturae et Silviculturae Mendelianae Brunensis, 67*(6), 1541–1550.

[30] Cambosu, D. (2017, March). *L'abc dell'insurtech, le parole dell'innovazione nelle assicurazioni.* www.insuranceup.it/it/scenari/l-abc-dell-insurtech-le-parole-dell-innovazionenelle-assicurazioni_1544.htm Accessed 30 March 2020. Reilly, M. (2016, July). *The future of the credit scoring process in the digital age.* insuranceblog.accenture.com/future-of-creditscoring-process-in-digital-age. Accessed 30 March 2020.

[31] insightsbenelux.com/publications/%2314_werkplaats_(ochtend)_EY_Finance_Robotics.pdf. Accessed 25 September 2020.

[32] eba.europa.eu/regulation-and-policy/customer-protection-and-financial-innovation/guidelines-on-creditworthiness-assessment. Accessed 20 January 2021.

[33] Wu, D. D., Olson, D. L., & Luo, C. (2014). A decision support approach for accounts receivable risk management. *IEEE Transactions on Systems, Man, and Cybernetics: Systems, 44*(12), 1624–1632.

environmental changes, it is necessary to process model change applications more quickly. For this reason, it is necessary to further develop the processes and procedures in supervision and expand AI competencies.

The credit risk department can use new data sources, including external data (for example, social data, web sentiment, the marketplace, and so on) and new data analytics tools such as machine learning to develop alternative models. The possible costs/benefits of the applications of these new data sources and tools come in terms of accuracy improvements, model explainability, and maintenance ability compared to the traditional models.

AI solutions allow financial institutions to offer prices that continuously adjust to customer behavior and preferences.[34] Simultaneously, financial institutions can respond to supply and demand laws, margin requirements, and external influences. Machine learning (ML) algorithms can predict the top price a customer should pay for a product. These prices apply to an individual customer at the engagement point, such as online platforms.[35] On one hand, AI can use dynamic pricing to the customer's benefit. On the other, customized pricing will be harmful if it involves unequal, distortionary, un-explainable, or exclusionary pricing.[36]

Neural network techniques can analyze vast quantities of data collected from credit reports. They can conduct a fine-grained analysis of the most relevant factors and of their relationships. AI algorithms, based on large datasets, automatically find the leveraging of neural networks, customer segments, and weights. Credit bureaus in the USA report that deep learning techniques that analyze data in new ways can improve predictions by up to 15%.[37]

Figure 12.2. shows an integrated scheme for the ICT support to risk management in banking 5.0. Figure 12.3 shows the AI support to risk management in banking 5.0

[34] OECD. (2018). *OECD science, solutions and innovation outlook 2018: Adapting to technological and societal disruption*. OECD Publishing, Paris, France.

[35] Waid, B. (2018, July). AI-enabled personalization: The new frontier in dynamic pricing. *Forbes*.

[36] Brodmerkel, S. (2017, June). Dynamic pricing: Retailers using artificial intelligence to predict top price you'll pay, *ABC News*.

[37] Press, G. (2017). Equifax and SAS leverage AI and deep learning to improve consumer access to credit. *Forbes*, 20.

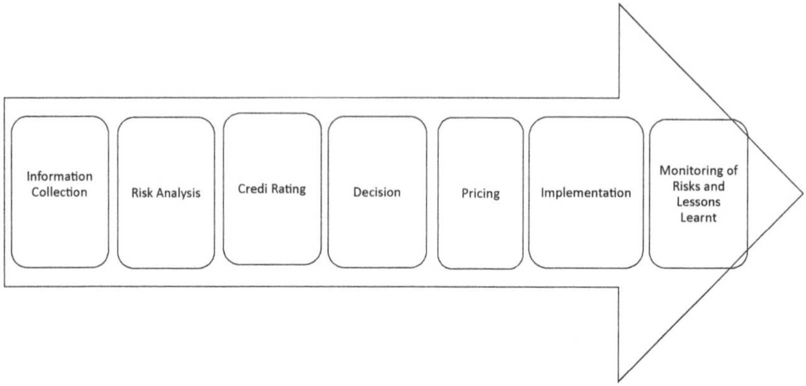

Fig. 12.2 Credit scoring process

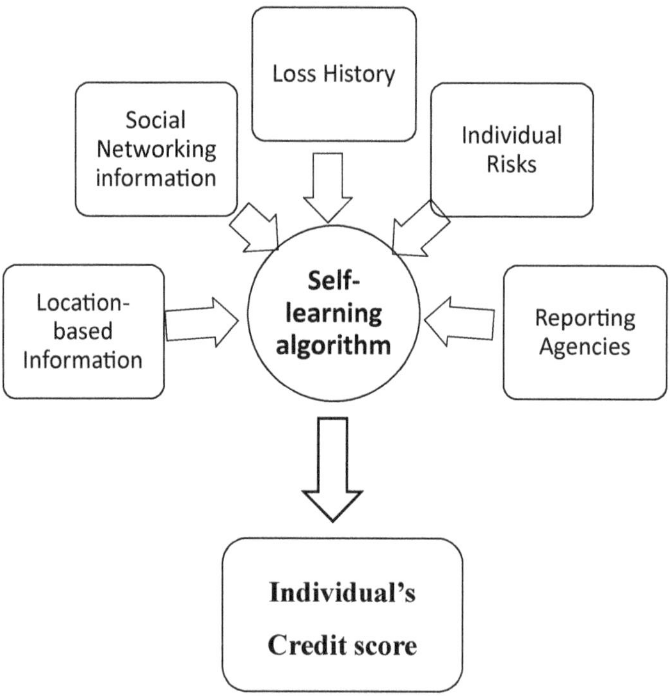

Fig. 12.3 Artificial intelligence in credit scoring

Société Générale

Société Générale uses Machine learning (ML) in the management of market risks.[38] It uses it to detect entry errors and non-compliant transactions based on a history of correct transactions. With this solution, they have resolved 15% of these problems and expect to correct 30 to 40% of them.

It is not acceptable to manage a portfolio of assets based on indicators that a person cannot explain. La Société Générale does not stop. It goes as far as to use voice recognition to analyze its market operators' conversations with a view to detecting any abnormal exchanges. They consider speech-to-text to retrieve (anonymously) data from telephone conversations with our customers relating to pricing to enrich our predictive models.

For some customers (for example, pension funds, editor's note), principal component analysis allows the bank to reduce the number of dimensions in the securities scoring matrix to make the model more interpretable.

Financial institutions are beginning to use predictive models that detect the customer risk profile in real-time, thanks to advanced solutions.[39] Intelligent analytics, predictive modeling, and connected telematics devices help financial institutions design their services and set prices based on how customers behave, rather than general proxies. Therefore, financial institutions can make policy and credit management more effective and efficient.[40] As new risks come up, in real-time financial institutions can improve eligibility, credit scoring, and credit risks monitoring.

[38] www.journaldunet.com/solutions/dsi/1494883-l-ia-est-en-train-de-revolutionner-la-gestion-d-actifs-des-banques-francaises/. Accessed 20 January 2021.

[39] Cappiello, A. (2020). The digital (r)evolution of Insurance Business Models. *American Journal of Economics and Business Administration, 12*(1), 1–13.

[40] OECD. (2017). *Solution and innovation in the insurance sector*. Organization for Economic Cooperation and Development, Paris, France.

Alipay
Alipay uses customer data points to find credit scores,[41] These items include purchase history, type of phone used, games played, and friends on social media. Using traditional credit scoring to grant loans, Alipay's social credit score can influence decisions like the deposit level on home rentals or online dating matches. A person playing video games for hours every day might, for example, get a lower social credit score than a person buying diapers who is assumed to be a responsible parent.[42]

Benefits and Challenges of Pricing

The opportunity to collect and analyze a large variety of data in real-time enables financial institutions to improve fraud detection, cut loss-adjustment costs, and reduce personal interactions. AI and big data analytics help to perform credit management correctly: This type of analysis makes it possible to prevent false accident frauds, automate credit scoring, and better manage correct payments.[43]

Financial institutions with innovative pricing models and information about individual risks can better find the lowest-risk customers.[44] Self-informed, higher-risk customers may seek out fewer involved providers offering more attractive rates based on fewer data. In this environment, late adopters of innovative solutions would be more susceptible to adverse selection.[45]

Pricing is essential for customers. The AI solutions can help quite a bit. Simon-Kutcher, in August 2017, conducted a quantitative study on the main reasons pushing customers to change their financial institutions. He

[41] O'Dwyer, R. (2018. May). Algorithms are making the same mistakes assessing credit scores that humans did a century ago. *Quartz*.

[42] Rollet, C. (2018, June). The odd reality of life under China's all-seeing credit score system. *Wired*.

[43] Cappiello, A. (2020). The technological disruption of insurance industry: A review. *International Journal of Business and Social Science*, *11*(1).

[44] Porter, M. E., & Heppelmann, J. E. (2014). How smart, connected products are transforming competition. *Harvard Business Review*, *92*(11), 64–88.

[45] Porter, M. E., & Heppelmann, J. E. (2014). How smart, connected products are transforming competition. *Harvard Business Review*, *92*(11), 64–88.

found that: 29% changed due to prices too expensive, 20% for prices going up without justification, 16% due to credit lines not adapted to customers' needs, and so on.[46] The benefits of signing online banking are 53% due to lower prices, 51% for simplicity and rapidity, 23% customization of the offer to customer needs.

Information can be analyzed and processed by algorithms to compute the credit reserves accurately in case of defaults. Financial institutions can use the resources available in a more effective, efficient, and economical way, directing them toward investments with a better return rate.

Suppose the core banking is based on risk selection and the price determination for taking it. In that case, the current trend toward using big data analytics and AI can change the data type itself, how data is analyzed, credit management, and relationships with customers.

Some researchers compared the performance of algorithms to forecast the default probability based on the traditional FICO (originally Fair, Isaac and Company)[47] score used in the USA and alternative data.[48] The FICO score alone had an accuracy rate of 68.3%. By using alternative data, another algorithm reached an accuracy rate of 69.6%. Using both types of data together, the accuracy rate went up to 73.6%. Alternative data complements, rather than substitutes, for credit bureau information. Financial institutions using traditional (FICO) sources and alternative data, can make better credit decisions.

Conclusions

Model risk management allows for innovation in risk pricing approaches in banking 5.0.[49] These models allow financial institutions to include many and up-to-date data on the customer into pricing calculations while respecting regulatory constraints. A banking service supplying continuous

[46] Sayegh, K., & Desoky, M. (2019). Blockchain Application in Insurance and Reinsurance. *France: Skema Business School*.

[47] Hurley, M., & Adebayo, J. (2016). Credit scoring in the era of big data. *Yale JL & Tech*, *18*, 148.

[48] Berg, T., et al. (2018). On the rise of FinTechs – Credit scoring using digital footprints. *Michael J. Brennan Irish Finance Working Paper Series Research Paper*, 18–12.

[49] Abdou, D. S. (2019). Using big data to discriminate charged price in the Car Insurance Industry: Evidence from United States. *Proceedings of Business and Economic Studies*, *2*(6).

monitoring of risk exposure during the credit period makes it possible to price adequately each risk.[50]

Banking 5.0 can change loss frequency and severity (sale, operations, and administration costs could decrease, the valued customer could increase due to more effective built-in solutions).[51] Applying cyber security tools is essential. Innovative solutions could increase threats through connectivity (cyber risks), raising many legal and ethical questions.

AI can contribute to model risk management, especially in a dynamic and increasingly regulated situation.[52]

[50] www.slideshare.net/matteocarbone/smart-home-procurement-144438351. Accessed 15 November 2020.

[51] The Impact of Digitalization on the Insurance Value Chain. slideheaven.com/the-impact-of-digitalization-on-the-insurance-value-chain-and-the-insurability-o.html. Accessed 12 June 2020.

[52] Catlin, T., Lorenz, J. T., Nandan, J., Sharma, S., & Waschto, A. (2020). Insurance beyond digital: The rise of ecosystems and platforms. www.mckinsey.com/industries/financial-services/our-insights/insurance-beyond-digital-the-rise-of-ecosystems-and-platforms. Accessed 21 March 2020.

CHAPTER 13

Payments for Costs and Investments in Banking 5.0

An investment in knowledge pays the best interest.
Benjamin Franklin

Introduction

According to an Ernst & Young survey of Swiss banks in 2019, the main priority, cited by 44% of financial institutions (previous year: 49%), is Growth and innovation. Aside from this, 39% (previous year: 32%) consider Cost efficiency to be the priority.[1]

Challenging economic situations might tempt financial institutions to suspend investment and cut costs. The crisis creates an incentive to do the reverse: invest in how they run and make a more agile, digitally enabled business. This approach is the only way to prepare for the future. The economic and pandemic crisis provides financial institutions the opportunity to test and ensure that their businesses have sufficient infrastructure to move to the "new normal"[2] with, for example, support from staff

[1] E&Y. (2020). EY Banking Barometer 2020. *EY Report.*

[2] Meinert, M. C. (2020). Navigating the 'new normal' of a global pandemic. *American Bankers Association. ABA Banking Journal*, *112*(3), 30–32.

B. Nicoletti, *Banking 5.0*, Palgrave Studies in Financial Services Technology, https://doi.org/10.1007/978-3-030-75871-4_13

working remotely and according to flexible ways and especially be resilient to un-expected events.[3]

The guiding principles of finance are the best reallocation of the wealth collected, pursuing a good combination of risk-return, and keeping ownership assets. This activity is complementary to technical-banking management, which relates to the coverage of the risks assumed. It is the core banking of financial institutions.[4]

AI benefits both customers and financial institutions within the front office (for example, automated customer proximity center), middle office (for example, support for front office), and back office (for example, accounting, human resources, compliance). The deployment of AI in the front, middle, and back offices could save financial institutions an estimated one trillion USD by 2030 in the USA alone, affecting 2.5 million financial services employees.[5] Advanced AI tools are reducing the need for human interventions.

Contracts Life Cycle Management

A contract is a legally binding agreement that recognizes and governs the parties' rights and duties as agreed. Correctly composing contracts is crucial to ensure their legal and economic validity. A banking process often neglected is Contract lifecycle management (CLM). This process is the proactive management of a contract from its creation to its renewal or termination. The implementation of an effective CLM can lead to significant improvements in effectiveness, savings, and efficiency. Understanding and automating the CLM can limit the probability of litigations and improve compliance with legal requirements.

Manual review of contracts is one of the most time-consuming duties for legal professionals, especially in third-party agreements. Stakeholders may view legal teams as bottlenecks in the contracting process. AI-based contract analytics solutions are maturing and becoming more reliable.

[3] home.kpmg/xx/en/home/insights/2020/03/do-financialinstitutions-have-covid-19-covered.html. Accessed 30 May 2020.

[4] Mallick, I. (2020). Financial system performance and economic dynamics. *Global Journal of Management and Business Research.*

[5] Sokolin, L., & Low. M. (2018). *Machine intelligence and augmented finance: How artificial intelligence creates $1 trillion dollar of change in the front, middle and back-office*, Autonomous Research LLP, London, UK.

Early AI applications varied in their ability to understand and mimic a lawyer's process for reviewing contract documents, limiting their applicability to high-volume, low-complexity documents.[6] However, these applications are evolving to deliver faster, more complex insights across more languages than before.

The CLM process can be managed in banking 5.0 using commercial software, available and robust. The contract management software is a program or set of programs related to the storage and management of legal agreements with customers and partners, such as deposit contracts, leases, credit, and license agreements. A contract management software aims to simplify the contract administration and reduce the workload by supplying a single, unified view of each contract's processes and documentation.[7] The goal is to have sound contracts and do Contract inconsistency checking (CIC).

JPMorgan Chase & Co.[8]

The financial institution JPMorgan employs lawyers and loan officers who spend about one hundred thousand hours per year tackling ordinary tasks, including interpreting commercial-loan agreements. The organization has successfully managed to cut the time spent on this work down to a matter of seconds using machine learning (ML).

JPMorgan implemented a program called COiN (COntract iNtelligence) that uses unsupervised machine learning, with minimal need of persons' support after its deployment. COiN can examine documents based on banking rules and data validation that would take a person 360, 000 hours of work to review.[9]

COiN runs on an ML system powered by a private cloud network that the financial institution uses for automating the document review process for a specific class of contracts. The first stage of testing the COiN platform included the review of the bank's credit contracts. The

[6] Gartner. (2020). Predicts 2021: Artificial intelligence in enterprise applications. *Gartner Report.*

[7] searcherp.techtarget.com/definition/contract-management-software. Accessed 30 April 2020.

[8] www.imaginovation.net/blog/ai-in-banking-jp-morgan-case-study-benefits-to-businesses/. Accessed 22 August 2020.

[9] Song, H. (2017, February 28). JPMorgan software does in seconds what took lawyers 360,000 hours. Bloomberg.com.

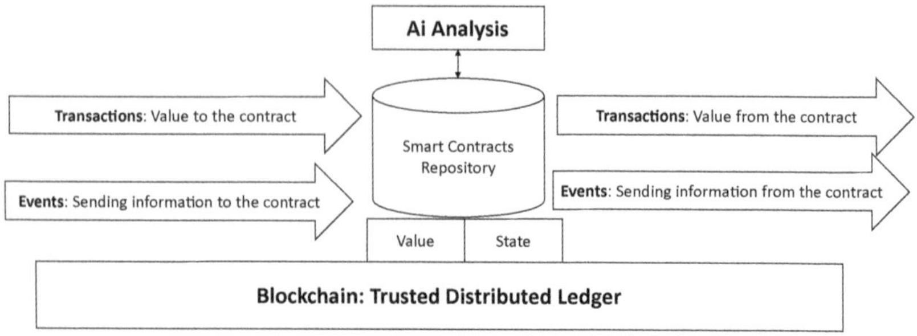

Fig. 13.1 Schema for smart contracts

primary tool used is image recognition: where the software can compare and distinguish between different agreements.

In the first implementation of this solution, the algorithm would extract about 150 relevant attributes from annual commercial credit agreements in seconds compared to 360,000 person-hours under manual review. The algorithm may find patterns based on wording or location in the contracts. This software proves to be cost-effective, more efficient, and less prone to errors.

Smart Contracts Architecture

One of the most exciting implementations of blockchain solutions is the so-called intelligent or smart contract.[10] This solution aims to make contracts "live" with the automatic application of some specific contractual provisions for self-execution in a blockchain solution (Fig. 13.1). In the context of banking 5.0, these programs can be self-executing smart contracts that manage the flows of funds based on the contract terms' automatic application. It is possible to apply effectively, efficiently, economically, and ethically (that is correct) contractual arrangements through a digital application. Potentially, there would be no need for person involvement in the execution of an agreement. It is possible to develop contracts algorithmically to clarify and enforce the rules of

[10] Xu, Z., Wang, Q., Wang, Z., Liu, D., Xiang, Y., & Wen, S. (2020, February). PPM: A provenance-provided data sharing model for open banking via Blockchain. In *Proceedings of the Australasian Computer Science Week Multiconference* (1–8).

the transaction independently. All interactions related, for example, to payments or trade finance, can be automated according to fixed rules and agreements.[11]

Smart Contracts Alliance lists 12 smart contract use cases[12]:

- Digital identity: controlling digital assets for individuals.
- Records: storing digitized files, enabling auto-renewal and release processes.
- Securities: enabling automated payment of dividends, removing operational risks.
- Derivatives: enforcing a standard set of rules and conditions for a transaction.
- Financial data recording: uniform, correct, and transparent recording of financial data.
- Mortgages: enabling automated payment processing and release of a mortgage.
- Land title recording: impeding fraud and assuring transparency of property transfers.
- Trade finance: faster approval and payment initiation.
- Supply chain: supplying reliable tracking of the products from the factory to their sale.
- Elimination of duplicate recording and verification processes of each party.

A smart contract ceases to be a static document filed on a computer.[13] The contract could become empowered to execute contractual agreements throughout the contract life. A smart contract, as an object, will know things about itself.[14] It will know its economic value. It simplifies the contract administration and reduces the workload by supplying a unified view of each contract's processes and documentation. With further

[11] Nicoletti, B. (2018). *Procurement finance*. Springer International Publishing, London, UK.

[12] Gatteschi, V., Lamberti, F., Demartini, C., Pranteda, C., & Santamaría, V. (2018). *Blockchain and smart contracts for insurance: Is the solution mature enough?*

[13] Chesebro, R. (2015). *A contract Which managed itself*. Working Paper. University Fort Belvoir, VA.

[14] Morabito, V. (2017). *Business innovation through blockchain: The B3 Perspective* (101–124). Springer, Cham, Switzerland.

developments in smart contracts, the agreement would be able to interact with other objects. This solution would allow all stakeholders to access the same source, the movements of funds between customers, partners, financial institutions, and when funds need to be released. If a problem occurs, such as unspent funds with the contractor no longer in business, the contract knows how to handle this situation based on its clauses.[15]

Many software vendors offer CLM applications. The main functions of a Contract lifecycle management/CLM) to automate contract management are (Fig. 13.2)[16]:

- Capture: The first step in a CLM is to centralize all current documents into a single central repository accessible to all authorized persons. The clear and complete knowledge of all contracts supports a comprehensive view of the potential exposure to risks.
- Tracking: The next step is to get the data from the contracts. The goal is to keep track of all the essential data not to miss any of them.
- Preparation of new contracts. The focus is on accelerating the process of creating a new contract. The authoring process involves creating contract templates and libraries to connect and create new agreements quickly but controlled.
- Draft: The drafting of a contract can occur in two ways. First, drafting by the legal and procurement officers. It is possible to empower users in the organization by creating self-service draft contracts based on intelligent templates pre-approved by the legal department.
- Approval: Organizations need an approval workflow to ensure that risky contracts are reviewed and approved by the correct parties. Some risks need to be approved by the legal department, some by the management, others by specific organization's entities such as finance, credit scoring officers, and so on. Ideally, a simple contract should be pre-approved once the clearance on the pricing is defined.
- Negotiation: The typical negotiator needs to include a list of potential control problems for each contract type. It is possible to track

[15] www.kinno.fi/en/smartlog. Accessed 30 May 2020.

[16] Nicoletti, B. (2017). *Agile procurement. Volume II: Designing & implementing a digital transformation*. Springer International Publishing, London, UK, ISBN 978-3-319-61085-6.

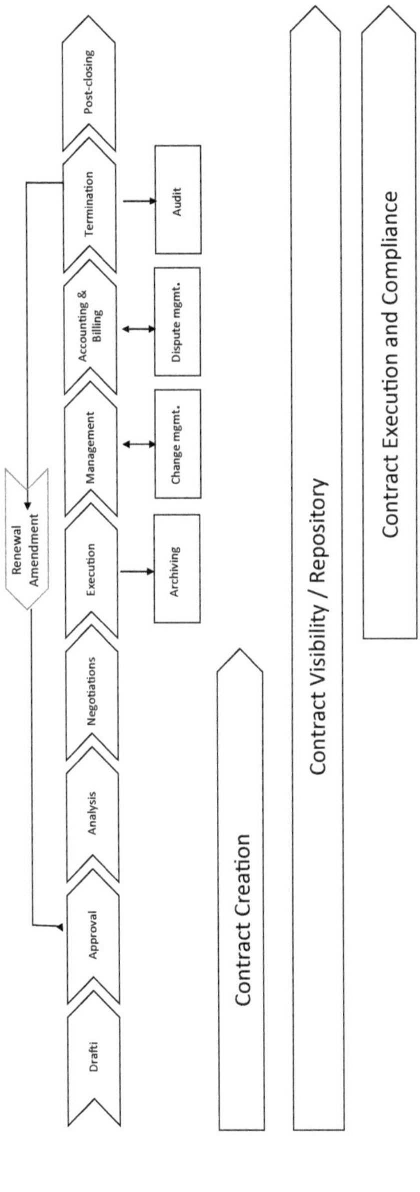

Fig. 13.2 Smart contracts process

the differences compared to the original or last draft, and capture and report these differences.

- Analysis: Organizations with many contracts need to analyze these contracts for potential risks, rights, and obligations. Possible threatening clauses should have contingency scenarios. Fast access to the terms and contractual information allows persons to react quickly to new situations and address the risks related, for example, to the time factor.
- Execution: When the contract is final and agreed upon, it must be signed (physically and increasingly digitally) by all subjects and the signed copies filed. Someone must ensure that the final approved version is not adjustable in any way after sending texts around for their execution.
- Management: Capabilities such as checking complex contracts with more applications, additions, amendments, and specifications for the power of changes or evolutions of the first agreements are critical and help prevent errors, litigations, or similar actions. Management of the contracts includes alerts on relevant dates.
- Termination or automatic renewal. Reminders of upcoming deadlines and closing tasks of contracts or basis for their renovation or extensions are critical not to incur in penalties.
- Support litigations, if necessary.
- Post-closing: Support for any defaults or disputes making available the contract history and all its variations and respect over time.

Smart Contracts in Banking 5.0

Start-up organizations and investors focused in the past on payments processing and banking. They are increasingly interested in banking solutions.[17] It is possible to use artificial intelligence (AI)-based capabilities, with natural language processing and machine learning tools that optimize and streamline the contract analysis process.[18] The tool analyzes the

[17] Stoeckli, E., Dremel, C., & Uebernickel, F. (2018). Exploring characteristics and transformational capabilities of InsurTech innovations to understand insurance value creation in a digital world. *Electronic Markets*, *28*(3), 287–305.

[18] Yang, D., Leber, C., Tari, L., Chandramouli, A., Crapo, A., Messmer, R., & Gustafson, S. (2013, November). A natural language processing and semantic-based

draft contract documents and automates the data analysis to find critical information and terms for the legal and vendor management teams' financial institution organization.

The tool adapts to each organization's unique jargon and contract type. This capability allows an AI analysis application to automatically customize itself to a financial institution's legal practices and learn which critical contract documents and data correspond to specific standard clauses and field values.

Smart contracts, based on a blockchain solution,[19] can ensure the execution of the terms of a contract using cryptographic code.[20] Blockchain smart contracts can manage complex rules among large numbers of customers. They can help develop peer-to-peer banking.

Blockchain solutions for the automation of the contracts allow reducing administration costs for reconciliation and errors. Smart contracts could supply customers and financial institutions with ways to manage credit, for instance, transparent, responsive, and indisputable. The process would be[21]:

- The blockchain solution includes an option contract and related transactions. The individuals involved are anonymous, but the agreement is in the public ledger.

system for contract analysis. In *2013 IEEE 25th International conference on tools with artificial intelligence* (707–712). IEEE.

[19] Price Waterhouse Coopers. (2017). Blockchain: A catalyst for new approaches in insurance. www.pwc.ch/en/publications/2017/Xlos_Etude_Blockchain_UK_2017_Web.pdf. Accessed: 30 March 2020.

Deloitte. (2016). Blockchain applications in insurance, www2.deloitte.com/content/dam/Deloitte/ch/Documents/innovation/ch-en-innovation-deloitte-blockchain-app-in-insurance.pdf. Accessed: 30 March 2020.

McKinsey & Financial institution. (2017). Blockchain solution in the insurance sector. In *Proceedings of the quarterly meeting of the Federal Advisory Committee on Insurance (FACI)*, New York, NY,

[20] Lorenz, J. T., Münstermann, B., Higginson, M., Olesen, P. B., Bohlken, N., & Ricciardi, V. (2016, July). Blockchain in insurance—Opportunity or threat? *McKinsey Co.* 1–9.

[21] www2.deloitte.com/content/dam/Deloitte/ch/Documents/innovation/ch-en-innovation-deloitte-blockchain-app-in-insurance.pdf. Accessed 30 March 2020.

- A triggering event, such as an end date and strike price, is hit. The contract executes automatically based on the coded terms confirmed by the network, completing only valid requests.[22]
- Regulators can use the blockchain solutions to check the activity in the market.[23] Simultaneously, they can keep the privacy of individual actors' positions.
- AI could support auditing of smart contracts:
- AI streamlines contract reviews for a heavily contracts congested banking environment so that banks can supply better forecast which terms have a higher default risk or have a compliance issue.[24]
- AI can perform a Contract inconsistency checking (CIC), which is an automatic contract analysis task with significant functionality to find inconsistencies.[25]

Current financial credit management systems work usually in a single service mode. The transactions are not transparent and traceable to many stakeholders. Their data privacy protection mechanisms are not sufficiently strong in facing various cyber attacks. To overcome these challenges, a proposal is Loan on blockchain contract (LoC), a financial loan management system based on smart contracts over permissioned blockchain Hyperledger Fabric.[26] It is possible to design a digital account model to transfer assets between centralized and decentralized ledgers and use locking and unlocking algorithms for smart contracts. Digital signature and oracle protect data privacy. Performance evaluations on chain code and unlocking codes show that such a system is applicable in a real financial loan setting.

[22] Blockchain and cryptocurrencies. https://www.carolinascashadventure.com/resources/Documents/2018/Presentations/CCA%202018%2007A%20-%20Wells%20-%20Blockchain%20and%20Cryptocurrencies.pdf. Accessed 05 May 2020.

[23] Cohn, A., Michael, J., & Butcher, J. R. (2018). Blockchain solution. *The Journal, 1*(7).

[24] www.elibrary.imf.org/view/IMF071/24304-9781484315224/24304-9781484315224/ch07.xml?language=en&redirect=true. Accessed 20 January 2021.

[25] Zhang, S., Zhao, J., Wang, P., Xu, N., Yang, Y., Liu, Y., & Feng, J. (2020). Learning to check contract inconsistencies. *arXiv preprint* arXiv:2012.08150.

[26] Wang, H., Guo, C., & Cheng, S. (2019). LoC—A new financial loan management system based on smart contracts. *Future Generation Computer Systems, 100*, 648–655.

McKennon[27]

McKesson is a USD 179 billion healthcare services and information solution. It employs 70,000 persons and several partners. It uses a discovery and analytics platform to find all their banking and sourcing contracts across the organization.[28] It stores the documents in a specific contract repository. It is possible to search the contracts easily and quickly in this repository, saving some staff time. The contract analysis's metadata enables the organization to find potential obligation risks and revenue opportunities, and savings from otherwise hidden unfavorable payment and renewable terms.

Benefits and Challenges of Smart Contracts

The potential savings with smart contracts could be significant. A smart contract allows a reduction of the administration costs, the reconciliation, and the elimination, or at least decrease, of the potential errors. It would be possible to reduce the risks and disputes related to contractual relationships. With the support of blockchain solutions, smart contracts could supply retrieval modes of information and agreements to manage credit transparently, responsive, and irrefutable. Contracts and complaints may be recorded on a blockchain solution and confirmed by this solution.[29] (Figure 13.3[30])

Smart contracts and blockchain solutions can help control process flows, the administration of banking protections, the authentication and verification of identities, methods, and documents, or contract auditing. The benefits are the possibility to avoid a further review or manual administration of the credits. Blockchain solutions and smart contracts can

[27] www.mckesson.com/. Accessed 20 June 2019.

[28] Burgess, A. (2017). *The executive guide to artificial intelligence: how to find and implement applications for AI in your organization*. Springer, Cham, Switzerland.

[29] Deloitte. (2016). Blockchain: democratized confidence in *Tech Trends 2016*: Innovating in the digital age.

[30] Adapted by the author from *Blockchain solution and its potential in taxes*, Deloitte (2017).

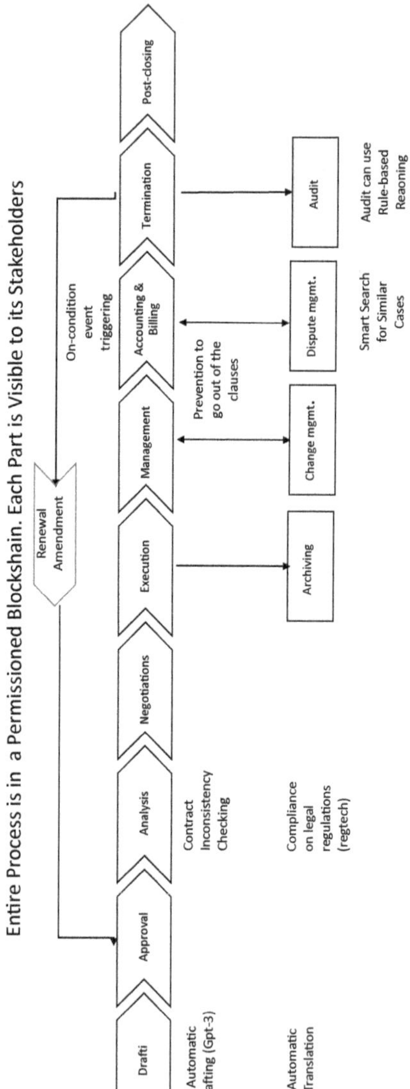

Fig. 13.3 Smart contracts in banking 5.0

simplify and accelerate the processing, checking, and finding defaults, shortening the processing time of credits.[31]

The CLM software category should grow, on average, between 15 and 20%.[32] The reasons are several. The implementation of the CLM can lead to significant improvements in savings and efficiency. These solutions do more than merely creating a legal archive. They optimize and automate contracts. They allow the organization to follow-up and support all the stages of the contract life cycle.

Some specific benefits to support a business case for their evaluation are[33]:

- Rationalize the authoring process. Use of clauses libraries and improved collaboration mode.
- Reduce time and costs for contract operations.
- Automate the tracking of compliance. The integration with transactional systems ensures the issuance of orders and payments with proper economic clauses. It alerts organizations to demand the agreed discounts or benefits associated with the agreement.
- Reduce total administrative costs. This reduction enables banking and legal entities to focus on more critical and complex tasks that add more value to the organization.
- Cognitive systems can continually scout the blockchain data to look for abnormal behavior and other exceptions that might signal non-compliance or fraud.[34]

Smart contracts require higher decentralization, an agile approach, and autonomous interactions.[35] There are liability issues. A technological

[31] Nicoletti, B. (2018). *Procurement finance*. Springer International Publishing, London, UK.

[32] wwwdigitaljournal.com/pr/3814597. Accessed 30 March 2019.

[33] www.bearingpoint.com/files/0553_WP_EN_Vertragsmgt_final_web.pdf. Accessed 30 March 2019.

[34] www.elibrary.imf.org/view/IMF071/24304-9781484315224/24304-978148431 5224/ch07.xml?language=en&redirect=true. Accessed 20 January 2021.

[35] Platform Industries 4.0: Aspects of the research roadmap for application scenarios. www.plattform-i40.de/I40/Redaktion/EN/Downloads/Publikation/asp ects-of-theresearch-roadmap.pdf?__blob=publicationFile&v=10. Accessed 20 March 2020.

failure or rigidity could result, for example, in less flexibility to correct errors once the contract has been closed.[36]

Other challenges are the absence of regulations and especially of standards. There are regulations of the economic activity in the financial sector at both national and regional levels through comprehensive compliance provisions. Smart contracts get compliance relevance when individuals or financial institutions use a blockchain solution related to the financial sector. On smart contracts and, in general, on blockchain solutions, there are still many compliance uncertainties and unanswered questions. Similarly, there are no European or American level approaches for the standardized compliance treatment of smart contracts.[37]

> **ROSS**[38]
> The American law firm BakerHostetler[39] uses Ross, a robot lawyer, to help in bankruptcy cases. Ross is based on IBM's AI solutions and serves as a legal researcher for the company.
>
> Lawyers have been using static software to navigate the law repositories. They are limited and take hours of information retrieval tasks from the lawyers. Ross examines relevant law documentation and then lets lawyers to interact with them. Lawyers can either confirm Ross' suggestions or get it to question its assumptions. Ross reduces costs and hence allows to charge lower fees.
>
> As an AI application built by a neutral third party, Ross is impartial. This characteristic implies that both sides could use it to look up relevant legal details and rulings of an ancient case from 50 years ago. A manual intervention can improve this search by a human ROSS communication in everyday English.

[36] Insurance: Models, digitalization, and data science. www.researchgate.net/publication/332801334_Insurance_Models_Digitalization_and_Data_Science. Accessed 30 March 2021.

[37] Drummer, D., & Neumann, D. (2020). Is code law? Current legal and technical adoption issues and remedies for blockchain-enabled smart contracts. *Journal of Information Solutions, 35*(4), 337–360.

[38] www.techtree.com/content/features/11019/meet-ross-world-s-first-ai-lawyer.html. Accessed 11 December 2020.

[39] www.bakerlaw.com/. Accessed 30 March 2021.

Conclusions

In the current highly turbulent times, it is critical to keep the necessary agility. This approach means strict control of the costs and investments. This chapter examines the structure of costs and contracts in financial institutions. This chapter suggests using AI tools to reach the goals of agility, feasibility, and profitability in contract administration using AI- and blockchain-based smart contracts. A smart contract is a computer application that can automatically execute, control, or document legally relevant events. The combination of artificial intelligence and smart contracts adds other interesting features to banking 5.0.

CHAPTER 14

Protection of Banking 5.0

There are risks and costs to a program of action — but they are far less than the long-range cost of comfortable inaction.
John F. Kennedy

Introduction

The first business model canvas did not consider the protection component. It has become dramatically important in the last few years. External actors are becoming more sophisticated and aggressive. Financial institutions are growing more vulnerable.[1] In banking 5.0, it is even more critical. Banking will depend increasingly on Artificial intelligence (AI) took kits, robotic process automation, and many regulations.

Three aspects are essential for the financial institutions' protection[2]:

- Attack and incident response.
- Third-party risk management.
- Change management and related exact testing.
- Data Privacy.

[1] Bank risk management in 2021: Issues for boards of directors | McKinsey. Accessed 10 February 2021.

[2] Bank risk management in 2021: Issues for boards of directors | McKinsey. Accessed 10 February 2021.

B. Nicoletti, *Banking 5.0*, Palgrave Studies in Financial Services Technology, https://doi.org/10.1007/978-3-030-75871-4_14

In such a situation, it is important to assure disaster recovery and business continuity. On this last aspect, resilient banking is important. In the past, resilience has not been particularly considered. It is now increasingly one of the critical elements to consider. Pandemic has proved the importance of ensuring the continuity of banking activities whatever could happen. The approach cannot be only to secure a prompt recovery. The goal is to assure as much continuity as possible.

The new tools and methods, especially AI, require a controlled development and deployment, full assurance about transparency, explainability, and fairness. While these aspects are essential, they will not come automatically with banking 5.0. It is necessary to work well in advance to assure their effective and continuous presence. These activities are not one-time. They must be a dynamic process to consider and implement continuously.

On all these aspects, it is essential to consider AI and robotic process automation not only as the objects to protect. It is necessary to consider them also as protection tools. In this respect, regtech organization can play a crucial role in supporting the planning, control, and monitoring of compliance respect.

Cyber Security

Cyber security organizes and keeps resources, processes, and infrastructures to protect cyber space and cyber space-enabled systems from malicious attacks and effects on property rights.[3] In banking 5.0, there are strong connections between several systems, making the overall system more fragile. This situation makes data and assets protection more difficult in the various processes that the organization carries either internally or externally. As a result, secure and reliable communications, protected identity, resilience, and access management of systems and users are essential in AI implementations.[4]

A UK government survey estimated that in 2014, 81 percent of large corporations and 60 percent of small organizations suffered a cyber security breach. A cyber security breach's average cost is GBP 600 k. GBP

[3] Craigen, D., Diakun-Thibault, N., & Purse, R. (2014). Defining cyber security. *Solution Innovation Management Review*, *4*(10).

[4] Rodrigues, M., Sousa, B., & da Costa, J. B. (2019). The improvement of the supply chain channel based on digital transformation: An exploratory study in the sustainable industry 5.0, *4th Regional Helix- Book of Abstracts* Parallel Session 4, Porto, Portugal.

1.15 m for large organizations and GBP 65 k–115 k for small- and medium-sized financial institutions.[5]

The increasing digitization of the processes has made cyber hackers highly active. They are working to penetrate the people and organizations' confidential information to gain financial and personal benefits. The threats to banking are severe. It is necessary to protect systems so that any malicious attack can be prevented, stopped, and, in the unlikely event that it has been able to create damages, remediated.[6] The organizations' competitors are using cyber crimes to steal intellectual property and harm their competitors so that the formers can gain a better position in the market.

AI can support all the cyber security functions, making them highly effective in protecting systems and data.[7] Their high accuracy and efficiency and the ability to enhance themselves automatically have made AI methods effective in cyber security.[8] AI is already used in digital security applications such as network security, anomaly detection, security operations automation, and threat detection and monitoring.[9] Simultaneously, the malicious use of AI increases. Such malicious activities include identifying software vulnerabilities. The goal is to exploit vulnerabilities to attack the availability, integrity, or confidentiality of systems, networks, infrastructure, applications, and data. The operational risk is remarkably high. It is necessary to manage vulnerabilities.

Two trends make AI systems relevant for security: the growing number of digital security attacks and the skills shortage in the digital security

[5] www.abi.org.uk/Insurance-and-savings/Products/Business-insurance/Cyber-risk-insurance. Accessed 20 April 2020.

[6] Ben-Asher, N., & Gonzalez, C. (2015). Effects of cyber security knowledge on attack detection, *Computers in Human Behavior, 48,* 51–61.

[7] Akbari Roumani, M., Fung, C. C., Rai, S., &. Xie, H. (2016). Value analysis of cyber security based on attack types. *ITMSOC: Transactions on Innovation and Business Engineering, 1,* 34–39.

[8] Alrajhi, A. M. (2020). A survey of Artificial Intelligence techniques for cyber security improvement. *International Journal of Cyber-Security and Digital Forensics, 9,* 34–41.

[9] OECD (2017). *OECD Digital Economy Outlook 2017*. Paris, France: OECD Publishing.

industry.[10] Malware continually evolves.[11] Machine learning (ML) has become essential to combat attacks such as polymorphic viruses, denial of service, and phishing.[12] Leading email services, such as Gmail and Outlook, have used ML at various levels of success to filter undesired or malicious emails.[13]

Computer code is subject to human errors. Nine out of ten digital security attacks are estimated to result from flaws in software code.[14] Despite the extensive development time, between 30 percent and 75 percent, this situation occurs on testing.[15] Given the billions of code lines being written every year and the reuse of third-party proprietary libraries to do it, detecting and correcting software code errors is challenging for humans. Countries like the USA and China are funding research projects to make AI systems that can detect and prevent software security vulnerabilities.[16] AI technologies can learn and become more effective as they go.[17]

The main concern until now has been on the protection. A field that will develop in the future is resilience and recovery. The next stage for cyber security will be the extensive protection of the AI ecosystem and the use of AI itself to improve the tools used.

[10] ISACA. (2016), *The State of Cyber security: Implications for 2016*, An ISACA and RSA Conference Survey, Cyber security Nexus.

[11] MIT. (2018, August), Cyber security's insidious new threat: Workforce stress, *MIT Solutions Review*.

[12] OECD iLibrary | Home. www.oecd-ilibrary.org/sites/eedfee77-en/1/2/3/index.html?itemId=/content/publication/eedfee77-en&_csp_=5c39a73676a331d76fa56f36ff0d4aca&itemIGO=oecd&itemContentType=book. Accessed 30 January 2021.

[13] OECD iLibrary | Home. www.oecd-ilibrary.org/sites/eedfee77-en/1/2/3/index.html?itemId=/content/publication/eedfee77-en&_csp_=5c39a73676a331d76fa56f36ff0d4aca&itemIGO=oecd&itemContentType=book. Accessed 20 January 2021.

[14] OECD iLibrary | Home. www.oecd-ilibrary.org/sites/eedfee77-en/1/2/3/index.html?itemId=/content/publication/eedfee77-en&_csp_=5c39a73676a331d76fa56f36ff0d4aca&itemIGO=oecd&itemContentType=book. Accessed 20 January 2021.

[15] FT. (2018, September). US and China back AI bug-detecting projects. *Financial Times, Cyber Security and Artificial Intelligence*.

[16] FT. (2018, September). US and China back AI bug-detecting projects. *Financial Times, Cyber Security and Artificial Intelligence*.

[17] FT. (2018, September). US and China back AI bug-detecting projects. *Financial Times, Cyber Security and Artificial Intelligence*.

Cyber Security Architecture

For the cyber security architecture, it is possible to refer to the NIST Cyber security framework (CSF). It includes the following functions[18]:

- Identify. Develop the organizational understanding to manage cyber security risks to systems, assets, data, and capabilities. The activities in "identify" are fundamental for the effective use of the CSF.
- Protect. Develop and implement the proper safeguards to ensure the delivery of critical services.
- Detect. Develop and implement the proper activities to find the occurrence of a cyber security event.
- Respond. Develop and implement the proper activities to act on a detected cyber security event.
- Recover. Develop and implement the proper activities for planning for resilience and being able to restore any damaged capabilities or services due to a cyber security attack.

Another aspect important for financial institutions relates to reporting to all interested parties in case of incidents. In some countries, such reporting is mandatory,[19]
Cyber security has developed over time. The generations have been the following ones,[20] based on the area of protection [21]:

- Cyber security 1: Disaster recovery and business continuity respond to cyber security incidents, which may cause a loss of data or outages in the services. Methods and tools introduced in this generation are: Uninterruptible power supply (UPS), Disaster recovery (DR) (including Disaster recovery sites (DRS) and Disaster recovery

[18] www.nist.gov/system/files/documents/cyberframework/cybersecurity-framework-021214.pdf. Accessed 20 January 2021.

[19] An example of mandatory reporting is the following: (2021, January) Computer-security incident notification requirements for banking organizations and their bank service providers, Federal Deposit Insurance Corporation, fdic.gov.

[20] Griffor, E. (2017). *Handbook of system safety and security*. Amsterdam, The Netherlands: Elsevier. .

[21] Akbari Roumani, M., Fung, C. C., Rai, S., & Xie, H. (2016). Value analysis of cyber security based on attack types, *ITMSOC: Transactions on Innovation and Business Engineering, 1*, 34–39.

plans (DRP)), and Business continuity (BC) (including Business continuity plans (BCP).

- Cyber security 2: Servers and end-point security protections keep the system aware and educated to secure and avoid cyber threats. Tools in this generation are antiviruses, firewalls, and forensic analysis.
- Cyber security 3: Network security protects the networks and keep communication networks of the organizations secure from intruders. Tools introduced are Intrusion detection system (IDS) and later Intrusion prevention system (IPS), Secure sockets layer (SSL), and penetration tests.
- Cyber security 4: Operational security: Organizations' operations usually require handling, storing, and transporting a large quantity of data. It is necessary to have a Computer emergency response team CERT) and a Security operations center (SOC) to monitor, check, detect, and take actions on the Indicators of compromise (IoCs) (for example, malware signatures, botnet IPs, and so on) through public sources (for example, blogs, forums, tweets, and so on) for the defense from attacks.[22] Tools used are Fraud and Threat prevention. Monitoring and Security Information and Event Management. (SIEM).
- Cyber security 5: Informational and application security keeps the databases safe from intruders and hackers. This cyber security protocols also ensures that the applications and software are secure from any malicious activity that can cause data loss or unintended software modifications. Tools introduced are application and database protection, and Next-generation firewalls (NGFW),
- Cyber security 6: In this phase, the concentration is on Identity access management (IAM), Security by Design, DevSecOps, Multi-factor authentication (MFA), Zero Trust, and vulnerability management.

One developing area for cyber security is biometrics. Biometrics refers to any reliable method that differentiates one person from another using

[22] Liao, X., Yuan, K., Wang, X., Li, Z., Xing, L., & Beyah, R. (2016, October). Acing the IoC game: Toward automatic discovery and analysis of open-source cyber threat intelligence. In *Proceedings of the 2016 ACM SIGSAC Conference on Computer and Communications Security* (pp. 755–766).

measurable qualities that may be physiological (fingerprints, hand geometry, retinas, iris, facial image) or behavioral (signature, voice, keystroke rhythms). They are used, for example, in financial transactions. Some ATMs (Automatic Teller Machines) and some ICT devices are equipped with fingerprint scanners, easing card-less transactions. Financial institutions need to be cyber secure from the inside. Since the emergence of AI, physical signatures are being outdated by biometrics and more secure ways.[23]

Biometrics are secure, but they are not fool proof. Since biometrics matches records. databases can be hacked into and can be tricked into, making it look like the biometric entered.

It is essential to remember the importance of the security of AI applications themselves.[24] Researchers have conducted many studies on malicious attacks and defense methods and produced satisfactory results. Malicious attacks are always possible. Two stages are particularly dangerous in the lifecycles of AI: the testing and the training stages.

Researchers have proposed some defense methods to deal with malicious attacks. They have achieved satisfactory results, reducing the success rate of malicious attacks by 70%–90%. They aim at a specific type of malicious attacks, and there is no defense method to deal with multiple or even all kinds of attacks.[25]The key to ensuring the AI solutions' security in various applications is to research the malicious attack protection solutions automatically, profoundly and continuously.

There is a continuous increase in the number of attacks and malicious messages. AI is essential to help to protect and to reduce the number of false positive IoCs to analyze.

[23] Iyer, A. P., Karthikeyan, D., Khan, M. R. H., & Binu, D. (2019). An analysis of artificial intelligence in biometrics—The next level of security. *Journal of Critical Reviews*, *7*(1), 2020.

[24] Szegedy, C., Zaremba, W., Sutskever, I., Bruna, J., Erhan, D., Goodfellow, I., & Fergus, R. (2013). Intriguing properties of neural networks. *arXiv preprint*. arXiv:1312.6199.

[25] Qiu, S., Liu, Q., Zhou, S., & Wu, C. (2019). Review of artificial intelligence malicious attack and defense technologies. *Applied Sciences*, *9*(5), 909.

Cyber Security in Banking 5.0

In banking, cyber security activities are not only necessary for protection. They are a tool to reinforce reputation in the market. In the last few years, financial institutions received more cyber attacks with respect to any other industry. Attacks on this sector accounted for 17 percent of all attacks in the top 10 attacked industries.[26] Financially motivated cyber hackers make up the most sizable part of active cyber threat actors targeting financial entities. Financial institutions' loss to a cyber hacker is potentially significant and with a rapid payout. It can reach the millions of dollars for a successful attack.[27]

Financial institutions should have more effective tools and processes to detect and hold threats before they turn into major incidents. Extensively testing incident response plans and teams against relevant scenarios proved effective at mitigating financial damages from data breaches, according to the 2019 Cost of a Data Breach Report conducted by the Ponemon Institute and sponsored by IBM Security.[28] Breached organizations that extensively tested their incident response plans lost on average USD 320,000 less than the overall mean cost of a data breach of USD 3.92 million.[29]

A Security operations center (SOC) receives on the average 10,000 alerts per day, but it has the workforce and resources to manage only part of them.[30] Two-thirds of security analysts investigate fewer than 30 alerts a day. Between three-quarters and half of these are false positives.[31] An

[26] www.ibm.com/security/digital-assets/xforce-threat-intelligence-index-map/#/. Accessed 20 August 2020.

[27] Stephens, J., & Valverde, R. (2013). Security of e-procurement transactions in supply chain reengineering, *Computer and Information Science*, *6*(3), 1–20.

[28] www.bluefin.com/bluefin-news/highlights-ibm-security-ponemon-institutes-2019-cost-data-breach-study/#:~:text=Overpercent20thepercent20lastpercent2014percent20years,frompercent202018'spercent20costpercent20ofpercent20percent24148. Accessed 20 October 2020.

[29] www.bluefin.com/bluefin-news/highlights-ibm-security-ponemon-institutes-2019-cost-data-breach-study/#:~:text=Overpercent20thepercent20lastpercent2014percent20years,frompercent202018'spercent20costpercent20ofpercent20percent24148. Accessed 20 October 2020.

[30] Klahr, R. (2017). *Cyber security breaches survey* (Doctoral dissertation). University of Portsmouth, Portsmouth, UK.

[31] www.helpnetsecurity.com/2019/08/29/soc-alert-overload/. Accessed 20 October 2020.

AI-based virtual security analyst can accelerate the process of accurately detecting and classifying attacks, investigating to find the possible source of the threat, the affected devices, and apply a suitable solution. The more data under monitoring, the better the detection.[32] With AI, financial institutions can continually improve their security posture. Machine learning (M) methods can analyze the data patterns and get trained to prevent or mitigate similar cyber attacks in the future.[33] They help the financial institutions to be prepared for the changing pattern of the cyber attacks by self-improving themselves, without the need for external intervention or programming.[34] These systems depend on the data, which can cause the problem of biases in their actions.[35] It is necessary to feed these systems with high-quality data so that the ML methods can better learn how to support cyber security.

A particular case in cyber security is fraud prevention. Financial institutions traditionally divide fraud into two main categories: external (for example, attacks on the financial institution or its customers related to money transfer, identity fraud, online payments, and so on) and internal fraud (for example, malicious actions from employees or contractors). External frauds relate to a wide variety of areas within financial institutions: non-cash payment over the internet, money transfer, documents (identity fraud), bank cheques, and so on. A Fraud detection system (FDS) is helpful to help with such threats. The process follows these steps: collect financial data, such as transactional data, analyze them, and learn from them or through the interaction with FDS operators in charge of implementing the detection rules. ML can, over time, improve the detection rules.

The cost of fraud associated with non-cash means of payment can be high. The Single European Payment Area (SEPA) estimated that non-cash

[32] Torabi, S., Boukhtouta, A., Assi, C., & Debbabi, M. (2018). Detecting Internet abuse by analyzing passive DNS traffic: A survey of implemented systems. *IEEE Communications Surveys & Tutorials, 20*(4), 3389–3415.

[33] Dua, S., & Du, X. (2016), *Data mining and machine learning in cyber security*. Boca Raton, FL: CRC Press.

[34] Bedi, P., Goyal, S. B., & Kumar, J. (2020, December). Basic structure on artificial intelligence: A revolution in risk management and compliance. In *2020 3rd International Conference on Intelligent Sustainable Systems (ICISS)* (pp. 570–576). IEEE.

[35] Jordan, M. I., & Mitchell, T. M. (2015). Machine learning: Trends, perspectives, and prospects, *Science, 349*(6245), 255–260.

payment frauds caused a 1.44 billion euros loss in 2013.[36] Fraudsters may take advantage of the innovative system's vulnerabilities and people's lack of digital awareness. Hackers offer hacking kits for tiny amounts of money on the "Dark Web."[37]

The risk of fraud has an impact on financial institutions' profitability. The most widely applied method for finding fraud is using computers to compare a particular set of structured data against a group of banking rules and limitations. With the help of cognitive analyzes, fraud finding models can become, over time, much more secure and correct. If a cognitive system finds a particular transaction as potential fraud, but a person later finds out this is not the case, the computer application can learn from personal insight. It will not make the same mistake again. This situation is an enormous change in the "rules of the game."[38] In this way, innovative solutions can help find emerging behavioral models and original fraudulent schemes, which persons could find very difficult to detect.[39] No less important is the role of AI in fraudulent practices identification and prevention.[40]

The vast imbalance between regular and fraudulent transactions means that a financial institution must be extra careful when estimating an anti-fraud system's performance. A bright and traditional way of checking is to measure two parameters:

1. Precision: the proportion of actual frauds among suspended or blocked transactions.
2. Recall: the proportion of frauds suspended or blocked.

[36] www.consilium.europa.eu/en/press/press-releases/2018/03/09/fighting-fraud-with-non-cash-means-of-payment-council-agrees-its-position/. Accessed 20 January 2021.

[37] Chen, H. (2011). *Dark web: Exploring and data mining the dark side of the web* (Vol. 30). Cham, Switzerland: Springer Science & Business Media.

[38] www.mygreatlearning.com/blog/what-is-artificial-intelligence/. Accessed 21 January 2021.

[39] Deloitte. (2016b). *Why artificial intelligence is a game changer for risk management*, www2.deloitte.com/content/dam/Deloitte/us/Documents/audit/us-ai-risk-powers-performance.pdf.

[40] Dzhaparov, P. (2020). Application of blockchain and artificial intelligence in bank risk management. *Икономика и управление*, *17*(1), 43–57.

Higher recall reduces the impact of fraud. Most of the time, it comes with low precision, meaning customer inconvenience is all but mitigated. Many more transactions will be suspended or blocked. AI algorithms are trying to balance both indicators.

Nonetheless, what is usually not considered is the cost associated with each event. The direct cost of fraud is easily measurable. The damage resulting from wrongly blocking an operation is not. The functioning cost of an investigation team is neither accounted for. Cost-sensitive learning starts a new way of dealing with fraud bearing in mind the whole picture.

Recently gaining relevance, reinforcement learning can improve the ways for dealing with fraud. Instead of waiting for the fraudsters to make the first move, reinforcement learning aims to model the fraudsters' behavior and continuously try to defend the system from their attacks.

Sometimes fraud detection looks ineffective. The reason is that the needed information is not available or that the attack happened upstream. For example, fraud is often connected with cyber attacks, which are challenging to deal with. ICT infrastructures (especially those of big financial institutions) are of great complexity. It is not easy to record logs into structured labeled data that is analyzable by supervised algorithms.

Collaboration is a crucial way to improve global performances against fraud. Such information sharing is essential for better tracking as finding links between people across financial institutions opens new horizons. More precisely, links are information about known people and their interaction on banking.

Building-up network-based AI models will reshape the way financial institutions are dealing with fraud by increasing the insights from real-world data.[41]

Advances in ML are enabling near real-time monitoring. This innovation is allowing the identification of anomalies at once. AI's ability to continuously analyze new behavior patterns and automatically self-adjust

Credit Suisse Group[42]
In 2016, the Swiss bank Credit Suisse Group AG launched an AI joint venture with Silicon Valley surveillance and security company Palantir Technologies. The goal is to help banks detect unauthorized trading.

[41] www.ebf.eu/wp-content/uploads/2020/03/EBF-AI-paper-_final-.pdf. Accessed 28 November 2020.

> The deployed solution catches employees with unethical behaviors before harming the bank.

Benefits and Challenges of Cyber Security

The new platforms are an exciting opportunity for hackers thanks to plenty of poorly protected devices to commit identity theft and infiltration in the organizations' ICT systems. It is critical defending access to these systems. Many organizations have limited experience and tools to detect or fix these types of attacks.[43]

Saving money for financial institutions, such AI applications are crucial in the fight against money-laundering and terrorism-financing, and other types of financial crimes.[44] Having a more secure system means increasing trust in the financial institution for both customers and financers.

Many applications are adopting machine and deep learning algorithms.[45] Some implementations are interesting for cyber security, mainly: intrusion detection, malware analysis, and spam detection. Machine and deep learning tools can support the security operator activities and automate some tasks. Hackers themselves turn to AI and use it to weaponize malware and attacks to counter the advancements made in cyber security solutions. For example, hackers use AI to conceal malicious codes in benign applications.[46]

[42] Voegeli, V. (2016, March). Credit Suisse, CIA-funded palantir to target rogue bankers. *Bloomberg*, 22.

[43] Atzei, N., Bartoletti, M., & Cimoli, T. (2017, April). A survey of attacks on Ethereum smart contracts (sok). In *International Conference on Principles of Security and Trust* (pp. 164–186). Berlin/Heidelberg: Springer. Germany.

[44] Genpact. (2018). *Transforming strategic risk management to realize competitive advantage: Genpact/ERMC FS Risk Management Survey*. www.genpact.com/downloadable-content/insight/transforming-strategic-risk-management-to-realize-competitive-advantage.pdf. Accessed 20 January 2021.

[45] Apruzzese, G., Colajanni, M., Ferretti, I., Guido, A., & Marchetti, M. (2018). On the effectiveness of machine and deep learning for cyber security. In *2018 10th International Conference on Cyber Conflict (CyCon)*.

[46] cisomag.eccouncil.org/hackers-using-ai/#:~:text=AI percent20Weaponization percent20by percent20Hackers,malicious percent20codes percent20in percent20benign percent20applications. Accessed 20 October 2020.

Regulation Compliance

The financial sector has a high cost for respecting standards and regulatory reporting requirements. New regulation in the USA and the European Union has further increased these costs. In recent years, US financial institutions spent an estimated USD 70 billion annually on regulatory compliance and governance software.[47] This spending reflects the costs of hiring lawyers, paralegals, and other consultants for verifying transaction compliance. Costs for these activities grew to nearly USD 120 billion in 2020.[48] Deploying AI technologies, for example, language processing could decrease financial institutions' compliance costs by 30 percent. It will significantly reduce the time needed to verify each transaction. AI can help interpret regulatory documents and run compliance rules.

Regulations

Since the 2008 crisis, the financial sector's regulatory requirements and controls have increased dramatically—both in volume (up to 1,503 standards in one year) and in complexity. The MiFID II regulation, for example, is divided into 1,400 measures, distributed over 7,000 pages.[49] This regulation introduced stringent requirements about the content and frequency of mandatory reporting. Adopting innovative solutions and the latest trends in a market in full transformation have contributed to this expansion. Small institutions are affected proportionately even more by new regulatory requirements. Based on 2017 data, the estimation is that it would take over 5,700 h (about eight months) for one individual to read all the relevant regulatory materials (at a continuous reading speed of 300 words per minute).[50] There are differences between reading lengthy literature works and reviewing regulatory rules. Many financial institutions problems are that reading and understanding regulations does not

[47] gomedici.com/a-report-on-global-regtech-a-100-billion-opportunity-market-overview-analysis-of-incumbents-and-start-ups/. Accessed 28 November 2020.

[48] Chintamaneni, P. (2017, June 26). *How banks can use AI to reduce regulatory compliance. burdens*, digitally.cognizant blog, digitally.cognizant.com/how-banks-can-use-ai-to-reduce-regulatory-compliance-burdens-codex2710/.

[49] Nicoletti, B. Future of Insurance 4.0 and Insurtech. In *Insurance 4.0* (pp. 389–431). Palgrave Macmillan, Cham, Switzerland.

[50] Financial Service Authority. (2019). Digital regulatory reporting: Phase 2 viability assessment. *Digit regul rep* (Phase 2 Viability Assessment): 44.

guarantee that the rules are implemented accurately and updated. Another example of the potential costs of regulatory breaches shows that the fines handed out by the Financial Conduct Authority (FCA) in the UK during 2019 totaled around GBP 392 million.[51]

Data Privacy

Data security and privacy is a significant concern with AI.[52] Reports on new concepts of digital monitoring are harmful (with reputational effects on the financial institutions). To manage these aspects and to avoid reputational risks, financial institutions should stick to a self-compliance framework and define which data to use for which purpose. They should limit their risk classification and pricing to specific criteria. This situation would mean that personal and susceptible information could not be collected or used by financial institutions.

A Gartner report says that by 2022, 70 percent of privacy breaches depend on a lack of privacy engineering.[53] To protect the personal information stored, transmitted, or accessed, vendors and financial institutions must use encrypted data.

As smart applications, such as AI ones, are becoming more ubiquitous, more opportunities for cyber hackers and fraudsters open. With data moved among systems, the risk of interception increases.[54] Smart products may lead to new types of applications and default fraud.

Financial institutions should not underestimate gaining and keeping customers' trust. Maintaining customers' data confidentiality should be a top priority for all financial institutions and intermediaries. The collection, use, and disclosure of data must be compliant with all applicable laws and regulations about data privacy, data security, data governance, and personal data protection.[55]

[51] FCA. (2019). Financial conduct authority. www.fca.org.uk/news/news-stories/2019-fines. Accessed 20 January 2021.

[52] iotinsobs.com/. Accessed 20 October 2020.

[53] www.gartner.com/en/documents/3877564/build-for-privacy. Accessed 3 March 2020.

[54] Smart Home Insurance. SlideShare. www.slideshare.net/matteocarbone/smart-home-insurance-144438351. Accessed 20 January 2021.

[55] Burdon, M. (2020). *Digital data collection and information privacy law*. Cambridge, UK: Cambridge University Press.

The compliance scenario for data privacy is getting clearer. In Europe, it is necessary to be compliant with the General Data Privacy Regulation (GDPR),[56] the Personal Data Privacy Regulation, and the European Data Protection Regulation.[57] In the USA, The California Customer Privacy Act (CCPA) allows enforcing actions since July 1, 2020.[58]

The European regulation on data protection has a relevant impact on banking. It aims to strengthen customer rights and supports substantial penalties for those who break the rules.[59] The users have more control over the data. The European regulations set standard rules on customers' right to know who has access to their data and how and why they are used. Financial institutions can no longer use data based on tacit consent. They must ask the customer's explicit consent. Financial institutions need to tell from which sources they get personal information, who and for what purpose have access to this information, and the legal basis for legitimizing these data.

PSD2

The revised Payment Services Directive with the official title: "Directive 2007/64/EC of the European Parliament and of the Council of 13 November 2007 on payment services in the internal market amending Directives 97/7/EC, 2002/65/EC, 2005/60/EC and 2006/48/EC and repealing Directive 97/5/EC" (PSD2) has preserved the structure of PSD1 and has kept much of the original text (for example, similar capital

[56] The General Data Protection Regulation 2016/679 is a regulation in the EU law regulation on data protection and privacy in the European Union and the European Economic Area. It addresses the transfer of personal data outside the EU and EEA areas. eur-lex.europa.eu/eli/reg/2016/679/oj. Accessed 28 November 2020.

[57] Carey, P. (2018). *Data protection: A practical guide to UK and EU law*. New York, NY: Oxford University Press.

[58] oag.ca.gov/privacy/ccpa#:~:text=The percent20California percent20Customer percent20Privacy percent20Act,that percent20is percent20collected percent20by percent20businesses.&text=The percent20Attorney percent20General percent20cannot percent20bringpercent20until percent20July percent201 percent2C percent202020,CCPA. Accessed 1 July 2020.

[59] Ponce de León, M. (2018, May 20). *Protección de datos: las aseguradoras apuran el plazo de adaptación a las nuevas exigencias*. www.expansion.com/empresas/2018/05/20/5b01966e22601db97f8b4613.html. Accessed 3 March 2020. European data protection: Impact of the EU data-protection. voxeu.org/article/european-data-protection-impact-eu-data-protection-regulation. Accessed 30 April 2020.

requirements). Some wording has been partially rewritten, and new provisions have been added. The structure is split into sections (Titles) and subdivision into content areas (chapters with related articles and points). The sections are:

- Title I: "Subject matter, scope and definitions."
- Title II: "Payment service providers" and specifically the regulation of payment institutions.
- Title III: "Transparency of conditions and information requirements for payment services;"
- Title IV: "Rights and obligations in relations to the provision and use of payment services."
- Title V: "Delegated acts and regulatory technical standards" where the power conferred on the EC to adopt delegated acts and technical regulatory standards appears.
- Title VI: "Final provisions."

PSD2 covers new services and players by extending the scope of existing services (payment instruments issued by Payment service providers (PSPs) that do not manage the account of the Payment service users (PSU). They enable third-parties access to customers' account data, start payments, and supply them with an overview of their various payment accounts based on explicit customer consent. Fresh players will be registered and licensed at the European Union (EU) level. The competition will increase by removing barriers for these organizations, leading to lower costs for customers. PSD2 updates the telecom exemption, extending the scope of currencies and geographical coverage. It enhances cooperation and information between authorities in the context of authorization and supervision of payment institutions. The European banking authority (EBA) develops a central register of authorized and registered payment institutions. To make digital payments safer and more secure, PSD2 introduces enhanced security measures compulsory for all PSPs.[60] EBA will develop the technical, regulatory standards that cover Strong customer authentication (SCA) provided by PSPs and Common and secure communication (CSC) between PSPs.

[60] EBF PSD2 guidance September 2016-Rev. www.ebf.eu/wp-content/uploads/2017/05/EBF_PSD2_guidance_September_2016.pdf. Accessed 20 January 2021.

Money Laundering
Money laundering has been a significant challenge for financial institutions globally. AI has proved to be some crucial solutions to fight this issue.[61] AI allows the financial institution to prevent potential money-laundering activity by analyzing internal, publicly available, and transactional data within the customer's comprehensive network. Some of the tools applied as combating measures include machine learning, deep learning, data mining and analytics, and other solutions.[62]

AI Regulations
A significant way to prevent or limit any negative impact and reimburse those who suffer from AI's negative consequences is to apply AI within specific ethical standards and in a socially responsible way.[63] There is a vast debate on the ethical concerns raised by AI. The literal interpretation of this principle ("no individual will ever be harmed") does not consider many situations where potentially individuals will be harmed in a "legitimate and reasonable" way. For example, access to an account might be refused based on potential money-laundering activities. A strict interpretation makes AI very restricted. Use-cases of potential benefit to other individuals, businesses, or society will be prevented, such as preventing a crime. Policymakers and society must remain neutral toward the solution. They should concentrate on its application, intent, and the goals behind it. The same solutions can be used differently and yield different results.

The European Commission issued some Ethical Guidelines on AI, characterized by a human-centric approach. They focus on some ethical principles and topics such as the security, confidentiality, and privacy of data and ICT solutions in this area.

To be ethically correct, AI must be reliable, which concretely translates into compliance with the law, respect for ethical principles and principles

[61] Chen, Z., Teoh, E. N., Nazir, A., Karuppiah, E. K., & Lam, K. S. (2018). Machine learning techniques for anti-money laundering (AML) solutions in suspicious transaction detection: A review. *Knowledge and Information Systems*, *57*(2), 245–285.

[62] Singh, C., & Lin, W. (2020). Can artificial intelligence, RegTech and CharityTech supply effective solutions for anti-money laundering and counter-terror financing initiatives in charitable fundraising. *Journal of Money Laundering Control*.

[63] Tsekeris, C., & Mastrogeorgiou, Y. (2020). Contextualizing COVID-19 as a Digital Pandemic. *Homo Virtualis*, *3*(2), 1–14.

capable of ensuring the significance of human dignity and freedoms. The Ethical Guidelines remind seven requirements[64]:

1. Human personnel should supervise AI systems to guarantee respect for fundamental rights and the user's well-being.
2. Robustness and safety are understood as the algorithms' security and reliability and sealing the control systems in hypothetical illegal operations.
3. Transparency should guarantee the traceability of the systems and to prove the operations carried out by the algorithms.
4. AI systems should consider different and distinctly human competencies and abilities while ensuring free access to these tools for all to respect diversity, fairness, and the absence of discrimination.
5. Social and environmental well-being requires considering the impact on the environment and on the social order, promoting AI only where its use can guarantee sustainable development.
6. Continuous verification of systems, both internally and externally.

There is a need to follow ethics and security by design approach when developing new systems.[65] "Fairness in AI" goes beyond the fairness principle provided under Article 5(1)(a) of the GDPR, which relates only to fair personal data processing. There is no standard definition of fairness for machine or individual decision-making.[66]

Addressing fairness and inclusion in AI covers all the use case life cycle: setting a concrete goal, using representative datasets to train and test the model, and the continuous testing of the final system for unfair outcomes. AI presents opportunities to conduct more goal decision-making. AI can help find, detect, and correct conscious and unconscious person biases or errors in judgment. Regarding unfair discrimination, the primary source of potential unfair discrimination is data. An algorithm and its result can only be as good as the data provided in the input. It is essential to

[64] ec.europa.eu/futurium/en/ai-alliance-consultation. Accessed 20 January 2021.

[65] d'Aquin, M., Troullinou, P., O'Connor, N. E., Cullen, A., Faller, G., & Holden, L. (2018, December). Towards an ethics by design method for AI research projects. In *Proceedings of the 2018 AAAI/ACM Conference on AI, Ethics, and Society* (pp. 54–59).

[66] Binns, R. (2018, January). Fairness in machine learning: Lessons from political philosophy. In *Conference on Fairness, Accountability and Transparency* (pp. 149-159). PMLR.

ensure access to high-quality and comprehensive data as a starting point. Running data through AI-based systems can help find such data quality and achieve high data quality and governance overall. To limit and avoid unfair bias, several types of measures can be implemented. Hacking large input data samples resulting from various sources can help improve accuracy and prevent discrimination from using a single specific source with limited data. It is essential to encourage employees to find potentially unfair bias and deploy policies, procedures, and control mechanisms.

Over time, many regulatory organizations started to control AI development and deployment. Some examples are in the following pages.[67]

In September 2019, the US Consumer Financial Protection Bureau (CFPB)'s Office of Innovation launched three new policies "to promote innovation and facilitate compliance" in the field of AI. The three guidelines included the No-Action Letter Policy (NAL), the Trial Disclosure Program (TDP) Policy, and the Compliance Assistance Sandbox (CAS) Policy. These policies enable financial service providers to interpret financial compliance standards in financial services innovation, streamline the regulatory application and ease existing compliance requirements. The CFPB's goal is to encourage innovation among financial service providers and therefore increase customer financial inclusion. In March 2020, US Congress introduced a bill to set up a national AI initiative. The National Artificial Intelligence Act of 2020 supports education and research and authorizes USD 391 million for a new risk assessment framework for AI systems developed by NIST.

The Bank of Canada Financial System Review proposed in 2020 Ensuring Appropriate Regulation of Artificial Intelligence: The Office of the Privacy Commissioner (OPC) has developed several proposals, or recommendations, about the AI regulation for both the public and private sectors.

In September 2019, the Brazilian Senate introduced a draft bill No. 5051/2019: The Use of AI supplies guidelines and principles for using AI in the Brazilian public sector. One of the core principles set up in this bill is the protection of privacy and personal data.

In December 2019, the Superintendencia Financiera de Colombia issued Circular 029 promoting the adoption of technologies such as blockchain, AI, and augmented reality to supply better financial services

[67]An introduction to the Global Partnership on AI's work on Responsible AI—OECD.AI. Accessed 12 December 2020.

to customers. It outlines the security requirements for biometric authentication. It calls for modifications to several chapters of the country's existing Basic Legal Circular, which is the set of general rules governing Colombia's financial institutions.

The European Union Commission issued a White Paper on AI: "A European Approach to Excellence and Trust." In March 2020, the European Commission released a white paper focused on the government's role in developing AI customer standards. The report poses questions about product safety and liability rules to address issues arising from AI systems. Some of the topics discussed include changing the existing regulatory framework to address changes brought on by AI systems.

UNESCO recently published the revised draft of a new document giving recommendations on AI ethics.

Russian State Duma issued a new bill in early 2020 on implementing an experimental legal framework for the development of AI projects. This bill aims to stimulate innovative solutions in the market and supply workable regulations for anonymized data.

In July 2020, the British ICO published new guidance on AI and data protection. The advice provides organizations using or developing AI technologies with practical recommendations on the steps they should take to follow the data protection law. Consistent with the ICO's general approach to compliance, the guidance emphasizes the importance of organizations taking a risk-based AI approach.

In July 2019, the United Arab Emirates (UAE) Financial Services Regulatory Authority (FSRA) issued new guidance, Supplementary Guidance: Authorization of Digital Investment Management ("Robo-advisory") Activities.

In November 2019, the Hong Kong Monetary Authority released guidance related to AI development and its use in the banking and fintech industries. This guidance proposes 12 high-level AI principles, including adopting an Ethical Accountability Framework for collecting and using personal data published by the PCPD.

In June 2020, the Reserve Bank of India published a notification to all authorized payment system participants and operators in the country, including banks and non-banks, directing entities to use multiple communication accesses to raise customer awareness of digital payment fraud.

The regulation of AI in China is governed by the State Council of the PRC's July 8, 2017 "A Next Generation Artificial Intelligence Development Plan". In this document, the Central Committee of the Communist Party of China and the State Council of the People's Republic of China urged China's governing bodies to promote the development of AI. Regulation of the issues of moral and legal support for developing AI is growing in importance.

In September 2020, the Taiwan government's legislative branch introduced a private bill to set up a framework to promote safe AI development within the country's economy. The law supplies legal certainty on critical definitions, core development principles supporting AI solutions, and ethical aspects.

The OECD Global partnership on AI (GPAI) has a mission to "support the development and use of AI-based on human rights, inclusion, diversity, innovation, and economic growth while seeking to address the United Nations Sustainable Development Goals." GPAI will bring together experts from businesses, government, civil society, and academia to advance innovative research and pilot projects on AI priorities. It is supported by four Working Groups looking at Data Governance, Responsible AI (including a subgroup on Pandemic Response), the Future of Work, and Commercialization and Innovation.

Regtech

The term regtech (REGulatory TECHnology) refers to technological solutions developed to support the management and regulatory compliance monitoring. Regtech organizations are part of the fintech organization world.[68] Regtech organizations are often start-ups characterized by lean business models and innovative solutions (for example, cloud computing, big data analytics, machine learning, and so on).

Regtech organizations appeared years ago. The British Financial Conduct Authority, for example, started to study this area in 2015.[69] In other countries, big consultancy organizations have offered services in

[68] Nicoletti, B. (2017), *The future of fintech*, Springer International Publishing, London, UK. ISBN 978-3-319-51414-7.

[69] www.fca.org.uk/publication/call-for-input/regtech-call-for-input.pdf. Accessed 10 May 2020.

the sector for several years. The market has proliferated over the past few years.

The sector most involved in the growth of regtech organizations is the banking sector. However, regtech organizations' interest has been directed toward large financial institutions or banking groups. Now, regtech organizations aim at the small- and medium-sized banking sector.[70] Four main factors motivate the use (and costs) of these new technological organizations in small or so-called minor institutions, which, for example, are estimated to manage 26 percent of Italy's assets.

1. The growing complexity of the legislation still has significant consequences on these actors' operations since they often lack the possibility of investments and the necessary resources and competencies.
2. Costs related to compliance are associated with the monitoring and compliance adjustment activity, which is estimated to be around 10–15 percent of operating expenditure in the financial services. These costs are growing. In 2018, 89 percent of the compliance officers in the financial services forecasted an increase.[71] US banks spend over USD 70 billion per year on regulatory compliance.[72]
3. The adoption and continuous updating of organization and control models in compliance with the principal corporate regulations (such as the European Data Protection Regulation, adopting a Legality Rating, and so on) is a challenge for financial institutions.
4. The diffusion of modern technologies has enabled the development of cheaper solutions. Still, there is an increase in the costs of more effective regtech solutions. Technologies such as AI, machine learning, robotic process automation, and blockchain solutions are implemented systematically and integrated.[73]

[70] Mulder, B. J. M. (2019). RegTech: Tackling regulation with innovation. *The RegTech Book*.

[71] www.finextra.com/blogposting/17167/4-trends-to-watch-in-regulatory-ai. Accessed 30 May 2020.

[72] gomedici.com/a-report-on-global-regtech-a-100-billion-opportunity-market-overview-analysis-of-incumbents-and-start-ups/. Accessed 28 November 2020.

[73] von Solms, J. (2020). Integrating Regulatory Solution (RegTech) into the digital transformation of a bank Treasury. *Journal of Banking Regulation*, 1–17.

In some countries, regtech organizations face challenges. Their solutions would require continuous and significant updates. Other challenges are with technological capabilities. These considerations are particularly relevant for small- and medium-sized financial institutions.

Regtech organizations can standardize, automate, and speed up several manual activities, making the regulatory process more robust and economical. Regtech solutions offer enhanced characteristics,[74]

- Cluttered and interlinked data sets can be decoupled and organized by using more intelligent agile technologies.
- Reports can be configured and generated faster.
- Integrated approaches allow for shorter timeframes to generate operational solutions and get them up and running in a brief time.
- Advanced analytics tools can intelligently process existing big data sets and unlock real value, for example, improved insights and use of the same data for multiple purposes.

There are now automated, flexible, dynamic, and modular solutions to support the financial institutions' needs. For example, the tool CR.AA.M. (Compliance Risk & Audit Activity Management) allows the management and monitoring of the compliance checks applicable to a financial institution, automating the risk status trend.[75] This web-based applications' strength is the reporting: CR.AA.M allows operators to configure and generate summary and analytical reports of a graphic, tabular, and descriptive type together with historical trend graphs on the state of compliance. Dashboards can be set according to specific organization requirements and generated in a brief time.

Machine learning (ML) is used in regtech solutions to reduce costs and increase compliance with various regulatory requirements. Some regtech tools based on ML have already been applied to better follow regulatory requirements at lower costs, and more solutions are under development.

An area of application of ML is the conduct and market abuse in trading. Carney said that global banks' misconduct costs had exceeded

[74] Copinni, I. (2016). RegTech is the new FinTech. *Deloitte Services*.

[75] www.ict-ss.net/?q=node/18. Accessed 10 May 2020.

USD 320 billion.[76] One of the responses of financial institutions is to develop automated systems that watch a variety of behavior by traders.[77] The behaviors may include trading patterns, email traffic, calendar items, and telephone calls. Often there is a lack of labeled data for supervised learning and the need to audit the results.[78]

ML solutions have become more interesting from a cost and practical perspective to combine with big data analytics with the expansion in computing power and distributed processing. Some of the emerging digital technologies to meet the increasing demands of the regulatory processes are[79]:

- AI can help deliver a more innovative and efficient onboarding process, find weaknesses in existing risk and control frameworks, and help guide the intelligent allocation of financial resources.
- Big data analytics can improve the insights from structured and unstructured data and support programmable reporting. This solution can learn more about customer actions along with their connections. Many regulatory issues, such as money laundering and fraud discovery, appear from behaviors or transactions that are not easy to discover through traditional risk and control models.
- Natural language processing can support heavy regulatory compliance tasks that include scanning for revised or new regulations and modified risk reporting. These algorithms can continuously and relentlessly perform these functions, share the impact with compliance process owners, and find decision-making drivers.
- Machine learning can help with the testing of computational models and improve the forecasting of cash flows.

[76] www.marketwatch.com/story/carney-says-bank-misconduct-has-cost-the-global-economy-5-trillion-in-lost-lending-2017-04-20. Accessed 28 November 2020.

[77] Van Liebergen, B. (2017): Machine learning: a revolution in risk management and compliance? *The Capco Institute Journal of Financial Transformation, 45*, 60–67.

[78] Van Liebergen, B. (2017): Machine learning: a revolution in risk management and compliance? *The Capco Institute Journal of Financial Transformation, 45*, 60–67.

[79] www.grantthornton.com/library/articles/financial-services/2018/BK/RegTech-future-compliance.aspx. Accessed 20 January 2021.

Podder, S., Pisanu, G., & Ghosh, B. (2018). RegTech for regulators. *World Gov Summit*.

- Robotic process automation can deliver productivity and efficiency gains by automating non-value-added manual activities like data extraction, formatting, and reconciliation tasks. Robotic process automation can produce the reports automatically,
- Application programming interfaces (API) can integrate fragmented activities and enable automated reporting to regulators.
- Distributed ledger solutions can minimize the dependency on back-office personnel and departments. By replacing traditional procedures with verifiable digital workflows, respects to compliance and regulatory practices are enhanced. A distributed ledger solution can help ensure that the report production is verified and checked throughout the process.
- Cloud computing allows the integration of fragmented data systems to produce a real-time standardized view of risk information that would require a significant upfront ICT investment and long development time. A cloud platform supplies organizations the flexibility to scale as requirements change and simplify incorporating other data methodologies and analytics, such as ML and big data analytics.

Going beyond its role in helping financial institutions complies and enforces the regulation, regtech organizations can bring significant benefits for the Regulators.[80]

Credit Suisse
Credit Suisse partnered with Palantir Technologies (an AI company, already backed by the CIA's venture capital arm) to use data-driven behavioral analysis to better monitor markets and avoid rogue traders and insider dealing.[81] "The venture tracks traders' activities and tries to find deviations both from their norms and from those of their colleagues. The new product analyzes those outliers and couple the data on them with behavior analysis, such as mobile phone usage and door key-card swipes to get hints on compliance."

[80] Anagnostopoulos, I. (2018). Fintech and regtech: Impact on regulators and banks. *Journal of Economics and Business*, *100*, 7–25.

[81] Voegeli, V. (2016). Credit Suisse, CIA-Funded Palantir to target Rogue Bankers. *Bloomberg*.

Resilient Solutions

With the spread of banking 5.0, financial institutions can connect all their systems and automation applications with management tools to support the banking processes. The information gathered can be shared in real-time directly with the partners in the same ecosystem.[82]

Resilience is an essential subject for two reasons. Financial institutions should analyze better their capabilities to reduce the probability of the risks and especially their potential impact. To defend their reputation, financial institutions should assure maximum resilience in such a way to be able to supply their services under any foreseeable conditions and events.[83] After the pandemic, what was"just in time" has become"just in case." It is essential to prepare to some unknown event that can affect on the existence itself of the financial institution.[84]

The resilience of ICT and automation systems is essential.[85] It must be an integral part of assessing potential risks, services, systems, and even more in evaluating workable solutions. The researchers are developing products with autonomic computing, a computer system of self-care, or self-unlock.[86] The products or services can autonomously detect and remediate failures/recover. For example, these solutions enable large ICT systems to supply services 24*7 to meet their targets with little or no personal intervention. Achieving self-care requires automated testing as it is possible using Jenkins' continuous integration.[87] and the implementation and maintenance of domain knowledge in problem determination,

[82] Rajola, F. (2019). *Customer relationship management in the financial industry organizational processes and solution innovation*. Berlin/Heidelberg, Germany: Springer-Verlag.

[83] Bitter, P., & Uphues, S. (2017, September). Big Data und die Versichertengemeinschaft– «Entsolidarisierung» durch Digitalisierung. *ABIDA-Dossier*.

[84] Brakman, S., Garretsen, H., & van Witteloostuijn, A. (2020). The turn from just-in-time to just-in-case globalization in and after times of COVID-19: An essay on the risk re-appraisal of borders and buffers. *Social Sciences & Humanities Open*, *2*(1), 100034.

[85] Nicoletti, B. (2016). Resilience & outsourcing, *Pmworld*, 2, 16.

[86] Montani, S., & Anglano, C. (2008). Achieving self-healing in service delivery systems software through case-based reasoning. *Applied Intelligence, 28* (2), 139–152.

[87] Smart, J. F. (2011). *Jenkins: The definitive guide—Continuous integration for the masses*. O'Reilly Media, Inc. Sebastopol, CA.

diagnosis, and repair models.[88] Case-Based Reasoning (CBR) is a learning paradigm that reduces many types of these bottlenecks thanks to automatic knowledge acquisition.[89] The application of CBR for the diagnosis and remediation in software systems looks promising. In this field, most errors are new occurrences of known issues. It is more challenging to develop an autonomic solution in services with a strong human presence in the service provision.

The future holds exciting developments in this area, thanks to AI. The expectation is that AI will play an increasing role in defensive and offensive measures to supply a rapid response to react to evolving threats. It is possible to imagine and design a general hybrid AI network resiliency system (ARS) that strikes the right balance between centralized and distributed security systems and may apply to different ICT environments.[90] The characteristics of a resilience are in Figs. 14.1 and 14.2.[91]

Conclusions

There is a concern for cyber security in banking 5.0 and risks for financial institutions in malicious attacks.[92] It is critical developing cyber security and related systems within banking 5.0. It is necessary to use a standard approach and include all stakeholders.[93]

[88] Yiran, W., Tongyang, Z., & Vidong, G. (2018, May). Design and implementation of continuous integration scheme based on Jenkins and Ansible. In *2018 International Conference on Artificial Intelligence and Big Data (ICAIBD)* (pp. 245–249). IEEE.

[89] Kolodner, J. (2014). *Case-based reasoning*. Morgan Kaufmann, Burlington, MA.

[90] Hussein, A., Chehab, A., Kayssi, A., & Elhajj, I. H. (2018, April). Machine learning for network resilience: The start of a journey. In *2018 Fifth International Conference on Software Defined Systems (SDS)* (pp. 59-66). IEEE.

[91] Nicoletti, B. (2016). Resilience & Outsourcing, *Pmworld*, N. 2, p. 16.

[92] Barron, S., Cho, Y. M., Hua, A., Norcross, W., Voigt, J., & Haimes, Y. (2016, June 10). Systems-based cyber security in the supply chain, *IEEE Systems and Information Engineering Design Symposium (SIEDS)* (pp. 20–25).

[93] Johnson, T. A. (2013). *Cyber security: Protecting Critical Infrastructures from Cyber Attack and Cyber Warfare.* Boca Raton, FL: CRC Press.

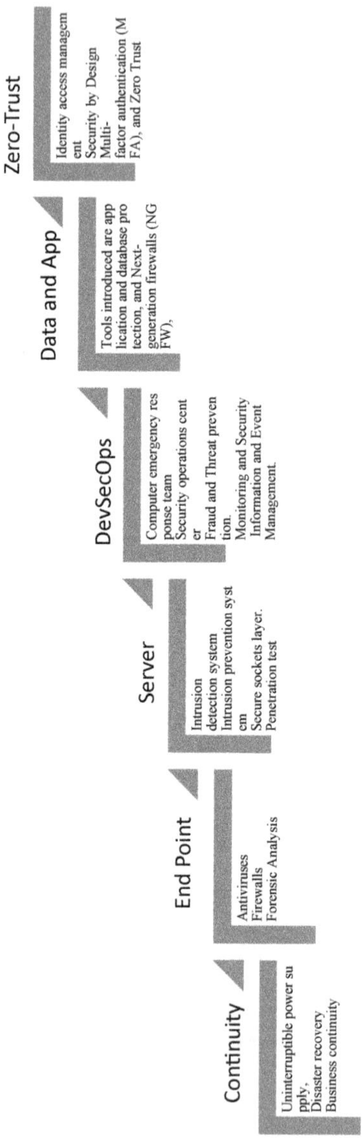

Fig. 14.1 Cyber security generations

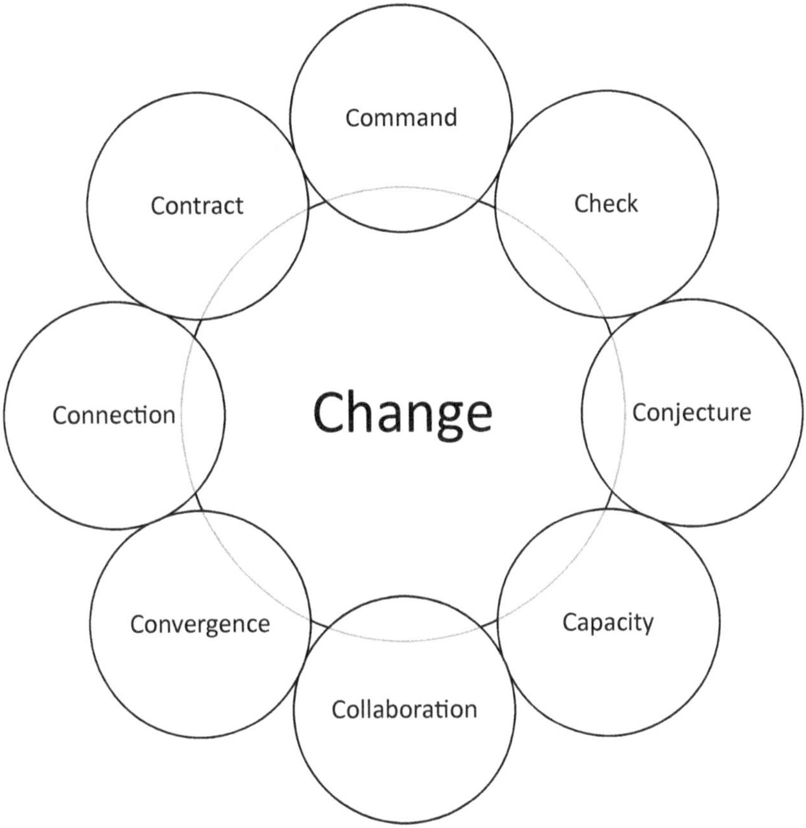

Fig. 14.2 Basic aspects of resilience

The cyber security tools are developing rapidly against threats that can take many forms. The sector is highly active, and innovative solutions arrive continuously.[94]

Digital resilience and security by design will be available in the not distant future. It is the ability to design customer applications, banking processes, solution architectures, and related cyber security defenses with

[94] www.grantthornton.com/library/articles/financial-services/2018/BK/RegTech-future-compliance.aspx. Accessed 30 March 2021.

the protection of critical information and assets of the organization in mind and the assurance of continuity of service,[95] The chapter dedicates attention to resilience.

[95] Kaplan J. M., Bailey, T., O'Halloran, D., Marcus, A., & Rezek, C. (2015), *Beyond cyber security: Protecting your digital business*. Hoboken, NJ: John Wiley & Sons.

CHAPTER 15

Future of Banking 5.0

We tend to overestimate the effect of a solution in the short run and underestimate the effect in the long run.
Roy Amara

Introduction

This chapter deals with the future of banking 5.0. The great physicist Niels Bohr said: "It is challenging to predict, mainly the future."[1] On the other side, it is critical to predict the future in the best conceivable way for surviving as persons and organizations. This observation holds true in general. It is even more so in banking because of its close links with the external environment. This interrelationship becomes vital in banking 5.0.

Banking will evolve in the short and medium term. Banking 5.0 not only changes current markets and business models.[2] The new technological possibilities, innovative solutions, and new services will bring substantial changes. Fintech organizations with new business models

[1] Camussone, P. F. (2017). Digital for job: The future of work—Solution. *Digital World*, *2*, 1–15.

[2] Prognos, A. G. (2017). Digitalisierung in der Versicherungswirtschaft. Studie. Hg. v. vbw *Vereinigung der Bayerischen Wirtschaft e.V*. München, Germany.

B. Nicoletti, *Banking 5.0*, Palgrave Studies in Financial Services Technology, https://doi.org/10.1007/978-3-030-75871-4_15

beyond the established financial institutions' core markets open entirely new scenarios.

Competitors could come from outside the banking world. Large internet organizations, the so-called bigtech organizations,[3] can find ways to go round the structural barriers to market entry in banking.[4] They have robust financial strength and data and information essential for risk and marketing calculations. Compliance and administrative burden are so high that fintech organizations or bigtech organizations' widespread market entry as digital financial institutions is unlikely in the short term. Big internet or bigtech organizations may occupy part of the value network currently covered by the traditional financial institutions. From the financial institutions' perspective, the loss of direct customer proximity is already starting to pose significant dangers.

Scenarios

To predict it is necessary to define scenarios. A prediction might be simple for the short term. Slower growth, pandemic, and other difficulties worldwide will make it challenging to resume the pre-crisis operational levels of 2008 or even 2019. Simultaneously, globalization is in crisis. There are several reasons. The acceleration of globalization was too fast. The result has been a revival of localism and sovranism (a new term to avoid the word nationalism, which evokes bad past times).

These changes will be reflected in the organizations and so on banking. The examination of what could happen to banking 5.0, is fascinating, referring to the classic four Ps of the marketing mix: product, price, promotion or advertisement, and place or location.

- From the product point of view, dematerialization is prevailing. This trend pushes the services toward a sharing economy, the sharing of material products, and consumptions. Outsourcing is the traditional mode of sharing economy for organizations. The expectation is that in a joint environment with complex ecosystems outsourcing will also grow for banking.

[3] Frost, J., Gambacorta, L., Huang, Y., Shin, H. S., & Zbinden, P. (2019). *BigTech and the changing structure of financial intermediation.*

[4] Prognos, A. G. (2017): Digitalisierung in der Versicherungswirtschaft. Studie. Hg. v. vbw *Vereinigung der Bayerischen Wirtschaft e.V.* München, Germany.

- From the price perspective, the trend will include in the economic balance of a product or service factors not connected with the price but with the general's financial gains.
- It is interesting to note the diffusion in the banking of some multimedia promotions to the customers.
- The place and the help in selling and delivery of banking will expand through online and mobile channels with a push to an omnniaccess approach.[5]

There are other socio-economic changes synthetized in the words globalization and robotics (globotics).[6]

Future Business Model Components

The organization can try to find how the future looks from some of the components introduced in this book's approach to the banking business model canvas (BMC). Each one of the main components of the BMC is analyzed in the following pages (Fig. 15.1).

Proposition of Value

New cryptocurrencies from private organizations such as Facebook threaten the current monetary power of the central banks. The central banks could counteract launching Central Bank Digital Currencies (CBDCs).[7] One of the most popular decentralized currencies is Stablecoin tied to the US dollar. For example. Tether is expanding. It is backed by the US dollar. The support of governments to the issue of digital currencies will be fundamental.

It means that most cryptocurrencies, including bitcoin and Ethereum, might lose value in the future. They might be replaced by digital currencies backed by central banks or Stablecoin-like currencies supported by

[5] Hu, T. I., & Tracogna, A. (2020). Multichannel customer journeys and their determinants: Evidence from motor insurance. *Journal of Retailing and Customer Services, 54,* 102022.

[6] Baldwin, R., & Forslid, R. (2020). *Globotics and development: When manufacturing is jobless and services are tradable* (No. w26731). National Bureau of Economic Research.

[7] thefinanser.com/2020/10/or-will-cbdcs-will-destroy-banking.html/. Accessed 25 October 2020.

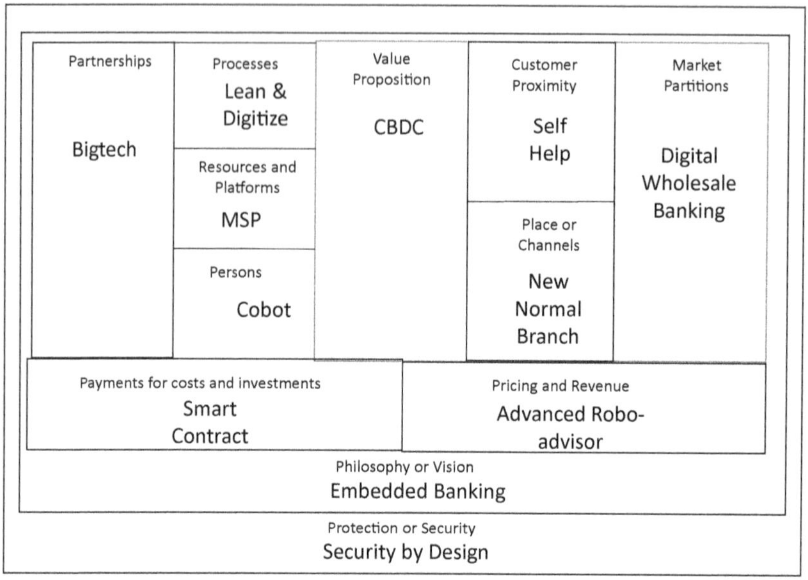

Fig. 15.1 Future banking

real assets, including US dollars, euros, yuan, gold, and other investable asset types.

The possible implementation of a CBDC is under consideration in many countries worldwide.[8] As cash use is diminishing and cryptocurrencies continue to increase in usage and value, there is a need for an alternative to fiat currency. The literature highlights two types of CBDC, retail and wholesale.[9]

A register-based CBDC would offer an effective solution to the possible troubles associated with transferring the money to citizens. The current inflation could be replaced through price-level targeting and offer a correct forecast of future price levels. A CBDC could affect the

[8] Brokke, O. G. J., & Engen, N. E. (2019). *Central Bank digital currency (CBDC): An explorative study on its impact and implications for monetary policy and the banking sector* (Master's Thesis). Bergen, Norway.

[9] Auer, R., Cornelli, G., & Frost, J. (2020). Rise of the central bank digital currencies: Drivers, approaches and technologies. *Bank for International Settlements Working Papers* (880), 1–41.

seigniorage a central bank earns through creating money. The potential effects would be primarily dependent on the construction of the CBDC. An interest-bearing design would be in higher demand, causing a larger volume of CBDC in the economy. However, as the seigniorage covers the interest, the total effects are dependent on the rate set by the central banks.

Commercial banks receive much of their funding from depositors. A CBDC built with an interest-bearing structure would act as competitor to deposit accounts, as they offer low-interest rates. The CBDC rate would act as a floor for how low the commercial banks can set their deposit rates.

The technical base of digital currencies is the blockchain solution. There are several reasons to consider blockchain solutions and deep learning together[10]:

- It appears that there is the emergence of a new class of global network computing systems.
- Blockchain solutions and deep learning are both necessary to ease the development of the other solution. This solution includes using deep learning algorithms for setting fees and detecting fraudulent activity. Blockchain peer-to-peer nodes might supply deep learning services as they already supply transaction hosting and confirmation, news hosting, and banking (payment, credit flow-through) services.

There is a debate about whether future CBDC will go around banks or go through banks.[11] This question is essential for the future of the financial system. Suppose central banks could run a techno-ledger using cryptocurrencies that they issue digitally. In that case, it becomes unclear the role of banks, SWIFT, MasterCard, Visa, or any of the systems currently in use. Those systems become redundant, and banks would change role. In a digital currency or cryptocurrency world, financial institutions' proper

[10] Swan, M. (2018). Blockchain for business: Next-generation enterprise artificial intelligence systems. In *Advances in computers* (Vol. 111, pp. 121–162). Amsterdam, The Netherlands: Elsevier.

[11] Tronnier, F., Recker, M., & Hamm, P. (2020). Towards Central Bank digital currency—A systematic literature review. In *PACIS* (p. 131).

role is to store and exchange value with trust. That is why they are regulated the way they are and why they exist the way they do.[12] That is not going away soon.

Proximity

It is interesting to look at the future of Customer proximity centers (CPCs). The trend is to design and implement customer proximity centers for self-help.[13] Some financial institutions are trying to first change the customers' attitude about the customer proximity centers: from the "welfare" approach (the center is necessary to solve problems, and at any cost) to cooperating, proactively and more demanding from the center. Some financial institutions are already moving in this direction due to the exciting revenue and cost savings that it brings. The tools that can help are self-diagnosis technologies, automatic identification of failure, the connection with monitoring and control systems, and databases of statistical information of the non-quality made available to the customers. These new tools focus less on accessing a customer proximity center and more on perfecting the system and preventing malfunctions.

Thanks to this self-help activity, financial institutions can save up to 40 percent on some support/maintenance contracts costs. Financial institutions agree: the higher the customer's self-service ability, the more financial institutions can expand their radius of action. All this should be a target for the banking 5.0 customer proximity centers. Self-help makes it more challenging to measure the quality of the service offered to the customers. It is interesting to deepen the financial goals associated with a policy of this type. It is interesting to explore the concept of complex support concerning simple advice. It is moving from servicing services to the provision of a service. There is a growing need for financial institutions to perfect the performance of the system. To do this, the support service must move toward constant monitoring and remote control. These actions allow the tuning of the system and the prevention of defects and not only of the interventions after the onset of a problem.

[12] Skinner, C. (2018). *Digital human: The fourth revolution of humanity includes everyone*. Hoboken, NJ: John Wiley & Sons.

[13] Mohapatra, S. (2013). Understanding e-commerce product design strategy. In *E-Commerce Strategy* (pp. 113–125). New York, NY, USA: Springer.

The CPC should look increasingly to improve the efficiency of the customers' use of banking services. All this implies that it is necessary:

- Change processes.
- Supply suggestions for the optimization of the services,
- Assure the customers with the continuity in their use of the services without harm.
- Change completely the characteristics of the CPC to be much more proactive and "outbound."

Partition

Until now (and in this book), the preference for AI, robots, and sustainability has been mostly limited to retail banking. Wholesale banking is essential. In the future, the solutions for retail banking will be applied to wholesale banking.

Wholesale financial services are mostly operators who supply coverage for risks outside of traditional financial institutions' risk preference or supply specialized capabilities. Digital transformation is spreading worldwide. Wholesale banking is no exception. It is slowly moving toward banking 5.0. Studies aim to create and describe an ideal business model for digital commercial banking.[14]

The spread of digital banking follows the so-called Information and Communication Technologies (ICT) consumerization path.[15] In the past, businesses were the first to use ICT innovations. Nowadays, more customers get priority in introducing ICT innovation. This sequence took place with physical products, like mobile phones and tablets. Initially, the target was the consumer market. Later they expanded in the businesses. Something similar is happening in financial services: mobile banking was initially introduced in retail banking. Now, there are solutions for corporate and small- and medium-sized financial institutions. It is now time to rethink this approach and understand how to use fintech organization initiatives for wholesale banking services. Some fintech organizations are moving in this direction. More will come.

[14] Digital Wholesale Insurance—The Future of FinTech. ebrary.net/79683/business_finance/digital_wholesale_insurance. Accessed 20 May 2020.

[15] Nicoletti, B. (2017). *The future of FinTech*. Springer, Cham, Switzerland.

To analyze how digital banking could support this sector, it might be interesting to refer to a sentence of Rudyard Kipling in his book: The Little Elephant.[16] Kipling considered complete the description of a problem if it is possible to respond to six questions starting with an interrogative character: 5 W's and 1 H. In the case of digital wholesale banking, this would mean to answer these questions:

- Why: The reason to go digital for wholesale financial institutions could be defensive. Fintech organizations might be able to invade their markets and introduce disruptive innovations. To go digital could help set up wholesale banking players to become more active, productive, efficient, and economical.
- Where: Thanks to cloud computing, commercial banking can expand the reach of concentrated markets quickly, undoubtedly fueling competition but increasing the size of markets.
- What: Big data analytics can help to improve the analysis of the risks. It is helpful for capital markets, security, customer insight, channel marketing, and new data sets for risk-based pricing and assets checking and tracking.
- Who: Artificial intelligence (AI) and robotics can help select the best alternatives also on wholesale banking? It is not easy to think about how social media, now spreading in financial services, could help with wholesale banking. On the other hand, comparators' websites could help business customers pick up their most convenient financial institution. Some similar "marketplace" could help in the wholesale banking market to find the best solutions for a specific customer's need.
- When: Mobile technologies can help reduce the time to decide and especially make decisions also when the operator works remotely.
- How: Another opportunity connected with innovative solutions is blockchain. It could change the wholesale banking environment thoroughly. Blockchain is a solution introduced with the virtual currency of bitcoin. Its base is an online, distributed ledger solution. Blockchain solutions help in setting up smart contracts with distributed ledger and AI solutions. It could help in managing

[16] Kipling R. (2013). *Just so stories*. Scotts Valley, CA: CreateSpace Independent Publishing Platform.

customer identities, reference data, and assets, with an increased and secure transparency.[17] It can ensure a seamless, reliable, and uninterrupted messaging service to the banking market, a cost-effective method of easing the availability and exchange of data between banking partners, and a trusted utility service that expands banking market competitiveness. Price Waterhouse Coopers is working on a long-term finance research project into the potential of blockchain solutions in wholesale banking.[18]

In this new commercial banking organization ecosystem, there is a need for innovative business models. For example, they could foster much closer collaboration and partnership between wholesale financial institutions and other organizations in the same ecosystem. The latter could receive help from digital solutions.

Retail financial institutions currently use chatbots. They are automated service assistants offering customers the convenience of resolving their queries via online messaging system using devices like personal computers, laptops, and mobile phones, limiting to necessary complex level support to human operators and the personal visits to their branches. An example is Nina, Swedbank's AI chatbot.[19]

AI algorithms can be developed to produce highly advanced investment strategies that ensure high-velocity data to outsmart the competition and enhance customer value. Management of customer data is a prominent area where the application of AI is continually progressing. Money laundering can be curbed with the application of AI.[20]

Global banking groups with retail and corporate banking segments are finding that they can no longer support parallel strategies for B2C and

[17] Or will CBDCs destroy banking?—Chris Skinner's blog. thefinanser.com/2020/10/or-will-cbdcs-will-destroy-banking.html/. Accessed 20 January 2021.

[18] www.finextra.com/pressarticle/64838/PwC-preps-research-into-blockchain-tech-for-wholesale-procurement. Accessed 20 August 2016.

[19] Ates, M. (2017). Artificial intelligence in banking: A case study of the introduction of a virtual assistant into customer service (Master thesis). Jönköping University, Jönköping, Sweden.

[20] Case, C. J., King, D. L., & Case, J. A. Blockchain: An empirical review of fortune 500 website postings and usage. *Journal of Business and Behavioral Sciences*, 42.

B2B regarding the user experience.[21] Chatbots will become common also in commercial banking.

Place

Many financial institutions are already making and reconfiguring the branch network, where demand has softened.[22] A McKinsey review supplies interesting data on trends.[23] In the past years, the use of cash and checks has eased in most markets. About 20–40% of customers report using significantly less cash.[24] In the meantime, customer interest in digital banking has increased in many markets, although this trend varies widely. In the UK and the USA, only 10–15% of customers are more interested in digital banking than before the pandemic crisis (and 5–10% are less interested). In Greece, Indonesia, Mexico, and Singapore, the "more interested" share ranges from 30 to 40 percent.[25]

To make the new digital behaviors stick, financial institutions can start with customer education about their attractive value propositions, combined with making the customer journey more manageable. Even before the crisis, relevant financial institutions in developed markets were able to get 25% less branch use per customer than their peers by migrating payments, transfers, and cash transactions to self-service and online accesses.[26]

Customers will not abandon the branches completely. Lower demand creates an opportunity to redesign the financial service's footprint. Branch

[21] www.finextra.com/researcharticle/161/digital-transformation-accelerated. Accessed 20 November 2020.

[22] www.mckinsey.com/industries/financial-services/our-insights/global-banking-annual-review. Accessed 4 January 2021.

[23] McKinsey's Global Banking Annual Review. www.mckinsey.com/industries/financial-services/our-insights/global-banking-annual-review. Accessed 4 January 2021.

[24] McKinsey's Global Banking Annual Review | McKinsey. www.mckinsey.com/industries/financial-services/our-insights/global-banking-annual-review. Accessed 10 January 2021.

[25] www.mckinsey.com/industries/financial-services/our-insights/global-banking-annual-review. Accessed 4 January 2021.

[26] www.mckinsey.com/industries/financial-services/our-insights/global-banking-annual-review. Accessed 4 January 2021.

networks have shrunk over the years. Pandemic pushed financial institutions much more in this direction. Leading financial institutions are using machine learning to study all the branches in their network, with particular attention to demographics, ATM proximity, and close competitors. One financial institution developed an algorithm that considered the ways branch customers accessed seven core products. It found that 15 percent of branches could be closed while keeping an acceptable service on all customers, keeping 97 percent of network revenue, and raising annual profits by USD 150 million.[27]

Financial institutions will need to re-train some branch bankers by designing flexible roles that merge on-site and remote work, such as the customer-experience officer. Traditional workers can be redeployed in distinct roles based on requirements of similar skills. Branch bankers can perform their regular teller tasks part-time. They can be trained on new skills to move to contact-center agents. Over time, some people can get a full set of skills and become jolly bankers, working well in various roles.

Platforms

AI and blockchain solutions are still at an early stage. Financial institutions are examining the areas in which they can apply these solutions. These tools will become more complex.[28]

Platforms Development

From a technical and business model point of view, and following some researches, it is reasonable to think of a future in which scientific and technological works focus on some of the following aspects:[29]

[27] www.mckinsey.com/industries/financial-services/our-insights/global-banking-annual-review. Accessed 4 January 2021.

[28] Özdemir, V., & Hekim, N. (2018). Birth of industry 5.0: Making sense of big data with artificial intelligence, the internet of things, and next-generation solution policy. *Omics: A Journal of Integrative Biology*, *22*(1), 65–76.

[29] Ruiz-Real, J. L., Uribe-Toril, J., Torres, J. A., & De Pablo, J. (2020). Artificial intelligence in business and economics research: Trends and future. *Journal of Business Economics and Management*, 1–20.

- Emergence of specific hardware for the implementation of AI solutions. (The current supply of this hardware is concentrated in a few organizations.) In the coming years, it will be possible to see the emergence of specialized hardware in the processing of AI applications to increase the solution potential.
- Standardization of the internal structures of neural networks that make up the deep learning algorithms, to be used and implemented more broadly and efficiently (like what happened with the architectures of neural networks last century).
- Development of realistic simulations of behaviors and attitudes considered to be human to improve the perception of AI applications in the interaction with the customers.
- In terms of economic activity, AI is a disruptive process, both in the financial institutions' activity and in their different departments' secondary activity. Its deployment in all fields of banking activity will continue and improve.
- Incorporation of AI-based services in more functions. A banking 5.0 financial institution is focused 24 hours a day on customers' needs, analyzing the data from its constant interaction with customers immersed in the digital world. AI is the perfect ally for this new form of financial institution–customer relationship.
- Improvement of the relations of all the departments with the finance departments and with other organizations in the exchange of information contextualized in accounting, fiscal data management, operations management with partners, financial services management, and the automation tasks that involve a significant volume of time and cost and do not generate real value to the organization.
- Incorporation of AI in decision-making at the highest level, such as the board of directors and auditing.

The process of social digitalization and the transformation that banking 5.0 is generating in the expectations and consumption habits of customers, together with the vast amount of data that needs to be analyzed, classified, and structured, leads also many high-level technical tasks, that is, ICT, carried out by specialized personnel, to AI.

Multi-Sided Platforms

Financial institutions have not yet made full use of innovative models and tools to streamline their value networks, increase transparency and speed, and reduce administrative costs and contract prices. Banking 5.0 platforms can bring significant savings and added revenue. Such a change process requires a new management culture and new tools. Several authors have shown that digital banking and e-commerce are the right tools to implement such changes. In connection with AI and Business process intelligence (BPI), these solutions can support significant improvements to cope with the banking's strategic and tactical challenges.[30]

One exciting development is the increasing diffusion of innovative Multi-sided platforms (MSP).[31] A multi-sided platform is a business model that allows multiple participants (producers and customers) to connect and interact with one another and create and exchange value.[32] Two critical functions that platform leaders aim to deliver are (1) bringing together disparate resources and knowledge from different organizations and (2) matching and connecting users with producers of products and services.

Multi-Sided Platforms Architecture

Multi-sided platforms are telematics platforms that allow the matching of four Ps (Fig. 15.2):

- The Proprietor of the platforms is the one that has founded and funded this type of online information system.
- The Provider of the platforms supplies the infrastructure, the service, and the software supporting the platform.
- The Producers supply the products and the services made available on the platform.
- The Purchasers buy the products or the services on the platform.

[30] Castellanos, M., De Medeiros, A. A., Mendling, J., Weber, B., & Weijters, A. J. M. M. (2009). Business process intelligence. In *Handbook of research on business process modeling* (pp. 456–480). Hershey, PA: IGI Global.

[31] Hagiu, A., & Wright, J. (2015). Multi-sided platforms. *International Journal of Industrial Organization, 43*, 162–174. Eling, M., & Lehmann, M. (2018). The impact of digitization on the insurance value chain and the insurability of risks. *The Geneva Papers on Risk and Insurance-Issues and Practice, 43*, 359–396. https://doi.org/10.1057/s41288-017-0073-0.

[32] Van Alstyne, M. W., Parker, G. G., & Choudary, S. P. (2016). Pipelines, platforms, and the new rules of strategy. *Harvard Business Review, 94*(4), 54–62.

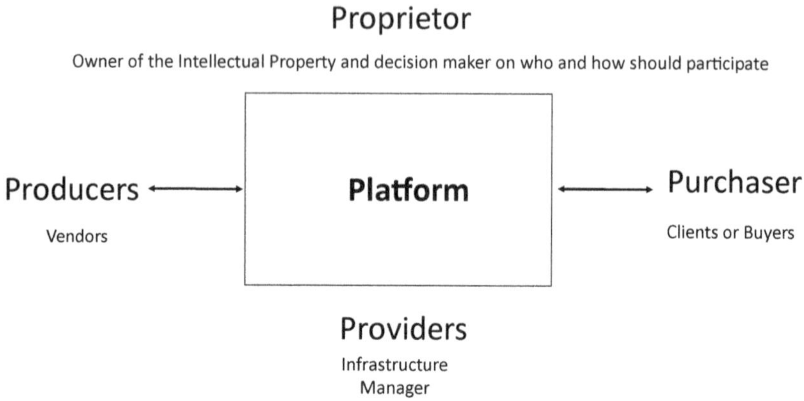

Fig. 15.2 Multi-sided platforms

These roles are interchangeable. For example, Producers can become Purchasers and vice versa.

These platforms are usually on the internet to make it easy to reach them. From a data management point of view, the support can be provided by a blockchain solution.[33] Blockchain solutions are open online ledgers in which it is possible to securely record every transaction in the network for a specific application. The blockchain is available for all participants. They can see it and check it. A standard log allows transparency of operations and services. This capability automates the secure exchange of data transfer among organizations. The blockchain solution can verify who is accessing and certify that the documents as accessed from an authorized user.

MSPs have two critical features beyond any other characteristics (such as indirect network effects or non-neutrality of fees)[34]:

- They enable direct interactions between two or more distinct sides.[35] The interactions involve trading. The critical terms of the commu-

[33] Nicoletti, B. (2017). *The future of fintech*. London: Springer. UK. ISBN 978-3-319-51414-7.

[34] Multi-sided Platforms. Harvard Business School Working Paper. hbswk.hbs.edu/item/multi-sided-platforms. Accessed 10 May 2020.

[35] Hagiu, A., & Wright, J. (2015). Multi-sided platforms. *International Journal of Industrial Organization, 43*, 162–174.

nication are the pricing, bundling, marketing, and delivery of the products or services traded, the ability to find the nature and quality of services offered, the terms and conditions, and so on.
- Each side has an association with the platform. Users on each side consciously take platform-specific actions necessary for them to interact with each other directly.[36] The actions could be getting a loan or an expenditure of resources.[37]

Considering the above, there are two economic theories at the base of a platform business model that are crucial. They are the main reasons that platforms thrive over traditional "pipeline" business strategies. These are the transaction costs and network effects theories.

- Transaction costs are the search, the coordination, the negotiation, and the information asymmetry cost an organization faces while choosing its processes. If the total costs are lower externally, the organization sources production outside in the market. According to transaction costs theory, economic institutions have as their primary function the optimization of transaction costs. A platform strategy can potentially be better than a hierarchy or a pure market transaction because it can further reduce the searching, matching, negotiation, and contracting costs and lower information asymmetries that are a potential risk to both customers and vendors.[38] In that context, the platform business model's critical value proposition is not about selling products but "selling reductions in transaction costs."[39]
- Network externalities or network effects describe the impact the number of network adopters has on each user's utility on a platform.[40] In other words, the marginal benefit (or cost reduction)

[36] Hagiu, A., & Wright, J. (2015). Multi-sided platforms. *International Journal of Industrial Organization, 43,* 162–174.

[37] Alonso, R., Dessein, W., & Matouschek, N. (2014). *Organizing to adapt and compete* (Working paper). University of Southern California, Los Angeles, CA.

[38] Williamson, O. E. (1975). Markets and hierarchies. *New York, 2630.*

[39] Munger, M. C. (2015). *The third entrepreneurial revolution: A middleman economy.* Duke University, Department of Political Science.

[40] Shapiro, C., & Varian, H. R. (1999). Networks and positive feedback. *Information rules: A strategic guide to the network economy* (pp. 173–225). Farrell, J., & Saloner, G.

> that platform users gain increases as the number of users on the platform increases.[41] Network effects are not always positive. Users' growth on an open platform can lead to situations where value is being subtracted from the network instead of increased. To avoid such a situation, the platform leader will need to moderate entry by applying filters, controlling, and limiting users' access onto the platform and potentially even their activities and connections. [42]

The open vs. closed dilemma is a difficult one to tackle. While having an open platform may create difficulties in monetizing the benefits, a closed system may restrain innovation and lead to isolation.

Multi-Sided Platforms in Banking 5.0
MSPs in the banking value network can[43]:

- Increase Competition among traditional financial institutions.
- Facilitate Coordination among financial institutions, customers, and other stakeholders.
- Enable Cooperation with financial institutions.
- Improve Collaboration among financial institutions and other organizations in the same ecosystem.

Value creation in banking can undergo a massive transformation due to the emergence of MSPs. This change has three main implications for banking: specialization, modularization, and higher complexity of the value network. It might become increasingly difficult for traditional

(1985). Standardization, compatibility, and innovation. *The RAND Journal of Economics* (pp. 70–83). Scott, S. V., Van Reenen, J., & Zachariadis, M. (2017). The long-term effect of digital innovation on bank performance: An empirical study of SWIFT adoption in financial services. *Research Policy*, *46*(5), 984–1004. Economides, N. (1996). The economics of networks. Zachariadis, M., Scott, S. V., & Barrett, M. I. (2010, December). Designing mixed-method research inspired by a critical realism philosophy: A tale from the field of IS innovation. In *ICIS* (p. 265).

[41] The Metcalfe's law states that a network's value grows as the square of the number of its users. Metcalfe, R. (1995). Metcalfe's law. *Infoworld*, *2*.

[42] Parker, G., Van Alstyne, M. W., & Jiang, X. (2016). *Platform ecosystems: How developers invert the firm* (Boston University Questrom School of Business Research Paper [2861574]).

[43] Pousttchi, K., & Gleiss, A. (2019). Surrounded by middlemen-how multi-sided platforms change the insurance industry. *Electronic Markets, 29*(4), 609–629.

financial institutions to structure and coordinate their value network, distribution, and communication activities. They might need to give up essential value creation activities and customer interactions to MSPs or other fresh players in the market. In the worst case, traditional financial institutions might become basic banking service vendors.

Banking's MSPs can decrease information asymmetries among traditional financial institutions, customers, and other value network stakeholders. Customers can interact with many vendors, assess information, compare, or buy banking services, and interact with their financial institutions. New ways of customer contacts might promote the development of new products or business models. Consequently, shifts in the value network and changing customer behaviors might lead to new customer ownership constellations.

The regulatory frameworks (PSD2 in the EU and open banking) offer a unique opportunity to apply some of the concepts in banking 5.0 across the entire banking sector. Opening the APIs (especially those of payment initiation service and account information service) of financial institutions, and instructing them to share customer data, supplies an opportunity for a platform business model to be implemented and its effects to be realized in banking. This move is called Banking-as-a-Platform (BaaP). BaaP describes the premises upon which financial institutions can adopt a platform strategy model and change competition rules. In doing so, financial institutions will need to revisit their role as financial intermediaries and prepare to become re-intermediaries by providing "online automated tools and systems that offer valuable new products and services to participants on [all] sides of the platform."[44] As part of this banking 5.0 transformation and the move to an open-API economy, financial institutions, and other licensed institution, that hope to become platform leaders will need to decide on the level of openness they wish to engage their community.

So far, many traditional financial institutions have not set up a comprehensive open banking model that allows application developers to tap into their APIs and develop value-added service applications on a "plug-and-play" mode. This situation naturally puts them with a platform that is only open for prospective demand-side users under specific terms. On

[44] Parker, G. T., Van Alstyne, M. W., & Choudary, S. P. (2016). *Platform revolution: How network markets are transforming the economy and how to make them work for you*. London, UK: W. W. Norton.

the other hand, challenger banks quickly set themselves up as "platform financial institutions."

For more details, refer to the literature on the applications of MSP in banking.[45]

Benefits and Challenges of Multi-Sided Platforms

Platforms change the nature of competition as businesses aim to help interactions between producers and customers, competing on network effects and value captured onto the platform to win market share. On that basis, the most attractive platform would be the most appealing value proposition for customers on both sides of the market, enhancing network externalities and customer retention.

Orange Bank[46]

Orange Bank works in France and Spain. It uses the Orange brand and distribution network to cross-sell high-volume products such as device insurance and device financing. It also uses its modern core and API network to orchestrate an ecosystem supported by a load balancing network solution. The bank collaborates with several players, such as the real estate services platform Nexity for real estate loans. The Orange Bank value proposition is to put the customer journey first, served through its network of stores (not branches), its mobile app, and mobile-first processes. The bank reports a 500,000-customer base (with 20,000 customers joining each month) and more than 60% of acquisitions originating from Orange stores.[47]

Processes

Processes will become increasingly integrated. For too long, financial institutions have leaned processes only with organizational or logistic

[45] Pousttchi, K., & Gleiss, A. (2019). Surrounded by middlemen-how multi-sided platforms change the insurance industry. *Electronic Markets*, *29*(4), 609–629.

[46] www.capgemini.com/news/world-retail-banking-report-2020/. Accessed 20 November 2020.

[47] Orange Bank celebrates its second birthday as it continues to grow, November 2019; www.orange.com/sites/orangecom/files/2020-06/CP_OrangeBank_2years_15112019_VENG.pdf. Accessed 20 November 2020.

measures. The lean and digitize method will become more used to make processes thinner and integrated into an increasingly digital world.[48]

Persons

Data analysis, customer relationship management, and the production processes of certain financial services will be highly conditioned applying an autonomous AI to make decisions. This situation has implications both in the labor relations and in the legal frameworks.

AI will need new job profiles: data scientists and, machine learning engineers, AI behavior analysts, and so on. There will be fewer persons in financial institutions. They will work more as consultants for customers or other organization functions rather than on operational tasks. Significant roadblocks for financial institutions include talent management and inadequacy in talent strategy.[49] Many traditional financial institutions organizations lack the proper competencies to upgrade their banking business model to banking 5.0.

AI is a disruptive solution, as were the other technologies at the base of the other industrial revolutions. Financial institutions should be aware of the value of the human workforce in solving unexpected problems and their *ad hoc* solutions situations in which automation of any kind cannot be able to cope.

One of the most important aspects is how people's civil rights can be preserved when AI systems manage certain activities. The preservation of the right to privacy, the responsible management of personal data, and the right to anonymity can be violated when AI applies analysis to the data. AI feeds on specific information.

Remote work will become very diffused, especially after the pandemic outbreak.[50] Financial institutions should ensure that employees can access the necessary files and conduct business from remote locations securely. Chief information security officers (CISOs) need to set up new cyber security policies and tools to support the secure exchange of confidential information among employees connecting from outside the office.

[48] Nicoletti, B. (2012). *Lean and digitize: An integrated approach to process improvement*. Farnham, UK: Gower Publishing. ISBN-10: 1409441946.

[49] SAP Ariba. (2018). *CPO Survey 2018. What's the next big thing in insurance*. www.ariba.com/resources/library/library-pages/cpo-survey-2018. Accessed 1 August 2019.

[50] DI_COVID-19-insurance.pdf (deloitte.com). Accessed 5 April 2020.

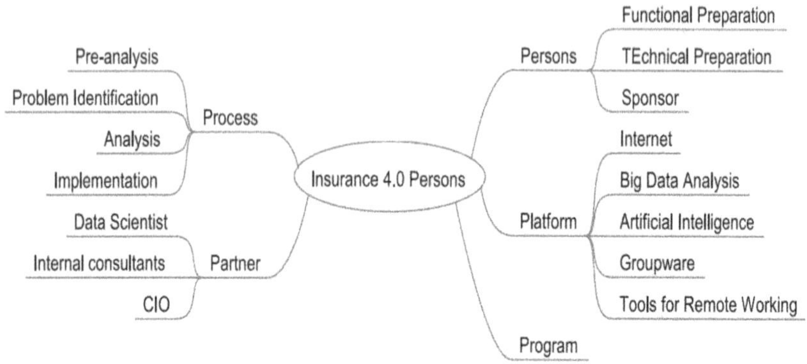

Fig. 15.3 Tools for remote working

Figure 15.3 shows some of the tools available for remote working.

Collaborative robots will become more interconnected thanks to Next generation web (NGW). NGW will revolutionize the Web application and banking 5.0 with the transformation of ecosystems from computers to mobile phones, starting from simple Web page viewing to complex robotics applications that will affect on everybody's life. The Next generation web (NGW) will change in basic assumptions. Web Speech APIs are at the draft state. WebUSB is still evolving. NGW does not need any other downloads or plugins or any intermediate server. WebRTC supports real-time ultra-low latency audiovisual media and non-media arbitrary data with a recording facility. Web Speech API includes speech recognition, speech synthesis, and audio processing on the Web browser. WebUSB will allow USB devices connected to the Web for collaborative robotics (Cobotics).

Partnerships

From the perspective of critical partners, future changes will be significant. There will be a move increasingly from internal supporting functions to partners. There will be a consolidation of the partners and their integration in the ecosystems. The partner location's importance, and then the proximity (physical or virtual) to the partners customers, will be relevant.

The digitization of the contracts is evolving rapidly. Smart contracts will become more used.[51] Smart contracts can ensure more security to the agreements and reduce the transaction costs associated with banking.

Financial institutions will connect more automatically with their customers and partners in the ecosystem. This connection is the correct and secure way after the terrible experience of the pandemic. Financial institutions that have invested in advancing their digital capabilities will be in good contact with their customers and with their ecosystem partners, who, in turn, should offer faster and more comprehensive services to their customers.[52]

Bigtech

Bigtech organization refers to large and capital-intensive solution organizations with a broad international reach.[53] The best known bigtech organizations in the Western world are Facebook, Google, Apple, and Amazon. Potentially, they have the power, knowledge, and capabilities to disrupt banking. As these organizations have worked on their terms with creativity and agility, banking inflexible and strict regulations reduce their ability to do so at the same pace. This bigtech organizations' ability to work and supply customers with the same products and services range as traditional financial institutions is not to be expected in big volumes, at least in the short term. Bigtech organizations can offer or "take over" some of the traditional financial institutions' services and products. Apple has launched Apple Pay in several countries that let users pay for customer products with their Apple device. Amazon sellers are provided with loans, Google allows to send money, and Facebook launched people-to-people payments within North America, with an ongoing application for an e-money license in Europe. In a similar situation, Ping An has been stopped to grow more in financial services by Chinese regulators.[54]

Understanding the competitive and comparative advantages of bigtech organizations in financial intermediation is a first step for evaluating

[51] Nicoletti, B. (2012). *Lean and digitize: An integrated approach to process improvement*. Farnham, UK: Gower Publishing. ISBN-10: 1409441946.

[52] file:/DI_COVID-19-insurance.pdf (deloitte.com). Accessed 5 April 2020.

[53] www.fsb.org/wp-content/uploads/P091219-1.pdf. Accessed 26 October 2020.

[54] www.europeanpaymentscouncil.eu/sites/default/files/inline-files/Paymentpercent20Methodspercent20Reportpercent202019percent20-percent20Innovationspercent20inpercent20thepercent20Waypercent20Wepercent20Pay.pdf. Accessed 26 October 2020.

the opportunities these technological developments may support in the banking value network, the role they may play for the economy, and the challenges this may have.

Capgemini's World Retail Banking Report 2019 shows the public's acceptance of fintech and bigtech organizations instead of traditional banks[55]:

- 75% of tech-savvy customers use at least one financial product from a bigtech organization.
- Customers choose non-traditional options for lower fees (70%), user experience (68%), and speed (54%);
- Over 80% of customers that would switch financial services providers in the next three years, use a banking service from a bigtech organization or a digital bank.

Bigtech Organizations Architecture[56]

Bigtech organizations present a distinctive business model due to the combination of two key features[57]:

- Network effects (generated by e-commerce platforms, messaging applications, search engines, and so on).[58]
- Solutions (for example, AI and big data analytics).

Because of their dimensions and digital nature, bigtech organizations could supply their services at almost zero marginal cost.[59] The provision of credit lines and other services to small vendors could be made without human intervention through a combination of AI and robotic process automation, in the spirit of banking 5.0.

[55] worldretailbankingreport.com/. Accessed 28 November 2020.

[56] Frost, J., Gambacorta, L., Huang, Y., Shin, H. S., & Zbinden, P. (2019). BigTech and the changing structure of financial intermediation. *Economic Policy.*

[57] Frost, J., Gambacorta, L., Huang, Y., Shin, H. S., & Zbinden, P. (2019). BigTech and the changing structure of financial intermediation. *Economic Policy.*

[58] Shapiro, C., & Varian, H. (1998). *Information rules: A strategic guide to the network economy*. Cambridge, MA: Harvard Business School Press.

[59] Metcalfe, B (2013). Metcalfe's law after 40 years of Ethernet. *IEEE Computer*. Nalebuff, B. (2003). *Bundling, tying, and portfolio effects* (DTI Economics Paper).

Bigtech Organizations and Banking 5.0

The financial services activities of bigtech organizations have snowballed in some countries, particularly in payments, lending to small and medium enterprises (SMEs), and other specific market segments, such as unbanked. Most bigtech organizations start in payments. There is considerable diversity in the sequencing of banking areas attacked and how bigtech organizations conduct payments services. Available data shows that China is the largest market, with bigtech organization mobile payments for consumption reaching CNY 14.5 trillion in 2017, or 16% of Gross domestic product (GDP).

The drivers of bigtech organization activity in finance, significantly beyond payments, may be like fintech organizational activities. In some cases, there might be unique drivers. There is a growing body of research in the past few years considering why investments in fintech organizations[60] or fintech credit have grown more in some jurisdictions than others.[61] Broadly, these drivers can be broken down into demand and supply factors.

On the demand side, crucial factors are:[62]

- Where organizations or customers are underserved by financial institutions, as shown by a low share of the population with a financial institution account or credit card, there may be an opportunity for the more rapid growth of lending by bigtech organizations.[63]
- Customers and small businesses are more likely to use the financial offerings of bigtech organizations when they are broadly comfortable with innovative solutions, significantly if financial institutions do not change their provision of financial services.

[60] Navaretti, G., Calzolari, G., & Pozzolo, A. (2017, December): FinTech and banks: Friends or foes? *European Economy: Banks, Regulation, and the Real Sector*.

[61] Davis, K., & Murphy, J. (2016). Peer-to-peer lending: structures, risks and regulation. *The Finsia Journal of Applied Finance, 3*, 37–44. Claessens, S., Frost, J., Turner, G., & Zhu, F. (2018, September): Fintech credit markets worldwide: Size, drivers and policy issues, *BIS Quarterly Review*. Rau, R (2017). *Law, trust, and the development of crowdfunding* (University of Cambridge Working Paper).

[62] www.iasonltd.com/wp-upload/all/2019_BigTech_and_New_Banking_Landscape_-_Evolution,_Benefits,_Risks_and_Oversights.pdf. Accessed 30 January 2021.

[63] Hau, H., Huang, Y., Shan, H., & Sheng, Z. (2018). Fintech credit, financial inclusion and entrepreneurial growth (Working Papers). Huang, Y., Lin, C., Sheng, Z., & Wei, L. (2018). *FinTech credit and service quality*. New York, NY: Mimeo.

- Traditional financial institutions with no innovation or entrepreneurial spirit.
- Customers might prefer to use tools that they often use, like Google or Amazon.

On the supply side, the principal factors are[64]:

- Bigtech organizations have access to a wide range of customer data, which may supply them superior information to assess the potential customers' habits and solvency, leading either to correct credit and insurance assessments or to lower costs of the intermediation process.
- Due to their extensive use of innovative solutions like AI and robot process automation,
- Securing adequate funding could be one limitation for bigtech organizations in expanding lending, even if they tend to be rich in cash thanks to their core activities.

Understanding the growth and potential of bigtech organization activities in finance is essential for several reasons. An analysis of such growth drivers helps understand better the changing market structure brought by innovative solutions. This understanding allows an assessment of the economic effects of changes, together with an assessment of the balance of risks and benefits.

By entering a widening range of financial services, bigtech organizations are increasingly competing with traditional financial institutions. There are other forms of interactions. For example, bigtech organizations are relevant third-party service providers to financial institutions.[65] Amazon Web Services is the largest vendor of cloud services in the world, including many financial institutions. Microsoft and Google are large cloud services providers. Ali Cloud (an affiliated organization of Ant Financial in the Ali Group) is a dominant player in Asia. Many bigtech organizations offer specific tools supported by AI and machine learning

[64] www.iasonltd.com/wp-upload/all/2019_BigTech_and_New_Banking_Landscape_-_Evolution,_Benefits,_Risks_and_Oversights.pdf. Accessed 20 January 2021.

[65] Sharma, M., Gupta, R., & Acharya, P. (2020). Analyzing the adoption of cloud computing service: A systematic literature review. *Global Knowledge, Memory and Communication*.

to corporate customers, including financial institutions. The activity of bigtech organizations as both vendors and competitors with financial institutions, raises several potential conflicts of interest. On the other side, their dominant market power in some markets is coming under greater scrutiny.[66]

Unlike financial institutions, bigtech organizations do not have a branch distribution network to interact with customers and get informal information through, for example, branch employees. Instead, those that offer credit use proprietary data from online platforms.[67] The loan onboarding process includes credit decisions based on predictive algorithms and machine learning.[68] The lack of widespread distribution is a limitation but a also big plus since bigtech organization exploited in a large way remote working, well before this became diffused thanks to the pandemic. A bigtech lender has an information advantage in credit scoring compared to a traditional credit bureau.

While the preliminary evidence is encouraging and sheds some light on these developments, much is still to be done to address the more significant economic questions. For example, what are the consequences of bigtech for relationship lending? A financial institution buys informal information from its customers by developing long-term relationships. By contrast, credit scoring with advanced analytics does not necessarily rely on long-term, one-to-one relationships.[69] It exploits patterns of customer preferences and behavior using big data analytics. Any judgment on these new credit scoring tools‘ abilities to find customer characteristics and resolve asymmetric information problems should be based on a complete cycle, evaluating the probability of these credits going into default under stressful situations.

[66] Khan, L. (2017). Amazon's antitrust paradox. *Yale Law Journal*, 126(3).

[67] BIS Working Papers. www.bis.org/publ/work779.pdf. Accessed 4 January 2021.

[68] Van Liebergen, B. (2017). Machine learning: a revolution in risk management and compliance? *The Capco Institute Journal of Financial Transformation, 45,* 60–67.

[69] BIS Working Papers. www.bis.org/publ/work779.pdf. Accessed 4 January 2021.

Benefits and Challenges of Bigtech Organizations

The rapid growth of bigtech services in finance will bring both benefits, challenges, and risks to the financial system.[70] Bigtech organizations may enhance competition and financial inclusion, particularly in emerging markets and economies. They can contribute to the overall efficiency of financial services. On the other side, such organizations may further concentrate market power or even give rise to new systemic risks. It is essential to understand how bigtech organizations fit within current financial regulation frameworks and under which principles regulation should be organized.

Given significant network effects and economies of scale and scope, bigtech organizations could lead to greater concentration also in banking. With a deep reliance on third-party service providers, especially for data storage, transmission, and analytics, operational failure or cyber events can more easily lead to systemic events.

Conclusions

The future is uncertain. Still, there are some scenarios for the role of banking and the actions to take to improve banking's future standing. Organizations will move from a linear supply chain to a value network, called an ecosystem. In other words, banking's role will be to build and coordinate an ecosystem composed of different actors with the partners' collaboration. It will not be an easy task, but it is an essential one. The ecosystem will facilitate the diffusion of embedded banking.

The world and banking will continue to change. Because of the forecasts and the variability of the environment, financial institutions need to plan carefully. It is, however, interesting to consider that "plans are made to change them." The secret for the organization's success in better banking will be the ability to be (or better become) agile and flexible to adapt to changes.

The banking role will grow, more out of the credit management activity, into creating alliances with partners and the customers. The latter

[70] BigTech Lending as a New Form of Financial Intermediation. voxchina.org/show-3-134.html. Accessed 4 January 2021.

will want to customize the products/services they buy. A key competence of partners will be in cognitive solutions.[71] They should create the environment and mobilize customers to generate value for themselves.

Due to the solutions' specificity and the need to adapt services to the customers' activities, the partners will have to work out effective, efficient, and economical methods and tools for creating customized versions of their services.[72] They will need to include banking in their processes. The support will come from the group's ability to categorize and find the best group of services for a given customer category.[73]

According to the MECSPE Italian Observatory, related to the second half of 2018, eight organizations out of 10 believe that their digital transformation occurred in recent years, and almost all (nine out of 10) believe they have a medium-high level of knowledge on the solution and digital opportunities on the market.[74] The future focus is on new enabling technologies, continuing in the direction toward cyber security (74%), connectivity (60%), cloud computing (33%), and collaborative robotics (28%), and at research and innovation: Sixty-one percent will invest up to 10% of their turnover for the digital transformation. Twenty-five percent will dedicate between 10 and 20% thereof. Targeted advice (51%), knowledge transfer (42%), confrontation with competing organizations (39%), workshops (21%), and tutorship from a university (15%) are considered tools for the development process.

An interesting question is if, with banking 5.0, the banking industry will lose parts of its value network to other sectors.[75] Organizations from other industries may have better access to the customer or the corresponding data. It helps follow these developments closely. Customers are increasingly willing to buy banking from non-traditional firms such as

[71] Wodecki, A. (2018). *Artificial intelligence in value creation: Improving competitive advantage*. Springer, Cham, Switzerland.

[72] Wodecki, A. (2018). *Artificial intelligence in value creation: Improving competitive advantage*. Springer, Cham, Switzerland.

[73] Wodecki, A. (2018). *Artificial intelligence in value creation: Improving competitive advantage*. Springer, Cham, Switzerland.

[74] www.mecspe.com/en/comunicati-stampa-en/osservatorio-mecspe-focus-nazionale/. Accessed 6 August 2019.

[75] Eling, M., & Lehmann, M. (2018). The impact of digitalization on the insurance value chain and the insurability of risks. *The Geneva papers on risk and insurance-Issues and Practice*, *43*(3), 359–396.

bigtech organizations or product manufacturers (for example, Tesla).[76] Still, now, it seems unlikely that bigtech organizations, for example, will take over substantial parts of the banking value network. This situation happens because a realistic return on equity is too small to justify investments in banking. More attractive alternatives exist (investment in other businesses, cooperation with traditional financial institutions, and so on). Regulation and lack of ability serve as entry barriers. These considerations hold for today, highly likely not for the future.

To end with another quote, attributed to Charles Darwin: "It is not the strongest of the species that survives, nor the intelligent, but the most open to change."[77] This message is also true for financial institutions.

[76] worldinsurancereport.com/. Accessed 30 May 2020.

[77] Girotto, V., Pievani, T., & Vallortigara, G. (2014). Supernatural beliefs: Adaptations for social life or by-products of cognitive adaptations? *Behaviour*, *151*(2–3), 385–402.

CHAPTER 16

Conclusions

Life grants nothing to us mortals without demanding work.
Horace

This book presents a business model highlighting the main components and solutions for effective, efficient, ethical, and economical banking 5.0.

Organizations are increasingly aware of the importance of implementing innovative solutions. They are struggling to analyze the scope of banking 5.0 transformation and how to do it in their specific environment. This situation is not limited to some organizations or certain business functions. It embraces every organization.

The main driver that pushes organizations to embrace banking 5.0 transformation is to supply a better customer journey. This goal is dynamic since customer expectations change fast and are diverse. This book aims to respond and support these needs of financial organizations. Organizations must adapt to the changing times, reviewing their internal processes and rethinking their business models. They must adapt to the digital age and look for innovative solutions that are increasingly attractive to a dynamic market and to reach a sustainable competitive advantage. Consequently, this book aims to improve readers' ability to go through the innovation cycle and optimize it.

One of the book's main topics is how to add value to the customer and not only change the distribution of the services, but the entire business model. The future will revolutionize the management of banking.

B. Nicoletti, *Banking 5.0*, Palgrave Studies in Financial Services Technology, https://doi.org/10.1007/978-3-030-75871-4_16

Banking 5.0 is an essential business model to make the future, described in this book's chapters, real.

Cultural change is critical to the success of banking 5.0. Digital education at all levels is crucial. The transformation will be completed successfully by implementing the lean and digitize approach to speed progress and making the organization agile. Simultaneously, financial institutions need to focus on customers and foster cross-functional teams with pool-specific competencies. Traditional financial institutions should start looking for ways to attract brilliant talents to set up a proper team, considering that the competition for bright digital talents is high. Fintech organizations are more attractive for talents for their characteristics.

The combination of all the ten components of the business model: provision of value, proximity to the customer, the partition of the customers, places of the distribution, processes, platforms, persons, partnerships, pricing, payments for costs and investments—plus the added two: philosophy or vision, and protection or security, supplies new opportunities for financial institutions and ecosystem players.

The traditional banks are in danger from this digital world. The world is moving quickly from physical to virtual. For example, how much cyber attacks should push investments in cyber risk protection? How can modeling and pricing of cyber risks be improved, given the lack of experience, continuous changes in these threats, and complex correlation structures?

The innovation must be integrated among the functions and follow top management strategy and cover the entire organization. Financial institutions in the first stage of change tend to apply innovative solutions working to improving current processes, often trying only to reduce costs. Organizations in an advanced innovation stage entirely rethink their business models around the digital opportunities and put their relationship with the customer at the center of their efforts, not cost-cutting.

Banking 5.0 model is an essential step for the innovation of financial institutions. To remain competitive in today's digital age, where the number of new competitors grows continuously, banking organizations must act quickly. Agile and individual policies are an added value for the customers. For financial institutions to offer this type of service, they must know their customers better to propose customized services, satisfy specific needs, to their manners, and gain their long-term trust. Fast and efficient big data analysis can help banking organizations to use the vast business potential of innovation in the best conceivable way. Many banking organizations still adopt a traditional business model. They need to transform it by moving to a banking 5.0 philosophy.

One of the book's main topics is how to add value to the customer and how to distribute these improved services. Particular attention is with the new type of distribution all-digital, born from customers' needs and digital evolution. The impressive sales rates of mobile phones worldwide supply evidence of how already today, and more shortly, both customers and banking organization partners must have fully embraced the logic of online and mobility. To take full advantage of innovation opportunities offered by innovative solutions, financial institutions must define a clear picture of how they want to be in customer proximity. Based on this perspective, financial institutions can design a business model and so develop marketing, sales, operations, and after-sales consistently by deciding to invest resources in innovative solutions. In this field, the highest returns are economic satisfaction and customer loyalty.

The future will revolutionize the management of banking. Banking 5.0 is an essential business model to make the future, described in the earlier chapters, real. The results included in this book prove that banking 5.0 can bring many benefits, including supporting the organization's activities and daily administrative tasks to perform complex decision-making, getting more focused strategic decisions and actions. There are barriers to the digitization of the banking processes. These challenges are in their legacy systems, procedures, processes, abilities, and talents availability. This book discusses several enabling solutions for supporting transformation to banking 5.0, methods, and tools to overcome these challenges.

Since innovation requires substantial amounts of investments, it must be secured.[1] This requirement will not be easy to satisfy in a situation of declining margins, if not losses.[2]

Banking 5.0 comes hand in hand with a customer-centric approach to implement across all the value networks. To gain novel support, traditional financial institutions should promote projects that deliver quick

[1] www.mckinsey.com/industries/financial-services/our-insights/the-age-of-innovation. Accessed 14 March 2020.

[2] www.mckinsey.com/industries/financial-services/our-insights/global-banking-annual-review. Accessed 12 December 2020.

rewards at manageable risk. For example, in the customer service activities and the redesign of credit processes, it is crucial building proper capabilities to modernize core operating platforms.

Long-term success will be dictated by the power, competencies, and knowledge of the financial institutions and of the ecosystem that financial institutions need to build around them. Ecosystems will create the competitive benefits necessary not only to survive but to grow in the markets. They will reduce the innovation gap between the current service offering and the possible competition by bigtech organizations. Traditional financial institutions must learn new ways of working, such as the agile approach, and adopt new methods, like design thinking, and lean and digitize.

The future of banking will be a complete immersion in the digital world. It will require acting on the entire business model. The industry is now ready to feel its impact. The innovation needs to cope with heavy regulations, overcome financial institutions' legacy, portfolios, and win customer loyalty.

There will be the need to improve AI[3]:

- Smarter learning algorithms, by making AI more creative and with less data needs.
- Explainable systems, with ethical, reproducible, visible, and secure use of AI.
- Shorter time to value by improving AI robustness, accessibility, productivity, faster development, and reliable operations.

The revolution of banking 5.0 will result in a much more agile and effective business model that will meet customers' needs and capitalize on the evolving commercial opportunities in a much more effective, efficient, economical, and ethical way to the present and past times.

[3] www.gartner.com/document/3996984?ref=TrackRecommendedEmail. Accessed 20 February 2021.

In conclusion, the future is challenging for banking.[4] There will be more opportunities to capture demand and evolve banking service portfolios, delivering higher value to the customers. Crucial will be to set up a suitable business model within the ecosystem.

The spreading of data and information enables financial institutions to analyze and turn them the as the basis for more imaginative solutions for customers, which must be winners in this transformation. Financial institutions need to keep integrity by protecting individuals from these innovations and by setting up the proper ethical bounds around these innovations. Banking has always been a representative and side player for regulation. It will be helpful to keep on doing that during these times of crisis and changes.

> This is the age of digital disruption. Across industries, insurgents with digitally enabled business models are challenging incumbents and their established business models. The incumbent has a choice to be disrupted or be the disruptor. Those that prosper in the digital future will be those that choose to be disruptors and invest in innovation today.[5]

Financial institutions need to consider few leadership principles when working toward banking 5.0[6]:

- Get the chief executive officer, board members, and top management to embrace the banking 5.0 approach and become the ones pushing and motivating the financial institution to evolve. This requires that those persons have either experience or an excellent knowledge of innovative solutions.
- Focus on solutions rather than technologies.
- Focus on critical values as a feature of innovative solutions rather than as a problem.

[4] www.mckinsey.com/industries/financial-services/our-insights/global-banking-annual-review. Accessed 12 December 2020.

[5] www.mckinsey.com/industries/financial-services/our-insights/the-age-of-innovation. Accessed 14 March 2020.

[6] Schwab, K. (2016). *Four leadership principles for the Fourth Industrial Revolution*. www.weforum.org/agenda/2016/10/four-leadership-principles-for-the-fourth-industrial-revolution. Accessed 22 July 2019.

- Empower the organization to manage innovative solutions and counter a fatalistic and deterministic view of the future.
- Prioritize a future by design rather than by default.

It is not easy to predict what the future holds. Banking 5.0 is a revolution compared to the past. Machine learning, cognitive solutions, robotic process automation, and sustainability are just some examples of implementations. Future innovative solutions will exceed imagination.

There are still many questions not answered. Hopefully, new research will clarify them.[7] There has been little academic research on digital transformation. This situation is surprising, given that digitization and big data analytics offer enormous potential for empirical research. One example is the impact of digital banking on moral hazard and adverse selection.[8]

The future of banking is full of questions and uncertainties. The fifth industrial revolution will potentially shape banking to new heights, enabling a fully autonomous value network with the power of solution advances.

Big data analytics and AI identification and evaluation open a new research field, for example, from actuarial science (pricing smart contracts). If, in the future bigtech organizations, like Apple or Google, gain access to even more information, how will they use it?[9] What is the role of financial institutions in such an environment? Which would be the product portfolio to win on the competition? How privacy and data protection laws and regulations interact with big data analytics and AI.

This book concentrates on a business model for banking. This starting point is essential. As digital networks and artificial intelligence increasingly capture the world, there is a fundamental transformation in the

[7] Eling, M., & Lehmann, M. (2018). The impact of digitalization on the insurance value chain and the insurability of risks. *The Geneva Papers on Risk and Insurance-Issues and Practice*, *43*(3), 359–396.

[8] Filipova-Neumann, L., & Welzel, P. (2010). Reducing asymmetric information in insurance markets: Cars with black boxes. *Telematics and Informatics*, *27*(4), 394–403. Hummel, T., Kühn, M., Bende, J., & Lang, A. (2011). Advanced driver assistance systems. *German Insurance Association Financial Institutions Accident Research*. Available on www. udv. de, accessed at, *6*(1), 2015. Bolderdijk, J. W., & Steg, L. (2011). Pay-as-you-Drive Vehicle Insurance as a Tool to Reduce Crash Risk. *Accident Analysis & Prevention*.

[9] The Impact of Digitalization on the Insurance Value Chain. slideheaven.com/the-impact-of-digitalization-on-the-insurance-value-chain-and-the-insurability-o.html. Accessed 20 June 2020.

nature itself of organizations. This requires a change in the relationships among organizations. The chapter on partnerships touches on this point. It is essential to take a broader vision. Simultaneously, industry 5.0, similarly to the earlier revolutions, changes traditional constraints on the scale, scope, learning, and creates both enormous opportunities and extraordinary turbulence and challenges. Some authors are questioning the consequences in socio-economic terms, such as the so-called globotics.[10]

Management needs to transform. Transformation requires what this book calls philosophy or vision. There is much more than that. Some chapters touch upon sustainability. It is necessary to rethink society. A big push has come up from the pandemic. It is essential to define the future rather than leave to a virus to force society into a "new normal." The challenges are too big, too complex, and too fluid to be solved by technologies (and much less by technologists) alone. Technologies are necessary but in conjunction with business model innovations. ICT and business teams need to work together to both develop innovative business models and deliver technology.[11] A McKinsey survey shows that top-quartile respondents are nearly three times as likely as their bottom quartile peers to say that business and ICT cocreate corporate and technology strategies.[12] And they are more than four times likelier than their bottom quartile peers to have a digitally integrated or fully digital operating model, in which digital and business-oriented teams or cross-functional teams all deliver technology across the organization.

Leading through these changing times will require new managerial wisdom, to drive organizations from full-scale organizations to flexible ventures, and from loose institutions to communities in an ecosystem.[13]

In the meantime, banking 5.0 brings several opportunities and challenges to the financial institutions: better customer delight, significant

[10] Baldwin, R., & Forslid, R. (2020). *Globotics and development: When manufacturing is jobless and services are tradable* (No. w26731). National Bureau of Economic Research.

[11] Naufal Khan, N., Lunawat, G., & Rahul, A. (2017, October). Toward an integrated technology operating model. McKinsey.com.

[12] Dhasarathy, A., Frazier, R., Khan, N., & Steagall, K. (2021, March). Seven lessons on how technology transformations can deliver value. *McKinsey Digital.*

[13] Iansiti, M., & Lakhani, K. R. (2020). *Competing in the age of AI: Strategy and leadership when algorithms and networks run the world*. Brighton, MA: Harvard Business Press.

financial investments, implementation and operational risks, strict infrastructure requirements, new levels of education and competencies of the persons involved, and so on. Simultaneously, this concept is changing because innovative solutions are continuously in development, and new solutions are available.

Interestingly, the time intervals for moving to the next industrial revolution decreases over time. If this is confirmed, banking 6.0 and more are not far in the future. The consequence is that applying the banking 5.0 concepts for the organizations is not a matter of choice (use it?) but a matter of time (when start?). The answer is one: NOW.

Glossary[1]

Accuracy. It is a quality parameter used in the classification tasks. It measures the proportion of correctly identified results (true positives plus true negatives) over the entire population of cases under consideration.

Active Management. Most robo-advisors follow a passive approach, that is, they follow indices as closely as possible. Some robo-advisors also apply active management in the sense that they try to outperform a given benchmark.

Adoption of Artificial Intelligence. It is the adoption of artificial intelligence in various industries and sectors. Successful adoption of AI in an organization's business process will depend on finding the right use cases, having a data culture, excellent talents, and having scalable solutions.

Agent Banking (Branchless Banking or Correspondent Banking). It is a third-party business arrangement of financial and non-financial institution payment service providers typically local entities, such as small

[1]These definitions are of necessity synthetic and not necessarily very accurate. Please refer to the text for a more proper presentation. This glossary includes a few terms based on the possible need to find a rapid clarification while reading this book. A helpful reference is Glossary—https://link.springer.com/content/pdf/bbm%3A978-3-319-61085-6%2F1.pdf. Accessed 10 May 2020.

B. Nicoletti, *Banking 5.0*, Palgrave Studies in Financial Services Technology, https://doi.org/10.1007/978-3-030-75871-4

shops, to supply basic payment and transaction account-related services on their behalf.

Agility. It is a metric to measure how quickly a solution responds to the customer's changes and resource load scales, distributing more and different resources to the activity.

Alan Turing Institute. It is UK's national Institute for data science and Artificial intelligence (AI). The Institute is named after the British mathematician, crypto analyst, and computing pioneer Alan Turing.

Algorithms. They are an essential part of modern advanced applications. They are used for certain tasks, from recommending products and services to automating the investments online. In stock markets, algorithms are connected directly into a digital exchange, and trading happens without intervention.[2] Pedro Domingos definition is. "An algorithm is a sequence of instructions telling a computer what to do."[3] He explains that algorithms are reducible to three logical operations—AND, OR, and NOT. While these operations can chain together in complex ways, algorithms are built out of a simple rationale at the core.

Analytics. It is a discipline that deals with finding, interpreting, and communicating relevant models in data sets. Analytics analyzes data to produce insights by applying statistical formulas, computer programming, and operations research tools. It is beneficial in areas characterized by substantial amounts of recorded information. The goal is to guide the decision-making process considering the business context. The analytical flow includes descriptive analysis. diagnostic analysis. predictive analysis. and strict measures.

App. It is short for application. It is a program or piece of software, as downloaded by a user into a mobile device.

Application. It is software that a user can run on ICT resources. to achieve a specific function related to the purposes of the user or the organization. These ICT resources could be programmable logic controllers, standard computers, mobile devices, or the cloud.

Application/App store. It is the virtual location for the distribution of digital applications. It is available on mobile devices.

[2] www.bbc.com/news/solution-14841018. Accessed 25 July 2020.

[3] Domingos, P. (2015). *The master algorithm: How the quest for the ultimate learning machine will remake our world*. Basic Books, New York, NY.

Application Programming Interfaces (API). They are programming interfaces that, by allowing the communication and sharing of data between applications, simplify the development of computer programs, supplying all the components that are developers then assemble. APIs also allow to access other applications in other systems, in a bidirectional way.

Artificial Intelligence (AI). It is a system that performs actions, reasoning, and behaviors that usually require the human being (visual perception, speech understanding, linguistic translation, learning, object management, decision-making ability, and so on).

Artificial Intelligence Bias and Human Bias. Like humans, artificial intelligence (AI) is prone to bias, not because it makes decisions based on illogical motivations, but because human errors can be latent in the machine learning process, from the training, the algorithm creation stage, up to the interpretation or completeness or correctness of the data and later interactions.

Artificial Intelligence System. It is a machine-based system that can influence the environment by making recommendations, predictions, or decisions for a given set of goals.[4] It uses machine and/or human-based inputs/data to (1). perceive environments; (2). abstract these feelings into models; and (3). interpret the models to formulate options for outcomes. AI systems are designed to run with varying levels of autonomy.

Asset Allocation. It is the distribution of assets in a portfolio to diversify the wealth of the investor. Typical asset classes include stocks, bonds, and cash. Other asset classes for robo-advisory may consist of real estate, commodities (gold), hedge funds, cryptocurrencies, and alternative investments.

Audit. It is the process by which an internal or external auditor independently verifies financial records, business processes, and information systems.

Augmented Reality (AR). It is the solution that allows enriching the perception of reality by superimposing on the vision of natural environments information or virtual objects by using a unique visor.

Authentication. It is the verification of the identity of a customer or another person by a system or service.

[4] An introduction to the global partnership on AI's work on responsible AI. OECD.AI. Accessed 12 December 2020.

Authorization. It is the procedure to check whether a customer or another person inside or outside the organization has the right to do a specific action, for example, to transfer funds or access sensitive data.

Automated Teller Machine (ATM). It is an electro-mechanical machine, which is run by the customer himself to make deposits, withdrawals, and other financial transactions. ATM facility is available to the customer 24*7.

Automation. It is the automated handling of services or products. It is the percentage of requests to the partner handled without any human intervention.

Availability. It is the metric that measures the percentage, usually computed over a periodical (such as a month) basis and net of planned or unplanned service downtimes.

Bancassurance. It is the partnership or relationship between a banking institution and an insurance organization The insurance organization uses the financial institution's sales accesses to sell its insurance products.

Banking. It is engaging in keeping or transferring money for savings and checking accounts, for exchange, or for issuing loans and credit and other financial products.

Banking as a Service (BaaS). It is the supply of complete banking processes, such as loans, payments, or deposit accounts, as a service. It is done using an existing licensed bank's secure and regulated infrastructure with API-driven platforms.[5]

Banks. It is an organization that accepts deposits, transfer money, and make credit.

Behavioral Analysis. It is a type of analysis that uses data on people's behavior to understand their intentions and predict their actions. It is the bulk of customer data produced by e-commerce platforms, games, web, mobile applications, and the internet of things powers predictive behavioral analysis algorithms. This data allows marketers to target the right offers to the right microsegment at the right time.

[5] thefinanser.com/2020/08/challenging-why-baas-open-banking-apis-is-all-a-confusion.html/. Accessed 33 August 2020.

Benchmarking. It compares processes and/or measures to other processes and/or measures implemented by well-organized entities or many of them to find best practices.[6]

Big Data. It is any collection of large and complex data such as difficult to process them using traditional data processing applications.[7] Big Data has 9Vs characteristics: (Veracity, Variety, Velocity, Volume, Validity, Variability, Volatility, Visualization, and Value). Big data technologies include data virtualization, data management and integration tools, and knowledge discovery and research tools.

Big Data Analytics. It examines large volumes of data of several types to find patterns, trends, correlations, and other helpful information to obtain insights that organizations can exploit to improve decision-making processes. Another definition is big data analytics is the science and engineering application of problem-solving where the nature, size, and conformation of data make it challenging to use traditional analysis tools.

Biometrics. It is an automated recognition of individuals based on their biological and behavioral characteristics.[8] It covers various technologies in which unique identifiable attributes of people are used for identification and authentication. These solutions include a person's fingerprint, iris print, hand, face, voice, gait, signature, or similar, used to confirm the individuals' identity.

Biometric Recognition. It is a computer system capable of finding people based on physiological and behavioral characteristics, such as fingerprints, iris, voice, or gestures. This solution uses algorithms that, by analyzing the data inputs from a specific subject, reconstruct and recognize his/her identity.

Bitcoin. It is a cryptocurrency, in other words, a token of value exchanged between two parties.

Black Box. It is a metaphor used to describe the inability to understand how technologies work and algorithms. While it is possible to

[6] Benchmarking—Open risk manual. www.openriskmanual.org/wiki/Benchmarking. Accessed 20 May 2020.

[7] Top Fintech terms you should know—Trulioo: Global. www.trulioo.com/blog/top-fintech-terms-know/. Accessed 30 May 2020.

[8] National Research Council, & Whither Biometrics Committee. (2010). *Biometric recognition: Challenges and opportunities*. National Academies Press, Washington, DC.

understand the results of artificial intelligence (AI) in terms of recommendations, decisions, and so on, the processes that lead to those results are often too complex to understand. Concerns about the AI black boxes relate to its apparent lack of accountability, the possible presence of hidden biases, and the inability to have a completely unobstructed vision of what drives the decisions.

Blockchain. It is a distributed database where trust is proven through consensus or mass collaboration. Each transaction is recorded continuously and sequentially on a public block creating a unique on-going chain. Blockchain solutions were introduced for bitcoin transactions.[9] It is still used to record cryptocurrency transactions. It runs like a distributed ledger where information, once entered, cannot be changed. There are several applications of blockchain solutions, including smart contracts and recording of digital assets. It can record data: a digital ledger of transactions, agreements, contracts, or anything that needs to be registered independently and verified as having happened. The blockchain solutions run across several or even thousands of computers in some applications. Every time a new batch of transactions is encrypted, it is added to the ledger "chain" as a "block." Blockchain solutions are in use in many applications, where data needs to be shared in a trustful way among organizations or persons.

Bot. It is any program or script that performs automated scripts or tasks.

Broad Network Access. It eases network capabilities and their access through standard mechanisms. Heterogeneous thin or thick customer platforms promote the use of the network. Personal computers (PCs), tablets, Personal digital assistants (PDAs), mobile phones, and other devices or objects can access networks.

Broadband. It is internet access via networks implemented as Digital subscriber line (DSL), television cable, or wireless solution (UMTS, WLAN, LTE, satellite, and so on).

Business Analytics. It is a term that shows the set of skills, technologies, statistical methods, and data-driven approaches that are used to explore and analyze the performance of an organization to obtain new knowledge that can support business planning. Data visualization, business

[9] Karajovic, M., Narula, H., Pandya, K., Patel, J., & Warring, I. (2017). *Blockchain: A manager's guide*. A Report for OMIS 3710 Schulich School of Business York University Toronto, ON.

intelligence reporting, and big data analytics are some examples of business analytics tools.

Business Continuity. It is an on-going process to ensure that the necessary steps are taken to find the impacts of losses and keep workable recovery strategies, recovery plans, and services continuity.[10]

Business Intelligence (BI). It is a broad category of applications and solutions for gathering, storing, analyzing, retrieving, and supplying data to help customers make better organizational decisions. BI applications include decision support systems, querying and reporting, online analytical processing, statistical analysis, forecasting, and data mining. Analytics has generalized and extended business intelligence. The use of artificial intelligence (AI) in big data and business intelligence is essential. Organizations use machine learning algorithms to find trends and extract insights from substantial amounts of data to make critical decisions quickly, or in real-time.

Business Model. It is a simplified representation of an organization and an abstraction of how its business and value creation make money. It describes the organization, cost structures, financial flows, value network, and organization's products compactly. The process of defining a business model is part of the business strategy.

Business Model Canvas (BMC). It is a strategic management and entrepreneurial tool. It allows describing, designing, challenging, inventing, showing, and pivoting a business model. Osterwalder and Pigneur introduced BMC.[11]

Business-to-Business (B2B). It refers to organizations that relate to other organizations, rather than individuals.

Business-to-Customer (B2C). It refers to organizations that relate to individuals rather than other organizations.

Business Web. It is the use of the internet by financial institutions or organizations in general. The speed of change inherent to the internet, and the existing international technical and semantic standards, open innovation potential to all areas of the organizations, their structures, and functions. This solution makes value-added networks flexible and

[10] NFPA 1600. (2013). Standard on Disaster/Emergency Management and Business Continuity Programs. https://www.nfpa.org/assets/files/aboutthecodes/1600/1600-13-pdf.pdf. Accessed 20 June 2019.

[11] Osterwalder, A., & Pigneur, Y. (2010). *Business model generation: A handbook for visionaries, game changers, and challengers*. John Wiley & Sons, Hoboken, NJ.

secure. Concepts such as cloud computing and social media support the business web.

Case-Based Reasoning. It is a process that tries to solve unfamiliar problems by applying solutions already found in the past for similar problems. Case-based reasoning algorithms can be used for both regression and classification analysis.

Cash Dispenser. Cash withdrawal is the primary service provided by the financial institution branches. The cashier or teller or the cash dispenses do it. The use of a cash dispenser is cheaper than manual operations. The customer accesses the cash dispenser with a plastic card, which is magnetically coated.

Central Processing Unit (CPU). It is the central processing unit, or central processor, of a computer. It carries out most of the data processing processes by interpreting program instructions. The CPU controls the instructions and the flow of data to and from the computer's other components and depends on a chipset placed on the main printed circuit board, known as the motherboard.

Challenger Bank. It is a smaller, newer financial institution that often aims to supply lower-cost banking services to customers. Challengers often lack a physical location or some standard services of a traditional bank.

Channel. It is a term that shows the various platforms that allow an organization to communicate with its customers or prospects.

Chatbot. It is an AI program. It simulates human conversations interactively, using pre-set sentences. It is used for assistance services (customer care) or marketing, such as social network and instant messaging. More complex than speech-to-text programs, chatbots communicate with people using text (text chatbot) and voice (voicebot). Text chatbots have been used before voicebots, holding a verbal conversation, understanding language, and supplying answers.

Checking Account. It is an account held at a financial institution in which account owners deposit and retrieve funds. Account owners can write checks or send money orders on their accounts and use ATM cards or debit cards to access funds.

Cloud. Short for cloud computing, it is a term that describes a network of remote servers that stores, manages, and processes data on the internet, cutting the need for a local server or personal computer. Cloud computing solutions have developed rapidly. Cloud providers, for example, have incorporated features such as facial recognition of online photos and automatic translation of spoken language into their respective cloud services. The next stage of cloud evolution will be creating AI-based platforms that can be used by any type of business, regardless of size or solutions level. Many Platform-as-a-Service (PaaS) solutions have already begun to incorporate AI capabilities.

Cloud Computing. It is a computing capability that provides convenient and on-demand network access to a shared pool of configurable computing resources.[12] These resources can be rapidly provisioned and released with minimal management effort or partner interaction. Cloud computing has six essential characteristics: pay-per-use, self-service, broad network access, resource pooling, flexibility, and measured service. In general terms, cloud computing enables four modes: Infrastructure as a Service (IaaS), Platform as a Service (PaaS), Software as a Service, and Business Process as a Service (BPaaS). It can be public, private, or hybrid.

Cognition. It is the mental action of getting knowledge and understanding through thought, experience, and senses.

Cognitive Automation. It is an intelligent software to process substantial amounts of information. What distinguishes cognitive automation from Robotic process automation (RPA) is the use of artificial intelligence.

Cognitive Computing. They are systems that learn at scale, reason with purpose, and interact with humans naturally. It is a mixture of computer science and cognitive science. By self-teaching algorithms that use data mining, visual recognition, and natural language processing, a computer can solve problems and optimize human processes. It includes machine learning, natural language processing, natural language understanding, and computer vision.

Cognitive Robotic Process Automation (RPA). Cognitive RPA uses artificial intelligence solutions such as machine learning and natural language processing (NLP) to augment RPA capabilities and enhance the customer journey by incorporating unstructured tasks into process automation.

[12] Liu, F., Tong, J., Mao, J., Bohn, R., Messina, J., Badger, L., & Leaf, D. (2011). NIST cloud computing reference architecture. *NIST special publication, 500*(2011), 1–28.

Cognitive Science. It is the interdisciplinary study of the mind and its processes based on psychology, linguistics, anthropology, and neuroscience. Together with artificial intelligence, it studies how to simulate human mental systems in machines.

Cognitive Search. It collects, analyzes, and supplies meanings to distinct types of data using rule-based or machine learning algorithms, often in a way that is like human cognition. It supports decision-making in complex situations.

Compliance. It is respect for the internal and external compulsory rules of the organization or of the government.

Compound Annual Growth Rate (CAGR). It is a measure of the average growth over many periods.

Computer Vision. It is the support of a computer to see and visually sense the environment around it. Computer vision supports the automatic extraction, analysis, and understanding of helpful information from a single image or a sequence of images. Machine vision uses visual data from the real world to produce numerical or symbolic information to support decisions or take other actions.

Consensus. It is a mechanism that allows computers to agree regularly on how to update the database, after which the modifications they have settled on are made unchangeable with the help of complex cryptography.[13]

Consent. It is the decision-making strategy based on the conviction and approval by all the members who undertake to support the decision.

Continuous Improvement. It is a structured method to improve the organization's performance or one of its processes by using arrangements proper to its problems.[14] Its scope may be the quality or social responsibility of the organization. Continuous improvement is called *Kaizen* in Japanese.

Conversational Artificial Intelligence. It is a type of AI trained to interpret human (everyday) language and communicate with people. Equipped with advanced Natural language processing (NLP) features, conversational AI is a logic that creates virtual conversations. An

[13] The blockchain in finance. Hype springs eternal | Finance. www.economist.com/finance-and-economics/2016/03/19/hype-springs-eternal. Accessed 22 June 2020.

[14] Bessant, J., & Caffyn, S. (1997). High-involvement innovation through continuous improvement. *International Journal of Solution Management*, *14*(1), 7–28.

example of an application is the voice control devices present on voicebots.

Convolutional Neural Network (CNN). It is a type of neural network that can find images and give them a sense that is used for image classification. Examples of everyday use of this type of network include Amazon buying recommendations and the Instagram search engine.

Core banking system. It is software, which stores and processes the core data of a bank.

Credibility. It expresses the believability, honesty, and trustworthiness of a person or an organization. It incorporates reputation, confidence, and general confidentiality.

Credit Risk Management. It is the practice of identifying and mitigating loss by understanding the limits of financial institutions loss reserves at any given time to maximize adjusted returns.[15]

Credit Scoring. It is used to evaluate the creditworthiness of a credit customer.[16] Usually, it is a numerical value with specific creditworthiness associated with an individual or a company. It describes the potential customers' ability to repay the credit. Credit scoring is based on several variables, such as income, personal and financial history, employment, and demographics.[17]

Credit Union. It is a non-profit financial institution owned by its members.

Crisis. It is a situation formally declared as service interruption or the deterioration of one or more critical processes or as systemically essential because of incidents or disasters.

Critical Success Factors (CSFs). They are the limited number of satisfactory results that will ensure successful competitive performance for the individual, initiative, or organization.[18] CSFs are the key areas where

[15] BIS. (2000). *Principles for the management of credit risk.* BIS book, Basel, Switzerland.

[16] Mpofu, T. P., & Mukosera, M. (2014). Credit scoring techniques: A survey. *International Journal of Science and Research*, 3(8).

[17] Mpofu, T. P., & Mukosera, M. (2014). Credit scoring techniques: A survey. *International Journal of Science and Research*, 3(8).

[18] Bullen, C. V., & Rockart, J. F. (1981). *A primer on critical success factors. Sloan School of Business.* MIT, Cambridge, MA.

"things must go right" for the organization to flourish and reach its goals.[19]

Crowdfunding. It is the practice of funding a project or venture by raising money from many persons. This transaction takes place most often via online platforms.[20] It works through mail-order subscriptions, benefit events, and other methods.[21] Equity crowdfunding is the process whereby persons (the "crowd") invest, in an early stage, in unlisted organization or initiative in exchange for shares in that organization. A shareholder has partial ownership of an organization and stands to profit should the organization perform well. The opposite is true. If the organization fails, investors can lose some, or all, of their investment. Seedrs is an example of an equity-based crowdfunding platform in the UK.[22] Debt-based crowdfunding is when persons lend to an organization. The lenders earn a rate of return based on the interest charged on the loan. Typically, loans are secured against assets, which partially protect investors should the borrower do not repay. Donation-based crowdfunding is when persons donate money to a project. Backers may receive in return token rewards that increase in prestige as the size of the donation increases.

Crypto Assets. It is a type of private asset that depends primarily on cryptography and distributed ledger or similar solutions as part of its perceived or inherent value.[23]

Customer. It is s/he who pays for the products, services, or activities. It is not necessarily the user of the product or the process or event. It can be external or internal to the organization. In the latter case, unless there is a system of internal prices, the internal customer does not pay for the product, the service, or the activity but uses it.

Customer Journey. It is the entire sequence of touchpoints in a customer journey when interacting with an organization's offering, from first awareness to buy to advocacy.

[19] CSF's, KPI's, Metrics, outcomes and benefits. www.itsmsolutions.com/newsletters/DITYvol6iss5.htm. Accessed 20 March 2021.

[20] Common Definitive Financial Solution (FinTech) Jargon. pupuweb.com/common-fintech-jargon-glossary-term/. Accessed 30 May 2020.

[21] Common Definitive Financial Solution (FinTech) Jargon. pupuweb.com/common-fintech-jargon-glossary-term/. Accessed 22 June 2020.

[22] www.seedr.cc/. Accessed 22 April 2019.

[23] www.fsb.org/wp-content/uploads/P101018.pdf. Accessed 30 December 2020.

Customer Relationship Management (CRM). It is an information system for managing relationships with customers. It can control the life cycle of the relationship with the customer, the acquisition of new customers, customer proximity, and customer loyalty based on the organization's relationships. It lowers transaction costs between customers and the organization and integrates the processes of customer management.

Customer Value Proposition. They are the benefits a product or service holds for a customer. It is the reason\why a customer might buy that product or service.

Cyber Crime. It is a crime when a computer system or one of its components is the object of the crime (hacking, phishing, spamming) or is the facilitator of a crime (such as theft of information or money).

Cyber Physical Services (CPS) Platform. It is the platform construct, the hardware, software, and communication systems with basic standardized CPS) mediation, interoperability, and quality of services for implementing and managing cyber physical systems and their applications and their integration in value networks.[24] CPS platform services, with their basic functionality for implementing reliable operation, and evolution of cyber physical systems, are an integral part of domain-specific CPS application platforms. They secure the cross-domain and cross-financial institution functionality and quality at the technological system level, for example, through Quality of service-(QoS) capable communication, services for ICT security or self-diagnosis, self-healing, and reconfiguration.

Cyber Resilience. It is a financial market infrastructure's ability to predict, withstand, hold, and rapidly recover from a cyber attack.

Cyber Risk. It is the combination of the probability of an event occurring within the realm of an organization's information assets, computer and communication resources, and the consequences of that event for the organization.

Cyber Security. It is the set of solutions and services aimed at protecting computers, other connected devices, equipment, and ICT systems from attacks of several types (malware, viruses, trojans, ransomware,

[24] Rojas, R. A., & Garcia, M. A. R. (2020). Implementation of industrial internet of things and Cyber-physical systems in smes for distributed and service-oriented control. In *Industry 4.0 for SMEs* (pp. 73–103). Palgrave Macmillan, Cham, Switzerland.

and so on), to prevent losses, compromise of data and information, or other types of malicious actions.

Cybernetics. According to Norbert Wiener it is the study of regulation or control systems. Much influenced by Ross Ashby and other systems theorists works, cybernetics has had a major influence in the development of intelligent systems, especially in the field of robotics.[25]

Cyber Physical Systems (Cps). They encompass embedded systems, production, logistics, engineering, coordination, management processes, and internet services that directly capture physical data using sensors and act on physical processes using actuators. They are connected using digital networks, use data, and services available worldwide, and have multimodal person–machine interfaces. Cyber physical systems are open socio-technical systems and enable several functions, services, and properties.

Dark data. It is known as "opaque data." This data is all the data that is not usually used—in many cases not even stored—and therefore does not interact with regular data. Typically, this is digital data generated from network devices, system logs but from email or other unstructured sources, which accumulate in the middle layers of every organization's operating systems.[26] Organizations often do not even realize the valuable insights in this unstructured, untapped, and/or unlabeled information, including server log file data and mobile geolocation data.

Data. It is a set of quantitative or qualitative variables. A novel, a video, or a chart of accounts are all examples of data. Artificial intelligence (AI) needs data to train, learn, and act. The more it has access to correct data, the better its chances of success.

Data Analytics. It is an end-to-end process that involves cleaning, inspecting, and modeling data to find helpful and actionable information to support decision-making. In a B2C context, this process includes qualitative and quantitative methods used to derive insights on buying behaviors, trends, and patterns.

[25] Ashby, W. R. (1961). *An introduction to cybernetics*. Chapman & Hall Ltd., London, UK.

[26] Narayanan, A., Toubiana, V., Barocas, S., Nissenbaum, H., & Boneh, D. (2012). A critical look at decentralized personal data architectures. *arXiv preprint* arXiv:1202.4503.

Data Collection. It is the process of collecting the data to generate information used to make decisions.[27] In manual data collection, persons use the so-called sheets check to collect and supply for their first classification.

Data Governance and Compliance. It defines who handles what and the policies and procedures that persons or groups need to follow in data management. Data governance requires governing the organization's infrastructure and the infrastructure that the organization does not control. Data governance has two critical components: understanding compliance and risk, healthy organization performance goals.

Data Mining. It is a process by which data is collected, aggregated by type, and sorted to find patterns and predict future trends.

Data Protection. It is the protection of the individual against impairment of his/her rights about personal data.

Data Science. It is a discipline that combines statistical systems and processes with computer science and information science to extrapolate insights through structured and/or unstructured data analysis. One of the most common data science applications (in AI and machine learning) is the development of predictive tools.

Data Source. It is a personal information database used by identity verification/identity proofing services to confirm an identity.[28]

Data Structured and Unstructured. In its most basic definition, a piece of data is an abstraction or measurement from a real-world entity. Structured data refers to data that can be stored in a table. Every instance in the table has the same set of attributes. Conversely, unstructured data refers to a type of data where each instance in the data set may have its internal structure.

Dataset or Database. It is a collection of data usually from a common source and assembled for a particular business or another purpose.

Debit Card. It is a card that allows an account owner to withdraw money or make payments directly from an account. It is normally connected with a password or other identification method.

Debits. They are charges to or withdrawals from an account. Debits are subtracted from the balance.

[27] Data collection. Open risk manual. www.openriskmanual.org/wiki/Data_Collection. Accessed 30 May 2020.

[28] Identity Insights—Global online identity verification .... www.trulioo.com/blog/top-fintech-terms-know. Accessed 20 March 2021.

Decision Model. It is a set of rules used to understand and manage the logic that drives business decisions. It involves applying sophisticated algorithms to large volumes of data. It can be used to recommend a course of action and predict its outcome.

Decision Tree. It is both a data representing a structure to support in deciding and a method used for data mining and machine learning.

Deep Learning. It is a machine learning method whereby a system recognizes the patterns present in the data through the automatic learning of a hierarchy of features or characteristics.[29] In deep learning, data is processed through a "deep" succession of activation levels. Each level creates a representation of the data, and the next groups use features from the earlier level to make more complex representations. The output of the final level is mapped to a category to which the data belongs. The goal of a deep learning algorithm is to make this final mapping correct. Superficial machine learning approaches rely on a significant amount of feature engineering processes performed by humans before the model can learn the relationships between features. In deep learning, on the other hand, the system gets the characteristics and their relationships simultaneously.

Deep Neural Networks (DNN). It is any neural network architecture that has multiple hidden layers of artificial neurons (nodes). These architectures allow the models to learn the multi-hierarchical, and therefore profound, interrelationships of the data characteristics.

Defects. They lack fulfillment in all customer expectations by a process, product, or service.

Descriptive Analysis. It is a type of historical data analysis aimed at quantifying what happened, as is the case with business reports that supply a historical perspective on performance.

Design Thinking. It is a method to find practical and creative solutions to problems through an approach like that adopted by designers.[30] Design thinking strategies have proven highly effective in the innovation sector because they allow organizations to develop creative thinking as the customer needs.

[29] Raschka, S., Patterson, J., & Nolet, C. (2020). Machine learning in python: Main developments and technology trends in data science, machine learning, and artificial intelligence. *Information*, *11*(4), 193.

[30] Martin, R., & Martin, R. L. (2009). *The design of business: Why design thinking is the next competitive advantage*. Harvard Business Press, Brighton, MA.

Digital Assistant. It is an AI system capable of understanding voice commands and performing various tasks, for example, supplying a customer support service.

Digital Banking. It is digitization (or moving online) of all the traditional banking activities and programs services that were historically were only available to customers when physically inside of a bank branch.[31] Any payment app or banking tool can adopt the term but lack the processes and customer-facing interface to complete banking tasks with minimal human attention.

Digital Banks. They are deposit-taking institutions that are members of a deposit insurance scheme and deliver banking services primarily through online channels instead of physical branches.

Digital Currency. It is a digital representation of virtual currency or e-money and is often used interchangeably with the term "virtual currency."[32]

Digital Financial Inclusion. It is the use of digital financial services to progress in financial inclusion.[33] It involves deploying in digital ways to reach financially excluded and underserved populations with a range of financial services suited to their needs and delivered responsibly at a cost affordable to customer, and sustainable for financial institutions.[34]

Digital Financial Product. A digital customer-facing financial service that a customer can interact with. For example, a bank app or an online stock market trading website.

Digital Financial Services (DFS). They are financial products and services, including payments, transfers, savings, credit, insurance, securities, financial planning, and account statements provided via digital

[31] ceo-insight.com/finance/the-road-to-true-digital-bank/.

[32] http://arthapedia.in/index.php?title=Crypto_Currency_/_Virtual_Currency_/_Digital_Currency. Accessed 30 May 2020.

[33] G20 high-level principles for digital financial inclusion. https://www.gpfi.org/sites/gpfi/files/G20%20High%20Level%20Principles%20for%20Digital%20Financial%20Inclusion.pdf. Accessed 30 May 2020.

[34] G20 high-level principles for digital financial inclusion. https://www.gpfi.org/sites/gpfi/files/documents/G20%20High%20Level%20Principles%20for%20Digital%20Financial%20Inclusion%20-%20Full%20version-.pdf. Accessed 22 June 2020.

solutions such as e-money, payment cards, and a regular financial institution account.[35]

Digital ID. It is a set of electronically captured and stored attributes and credentials. They can uniquely find a person or an organization.

Digital Payment Services (DPS). They are solutions to ease payment transactions by transferring money, clearing, or settling balances digitally, without physical cash.

Digital Transformation. It is a change in the business model, considering digital solutions. It is the set of social, cultural, and technological changes associated with digital solutions.[36]

Digital Wallet or E-wallets. It is an e-Money product, where the record of funds is stored on a particular device, typically in an Integrated circuit (IC) chip on a card or mobile phone.

Disruptive Innovation. It is an innovation that completely changes how persons or organizations do something.[37] It describes innovations that unexpectedly improve products or services and change both how things are done and the market. The mobile phone is an example of disruptive innovation.[38] It has completely changed how users connect to ICT services. Disruptive innovation affects the persons, businesses, and society at large.

Distributed Ledger Solution (DLT). Distributed ledgers use independent computers (referred to as nodes) to record, share, and synchronize transactions in their respective digital ledgers (instead of keeping data centralized as done traditionally).[39] Blockchain is one type of a distributed ledger that organizes data into blocks, which are chained together in an append-only mode, once encrypted.

[35] G20 high-level principles for digital financial inclusion. https://www.gpfi.org/sites/gpfi/files/documents/G20%20High%20Level%20Principles%20for%20Digital%20Financial%20Inclusion%20-%20Full%20version-.pdf. Accessed 22 June 2020.

[36] Matt, C., Hess, T., & Benlian, A. (2015). Digital transformation strategies. *Business & Information Systems Engineering*, *57*(5), 339–343.

[37] Disruptive innovation—Open risk manual. www.openriskmanual.org/wiki/Disruptive_Innovation. Accessed 40 May 2020.

[38] Disruptive innovation. Open risk manual. www.openriskmanual.org/wiki/Disruptive_Innovation. Accessed 22 June 2020.

[39] Blockchain & distributed ledger solution (DLT). www.worldbank.org/en/topic/financialsector/brief/blockchain-dlt. Accessed 22 June 2020. Blockchain & distributed ledger solution (DLT). www.worldbank.org/en/topic/financialsector/brief/blockchain-dlt. Accessed 22 June 2020.

Distributor. It is a person or entity that supplies products on a wholesale basis to retail outlets or organizations. It may be an organization entity, an arm of an organization entity, or an independent entity. It can be physical or virtual.

Ease of use. It means easing out the users in search, navigation, and connectivity such as a service/website. It includes the system flexibility and user-friendliness in the offered services.

Ecosystem. It is a network of organizations, including partners, distributors, customers, competitors, government agencies, and others, involved in delivering a specific product or service through cooperation.[40] An ecosystem is an interconnected set of services that allows users to fulfill various needs in one integrated experience.[41] Customer ecosystems tend to concentrate on requirements such as travel, healthcare, or housing. Business-to-business (B2B) ecosystems revolve around a specific function, for example, marketing and sales, operations, procurement, or finance.[42] One of the main benefits of ecosystems is supplying better solutions to those offered by the platform developer. In this sense, they can solve the problems of a sector but open new growth opportunities.

Ecosystem Participants. They are a set of organizations or individuals that can work together to get synergies.

Efficiency. This dimension includes ease and speed of accessing and using, for example, e-banking service, and availability and functionality of the service that ease completion of all the transactions in a convenient way.

Electronic Data Interchange (EDI). It is the computer-to-computer exchange of documents in a standard format between organizations.

Electronic Money or E-Money. It is a record of funds or value available to a customer stored on a payment device, such as chips, prepaid cards, mobile phones, or computer systems as a non-traditional account with a financial or non-financial institution.[43]

[40] Anitha, C., & Reddy, D. (2017, October). Evolution and emerging role of MFIs in Indian microfinance sector. *Sumedha Journal of Management*, *6*(4), CMR College of Engineering & Solution, 87.

[41] Insuritas | NSC | NAFCU. www.nafcu.org/insuritas. Accessed 30 May 2020.

[42] www.mckinsey.com/industries/financial-services/our-insights/insurance-beyond-digital-the-rise-of-ecosystems-and-platforms. Accessed 10 January 2020.

[43] Glossary GitBook. docs.mojaloop.io/mojaloop-specification/fspiop-api/documents/Glossary.html. Accessed 20 March 2021.

Embedded Banking. It refers to non-financial products or services with value propositions that are significantly enhanced or even transformed through the associated financial products and services embedded within them.[44]

Embedded Finance. It refers to non-financial organizations with value propositions that are significantly enhanced or even transformed through the associated financial products and services embedded within them.[45]

Embedded Systems. They are hardware and software components that are integrated into a comprehensive system to implement system-specific functional features.

Emerging Technologies. They are a set of technologies that are being generated and tested because of successive innovations. It is an important part in digital transformation.

E-money Services. It is the issuance of debt-like instruments to ease payment transactions.

Encryption. It is the process of encoding messages or coding to protect the customer's information assets. Encryption is vital to organizations, to the blockchain, and anything else that needs to be secure. Documents or data, like names and numbers, are turned into code using algorithms. A key is needed to turn that code back into readable, helpful data or decrypt it.

End-User. It is the end or final user of an application.

Enterprise Resource Planning (ERP). It is the extension of the Manufacturing Resource Planning II to the organization's remaining functions, such as engineering, finance, personnel administration, and management.[46] Some ERP components are accounting, industrial accounting, Human resource (HR) management, payrolls, sourcing, warehouse management, operations, project control, sales, distribution, and maintenance.

Equator Principles (EPs). They are a risk management framework adopted by financial institutions for figuring out, assessing, and

[44] King, B. (2018). *Bank 4.0: Banking everywhere, never at a bank.* John Wiley & Sons, Hoboken, NJ.

[45] http://medium.com/swlh/an-introduction-to-embedded-finance-a4d64302757d. Accessed 20 January 2021.

[46] Enterprise resource planning—Open risk manual. www.openriskmanual.org/wiki/Enterprise_Resource_Planning. Accessed 22 June 2020.

managing environmental and social risks in projects.[47] The goal is to supply a minimum standard for due diligence and checking to support responsible risk decision-making. The EPs apply globally, to all industry sectors and five financial products: (1) Project Finance Advisory Services, (2) Project Finance, (3) Project-Related Corporate Loans, (4) Bridge Loans, and (5) Project-Related Acquisition Finance and Refinance.[48]

Equity Crowdfunding (EC). It is an activity where investors supply funding to private organizations in the form of equity. The EC platforms match investors with organizations they want to invest in, enabling them to take part in the early capital-raising activities of start-ups and other organizations.

Exchange-Traded Fund (ETF). It is also called an index fund. It is an investment fund, which tries to minimize the tracking error compared to a given benchmark. It is used for passive investing and is part of many robo-advisory portfolios.

Expert Systems (Inference). They are computer systems that emulate the decision-making competencies of human experts. In these systems, inference applies rules of logic to a knowledge base to infer new knowledge.

Facial Recognition. It is a solution that can name or verify the identity of a person from a digital face image or video frame. The application extracts the facial features and classifies them by comparing the image with the faces in a database.

Facilitator. It is a person who helps a group to achieve its full potential through the identification and removal of barriers. S/he leads the group to carry out its mission.

Federation. In the context of federal CPS platforms, federation means that CPS platforms, services, and applications from different participants are used jointly for cooperative activities. The individual component or context stays secured for each of the participants. Only the data and information that are necessary for joint action are exchanged between the participants. The various parts can be accessed directly within the applications, services, or platform without central, dominant control. The individual components stay in control of their data.

[47] equator-principles.com/. Accessed 26 October 2020.

[48] Sarro, D. (2012). Do lenders make effective regulators? An assessment of the equator principles on project finance. *German Law Journal*, *13*(12), 1525–1558.

Fees. It is the money charged for services. Examples of banking fees are fees associated with checking and savings accounts, such as if an overdraft occurs and the account owner has asked that the financial institution accepts overdrafts.[49]

Financial Inclusion. It is the uptake and usage of a range of financial products and services by individuals and Micro, small, and medium enterprises (MSMEs), provided in a manner that is accessible and secure to the customer and sustainable to the provider.

Financial Institution (FI). It includes all organizations that supply financial services. Financial institutions run at all scales, including large and small incumbent banks, brokerages, insurance organizations, or fintech organizations.

Financial Market Infrastructure. It is a multilateral system among participating institutions, including the operator of the system. It is, used for clearing, settling, or recording payments, securities, derivatives, or other financial transactions.[50]

Financial Product. It is a financial instrument that allows for saving, spending, planning, or borrowing. For example, a credit card, or Registered retirement savings plan (RRSP) account, or a checking account are three examples of financial products.

Financial Service. It is an action or work that is done for a customer by their financial institution. An example of financial services includes managing and moving money between accounts. Financial services are not to be confused with a financial product. Financial services are what is done for a customer, while financial products are what a customer can use.

Fintech Balance Sheet Lending. It is a credit activity eased by internet-based platforms that use their balance sheet in the ordinary business course to intermediate borrowers and lenders.[51]

[49] PAGE ONE Economics. files.stlouisfed.org/files/htdocs/publications/page1-econ/2020/10/01/banking-basics_SE.pdf. Accessed 20 March 2021.

[50] Rosner, M., & Kang, A. (2016, February). Understanding and regulating twenty-first century payment systems: The ripple case study. *Michigan Law Review*, *114*(4), 649.

[51] Digital finance innovation road map and action plan 2020–2024. www.ojk.go.id/id/berita-dan-kegiatan/publikasi/Documents/Pages/Publikasi-Materi-Digital-Finance-Innovation-Road-Map-dan-Action-Plan-2020-2024-serta-Digital-Financial-Literacy/Digital%20Finance%20Innovation%20Road%20Map%20dan%20Action%20Plan.pdf. Accessed 20 March 2021.

Fintech Organization. It is the emerging financial solution sector whose name is composed of the words "FINance" and "TECHnology." A fintech organization is an organization or digital service that automates the delivery and use of financial products and services. Fintech organizations are often quite different from traditional financial institutions in organizational structure and personnel and often consider themselves technology firms. Some fintech organizations may offer similar services compared to traditional banks and interact directly with individual consumers. Some fintech organizations only supply Business-to-Business solutions to other financial institutions.

Fintech Platform Financing. It is a funding activity eased by internet-based platforms (not run by commercial banks). Fintech platform financing includes balance sheet lending, loan crowdfunding, or equity crowdfunding.

Float. It is the amount of funds withdrawn from the payer's account but not reflected at once in the recipient account. In the e-money context, a float is typically referred to as the total value of outstanding customer funds.

General Artificial Intelligence. It is a form of artificial intelligence that can perform a wide range of human-made tasks in various environments.

General Data Protection Regulation (GDPR). It is an EU regulation, that takes care of personal data protection and privacy in the European Union.

General Purpose Technologies. The importance of general-purpose technologies lies in the overall impact on persons, businesses, and society and in the wide range of complementary innovations they support. To date, the most powerful technologies are the engine, electricity, computer, the internet. Artificial intelligence is another essential turning point in the development of this type of technology.

Generative Pre-trained Transformer 3 (GPT-3). It is an AI that can create content that has a language structure: human or machine language.[52]

[52] www.forbes.com/sites/bernardmarr/2020/10/05/what-is-gpt-3-and-why-is-it-revolutionizing-artificial-intelligence/?sh=5cd94741481a. Accessed 21 January 2021.

Globalization. It is a worldwide movement toward economic, financial, trade, and communications global integration.[53]

Globotics. It is the synthesis of globalization, robotics, and the future of work. This combination has disruptive effects from a socio-economic perspective, with an explosive pace of developments in robotization and tele-migration. It threatens to overwhelm persons' ability to adapt.[54]

Goals. Goals are specific targets that are intended to be reached at a given point in time.[55] A goal is thus an operational transformation of one or more goals.

Governance. It refers to the controls and processes that ensure the effectiveness, efficiency, economics, and ethics of a sector.[56] The sector might refer to the entire organization or an organization unit, a process, or data.

Hackathons. They are moderated, multi-day activities designed to generate many innovative ideas and address critical customer challenges.[57] Operators, developers, and subject matter experts with various backgrounds are brought together to push lateral thinking boundaries and challenge current solutions in an innovative way. These teams do not focus on designing new products through a collaborative competition.

Heuristic Search Techniques. They are practical troubleshooting methods that restrict the search for best solutions by discarding the wrong options. In artificial intelligence, empirical search tools classify/rate alternatives in search algorithms at each decision branch using available information to decide which branch to follow.[58]

[53] businessdictionary.com. Accessed 20 June 2019.

[54] Baldwin, R. (2019). *The globotics upheaval: Globalization, robotics, and the future of work*. Oxford University Press, New York, NY.

[55] Bullen, C. V., & Rockart, J. F. (1981). *A primer on critical success factors. Sloan School of Business*. MIT, Cambridge, MA.

[56] Governance. Open risk manual. www.openriskmanual.org/wiki/Governance. Accessed 30 May 2020.

[57] www.softserveinc.com/en-us/blog/hackathons-fueling-banking-innovation. Accessed 30 March 2021.

[58] Applied Intelligence Glossary | Accenture. www.accenture.com/no-en/insights/applied-intelligence/artificial-intelligence-glossary. Accessed 20 March 2021.

High-Frequency Trading (HFT). It is an algorithmic trading solution. It is based on an infrastructure that minimizes network and other types of latencies using specific facilities as co-location, proximity hosting, or high-speed direct access and by a system determination of order initiation, generation, and execution without human intervention for trades or orders.[59]

Human-in-the-Loop (HITL). It is an expression that shows the integration of a person in automatic learning processes to optimize outputs and increase accuracy. The tool is recognized as a best practice of machine learning.

Human–Machine Interaction/Man–Machine Interaction (MMI)/ Human–Computer Interaction (HCI). It is the computer science part that deals with the user-friendly design of interactive systems and their human–machine interfaces. In addition to computer science findings, those from psychology, ergonomics, cognitive science, ergonomics, sociology, and design are used. Important sub-areas of human–machine interaction are, for example, usability engineering, interaction design, information design, and context analysis. The last aspect is vital for CPSs to ensure that the interaction is optimally adapted to the user in every situation.

Hybrid Robo-Advisor. It is a robo-advisor that integrates a human advisor as well in their automatic process. It is called hybrid because it links two different approaches: the robot's strength by implementing an automatized investment process and a human for personal contact and empathy whenever necessary.

Identity Verification. It identifies individuals by using their physical and behavioral characteristics to set up a mapping from a person's online identity to their real-life identity.[60]

Image Analysis. It is the extraction and analysis of information from image data by digital image processing. In addition to finding faces to prove age, gender, and sentiment, the image analysis algorithms can simultaneously recognize distinctive features (logos, objects, scenes, and so on). Barcodes and QR (Quick Response) codes are two simple

[59] MiFid II (2014). Directive 2014/65/Eu of the European Parliament and of the Council of 15 May 2014 on Markets in Financial Instruments and Amending the Insurance Mediation Directive and Aifmd. Article, 4(1)(39).

[60] Top Fintech terms you should know. Trulioo: Global. www.trulioo.com/blog/top-fintech-terms-know/. Accessed 22 June 2020.

examples of these types of applications. Among the more complex applications there are facial recognition and the analysis of position and movement.

Image Recognition. It is a solution capable of finding objects, places, people, writing, and actions present in images using computer vision combined with cameras, statistical methods, and artificial intelligence.

Incident. It is an event that is not part of the standard operation of a service. It causes or may cause an interruption to, or a reduction in, the quality of service.

Incumbent. It is a financial institution that has an established record of accomplishment and history.

Indicator of Compromise (IoC). It is forensic evidence of potential intrusions on a system or network. IOCs supply actionable threat intelligence shared within the cyber security community to improve incident response and remediation strategies further.

Inductive Reasoning. It is a process in which tests and datasets are used as the basis for reaching a specific conclusion. Given the evidence provided, the deduction may be probable since it is not inevitable.

Industry 4.0. It denotes the merge of ICT with automation, having at its base the internet solutions.

Industry 5.0. It is the increased collaboration between humans and intelligent systems like robots, especially in manufacturing.[61] With this revolution, machines take over all monotonous, repetitive tasks while humans take the creative side with more responsibility and increased supervision of systems. The result is an elevation of the quality of the outputs across the board and improvement in the quality of work.

Information and Communication Technologies (ICT). It is the combination of computers, storage, network, applications, and so on, which supplies integrated and remote access of computer-based services.

Information Retrieval. It is a field of information solutions that deals with tools, processes, and capabilities to extract, order, and organize relevant information from disparate sources, to fill an information need.

[61] Paschek, D., Mocan, A., & Draghici, A. (2019, May). Industry 5.0-The expected impact of next industrial revolution. In *Thriving on future education, industry, business, and society, Proceedings of the make learn and TIIM International Conference, Piran, Slovenia* (15–17).

Information Theory. It is a field that studies mathematical quantification, transmission, and coding of information. It is one of the foundations of modern computer design.[62]

Innovation. It describes the event when a new product (or idea or concept or process) is brought to market and adopted by some customers. More broadly, innovation is a novel idea that affects and creates impact.

Input. It is a resource introduced into the system or consumed in its operation, which helps get a result or output.

Integration. It is the process of combining components or systems into one integrated entity.

Intelligent Automation. It indicates an automation solution enhanced with cognitive abilities that allow programs and machines to learn, interpret, and respond.

Intelligent System. It is a machine integrated with a computer connected to the internet to collect and analyze data and communicate with other systems. It is an intelligent artificial system that can think and learn independently and adapt to current data.

Internet Banking or Online Banking or Virtual Banking. It enables a customer to do banking transactions through the bank's website on the internet. It is a remote access system. It transacts on accounts and general information on financial institution products and services through a computer. All transactions are encrypted, using complex multi-layered security architecture, including firewalls and filters. One can rest assured that one's transactions are secure and confidential.

Internet. It is a global computer network supplying various information and communication facilities, consisting of interconnected networks using standardized communication protocols.

Internet of Everything. It is the internet of everything. It goes beyond the interconnection of devices involving everything: persons, objects, processes, and services. It is the basis for a hyper-connected world that includes things, processes, data, and persons.

Internet of People. It means the internet of human beings. It refers to direct or indirect interactions between devices or persons and persons, generating a set of information to understand and improve persons' operations.

[62] MacKay, D. J., & MacKay, D. J. (2003). *Information theory, inference and learning algorithms*. Cambridge University Press, Cambridge, UK.

Internet of Services. It is the part of the internet that maps services and functionalities as granular, web-based software components. Providers make these functions available on the internet and offer their use on request. Financial institutions can orchestrate the different software components into complex yet flexible solutions. It is called Service-oriented architecture (SOA). Many market players can quickly develop and offer internet-enabled services via cloud-based development platforms. Service platforms are created to find a complete, needs-based, or process-oriented offer instead of having to search, compare, and compile individual recommendations.

Internet of Things (IoT). It is an expression that indicates an ever-expanding network of detection equipment such as sensors, cameras, and other devices connected via the internet and able to communicate and exchange information. It allows communication between objects over the internet, allowing data to be exchanged, modified behavior based on input received, instruction memory, and learning from the interactions.

Internet Protocol (IP). It is the primary protocol for transmitting data or information over the internet.

Interoperability. It is the ability of independent, heterogeneous systems to work together (as far as possible) seamlessly to exchange information in an efficient and usable manner, to cooperate, and to supply services to users without the need for separate agreements between the systems.

Interpretable Artificial Intelligence. It is a framework that provides non-data scientists with a rigorous method of interpreting artificial intelligence models, which goes beyond quality metrics and statistical measurements.

Key Performance Indicators or Key Process Indicators. They are the metrics (or measures) used within corporations to measure one department's performance against another concerning revenue, sales, lead conversion, costs, customer support, and so on.

Know Your Customer (KYC). It is the process of an organization verifying the identity and the standing of its customers and the character of the business or transactions they generate. The term refers to the legal regulations which govern these activities.

Lean and Digitize. It is the method used to make the processes simultaneously streamlined and digitized, wherever it helps improve the processes.[63]

Lean Six Sigma. It is a complete, flexible, and highly structured method, aimed at achieving, keeping, and increasing customer value.[64]

Learning the Time Difference. It is a reinforcement learning system designed to predict future values.

Lightweight automation (Robotic Process Automation / RPA). It is an expression that refers to software with artificial intelligence and machine learning functionalities for the automation of repetitive and bulky tasks and ordinary processes (such as customer assistance, calculation operations, and register maintenance) without having to transform existing ICT systems.

Loan Crowdfunding. It is a credit activity eased by internet-based platforms (not run by commercial financial institutions) that matches borrowers with lenders. Individual loan contracts are set up between borrowers and lenders.

Machine Intelligence. It is a term that describes the self-learning abilities obtained by a computer thanks to artificial intelligence, machine learning, and cognitive solutions.

Machine Learning (ML). It is a set of algorithms used to make a system artificially intelligent. ML is a subcategory of AI. By gathering and classifying information, machine learning can find types and patterns of data with few or no hard coded rules.[65] It is a set of algorithms, or execution rules, to solve a problem(s) whose performance improves with experience (data) without hindsight. Machine learning is an interdisciplinary field that embraces information theory, control theory, statistics, and computer science. Machine learning is used in banking for scoring, fraud detection, portfolio management, and risk assessment.

Machine Translation. It is a translation of text or speech from one language to another performed by a computer. There are two types

[63] Nicoletti, B. (2012). *Lean and digitize: An integrated approach to process improvement*. Gower Publishing, Farnham, UK. ISBN-10: 1409441946.

[64] Dahlgaard Park, S. M., Andersson, R., Eriksson, H., & Torstensson, H. (2006). Similarities and differences between TQM, six sigma and lean. *The TQM magazine*.

[65] Artificial-Intelligence-Sep2017.pdf. Artificial. www.coursehero.com/file/43001568/Artificial-Intelligence-Sep2017pdf/. Accessed 22 June 2020.

of machine translation: that performed by knowledge-based systems, which draws on dictionaries, grammars, and similar tools and statistical machine translation, which derives meanings from the deep learning analysis of bilingual texts.

Mainframe. It is a system used by large organizations to perform various data processing tasks that may include statistical analysis, ERP functions, and financial transactions. In the 1990s, mainframes were associated primarily with IBM, which still dominates the market. Mainframes are still a key resource for many large organizations and are likely to remain for many years.

Management Process. It is a method to optimize the organization as a system, finding which processes need improvement and/or control, defining priorities, and supplying leadership to start and support efforts for improving processes. It is the management of the information obtained because of these processes.

Marketing. The American Marketing Association (AMA) defines marketing as the activity, set of institutions, and processes for creating, communicating, delivering, and exchanging offerings that add value for customers, partners, and the society.[66]

Markets in Financial Instruments Directive (MiFID). It is a European directive to improve the transparency and efficiency of the European financial markets. It also decides standards for regulatory disclosures. Meanwhile, there is an updated regulation called MiFID 2.

Measures. They are specific standards that allow the calibration of performance for each critical success factor or goal.[67] Measures can be either "soft," which are subjective and qualitative, or "hard," which are objective and quantitative.

Metrics. It is an index of the performance of an organization's performance that shows whether it reaches a goal.

Millennial (or Generation Y). It refers to the customer segment between 18 and 34 years. This segment is highly active on the web, social media, and mobile phone. Generation Y is a quarter of the world population. It is a significant challenge for financial institutions to try and get this market, as they are the customers of the near future.

[66] www.ama.org/the-definition-of-marketing/. Accessed 30 May 2020.

[67] Bullen, C. V., & Rockart, J. F. (1981). *A primer on critical success factors. Sloan School of Business*. MIT, Cambridge, MA.

Mission. It is how to go ahead toward the vision.

Mobile. It refers to the access to the internet via mobile phone or other mobile devices, and the entire range of online products (services, voice calls, applications, information, and content). Mobile is often used to choose a market sector.

Mobile Banking. It is an extension of online banking. The financial institution in association with the cellular service providers offers this service. Mobile phones should either be SMS, WAP enabled, or use a specific App. These facilities are normally available to those customers with credit card accounts with a bank.

Mobile Device. It includes mobile phones, satellite phones, feature phones, and tablet computers. The term "mobile device" is used interchangeably with "mobile handset" or "handset."[68]

Mobile Money or m-Money. It is a digital money product where the record of funds is stored on the mobile phone or a central computer system. It can be drawn down through specific payment instructions to be issued from the customers.

Mobile Money Platform. It is hardware and software that enables the provision of mobile money service.

Mobile Payments. It is a type of e-payment, where the payment instrument used is a mobile money product. Mobile money is a type of e-money product where the record of funds is stored on a central computer system. It can be drawn down through specific payment instructions to be issued from the customers' mobile phone and increasingly found through Multi-Factor Authentication.

Mode. In this book, it is a possible, customary, or preferred way of doing or a particular functioning arrangement or condition.

Model. In this book, in the context of machine learning, a model is a representation of a pattern extracted using machine learning from a data set. Consequently, models are trained, fitted to a data set, or created by running a machine learning algorithm on a data set. Popular model representations include decision trees and neural network. A prediction model defines a mapping or function from a set of input attributes to a target attribute value. It is possible to apply a model once created to new instances from the domain. A model can be used for simulations.

[68] Mobile Device. Open risk manual. www.openriskmanual.org/wiki/Mobile_Device. Accessed 30 May 2020.

Model training. It is how artificial intelligence (AI) is trained to perform its tasks, and, in many ways. It is like the process of training human personnel. To be compliant it is necessary to ensure that AI decisions and actions do not unintentionally disadvantage a category of people, Consequently, data used for training the AI models must be without bias and comprehensive. A key feature of responsible AI is the ability to prove how AI was trained.

Money Transfer Operator (MTO). It is a service provider non-deposit-taking payment where the service involves payment per transfer (or payment for a set or series of transfers) by the sender to the payment service provider.[69]

Narrow Artificial Intelligence. It is an artificial intelligence application in which the model is optimized to perform a limited number of tasks. A concrete example could be that of a chatbot that is assigned routine tasks that require accuracy and speed of execution, such as retrieving information from a banking database.

National Institute of Standards and Solution (NIST). It is a measurement standards laboratory part of the USA Department of Commerce non-regulatory agency. It also promotes the effective and secure use of cloud computing within organizations.

Natural Language Processing (NLP). It is the interacting in human language, including Natural language understanding (NLU) (Sentimental Analysis, Conversational AI bots.) and Natural language generation (NLG) It is a field of computer science aimed at understanding or generating human languages, both in the form of text and speech.

Natural Language Understanding (NLU). It is a subfield of NLP aimed at building machines that have a reading comprehension ability to allow humans to communicate with them in a natural way and receive proper answers.

Near Field Communication (NFC). It is the solution that allows the exchange of data and information without wires between close devices.

Neobanks. They are online-only financial institutions that are like banks.[70] The offerings of a neobank are usually limited compared to traditional banks, sometimes no more than a simple checking and

[69] Institutional information concepts and definitions. unstats.un.org/sdgs/metadata/files/Metadata-10-0C-01.pdf. Accessed 20 March 2021.

[70] www.thebalance.com/what-is-a-neobank-and-should-you-try-one-4186468. Accessed 20 January 2021.

savings account. The slimmed-down model allows neobank customers to enjoy smaller fees and higher-than-average interests.

Neural Networks. It is a type of of machine learning, composed of several layers of networks requiring intensely supervised or unsupervised learning. The neural networks of machine learning consist of interconnected "nodes" that mimic the functioning of the brain's neuronal network. Optical character recognition is among the most common applications of neural networks,

Node. In this book, it is a component of the blockchain solution that receives/sends transactions.

Objectives. They are general statements about the directions in which an organization intends to go, without telling specific targets to be reached at points in time.[71]

Omniaccess. It is a generalization of omnichannel to access in general.[72]

Omnichannel. It is a cross-channel content strategy that organizations use to improve their user experience and drive better relationships with their audience across different channels or contact points. The design of the channels and their supporting resources can help communication to allow the synchronization of the customer's information.[73]

Online (only) Bank. It is a financial institution where customers access only through the internet or web. It does not have physical branches.

Online Banking. It is a digital banking system that allows customers of a financial institution to conduct a wide variety of financial transactions through the financial institution or website.

Open Banking. It is the sharing and leveraging of customer-permissioned data by financial institutions with third-party developers and other organizations to build applications and services. These services include, for example, those that supply real-time payments, improved financial

[71] Bullen, C. V., & Rockart, J. F. (1981). *A primer on critical success factors. Sloan School of Business.* MIT, Cambridge, MA.

[72] Skinner, S. (2020, March). *Doing digital. Lessons from leaders.* Marshall Cavendish International (Asia) Pte Ltd., Singapore.

[73] Beaudon, G., & Soulier, E. (2019, February). Customer experience analytics in insurance: Trajectory, service interaction and contextual data. In *International Conference on information solution & systems,* 187–198. Springer, Cham, Switzerland.

transparency options for account holders, marketing, and cross-selling opportunities.[74] EU sponsors them in Europe.[75]

Optical Character Recognition (OCR). It is a solution that converts images of typed, handwritten, or printed text into digitally encoded text. Sources can be a scanned document, a photo of a form, a picture of a scene, or text superimposed on an image.

Orchestration. It describes the setup and networking of software services to form a business process. It is possible to combine internal and external services. Each service realizes only one specific activity within the process. With conventional web services, a participant controls the process flow. In banking 5.0, business processes will emerge *ad hoc,* and decisions made dynamically to control process flows. In this respect, the term orchestration is broader in this context than with conventional web services. It refers to the setting up of federated services used in several business processes. Simultaneously, they ensure the own context for each software process.

Organization. In this book, it includes financial institutions, public or private institutions, either central or local, a department, or a non-profit organization.

Output. It is the result produced by a system or process. The final output is usually a product, a service, or an initiative.

Outsourcing. The term defines an operation with an organization getting from an outside partner the management and operations of a specific process, sub-process, or activity.

Overdraft. It occurs when an account holder authorizes a withdrawal through a check, ATM withdrawal, debit card purchase, or digital payment, and the account does not have enough funds to cover the transaction.

Pandemic. It is an epidemic of disease that spreads across a vast region or globally.

Passive Robo-Advisor. In contrast to active portfolio management, passive management robo-advisor tries to track a given benchmark as closely as possible. The aim is to recreate, for example, an index

[74] Emerging payments association Asia outlines how Asia can. www.jumpstartmag.com/emerging-payments-association-asia-outlines-how-asia-can-lead-innovation-in-open-banking/. Accessed 30 May 2020.

[75] www.openbankingeurope.eu. Accessed 27 February 2021.

returns as exact as possible and to avoid any deviations. Exchange-Traded Funds (ETFs) are a popular instrument for passively managed portfolios.[76]

Payment Service Provider (PSP). It is an entity that supplies payment services, including remittances. Payment service providers include financial institutions, other deposit-taking institutions, and specialized entities such as money transfer operators and e-money issuers.

Payment Services Directive 2 (PSD 2). It is an EU directive aiming at furthering the integration of the markets for digital payments within the EU to increase competition and reach better prices for customers.

Perceived Risk. It is a customer's subjective belief of suffering a loss in the pursuit of desired outcomes.

Perceived Use. It is an individual's perception that an innovative solution will enhance or improve his or her performance.

Personalization. It refers to supplying individual designs to customers following their set of needs, wants, and preferences.

Phone Banking. It is the possibility for the customers to dial up the financial institution's designed telephone number and dial or share some personal identification data to get access to the financial institution's designated computer application. By using an Automatic voice recorder (AVR) for simple queries and transactions and staffed phone terminals for complex questions and transactions, the customer can do banking transactions on the telephone: anywhere and anytime.

Platform. It is a group of technologies used as a base upon which other applications, processes, or technologies are developed. In this book, the term indicates any information and communication system or automation support.

Predictive Analytics. It combines data, statistical algorithms, and machine learning tools to find the likelihood of future outcomes based on historical data and improve the predictions' reliability. It is the practice that uses historical data to predict future results. By combining mathematical models (or "predictive algorithms") with historical data, predictive analysis computes the values and the probabilities with which events can happen. Machine learning-based predictive analytics have been around for some time. Until recently, it lacked three features

[76] Millennials don't trust us, investment advisers say. www.theglobeandmail.com/globe-investor/advisers-view/millennials-an-elusive-target-for-investment-advisers/article25845221/. Accessed 20 March 2021.

that are crucial to generating marketing value: scalability, speed, and explainability.

Predictive Search. Based on the frequency of searches, it is a function that, can predict a user's search query as it is typed. It supplies a drop-down menu of suggestions that changes if the user adds words to the question.[77]

Predictive Systems. Among the most adopted machine learning applications, predictive systems use intelligent technologies that allow, for example, banking sites to display the products or services that are most likely to please customers. Using machine learning to track interactions and learn preferences and behaviors, the system personalizes following customer visits with targeted recommendations.

Predictor. It is a term that indicates an observed variable which, being related to another variable, can be used to predict its value through an AI model.

Prepaid Card. It is a payment card that supplies e-money in exchange for preliminary deposit of funds specifically for use through this card product.

Problem. It is the cause that creates an incident. Incidents not resolved due to the lack of an available solution, and repeated incidents related to a known issue ("known problem/error"), pass through problem management. A workaround could remediate the problem before finding the root causes and resolving them.

Process. It is a set of interrelated activities that change inputs on one or more results or outputs with a specific goal. Sometimes the process is identified with a system. It would be correct to regard it as a component of a system.[78]

Process Improvement. It is a continuous effort to learn the causes and effects to reduce the complexity, variations, and shorten the times. The process gets better by removing incorrect root causes. Through the redesign of the process, it is possible to reduce the variations in common causes. It is a continuous effort to learn from the causes and effects of a process, aiming to minimize the complexity, variations,

[77] Applied intelligence glossary | Accenture. www.accenture.com/no-en/insights/applied-intelligence/artificial-intelligence-glossary. Accessed 20 March 2021.

[78] Process—Open risk manual. www.openriskmanual.org/wiki/Process. Accessed 33 June 2020.

and cycle times. Eliminating or reducing the impact of the root causes improves the functions.

Process Management. It is a method to optimize the organization as a system, determine which processes need to be improved and/or controlled, define priorities, and encourage leadership to start and sustain process improvement efforts. It manages the information obtained in these processes.

Program. In this book, it is a set of projects with similar goals. An example is the set of projects to improve systems installed at different subsidiaries of the same group.

Project Team. It is a group of persons from different fields (and in some cases, from various organizations) working for a certain period as a team to improve the process or reach its goal.

Python. It is a high-level programming language widely used in machine learning. With Python it is possible to program an AI application with a few code lines, thanks to libraries of data manipulation and artificial intelligence. Python is often used for clustering, predictive modeling, and learning concepts and functions.

Quality. It is not easily defined, several variants are specified, at times specified by an adjective or specification added to the name. In general, quality is customer delight profitably for the organization.

Quantum Computing. It is an emerging field of computer science that uses quantum mechanics as an information processing system. As with traditional information sciences, this field includes both the theoretical study of quantum computing and the physical development of systems that exploit its potential. They have capabilities in the millions over traditional computers. Financial institutions can get significant benefits from quantum computers.[79] They will be able to analyze large or unstructured data sets more effectively. In an increasingly commoditized market, this can be a way to get competitive advantages. Quantum computers are particularly promising where algorithms are powered by live data streams, such as real-time equity prices, which carry an elevated random noise level.

[79] www.mckinsey.com/industries/financial-services/our-insights/how-quantum-computing-could-change-financial-services?cid=other-eml-alt-mip-mck&hdpid=19541661-bf69-4b6a-9250-,1447f7be5056&hctky=9204549&hlkid=793d02a949cb4fd3857936ec02b09ca8. Accessed 20 January 2021.

Recurrent Neural Network (RNN). It is a type of artificial neural network used to understand sequential information and predict resulting probabilities.[80] Recurrent neural networks are used in natural language processing, with applications in language modeling and speech recognition.

Reference Architecture or Architecture Framework. It is a concept and method structure that forms a uniform basis for the description and specification of system architectures. The aim of reference architectures is, on the one hand, to create a standard structure and language for architectural stories. On the other hand, they supply a method to get a detailed structural description.

Regtech Organization. It is a start-up that uses solutions to help and implement regulatory compliance.[81]

Reinforcement Learning. It is a type of machine learning based on an algorithm that tries to adapt to the environment. Learning takes place through a feedback loop of appropriately distributed (virtual) rewards.

Reliability. It refers to the commitment to accessibility and accuracy of the services being provided to the users.

Reporting. It consists of supplying and updating representative data, indicators, and dashboards. The degree of detail depends on the person or organization for whom the report is prepared.

Representation Learning. It is a class of machine learning methods in which features are learned automatically by an algorithm. Deep learning is a form of representative learning.

Resilience. It is the capability to predict risks, limit impacts, and bounce back rapidly through survival, adaptability, evolution, and growth in the face of turbulent changes.[82]

[80] Wang, H. (2020). *Dynamic analysis of recurrent neural networks*, Doctoral dissertation.

[81] Discussion note from spreadsheets to Suptech. documents.worldbank.org/curated/en/612021529953613035/pdf/127577-REVISED-Suptech-Solution-Solutions-for-Market-Conduct-Supervision.pdf. Accessed 30 May 2020.

[82] Community and regional resilience Institute (CARRI) (2013). Definitions of community resilience: An analysis. www.resilientus.org/wp-content/uploads/2013/08/definitions-ofcommunity-resilience.pdf. Accessed 30 July 2019. infoprosolution.com/. Accessed 30 May 2020.

Response. In this book, it is an immediate and on-going set of activities, actions, programs, and systems to manage the effects of an incident affecting life, property, operations, or the environment.[83]

Responsible Artificial Intelligence. It is an important emerging capability for organizations. Its goal is to make artificial intelligence systems more transparent, reliable, and interpretable, to address ethical and compliance issues systematically.

Responsible Banking. It encompasses a strong commitment by financial institutions to sustainable development and the fact that a financial institution addresses corporate social responsibility as an integral part of its banking activities.[84]

Responsiveness. It refers to the prompt responsiveness to the customers' inquiry, information retrieval, and navigation speed. It is a critical factor in assuring customers' delight.

Retail Banking. It is banking that takes place between individuals and their financial institutions.[85] A retail financial institution offers consumers essential banking services, including checking accounts, savings accounts, money transfers, and loans.

Risk. In this book, it is defined in financial terms as the chance that an outcome or investment's actual gains will differ from an expected outcome. Risks include the possibility of losing part or all an original investment.[86]

Risk Tolerance. It is the amount of risk an investor could bear based on his or her risk appetite: from risk-averse to risk-loving, depending on individual preferences. However, people who love to take risks do not necessarily prefer risk in every field.

Robo-Advice. It is a digital investment advice tool that matches customers based on their personal preference for financial products.

Robo-Advisor. It is a financial service based on two components: investment advice and automatization through robots. The term robo-advice

[83] www.nfpa.org/codes-and-standards. Accessed 20 June 2019.

[84] Scholtens, B. (2009). Corporate social responsibility in the international banking industry. *Journal of Business Ethics*, *86*(2), 159–175.

[85] www.thebalance.com/what-is-a-retail-bank-315209. Accessed 20 February 2020.

[86] www.investopedia.com/terms/r/risk.asp#:~:text=Risk%20is%20defined%20in%20financial,all%20of%20an%20original%20investment.&text=In%20finance%2C%20standard%20deviation%20is%20a%20common%20metric%20associated%20with%20risk. Accessed 22 June 2020.

may include various levels of automatization: while algorithms typically supply the onboarding and risk profiling, the investment process can either be completely rule-based or driven by human advisor.

Robotic Process Automation (RPA). It is a solution that allows, through software or a virtual robot, to implement applications to process transactions, manipulate data, generate responses, and communicate with other digital systems. In the financial sector, RPA can handle many repetitive tasks and processes.

Rule-based Algorithms. They are the algorithms that take advantage of a series of "if-then" statements that use a set of assertions from which rules are created. The rules determine how to act based on those assertions. Rule-based algorithms enable intelligent and repeatable decision-making. They are used to manage knowledge.

Rule-based Reasoning. It is a set of algorithms used to store and manipulate knowledge to interpret information helpfully.

Savings Account. It is an account at a financial institution in which account owners deposit funds. Account owners are paid interest on the amount deposited in their accounts. Account owners can withdraw funds but do not write checks on these accounts.

Scalability. It is the ability of a system to scale up or down as needed. With artificial intelligence, it is possible to create models capable of handling vast amounts of data, supplying unparalleled real-time predictive performance and much more exact, valuable, insights from the decision point of view.

Securities and Exchange Commission (SEC). It is the U.S. Securities and Exchange Commission (SEC). It is a federal agency responsible for the regulation of markets and exchanges.

Security. It involves protection from any kind of risk and fraud or financial loss.

Semantic segmentation. It is a complex form of image segmentation that groups the parts of an image belonging to the same object and labels them choosing from hundreds of categories. This ability allows users to enable many applications.

Semantic Technologies. They enable an explicit representation of the semantics (meaning) of data.[87] These technologies allow for defining

[87] www.sintef.no/en/expertise/information-and-communication-solutions-ict/ict-general/semantic-technologies/. Accessed 20 January 2021.

the meaning of entities in a domain standing for and storing the entities according to such definitions and capture meaningful information related to the entities once they are stored.

Sentence. It is any input from a human user to a chatbot or other conversational AI system. Sentences can be both written and spoken. To understand what to do, a chatbot must understand the intent of the statement.

Service Vendor. An organization such as a financial institution, a telecommunication organization, a merchant, and so on provides services to be integrated, for example, with Near field communication (NFC) mobile payments for credit card transactions.

Service. In computer science, it is the bundling of specialist functions of a program, in networks, supplying an application on a server, and in telecommunications, data transmission. Services refer to the provision of services to meet a defined need. Services is also a product as the ones offered by financial institutions.

Sharing Economy. It is an economic model based on sharing, swapping, trading, or renting products and services, enabling access or use instead of owning them.[88] It is reinventing not just what is consumed but how it is consumed.

Short Message Service (SMS). It is a system of communicating with short messages over the mobile telephone network. It can be secure if encrypted.

Sigma (σ). It is the eighteenth letter of the Greek alphabet. In statistics, it relates to the variance. It is a metric based on the number of defects that occur per million of opportunities.

Signal Processing. It is a tool to sample and change signals to improve them, implemented through various processes and algorithms, such as the Fourier Transform or the Kalman Filter.[89]

Six Sigma. It is a method and performance goal.[90] The method is a structured approach to continuous process improvement. The goal is

[88] Geissdoerfer, M., Savaget, P., Bocken, N. M., & Hultink, E. J. (2017). The circular economy–A new sustainability paradigm? *Journal of Cleaner Production*, *143*, 757–768.

[89] Hanlon, P. D., & Maybeck, P. S. (2000). Multiple-model adaptive estimation using a residual correlation Kalman filter bank. *IEEE Transactions on Aerospace and Electronic Systems*, *36*(2), 393–406.

[90] Schroeder, R. G., Linderman, K., Liedtke, C., & Choo, A. S. (2008). Six sigma: Definition and underlying theory. *Journal of Operations Management*, *26*(4), 536–554.

to measure a process's performance versus the target of several 3.4 defective parts per millions of opportunities.

Smart Application. It is a software program designed to perform certain functions directly for the user or, in some cases, for another application.

Smart Assistants. They are virtual assistants who process user requests in the form of a dialogue system and perform tasks for them.[91] They can act audibly as voice assistants ("voice banking") and in text form as chatbots and can be found in electronic end devices.

Smart Contracts. They are computer programs that automatically execute a contract or part of it. These contracts are automated and often blockchain-based. They could save time and reduce costs in standard transactions. Smart contracts are computer protocols that ease, verify, or enforce a digital agreement. The idea is that these programs potentially replace notaries, lawyers, and financial institutions when handling standard legal and business transactions. Technically, it is a code stored on a blockchain solution, triggered by blockchain transactions, and reads and writes data in that blockchain database.

Smart Machines. It is a solution which enables devices through machine-to-machine and/or cognitive computing technologies to run. Smart machines can reason, solve problems, make decisions, and take some actions.

Smart Products. They are products capable of communicating with each other and humans on a global network such as the internet.

Social Media. It is a platform, that allows internet users to communicate and share user-generated content like knowledge, opinions, evaluations, impressions, and so on.

Society for Worldwide Inter-bank Financial Telecommunications (SWIFT). SWIFT, as an international cooperative organization with its headquarters in Brussels, Belgium. SWIFT supplies standards for rapid, secure, reliable, and cost-effective mode of transmitting financial messages worldwide. At present more than 3,000 financial institutions are members of the network. SWIFT is a highly cost-effective, reliable, and secure means of fund transfer. It eases the transfer of messages relating to securities, trade finance, interest payment, debit-credit statements, foreign exchange, and so on.

[91] Bendel, O. (2020). Die Maschine an meiner Seite. In *Mensch-Roboter-Kollaboration* (pp. 1–14). Springer Gabler, Wiesbaden, Germany.

Socio-Technical System. It is the interaction of employees, technologies (machines, infrastructure, systems), and work organization to carry out a task.

Software as a Service. It is a model for using the software in which applications are hosted by a partner or service partner and made available to customers over a network, usually the cloud.

Software. It is the set of programs and other operational information used by a computer.

Speech Analytics. It is a process that, through the analysis of voice sources such as recorded customer calls, obtains insights that allow for improved communication and future interactions with customers. It is a method widely used in call centers, where it allows operators to collect information such as customer delight, abandonment rate, agent performance, and campaign effectiveness.

Sponsor. It is a person in the organization, usually at a significant level, that sponsors the project or an initiative, having the necessary authority and power. It is typically a member of the executive. It is an essential success factor for a project.

Stakeholder. It is an individual, group, or organization that is likely to be affected, directly or indirectly, by an activity, a program, or an organization's particular arrangement. Stakeholders include all those groups that take part or are involved in its economic life (employees, customers, partners, shareholders), those who see the organization (unions, regulators, non-governmental organizations), and those that it affects either directly or indirectly (civil society, local authorities, and so on).

Standards. They are indications of voluntary or compulsory standardization.

Statistical Machine Translation. It is a document translation process that statistically analyzes a corpus of bilingual texts and extracts user models. The most significant benefit of this method over a rule-based approach is the efficient use of both human and data resources.

Steering Committee. It is a group that assembles periodically. It includes representatives of the executives, the project leader, and the facilitators. Its primary responsibilities are the management of the improvement process or project's, efforts, the assessment of the needs and overseeing the support and training within its area of responsibility, the communication of the progress to all stakeholders, and agreement on the goals.

STEM. It is an acronym of "science, solutions, engineering, and mathematics," STEM indicates the integrated approach applied to scientific subjects, which have come to the fore as essential areas of study to technological organizations' development. Politicians and other leaders have expressed fears that students are not sufficiently prepared to work in the currently expanding career sectors and have policies and programs to encourage greater uptake of STEM subjects.

Straight-Through Processing (STP). It is a system that requires no human intervention for the approval or processing of a customer application or transaction.

Strategy. It is an essential component in the digital transformation process that includes the business model. It defines the impacts and opportunities of the business to be able to create value-added services by using digital technology and data-based products and services.[92]

Strong Artificial Intelligence. It is the idea that a computer program can function similarly to the human mind in terms of perception, beliefs, and other cognitive abilities associated with the human being.

Structured Data. It is a set of data with a high degree of organization, which can be consistently included in a relational database and quickly examined through elementary search algorithms and/or other search operations. Structured data generated by machines is on the rise and supplies data sensory and financial ones.

Supervised Learning. It is an algorithm which tries to model relationships and dependencies between the target prediction output and the input features.[93] In this way, it is possible to predict the output values for new data based on those relationships which the algorithm learned from the earlier data sets.

Suptech Organization (SUPervisory TECHnology). It refers to organizations that use a solution to ease and enhance supervisory processes from supervisory authorities' perspective. This organization differs from Regtech organization, as Suptech organizations are not focused on complying with laws and regulations, but on supporting supervisory agencies in their assessment of that compliance.

[92] Enterprise resource planning—Open risk manual. www.openriskmanual.org/wiki/Enterprise_Resource_Planning. Accessed 22 June 2020.

[93] owardsdatascience.com/types-of-machine-learning-algorithms-you-should-know-953a08248861. Accessed 23 March 2021.

System. It is a network of interacting components that cooperate to achieve specific goals.[94]

Tablet. It is a general-purpose computer contained in a single panel, with a touchscreen as the input device.

Tele-banking. It supplies the facility to the customer of doing 24*7 banking. Tele-banking is based on the voice processing facility available on financial institution computers.

Telematics. It is the set of technical and methodological solutions adopted to allow remote data processing or to communicate with applications based on remote computing systems and connected. It denotes the cooperation between Telecommunications and Information Technology. In this book, it is shown as ICT.

Template. It is a representation or simulation of real-world phenomena. There are several types of models: iconic, analog, analytical. In machine learning, analytical models are produced through the process of a learning algorithm by a set of data.

Total Cost of Ownership (TCO). It is a metric considering the costs all along the lifecycle of a solution. Typically, it includes procurement costs, installation, testing, maintenance, use, and disposal at the end of the useful life.

Training Data. It is the data used to train a machine learning algorithm. In machine learning, data is typically divided into three sets: training, validation, and test data. In general, the more unbiased, correct, and complete the training data, the better the algorithm will perform.

Transaction. It is the action of executing a function or an application. An example of a transaction is the execution of a money order and the processing of authorization and clearing messages.

Transparency. Artificial intelligence (AI) must be transparent both in the actions it performs and its decisions.[95] For this to happen, an AI application needs a capability that documents how it gets to make its decisions. Transparency means that there must be governance structures suitable to watch AI and, if necessary, to optimize its decision-making process and make it compliant with regulations.

[94] Deming, W. E. (1994). *The new economics for industry, government, education*. MIT Press, Boston, MA.

[95] van Nuenen, T., Ferrer, X., Such, J. M., & Cote, M. (2020). Transparency for whom? Assessing discriminatory artificial intelligence. *Computer*, *53*(11), 36–44.

Trust. It is the ability of two parties to define a positive relationship with a proper authentication of the two parties.

Tuning. In this book, to implement artificial intelligence models on a large scale, it is necessary to tune them, a non-intuitive process that takes a long time, and in which the best values of the parameters (called hyperparameters) are looked for, which can significantly affect the accuracy of the model.

Turing Test. Invented by Alan Turing, it is called the "imitation game," and allows a person to decide if a machine is intelligent.[96] During the test, an adviser needs to judge the conversation between a machine designed to supply human responses and a human being. The solution passes the test if the evaluator cannot distinguish between the two. Since its start, the Turing test has always been a theoretical pillar of AI.

Unstructured Data. It is information that does not have a predefined data model or is not organized by default. Unstructured data can be non-textual (for instance, JPEG images and MP3 files) and includes emails, videos, photos, audio files, word processing documents, presentations, and web pages. Unstructured data analytics tools, like natural language processing, conversation analytics, and video analytics, allow solutions to analyze the large volumes of unstructured data that organizations have access to.

Unsupervised learning. It is a type of machine learning in which the algorithm does not need data with predefined labels. It classifies them by examining similarities or anomalies and grouping them accordingly.

User Interface (UI). It is a platform that allows a user to communicate with a computer that simulates a human conversation. Natural language processing (NLP) allows a conversational system to interact that considers the user's feelings and the conversation context.

Validation. It is a method to supply specific personal information to prove ownership of the identity for identity verification.

Value Network. It is the sequence of activities that brings value to the customer (and indirectly to the organization). It is the process used to deliver a good or service. It is a set of activities and organizations needed to design, order, manufacture, and supply (or supply a given product or service in the case of a service). These activities cover

[96] Neufeld, E., & Finnestad, S. (2020). In defense of the Turing test. *AI & Society*, 1–9.

the entire cycle of the product/service organization down to the end customer.

Value. It is the relationship between benefits and cost/damage of a product or service, as defined by the customer. In the case of a product/service, it is expressed, in its ability to meet the customer's needs at a given price and at a given time.[97] The value perceived by the customer is all the features of the product/service that the customer considers necessary and valuable. Any activity that consumes resources (including time) and does not create value is a waste (*muda* in Japanese).

Value-Added Network (VAN). It is a decentralized polycentric network, which is characterized by complex mutual relationships between autonomous, legally independent actors. It forms an interest group of potential value creation partners who interact in standard processes, if necessary. The creation of value-added networks is geared toward sustainable economic added value. Forms of value creation networks are referred to as business webs.

Variance. In statistics, it is the average of the squared deviations. It is a distribution or variability index.

Variations. They are changes in the quantity or time value between cases caused by acts and not predictable.

Verification. It is a programming procedure used to check if an algorithm produces the correct output (based on the defined parameters).

Video Analytics. It is a solution that automatically analyzes video images with deep learning algorithms to detect and decide temporal and spatial events. It is used in many industries (entertainment, security, healthcare, retail, and transportation).

Virtual Agent. It is an artificial intelligence system that supplies a human-like user interface and executes transactions. Virtual agents can hold a conversation, intelligently answer questions, and nod as they speak.

Virtual Reality (VR). It is a solution that simulates reality, replacing it with a digital environment, whose input is made possible by unique accessories that allow an operator to interact within virtual reality.[98]

[97] Value proposition—Open risk manual. www.openriskmanual.org/wiki/Value_Proposition. Accessed 30 May 2020.

[98] ACETİ6, M. (2020). The use of information and communication technologies (ICT) in the Banking Sector in Turkey. *In traders 2019: Academic studies in social, human and administrative sciences*, 27.

Virtual reality applications create very engaging experiences, which are seen, and experienced by the user through a viewer. The user finds himself immersed in a 3D virtual environment of natural dimensions that breaks the barriers imposed by wearing it. To increase the feeling of reality, interactive handheld devices, such as motion trackers, respond to the user's physical movements.

Virtualization. It is producing a virtual (instead of a physical) version, detached from the specific resources, such as a hardware platform, an operating system, a storage medium, or network resource.

Vision. It is the expression of what would stand for a success for the organization. A vision defines the goal to implement to ensure that the organization supplies the creative tensions between the current reality and the vision. It is an expression of what would be a success for the organization. The vision's goal is to produce a mental image for generating creative tensions between the current reality and the organization's future. To be valuable, the whole organization should know and accept the vision. Implementing the vision usually requires much effort and patience.

Visual Recognition. It is the application of pattern recognition to find what is in each photo/video. Based on this, the solution can produce recommendations or even make decisions.

Visual Search. It is a search that uses an image instead of text in a search query. Advanced visual search can find the content of a photo or a video.

Visualization. It is the representation of abstract data arising in administrative and production processes. Numbers are displayed in their context and a suitable visual form, for example, as a graphic. This contextual representation is based on prioritization, which means that less meaningful data is omitted in the given context.

Voice of the Customer. It is the customer's voice, or the citizen's voice, in the case of public organizations.

Vulnerability. It consists of a system's intrinsic properties resulting in vulnerability to a risk that can lead to a damage.

Weak Artificial Intelligence. It is known also as restricted AI. It is an AI application in which the model has been perfected to perform a limited number of tasks. It applies to all routine tasks that require precision and speed of execution.

Wholesale Banking. It is banking that covers three broad segments.[99] They are commercial banks (for smaller corporate clients), corporate banks (for upper-midmarket corporate clients), and investment banks (for large multinational corporate clients and financial-institution groups).

Withdrawal. It is a sum of money taken out of an account.

Working Capital. It is the set of financial resources invested by an organization in financing its current trading operations. They are usually expressed as the difference between current assets (receivables, inventory, and operating cash balances) and current liabilities (payables and short-term debt).[100]

[99] www.bcg.com/publications/2019/new-reality-wholesale-banks. Accessed 20 February 2021.

[100] Working capital. Open risk manual. www.openriskmanual.org/wiki/Working_Capital. Accessed 30 May 2020.

References

Acemoglu, D., Restrepo, P., & LeLarge, C. (2020, May). Competing with robots: Firm-level evidence from France. *American Economic Review Papers and Proceedings*.

Armbrüster, C. (2020). Innovative solutions. Political, legal, economic, and factual impact in Germany. *ZVersWiss*.

Belozyorov, S., Sokolovska, E., & Kim, Y. (2020). Fintech organization as a precondition for transformations on global financial markets. *Foresight and STI Governance, 14*(2), 23–35.

Bhalakrishnan, M., & Krishna, M. R. V. (2020). Awareness and use of industrial revolutions. In *Msme Manufacturing Sectors*. Editorial Board, *9*(6).

Boobier, T. (2020). *AI and the future of banking*. John Wiley & Sons, Hoboken, NJ.

Chen, T. H., & Chang, R. C. (2020). Using machine learning to evaluate the influence of FinTech patents: The case of Taiwan's financial industry. *Journal of Computational and Applied Mathematics*, 113215.

Cristea, L. M. (2020). Emerging IT technologies for accounting and auditing practice. *Audit Financial*, *18*(4), 731–751.

da Costa Tavares, M. D. C., & do Carmo Azevedo, G. M. (2020, October). Society 5.0 as a contribution to the sustainable development report. In *International conference on tourism, solutions and systems* (pp. 49–63). Springer, Singapore.

1

B. Nicoletti, *Banking 5.0*, Palgrave Studies in Financial Services Technology, https://doi.org/10.1007/978-3-030-75871-4

Donepudi, P. K., Banu, M. H., Khan, W., Neogy. T. K., Asadullah, A. B. M., & Ahmed, A. A. A. (2020). Artificial intelligence and machine learning in treasury management: A systematic literature review. *International Journal of Management*, *11*(11).

Eminente, G., & Nicoletti, B. (1985). *Strategia organizzazionale & sviluppo tecnologico*. Il Mulino, Bologna, Italy.

Gasiorkiewicz, L., & Monkiewicz, J. (Eds.). (2021). *Innovation in financial services: Balancing private and public interests*. Routledge, London, UK.

Gąsiorkiewicz, L., Monkiewicz, J., & Monkiewicz, M. (2020). Solution-driven innovations in financial services: The rise of alternative finance. *Foundations of Management*, *12*(1), 137–150.

Hazik, M. (2021). *Central Bank digital currency (Cbdc) formats and their implications, World scientific book chapters, in: Beyond fintech solutions applications for the Islamic economy* (chapter 9, 165–176). World Scientific Publishing Co. Pte. Ltd., Singapore.

Kabza, M. (2020). Sztuczna inteligencja w usługach finansowych (Artificial intelligence in financial services). In L. Gąsiorkiewicz, & J. Monkiewicz (Eds.), *Innowacje na rynkach finansowych (*Innovations in Financial Markets*)* (pp. 128–153). Oficyna Wydawnicza PW, Warszawa, Poland.

Kaczmarek-Heß, M., & de Kinderen, S. (2017). A multilevel model of IT platforms for the needs of enterprise it landscape analyzes. *Business & Information Systems Engineering, 59*(3), 315–329.

Kadyrbayeva, N. (2020). Identification of threats arising from financial technologies (*Master Thesis on Electronic Business management*). Faculty of economic and business, Mykolas Romeris University, Vilnius, Lithuania.

King, B. (2020). *Bank 4.0 banking every where, never at a bank*. John Wiley & Sons, Hoboken, NJ.

Knewtson H. S., & Rosenbaum Z. A. (2020). Toward understanding FinTech and its industry. *Managerial Finance*.

Monett, D., Lewis, C. W., & Thórisson, K. R. (2020). Introduction to the JAGI special issue on defining artificial intelligence—Commentaries and author's response. *Journal of Artificial General Intelligence*, *11*(2), 1–100.

Mühl, K. Y. (2020). *Bank 4.0: Wie digital leader Gewinne steigern, Kosten senken und neue Ertragsquellen erschließen* (Vol. 1). BoD–Books on Demand.

Nicoletti, B. (2006, December). Nuovo Pignone, l'arte di fondere Lean Management e Six Sigma, *Computerworld Italia*, 1–2.

Nicoletti, B. (2008, October 10–13). Project Management 2.0. *IPMA Congress*, Rome, Italy.

Nicoletti, B. (2012). *The method of lean and digitize*. Gower Press, Farnham, UK.

Nicoletti, B. (2013). Innovazione, una ricetta per la crescita. *Strategie & Procurement*, Lug. (18–19).

Nicoletti, B. (2017). *The future of fintech organization*. Springer, London, UK.

Nicoletti, B. (2021). Insurance 4.0 and digital transformation. In *Insurance 4.0*. (pp. 361–387). Palgrave Macmillan, Cham, Switzerland.

Omarova, S. T. (2020). «Dealing with disruption: Emerging approaches to FinTech regulation». *Washington University Journal of Law and Policy, 61*, 25–54.

Pedersen, N. (2020). *Financial solutions: Case studies in fintech innovation*, Google books.

Salgues, B. (2018). *Society 5.0: Industry of the future, technologies, methods and tools*. John Wiley & Sons, Hoboken, NJ.

Sarfraz, Z., Sarfraz, A., Iftikar, H. M., & Akhund, R. (2021). Is COVID-19 pushing us to the fifth industrial revolution (Society 5.0)? *Pakistan Journal of Medical Sciences, 37*(2), 591.

Scholz, P. (2021). *Robo-advisory: Investing in the digital age*. Palgrave Macmillan, London, UK.

Skinner, C. (2020). *Doing digital: Lessons from leaders*. Marshall Cavendish International, Singapore.

Smith, A., & Nobanee, H. (2020). Artificial intelligence: In Banking a mini-review. *Available at SSRN 3539171.*

Sundqvist, A., Berget, G., Nolin, J., & Skjerdingstad, K. I. (Eds.). (2020, March 23–26). *Sustainable digital communities: 15th International conference, iConference 2020, Boras, Sweden, Proceedings* (Vol. 12051). Springer Nature, Cham, Switzerland.

Verhoef, P. C. (2020). 7 customer experience creation in today's digital world. *The Routledge companion to strategic marketing*. Routledge, London, UK.

Webster, C., & Ivanov, S. (2020). Robotics, artificial intelligence, and the evolving nature of work. In B. George & J. Paul (Eds.). *Digital transformation in business and society theory and cases* (127–143). Palgrave-MacMillan, London, UK.

Xu, L., Lu, X., Yang, G., & Shi, B. (2020, March). Identifying fintech innovations with patent data: A combination of textual analysis and machine-learning techniques. In *International conference on information* (pp. 835–843). Springer, Cham, Switzerland.

Yıldırım, A. C. (2020). *The impacts of digitalization and covid-19 on the business model of banking: A qualitative study on Turkish banks* (Master's thesis, Middle East Technical University).

Zacpal, M. (2020). *FinTech a AML z právní perspektivy* (*Master thesis*), Karlova University, Prague, Czech Republic.

Sitography (Accessed 20 March 2021)

data.gov.uk.
emeia.ey-vx.com.
fintechorganizationnews.ch.
home.kpmg.com/content.
myhippo.com.
openparliament.ca.
searchmanufacturingerp.techtarget.com.
ssrn.com.
www.3isite.com.
www.aaai.org.
www.aberdeen.com.
www.accountingtools.com.
www.advisorevolved.com.
www.agendadigitale.eu/cloudmate.com/about.
www.altimate.ca.
www.amfam.com.
www.amodo.eu.
www.bain.com.
www.bernardonicoletti.com.
www.bershka.com.
www.briansolis.com.
www.businessdictionary.com.
www.capgemini.com.
www.carriermanagement.com.
www.ceclass.com/.

B. Nicoletti, *Banking 5.0*, Palgrave Studies in Financial Services Technology, https://doi.org/10.1007/978-3-030-75871-4

www.chaseperformance.com.
www.cloudmate.com.
www.con-way.com.
www.cordis.lu.
www.cscmp.org.
www.data.com.
www.dcvelocity.com.
www.eccellere.com.
www.en.wiktionary.org.
www.esisinc.com.
www.europarl.europa.eu/.
www.expansion.com.
www.ey.com.
www.financial-dictionary.com.
www.fostec.com.
www.fraunhofer.de.
www.freedomdefined.org.
www.fujutsu.com.
www.georgia-associates.com.
www.gformula.com.
www.grin.com.
www.hem.com.
www.hrpub.org.
www.ibm.com.
www.ieee.com.
www.impind.de.
www.inditex.com.
www.industryweek.com
www.investopedia.com
www.iotinsobs.com/.
www.isixsigma.com
www.ispo.cec.be/ecommerce/.
www.istitute-of-logistics.org.uk.
www.kin.com.
www.kpmg.com.
www.laserfiche.com.
www.leanmanufacturing.it.
www.logility.com.
www.ltdmgmt.com.
www.managementstudyguide.com.
www.mckinsey.com.
www.metromile.com.

www.microsoft.com.
www.newagepublishers.com.
www.novell.com.
www.ohio-state.edu/index.php.
www.opendefinition.org.
www.optimialelectronics.com.
www.organizzazioniaziendali.it/index.asp.
www.oysho.com.
www.pacificlifere.com.
www.pewresearch.org.
www.prophet.com.
www.pullandbear.com.
www.rgare.com.
www.ru.coursera.org/lecture/matematicheskiye-metody-v-psikhologii.
www.ryder.com.
www.sas.com.
www.sciencedirect.com.
www.scmr.com.
www.skillprofiles.eu.
www.stradivarius.com.
www.strategyzer.com.
www.svv.ch.
www.thebalancesmb.com.
www.theinstitutes.org.
www.timreview.ca.
www.uterque.es.
www.uwplatt.edu.
www2.deloitte.com.

Web Places of Banking Cases (Accessed 20 March 2021)

www.americanexpress.com.
heyguevara.com.
manulife.ca.
www.cii.co.uk.
statista.com.
www.crunchbase.com.
www.friendsurance.com.
www.hioscar.com.
www.lemonade.com.
www.shopify.com.

B. Nicoletti, *Banking 5.0*, Palgrave Studies in Financial Services Technology, https://doi.org/10.1007/978-3-030-75871-4

Index

B. Nicoletti, *Banking 5.0*, Palgrave Studies in Financial Services Technology, https://doi.org/10.1007/978-3-030-75871-4

I

S

U

Printed in the USA
CPSIA information can be obtained
at www.ICGtesting.com
CBHW032124090924
14324CB00001B/1